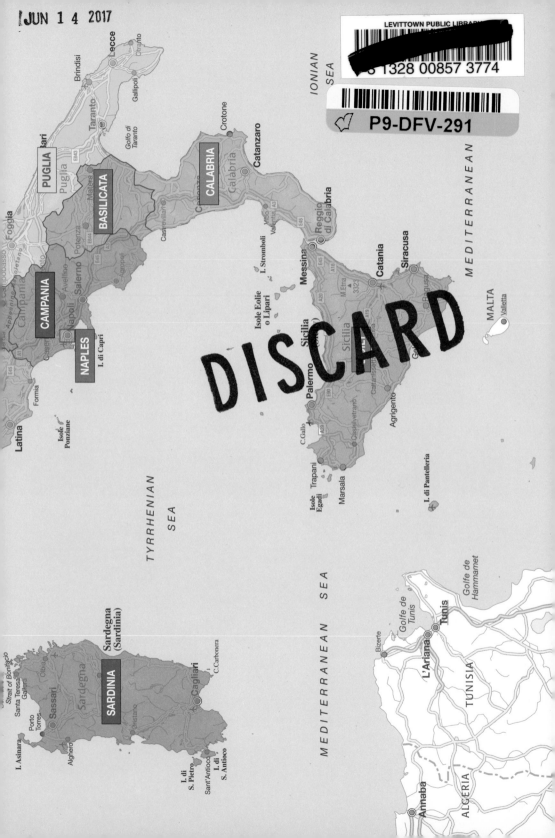

INSIGHT ⊙ GUIDES

ITALY

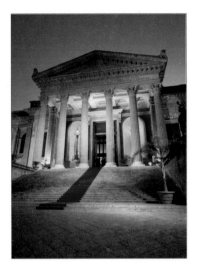

◉ Walking Eye App

YOUR FREE DESTINATION CONTENT AND EBOOK AVAILABLE THROUGH THE WALKING EYE APP

Your guide now includes a free eBook and destination content for your chosen destination, all for the same great price as before. Simply download the Walking Eye App from the App Store or Google Play to access your free eBook and destination content.

HOW THE WALKING EYE APP WORKS

Through the Walking Eye App, you can purchase a range of eBooks and destination content. However, when you buy this book, you can download the corresponding eBook and destination content for free. Just see below in the grey panels where to find your free content and then scan the QR code at the bottom of this page.

Destinations: Download your corresponding essential destination content from here, featuring recommended sights and attractions, restaurants, hotels and an A–Z of practical information, all for free. Other destinations are available for purchase.

Ships: Interested in ship reviews? Find independent reviews of river and ocean ships in this section, all available for purchase.

eBooks: You can download your free accompanying digital version of this guide here. You will also find a whole range of other eBooks, all available for purchase.

Free access to travel-related blog articles about different destinations, updated on a daily basis.

HOW THE DESTINATION CONTENT WORKS

Each destination includes a short introduction, an A–Z of practical information and recommended points of interest, split into 4 different categories:
• Highlights
• Accommodation
• Eating out
• What to do

You can view the location of every point of interest and save it by adding it to your Favourites. In the 'Around Me' section you can view all the points of interest within 5km.

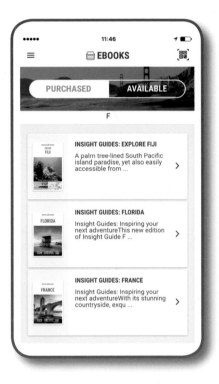

HOW THE EBOOKS WORK

The eBooks are provided in EPUB file format. Please note that you will need an eBook reader installed on your device to open the file. Many devices come with this as standard, but you may still need to install one manually from Google Play.

The eBook content is identical to the content in the printed guide.

HOW TO DOWNLOAD THE WALKING EYE APP

1. Download the Walking Eye App from the App Store or Google Play.
2. Open the app and select the scanning function from the main menu.
3. Scan the QR code on this page – you will then be asked a security question to verify ownership of the book.
4. Once this has been verified, you will see your eBook and destination content in the purchased ebook and destination sections, where you will be able to download them.

Other destination apps and eBooks are available for purchase separately or are free with the purchase of the Insight Guide book.

Contents

THE BEST OF ITALY: TOP ATTRACTIONS

From Roman ruins to Renaissance masterpieces, Italy offers scenery of equal magnitude; mountains, volcanic islands, vineyards and beaches – there's something for everyone.

◁ **Lake Como**. Arguably Italy's loveliest lake, Como promises gorgeous villas and gardens, charming ports of call, fish dinners – and possible sightings of local resident George Clooney. See page 232.

△ **The Dolomites**. Walk or cycle through Europe's loveliest peaks, now a Unesco World Heritage site. Scenic trails may end at an Alpine inn, ideally with a concert in the meadows. See page 212.

▽ **Ancient Rome**. The majestic ruins of the Colosseum, the Forum and the Palatine Hill speak to us all as potent symbols of the power centre that was Ancient Rome. See page 133.

△ **Tuscan spas**. Whether simple or luxurious, the spas command seductive settings, which provide a pretext for lapping up a landscape of olive groves, vineyards and cypress-clad hills. See page 377.

△ **Island-hopping near Sicily**. The Aeolians, seven volcanic specks off Sicily, offer sheer escapism, from barefoot luxury in boutique hotels to a back-to-nature experience. See page 377.

◁ **Truffles in Alba**. Italy abounds in foodie feasts, but finely grated truffles transform the simplest dish into a sensation that some Piedmontese say is better than sex. See page 242.

▷ **Florence**. No other city boasts such a concentration of Renaissance art. But beyond the Uffizi Gallery, the city itself is a Renaissance masterpiece of piazzas and palaces. See page 267.

▽ **The Amalfi Coast**. Even without a vintage Alfa Romeo, this is the drive of a lifetime. Vertiginous views await on the winding, cliff-top coastal road linking Positano, Amalfi and Ravello. See page 340.

△ **Le Cinque Terre**. Ramble your way through a cluster of five fishing villages which cling to the rocky coast. Byron praised this pocket of Liguria as "paradise on earth". See page 247.

▽ **Venice**. Sweep down the Grand Canal on a number one vaporetto; smooch in a gondola or shun romance for an island ferry – or even a lagoon kayaking adventure. See page 177.

THE BEST OF ITALY: EDITOR'S CHOICE

Unique attractions, festivals and events, piazzas and parks, art and culture... here, at a glance, are our recommendations to make the most of your stay in Italy.

Sicily's Valle dei Templi (Valley of the Temples) boasts the best-preserved Greek temple in the world.

BEST LANDSCAPES

The Abruzzo. One of Italy's last untamed wildernesses, where bears and wolves still roam. See page 313.
The Maremma. A mixture of marshland, mountains and virgin coast, with trails and riding

Frescoes at Pompeii.

opportunities in the Parco della Maremma. See page 289.
Chianti country and the Val d'Orcia. The landscape of gentle hills, stately cypresses, vineyards and olive groves is the Tuscany of postcards. See page 286.
Parco Nazionale del Gran Paradiso. An area of outstanding natural beauty, this Alpine park is fabulous trekking country. See page 243.
Parco Nazionale del Pollino. Italy's largest national park straddles Basilicata and Calabria. See page 358.
Monti Sibillini and the Nera Valley. A wild Umbrian landscape of gorges, mountains and vertiginous views. See page 305.

BEST ANCIENT SITES

Pompeii and Herculaneum. Remains of two thriving Roman towns set against the backdrop of Vesuvius, their slayer. See page 337.
San Vitale, Ravenna. Mosaics that are the

crowning glory of Byzantine art – started under a Roman emperor, and finished under the Byzantines. See page 261.
Paestum. Magnificent standing temples of an ancient Greek settlement. See page 341.
Selinunte. The scattered remains of a once powerful and rich Greek colony in Sicily. See page 372.
Valle dei Templi. Classical temples and tombs in Agrigento, Sicily. See page 372.
Ostia Antica. Once the commercial port of Rome, two-thirds of the excavated Roman town can now be seen. See page 166.

Dancing faun statue at Pompeii.

GREATEST PIAZZAS

Piazza Navona.

Piazza Navona, Rome. A Baroque extravaganza of fountains and churches. See page 151.

Piazza San Marco, Venice. The city's ceremonial stage-set of a square. See page 179.

Piazza della Signoria, Florence. Outdoor sculpture gallery, dominated by *David*. See page 269.

Campo dei Miracoli, Pisa. The aptly named "Field of Miracles" is home to the iconic Leaning Tower of Pisa. See page 292.

Piazza del Campo, Siena. Fan-shaped medieval square, the stage for a thrilling annual bareback race. See page 283.

Piazza Pretoria, Palermo. Its centrepiece is a legendary fountain with a sensuous abundance of near-naked nymphs, tritons and gods. See page 374.

Piazza IV Novembre, Perugia. The hub of Umbria's dynamic capital. See page 301.

Palermo's Piazza Pretoria was once nicknamed Piazza Vergogna (Square of Shame), due to the saucy nudes cavorting in its fountain.

MOST SEDUCTIVE ISLANDS

Capri. A capsule of Mediterranean beauty, with legendary status. See page 338.

Ischia. The volcanic "green island" is renowned for its spas. See page 339.

Procida. The unique charm of Procida is a magnet to filmmakers. See page 339.

Giglio. Popular with weekending Romans and day-trippers alike. See page 290.

Elba. Dramatic scenery and lots of small beaches make this ideal for families. See page 289.

Sicily. Italy's most enigmatic island is a kaleidoscope of ancient civilisations. See page 367.

Aeolian Islands. Seven volcanic islands off Sicily; some offer luxury, others a back-to-nature experience. See page 377.

Sardinia. For a sun-worshipper's beach holiday. See page 381.

Views from the island of Capri.

GOURMET ITALY

Emilia Romagna. The culinary region par excellence produces balsamic vinegar from Modena, Parma ham and Parmesan cheese. See page 258.

Pizza in Naples. Birthplace of the authentic thin-crust pizza cooked in a wood-fired oven. See page 328.

Piedmont. For Barolo wine, rice, gorgonzola, chocolates and white truffles. See page 240.

Tuscany. For wine, olive oil, tagliatelle and Chianina cattle that provide meat for the classic *bistecca alla fiorentina*. See page 282.

Milan. Risotto, *osso bucco* (stewed veal shank), polenta and salami are all local specialities. See page 220.

Naples is the birthplace of pizza.

CULTURAL ITALY

Accademia, Florence. Originally the world's first school of art, the gallery is now home to Michelangelo's most famous work, *David*. See page 276.

Cenacolo Vinciano, Milan. Make an advance booking to see Leonardo da Vinci's *Last Supper*. See page 217.

Uffizi, Florence. Countless rooms and corridors in this palace hold Italy's highest concentration of Renaissance masterpieces. See page 271.

Capitoline Museums, Rome. A rich collection of ancient sculpture. The Etruscan statue of the she-wolf nursing Romulus and Remus can be seen here. See page 138.

Guggenheim (Palazzo Venier), Venice. A superb modern art collection representing most major art movements, housed in a palazzo along the Grand Canal. See page 183.

Vatican Museums, Rome. The glorious Sistine Chapel is the inner sanctum of the papal treasure house. See page 159.

Archaeological Museum, Naples. Rich repository of Roman and Greek antiquities, including treasures from Pompeii and Herculaneum and the colossal Farnese sculptures. See page 329.

Santa Giulia Museo della Città, Brescia. Over 3,000 years of history covered in a Benedictine monastery, itself a major monument. See page 234.

Cinema Museum, Turin. Star-studded museum set in a cavernous former synagogue. See page 239.

Etruscan Museum, Volterra. Some of the best Etruscan art to be found outside Rome, housed in a papal villa. See page 291.

Archaeological Museum, Palermo. Great classical finds excavated from all over Sicily and displayed in a late-Renaissance monastery. See page 375.

Pinacoteca di Brera, Milan. Contained within a handsome 17th-century Jesuit palace, the Pinacoteca di Brera houses one of Italy's finest art collections, with works by Mantegna, Raphael and Piero della Francesca. See page 216.

Venaria Reale, Turin. Dubbed Italy's Versailles, this sumptuous, superbly restored royal residence was created in 1658 for the Savoy dynasty. See page 241.

Palazzo dei Conservatori statue, Rome.

TOP HILL TOWNS

Assisi. Birthplace of St Francis, whose life is portrayed in Giotto's frescoes that decorate the great Basilica. See page 302.

Bergamo. Rising out of the plain of the Po Valley on a steep hill, not far from Milan. See page 229.

Gubbio. The best preserved of Umbria's many medieval hill towns. See page 308.

Matera. Hill town in deepest Basilicata, famous for its cave dwellings or Sassi. See page 355.

Montalcino and Montepulciano. Quintessential Tuscan hill towns, both famed for their wines.

See page 287.

Ostuni. Whitewashed Puglian town with a distinctly Middle Eastern feel. See page 351.

Urbino. A remarkably well-preserved Renaissance town set amid spectacular mountains. See page 309.

San Gimignano. Medieval Manhattan in Tuscany. See page 290.

San Marino and San Leo. Medieval citadels in Rimini's rugged hinterland. See page 310.

Santo Stefano. An ancient hamlet in the wilds of Abruzzo, transformed into a model for rural tourism. See page 317.

The medieval towers of San Gimignano.

GREATEST CATHEDRALS

Duomo, Siena. Perched on a hill, Siena's Duomo is a dazzling mix of styles. See page 284.

Duomo, Milan. This is the most grandiose of Italy's Gothic cathedrals. See page 215.

Basilica di San Marco, Venice. The onion-domed and mosaic-covered cathedral dominates the square. See page 179.

Basilica di San Pietro, Rome. Its giant cupola is a Roman landmark. See page 159.

Duomo, Monreale. Glittering mosaics adorn Sicily's finest cathedral. See page 373.

Duomo, Orvieto. Hilltop cathedral with a stunning facade. See page 306.

Costa Smeralda resort, Sardinia.

The view from the top of Milan's Duomo.

BEST FESTIVALS

Il Palio, Siena. A climactic bareback horse race round the Campo.

Carnevale, Venice. A 10-day extravaganza of masked balls, pantomime and music.

Arena di Verona, Verona. The magnificent open-air summer opera festival in the Roman Arena.

Easter, Sicily. Celebrations include "The Mysteries" at Trapani and the "Easter Devils" at Prizzi.

Suoni dei Dolomiti, Trentino. The Sounds of the Dolomites is a summer music festival in the peaks.

Torre del Lago, Tuscany. A celebration of Puccini's operas by his lakeside home.

Siena's Palio race in full swing.

COASTAL ITALY

Po Delta, Emilia-Romagna. The Italian Camargue, a mosaic of marshes, dunes and mudflats, with cycle tracks along raised banks. See page 260.

Portofino Promontory, Liguria. This coastal reserve embraces a chic resort, a marine reserve, and pine and olive groves on rugged slopes. See page 247.

Costa Smeralda, Sardinia. Beautiful emerald waters that draw a moneyed crowd.

See page 381.

Cefalù, Sicily. Clean, picturesque and an ideal family-friendly resort. See page 377.

The Gargano promontory, Puglia. The most attractive stretch of coastline on Italy's eastern seaboard. See page 345.

The Calabrian Coast, Tropea. Known as "the Capri of Calabria", is the most picturesque of a string of resorts with some fine beaches. See page 362.

Colourful Burano, an island in Venice's lagoon.

Il Gesù, also known as Casa Professa, Sicily's first Jesuit church.

Milan's exquisite Galleria Vittorio
Emanuele II shopping arcade.

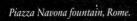
Piazza Navona fountain, Rome.

THE ETERNAL SEDUCTRESS

Italy, with her unrivalled beauty and baffling contradictions, continues to seduce and enchant those who are drawn to her.

Mask at Cagliari's Archaeological Museum, Sardinia.

taly, like the sorceress Circe, tantalisingly beautiful and at the same time treacherous, has attracted kings, scholars, saints, poets and curious travellers for centuries. This is the spell of the "Eternal Seductress".

Italy has always seemed somewhat removed from the rest of Europe: physically by mountains and sea, spiritually by virtue of the Pope. In the eyes of outsiders, the Italians themselves are characterised by extremes: at one end of the spectrum, the gentle unworldliness of St Francis, and, at the other, the amoral brilliance of Machiavelli; on the one hand, the curiosity of Galileo or the genius of Michelangelo, on the other, the repressive dogmatism of Counter-Reformation Jesuits.

Here you can explore the land and its people, from Calabrian villagers to Milanese sophisticates, and delve into their treasures, from Etruscan statues to Botticelli's radiant *Birth of Venus*. Special features celebrate Italian passions – films, fashion, opera and food – while the history section threads its way through a tumultuous past, from the legendary founding of Rome by Romulus and Remus to the Renaissance, reunification, Mussolini and the Mafia.

Mosaic inside Rome's Palazzo Massimo.

In Italy the past is always present: ultra-modern museums display pre-Roman artefacts; old people in tiny mountain villages preserve customs which are centuries old while their grandchildren roar into the future on shiny new Vespas.

This is the country that inspires imagination in the dull, passion in the cold-hearted, rebellion in the conventional. Whether you spend your sojourn in Italy under a brightly coloured beach umbrella on the Riviera, shopping in Milan or diligently examining churches and museums, you cannot be unchanged by Italy. At the very least, you will receive a highly pleasurable lesson in living. Whether you are struck by the beauty of a church facade rising from a perfectly proportioned piazza, the aroma of freshly carved *prosciutto*, or the sight of a stylish passer-by, there is the same superb sensation: nowhere else on earth does just living seem so extraordinary.

High-perched Calascibetta, Sicily. Sicily's diversity of landscape is unmatched by other Mediterranean islands.

WILD PLACES

**Italy is more than a glorified art museum.
Exploring its diverse landscapes can be just
as rewarding as the Renaissance art.**

Italy is full of Leonardo da Vinci landscapes
and Piero della Francesca views. The secret
is to choose an area that is off the beaten
track, but well mapped, well marked and not
too remote. If this sounds obvious, bear in
mind that Italian maps are notoriously unre-
liable outside the most popular walking areas
– meaning the Dolomites, Lombardy and parts
of Tuscany and Umbria – with the south largely
uncharted. The majority of Italy is mapped
with old Military Institute maps, designed for
aligning an artillery bombardment rather than
lining up a pretty view. If footpaths are marked,
there is no indication as to whether they are
private or public. With this in mind, companies
that organise walking holidays tend to produce
their own maps or take their own guides.

On the upside, there is little risk of being outnumbered by Italians on most trails. Curiously, as
far as independent walking is concerned, serious
hikers are better served than "Sunday walkers":
long-distance trails in the Dolomites are generally better marked and mapped than meanders
around Tuscany's hilltop hamlets. By the same
token, Italian hikers, where they exist, tend to be
found in "sporty" regions, especially in the north.
The rest can be found following the local *strada
dei sapori*, the food and wine trail – by car.

Charting the country

Before heading for the hills, lakes or coastal
marshes, get to grips with the geography. The
boot-shaped Italian peninsula spans 1,000km
(620 miles) from the Alps to the Mediterranean
and is bordered by the Ligurian and Tyrrhenian
seas to the west, the Ionian to the south and the
Adriatic to the east. If the Alps represent the
top of the boot, the jagged seam is formed by
the Apennines, while the toe, heel and spur are

Lago Toblino in the Italian Lakes.

represented by the Calabrian, Salento and Gargano peninsulas. Much of Italy is covered by
peaks, notably the Dolomites, which form part
of the Alps, the country's northern boundary.
These Alpine borders are shared with France,
Austria, Switzerland and Slovenia, with Monte
Bianco (Mont Blanc; 4,810 metres/15,780ft) on
the border with France marking the highest
point in Italy. The Dolomites are the defining
feature of Italy's Tyrolean Trentino-Alto Adige
region, and neighbouring Veneto, with the peaks
forming part of the world's largest integrated ski
network, the Dolomiti Superski. Instead, the
Apennines, the spine of Italy, stretch from north
to south, dividing the east and west coasts, and
bring a rugged climate to part of central Italy.

For lovers of seductive scenery, Italy dazzles: the north's national parks, true Alpine wilderness areas, give way to Piedmont's undulating farmland and patchwork of wine estates. The glittering lake district, framed by the jagged pinkish peaks of the Dolomites, creates the illusion of the Mediterranean meeting the mountains. Emilia's mundane farmland, coastal wetland and mountains lose out to Tuscany's Chiantishire, a gentle vision of olive groves, cypresses, vineyards and Medicean villa gardens. The rolling slopes are planted with olive groves that shimmer dark green and dusty silver.

Domesticated Tuscany melds with the hazy spirituality of Umbria's green hills, the serenity only frayed at the edges by wild stretches of the Apennines where wolves still roam.

Further south, Campania's natural wonders are as wild as Italy gets, from a smouldering volcano to belching, sulphurous springs and eerie lakes that myths refer to as the gateway to Hades.

The north

The Valle d'Aosta, concertinaed against the French border, is a patchwork of towering peaks and valleys in the northwestern corridor.

Odle Mountains and Val di Funes, South Tyrol.

HIKING AND CYCLING HEAVEN

The Giro d'Italia, Italy's version of the Tour de France, is proof of the country's passion for cycling. This now translates into thrilling new trails and cyclist-friendly schemes, particularly in the Dolomites, which abound in hotels and holidays designed with cyclists in mind. In central Italy, Emilia-Romagna is blazing a trail with cycle routes between "cities of art", such as Ravenna and Faenza. It is also home to Italy's most cycle-mad cities, Ferrara and Modena, and offers easily downloadable routes (www.ferraraterraeacqua.it). The south is less well served, but has the long-distance Bourbon Cycle Route, linking Bari and Naples via Matera. Liguria is superb cycling country but also has hiking trails of the stature of

the Cinque Terre paths (see page 25). The celebrated Poets' Trail, in the footsteps of Byron and Shelley, runs from Porto Venere to Lerici, through vineyards and olive groves, overlooking coastal cliffs and islands. Neighbouring Tuscany, Emilia and Umbria offer some of the country's most beguiling hikes, ranging from the Via Francigena pilgrimage route to foodie rambles between medieval abbeys and homely inns. Further south, Puglia embraces whitewashed villages, Adriatic seascapes and stays in the conical "beehive" homes known as *trulli*. Whether opting for a guided or self-guided break, book through a specialist operator, such as Headwater (www. headwater.com) or Inntravel (www.inntravel.co.uk).

Abutting it, Piedmont's craggy peaks loom over the region, which mellows into fertile foothills and feasts of truffles, nuts, fruit and powerful Barolo and Barbaresco wines. South of Turin, the Po Valley rises into the rolling Langhe and Roero hills, creating a carpet of vineyards and orchards. Further north lies metropolitan Milan, the gateway to Lombardy's lake district, watched over by the peaks and Alpine resorts beyond. Close to Lake Iseo, Franciacorta represents a chequerboard of prestigious vineyards while, to the south, Lombardy's fertile farmland comes into its own.

Italy's easternmost region, Friuli-Venezia Giulia, is a sliver of coastline across the Adriatic Sea from Venice. Were it not for the border-juggling that followed World War I, the region would probably be part of Slovenia today.

Lake Garda to the west and the River Po to the south. Orchards, river valleys and vineyards dot the region, which is noted for sparkling Prosecco, Valpolicella and Merlot. The bucolic

The stunning vista at Lake Maggiore in the Lakes district.

Bounded by Lombardy and the Veneto, Trentino-Alto Adige is serrated by soaring mountain ranges. The towering peaks of the Alps and the Dolomites preside over forested wilderness, Alpine pastures, meadows carpeted with wild flowers, vineyards in the foothills and orchards in the valleys. Alto Adige, the northernmost province, is Italy's South Tyrol, which belonged to Austria until the end of World War I. The area still resembles the Austrian Tyrol, while Trentino, the southern province, prides itself on looking more Italian.

East of Trentino, the Veneto stretches up into the apricot-tinged Dolomites and Cortina d'Ampezzo, the country's premier ski resort, but is bordered by the Adriatic to the east,

Brenta Canal winds languidly through the noble countryside, with Palladian villas lining the banks.

Framed by the Alps, and stretching from Piedmont across northern Lombardy to the Veneto, the lake district offers stunning scenery. West of Bergamo, the most appealing lakes are Como, Maggiore and Orta, matched by Iseo and Garda to the east. In terms of scenery, cognoscenti consider Como the most beguiling lake, Maggiore the most stately and Orta the most mystical. With its snow-clad peaks, romantic scenery and sluggish steamers, Como still stirs visitors, while on the Borromean Islands, Lake Maggiore boasts the grandest gardens. Pocket-sized Iseo possesses the biggest lake island in

Europe but is Alpine in character, with olives and horse chestnuts rather than lemon groves and palm trees. Lake Garda remains a Mediterranean hothouse in northern climes. The old charm lingers on in the avenues lined by palms, oleanders and camellias, as well as in the profusion of lemon groves, vineyards and Italy's most northerly olive groves.

Protected by the Alps and perched on a crescent-shaped sliver of coast, Ligurian resorts enjoy balmy weather, with the Riviera di Levante, east of Genoa, comprising the rockier, wilder stretch, especially around Le Cinque Terre.

lives up to its name in densely forested slopes, misty valleys, tufa-stone outcrops and its sense of remoteness.

Compared with the brooding, dramatic landscape of Abruzzo, one of Italy's last wildernesses, Lazio is less homogeneous, from the Apennine peaks in the north to marshland in the south, via volcanic lakes, vineyards and misty, undulating hills reminiscent of Umbria, which it borders.

The south

In Campania, south of Rome, the crescent-shaped Bay of Naples contains unspoilt Capri

Tuscan landscape south of Siena.

The centre

Just east, Emilia-Romagna embraces the Po Valley, from coastal marshes to vineyards, as well as farmland dedicated to the production of Parmesan cheese and Parma ham. Its neighbour, Tuscany, has been landscaped since time immemorial, with the Val d'Orcia, south of Siena, representing quintessential Tuscany: clusters of cypresses, ribbons of plane trees, vineyards on the slopes, farms perched on limestone ridges. Towards the Emilian border, Tuscany becomes more rugged, dramatised by deep forests, Michelangelo's marble quarries and the Apuan Alps around Garfagnana.

Umbria, "the green heart of Italy" (and the only landlocked region of the Italian peninsula)

THE PEACE PATH

Head to the hills, where diversity in landscape is matched by the drama of the human story. The most poignant long-distance trail has to be the Peace Path, a 350km (217-mile) trail that hugs what was the Austro-Italian frontline during World War I. The landscape runs from jagged rocks to cool lakes and meadows, passing lofty forts with gun emplacements built into the rock. For information on the Dolomites trails and "The Legendary Trails" (one of the country's best series of mountain hikes), contact www.visittrentino.it. For information on all long-distance trails, contact the CAI, the Italian Alpine Club (www.cai.it).

The locals generally only see walking as an adjunct to eating, with family expeditions focused on finding the best funghi porcini rather than the best view. The countryside is a larder rather than a living landscape.

and volcanic Ischia, two of Italy's loveliest islands. On the Amalfi Coast, buildings are cantilevered above rock-studded cliffs and overlook the country's most romantic coastal drive. Campania's Cilento national park is a patchwork of wheatfields and olive groves, though wolves and wild cats survive in remote corners.

Further east, Puglia, the "heel" of the Italian boot, is the gateway to Greece, and is washed by both the Ionian and Adriatic seas. Puglia produces more wine and olive oil than any other region yet is also a riot of carob trees and rosemary, with marine grottoes and turquoise seas framed by sun-bleached beaches and wind-twisted pines.

Forming the toe of the Italian peninsula, sparsely populated Calabria is crushed between the mountains and the sea. It is notable for the Pollino park, the richest repository of wildlife in the south, in a wilderness setting ranging from canyons to rivers, high plains to soaring peaks.

Just over the Strait awaits Sicily, as mountainous as it is mysterious. Partly thanks to its volcanic soil, the island is a major wine producer, including around Mount Etna.

The Mount Etna volcanic park presents myriad safe and accessible options for exploring this most haunting of sites. Volcanic activity is the earth's indigestion, with deep rumblings producing sudden eruptions, emitting sulphurous gases and scalding vapours through cracks in the earth's surface. Further along the Tyrrhenian Coast, the compact Zingaro reserve, west of Palermo, is a gentle introduction to Sicily's charms.

Walking country

Foremost among Italy's long-distance trails is the Via Alpina, which links Trieste and the Adriatic to the Mediterranean. This great transalpine trail crosses eight countries but, in the Italian Dolomites, touches upon Europe's shared Alpine heritage. It runs through the legendary landscape of the Fassa Dolomites, linked to the Ladin people, who speak an archaic version of Latin. Beyond is the land of Oetzi the Ice Man, taking us back to prehistoric times, a reminder that this path traces a common Alpine heritage. Just north of Canazei, the trail crosses Passo Pordoi, the majestic Alpine pass that marks Trentino's borders with the Veneto, revealing vestiges of World War I fortifications and views over the Sella group. Rewards come in the form of rosy-hued sunsets, the striking Marmolada glacier and the lunar landscape of the Catinaccio group. Fortunately, this Alpine area is blessed with exceptional lodges and cable-car networks –

Hiking in the Dolomites.

the answer to your prayers when your bed is at the top of the next peak.

In Liguria, the best-known trails lie in the rugged Cinque Terre, the Unesco-protected stretch of coast that encompasses olive-growing terraces and quaint fishing villages. The "Blue Trail" (Sentiero Azzurro) clings to the coast for 13km (8 miles) from Riomaggiore to Monterosso. Its popularity means that it is best not undertaken in the height of the summer.

Further down the coast, in Tuscany, the drained marshes of the Maremma include an unspoilt coastal park with deep Etruscan roots, and white cattle watched over by the *butteri*, Tuscan cowboys. Umbria's Sibillini park, which marks the watershed between the Adriatic and the Tyrrhenian, is home to wild boar, wolves and peregrine falcons, though botanists are keener on the orchids and Alpine anemone. Both parks have way-marked trails.

On the Adriatic Coast, the Po Delta coastal wetlands, studded with nature reserves and abbeys, form a Unesco heritage site and one of the wildest areas in central Italy. This mosaic of marshes, dunes, mudflats and islands is dubbed the Italian Camargue: sturdy white ponies share the marshes with migratory birds and waterfowl. Birdlife abounds on the

peaches and strawberries took over. Since this is farming and wine-growing country, walkers will spot asparagus beds, rice paddies, hemp-growing and even vineyards.

The peaks, forests and lakes of the Parco d'Abruzzo, dominated by the Apennines and laced with trails, are home to 40 species of mammal and 300 types of bird, from Apennine wolves to golden eagles.

Further south, in Puglia's Gargano promontory, the northern salt lakes provide a haven for wildfowl. The Gargano – a thickly wooded peninsula that juts out into the Adriatic to form

Hiking trail on Capri.

In terms of gentle walks though coastal scenery, chic Capri has, paradoxically, one of the wildest trails, embracing macchia mediterranea shrubland, as well as ocean views, glimpsed through exotic agave and bougainvillea.

mudflats, from cormorants, coots and reed warblers to white egrets and purple herons. Scenic trails criss-cross the park between Ferrara and Comacchio, from locks and flood plains to the raised canal banks which serve as cycle trails. The salt pans are flanked by wind-mills, a reminder of the time before pumpkins,

the spur of Italy's boot – was an island until river sediment formed a "bridge" linking it to the mainland. Reached via an old pilgrimage route, the wilder parts of the peninsula have a timeless quality, from the pine groves to the coastline of cliffs, rocks and caves.

In the south, the best trail is the Sentiero Italia, which begins in Montalto, in Calabria's Parco dell'Aspromonte, and runs along the spine of the Apennines until Umbria and even as far as Trieste.

Volcano-watching

Italy's volcanic parks make fascinating places to explore, from the eerie lunar landscape of Etna to the mud baths on the gorgeous Aeolian

Italy's wildlife has been decimated by hunting, but this trend is being fought fiercely in Abruzzo. In the Parco d'Abruzzo bears have been successfully re-introduced, as have chamois in Gran Sasso, while wolves are protected in the Majella park.

Set off the north coast of Sicily, the seven Aeolian Islands have a stark volcanic allure and a striking natural beauty. The archipelago's appeal lies in the marine life and underwater lava formations, as well as sulphurous Vulcano and Stromboli, "the lighthouse of the Mediterranean", which glows incandescently at night and shoots fireballs. Locals refer to Stromboli as "Iddu, a good friend with a volcanic temper; he sleeps just like us, he lives just like us." Iddu's intoxicating explosions have occurred every 15 minutes for the past 2,500 years.

archipelago. Although Vulcano is set in one of the most beautiful archipelagos in the Mediterranean, visitors are assailed by a sulphurous, rotten-egg stench. Ignoring the limpid

Sicily has a volcanic hinterland.

seas, bathers squat in a stinking mud hole and smear smelly gloop over their bodies. This yellow volcanic soup and foul-smelling mud are common to many volcanic areas. As for Naples, Vesuvius may be an active volcano, but you can still visit the rim of the crater's mouth and gaze down into its smouldering core. The approach is dramatic, passing vineyards that produce the amber-hued Lacrimae Christi (Tears of Christ), a wine favoured by the ancient Etruscans. The puce-tinged summit induces a feeling of foreboding, but when gazing into the volcano's core, spare a thought for Spartacus, who, a century before the eruption that buried Pompeii, hid in the hollow of the crater, which was then covered with vines.

THE SAN REMO COASTAL TRAIL

A spectacular cycle-pedestrian path hugs the picturesque Ligurian Coast close to the French Riviera. The first 24km (17-mile) stretch, from Ospedaletti via San Remo to San Lorenzo al Mare, offers an exhilarating Riviera route. Divided into five sections, the coastal path follows a disused railway line and wends its way through former fishing villages. The path provides access to previously unreachable beaches and a marine park, which acts as a whale sanctuary. With the Mediterranean on one side and the Alps on the other, the cycle path is one of the loveliest in Europe, and the first on the Italian coast (www.area24spa.it).

The Pantheon, Rome.

DECISIVE DATES

Romulus and Remus, the mythical founders of Rome.

Origins to the Roman Empire

2000–1200 BC
Tribes from Central Europe and Asia, the Villanovans, settle in northern Italy.

c.800 BC
Etruscans arrive in Italy.

753 BC
Legendary date of Rome's founding.

750 BC
Greeks start to colonise southern Italy.

509 BC
Rome becomes a republic.

390 BC
Gauls sack Rome, but are expelled.

343–264 BC
Rome gains ascendancy in Italy.

264–146 BC
Punic Wars; Rome extends conquests abroad.

58–48 BC
Caesar conquers Gaul, then crosses the Rubicon, occupies Rome and is made dictator.

44 BC
Caesar assassinated.

27 BC
Octavius proclaimed Princeps, as Augustus Caesar; start of Pax Romana.

AD 96–180
Golden century of peace; empire reaches its greatest extent.

303
Persecution of Christians under Diocletian.

306–337
Constantine makes Christianity the state religion and Constantinople the capital.

393
The empire is divided into Eastern and Western halves.

5th century
Invasions by Visigoths, Huns, Vandals and Ostrogoths.

410
Sack of Rome by Alaric the Goth.

476
End of the Western Roman Empire.

Medieval Italy

535–53
Justinian brings all Italy within rule of Eastern emperor.

568
Lombards overrun much of Italy; peninsula divided into Lombard state, ruled from Pavia and Byzantine province centred at Ravenna.

800
Charlemagne crowned Holy Roman Emperor and founds Carolingian Empire.

Charlemagne.

Benozzo Gozzoli's Journey of the Magi (1459), in which members of the Medici family are depicted among the royal retinue.

827
Saracens capture Sicily.

9th century
Carolingian Empire disbands, leaving behind rival Italian states.

951
951 Saxon King Otto I becomes King of the Lombards; the following year he is crowned Holy Roman Emperor.

11th century
Normans colonise Sicily and southern Italy.

1076
Pope Gregory VII and Emperor Henry IV become embroiled in a power struggle that marks the start of a 200-year conflict between the papacy and imperial powers.

1155
Guelphs, supporting the Pope, clash with the Ghibellines, who follow the emperor.

1167
Lombard League of cities formed to oppose the emperor.

1227–50
The papacy is the victor.

Late Middle Ages and Renaissance

1265
Charles of Anjou becomes King of Sicily.

1302
Anjou dynasty established in Naples.

1309–77
Papacy established at Avignon then returns to Rome.

1442
Alfonso V, King of Aragon, is crowned King of the "Two Sicilies" (Naples and Sicily).

1469–92
Lorenzo de' Medici leads Florence; apogee of the Renaissance.

1494
Wars of Italy begin with invasion by French King Charles VII invades; Medici driven from Florence.

Centuries of Foreign Despotism

1503–13
Julius II is pope; Rome is centre of the Renaissance.

1527
Rome sacked by Charles V's imperial troops; Venice is the centre of artistic activity.

1559
Treaty confirms Spanish control of Italy.

1700–13
Austria becomes main foreign power on peninsula.

1796–1814
Napoleon invades Italy, brings ideals of French Revolution and founds several republics.

1814
Overthrow of French rule.

Towards Italian Unity

1815
Congress of Vienna; Venice given to Austria.

1848
Uprisings against Austria led by Charles Albert, Duke of Savoy.

1859–60
With the help of France, Savoy annexes most of northern Italy. Garibaldi's "Thousand" conquer Sicily and Naples.

1861
Victor Emmanuel II of Savoy proclaimed King of Italy.

1870
Unification completed; Rome becomes capital.

Modern Italy

1882
Triple Alliance agreed between Italy, Germany and Austria.

1900
Anarchist assassinates King Umberto I. Victor Emmanuel III is crowned king.

1915
Italy joins Allies in World War I.

1919
Rise of Fascism.

1935
War against Ethiopia.

1940
Italy joins Nazi Germany in World War II.

1943
Allies land in Sicily. Mussolini deposed, rescued by Germans to found puppet government in the north.

1944
Liberation of Rome; abdication of King Victor Emmanuel III.

1946
Italy declared a republic.

1957
Treaty of Rome: Italy joins the Common Market as one of six founder members.

1950s–60s
Italy's "economic miracle".

1966
Floods in Venice and Florence.

1978
Former premier Aldo Moro is kidnapped and killed. Period of political instability.

1980
Earthquake strikes Campania.

1990s
Rise of the Northern League and corruption scandals.

2000
Millions flock to Rome for Holy Year.

2001
Silvio Berlusconi elected prime minister.

2002
The euro becomes the official currency in Italy.

2005
Pope John Paul II dies and is succeeded by Benedict XVI.

The 1922 March on Rome saw Mussolini's Fascist Party take over control of the country.

Matteo Renzi, prime minister from 2014 to 2016.

2009
A 6.3-magnitude earthquake strikes L'Aquila killing 308 people.

2010
Pompeii's House of the Gladiators collapses. State neglect is blamed.

2011
Berlusconi resigns and Mario Monti appointed as prime minister.

2012
Earthquake in Emilia-Romagna kills 16, more than 200 injured. Spain and Italy are bailed out as euro debt crisis deepens.

2013
Pope Francis succeeds the resigning Pope Benedict XVI. Enrico Letta becomes prime minister; Giorgio Napolitano is re-elected president. Former PM Silvio Berlusconi is expelled from parliament after his conviction over tax fraud is upheld by Italy's Supreme Court. Over 300 immigrants die as their boat sinks near the Italian island of Lampedusa.

2014
Matteo Renzi becomes prime minister of a left-right coalition government and embarks on major political and economic reforms.

2015
Sergio Mattarella is the first Sicilian to become Italy's president following Giorgio Napolitano's retirement. Parliament passes an electoral reform granting the largest party an automatic majority of seats in the lower house. Immigration crisis intensifies as more than 1,500 immigrants perish trying to reach Italy by boat.

2016
A 6.2-magnitude earthquake destroys Amatrice, a town in central Italy, killing nearly 300 people; a few months later a 6.6-magnitude earthquake strikes in nearby Norcia. Same-sex union is legalised. PM Matteo Renzi resigns after losing the referendum he called on proposed major constitutional reforms. He is replaced by fellow centre-leftist Paolo Gentiloni and early elections to be called in 2017.

Posters for the 2016 referendum, which resulted in the resignation of Matteo Renzi.

An Etruscan statue of Apollo.

BEGINNINGS

Many primitive tribes settled in Italy, but under the Greeks and the Etruscans it became the centre of the ancient world.

As schoolchildren often observe, Italy looks like a boot. The long, narrow peninsula sticking out of Europe's underbelly is perpetually poised to kick Sicily westward. This peculiar shape made Italy a natural site for settlement. The Alps, which cut across the only land link with the rest of Europe, protected the peninsula from the barbarians who roamed northern Europe, while the Mediterranean, which surrounds the three remaining sides, served as a highway, first to bring civilisation to the peninsula and later to export it.

The Apennine range, the so-called backbone of Italy, dominates the peninsula. These mountains zigzag down from the French Alps and Ligurian Coast in the northwest, through northern Tuscany and southeast to the Adriatic Coast, and veer west again to the Strait of Messina, between Sicily and the toe of the boot. In the central Abruzzo region, the peaks of the Gran Sasso soar as high as 2,912 metres (9,700ft).

The Tiber, Arno, Livi and Volturno are easily navigated by small craft, and their valleys provide easy communication between the coast and the interior. What is more, the plains of Tuscany, Latium and Campania comprise fertile farmland, thanks to rich deposits of volcanic ash.

Villanovan civilisation

Around 200,000 years before the founding of Rome, only cave-dwelling hunter-gatherers lived on the Italian peninsula. However, with the Indo-European migrations (2000–1200 BC), tribes of primitive peoples poured into Italy from Central Europe and Asia. The Villanovan tribes were farmers who lived in round

Greek temple at Selinunte in Sicily.

THE ETRUSCANS

The Etruscans were skilled craftsmen, seafarers and merchants who traded with the Greeks and later the Romans, who assimilated them. Etruria, the Etruscan civilisation, flourished as a confederation of 12 city-states, tribes which gathered together to celebrate sacred rites. Divination and sacrifice were used to stave off divine retribution. Spirituality was balanced by a hearty appetite for life. Hundreds of Etruscan tombs have survived, with wall paintings depicting dancing, banqueting, music-making, battle and hunting scenes. The Etruscans exerted a dynamic influence on Roman art and were praised as "founders of cities".

huts clustered in small villages in central Italy. These Italic, Iron Age settlers worked tools and cremated their dead, placing the ashes in tall, clay or bronze urns.

Villanovan culture spread from its original centre around Bologna south to Tuscany and Latium. Nowhere, however, did settlements grow to the size of towns, and Villanovans are not known for any great artistic achievements.

The Greeks and the Etruscans established communities on the peninsula in the early 8th century BC. Greek colonists settled in Sicily and on the west coast near modern-day Naples.

The colonists prospered, farming the land around their cities, and trading with mainland Greece.

During the 5th century, both Syracuse and Athens tried to establish rival empires out of the Greek colonies in Italy. Numerous battles were fought and many Italian natives were drafted as soldiers. But after years of inconclusive fighting the Greek leaders gave up the struggle.

The colonists still argued among themselves, and therefore failed to become a dominant political power in Italy. They did, however, become the major cultural and artistic force.

Men enjoying a banquet in a fresco at Paestum.

Most came in search of land to farm, for Greece had insufficient arable land to feed its entire population. Others were political refugees: whenever a Greek king was overthrown, all his followers were forced to flee.

On arriving in Italy, Greek settlers formed independent cities, each loosely linked to their city of origin on the Greek mainland. One of the earliest colonies was at Cumae, by the Bay of Naples. Greeks from Euboea, an island northeast of Athens, settled there in about 770 BC. Other Euboeans founded Rhegion (modern Reggio di Calabria), at the tip of the boot, a few years later. The Corinthian city of Syracuse on Sicily ultimately became the most powerful of the Greek colonies.

> It is no coincidence that the early inhabitants of Italy flourished in the west, on the lowland plains north and south of Rome. Here there are a few natural harbours and long rivers.

Italian natives were eager to trade for Greek luxury goods, the like of which they had never seen. Soon Greek bronze and ceramic ware became widely available in Italy and provided the natives with sophisticated new art forms to imitate; the architecture and sculpture in the Greek cities also served as models. The civilising influence of the Greeks went beyond the visual arts. The natives adapted the

The transformation of Italy from a primitive backwater to the centre of the ancient world was due to the Greeks and the Etruscans. Both sailed across the sea in search of rich new land and sowed the first seeds of civilisation.

Greek alphabet for their own Indo-European tongues and each native group soon had its own letters. Through example, the Greeks also taught the Italian natives about modern war-

by DNA analysis on Etruscan bones, suggests Middle Eastern origins. But wherever the migrants came from, it was the intermingling with the Italic tribes that created the uniquely Etruscan civilisation.

Vital trade routes

Each Etruscan city supported itself by trade. Eager to obtain luxury goods from the Greek colonists, the Etruscans developed overland routes to reach the Greek cities. These cut straight through Latium, the plain south of the Tiber occupied by Italian natives called Latins.

Remains of an Etruscan necropolis in Sutri, Lazio.

fare, lessons that they later used against their Greek teachers. The Italians learnt how to fortify towns with high walls of smooth masonry, and discovered the value of shock-troop tactics with armoured spearmen.

But exceptional wealth and knowledge did not enable the Greeks to control Italy, and failure to unify the natives under Greek leadership left great political opportunities wide open.

In about 800 BC, Etruscans settled on the west coast where Tuscany (Etruria) and Lazio are today. The origins of the Etruscans still puzzle scholars. The Greek historian Herodotus claimed that they came from Asia Minor, driven by revolution and famine at home to seek new lands. More recent research, backed

One of their trading posts on the route south was a Latin village called Rome, originally only a cluster of mud huts. Under the influence of the Etruscans, the settlement flourished. They drained the swamp that became the Roman Forum and built grand palaces and roads.

For 300 years from the late 8th century BC, Etruscan kings ruled Rome. But, by the 5th century BC, their power was fading. In the north, Gauls overran Etruscan settlements in the Po Valley. Next, Italic tribesmen from Abruzzo threatened the main Etruscan cities. Then, in the south, the Etruscans went to war against the Greeks. The Romans chose this moment to rebel against their Etruscan masters.

The *Augustus of Prima Porta* shows a youthful emperor looking to Rome's future of *imperium sine fine* (rule without end).

ROME RULES THE WORLD

Between its legendary founding by Romulus and its sacking by barbarians, Rome presided over one of the world's greatest civilisations.

The historians of Ancient Rome wrote their own version of events leading to the overthrow of the Etruscan kings. They drew upon legends of Rome's past and claimed that the city had only temporarily fallen under Etruscan rule. According to legend, Rome was founded by the descendants of gods and heroes.

In his epic, the *Aeneid*, Virgil tells how Aeneas, a hero of Homeric Troy, journeyed west after the sack of Troy to live and rule in Latium. In the 8th century one of his descendants, the Latin princess Rhea Silvia, bore twin sons, Romulus and Remus, fathered by the god Mars. Her uncle, King Amulius, angry because the princess had broken her vow of chastity as a Vestal Virgin, locked her up and abandoned the boys on the riverbank to die. They were found there by a she-wolf which raised them. As young men, the brothers led a band of rebel Latin youths to find a new home. As they approached the hills of Rome, a flight of eagles passed overhead – a sign from the gods that this was an auspicious site for their new city.

Rape and revolt

Rome was ruled by Etruscan kings until 509 BC when the son of King Tarquinius Superbus raped a Roman noblewoman, Lucretia. She killed herself in shame and Roman noblemen rose in revolt against the Etruscans.

The leader of the Roman revolt, Lucius Junius Brutus, may have been an actual historical figure. In Roman legend he is the founder of a republic, a vigorous leader, and a puritanical ruler. The historian Tacitus wrote that he was so loyal to Rome that he watched without flinching as his two sons were executed for treason.

In the war against the Etruscans, Rome was also aided by Cincinnatus, a simple Roman

Hannibal's Carthaginian forces cross the Alps during the Second Punic War.

farmer who left his plough to help his city. He was so able that he rose quickly to the rank of general. But once the fight was won, he surrendered his position of power and returned to his life as an ordinary citizen.

These stories of Rome's early heroes reveal a lot about the Roman character. For the Romans, *pietas* – dutiful respect to one's gods, city, parents and comrades – was all-important. Because of this, the heroes of legend were very useful propaganda tools within the empire.

Upon the overthrow of the Etruscans, Rome's leaders founded a republic based on the Greek model, and the Senate took control of the city.

Roman conquests

During the next 200 years Rome conquered most of the Italian peninsula. But Carthage, a city in North Africa founded by the Phoenicians, controlled the western Mediterranean. If Rome was to expand, Carthage had to be defeated.

The initial clash between the two cities, the First Punic War (264 BC), began as a struggle for the Greek city of Messina on Sicily. By the time it was over, in 241 BC, the Romans had driven the Carthaginians out of Sicily completely. The island became Rome's first province. Three years later Rome annexed Sardinia and Corsica,

Julius Caesar was not the first to put his face on a coin, but he is the most famous.

and further military triumphs followed. When Rome conquered Cisalpine Gaul (northern Italy) and extended its borders to the Alps, it alleviated the threat of invasion by the Gauls.

War broke out again in 218 BC when the brilliant Carthaginian general Hannibal embarked on an ambitious plan to attack Rome from the north via Spain, the Pyrenees and the Alps. Rome eventually counterattacked Carthage, and Hannibal was forced to return and defend his homeland. He was defeated in 202 BC.

Final defeat of Carthage

The Third Punic War was almost an afterthought. Carthage, stripped of many of its

> *Carthage represented Rome's most formidable opponent, and took the Romans to the brink of defeat. The battles between the two powers helped forge the Roman legions and navies into the Mediterranean's supreme fighting force.*

possessions 50 years earlier, had regained its commercial power. When the Carthaginians challenged Rome indirectly, the Romans razed the city of Carthage and ploughed salt into the soil. The Carthaginians were sold into slavery.

Rome was now more prosperous than ever before, but only the middle class and the rich benefited. For the common people, many of whom had served their city faithfully during the wars, peace meant greater poverty as the menial jobs on which they had depended were now filled by slaves. Independent farmers, who traditionally formed the backbone of the Roman state, sold their land to the owners of great estates, who used slaves to work it. These displaced farmers joined the Roman mob or wandered through Italy seeking work.

The Senate's usual way of dealing with potentially explosive situations was to feed the masses bread and entertain them with circuses. But eventually a patrician, Tiberius Gracchus, challenged the exploitative system. Elected tribune in 133 BC, he campaigned to reintroduce a law limiting the size of the great estates, and proposed redistributing state-owned farming and grazing land among the poor. The Senators, many of them wealthy landowners, blocked Gracchus' plan, and when he persisted and ran for re-election as tribune they engaged assassins to murder him and his supporters.

Gaius the populist

Gracchus' spirit did not die with him. Eleven years later, his brother Gaius was elected tribune. An effective speaker, he was popular with the Roman masses. Once in office, he called for sweeping land reform. Again the Senate struck back viciously. The Roman people were incited to riot, and Gaius was blamed. He was killed or forced to kill himself (the records are not clear), and his followers were imprisoned.

The power of the army commanders now became the determining factor in Roman politics. The general Gaius Marius, son of a farmer, returned to Rome from triumphant campaigns in Africa determined to smash the power of the despised Senate. To the Roman people, Gaius Marius was a god-like figure who had transformed the Roman citizen legions into a professional army. He and his supporters butchered the senatorial leaders and thousands of aristocratic Romans.

This fateful action, taken in the name of liberty, opened the way to dictatorship. The Senate turned to Sulla, a rival general and a patrician by birth, who answered Marius' violence with a bloodbath of his own. Sulla returned to Rome and ruled as absolute dictator. The Senate could

agreement aimed at preserving their power. This arrangement was successful until Crassus died in 53 BC, and the two remaining leaders quarrelled. For several years Pompey and Caesar eyed each other warily. Then, in 49 BC, Caesar, after his successful campaign in Gaul, led his army across the flooded Rubicon River (the border between Cisalpine Gaul and Italy), against the orders of the Senate. With Caesar heading for Rome, Pompey left for Greece, taking his own army and most of the Senate with him. But Caesar moved first. He attacked Pompey's allies in Spain, then in Greece, forc-

Emperor Augustus built the Ara Pacis to celebrate peace.

put no check on him for it had opened the door for him to take power. The Republic was effectively dead, the victim of three centuries of empire building.

Enter Pompey the Great

For two years the streets of Rome ran with blood. But in 79 BC Sulla grew tired of ruling and retired to his estate near Naples. Civil war broke out again. Sulla's successor was another general, Gnaeus Pompeius, called Pompey the Great. He restored many liberties suspended by Sulla, but failed to go far enough for the rioting masses.

Pompey's solution was to join forces with two other military men, Crassus and Julius Caesar, and form Triumvirate, an unofficial

ing Pompey to flee to Egypt, where he was eventually killed in 48 BC.

Caesar returned to Rome in triumph. The masses thought his victories proved he was divinely appointed to rule Rome. For the first time in decades there were no riots in the capital. But the upper classes were wary of Caesar's autocratic tendencies. A conspiracy formed against him.

After Caesar's death, Mark Antony, Caesar's co-consul, and Octavian, his grand-nephew, joined forces to pursue and kill the conspirators. Despite their cooperation, the two were never good friends. Initially they collaborated with a Caesarian patrician, Lepidus, to form a formal but uneasy Second Triumvirate, but the arrangement faltered when Antony fell in love with the Egyptian queen Cleopatra and rejected his wife, Octavian's sister, to marry her. In revenge, Octavian turned the Senate against Mark Antony, then declared war on his former partner. When defeat was imminent, Antony and Cleopatra committed suicide.

Augustus and the Pax Romana

Octavian's triumphant return to Rome marked the beginning of a new era. He called himself simply "Augustus", meaning "the revered one", but in fact he was the first emperor of Rome.

this challenge Augustus created a personal bureaucracy within his household. In addition to footmen and maids, he also had tax collectors, governors, census takers and administrators as his "servants". He allowed this personal civil service to grow to a size sufficient to run the empire, but kept it under tight control.

With peace, art and literature flourished. The poet Virgil, who had lived through the civil wars and military dictatorships, paid tribute to Augustus' achievements in the *Aeneid*; the poet Horace likened the emperor to a helmsman who had steered the ship of state into a safe

Pollice Verso ('Thumbs Down') by Jean-Léon Gérôme, 1872.

Unlike his grand-uncle before him, he took care not to offend the republican sentiments of the Romans, and therein lay the key to his success. He allowed the Senate the outward trappings of power and influence, but little of the reality. Uninterested in status symbols or ostentation, he lived and dressed simply. The competence and sensitivity with which Augustus reigned made for an unprecedented period of peace, order and prosperity; for some 200 years after Augustan reform, the Mediterranean world basked in a *Pax Romana*, a Roman peace.

Before Augustus assumed power, the republican institutions had been unable to administer the vast territories Rome now controlled. Military dictatorship had been the result. To meet

BEWARE THE IDES OF MARCH

An Etruscan soothsayer had warned Caesar to beware of misfortune that would strike no later than 15 March 44 BC. On that day – the Ides of March – Caesar was scheduled to address the Senate. On his way to the Senate chamber he passed the soothsayer. Caesar remarked that the Ides had come safely. The Etruscan replied that the day was not yet over. In the chamber, Caesar was surrounded by conspirators and stabbed 23 times. When he saw that Marcus Junius Brutus, a patrician he had treated like a son, was among his murderers, he murmured "Et tu, Brute?" ("You too, Brutus?") and died.

port. Augustus himself took part in the artistic resurgence and set about rebuilding the capital. He claimed that he had found Rome a city of brick and left it a city of marble.

Augustus reigned for 41 years and set the tone of Roman leadership for the next 150. None of his successors had his ability, but his institutional and personal legacy did much to preserve peace in the flourishing Roman world.

The mad and the bad

The Emperor Tiberius had none of his step-father's sense of proportion, nor his steadiness. He began his reign with good intentions, but he mismanaged many early problems. He spent the last 11 years of his reign at his villa on Capri, from where he issued a volley of execution orders. The historian Suetonius wrote (in the translation by Robert Graves), "Not a day, however holy, passed without an execution; he even desecrated New Year's Day. Many of his victims were accused and punished with their children – some actually by their children – and the relatives forbidden to go into mourning."

Rome was relieved when Tiberius died, only to find that there was worse to come. Caligula, his successor, ruled ably for three years, then ran wild. He insisted that he was a god, formed his own priesthood and erected a temple to himself. He proposed his horse be made consul. Finally a group of his own officers assassinated Caligula, and Rome was rid of its most hated ruler.

The officers took it upon themselves to name the next emperor. Their choice was Claudius, grandson of Augustus, whom they found hiding behind a curtain in the palace after the assassination. Many thought Claudius a fool, for he stuttered and was slightly crippled, but he proved a good and steady ruler. He oversaw the reform of the civil service, and the expansion of the Roman Empire to include Britain.

Claudius was poisoned by his ambitious wife Agrippina, who pushed Nero, her son by a previous marriage, onto the throne. Like Tiberius before him, Nero started out with good intentions. He was well educated, an accomplished musician, and showed respect for the advice of others, especially senators. But the violent side of his nature soon became apparent. He poisoned Britannicus, Claudius' natural son, and tried to do the same to his mother, but she had taken the precaution of building up an immunity to the

poison. In the end Nero accused her of plotting against him, and had her executed.

Nero's excesses caused alarm among Rome's citizens. When a fire destroyed the city in AD 64, he was accused of starting it. In fact, he was away from the city at the time and stories of him fid-

> Augustus, first emperor of Rome, outlawed prostitution and drunkenness and strengthened divorce laws. He also built a vast civil service to administer his harmonious realm.

Villa Jovis, on the isle of Capri, where Tiberius spent the last years of his life.

dling while Rome burned are probably untrue.

Nero lost his throne after the Roman commanders in Gaul, Africa and Spain rebelled. With no hope left, Nero killed himself in AD 68. His suicide threw the empire into greater turmoil. He left no heir and therefore the rebellious commanders fought amongst themselves for a year until a legion commander, Flavius Vespasian, emerged as emperor.

Vespasian proved a wise emperor, and his rule ushered in a period of peace. There was a short time of troubles when his son, Domitian, became emperor but, by the time he died, the Senate was powerful enough to appoint its own emperor, Nerva, a respected lawyer from Rome.

Nerva was the first of the "five good emperors" who reigned from AD 96 to 180, a period known as Pax Romana. He was followed by Trajan, Hadrian, Antoninus Pius and Marcus Aurelius – all educated men, interested in philosophy and devoted to their duties. They were loved by the people of Rome for administering their vast empire well and successfully defending its borders.

Decline and fall

During the period between the death of Marcus Aurelius and the sack of Rome in the 5th cen-

Fragments of an enormous statue of Constantine in the Musei Capitolini.

"Within a short time you forget everything, and everything forgets you," declared Marcus Aurelius. But the glories of Rome have survived as the finest memorial to the imperial builders.

tury, it became increasingly difficult to defend the empire from barbarians. Between AD 180 and 285, Rome was threatened in both the east and the west by barbarian tribes. The empire doubled the size of the army. The drain on manpower and resources caused an economic crisis, and the powerful army could place emperors on the throne and remove them at will. Most of these "barracks emperors" served for less than three years and never even lived in the capital. Plague also struck Rome, which weakened the empire and made it more vulnerable to enemy

Constantine's conversion established Christianity, which had been spreading through the empire since the time of Nero, as the religion of the Roman state and thus of the Western world.

attack. On all sides wars raged. In the east, the revived Persian Empire threatened Syria, Egypt and all of Asia Minor. In the west, Franks invaded France and Spain.

Major political reform was undertaken by Emperor Diocletian in 286. He believed the empire could no longer be ruled by one man, so he divided it into eastern and western region. He chose Nicomedia in Asia Minor as his capital and appointed a soldier named Maximinus to rule the west from Milan.

Unfortunately this arrangement did not end quarrels about the succession. Constantine marched on Rome in 311 to assert his right to the throne. While on the road, however, he claimed he had a vision. The sign of the cross appeared in the sky with the words: "By this sign win your victory." As a result, when Constantine defeated his rival, Maxentius, and emerged as the sole emperor, he ruled as a Christian and granted religious freedom to existing Christians.

In 324, Constantine confirmed Christianity as the state religion. Not all citizens followed the new faith; some notable families remained true to their pagan beliefs. Under his auspices, and in the decades that followed, the first Christian churches of Rome were built. These included the earliest constructions of the five patriarchal churches of which the Pope himself was the priest: San Pietro (St Peter's), San Giovanni in Laterano, San Paolo fuori le Mura, San Lorenzo fuori le Mura and Santa Maria Maggiore.

Despite the conversion to Christianity, the empire continued to decline. In 330, Constantine decided to move the capital east, and make a fresh start in his new city of Constantinople. Back in Italy, the barbarians gradually moved closer. The city of Rome was sacked in 410.

Life in the Empire

Ancient Rome was a codified, class-conscious society, but beneath the veneer lay a devotion to pleasure and property – like Rome today.

In more than 60 treatises on morality, Plutarch (AD 46–126) laid down what was expected of a Roman gentleman. It was a damnable luxury to strain wine or to use snow to cool drinks. It was "democratic and polite" to be punctual for dinner; "oligarchical and offensive" to be late. Conversation over dinner ought to be philosophical, like debating which came first, the chicken or the egg.

It would be naive to think that all Romans obeyed Plutarch's strictures. Life was as diverse as in any modern capital, with an elegant high society at one end of the scale, more unruly elements at the other. The one common factor was probably a passion for bathing. With underground furnaces heating the water, the baths got bigger and bigger. The well-preserved Baths of Caracalla could disgorge 1,600 glowing Romans per day.

Rules of society

In the early days, relations between patricians and plebeians were codified, as were family matters. Patricians were the source of "tranquillity", mainly by lending an ear to plebeians' problems and dispensing advice. In return, plebeians had to stump up money when the patrician was held to ransom or could not settle his debts. Money made available in such circumstances was not a loan but a plebeian's privilege, for which he was supposed to be grateful. Yet plebeians were not enslaved and could switch allegiance to more suitable patricians.

Divorce was introduced relatively late. At first, marriage was permanent and wives automatically acquired half the conjugal property. However, husbands exercised the ultimate sanction in that they were legally entitled to murder wives for serious offences, such as poisoning the children or making duplicates of their private keys. Fathers were prevented from selling sons into slavery once the boys had married.

In a spiritual context, the lives of the Romans were wrapped up in astrology and mysticism. The spread of Bacchic rites in republican Rome alarmed the government, which called them "this pestilential evil... this contagious disease". Senators "were seized by a panic of fear, both for the public safety, lest these secret conspiracies and nocturnal gatherings contain some hidden harm or danger, and for themselves individually, lest some relatives be involved in this vice".

Problems and wrong-doers

Citizens bombarded bureaucrats with complaints about the quality of life in Rome: disgraceful traffic congestion and refuse collection; escalating inflation; homosexuals getting too big for their boots; the filthy habit of smoking dried cow dung. The most castigated men in Rome were unscrupulous property developers who set fire to a building they wanted and

Plutarch, Greek biographer and historian.

then, as the flames went up, offered the uninsured owner a pittance. As soon as the deal was struck, the developer summoned a private fire brigade parked around the corner.

The social decadence supposedly behind the downfall of Rome had its own decorum. Petronius Arbiter, author of the Satyricon, orchestrated Nero's orgies. He later fell out with Nero and was ordered to take his own life. Petronius invited friends to a farewell banquet where he sat with bandages wrapped around wrists which he discreetly slashed as the evening progressed. The controlled bleeding enabled him to sustain repartee up to the moment his head slumped. It is not known whether he expressed a parting thought on the interesting question of the chicken and the egg.

THE MIDDLE AGES

A period that saw Lombard, Saracen and Norman
invasions and clashes between emperor and pope.

For four centuries after the sack of Rome in AD 410, barbarian invaders, including the Goths and the Lombards, battled with local military leaders and the Byzantine emperors for control of Italy. Under these conditions, the culture and prosperity that had characterised ancient times faded. The Roman Empire had unified Italy and made it the centre of the world, but after its demise Italy became a provincial battlefield. Since none of the rival powers could control the whole of Italy, the land was divided, and it remained so until the 19th century.

The Dark Ages began with a series of Visigothic invasions from northern and eastern Europe. The emperors in Constantinople were still in theory the rulers of Italy, but for decades they accepted first the Visigoth and later the Ostrogoth leaders as *de facto* kings. Justinian I, who became emperor in Constantinople in 527, longed to revive the splendour of the empire and sent the brilliant general Belisarius to regain direct control of Italy. But, although he met with initial success – he captured Ravenna from the Goths in 540 – a new group of barbarians soon appeared on Italy's borders: the Lombards.

Gregory I, c.540–604, later canonised.

Invaders from the north

The Lombards were German tribesmen from the Danube Valley. They swiftly conquered most of what is now Lombardy, the Veneto and Tuscany, causing the inhabitants of the northern Italian cities to flee to eastern coastal regions where they were protected by the Byzantines, who still controlled the seas. Many settled around the lagoon of Venice.

Meanwhile, the Lombards altered the system of government. They replaced the centralised Roman political system with local administrative units called "duchies", after the Lombard

army generals who were known as *duces*. Within each duchy a *dux* ruled as king. The land was distributed to groups of related Lombard families, each headed by a free warrior, who owed limited feudal allegiance to his king but had a free hand on his own land. This, along with the Byzantines' continuing control of many provinces, meant Italy was effectively divided.

The radical changes that the Lombards brought to Italy's administration did not affect the Church. Indeed, in Rome the bishopric rose to new prominence because the emperors in Constantinople were too distant to exert any temporal or spiritual authority.

Greatest among the early popes was Gregory I (589–603), a Roman by birth, a scholar by instinct and training, and a great statesman. He persuaded the Lombards to abandon the siege of Rome, and helped achieve peace in Italy.

He sent missionaries to northern Europe to spread the word of God and the influence of Rome, and sent the first missionaries to the British Isles.

Gregory's successors reorganised the municipal government of Rome, and effectively became rulers of the city. It was inevitable that the popes would eventually clash with the emperor in Constantinople. In 726, Emperor Leo decreed that veneration of images of

After the imperial capital, Ravenna, fell to the Lombard army in 751, the popes, feeling more directly threatened by the powerful Lombards than by an absent emperor, sought a new ally and turned to the Franks for help.

Pepin, king of the Franks, invaded Italy in 754. He reconquered the imperial lands but ceded control to the Pope. Twenty years later, Pepin's son, Charlemagne, finished his father's work by defeating and capturing the Lombard king, confirming his father's grant to the papacy, and assuming the crown of the Lombards.

Mosaics, such as this one of the Emperor Justinian, are glittering reminders that Ravenna was once the capital of the Western Roman empire.

The Lombard League, founded in 1167, an alliance of northern Italian cities, has been used as a rallying cry by secessionist movements in modern times.

Christ and the saints was forbidden and that all images were to be destroyed. The Pope opposed his decree on the grounds that the Church in Rome should have the final say on all spiritual matters, and organised an Italian revolt against the emperor. The Lombards joined the revolt on the side of the popes and used the opportunity to chase the Byzantines out of Italy.

Charlemagne then returned to the north and campaigned against the Saxons, Bavarians and Avars, making himself ruler of much of western Europe. To unify his vast territories under Christian auspices, he had Pope Leo crown him Holy Roman Emperor at St Peter's in Rome on Christmas Day 800.

Charlemagne lived only 14 years after his coronation, and none of his successors matched him in ability; authority fell into the hands of Frankish counts, Charlemagne's vassals who had accompanied him south and been granted land of their own.

A period of ensuing feudal anarchy was also marked by invasions. In the south the Saracens invaded Sicily in 827, and for the next 250 years Sicily was an Arab state. Sicily also became a base for raids on the Italian mainland, and Charlemagne's great-grandson, Louis II, who was emperor for 25 years, failed to raise an organised defence against them. The Lombard dukes in the south allied themselves with these invaders against the Carolingian emperor.

The Normans in the south

In the early 11th century, small groups of Normans arrived in southern Italy. As adventurers and skilled mercenaries, they fought for

candidate. But, by reforming the papacy, the emperors started a trend that would have far-reaching consequences.

In the 11th century, the popes strove to reform the Church further by imposing a strict clerical hierarchy. Throughout the Holy Roman Empire, bishops were to be answerable to the Pope, and priests to bishops. A single legal and administrative system would bind all members of the clergy together. These reforms immediately angered all lay rulers from the emperor down.

The struggle reached a climax when Emperor Henry IV invested an anti-reform candidate as

Marble columns adorned with mosaics inside Monreale's Duomo, Sicily.

Greek, Lombard and Saracen alike, in return for land.

Soon landless men from Normandy arrived to fight, settle and conquer for themselves. The papacy lost no time in allying itself with this powerful group of Christians. In the 1050s, the Norman chief, Robert Guiscard, conquered Calabria. Pope Nicholas II "legitimised" Norman rule of the area by calling it a papal fief. Guiscard was invested as king, a role that passed to Roger II in 1130 (see page 48).

During the 9th and 10th centuries, the papacy was controlled by Roman nobles, who were often corrupt. After Emperor Otto I arrived in Rome in 962, he insisted that no pope could be elected until the emperor had named a

THE NORMAN CONQUEST

On his accession in 1130, the Norman Roger II became the richest king in Christendom. Centred on Sicily, his realm stretched to southern Italy and North Africa. A tolerant ruler, Roger acted as an oriental sultan, indulging his love of Arab culture as well as welcoming Jewish, Greek and Arab scholars; the court included Koranic astronomers, French balladeers and Sicilian poets. Arab-Norman architecture flourished in a fusion of oriental and Western styles. Moorish masterpieces can be seen in Palermo and in the cathedrals of Monreale and Cefalù. Norman control of southern Italy only came to an end with the death of William II in 1189.

archbishop of Milan in 1072. As a result, Pope Gregory VII decreed that an investiture by a non-cleric was forbidden and excommunicated Henry. The emperor was forgiven but failed to keep his promise to recognise the claims of the papacy, and a new civil war broke out. Gregory's supporters were defeated initially and he was

> The great Pope Gregory, who made peace with the Lombards to save Rome, also gave his name to the Gregorian chant, and sent the Benedictine monk Augustine to England.

carried off to Salerno and death, but his successors ensured the triumph of Gregory's cause, and the emperors were forced to concede their rights of investiture in 1122.

During the years of the investiture controversy and the ensuing civil wars, the cities of northern and central Italy grew rich and powerful. The emperors were too distracted to administer them directly. Around the same time, Mediterranean commerce was revived. With new wealth at their disposal, the cities forced the nobles in the countryside to acknowledge their supremacy. The Italian city-states were born. The strong and separate identity of the city-states is one of the leitmotifs of Italian history, influencing the pattern of future political affiliations, fostering separate schools of art, architecture and music, and largely determining regional attitudes today.

The maritime republics of Venice, Genoa and Pisa were foremost among the Italian cities, but inland cities that were situated on rich trade routes also prospered. Milan and Verona lay at the entrance to the Alpine passes, Bologna was the chief city on the Via Emilia, and Florence had sea access via the River Arno and controlled two roads to Rome.

The growing political power of the city-states was an important factor in renewed conflict between emperor and Pope during the 13th century. Emperor Frederick II (1197–1250) tried to build a strong, centralised state in Italy. The cities that opposed him, wanting complete political autonomy, found an ally in Pope Gregory IX, who harboured imperial designs of his own. Northern Italy became a battlefield for civil war between the Guelphs, supporters of the Pope, and the Ghibellines, allies of the emperor.

By the time Frederick died in 1250, without instituting his reforms, the Guelf cause had won. The alliance of Pope and the city-states had ruined imperial plans for a unified Italy.

The age of Dante

The Guelphs beat the Ghibellines decisively, but a feud broke out between two Guelph factions: the Blacks and the Whites. This split was especially severe in Florence, where the Blacks defended the nobles' feudal tradition against the Whites, rich magnates who were willing to give merchants a voice in government.

Dante Alighieri, by Andrea del Castagno.

Pope Boniface VIII sided with the Blacks and worked to have all prominent Whites exiled from Florence in 1302. Among the exiles was Dante Alighieri, who went on to write *La Divina Commedia* (*The Divine Comedy*), a literary masterpiece that promoted Tuscan Italian to the status of a national tongue and also reveals much about the politics of the period.

When Henry VII became Holy Roman Emperor in 1308, he wanted to revive imperial power in Italy and set up a government that was neither Guelph nor Ghibelline. But the cities refused to support him. Dante's home town, Florence, was the centre of the resistance to his plans.

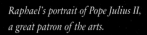
Raphael's portrait of Pope Julius II,
a great patron of the arts.

THE RENAISSANCE

**Free from foreign interference,
the city-states flourished and witnessed
an unprecedented cultural awakening.**

The constant fighting in northern Italy subsided in the early 14th century when both the popes and the emperors withdrew from Italian affairs. After Henry VII's demise, the emperors turned their attention to Germany. Meanwhile, the influence of the papacy declined after a quarrel between Pope Boniface and King Philip of France in 1302. Pope Boniface insisted that Philip had no right to tax the French clergy; the king's response was to send his troops to capture the pope. French pressure ensured that the next pope was a Frenchman, Clement V, and he moved the papacy from Rome to Avignon, where it stayed until 1377.

The people of Italy were thus free from outside interference during the 14th century and the Italian cities grew stronger, richer and bigger than any in Europe. Against the political background of the supremacy of the city-state, a new culture bloomed and new ideas flourished. Rulers tried new methods of administration. Scholars were allowed to rediscover the pagan past. Wealthy merchants became lavish patrons of the arts. Through their commissions, artists experimented with a new, more realistic style.

Plague and depression

Not even the Black Death – the terrible outbreak of bubonic plague that ravaged Europe in the 14th century – could smother the new cultural awakening. The merchants' solution to the declining profits of the period was to change the way they did business. Their innovations included marine insurance, credit transfers, double-entry book-keeping and holding companies – all of which eventually became standard business practice.

Detail of Raphael's School of Athens in the Stanza della Segnatura, Vatican Museum.

To be a good businessman in the Early Renaissance required a basic education: reading, writing and arithmetic. But the more complicated business became, the more knowledge was needed, including an understanding of law and diplomacy, and of the ways of the world. Thus the traditional theological studies of the Middle Ages were replaced by the study of ancient authors and of grammar, rhetoric, history and moral philosophy. This education became known as *studia humanitatis*, or the humanities.

Humanism grew partly out of the need for greater legal expertise in the expanding world of Mediterranean commerce. To learn how to administer their new, complex societies, lawyers looked back at the great tenets of Roman law. As they studied the codes of the ancients, they grew to appreciate the cultural riches of that long-buried civilisation. All aspects of Italian life were re-examined in the light of this new humanism. One way of life was thought to be ideal – that of the all-round man based on classical models. The Renaissance man was in fact a reincarnation of rich, talented Roman philosophers.

Despots and republics

Italians of the 14th century were citizens of particular cities, not members of a national unit.

eventually made his office hereditary. This was how the della Scala (Scaligeri) family in Verona, the Gonzaga in Mantua and the Visconti in Milan came to power.

Some cities, including Venice, Florence, Siena, Lucca and Pisa, did not succumb to despotism until quite late in their history: the merchants were so powerful that rulers such as the Medici only survived by winning their support. In these cities republicanism flourished briefly, but even so the merchants dominated the organs of the republican government.

The Battle of San Romano by Paolo Uccello, showing the victory of Florence over Siena in 1432.

Rulers encouraged artists and writers to glorify their towns. There were a few experiences and conditions that many cities shared.

As the authority of the popes and emperors declined, life in the cities became increasingly violent and leading families fought each other constantly. The remedy to this bloody civil strife was the rule of one strong man. The pattern was repeated over and over again in northern Italy. Traditional republican rule which could not keep order was replaced by a dictatorship. The future despot was often originally a *capitano del popolo* – the head of the local police force and citizens' army. Over time, this captain would extend his powers until he controlled the entire city and

The eminent Renaissance historian Jacob Burckhardt admired the "strict rationalism" of Visconti's Milan and called its government a work of art.

During the 14th and 15th centuries, northern and central Italy changed from an area speckled with tiny political units to one dominated by a few large states. The most successful and the most powerful was Milan. During the 14th century, the authoritarian Visconti family dominated Milan, and led the city to innumerable military and political victories until it was the largest state in northern Italy.

The Visconti regime may have been, in its efficiency, unlike anything Europe had seen for centuries, but for the Milanese people it had great drawbacks. The personal brutality

> The historian Guicciardini extolled life under the Medici: "Talented men were assisted in their careers by the recognition given to arts and letters... tranquillity reigned within her walls, and externally the city enjoyed high honours."

of the Visconti controlled Milan. The regime could not rely on the loyalty of the populace for its survival. When the Visconti line died out in 1447, the Milanese declared a republic, but it was not strong enough to rule over all the restive towns Milan now controlled. When, in 1450, Francesco Sforza, a famous general who had served the Visconti, overthrew the republic and became the new duke, ruling with his wife Bianca Visconti, many Milanese were relieved.

The Republic of Florence

The spectacular transformation of Florence from a small town in the 1100s to the commercial and financial centre it had become by the end of the 14th century was based on the profitable wool trade. The wool guild of Florence, the Arte della Lana, imported wool from northern Europe and dyes from the Middle East. Using the city's secret weaving and colouring techniques, guild members produced a heavy red cloth that was sold all over the Mediterranean area. Wool trade profits had provided the initial capital for the banking industry of Florence. Since the 13th century, Florentine merchants had lent money to their allies, the Pope and powerful Guelph nobles. This early experience led to the founding of formal banking houses, and made Florence the financial capital of Europe.

The rich men of Florence controlled the city government through the Parte Guelfa. With membership came the right to find and persecute anyone with "Ghibellistic tendencies". Other political non-conformities were also not tolerated. Members of lesser guilds who demanded a greater share of power, or joined with the lower classes to fight the Parte

Guelfa, were annihilated. However, in the early 15th century the violence of class war escalated. The disenfranchised artisans struck back repeatedly. At this point the rich merchants allowed Cosimo de' Medici to rise to the leadership of Florence.

The 15th century was the golden age of the Renaissance. The stage was set for a period of unprecedented artistic and intellectual achievement. To live in Italy at this time was to live in a new world of cultural and commercial riches. Italy was truly the centre of the world.

Cosimo de' Medici in the Uffizi, Florence.

BUILDING BOOM

The merchant guilds of Florence spent their wealth on art, helping to turn the city into a showcase of Renaissance sculpture, painting and architecture. Clarity, rigour and geometry were the watchwords of Florentine architecture. In the second half of the 13th century construction began on the Bargello, the Franciscan church of Santa Croce and the Dominican church of Santa Maria Novella. Arnolfo di Cambio designed the cathedral, (funded by the wool guild), and the Palazzo Vecchio, the emblem of Florentine power. The city also hired Giotto to design the cathedral bell tower, and in 1434 chose Brunelleschi to finish the great dome.

The political history of the century divides into two parts. Until 1454 the five chief states of Italy were busy expanding their borders, or strengthening their hold on territories, which meant fighting many small wars. The soldiers who fought them were mostly *condottieri* (mercenaries). After 1454 came a period of relative peace, when the states pursued their interests through alliances. These years saw the greatest artistic achievement, when Italian states of all sizes became cultural centres.

Italian wars of the Late Middle Ages and Early Renaissance had traditionally been

Portrait of a condottiere by Andrea del Castagno.

fought by foreign mercenaries, but by the 15th century the mercenaries were more likely to be Italian. Men of all classes and from all parts of Italy joined the ranks of the purely Italian companies to fight northern wars for rival nobles. The *condottieri* looked upon war as a professional, technical skill. The countryside, however, suffered heavily as village after village was plundered. The *condottieri* were bound by no patriotic ties, only by a monetary arrangement, so an important captain could always be bought by the enemy.

One of the greatest *condottieri* was Francesco Sforza, who had inherited the command of an army upon his father's death in 1424. He fought first for Milan and then for Venice until

Filippo Visconti sought to attach him permanently to Milan by marrying him to his illegitimate daughter, Bianca.

Visconti died in 1447 leaving no heir, and Milan declared itself a republic. But when the

> Macchiavelli was inspired by Lorenzo de' Medici when he wrote in The Prince:
> "A ruler must emulate the fox and the lion, for the lion cannot avoid traps and the fox cannot fight wolves."

republican government proved incompetent, Sforza turned his forces on the city and starved Milan into surrender. The chief assembly of the republic invited him to be the duke of the city.

Peace and the Italian League

Sforza, the great soldier, was key to bringing peace to northern Italy. He signed, and encouraged others to sign, the Treaty of Lodi, which led to the Italian League of 1455. This was a defensive league between Milan, Florence and Venice that the King of Naples and the Pope also respected. It was set up to prevent any one of the great states from increasing its powers at the expense of its weaker neighbours, and to present a common national front against attack. The smaller states benefited most from the new league.

During the decades of peace in Italy, Florence experienced its own golden age under the rule of the Medici family. The historian Guicciardini described the Florence of Lorenzo de' Medici as follows: "The city was in perfect peace, the leading citizens were united, and their authority was so great that none dared to oppose them. The people were entertained daily with pageants and festivals; the food supply was abundant and all trades flourished."

In part, the success of the Medici was a public relations coup. They allowed the Florentines to believe that the city government was still a great democracy. Only after Lorenzo's death, when Florence was briefly ruled by his arrogant son, did the citizens realise that their state, for all its republican forms, had drifted into the control of one family. They then quickly exiled the Medici and drafted a new constitution. Until then, both Cosimo and Lorenzo de' Medici had dominated Florence while shrewdly never appearing to be more than prominent citizens.

An end to the peace

When Lorenzo de' Medici died in 1492, the fragile Italian League that had kept Italy at peace and safe from any foreign attacks died with him. Ludovico il Moro, the lord of Milan, immediately quarrelled with the Neapolitan king and proposed to the King of France that he, Charles VIII, conquer Naples and the surrounding states. Ludovico offered finance and safe passage through the north of Italy. Charles readily accepted and so began a truly demoralising chapter of Italian history.

The internal disarray in Italy at the time was

one, and they could launch a surprise attack against their enemy. But the Italian strategy fell apart. When the battle ended, four thousand men had died – the majority of them Italian.

"If the Italians had won at Fornovo, they would probably have discovered then the pride of being a united people... Italy would have emerged as a respectable nation... a country which adventurous foreigners would think twice before attacking," wrote Luigi Barzini in *The Italians*. Instead, the defeat at Fornovo broke the Italian spirit and led to 30 years of foreign interventions, bloody conflicts, civil wars and revolts.

Francesco Sforza married Bianca, natural daughter of the last of the Visconti rulers, to become despot of Milan.

Bianca Maria Sforza.

so great that the French troops faced no organised resistance. The new leader of Florence, a Dominican friar named Girolamo Savonarola, preached that Charles was sent by God to regenerate the Church and purify spiritual life. Other Italians also welcomed the French. They believed that the invaders would rid Italy of decadence and set up governments with native Italians in key posts. Only when these ideas proved illusory could Italian patriots recruit an army and challenge the French.

The French and Italians met near the village of Fornovo on 6 July 1495. The Italians, led by General Francesco Gonzaga, looked certain of victory: they outnumbered the French two to

MEDICI MIDAS TOUCH

Wherever you look in Florence, you encounter the Medici – not just their busts and coat of arms but the magnificent churches, palaces and works of art they commissioned and the art and culture they promoted. When the humanist Niccolò Niccoli died, Cosimo de' Medici acquired his book collection and attached it to the monastery of San Marco, creating the city's first public library. Cosimo also created a Platonic Academy and made Florence a centre of Platonic studies. He supplied Donatello with classical works that inspired his sculpture. Lorenzo de' Medici singled out a young Michelangelo, whose statues still adorn the city.

RENAISSANCE ART

**The revolution in art and architecture which began
in Florence in the 15th century gave us our greatest
treasures and transformed the way we see the world.**

Italian art shone brightest during the Renaissance when, as in most disciplines, a revolution took place. The Early Renaissance (1400–1500), the *Quattrocento*, introduced new themes that altered the future of art. Ancient Greece and Rome were rediscovered and with them the importance of man in the here and now. The human body surfaced as a new focal point in painting and sculpture. The discovery of perspective changed architecture.

First in Florence was Lorenzo Ghiberti's commission for sculpting the gilded bronze north doors (1403–24) of the Baptistery, won in a competition with Filippo Brunelleschi in 1401. Ghiberti's more famous east doors (1424–52) are so dazzling that Michelangelo called them "the Gates of Paradise".

*The Early Renaissance centred on Florence.
The city wanted to be seen as "the new
Rome", and public works flourished.*

*The anguish of Adam and Eve, from Masaccio's Expulsion
from Paradise.*

Classical architecture

It was Filippo Brunelleschi (1377–1466) who championed the new classically inspired architecture. After losing the Baptistery door competition, he went to Rome to study the proportions of ancient buildings.

His studies led him to design such masterpieces as the dome of Florence cathedral, the arcade fronting the Innocenti orphanage, the church of San Lorenzo (1421–69), the Pazzi Chapel of Santa Croce (begun 1430–33) and Santo Spirito, all in Florence. You need no yardstick to appreciate the use of mathematical proportions. The overriding impression is of harmony, balance and calm.

If Brunelleschi was the most noted architect, Donatello (1386–1466) excelled in sculpture. His work expresses a new attitude to the human body. The figure of St George, made for the church of Orsanmichele and now in the Museo del Bargello, is not only a realistic depiction of the human form, but also a work of psychological insight. His *Gattamelata* (1445–50) in Padua was the first equestrian statue cast in bronze since Roman times, and his bronze *David* (1430–32), in the Bargello, was the first freestanding nude statue since antiquity.

The groundwork for the revolution in painting was laid a century earlier by Giotto

(1267–1337). His frescoes – in Florence's Santa Croce, Padua's Cappella degli Scrovegni and Assisi's Basilica di San Francesco – depart from the flat Byzantine style and invest the human form with solidity and volume, and

> In architecture, Andrea Palladio (1518–80) designed classically inspired churches, villas and palaces, including Villa Rotonda, Vicenza (1567–70), and San Giorgio Maggiore, Venice (1565).

mathematics – heads and limbs as geometric shapes: spheres, cones and cylinders.

The artistic revolution in Florence soon spread to other parts of Italy. Leon Battista Alberti (1404–72), an author of treatises on sculpture, painting and architecture, introduced the tracing of classic motifs (columns, arches) on the exteriors of buildings, such as on the Malatesta Temple in Rimini (1450). Giovanni Bellini (1430/1–1516) triumphed in Venice. In his *Madonna and Saints* in San Zaccaria (1505), the grandeur of Masaccio's influence is tempered by Flemish detail. Detail

Botticelli's Primavera in the Uffizi in Florence.

the setting with a sense of space and depth. His breakthrough was carried further by the Early Renaissance's most noted painter, Masaccio (1401–28). His Florentine frescoes of *The Holy Trinity with Virgin and St John* in Santa Maria Novella (1425), and his frescoes in the Brancacci Chapel (1427) display all the traits characteristic of the Renaissance: attention to the human form, emotion and the use of perspective.

Domenico Veneziano moved to Florence in 1439 and introduced pastel greens and pinks awash with cool light. The palette was picked up by his assistant, Piero della Francesca (1416–92), for his frescoes at San Francesco in Arezzo (1466), marvels of pale tone as well as

most delicately expressed is the hallmark of Sandro Botticelli (1444/5–1510). The Uffizi Gallery houses the allegorical *Primavera* (1480) and the lovely *Birth of Venus* (1489).

The High Renaissance

The High Renaissance (1500–1600) was the heyday of some of the most celebrated artists in the entire history of art: Leonardo da Vinci, Michelangelo, Bramante, Raphael and Titian. Unlike their predecessors, who were thought of as craftsmen, they were considered to be creative geniuses capable of works of superhuman scale, grandeur and effort. Their extravaganzas were made possible by a new source of patronage – the papacy.

Having returned to Rome from exile in Avignon, the popes turned the Eternal City into a centre of culture. The art of the High Renaissance is marked by a move beyond rules of mathematical ratios or anatomical geometrics to a new emphasis on emotional impact. The increasing use of oil paints, introduced to the Italians in the late 1400s, began to replace egg tempera and opened new possibilities for richness of colour and delicacy of light.

Leonardo da Vinci (1452–1519) was born near Florence but left the city to work for the Duke of Milan, primarily as an engineer and

In 1503, Pope Julius II, a great patron of the arts, commissioned the most prominent architect of the day, Donato Bramante (1444–1514), to design the new St Peter's. Bramante had earlier made his mark with the classically inspired gem The Tempietto (1502), in the courtyard of Rome's San Pietro in Montorio. The Pope's directive for the new project was to create a monument which would surpass any of Ancient Rome. Working with a stock of classical forms (domes, colonnades, pediments) Bramante revolutionised architecture with his revival of another classical technique,

Raphael's Entombment, in the Borghese Gallery, Rome.

only secondarily as a sculptor, architect and painter. In Milan, Leonardo painted the *Last Supper* (1495–98), in Santa Maria delle Grazie. The mural – an unsuccessful experiment in oil tempera, which accounts for its poor condition – is a masterpiece of psychological drama.

Leonardo also exploited new techniques in painting. *Chiaroscuro* (literally, light and dark) – the use of light to bring out and highlight three-dimensional bodies – is vividly seen in the whirl of bodies in the *Adoration of the Magi* (1481–2) in the Uffizi. Another invention was *sfumato*, a fine haze that lends a dreamy quality to paintings, enhancing their poetic potential.

concrete, which enables greater flexibility and monumental size.

Bramante died before his design was realised. In 1546, Michelangelo was put in charge of the project, and St Peter's gained its present form.

Michelangelo and Raphael

Michelangelo Buonarroti (1475–1564) first astounded the world with his sculpture: human figures with a dignity, volume and beauty inspired by Hellenistic precedents, yet given new emotional impact. It has been said that Michelangelo sought to liberate the form of the human body from a prison of marble: an allegory for the struggle of the soul, imprisoned in an earthly body, and a condition ripe for themes of triumph and tragedy. The tension imbues his best-known works: *David* (1501–04) in Florence's Accademia, *Moses* (1513–15) in Rome's San Pietro in Vincoli, and the beloved *Pietà* in St Peter's.

Julius II commissioned Michelangelo to paint the Sistine Chapel ceiling. The result, which was completed in only four years (1508–12), is a triumph of emotions unleashed by the human condition: man's creation, his fall, and his reconciliation with the Lord. Michelangelo returned to the Sistine Chapel in 1534 to paint the spectacular *Last Judgement*. In the intervening years he went to Florence to complete the Medici Chapel of San Lorenzo (1524–34) and the Laurentian Library (begun 1524), where the drama of the design outweighs many functional considerations. Michelangelo's architectural genius culminates in his redesign of Rome's Campidoglio (1537–39). This open piazza, flanked by three facades, became the model for modern civic centres.

While Michelangelo was busy on the Sistine Chapel ceiling, a young artist from Urbino was working nearby, decorating rooms in the Vatican Palace. This artist, soon to be known as the foremost painter of the High Renaissance, was Raffaello Sanzio, or Raphael (1483–1520). His masterpiece here is the *School of Athens* (1510–11), where the dramatic grouping of philosophers suggests the influence of Michelangelo, yet the individualised intention of each recalls Leonardo's *Last Supper*.

Venetian masters

In Venice, the paintings of Giorgione da Castelfranco (1476/8–1510) have all the charm and delicacy of Bellini's; they also favour poetic mood over subject matter (*The Tempest* of 1505 in Venice's Gallerie dell'Accademia is a perfect example), prefiguring the Romantic movement. Also looking ahead to the freer brushwork and shimmering colours of the Impressionists is the Venetian Titian (1488/90–1576). He mastered the technique of oil painting, and left a legacy of richly coloured, joyously spirited religious and mythological pictures as well as masterful portraits.

Detail of Raphael's School of Athens in the Vatican Museum.

THE MANNERISTS

The drama of Leonardo, the theatricality of Michelangelo, the poetic moodiness of Giorgione: all set the stage for the Mannerist phase of High Renaissance art, when the serene classicism that characterised the works of Raphael were abandoned. In Mannerism the human form is paramount, yet it is depicted in strained, disturbing poses and violent colours. This unnatural look grew out of the work of artists such as Michelangelo, whose exaggeration of human features creates drama in the overlarge head and hands of David. Expression of an "inner vision" at the expense of reality was vital to Mannerism. In Fiorentino's *The Descent from the Cross* (1521) in Volterra's Pinacoteca,

the angular figures bathed in an unreal light stir feelings of anxiety. His friend Pontormo (1494–1557) displays unexpected colour, unnaturally elongated figures and disquieting mood. Bronzino (1503–72) epitomises this style in his psychological portraits of Cosimo I. Parmigianino (1503–40) used distortion merely for effect, despite being inspired by Raphael's fluid grace. In Venice, Tintoretto (1518–94) combined the bold style, rich colours and glowing light inspired by Titian with a mystical bent. His depiction of the transubstantiation of bread into the body of Christ results in the haunting *Last Supper* (1592–94) in San Giorgio Maggiore, Venice, with its swirling angels created out of vapours.

Giuseppe Garibaldi, a prominent leader of the Risorgimento.

BIRTH OF A NATION

**After centuries of foreign domination and a
prolonged struggle, Italy emerged in 1870
as a united independent kingdom.**

The seeds of Italian patriotism, crushed
by the battle of Fornovo in 1495, lay
virtually dormant for three centuries.
After Fornovo, all the armies of Europe came
to Italy and fought among themselves for a
share of the spoils. Spain, the most powerful nation in Europe at the time, eventually
emerged as the clear master of Italy. The
country was burdened by heavy taxation,
and under Spanish influence liberty and
native energy and initiative declined. The
papacy was no less oppressive; the rules of the
Inquisition, the Index and the Jesuit Orders
forced many Italians to flee.

Under the Spaniards and later (after the
1713 Treaty of Utrecht) under the equally
oppressive Austrians, Italy lost its reputation
as a cultural centre. But the 1789 French Revolution inspired many Italians, and patriots
dreamt of an independent Italian republic
modelled on France.

> The Pope crowned King Charles I of Spain
> Holy Roman Emperor in 1530, and Charles
> and his descendants ruled Italy for more than
> 150 years.

When Napoleon invaded Italy in 1796, the
people rose against the Austrians and a series
of republics was founded. For three years the
whole peninsula was republican and under
French rule. But in March 1799, an Austro-Rus-
sian army expelled the French from northern
Italy and restored many local princes.

To work against the foreign oppressors, Italian patriots joined secret societies, such as the
Carbonari. In their love of ritual they resembled

Camillo Benso, Count of Cavour, Italy's first great statesman.

the Freemasons, but they had a serious goal: to
liberate Italy.

The Risorgimento

In 1800 Napoleon won back most of Italy. The
kingdom that he founded lasted only briefly
but, by proving that the country could be a single unit, it gave Italian patriots new inspiration.
From the Congress of Vienna in 1815, which
reinstated Italian political divisions, until Rome
was taken in 1870 by the troops of King Victor Emmanuel II of Savoy (who also ruled over
Piedmont and Sardinia), the history of Italy was
one continuous struggle for reunification.

The period is a complex one. Many northern
and southern Italians wanted the peninsula to

become one nation, but there was no agreement as to how it should be achieved. Some, like Giuseppe Mazzini, wanted to revive the Roman Republic. Others were for a kingdom of Italy under the House of Savoy.

In 1848, a year of revolt all over Europe, the first Italian war for independence was fought. First, rebellions in Sicily, Tuscany and the Papal States forced local rulers to grant constitutions to their citizens. In Milan, news of Parisian and Viennese uprisings sparked the famous "five days" when the occupying Austrian army was driven from the city. A few days

commander of the city's armed forces was Giuseppe Garibaldi, a lifelong Italian patriot who had honed his fighting skills as a mercenary in the revolutions of South America, where he had fled after being convicted of

> Giuseppe Mazzini (1805–72) was a great patriot and, with Cavour and Garibaldi, one of the founders of Italian independence. As a true republican, he never accepted the monarchical unification of Italy.

Garibaldi and Victor Emmanuel II of Savoy join forces at Teano.

later, Charles Albert of Savoy sent his army to pursue the Austrians, and the revolution began in earnest.

Charles Albert was soon supported by troops from other Italian states; however, the tide turned when the Pope refused to declare war on Catholic Austria. The newly confident Austrians drove Charles Albert's army back into Piedmont. He abdicated months later, and the House of Savoy signed a peace treaty.

Garibaldi and Cavour

Venice and the Roman Republic continued the fight. In Rome, Mazzini led a triumvirate that governed the city with a true democratic spirit despite the siege conditions. The

subversion in Piedmont. Now he and his men faced the combined strength of the Neapolitans, the Austrians and the French. It was French forces that entered the city on 3 July 1849, the day after Garibaldi escaped into the mountains. The following month the Venetians succumbed to an Austrian siege.

The treaty the Austrians had signed with the House of Savoy kept them out of that region, so it was now the only Italian state with a free press, an elected parliament and a liberal constitution. Piedmont-Savoy was also blessed, from 1852, with a brilliant prime minister, Count Camillo di Cavour, who was devoted to the cause of Italian unity. Cavour went to England and France to raise support for the Italian cause. He contributed Piedmontese troops to the Crimean War, and thus won a seat at the peace conference, where he raised the Italian question. Although Cavour made no tangible gains at this meeting, he won moral support.

Europe was thus not surprised when France and Piedmont went to war with Austria three years later. The French emperor, Napoleon III, and Cavour had agreed that, after the expected victory, an Italian kingdom would be formed for the Piedmontese king, Victor Emmanuel, and Nice and French Savoy

rule on the island. Garibaldi declared himself dictator in the name of Victor Emmanuel. After fierce fighting, with the aid of Sicilian rebels Garibaldi entered Palermo in triumph. Men from all over Italy now came to help him and, on 7 September, Naples fell to the patriots.

Meanwhile, Victor Emmanuel gathered troops and marched south to link up with Garibaldi and his men. The two groups met at Teano, and the Kingdom of Italy was declared. The new kingdom excluded Rome: the Pope preached against the patriots, and French garrisons protected the city.

Celebration of Italian unity in Turin.

would be returned to France. The people of the Italian dukedoms proclaimed their allegiance to Victor Emmanuel.

Unfortunately, the French tired of fighting and made peace with Austria. The Austrians agreed to let Lombardy become part of an Italian Federation, but the Veneto region went back to Austria and the dukes of Modena and Tuscany were reinstated.

In Italy, there was outrage. Cavour resigned in protest, but first arranged plebiscites in Tuscany and Modena. Citizens refused to have their dukes back and voted to become part of Piedmont.

Garibaldi and 1,000 red-shirted volunteers sailed for Sicily from Genoa on 5 May 1860. His arrival was a signal for the overthrow of Bourbon

Finally, in 1870, Italian troops fought their way into Rome. The Pope barricaded himself in the Vatican. For half a century, no pope emerged to participate in the life of the new Italy.

The new government of all Italy was a parliamentary democracy with the king as executive. The most powerful men in the early days of the Italian state were the loyal Piedmontese parliamentarians who were largely responsible for its creation and for designing the administration of the whole peninsula.

However, once the government moved down to Rome, this group began to splinter. This was the start of the breakdown of the party system in Italy, the effects of which are discernible even today.

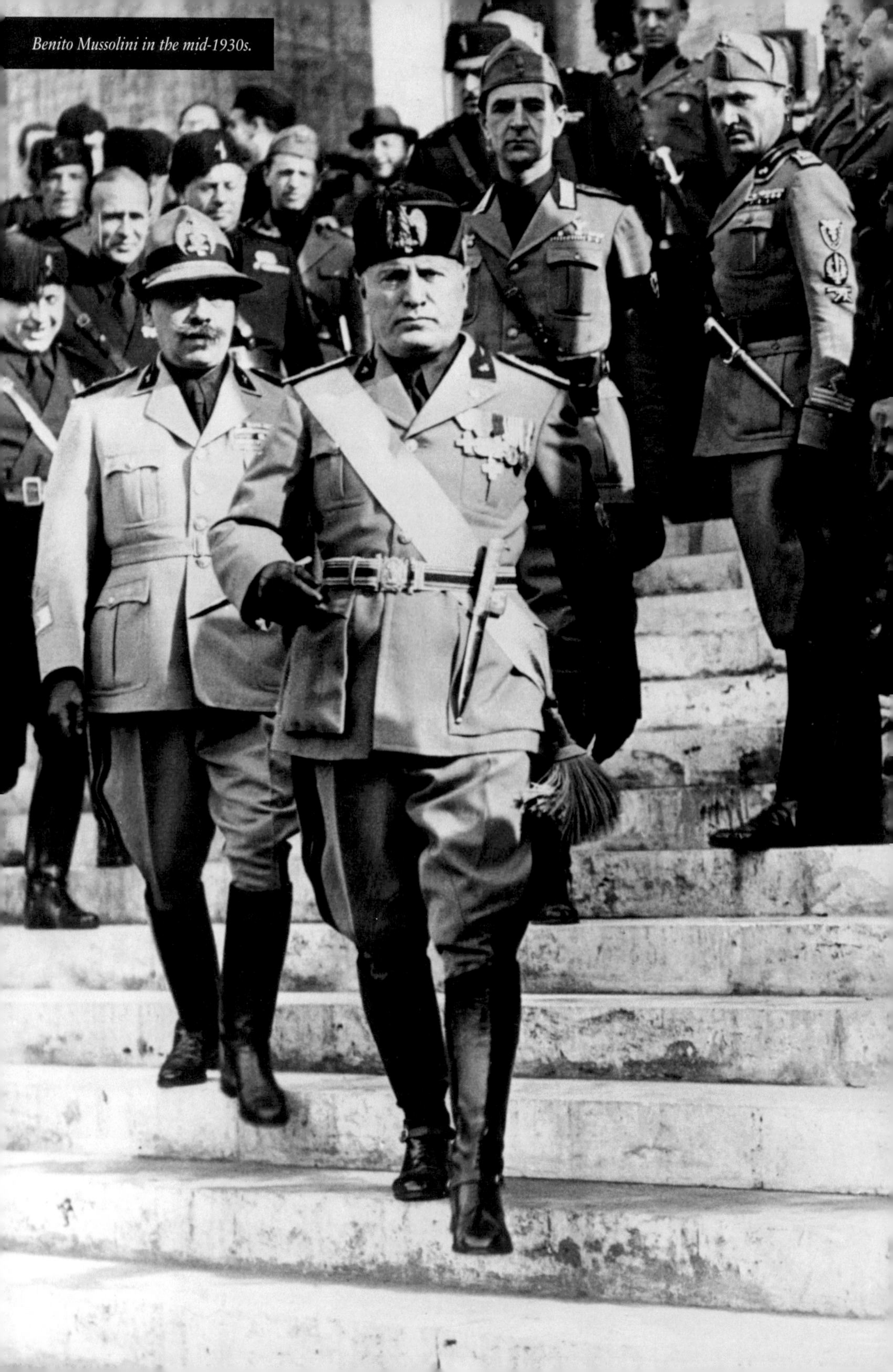

Benito Mussolini in the mid-1930s.

THE MAKING OF MODERN ITALY

**Wars, Fascism, corruption scandals...
with remarkable resilience, Italy survived
every challenge the 20th century presented to it.**

Statue of Victor Emmanuel II in Sardinia.

As governments so often do during times of rapid change and relative instability at home, Italy's began to look abroad for confirmation of its hard-won independence. Relations with France had cooled during the final fight for unification; when France occupied Tunisia, a traditional area of Italian influence, they became positively chilly. Italy's response was to sign the Triple Alliance with Germany and Austro-Hungary, providing mutual defence in the event of war.

Under the Conservative governments of Francesco Crispi (1887–91, 1893–6), Italy also joined the scramble for colonies in North Africa. Crispi successfully colonised Eritrea, but when he tried to subdue Ethiopia (Abyssinia), the Italian army suffered a humiliating defeat at Adwa, which led to Crispi's resignation. A later colonising attempt during the Italo-Turkish War (1911–12) ended in victory and the Italian occupation of Libya and the Dodecanese Islands.

North–south divide

At home, the years leading up to World War I were marked by the division that still plagues the country today: relative wealth in the north and extreme poverty in the south. The economy was overwhelmingly agricultural, and the government's protectionist policies left Italy increasingly isolated from other European markets. The industrial boom of the late 1800s, mostly in textiles and refining, was confined to the north. The crushing economic conditions in the south fuelled a wave of emigration. In the last years of the 19th century, nearly half a million people a year set out for the New World.

When World War I began with Austria's attack on Serbia in July 1914, Italy had not been consulted, in breach of the terms of the Triple Alliance. In consequence, on 2 August, Prime Minister Antonio Salandra declared Italy's neutrality. Public opinion began to swing in the direction of the Allies. To help win Italy over, the Allied governments dangled the possibility of territorial gains: Rome was offered the chance to gain the "unrecovered" provinces of Trieste and Trentino, long held by the Austro-Hungarian Habsburg Empire. In addition, Italy would receive the Alto Adige, plus North African and Turkish enclaves. Finally swayed, in April 1915 Italy signed the secret Treaty of London and, a month later, broke the Triple Alliance and entered the war on the Allied side.

Seldom had a country been so ill prepared for war. Italy's army was poorly equipped, and

Austrian troops had already dug into defensive positions in Alpine strongholds along the 480km (300-mile) shared border. For Italy the war was a costly stalemate; of the 5.5 million men mobilised, 39 percent were killed or wounded.

At the post-war conference table, the Treaty of St-Germain (10 September 1919) gave Italy Trentino, the Alto Adige (South Tyrol) and Trieste. But Fiume, Dalmatia and the other promised territories were negotiated away by the Allies.

Disappointment in the peace talks, combined with the social and economic toll of the war, produced chaotic domestic conditions.

The Palazzo della Civiltà del Lavoro in Rome's EUR district, a prime example of Fascist architecture.

Soon there was talk that Italy had won only a "mutilated victory", despite its wartime sacrifice. Inflation soared. Factory workers took to the streets, and peasants clamoured for land reform.

Into this power vacuum marched Benito Mussolini and his Fascist Party. When he founded the party in 1919, Mussolini played on the worst fears of all Italians. To placate the rich he denounced Bolshevism. To the middle classes he pledged a return to law and order, and a corporate state in which workers and management would pull together for the good of the country.

By mid-1922, Fascism had become a major political force. When workers called for a general strike, Mussolini made his move. On 28 October,

50,000 members of the Fascist militia converged on Rome. Although Mussolini's supporters held only a small minority in parliament, the sight of thousands of menacing Fascists flooding the streets of the capital was enough to topple the tottering government of Prime Minister Luigi Facta. Refusing to sanction a state of siege, King Victor Emmanuel III instead handed the reins of government to Benito Mussolini.

Once in control, Mussolini quickly pushed through an act assuring the Fascists a permanent majority in the parliament. After questionable elections in 1924, he dropped all pretence of collaborative government. Italy was now a dictatorship. In Christmas of that year, he declared himself head of the government, answerable only to the king. Within two years all parties except the Fascists were banned, and opposition activists were jailed or forced into exile or underground.

Fascist rule

Despite its ugly underbelly, on the surface Fascism seemed to work. Weary of inflation, strikes and street disturbances, Italians eagerly embraced their severe new government and its charismatic *Duce*, or leader. This spontaneous response to Fascist rule was reinforced by a strong propaganda campaign. Mussolini promised to restore to Italy the glories of Ancient Rome, and for a time promises were enough. Soon, however, the government could show results. The economy stabilised, huge public works projects were launched, and Mussolini even made peace with the Vatican, hammering out the Lateran Treaty (1929), which ended the 50-year rift between Rome and the Catholic Church. He also set out on an imperial campaign, restoring control over Libya, which had been ignored during and after World War I. In October 1935, Italian troops crossed the border of Eritrea and headed for the Ethiopian capital of Addis Ababa. The League of Nations protested, but took no action. Six months later, *Il Duce* announced to a hysterical Piazza Venezia crowd that, finally, Rome had begun to reclaim its empire.

The international outcry over the Ethiopian occupation left Rome isolated. The one government willing to overlook Mussolini's expansionism was in Berlin, where Adolf Hitler's Nazis had held power since January 1933. Both Germany and Italy had supported General Francisco Franco's nationalist troops in the

Spanish Civil War (1936–9), and this cooperation led eventually to the signing of the Pact of Steel between Berlin and Rome in May 1939.

Three months later, Hitler invaded Poland. Within days, Britain and France declared war on Germany. At first the Rome government remained neutral, as it had in 1914, arguing that Berlin's surprise attack on Poland did not require an automatic military response. In any case, most Italians opposed intervention, and the army was ill-prepared for war. But as Hitler claimed victory after victory – in Denmark, Norway and Belgium, and with France on the

morale sank to a new low. On 25 July 1943, the Grand Council of Fascism voted to strip *Il Duce* of his powers. Mussolini refused to step down, but the next day, King Victor Emmanuel ordered his arrest. Mussolini was detained in the Abruzzo Mountains, but in September, German air commandos airlifted him to Munich.

Chaos broke out in the final days of the war. To placate the Germans, who would otherwise have occupied the entire country, Prime Minister Marshal Badoglio publicly declared that Italy would fight on. In secret, however, he entered negotiations with the Allies, who by then had

Axis allies – Mussolini and Hitler.

verge of collapse – the lure of sharing the spoils of war proved irresistible. On 10 June 1940, Italy entered the war, just before the fall of France.

Eager to pull off his own battlefield coup, in the autumn of 1940 Mussolini set his sights on taking Greece. But the Greeks fought back fiercely. The Italians suffered many casualties, and only Nazi intervention prevented a likely Italian defeat. The war was also going badly for the Axis Powers in North Africa, and eventually even the Nazi General Rommel could not prevent the collapse. In 1943 US and British troops captured Sicily.

The beginning of the end was in sight. From their base in Sicily, the Allied forces began to bomb the Italian mainland, and Italian public

fought their way as far north as Naples. Above that line was the hastily organised *Repubblica Sociale Italiana*, headed by the liberated *Duce*. Better known as the Republic of Salo, based on Lake Garda, this was a puppet regime of Berlin, and Mussolini spent most of his time brooding on the judgement history would pass on him.

As the Allies fought northwards, the Italian Resistance felt safe enough to begin widespread activities. Combined, the forces managed to liberate Rome on 4 June 1944; the liberation of Florence followed not long after, on 12 August. The Germans and Mussolini lasted out the winter behind the so-called "Gothic line" in the Apennines, but by spring 1945 that effort, too, had collapsed.

Mussolini tried to escape into Switzerland disguised as a German soldier, but Italian partisans found him, and he was shot. His body was hauled into Milan and hung by a rope for the public to see.

> After World War I, Italian politicians focused on the negative elements of the peace treaties, and so the myth of the "mutilated victory" spread, fuelling Fascist propaganda and helping Mussolini seize power.

Fuelled by cheap labour, the economy developed rapidly. The 1950s witnessed a steady migration from rural areas to the cities and from south to north. Heavy industry such as chemicals, iron, steel and cars took off. In 1957, Italy became a founding member of the European Community. By the mid-1960s, manufacturing overtook agriculture, and observers hailed Italy's "economic miracle".

Terrorism and scandals

A few years later, however, the boom had gone bust, Italy was dubbed the "sick man of Europe",

The liberation of Rome.

Recovery and resiliency

In the immediate post-war period, Italy suffered greatly. The Italian colonies were taken away and reparations paid to the Soviet Union and Ethiopia. The political system needed a complete overhaul. In the 1946 elections, voters opted for a republic, thus formally ending the days of the monarchy. The economy was in disarray, but US aid in the form of the Marshall Plan helped to ease the burden.

For over a decade after the war, centrist coalitions ran the country. Then, in the early 1960s, the Christian Democrats, Socialists, Social Democrats and Republicans formed a coalition and ruled, in various combinations, until 1968.

and terrorism reared its ugly head. From the late 1970s, kidnappings, knee-cappings and murders were a fact of life. The murder, in 1978, of former Christian Democrat prime minister Aldo Moro by the left-wing *Brigate Rosse* (Red Brigades) spurred new anti-terrorist measures, and eventually 32 Red Brigade members were imprisoned for the deaths of Moro and 16 others. Neo-Fascist terrorism also plagued the country, culminating, in 1980, in a bomb blast at Bologna station, killing 84 people.

In the 1980s the economy grew, and Italy briefly overtook France and Britain in the economic league. Troubles were in store, however. In the 1990s a wave of corruption scandals rocked the state. In 1992, it was alleged that some £67 million (US$100 million) had been shared out among the leaders of the five coalition parties governing Italy in 1990. Two former premiers were convicted of being chief recipients, while veteran prime minister Giulio Andreotti was charged with Mafia links (see page 73), as were other leading figures, from fashion designers to industrialists. The short-lived first premiership of media magnate Silvio Berlusconi, in 1994, also stumbled over accusations of corruption. These scandals unleashed a volley of reforms spearheaded by the first left-wing government in Italy's post-war history. In order to create stronger, more durable governments, the system of proportional representation was changed to a largely first-past-the-post system.

Into the new millennium

In a landslide victory in 2001, Silvio Berlusconi's centre-right government came to power on a tide of populism, nationalism and reforming zeal. Perceived as a free-marketeer, the media mogul was elected to slash red tape and reform the tax system. However, by 2006, when he left office, he had singularly failed to resolve the conflict of interest between his public and business roles, and, as a convicted fraudster, evoked the tainted world of the Italian kickback culture. Commentator John Carlin likened the Milanese mogul to a megalomaniac Roman ruler: "The Roman emperors knew that the secret to exercising peaceful rule over the people was to provide them with bread and circuses. Berlusconi owns the circuses, pretty much all of it – the TV, the football, the magazines, the books. And as a head of government, who also happens to own

Italy's biggest supermarket chain, he also controls, in the widest sense of the word, the bread."

After a left-wing coalition under Romano Prodi collapsed in disarray, Berlusconi was re-elected in 2008 for his third term. Formerly known as Forza Italia, his People of Freedom party (PdL), a centre-right coalition, embraced the heirs of the newly respectable post-Fascist movement. It also relied on the support of the Northern League, the secessionist-leaning party. The League, with its power base in Lombardy, the Veneto and Piedmont, strived for greater autonomy for the wealthy, industrialised north, and resented supporting the

10.25am, on the day in 1980 when a terrorist bomb ripped through Bologna train station.

A MARXIST PARTY WITHOUT MARX

A distinctive feature of Italian politics has been the influence of the Italian Communist Party (PCI). In the post-war years, the party cleaved to the Soviet Union's political line, and Rome's centrist government kept the communists at arm's length. Under Enrico Berlinguer, PCI secretary 1972–84, the party's orientation changed. It often led the Eurocommunism movement, favouring more independence from Moscow; it scolded the Soviets for human rights abuses and the Russian invasion of Afghanistan. On economic issues it grew ever more centrist, prompting some to dub it a "Marxist party without Marx". By 1981 the PCI attracted a third of the popular vote, and it was second only to the

Christian Democrats (DC) in size. Catholicism and communism were the two dominant political cultures of the post-war years. The collapse of communism in Eastern Europe led to the PCI splitting into the mainstream Democratic Party of the Left (DS) and a hard-line splinter group. After the upheavals of the 1990s, the DC was dissolved while the DS has seemingly lost its way and succumbed to infighting. Today's political scene is awash with new parties, even if many old faces remain. Tuscany and Emilia-Romagna remain left-leaning and liberal – but sleekly consumerist. This "Red Belt", once the communist heartland of central Italy, is nowadays more "pretty-in-pink" than radically red.

poorer south, an area which continues to struggle for economic survival.

Berlusconi's premiership was tainted by allegations of sex and sleaze scandals; in 2011 Berlusconi was being investigated for paying for sex with one of his guests (aged 17), and for "charitably" housing young female escorts in return for performances at his so-called "bunga bunga" parties. Throughout his political career he has appealed against charges of fraud, false accounting and corruption. Despite a suspended sentence for fraud in 1997, Berlusconi managed to maintain his media empire, high political profile and

the surprise rise of comedian Beppe Grillo's Five Star Movement who gained one in four of Italian votes. His anti-austerity policies had caught the people's imagination. Globally there was a loss of faith in Italy and share prices, both

> *The much-derided Northern League came up with a crazy proposal to increase the speed limit on Italian motorways from 130 to 150 km/h (93 mph) – but only if applied to big cars, and on motorways with speed traps.*

The indomitable Silvio Berlusconi.

ownership of AC Milan football club. In total to date he has been on trial over 20 times in 25 years and it is alleged he has links to the Mafia.

Berlusconi finally resigned in November 2011 as a result of a no-confidence vote brought about by controversy over budget reforms. Technocrat Mario Monti formed the new government and brought in further austerity cuts. Monti was an unpopular choice, and Berlusconi announced he would run again for prime minister in the 2013 elections, despite a jail sentence hanging over him for tax evasion. In February 2013 Italy went to the polls and two months of political chaos ensued. Neither centre-right nor centre-left gained an outright majority in the upper house, the Senate. Amid the chaos was

international and Italian, fell and the value of the euro dropped. Finally on April 24th Enrico Letta was designated prime minister, and he managed to form a grand coalition of his centre-left Democratic party with four other parties.

An uncertain legacy

It may be too early to assess Berlusconi's legacy and he continues to divide opinion. Detractors point to Berlusconi's ruthless pursuit of self-interest, his lack of probity and unstatesmanlike behaviour. However, while Berlusconi's gaffes regularly made him a laughing stock on the world stage, fans claim that he has proved a loyal ally to the United States and Britain, and tried to liberalise the economy and reform the fossilised state of Italian bureaucracy. His political career took another bad turn in 2013, when Italy's highest court – the Court of Cassation –convicted him for tax fraud. Due to his advancing age, Il Cavaliere escaped prison, receiving a year-long community service sentence instead (which was later cut short). As a result of this conviction, Berlusconi was forced to resign his seat at the Senate and barred from serving any legislative office for six years, all of which could finally put an end to his political career.

Italy has been facing an even more unstable future than usual, with towering national debt and reduced industrial output. Economically, Italy is highly exposed to the challenges of globalisation as a disproportionate share of its manufacturing is concentrated in clothing, footwear and white goods, where it cannot compete with the Asian Tiger economies. The challenge is to liberalise the economy and weaken the straitjacket of guild-like rules that have their origins in the Middle Ages.

But Italy's greatest task has been to reduce the public deficit, which was the highest in the EU. Austerity cuts were imposed in 2010 and the belt tightening measures continue to cause waves of strikes and unrest. The short-lived government under Enrico Letta promised growth policies and to scrap the planned increase in VAT. But Letta was quickly deposed and replaced by a much younger member of his own party – Matteo Renzi.

In 2014 the former major of Florence formed a new coalition government and embarked on an ambitious programme of reforms aimed at reviving the stagnant economy, cutting red tape to make the political system more efficient. Renzi pushed through a series of controversial institutional and political reforms which included curtailing the powers of the Senate and reducing the number of senators. He also scrapped some smaller taxes, overhauled the public administration and relaxed labour and employment laws. He even forced the heads of the largest state-owned companies to resign (claiming loss in public confidence) and replaced them with female managers. He also put forward an economic programme dubbed "Millegiorni" (Thousand Days), aimed at 'unblocking' Italy's economic powers in order to make it easier and quicker for major civil works and infrastructure projects to be implemented.

These radical moves had some positive effects: in mid-2015 the Italian economy registered a minimal growth, effectively ending the long recession. In 2016, Renzi endeavoured to push through even more radical changes to the Italian political system. These were approved by parliament but by a slim margin, thus requiring that they also be passed by referendum. In December, Renzi lost the popular vote and resigned as prime minister. He was replaced by Paolo Gentiloni and elections are likely to be scheduled for early 2017. One can can only hope that this time Tomasi di Lampedusa's famous claim that 'everything must change so that everything can stay the same' will prove to be wrong.

Matteo Renzi resigns after losing the referendum on proposed constitutional reforms.

GRAND DESIGNS

During his first premiership, Berlusconi was drawn to "grand projects". Saving Venice for posterity was a big enough project for any megalomaniac. The first stage of MOSE, the controversial mobile flood barrier, was met with a mixed reception. The project won support from Venice in Peril, but critics fear that the barrier is not reversible and could affect the delicate ecological balance, turning the lagoon into a stagnant pond. MOSE was also marred by a corruption scandal and 35 of its officials were arrested. When MOSE starts operating in 2018–20, flooding should be controlled, but it can do nothing to counteract the chronically raised water level, the city's next great challenge.

The Mafia

With its tradition of brutal private justice and its code of silence, or *omertà*, the Mafia remains Italy's biggest blight.

The Mafia still colours Sicilian life, but local attitudes are changing. Not that the Mafia is a unified entity confined to Sicily, where it is known as the "Cosa Nostra"; in Naples it mutates into the "Camorra", and in Calabria the "'Ndrangheta".

phenomenon of *pentitismo*, infiltrating bogus turn-coats, and weaving in false evidence to discredit witnesses and sow uncertainty.

As the old Mafia guard languishes in jail, the women have stepped into the breach, acting as messengers or enforcing extortion rackets. The last Mafia taboo has been broken. But some have turned state's evidence too. In 2009 the wife of a Sicilian gangster betrayed her husband at their daughters' request, and appealed to mob women to leave their men. Carmela Luculano's evidence sent her husband, Pino Rizzo, to jail, but is relatively rare in an organisation that expects submission and respect of the code of silence.

One of the maxi-trials held in the 1980s in Palermo.

The revulsion of Sicilians to the 1992 murders of the anti-Mafia judges Giovanni Falcone and Paolo Borsellino weakened the Mafia's grip on public opinion, its greatest weapon, and dented the age-old code of silence, or *omertà*. Pentiti ("the penitents"), as Mafia turncoats are called, grew from a handful in 1992, when Falcone was killed, to 500 a year later. As a result dozens of Dons, including "Toto" Riina, the Godfather of Corleone, were jailed, and the Sicilian Mafia has gone underground.

The new generation of gangster is as ruthless on the stock exchange as on the streets of Palermo, and is adept at money-laundering via the web, along with arms-dealing, drugs-dealing, extortion of public funds (particularly the European ones) and property speculation. The Mafia also exploits the

The Mafia's good old days

The Mafia emerged in the early 19th century, in the guise of brotherhoods formed to protect Sicilians from corruption, foreign oppression and feudalism, but which thrived on human misery. Between 1872 and World War I, poverty forced 1.5 million Sicilians to emigrate to the Americas, where many joined brotherhoods, and the foundations of Cosa Nostra were laid. During Prohibition, US bootlegging marked the Mafia's graduation from rural bands to urban gangsterism. In 1925, Mussolini tried to crush the Mafia but it won a reprieve in 1943, when the Allied invasion essentially reinstated the Mob, in exchange for help in paving the way for the invasion.

Naples became a fiefdom of Cosa Nostra, and was chosen by US gangsters as the site of Italy's first heroin refinery. Sicily's "Americanised" Mafia achieved its quantum leap in the late 1950s with the emerging drugs trade. In 1957, after a US crime crackdown, American bosses entrusted their Sicilian counterparts with the importation of heroin, linked to Lucky Luciano and Luciano Liggio.

Clan warfare

Liggio, a wartime marketeer, elevated his Corleonese family to the pinnacle of the Cosa Nostra. After being jailed in 1974, he was eclipsed by "Wild Beast" Toto Riina. The Corleonesi tactics were simple: the removal of mafiosi who coveted power or caused trouble. The 1980 clan wars left Palermo's streets bathed in blood, the Corleonesi undisputed victors, and Riina linked to 1,000 murders. The list of "illustrious corpses" included Palermo's prefect, dalla Chiesa, thought to have stumbled on the "Third Level", a top politician who protected the Mafia. Supergrass Tommaso Buscetta claimed that former premier Giulio Andreotti ordered the Mob to kill dalla Chiesa and a journalist, because they knew too much. His evidence led to "maxi-trials" in the 1980s, where hundreds of mafiosi sat in the dock, and launched magistrate Falcone's fight against the Mafia.

In 1992, the murder of Salvo Lima, the Sicilian leader of a faction led by Andreotti, provoked a terror campaign that saw the assassination of the public prosecutors, Falcone and Borsellino. Even if their "heroic" deaths marked a turning point, the terror continued in 1993 with bombs in Milan and Rome, and an explosion at Florence's Uffizi Gallery. The assassinations and attempt to destroy the nation's cultural treasures strengthened Italian resolve against the Mafia. Sicily even saw the rise of the Addiopizzo ("Goodbye *pizzo*") grassroots movement uniting businessmen and consumers who refuse to pay *pizzo* – a mafia extortion 'tax'.

In 2006, the fugitive Mafia Godfather, Bernardo Provenzano, was captured after 43 years on the run. The capture of the "Phantom of Corleone", also nicknamed "The Tractor" due to his propensity for mowing people down, provoked celebrations, even if cynics suspected the mobster had long been protected in his Corleone power base. After the arrest of Godfather Toto Riina in 1993, Provenzano led the Mafia underground, consolidating the crime syndicate and abandoning overt violence. He allegedly passed the leadership to Salvatore Lo Piccolo, a Palermitan Mafia boss, who was himself arrested in 2007. This left the way clear for ruthless rival boss Messina Denaro from Trapani to take over and reform the "Mafia Commission" or "Cupola", which instructs the clans and acts as arbiter in turf wars.

After the Sicilian Mafia dropped the baton in the 1990s, the Neapolitan Camorra and the 'Ndrangheta from Reggio Calabria picked it up. Unlike the more centrally controlled Sicilian Mafia, the Camorra, with its 20 rival clans, has always been volatile. Since 2004, hundreds have died in turf wars related to an annual £11 billion (US$20 billion) drugs trade. Naples' poverty-stricken northern suburbs have become a battleground, with protection rackets endemic, drug dealers executed and businesses torched. In 2006, Roberto Saviano's bestselling book *Gomorrah* offered a personal insight into the ruthless world of the Camorra. It must have been quite an accurate picture as the writer

Mafia godfather Bernardo Provenzano is arrested in Corleone.

now lives under police protection.

As for the 'Ndrangheta, in 2004 Italy's biggest anti-Mafia operation for a decade discovered that a drug-running clan had built an underground village below Plati. A year later, the vice-president of Calabria's regional council was gunned down.

Criminal practices remain entrenched, from illegal building in beauty spots to protection rackets. The mafia also funnels its illicit profits into legitimate businesses such as supermarket and hotel chains across the country. It is also very efficient in high-jacking EU funding. In 2012 it was reported that the Italian *mafiosi* had joined forces with the Mexican drug cartels to bring cocaine into the European market. It is believed the Calabrian mafia now controls up to 80 percent of the cocaine supply in Europe.

*A breathtaking view of Manarola,
Le Cinque Terre.*

THE CONTEMPORARY SCENE

Tradition and rebellion, conformity and
individuality, chaos and over-regulation...
Italian life is riddled with paradoxes.

According to Sergio Romano, a political journalist on *La Stampa*, "Italy is a constellation of large families, whether ideological, political, professional or criminal – the Church, the business community, the trade unions, the professions, state bureaucracies and the Mafia." He observes that "each family strives for sovereignty", acting as a fierce lobby group and dooming most national reforms to failure.

At the simplest level, Italians create a cosy little world of "their" baker, dressmaker and picture-framer, conveying the social status of a patron rather than of a mere consumer. Personal recommendation is everything. And beyond lies the arbitrary world of bureaucracy, in which citizens feel powerless in the face of state indifference. Many commentators conclude that Italy would be a paradise if it could only reinvent the relationship between citizen and state. Yet without political chaos and conflicting social groups, the Italians would cease to be Italians and become Swiss.

Italians are Catholic.

The political picture

The Italian mindset precludes a modern democracy, seeming to favour an abyss between the state and its citizens. The people swing between political disaffection and an obsession with politics. Fortunately, however, they also have an innate talent for brinkmanship, coupled with an ability to conjure compromise out of conflict. But if Italy totters along in an amiable

> *Politics rarely impinge on social divisions: a member of the DS, the former Communist Party, may be a Catholic, wear Armani and have a Romanian maid.*

state of chaos, it may be because Italians like it that way. "Controllers and controlled have an unspoken agreement," notes columnist Beppe Severgnini. "You don't change, we don't change, and Italy doesn't change, but we all complain that we can't go on like this."

The country positions itself as the new Italy, turning its back on a baroque political structure steeped in *clientelismo* (nepotism). Even so, one in three people finds a job through a relative. Italy remains deeply old-fashioned, despite its faddism. Italians pride themselves on their free spirit, yet society remains static, while protectionism has preserved many monopolies, including limiting the growth of super-pharmacies, even if shopping malls are slowly moving in. Despite their sense of tradition, Italians have a mania for modernity, novelty and new-fangled gadgetry, from the latest mobile phones to shopping malls.

Milan is the business capital, a sophisticated metropolis dedicated to moneymaking and pleasure. Most wealth is still created in northern and central regions, such as Lombardy, the Veneto and Emilia-Romagna. However, although the Ferrari, Prada and Armani fiefdoms are well known abroad, most Italian companies are small, family-run firms. These provide more than two-thirds of indus-

Murals in Italy often have political or socially critical statements, here 'fertiliser not bullets'.

trial employment, from textiles in Tuscany to designer sunglasses in the Veneto or bathroom taps in Piedmont. Even so, high unemployment and low consumer demand mask a thriving black economy. In the workplace, industrial action is commonplace.

The recession and the country's uncompetitiveness are major concerns. Privatisation of the public utilities did not end state interference. Given the traditional monopoly of top jobs in state companies by the political parties, politicians remain reluctant to give up their power. By the same token, the family dynasties who dominate the economy still hold sway. With his patrician charm and playboy reputation,

> *"It is not impossible to govern Italians, it is pointless." Mussolini's judgement has been borne out by the country's perpetual sense of teetering on the edge.*

the late Gianni Agnelli epitomised the closed, dynastic style of Italian capitalism. After his death in 2003, the Turin football stadium was renamed in his honour, and the Fiat family empire survives.

A complex but coherent society

The social system is a rich landscape, not calibrated on class, success or wealth but on subtle distinctions. In conventional terms, a class system exists but has different connotations. The aristocracy thrives, thanks to its adaptability. Many *marchesi* (marquesses) are entrepreneurs, carving niches in the fashion, art, wine and food industries. The Tuscan Frescobaldi and Sicilian Tasca are still big wine dynasties, while the Ferragamo fashion and hotel empires thrive in Florence.

While class-consciousness and accent are essentially immaterial, the *borghesi* (middle classes) form a cohesive group, as do the *agricoltori* (encompassing peasants and farmers). The ranks of the middle classes are swelling, even among the criminal caste. A recent Mafia round-up revealed that many new-generation Dons are doctors or lawyers, in sharp contrast to the Cosa Nostra's agrarian roots, and even to recent Godfathers, who were barely literate. Whatever one's profession, honorific titles count, especially in

IN GOOD FAITH?

Curiously, the phrase often used to bemoan declining standards is: "There's no religion left any more." Jonathan Keates describes the Italian attitude to religion as "a lackadaisical Catholicism taken out of mothballs at christenings, first communions, weddings and funerals". Increasingly, Italy's practising Catholics prefer to take their cue not from the pope but from personal conscience or the liberal wing of the Church. Civic culture, regional pride and fierce individualism form the real Italian faith today. Even so, the election of Pope Francis in 2013 brought huge crowds to the Vatican and a keen sense of involvement.

the south: an engineer is addressed as *"ingegnere"*; *dottore* (doctor) is a mark of respect bestowed on anyone with gravitas.

Apart from the north–south divide, the key distinction is between *statali*, civil servants, and non-*statali*, the rest. Civil servants are seen as cosseted, with a protected pension and a job for life. Ranged against them are the *dipendenti* (company employees), *autonomi* (self-employed), *imprenditori* (entrepreneurs) and, lastly, the *liberi professionisti* (professionals). The employees claim the moral high ground, charging civil servants with exploiting the system and accusing the self-employed and professionals of tax evasion. This is a strange Italian stalemate in which private-sector workers (non-*statali*) justify tax evasion on the grounds that their taxes would only perpetuate the bloated state bureaucracy and southern incompetence. Tax evasion is a sport and a duty. If he were to cheat on his taxes in Italy, remarks Beppe Severgnini, "Two neighbours would come round to ask me how I did it, and two more would loathe me in silence."

A recent pressure group are the *precari*, workers on temporary contracts who crave security. Around 3.3 million people, mostly young, fall into this category, from language teachers to hotel workers. Without holiday pay, overtime or job security, many resort to "cocooning", concentrating on their private lives and opting out of the rat race. Over 35 percent of these workers are based in the far south and the islands of Sicily and Sardinia, an area hard pressed with severe austerity cuts.

Despite a country mired in recession with record high unemployment, a banking crisis and pressure from international financial markets, only 75 percent of the population turned out to vote in the 2013 elections. Corruption is still endemic, even seen as getting worse with more high profile scandals emerging. After the resignation of Berlusconi in 2011, the interim Prime Minister, Mario Monti, put forward new anti-corruption laws, bringing new crimes into the penal code and improving accountability. In 2013, with the government under Prime Minister Enrico Letta, further austerity cuts caused widespread unrest. Letta quickly lost support of his own Democratic Party members and was forced to resign. In 2014, he was replaced at the helm of the party and the government by Matteo Renzi, the young, left-leaning former mayor of Florence, who launched an ambitious programme

of political and institutional reforms. Dubbed "demolition man", Renzi pushed through parliament a controversial labour market reform, changed the electoral system, curtailed the powers of the Senate and reduced the number of senators. He also passed a law legalising same-sex civil unions. On the downside, he struggled with high youth unemployment (over 39 percent in July 2016) and a deepening immigration crisis caused by the constant flow of immigrants from war-torn Libya and Syria. In 2015 alone, more than 1,600 migrants died while trying to get to Italian shores. Other pressing issues that will

Pope Francis in St Peter's Square.

need addressing by Renzi's successor include a weak economy (which shrunk by 10 percent in 2007–2014 only to start a weak recovery in 2015), a rising popularity of the populist Five Star Party and the banking crisis.

Popular culture and the arts

Both in the art world and in the broader cultural arena, Italian genius thrives on dissension, diversity and unbridled rivalry. However, music and the performing arts are more dynamic than the literary scene: Italy has always been a musical, visual and verbal culture more than a literary one. Contemporary fiction is an acquired taste, one that few acquire. A recent survey reports that a third of Italians never read, and

Heritage Industry

Italy has more Unesco World Heritage sites than any other country – the challenge is to maintain them, without selling off the family silver.

There is a price to pay for Italy's historic cultural riches. Air pollution, illegal building and sewage-laden water are endangering a third of Italy's Unesco sites, including such treasures as Pompeii's ancient ruins.

A city tour of Noto, Sicily.

Burdened by its costly heritage, towns in Italy often resemble a cultural building site, with many buildings and monuments under wraps. That's without considering the cost of natural disasters, such as the earthquakes in L'Aquila and Amatrice in 2009 and 2016 respectively (see page 319).

Vandalism is another problem, with Italy's sculptural treasures particularly vulnerable. As the despairing head of the Carabinieri's art-theft unit says: "Italy is an open-air museum, with many of its most celebrated works of art standing on streets and squares, and nowhere is this truer than in Florence."

The state is also under pressure to "sell the family silver" to the highest bidder. State assets, ranging from palaces to prisons, monasteries to islands, have already been auctioned. In the case of Venice, this Unesco gem has already "lost" numerous islands to hotel developers, as the council has sold some Grand Canal palaces to fill depleted city coffers.

Recent developments

Despite the threats to the nation's heritage, unqualified success stories abound. Amid the frantic fire-and-ice effects of the 2006 Winter Olympics, Turin was rebranded as a cinematic capital, Baroque stage and cutting-edge design centre. Key sites underwent makeovers, from the Egyptian Museum to the star-studded Cinema Museum. Turin's renaissance continued with the restoration of the Unesco-listed Venaria Reale, Italy's Versailles, and projects celebrating the Unification of Italy in 2011.

In the meantime, the country continues to open major museums and stage dazzling art extravaganzas. All over Italy, seemingly mundane restoration work ensures that masterpieces survive, such as Caravaggio's *Adoration of the Shepherds in Messina* or the restoration of Baroque Noto, also in Sicily. Elsewhere, archaeologists are constantly unearthing Etruscan or Roman treasures, most recently in Lombardy, Tuscany and Rome. In Brescia, the discovery of frescoed Pompeian-style villas confirm that the city boasts the greatest concentration of Roman remains north of the Rome.

Rome's solution has been to allow luxury brands to fund the restoration of its most iconic landmarks. The Colosseum got a new façade courtesy of Tod's and the Trevi Fountain gleams again thanks to Fendi.

Aristocratic entrepreneurialism

Given the heavyweight nature of Italian heritage, stately homes tend to be treated as a burden, with little incentive for owners to turn their properties into public attractions. However, local landowners are increasingly taking the initiative. In Tuscany, country seats have been reborn as wine estates or rural resorts, but even the Sicilians are showing enterprise: princesses in Palermo are staging cookery courses and masked balls to save the ancestral seats.

Near Trieste, Duino Castle, home of the princes Torre and Tasso, inventors of the modern postal service, is a model of entrepreneurial flair. The family, who trace their lineage back to Bonaparte, still live in the medieval castle yet welcome visitors, happily throwing their towers open to wedding banquets or corporate retreats. Few can resist celebrating an event on Roman ruins, overlooking a Druidic site dedicated to the sun god, or on a medieval terrace overlooking the Gulf of Trieste. The Italian heritage industry looks safe for some time to come.

that a mere 8 percent can be considered regular readers. This is either confirmation that Italy is a predominantly visual culture, or linked to the fact that pleasure lies elsewhere – on the beach or on "the box". Italians watch more (bad) television than any other nationality in Europe.

The classical music scene is thriving and not restricted to the great opera houses: Italy boasts some of the best musical festivals in Europe, from the operatic masterpieces performed in Verona's lovely Roman amphitheatre, the Arena di Verona, to the Puccini Festival at the composer's lakeside home in Tuscany's Torre del Lago.

Italian high culture tends to be buffeted by perennial funding crises. The Berlusconi government urged citizens to take responsibility for their heritage. A shock advertising campaign showed images of mutilated artistic icons, such as Leonardo da Vinci's *Last Supper* with the Disciples scratched out. The provocative slogan was: "Without your help, Italy could lose something," which singularly failed to elicit mass donations to save the country's treasures. Fortunately, local businesses and banks see themselves as stakeholders in their city's cultural identity, so pride and political pressure usually prompt a rescue bid. Banks, such as Monte dei Paschi in Siena, can sometimes single-handedly fund "their" city's cultural life, from sponsoring blockbuster Renaissance art exhibitions to saving small museums from ruin.

The media moguls

Popular culture is dominated by television and by the power of monopolies. American-style anti-trust laws do not exist in Italy: telecommunications, publishing and the mass media are aces held in a few family hands. Berlusconi still dominates the airwaves by owning the three most popular channels and influences RAI TV's three "public" channels. Mediaset, his media arm, controls channels that draw 60 percent of the audience share to "trashy TV". With a few exceptions, the output is devoted to propaganda, poor-quality American imports and platitudinous game shows, although standards on RAI 3 are distinctly higher.

"Arriverderci to cleavage" were the headlines on a crusade to clean up sexism on state-funded television. This was in response to a shift in public mood to the way women are portrayed on television. Yet sexism on television simply reflected the tawdry realities of political life, where the former premier was seen to promote beautiful babes as political candidates, irrespective of ability.

About a year after the fall of Berlusconi a new head of Italy's state television, the formi-

> Jorge Mario Bergoglio was inaugurated pope in March 2013 after Pope Benedict XVI renounced the papacy. Taking the papal name of Francis, he is the first pope from a Latin American country and the first Jesuit too.

Palazzo di Montecitorio, the seat of the Italian Chamber of Deputies.

dable Anna Maria Tarantola, launched a crusade against the "bunga, bunga" Berlusconi era. Appointed by Mario Monti to clean up the media, she was part of a distinct shift in attitude towards women in public life in both politics and business.

Health and happiness

Despite its weaknesses, Italy appears in robust health. The World Health Organization rates the Italian national health service highly, even if there can be huge disparities between the north and south in terms of facilities and care.

The successful smoking ban has seen smoking decline by a further 2 million people, down

> *It seems the country enjoys a flexible moral code, except when it comes to drugs. Italy operates a zero-tolerance policy, with anyone found in possession of hard or soft drugs open to prosecution for dealing.*

to a current 10.3 million smokers (about 19 percent of the population) and the incidence of death from heart attacks significantly lowered. Further stringent anti-tobacco laws introduced in 2016 are likely to reduce the number of

Sardinian elders.

smokers even more. These include hefty fines for throwing cigarette butts on the ground or smoking in a car (even parked) as well as in and around hospitals. Surveys also show that Italians are models of moderation, the most sensible drinkers in Europe. Ninety percent claim never to consume more than two alcoholic drinks in one session. Coffee is the real vice: the Italians are reportedly the keenest consumers in Europe.

Even so, health scandals abound, with clinics, particularly in Sicily and Calabria, often linked to crime syndicates and substandard services. Second only to drug-trafficking, the control of public and private contracting is the most lucrative activity for organised crime, with a

turnover of £11.8 billion (US$23 billion). Fortunately, the Mafia also cares about its own members' health and happiness: criminal gangs have resorted to cheese raids, hijacking lorries containing wheels of Parmesan cheese. The love of the good life is not restricted to the virtuous.

Not that the *dolce vita* is dead in society at large. Italians have always ranked well in the quality of life reports. An Italian version of the survey, by the respected *Il Sole 24 Ore* newspaper, rates northern Italian cities as being home to the smuggest citizens. The Alpine arc of Trieste, Belluno and Sondrio score highest for quality of life, but medium-sized towns in Tuscany and Emilia-Romagna also score highly on the happiness scale. Curiously, the sunnier the place, the less contented the population, so the south fares badly, apart from Sardinia. Austerity cuts, too, have played their part in dissatisfaction in the south. Facile conclusions suggest that happiness means mountain air or medium-sized, medieval towns, aided by copious amounts of coffee.

The notion of happiness is inextricably linked to *allegria,* fun, second cousin to festivity. Foremost among the reassuring rituals of Italian life is the love of spectacle. During the opera season, La Scala's marbled and mirrored lobby is awash with Milanese matrons in furs, a spectacle matched by operatic Sicilians in Palermo's Teatro Massimo. The love of display cuts across regional and social divides, from the chic Venice Carnival to the smallest Umbrian truffle festival.

Tellingly, there is no Italian term for privacy. The emphasis is on the everyday values of sociability, simplicity and pleasure. The essence of Italian sociability is the *passeggiata*, the evening parade, with pauses for preening, flirting and gossiping. Social life is neatly ordered, even underpinned by excessive planning. Commenting on the cloying social packaging of Italian life, novelist and long-term Italian resident Tim Parks says: "Cappuccino until ten, then espresso; aperitivo after twelve; your pasta, your meat, your dolce in bright packaging; light white wine, strong red wine, prosecco; baptism, first communion, marriage, funeral."

> *After a bitter court battle with his cousin, Prince Victor Emmanuel has been recognised as the rightful heir to the throne of Italy. The Savoy title can only be used by himself and his son.*

Football Fever

Football is huge in Italy. Although they crashed out of the 2014 World Cup, the Italians have won the trophy four times.

Football, like fashion, is at the heart of Italian life. Dolce & Gabbana declare: "We have always been football fans and footballers are, for us, the new male icons." The design duo have dressed the World Cup national team and featured the stars in steamy locker-room scenes for their collections. Dolce supports (and dresses) AC Milan, while Gabbana favours rivals Inter Milan, who have had more success in recent years.

Italy has a fine World Cup record, even if there was no jumping into fountains after the 2014 tournament. Italy won the 2006 World Cup but victory came during the Calciopoli ("Footballgate") match-fixing furore, one of the biggest scandals in sporting history. Phone taps revealed sporting fraud perpetrated by managers and referees, leaving Juventus stripped of its Championship titles and relegated to Serie B, while AC Milan and other teams were docked points. Despite the sacking of managers and the prosecution of match officials, probity has not dribbled down the wings of the Italian game. Referees face a struggle to regain their credibility. Still, recalling the notorious Rolex scandal, when the watches found their way onto the wrists of key referees, courtesy of Ast Roma, lavish gifts are now considered bribes, a first for Italian football.

Subversively, football often lobs an own goal at its political masters, unsurprising in a country where the beautiful game is a metaphor for political success. Berlusconi rose to prominence on the back of his ownership of AC Milan, and named his party after a football chant. Italy's top teams have always been the ultimate boy's toys for the country's power-brokers. While AC Milan belongs to media mogul Berlusconi, Juventus remains a plaything for the Agnelli car dynasty.

At home, Italian football is not the success story it once was, even if Buffon (Juventus) is rated the world's best goalkeeper. In the 1980s these stadia drew Europe's largest crowds, with averages of nearly 40,000 a match. Since then, attendance has fallen, possibly linked to the predictability of certain fixtures rather than to the Calciopoli scandal. It is a different story abroad, where Italian

coaches are greatly prized, especially in England, where Fabio Capello coached the English side in 2008–12 and Claudio Ranieri won the Premier League title in typical underdog fashion with Leicester in the 2015/16 season.

Controversy is never far from Italian football, especially in home derbies. Given the sectarian nature of society, rival teams in the same city are commonplace. In the case of bitter rivals Roma and Lazio, the clash is underscored by a polarised fan base: Roma supporters see themselves as liberal-minded urbanites and, unfairly, dismiss Lazio fans as country bumpkins or Fascistic thugs.

Devoted Italian fans.

The jury is still out on whether endemic corruption is being tackled, but football violence seems to be on the wane. In 2007, the death of a policeman during violent clashes following a Sicilian derby led to the temporary closure of stadiums, and probably cost the country the chance to stage Euro 2012. The Italians pay lip-service to the lessons learnt by the British experience of hooliganism, Even so, weapons searches, harsher penalties for hooliganism, and the introduction of all-seater stadiums have been accepted.

On the pitch, a new law forbids swearing at opponents: perpetrators are sent off. With their renewed commitment to "the beautiful game", Italians were disappointed to lose the bid for Euro 2016 to France where they lost to Germany in the quarterfinals.

THE ITALIANS

Individualism, a sense of survival and natural ebullience are qualities almost all Italians share – but there the similarities end.

It has been said that Italians do not exist, that those who are thought of as Italian regard themselves as Piedmontese, Tuscan, Venetian, Sicilian, Calabrian and so on. No one has ever classified the Italians convincingly: to be born in Palermo, Sicily, or in Turin, Piedmont, is a classification in itself. Sometimes even fellow-countrymen feel like foreigners. In Pietro Germi's film *Il Cammino della Speranza (The Path of Hope)*, a peasant says: "There's bad people in Milan, they eat rice."

Generations have learned the art of *arrangiarsi*, of getting along in difficult situations. Adjusting to political change and foreign conquest has generated a flexible mentality and a detached attitude towards political regimes, all of which are considered ephemeral. The forest of rules, statutes, norms and regulations has engendered distrust of the state.

North versus south

"Southerners tend to make money in order to rule, northerners to rule in order to make money," declared the writer Luigi Barzini. The conflicting values of north and south reflect different cultures and history. Compared with the industrialised, progressive north, the agrarian, conservative south experienced feudalism, oppression, corruption, poverty and neglect. Known as the Mezzogiorno, the region has suffered grandiose white elephants, called "cathedrals in the desert": steelworks sited in remote places with no proper infrastructure. Cut off from the progress and markets of northern Europe, southerners were left for their own survival. Before 1914, more than 5 million emigrated to North America alone.

Although emigration is on the wane, the south still suffers from depopulation, perceived backwardness and a great gap between rich and

A passion for good food unites Italians.

poor. Southerners, known as *meridionali*, often encounter prejudice, with northerners resenting "subsidising" the south through taxation. Indeed, some northerners see such aid as pouring their hard-earned money into the pockets of the Camorra in Naples or the Mafia in Sicily. The north–south divide, in all its tragicomic aspects, remains at the heart of Italian life.

Navel-gazing about what it means to be Italian is not a common pastime. However, the marking of the 150th anniversary of Italian Unification in 2011 put the issue of *Italianita* (Italian-ness) on the agenda. The conclusions suggest that in an intensely parochial nation, regional differences are, in themselves, a defining feature of being Italian. As for unity and shared values, all the natives will agree on is a devotion to Italian cuisine, in all its forms, and feverish support for *gli azzuri*, "the boys in blue" in international football matches.

Politics and individualism

The average person in the street expresses a revulsion for politics: *la politica è una cosa sporca* (politics are a dirty thing) is a typical view. This is based on a belief that all parties are the same, and that politics work only for politicians. The Italians remain sceptical of the state, and cannot conceive of abstract solutions or trust in ideologies. Behind such opinions lurks an unrestrained individualism that denies civic responsibility. Yet hand in hand with individualistic entrepreneurship, there is a nostalgic yearning for "the strong man" whose power and will is stamped on his face, whose voice captures the nation's mood. It was a wave of such nostalgia for authoritarian answers that swept Alessandra Mussolini, grand-daughter of Benito, into parliament in 1992, and helped Silvio Berlusconi to his third term as premier in 2008.

The strong sense that Italians have of their own self-importance is evident in their dislike of queuing or of respecting rules. "We think it's an insult to our intelligence to comply with a regulation," writes commentator Beppe Severgnini.

"Obedience is boring. We want to think about it. We want to decide whether a particular law applies to our specific case. In that place, at that time." Hence red traffic lights rarely mean stop. A pedestrian crossing at 6am might count as a "negotiable red", a "weak orange" at a busy traffic junction might be a *rosso pieno*, a full red. It all depends. Only a cappuccino after 10am is non-negotiable.

Italians are far more conformist than they would wish, whether with regard to drinking coffee at set times, obeying non-smoking laws or wearing orange, if deemed the season's colour. Self-regard is reflected in the way Italians dress. Shoes, ties, lovely fabrics and liberty of the imagination all contribute to the *costume*. Fastidious care is lavished on cars, seen as extensions of their owners' personalities. Yet beyond the surface gloss, there is a sense of humanity that transcends differences. As Severgnini wrily points out, Italian air hostesses are hopeless at serving you coffee but good at cleaning it up and sympathising when you spill it. Giulio

Customers queue up in this popular Roman pizzeria.

Andreotti, the machiavellian seven-times premier, also singles out this sense of common humanity: "In Italy there are no angels nor devils, only average sinners." This tolerant Roman Catholic society is nurtured on the concept of original sin, universal temptation and redemption, so penitence can erase sins, even crimes.

Despite an authoritarian pope, same-sex civil unions, abortion and divorce are legal, while contraception is widely accepted. Indeed, much to the chagrin of the Vatican, Italy has the lowest birth rate in Europe. Catholicism has a stronger hold in the south and in the Veneto than in the former "red belt" of Emilia-Romagna, Umbria and Tuscany. According to a recent survey, more than 85 percent of Italians claim to be Catholics, but only a quarter attend Mass regularly. Nonetheless, Catholicism still plays an important role in rituals, from first holy communion to the marriage ceremony and Christian burial.

Sex and the family

While the family remains the bedrock of traditional Italian society, *mammismo*, the cult of the mother, is its cornerstone. The iconic image of the mother pervades the male approach to courtship and his choice of bride. Once married, however, male infidelity is often quietly condoned, provided that the family is supported and appearances preserved.

A recent report reveals that divorce happens every four minutes in a country once regarded as a bastion of marriage. Tellingly, three out of 10 marriages fail because of the unhealthily close attachment of Italian men to their mothers. An intrusive mother-in-law may expect her adult offspring to eat with her every Sunday, or may deal with her married son's domestic chores. Moreover, disillusioned daughters-in-law help account for the popularity of the therapist's couch, a trend exacerbated by the "superwoman" syndrome, which is, in turn, linked to the low birth rate, one of the lowest in Europe: if so much is now expected of working women, having one child is challenging enough.

In terms of morality, a north–south divide prevails, with southern values more traditional and northern mores similar to those of northern Europe. Even here, appearances are more

A Sicilian wedding.

BIG BABIES

Italy is full of "big babies", a social phenomenon steeped in significance for family-minded Italians. Known as *bamboccioni*, these "big babies" live at home until they marry – and then move next door, to a flat bought by their parents. The concept of *mammoni*, sons who cling to apron strings, is common, with boys over-indulged into adulthood. But girls can also be "big babies", reluctant to flee the nest.

Renato Brunetta, a minister in the last Berlusconi government proposed a law in 2010 to oblige children to leave home at 18, a ploy designed to stimulate debate about the fact that three-quarters of Italians in the 18–35 age group still live at home.

In their defence, some "big babies" claim that their studies or finances preclude them from renting a flat. They might even be *precari*, part-timers, seasonal workers or freelancers, with no job security. This in a country where job security is traditionally seen as one's birthright. There is still no social stigma in being supported by the family. In 2010 a 32-year-old student from Bergamo won a court case against her father after he had decided to stop funding her tuition – after eight years and no degree in the offing. In fact the statistics point to a further rise in the numbers staying at home, with the continuing problems with the economy and unemployment highest among this age group.

important than reality. A slick young Milanese banker attaches as much importance to family ties as does the humblest Calabrian peasant, and neither would dare miss Sunday lunch with their parents.

As for sex, discretion counts for much, and provided premarital relationships are not flaunted, honour is maintained. Since students tend to live at home, and offspring are reluctant to flee the nest, romantic assignments can take on the complexity of a Pirandello farce. Male offspring may also rely on a doting mother to act as a domestic drudge.

on enjoyment. Simple things, such as eating a meal, taking a walk, having an ice cream, watching the world go by, become special in Italy. Life is enjoyed to the fullest, with a flair gained over centuries of practice.

The new Italians

For a country with its roots in so many races, Italy is far from being a multiracial society, and Italian culture predominates. Settlers linked to Carthage, Constantinople, Normandy, North Africa and Moorish Spain have all made their mark in Italy, whether as colonisers or plunder-

Sicilian smiles.

A style of life

The Italian style of life is beset by intractable problems, from officialdom to a barely functioning legal system and dysfunctional governments. In the workplace, fear of failure stymies innovation, as does the Italians' reluctance to relocate, should a better job beckon. At the deepest level, Italians seem unable to believe in the possibility of constructive change. But merely listing the ills is missing the point. Italian life is not about work and progress, but about survival and individualism, family and friends, roots and relaxation. Italian life sparkles with a brilliance unmatched anywhere else in Europe. The Italians have perfected a lifestyle that may be short on efficiency but is long

ers. But given Italy's lack of significant empire since Roman times, the colonial lessons have been lost. Italians have been slow to accept that someone can be visibly non-European yet fully assimilated, or even an Italian citizen.

In the last decade or so, the influx of newcomers has made an impact, both in the northern cities and in the southern countryside. Cosy assumptions have been shattered by the existence of ethnic-looking children, born in Italy, who speak Italian with a Roman accent, or by Romanian therapists who have taken Italian citizenship and integrated perfectly. More usually, the different ethnic groups lead parallel lives in their own communities, and there are few mixed marriages and little assimilation.

Italy's historic ethnic groups comprise the Greek, Jewish, Armenian and Albanian communities who have had footholds in Italian towns since medieval times. In many cases, local traditions are retained, as happens with the Greeks and Albanians in Sicily and Calabria.

Officially, foreigners make up less than 8 percent of the population. Albanians, Romanians, Moroccans, Ukrainians and Chinese are the biggest ethnic minority groups, along with the French and South Americans, but recent waves of migrants have been from Africa and Eastern Europe. Most immigrants remain second-class citizens, unable to vote and unlikely to gain Italian citizenship. Moreover, immigrants do the jobs that Italians shun, whether on factory production lines or in the tomato fields of the south. Racist incidents occur sporadically in immigrant "hotspots", including street battles

> During Lent, the Vatican has encouraged Italy's faithful to give up texting rather than more traditional treats. Italians send an average of 50 texts a month, second only to the British.

between North African and South American immigrants in a deprived Milanese suburb.

As the back door to Europe, Italy struggled to cope with the influx of boat people, especially from Albania and Africa. First it was Puglia, caught in the eye of the "Albanian Hurricane". Then it was Sicily's turn in 2006, with thousands washed up on the remote island of Lampedusa, sandwiched between Sicily and Libya, and the influx continues to this day. Even if the European Union was the goal, many stayed in Italy nonetheless, particularly given the magnetic pull of the wealthy northern cities, including Milan and Brescia.

Integration and segregation

In 2009 Italy cracked down on illegal immigration, declaring it a crime for the first time. Immigrants caught without a permit can now be expelled immediately, as well as being heavily fined. Certain categories, such as doctors, are to be treated more leniently. Other measures

This Roman policeman has his work cut out.

THE ITALIAN LANGUAGE

Of the Romance languages, Italian is one of the closest to Latin. Modern Italian owes much to writers such as Dante and Manzoni, who assumed as their standard the educated language of Tuscany. Today the finest form of speech is said to be *la lingua toscana in bocca romana* ("the Tuscan tongue in the Roman mouth").

In the 16th century, the Holy Roman Emperor, Charles V, is said to have spoken Spanish with God, French with men, German with his horse, but Italian with women since it was capable of expressing such subtleties of thought and feeling. Italian can be as precise as any other language, yet the style of newspaper editorials, art criticism and political speeches, in particular, is often pretentious and wilfully obscure.

Until recently, more than 1,500 dialects existed alongside Italian, most virtually incomprehensible beyond their own village. The advent of television has done much to further the cause of "standard" Italian but has not dealt a death blow to dialects. Although on the decline, dialects are still spoken by the elderly. Many dialects contain foreign terms introduced by past occupiers, including borrowings from Arabic in Sicilian dialects, or French influences in the Piedmontese dialect. All dialects are a way of staying in touch with one's roots, and there is little stigma attached to regional accents either.

include tough fines for landlords who rent to illegal immigrants, and a longer waiting period for foreigners seeking citizenship through marriage. The wearing of a *burqa* can incur a fine. All these measures followed equally controversial policies to repatriate "boat people" to Libya, which critics say violated their rights. Those not granted asylum can be held in detention centres for up to six months prior to deportation.

Despite these restrictions, recent years saw a new wave of immigrants pouring into Italy, mainly from worn-torn Syria and Somalia. In 2015 alone, some 170,000 immigrants made it

regions. A *straniero* can be a foreigner or someone from the next village, so ingrained is the sense of belonging to one's own village, town or region. Moreover, the political agenda of separatist groups has exploited the resentment of the wealthy north towards the impoverished south.

However, there is implicit racism in the word *extracomunitari*, common parlance for non-white immigrants, and the *vu compra*, the pejorative term for African street vendors, who traipse tourist haunts, selling fake designer bags. People-trafficking, prostitution and gangsterism are attributed to "foreigners", even if

Indian men shopping at the Mercato Esquilino in Rome.

to the Italian shores, putting an unprecedented strain on the Italian economy and fomenting social tensions. In the first three months of 2016, the number of illegal immigrants arriving in Italy was 60 percent higher than the same period the previous year. PM Matteo Renzi has called upon the EU to help Italy and other frontier countries deal with the crisis and adopt a common asylum and immigration policy.

With little recent history of empire, the Italians veer between demonising and fetishising foreigners, particularly non-EU citizens. The typical professional workplace is still closed to ethnic minorities, but to dub the Italian majority racist misses the point: Italians are most scathing about their fellow-countrymen from "rival"

> In a classic Berlusconi gaffe that passes for immigration policy among his devoted fans, the premier once told his Albanian counterpart: "We will only accept the pretty girls from Albania".

the natives have proved perfectly competent at drug-running and Mafia murder themselves.

On a positive note, even in cities where racial tensions are most felt, such as Brescia and Milan, there is nothing resembling a ghetto, and none of the race riots that have scarred France. Ethnic restaurants and bohemian bars have been slow in coming, but Italians have finally acquired a taste for them.

THE ITALIAN LOOK

Supreme visual sense, a feeling for fashion and a creative twist on classic lines form the essence of the Italian look.

Only an Italian fashion editor could be so sweeping: "The Versaces and Armanis are our modern-day Michelangelos, helping dress our dreams. Anything else isn't *moda* – it simply serves to cover us." In other words, from the Renaissance to Romeo Gigli is but a small step, preferably taken in Ferragamo footwear, La Perla lingerie and Prada sunglasses. On Planet Fashion, you don't so much name-check the designer brands as breathe them, eat them, sleep them, and even live their dreams. Milan is at the cutting edge of consumerism and bombards us with beguiling messages. Brand brainwashing has fashionistas going to bed with Bulgari, waking up with Armani, and breakfasting with Gucci. The designers are getting in on the lifestyle act, beguiling us with branded bars, spas, bars and galleries.

Secret conformists

Italians may pride themselves on their individuality and exhibitionism but are often bound to brands or conventions. Dressing appropriately for the occasion is more important than dressing to please one's mood. To be accidentally overdressed for a visit to a park or pizzeria can be a cardinal sin; equally, a mere "stroll" can be code for parading in one's finery. If in doubt, the look of de luxe anonymity is the safe sartorial badge.

In a country that worships visual display, style is an emblem of high seriousness, with great attention accorded to the simple purchase of a picture or a place mat. The world remains in awe of Italian taste, inviting native talent to style American furniture, Japanese cameras, German limousines and French family cars. As a result, *la linea italiana*, Italian style, has a continuing impact on international design.

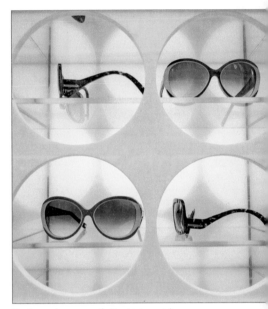

Prada sunglasses are a fashionista's must-have.

Milan: fashion mecca

The contribution of fashion to Italy's balance of payments is second only to tourism. Commercially, the industry is more successful than its French counterpart, with the Milan collections considered more wearable.

Italian fashion thrives on a long craft tradition, a ready supply of homegrown talent and a contemporary feel, essentially a creative twist on classic lines. Its deep design roots lie in medieval craftsmanship, traditional skills which are prized *in haute couture* (*alta moda*) as well as in the making of quality fabrics, jewellery, bags and shoes. Native designers also have a highly developed aesthetic sense dating back to the Renaissance.

Florence was Italy's original fashion capital

but, for cognoscenti, Milan now has a monopoly on "the Italian look". Milan's fashion and design status has developed not by chance but by design. An innovative industrial culture and sound mass-production techniques set the city on its successful course, particularly after World War II, when the design industry came into its own. The Triennale, the Italian "temple of design", is now in the 1940s premises that pioneered mass production of household objects; it also boasts an exhibition of Italian design, from vintage scooters to early Olivetti computers.

As the country's design capital, Milan remains

The Prada look.

a well-tailored, cosmopolitan city that knows how to put on a show, whether during Fashion Weeks or at the equally celebrated Furniture Fair.

Cutting-edge Turin

Yet Turin also sees itself as a vibrant, visionary city, proud of its cutting-edge culture and museums of contemporary art. As the centre of the car industry and first ever Capital of Design (in 2008), Turin is currently Italy's leading city of contemporary art and design. The Luci d'Artista art festival and Artissima art fair appeal to the general public as well as to art buffs. The 2006 Winter Olympics put the city on the design map, including showcasing Pininfarina, the greatest car-design studios on the planet. During the opening ceremony, the sight of a red Ferrari doing tight spins on the ice reminded the world that the Italian car industry was born here. Futurism thrived in Turin, and at its core was the cult of speed. "Italian design has become a universal language of car design," says Lorenzo Ramaciotti, general manager of Pininfarina: "An American car is expected to be solid and a little flamboyant. An Italian car is expected to be aggressive, sporty and very sexy."

A sense of style

A sense of style and design is in the Italian genes. In 1946, the Italian architect Ernesto Nathan Rogers stated that design should be all-embracing, "from the spoon to the city". Italian designers dutifully filled our world with high-tech telephones and computers, office furniture in fluid shapes, sleek chrome kitchen appliances and twirly pasta quills. Giandomenico Belotti's Spaghetti Chair was literally inspired by pasta.

VESPA VERSUS LAMBRETTA

The Vespa, the most celebrated scooter on the planet, was created after World War II by the Italian manufacturer Piaggio, which turned its back on warplane production after its factory was destroyed by American bombers. Amid the wreckage, the workers found a German scooter that had been used by paratroopers, and it became the prototype Vespa. The thinking behind the brand was to create a form of transport that was practical, cheap, easy to handle and simple to repair. The Vespa ("Wasp") was a runaway success from its first launch and is now the height of retro-chic.

The Lambretta, another design classic, was the rival to the Vespa, and produced in 1947, a year after the Vespa. The wartime engineer Pierluigi Torre was commissioned to design a scooter boasting a tubular steel frame construction. The Lambretta A 125cc scooter came with a three-speed gear box and foot-operated gear changer, but had no body panels to cover the frame or engine. The brand returned to Grand Prix racing in 2010 with its new 125cc bike and catchphrase, "Lambretta – it's an Italian thing."

Lambrettas and Vespas are as popular as ever, whether in car-clogged cities or with hobbyists – there are owners' clubs worldwide and 17 million users. Vespas have featured in many films, including *Roman Holiday*, *American Graffiti* and *The Talented Mr Ripley*.

Italian design encompasses the austere, the provocative, the restrained and the kitsch. The roll-call of honour includes the Olivetti typewriter and the Artemide lamp, as well as the Ferrari, a symbol of national pride. Italy has a reputation for inspired car and motorbike design, from chic Maseratis to cheap Vespa scooters. In reply, the fashion world fields designers with the aspirations of Renaissance princelings: Armani's fluid lines clash with Roberto Cavalli's camp eroticism and Dolce & Gabbana's Sicilian kitsch.

Aesthetically, Italy is known for its smooth, streamlined objects, from washing machines to motorbikes and coffee machines – designed in 1938, the Gaggia was the first modern steamless coffee machine, and swiftly became recognised as a design icon thanks to its sleek lines and sheer functionality.

Design diversity

The design field has traditionally cultivated cross-fertilisation between the craftsman and architect, designer and artist. Giò Ponti, the 20th century's greatest Modernist, believed that Italy had been created half by God and half by architects. He detested the superfluous and favoured practical, perfect forms such as his Superleggera, the consummate chair, a sculpted lightweight piece. Ponti designed Milan's Pirelli Tower (1956) as well as creating the espresso machine.

The highlights of Italian design history reveal both its readiness to innovate and its essential classicism. In the 1950s, the Modernists abhorred meretricious designs, but eclectic designers were eager to experiment. The 1960s avant-garde relished visual disorder and inflatable fantasies. Yet even during the Pop Art period and Swinging Sixties, designers did not abandon their love of craftsmanship or use of high-quality materials such as leather. The 1970s represented the high point of Italian minimalism, with austere tubular steel chairs. Even so, minimalism remains a Milanese default mechanism, even in the new millennium.

The belief in *bellezza*, beauty for its own sake, means that even high-tech must be aesthetically pleasing. High-tech in the home has a distinguished pedigree, with cult objects by Aldo Rossi, Ettore Sottsass and Robert Venturi, including coffee pots, chairs and trays in severe metallic designs. Particularly prized are stainless-steel kettles by Alessi, or Achille Castiglioni cutlery and lamps. The Italians broke the mould of lighting design: "Light does not simply illuminate, it tells a story," says Sottsass. The modern lighting heyday was the 1970s, but certain lamps, from 18th-century Murano chandeliers to Pietro Chiesa's Art Deco funnel lamps, stand the test of time.

Temples of consumerism

Milan may be the design showcase, but most cities are citadels of good taste, with smart shops and shiny people. If the authentic article is too costly, then dedicated shoppers will settle for a fake: appearances are everything. Naples is the capital of counterfeit culture, where painted marzipan fruit looks finer than real peaches.

Clean lines and a splash of colour in Rome.

The fashion and design showrooms are located between the Brera and Piazza San Babila in the Quadrilatero, Milan's chicest shopping district.

It is invidious to single out the most prestigious designers, but Armani, the master of deconstruction, wins accolades for his sleek, sophisticated look and minimalist colours. Armani's polar opposite is Versace, which opted for vulgarity, glamour and sex appeal. The coolly intellectual approach of Prada chimes with jaded fashionistas, while the duo Dolce & Gabbana hails retro red-carpet glamour. As always, Italians are beguiled by *la bella figura*, a fatal weakness for beauty and surface gloss.

Who's Who in Italian Design

With its supreme grace, craftsmanship and lovely lines, Italian design leads the world in lifestyle – here we highlight its biggest names.

Alberta Ferretti

The designer champions ultra-feminine styles. With its love of floaty fabrics, the label attracts romantics rather than adventurous fashionistas.

The fun and useful Anna G. Corkscrew, designed by Alessandro Mendini for Alessi.

Alessi

Based by Lake Orta, this family-run design house is known for its playful products, ranging from quirky cutlery to colourful kettles and corkscrews. Alessi has always drawn on the skills of top designers of the calibre of Castiglione, Sottsass and Philippe Starck.

Armani

With its sleek yet understated look, Armani is the epitome of Italian chic. Giorgio Armani's alluring womenswear transcends boring beige. The look works for rock royalty and real royalty. "Women want to be more grown up," claims Giorgio. The designer has fully embraced lifestyle, with his own bars, restaurants and hotels.

B&B Italia

The market leader in luxury furniture design was founded in 1966 on the innovative principle of streamlining research, manufacture and marketing into a seamless whole. The company attracts leading designers, from Gaetano Pesce to Patricia Urquiola and designs hotels, stores and even cruise ships.

Benetton

Luciano Benetton is dubbed "the prince of pullovers" yet the company's real success was to introduce mass production to the sleepy Italian textile industry. This close-knit Treviso-based firm is a global casual-clothing brand, but remains innovative, sponsoring Fabrica, its creative think-tank.

Bottega Veneta

Once a moribund Venetian family accessories firm, the luxury brand is now part of the Gucci Group. Classic rather than trend-driven, it offers pared-down clothes that sell on fabric and cut alone. Menswear favours the Milanese gentleman look, while womenswear is timelessly elegant.

Dolce & Gabbana

Sicilian Domenico Dolce and Venetian Stefano Gabbana may no longer be a couple, but the creative partnership survives. Arguably the glitziest of Italian fashion labels, its strengths are sharp tailoring, cutting-edge styling and a Latino sensibility, part peasant, part Sicilian gigolo. "Molto sexy" is the only instruction to the D&G catwalk models.

Ermenegildo Zegna

Steeped in history, this family firm are the fashion designers with the deepest roots in fabric production and design. Based in Biella's "textile valley," Zegna is both the luxury menswear brand and a supplier of fabrics to its rivals. The family puts a lot back into the local community.

Fendi

Under Karl Lagerfeld, Fendi has had a resurgence and produces chic collections for city sophisticates. Fendi's legendary love of fur can make the label controversial abroad, but to Italians, the Fendi femme fatale is still a seductive fashion icon.

Ferragamo

This Florence-based fashion dynasty started with Salvatore, a Neapolitan shoemaker to the stars, who invented the wedge. Leatherware and accessories are no longer the essence of the brand:

glamour-puss cocktail dresses feature, along with hotels, boat companies and wine estates.

Gucci

Gucci began as humble Florentine saddle-makers but its leather range, made from honey-cured hides, was a stepping stone to stardom. Family feuds led to the collapse of the dynasty, and the firm is now a mega-brand, with a glam-rock style that appeals to footballers' wives and celebrities.

Lagostina

For generations of Italian mammas, Lagostina is synonymous with the best stainless-steel Italian kitchenware. Known as the "Michelangelo of stock-pots", it is still on most Italians' wedding lists.

Marcolin

This Veneto-based firm is one of the major producers of eyewear, both spectacles and sunglasses, and is owned by both the family and the Florentine design-ers behind Tods, Diego and Andrea della Valle.

Missoni

Missoni are the knitwear masters, and produce intri-cate, imaginative and eye-catching designs, with clothing and homeware collections. This family-run firm is now headed by Angela Missoni, who has reworked her parents' hippy-chick knitwear by creat-ing equally vibrant, swirly designs. In recent years they have also created a stylish hotel chain.

Moschino

Noted for its visual tricks and bold spirit, Moschino boasts a sexy yet daring look and bucks many fash-ion trends. Moschino's biggest fan is the burlesque striptease artiste, Dita Von Teese, who embodies the label's Forties silhouette and retro glamour.

Pininfarina

The world's pre-eminent car design firm dates back to the 1930s, when car chassis and bodywork were assembled separately. "Pinin" Farina (succeeded by his son) created car concepts for Alfa Romeo, Lancia and Ferrari, as well as the design of coffee machines, aircraft and even the Olympic Torch.

Prada

Husband and wife team Miuccia Prada and Patrizio Bertelli have propelled the brand to fame. Prada is an intellectual yet classless brand with a "less is more" ethos. Arguably the coolest, most sought-after brand of recent years, Prada prides itself on its contemporary styling and well-cut, fuss-free designs, with the focus on crisp, demure shapes.

Pucci

Founded by the eccentric Florentine aristocrat Emilio Pucci, the brand revels in swirling, Sixties-inspired silk prints, a spirited hippy-deluxe style.

Roberto Cavalli

The Cavalli attitude evokes man-eating sexiness and red-carpet glamour. The Cavalli dress is a red-carpet show-stopper, but the Florentine fashion house is shifting away from thigh-high splits and animal

Monochrome geometric designs at Missoni.

prints. Cavalli also brands his own wine and bars, including funky Café Giacosa in Florence.

Valentino

The couturier caters for a sleekly sophisticated and ultra-groomed clientele. Rarely a trendsetter, the label excels at romantic eveningwear. Despite selling the company, Valentino's brand survives.

Versace

Founded by Gianni Versace, the flamboyant fashion house has been run by his sister Donatella since his death. The label's glitzy vulgarity has been toned down to create elegant, well-cut collections but its menswear remains the sexiest of top Italian brands. Also designs hotels, jewellery and homeware.

DESIGN CLASSICS

Furniture, clothes, cars, typewriters, even kitchen appliances – the influence of Italian design has permeated the way we live and work today.

Italian designers bask in their reputation for refinement, innate good taste and eye for colour and line. "Quite simply, we are the best," boasts architect Luigi Caccia. "We have more imagination, more culture, and are better mediators between the past and the future." The distinction between architect and industrial designer is blurred, with practitioners dabbling in factory building and furniture design, office lighting and graphics. In the words of the late Ettore Sottsass, one of the most influential designers: "Design should be a discussion of life, society, politics, food and the design itself."

Modernism to Pop-Art

Since the beginning of the 20th century, Milan has led industrial design, reaching its apogee in the 1970s and 1980s. The Italians produced seminal designs for cars and lamps in the 1930s, matched by radios and motorbikes in the 1940s. Milan also pioneered innovative design in the 1950s, with the mass production of household appliances, from cookers and washing machines to kitchen utensils. Italian modernism supplanted the post-war European taste for the safe, handcrafted homeliness of Scandinavian design. Stylish kettles and coffee percolators became cult objects in the 1960s, followed by quirky Pop Art furniture and the fashion-designer chic of subsequent decades, from cool Armani to pared-down Prada. The inimitable character of *la linea italiana*, Italian style, sets the standard for international design values.

The Ferrari Spider (F430 model shown here) is in a long line of fabulous cars from the most admired Italian manufacturer. Enzo Ferrari (1898–1988), the firm's founder, was also a racing-car designer.

Prada stiletto heels in Milan's fashion district. Prada is the fashion company that best captures the Zeitgeist of the new millennium. Its designs have made it the most copied label on the city streets.

The Piaggio Vespa ("wasp"), first produced in 1946, became the symbol of freedom for the post-war generation.

A classic Alfa Romeo 1900 S Sprint (1956 model).

CLASSIC CAR STYLE

Ever since the 1930s, Italian car design has been characterised by stylistic restraint, versatility and timeless elegance. At one end of the scale, the Italians still produce some of the greatest status symbols in the world. In the 1950s, the beautiful Alfa Romeo convertibles spelt playboy raffishness; Ferrari's Spider, the ultimate in glamour, was produced from 1966 to 1992, making it the only sports car to have a longer production run than Germany's Porsche 911.

Yet the Italians have also had great success with Fiat's bland but eminently practical models. Topolino ("the little mouse") was launched to great acclaim in 1939, and continued into the 1950s. The late Giovanni Agnelli studied North American mass-production techniques and from the 1950s the family dynasty had a captive market, with customers eager for Fiat 500, which was relaunched in 2007 with great success. The car industry is based in the north, with Fiat in Turin and Ferrari in Modena. Alfa Romeo is now owned by Fiat but still produced in the north. The huge Fiat Lingotto plant was set up near Turin in the 1920s, and today, the city's fortunes are still inextricably linked to Fiat.

Postmodernist bookcase in laminated plastic, a bold design for the Memphis studio by Sottsass (1981). Memphis was the design event of the 1980s, inspired by Bob Dylan's song, Memphis Blues.

Cesare Casati's classic Pillola lamps (1968). Casato designed his 'pill' lamps at the height of the pop art movement. They are now rare and out of production but can be admired in the permanent collection of the MoMA New York.

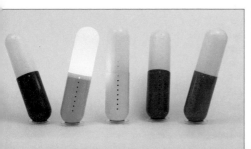

Zanussi's rigorous designs, streamlined look and user-friendly features have long made it a European market leader in the field of white goods.

A wide selection of salami for sale at Nemi, in Castelli Romani near Rome.

ITALIAN CUISINE

Each region is a culinary adventure, from velvety pasta in Emilia-Romagna to earthy Tuscan soups or the spicy flavours of Sicily.

For Italians, a meal is a celebration of life itself – less of man's art than of nature's wondrously bountiful providence. A deep respect and admiration for ingredients is found throughout the country, although both history and geography have played their part in making the cooking of Italy so strongly regional.

One of the secrets of Italian cuisine, impossible to replicate elsewhere, lies in Italy's soil. After making pulp of Mexico, the Spanish conquistador Hernando Cortés returned to the Old World laden with strange new fruits and vegetables, among them a humble, fleshy yellow sphere smaller than a ping-pong ball which, in 1554, the Italians dubbed the *pomo d'oro* (golden apple). Two hundred years on, thanks to the rich Italian soil, these jaundiced cherries had become huge, lush tomatoes in deep ruby hues.

These days, as well as being a key ingredient in many more elaborate Italian dishes, tomatoes are stuffed with beans or rice, offered as an antipasto with alternating slices of fresh mozzarella cheese, or simply served lightly dressed in olive oil and topped with sprigs of basil.

A savoury history

Until the Renaissance, the history of Italian cooking largely corresponded with Italy's military fortunes. In the 9th century, the Arabs invaded Italy, introducing Eastern sherbets and sorbets, originally served between courses to refresh the palate. Sicily, where Arab influence was most entrenched, is still noted for its sorbets and sumptuous sweets, including *cassata siciliana*, sweet sponge filled with ricotta cheese or pistachio cream and decorated with candied fruit. Two hundred years after the Arabs left mainland Italy, the Italians set off on their own

Mouthwatering spaghetti alle vongole.

holy wars. Their return was sweetened by the presentation of sugar cane which they had discovered in Tripoli.

As for pasta, the Roman gastronome Apicius, writing in the 1st century AD, describes a *timballo* (a sweet or savoury pie made with pasta). Later, in the Middle Ages, Boccaccio recommended the combination of macaroni and cheese.

It was during the Renaissance that cooking became a fine art and evolved along the lines familiar to us today. Bartolomeo Sacchi, a Vatican librarian also known as Platina, composed a highly sophisticated cookbook entitled *De Honesta Voluptate ac Valetudine* (Concerning Honest Pleasures and Well-Being); within three decades the volume had seen six editions. Florentine merchants spent huge sums on establishing schools for the promotion of culinary knowledge.

Consolidation of the Venetian Spice Route led to fragrant innovations. New pastry cooks invented macaroons, *frangipane* (filled with cream and flavoured with almonds) and *panettone* (a spicy celebration brioche incorporating sultanas). Conquistadors bombarded the Old World with its first potatoes, pimentos and, of course, tomatoes. When Catherine de' Medici, a keen gourmet, married Henry II of France,

Naples). Distinctive culinary identities evolved as naturally as particular painting styles. Even more influential than political boundaries were natural variations in soil type, climate and proximity to the sea.

> The only authentic Parmesan cheese is Parmigiano-Reggiano, produced around Parma, Reggio nell'Emilia and Modena. It is sold as young (under 18 months), medium (18–24 months) or mature (24–36 months).

Zucchini (courgette) flowers are either fried or stuffed with ricotta-based fillings.

she took with her to France her Italian cooks, thus laying the foundations for French cuisine. Until then, France had no cuisine of its own. Even *Larousse Gastronomique* honours Italy as the "mother" cuisine.

Regional divides

The concept of an Italian national cuisine is highly treacherous. Italy offers the world 20 regional cuisines, a diversity reflecting the country's pre-unification history and the importance of locally available produce (for example, beans, boar, rabbit and chestnuts in Tuscany; pork and truffles in Umbria; buffalo mozzarella, squid and *polpo* – octopus – in

Although there are territorial distinctions between the north and the south, the distinctions between individual regions are even more marked. Compared with the olive oil-loving south, there is a preference for butter in certain northern and central regions, notably in Emilia-Romagna, but not, for instance, in Tuscany or Liguria. As for pasta, in the Austrian-influenced Alpine regions of Trentino-Alto Adige, polenta takes the place of pasta, while in French-influenced Piedmont, rice is favoured. Traditionally, northerners tend to eat more flat, ribbon-shaped pasta, while southerners prefer more tubular-shaped pasta. By the same token, much northern pasta is prepared at home with eggs and eaten immediately, while southerners are more associated with 'dried' pasta, made without eggs, a tradition stemming from the days when pasta was dried in the warm sea breezes around Naples. Not that one should generalise about pasta in a country where most regions boast a full complement of local styles and sauces.

A feast of fish

Situated between the Adriatic and the Tyrrhenian seas, Italy hauls in well over 320 million kg (700 million lbs) of fish a year. Alpine streams make the Adriatic significantly less salty than most oceans, and it is therefore an ideal habitat for turbot (*rombo*), sea bass (*spigola*), sea bream (*orata*) and grouper (*cernia*). Seafood dishes, whether linked to grills, pasta or soups, will often include clams, mussels, lobster, octopus, cuttlefish and, in the south, swordfish.

Zuppa di pesce, which is more of a stew than a soup, is a stalwart of many menus and usually served in an enormous tureen. Luxurious versions include *buridda alla Genovese*, incorporating octopus, squid, mussels, shrimps and clams.

Anchovies and sardines are classic Mediterranean fish. *Pasta con sarde*, a speciality of Palermo, is pasta with a sauce of wild fennel, pine nuts, raisins and fried sardines. A more intricate dish, often found as an *antipasto*, is sardines stuffed with capers, pine nuts, Sardinian pecorino cheese, bread and eggs.

Meat and game

Italy also produces some of the finest meats in the world, which may explain why the Italians don't find it necessary to add sauce to their national specialities. Tuscany's Chianina cattle are alabaster in colour and grow to weigh 1,800kg (4,000lbs). Chianina beef is used to best advantage in *bistecca alla fiorentina* – a recipe in which the steak is marinated in a little olive oil, wine vinegar and garlic, then rapidly grilled. Lamb and kid are popular in hilly regions, including Sardinia.

Game birds are also used extensively (Italians are said to eat anything which flies, however small), and warbler, bunting, lark, quail and pheasant are favourites on regional menus. However, even more prized is wild boar *(cinghiale)* which features on many autumnal menus,

Fishmonger at Catania's fish market.

SLOW FOOD

Founded in Piedmont in 1986, the Slow Food movement has conquered the world with its crusade against junk-food culture. Its manifesto declared: "Let us rediscover the flavours and savours of regional cooking and banish the degrading effects of fast movement." The movement now has more than 100,000 members spread across five continents. Carlo Petrini, the founder, explains: "The goal of this movement is the propagation of leisurely, more epicurean eating habits, and a more enlightened and patient approach to life."

Italy remains one of the leaders in food and wine tourism, with hundreds of *strade dei sapori* (food trails) and *strade del vino* (wine trails). The bewildering choice runs from Parmesan cheese and Parma ham trails to routes dedicated to Calabrian leeks, Puglian olive oil, Modena's balsamic vinegar, Barolo wine or Asti truffles. Whether it's Tuscany's Chianti country, the Amalfi Coast wine route or Treviso's radicchio trail, there is ample fodder for gastronomes.

Depending on the region, the trails may be nothing more than a clutch of inns, growers and wine estates, or a well-trodden path through gorgeous scenery, with welcoming food and wine outlets en route.

including in Tuscany, and venison, which is favoured in regions such as Trentino.

Local specialities

Rome's cuisine comes nearest to that associated with feasting. Suckling pigs and suckling lambs are mouth-watering specialities. The justly famous *saltimbocca alla romana* (a thin slice of veal wrapped around a slice of *prosciutto* and a sage leaf, browned in butter and simmered in white wine) lives up to its name – "jump into the mouth". Romans also thrive on gnocchi – feathery dumplings

Making pizza in Naples, where it all started.

LEARNING TO COOK ITALIAN

Attending a cookery course in Italy is about getting to know its underbelly and coming home with a new skill. In Piedmont, chef and sommelier Carlo Zarri (www.hotelsancarlo.it) can guide you through truffle and Barolo country and teach you the secrets of a silky risotto. In Florence, Silvia Maccari of The Florence Chefs (www.theflorencechefs.it) can take you through the food markets to taste oils, wines and cheeses before conjuring up stuffed pasta and Tuscan biscuits with your help. In medieval Certaldo, Cucina Giuseppina (www.cucinagiuseppina.com) passes down her Tuscan family recipes, from pasta to truffle dishes, with wine appreciation and truffle-hunting experiences optional.

incorporating butter, eggs, nutmeg and Parmesan – while their poor relation, polenta, made from yellow maize flour, is popular in the Veneto and Trentino.

Emilia-Romagna, long celebrated for its gastronomy, is home to the country's most opulent cuisine. Bologna, the capital of Italian cuisine, relishes its reputation as "the fat" (*la grassa*), but foodies regard the stuffed pasta as supremely rich rather than fattening. *Prosciutto* is synonymous with Parma, while Bologna claims *mortadella*, a classic cold cut, as well as meaty *ragu*, the true Bolognese sauce, rather than the bastardised versions served abroad. Parma has also patented Parmesan cheese while neighbouring Modena guards the secrets of its renowned artisanal vinegar, *aceto balsamico*.

Bologna is also the home of tortellini, rosebud-shaped pasta filled with spinach and ricotta cheese. "If the first father of the human race was lost for an apple, what would he not have done for a plate of tortellini?" goes a local saying. Legends as to tortellini's origins abound. One version gives credit to a young cook of a wealthy Bolognese merchant who modelled the curiously shaped pasta on the navel of his master's wife, whom he had seen sleeping naked.

Certain regions are intrinsically dedicated to healthy eating – including Tuscany, whose staples are inspired by peasant cuisine and hearty bean soups, or Liguria, which depends on pesto, vegetables and fresh fish.

Lombardy produces more rice than any other European region, and the famous *risotto alla milanese*, seasoned with saffron, does justice to the native grain, which is ideally suited to slow cooking. Variations on risotto include *risotto nero*, in which the rice is coloured black by cuttlefish ink. Another way to transform a risotto is to shave a little truffle over the top. The best white truffles are found in the Alba area of Piedmont, where they are sniffed out by specially trained dogs; white and black truffles are also found in Tuscany, while black truffles are associated with Umbria.

Bread and pizza

Naples is the place to eat pizza baked over wood in a brick-lined oven – traditionally, *pizza napoletana* (tomatoes, mozzarella, anchovies and oregano), *pizza Margherita* (topped with mozzarella, tomatoes and basil leaves) and *pizza marinara* (topped with tomatoes, garlic, clams, mussels and oregano).

> Sometime in the late Middle Ages, pasta appeared. Nobody knows exactly how or where it was invented, but the legend of Marco Polo bringing it back from Cathay (as China was called) is firmly refuted by Italians.

consists of a pasta or rice dish (especially in the north) or soup. (Antipasti, such as toasted bread with olive oil and garlic, seafood salad or grilled vegetables, are generally served only in restaurants or at banquets.)

The second course (*il secondo*), comprising meat or sometimes (especially on Friday) fish, complements or elaborates the theme begun by the first. For example, if the first course was tortellini filled with parsley and ricotta, the second would probably be something light – such as a sautéed chicken dish with lemon and a little more parsley, echoing the first course. The

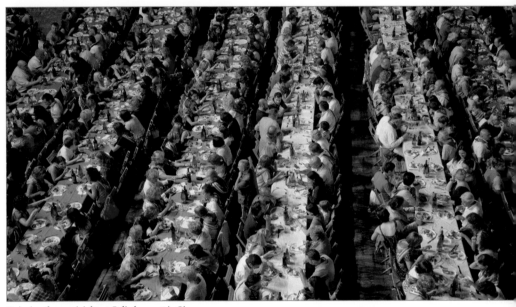

Enjoying the convivial post-Palio banquet in Siena.

Bread, eaten without butter, accompanies most meals, and comes in myriad varieties. Speciality breads include focaccia, a flat bread drizzled with olive oil and sprinkled with salt, or topped with olives or onions. Sardinia is noted for its *carta da musica* (music-paper bread), a wafer-thin unleavened bread, which is crunchy and long-lasting. Shepherds traditionally took it with them on long expeditions into the hills with their flocks.

The ritual of the feast

Wherever you are in Italy, the rituals surrounding food and eating remain the same. Though their specialities differ greatly, all regions eat their particular dishes in a remarkably similar order. The first course (*il primo*) invariably

second course is usually enhanced by at least one, often two or three vegetable dishes, such as *funghi trifolati* (mushrooms sautéed with garlic and parsley), *fave in salsa di limone* (broad beans in lemon sauce) and *cicoria all'aglio* (chicory with garlic sauce).

Afterwards comes the grand finale: the desserts (*dolci*), not forgetting an array of Italian cheeses (*formaggi*), perhaps served with pear. While *tiramisu* and ice cream are now widespread, many desserts still remain intensely regional. Depending where you are, tuck into Tuscan *cantuccini* biscuits dipped in Vin Santo, or sample sweet Sicilian *cassata* or *cannoli*. Needless to say, each course is washed down with copious quantities of wine.

Rossese di Dolceacqua is arguably the finest red wine made in Liguria.

WINE IN ITALY

In Italy wine is intensely regional – and a compelling social ritual that transforms any occasion into a pleasurable celebration of life itself.

J ust as there is hardly any such thing as Italian cuisine, so the wines of Italy, too, are distinctly regional. Vine-growing echoes the north–south divide, largely for climatic reasons; as one travels south, the grape varieties become increasingly exotic, even if unusual grape varieties are not the preserve of the south.

Northern varieties

The Veneto region – from Venice to Lake Garda – is a major wine producer of DOC wine (see page 107). *Soave*, the country's biggest-selling dry white DOC, can be bland, so choose a *Soave Classico* instead, made by first-rate producers. The same broad range is true of *Valpolicella*, where one billed as *Ripasso* will have more character.

There has been a revival of the ancient Venetian vineyards focussing on the island of Mazzorbo, off Burano. The limited-edition wine, known as Venissa and created by the Bisol wine dynasty, can be sampled locally.

To the north and east of Venice, Friuli-Venezia Giulia produces some of the country's finest crisp, white wines, including in the Collio area, near the Slovenian border, where Marco Felluga is a noted producer.

Up above Lake Garda, in mountainous Trentino-Alto Adige, the vineyards cling to precipitous slopes under peaks that are snow-covered until well into the spring. The Alto Adige, or South Tyrol, was once part of Austria, and many growers have distinctly un-Italian names. Reds from here can be chewy and plummy, or strawberry-fresh; whites are as crisp as the mountain air, light and refreshing.

Sardinian vineyard.

TOP WINE TRAILS

Italy abounds in appealing wine trails, which are increasingly linked to foodie routes and charming inns. Enquire about the local Strada del Vino (wine route) wherever you happen to be. In Tuscany, the Chianti Trail, set among Renaissance scenery is the best known. Lake Garda offers Valpolicella, Bardolino and Soave trails, but the Valtenesi wine and olive oil route north of Desenzano is the most engaging. Sometimes, as in Franciacorta, near Lake Iseo, the wine trail combines culture, food and wine tastings. Here, the rolling countryside is dotted with wine estates centred on castles, villas and manor houses.

Trentino is also a major wine region, producing almost a third of Italian sparkling wines (*Spumante*), including some which rival champagne. Other distinctive wines include ruby-red *Marzemino*, Mozart's favourite tipple, purplish *Teroldego*, as well as aromatic white *Muller-Thurgau* and elegant *Pinot Grigio*.

> Italy grows over 2,000 grape varieties, more than any other country, so the wine map is a challenge – but an infinitely rewarding one.

Castello di Brolio, on the Chianti wine trail.

In Lombardy, Franciacorta, the area near Lake Iseo, produces the country's most prestigious sparkling wines, a world away from supermarket *Spumante*, and a genuine alternative to French bubbles. Piedmont is prestigious wine country and a wonderful place to visit in autumn, when the early morning fog that hangs over the vineyards clears slowly, and the streets of Alba smell of white truffles. The main red grape variety, *Nebbiolo*, ripens very late, so it can cope with the humid climate that would threaten thinner-skinned varieties; it is also responsible for the wine's deep colour, and for mouth-puckering tannins that make *Barolo* and *Barbaresco* such big, powerful wines. These are perfect for a leisurely dinner, leaving a less full-bodied red, such as *Nebbiolo d'Alba*, better for a lighter lunch.

Chianti country

Tuscany challenges Piedmont as producer of the country's most aristocratic wines. Some of the noble families in the business today (Antinori and Frescobaldi, for example) have been making wine since before the Renaissance. *Chianti* is the staple, Italy's best-known red wine, made mostly from the Sangiovese grape. The "blood of Jove" manifests itself in varying forms, from light and fruity to capable of ageing in the bottle. Standards of winemaking have improved dramatically, and there has been a shift in emphasis from quantity to quality, so that most *Chianti* is gratifyingly good.

Brunello di Montalcino and *Vino Nobile di Montepulciano*, both Sangiovese-based wines, have traditionally represented the heights to which Tuscan reds could aspire. *Morellino di Scansano* is a fruity, juicy red made from Sangiovese grapes. But Super-Tuscans, a loose-knit family of brilliant wines that burgeoned in the 1980s, also represent some of Tuscany's greatest stars. Each has its individual style: they sprang from the desire of certain winemakers to produce their dream wine outside the stultifying conventions of the time. They have snappy names like *Sassicaia* or *Solaia*, and are pricey, but with inimitable richness and complexity. Dry white wines from Tuscany are less exalted. *Galestro* is a brave attempt to show that Italy's high-yielding Trebbiano grape can turn into something tasty, especially when blended with *Sauvignon blanc*, *Chardonnay* and others. *Vernaccia*, from the medieval town of San Gimignano, is made in more traditional style.

In Emilia-Romagna, where dishes are gloriously rich and sticky, *Lambrusco*, an acquired taste, can be a natural partner, especially the dry, red version, with the best vastly superior to its reputation as cheap fizz. Look out for Lambrusco di Sorbara to get a taste of the real thing. Although not exported widely, the regional wines can be eccentric or distinctive, not just made from *Sangiovese*.

Further south

Most of the best wines of central and southern Italy are red, although regions such as Sardinia and Sicily also produce notable whites. The centre and south are associated with quaffable wines,

The fog (nebbia) in the wine-growing region of Piedmont gives its name to the main red grape variety, Nebbiolo, which ripens very late. The thick skin enables it to survive the humidity and avoid rot.

such as *Montepulciano d'Abruzzo*, with southern wines historically cheaper. But don't be fooled: a winemaking revolution has taken place in these sun-baked villages, including in Sicily and Sardinia, with a shift away from high yields. Sicilian wine was once synonymous with insipid blending but now native grape varieties are appreciated by discerning drinkers. There are 23 DOC zones in Sicily and one DOCG. Full-bodied red *Nero d'Avola* is one of the stars, but good whites and blends are prospering, including at such reputable estates as Planeta and Regaleali.

The whites generally don't live up to the reputation of the reds but tend to be clean, fresh, well made, perfect for a summer's day, with *Frascati* a typical example. More notable are *Orvieto Classico*, from Umbria, which can have good nutty fruit, and *Vermentino* in Sardinia, with Sella & Mosca one of the best names in general. Much white wine is Trebbiano-based and quaffable, but the better producers often use *Malvasia*.

Sweet wines

Southern Italy abounds in sweet or fortified wines, especially Sicily and the Aeolian Islands – although calling them whites seems perverse when most age to a rich tawny colour. Look for the names of the *Malvasia* or *Moscato* grapes on the label. *Marsala*, a Sicilian fortified wine, has made a resurgence, either served as a sweet dessert wine or chilled as an aperitif.

In Tuscany, try the *Vin Santo* ("holy wine") made from grapes which have been hung to dry for months or even years.

One of the pleasures of Italy is to follow local drinking rituals. Traditionally, Italians drink an *aperitivo* (such as *Prosecco* or *Spritz* in the Veneto) before a meal and might follow a heavy dinner with a *digestivo*, such as *Vin Santo* in Tuscany, *Limoncello* on the Amalfi Coast, or *grappa* in the Dolomites. *Cin cin!*

A refreshing Sardinian white wine.

HOW TO READ AN ITALIAN WINE LABEL

Given a mixture of individuality, marked regionalism and outdated demarcations, Italian wines are notoriously difficult to classify. *Denominazione di Origine Controllata* (DOC) is a delimited wine region, the equivalent of the French *Appellation Contrôlée*. Not all DOC wines are very good, though, and some top wines are in fact not DOC; the producer's name is often a surer guide. DOCG (the g standing for *e garantita*) is meant to be a better wine than a straight DOC. *Indicazione Geografica Tipica* (IGT) is a classification between DOC and *vino da tavola*, that ranges from cheap everyday wine to some high-quality, expensive wines made by producers dissatisfied with DOC restrictions. *Classico* refers to the heartland of a wine region, often producing the best wine. Other words to look for are *abboccato* (semi-sweet), *amabile* (sweet, usually in reference to sparkling wine), *secco* (dry), *frizzante* (pétillant) and *spumante* (sparkling), which may be made by the *metodo classico* (champagne method). *Passito* is sweet wine made from semi-dried grapes to concentrate the flavours, *recioto* a sweet or dry wine made from dried grapes, and *ripasso* a rich red wine fermented in the barrels previously used for a *recioto*. In Valpolicella, *amarone* is a dry, full-bodied wine of great character made from dried grapes fermented for a longer period. *Riserva* is wine given extra ageing in the barrel.

Marcello Mastroianni, Italy's most
sophisticated leading man.

ITALIAN CINEMA

As windows of the nation's soul, Italian films showed veracity and vitality once freed from the fictions of Fascism.

talian cinema runs the gamut from gritty realism to epic drama, often tinged with satire or sentimentality. From the outset, the Italians blazed their own trail. In Britain, the United States and France, the early directors were steeped in vaudeville or music hall, and their output was generally classed as lowbrow entertainment. By contrast, Italy's first film-makers were from the aristocracy or intelligentsia, intent on creating highbrow epics or art-house cinema. At a time when most countries saw film as an amusing novelty, Italy was using it to express the meaning of life.

Directors soon had a sense of themselves as *"auteurs"*, as masters of the medium, not that Italian cinema is a story of unqualified success. The heyday of Italian cinema, in the 1960s and 1970s, coincided with Federico Fellini working at the height of his powers. Since then, Italian cinema has been more a case of light and shade, although the annual Venice Film Festival is as glamorous as ever.

Maciste, an earlier heart-throb.

ITALY IN THE MOVIES

Rome, Tuscany, Venice and Sicily provide seductive backdrops to the cinematic illusion of Italy. Of non-Italian directors, Peter Greenaway's *Belly of an Architect* (1987) arguably best captures the elusive character of the Eternal City. *Eat, Pray, Love* (2010), starring Julia Roberts, delights in the sexiness of the dolce vita capital, as does a Daniel Day Lewis harem in the bitter-sweet musical *Nine* (2010). Rome steals the show in Paolo Sorrentino's Oscar-winning *La Grande Bellezza* (The Great Beauty; 2013). Tuscany evokes the Merchant-Ivory *Room with a View* (1985), both a classic and a cliché, shot in Florentine villas. Quirkier are Jane Campion's *Portrait of a Lady* (1996), set near Lucca, and Tarkovsky's *Nostalgia* (1983), filmed in Bagno Vignone's moody Roman baths south of Siena. Anthony Minghella's *The English Patient* (1996) and *The Talented Mr Ripley* (1999) are paeons to Tuscany and Ischia, while Ridley Scott's *Gladiator* (2000) lingers on Tuscany's Val d'Orcia. Venice is at home with costume drama, art-house or action flick. The cult *Don't Look Now* (1973) by Nicolas Roeg brings a couple to an eerily deserted Venice; Al Pacino is Shylock in Michael Radford's *The Merchant of Venice* (2004), while 007 Daniel Craig survives drowning in the lagoon in *Casino Royale* (2006). Sicily is not just *The Godfather* but Rossellini's *Stromboli* (1950) set on a volcanic outpost, and *The Leopard* (1968) Visconti's hymn to princely grandeur and Sicilian pathos.

Early extravaganzas

When the Alberini-Santoni production company released *La Presa di Roma* in 1905, the Italian feature film was born. The subject is the 1870 rout of the Pope by Garibaldi's troops. In its most famous scene, Bersaglieri rallies his forces to breach the wall at Rome's Porta Pia. Because so much of it was shot on location, the film anticipates two dominant themes in Italian cinema: realism and historical spectacle.

Early in the 20th century, two directors, Enrico Guazzoni and Piero Fosca, revolutionised Italian films. Both directors' melodramatic tastes were

Federico Fellini, the godfather of Italian cinema.

in tune with Italy's burgeoning nationalism, and both glorified the martial exploits of Ancient Rome. Guazzoni's significance was as much for his business acumen as for his cinematic talent. *Quo Vadis?* (1913), which established his reputation, used the world's first gargantuan sets. Guazzoni limited distribution to art-house theatres, and in New York *Quo Vadis?* received its first star-studded première. Shrewd marketing set a precedent for producers to raise huge financial backing for future films.

Piero Fosca's contribution was more aesthetic. His major opus, *Cabiria* (1913), depicts the adventures of virtuous maidens, villains and heroes during the legendary wars between Rome and Carthage. Fosca was one of the first

> *Founded as a showcase for Fascist Italy in 1932, the Venice Film Festival is the world's oldest, and rivals Cannes in terms of prestige and glamour.*

to pan cameras across vast scenes, and introduced live orchestras at screenings. More importantly, *Cabiria* introduced subtle characterisation to the epic genre.

After the success of *Quo Vadis?* and *Cabiria*, Italy woke up to cinema as a medium. Industrialists realised the moneymaking potential of movie-making. Equally intrigued were the aristocracy, the natural milieu of many of Italy's filmmakers and patrons. Luchino Visconti, a first generation neo-realist, was from an aristocratic Sicilian background. Roberto Rossellini, instead, was bankrolled by a Roman countess, enabling him to make the celebrated *Roma, Città Aperta*.

The aristocratic influence is one explanation for the high production standards of early Italian cinema. While directors in France and the United States were still pinning up painted backdrops, Italians hired the nation's finest architects to design full-scale sets. Furnishings in period dramas were often borrowed from the private collections of the dynasties depicted in the movies; and if a film included aristocrats, authentic aristocrats were invited to make guest appearances.

This first golden age of Italian cinema barely had time to blossom before the Fascists came to power. Mussolini "regulated" the film industry, so convinced was he of the power of the medium. Directors deemed ideologically sound were eligible for state financing, with particularly patriotic endeavours, such as *Scipione l'Africano*, often fully funded.

Neo-realism

In 1944, while the Germans were still retreating from Rome, Roberto Rossellini made *Roma, Città Aperta*, a film whose unflinching truthfulness unnerves audiences to this day. The film, co-written by Federico Fellini, is about a Resistance leader tracked down by the Nazis. Every scene, except those set in the Gestapo headquarters, was shot on location. *Roma, Città Aperta* has a rough, visceral feel that was ground-breaking for the times, with sequences that resemble documentary footage.

Despite its sense of immediacy, *Roma, Città*

Aperta has a hidden meaning. The film elevates drug addicts, priests, German lesbians and Austrian deserters without sacrificing their unique personalities. Pina (Anna Magnani), an anguished matriarch, is both utterly convincing and representative of the desperate plight of Italian housewives during the war.

Rossellini, along with Visconti and Vittorio de Sica, developed a new kind of cinema. Neorealism remains the core of what is considered modern in film. The movement arose from the remarkable homogeneity Italy achieved just after World War II, with the widespread conviction that Fascism was wrong. Neo-realist directors spoke from – and for – an Italy which could admit to contradictions.

A golden age

During the 1960s and early 1970s, prosperity helped to usher in a new wave of Italian filmmaking. The leading lights were Federico Fellini, Michelangelo Antonioni and Francesco Rosi. This was also the era of Luchino Visconti's *The Damned*, Bernardo Bertolucci's *The Conformist* and Paolo Pasolini's *The Decameron*. Rosi was born in Naples, and southern Italy is a dominant

Still from Cinema Paradiso (1988), Giuseppe Tornatore's nostalgic tribute to cinema.

CINEMA IN THE SOUTH

Southern Italy is a self-conscious movie in the making. Cinematically, the two poles of attraction remain Sicily and Naples, confirming their cultural superiority. As well as being intensely visual, the south is seen as a place of extremes, of exquisite morality and cold-blooded Mafia murder. Movie fans have long been enthralled by a mob mythology of sharp-suited Dons wearing fedoras and carrying machine-guns in violin cases. The sun-bleached image of Sicily is the land of *The Godfather*. Mafia-infested Corleone lends its jagged rocks and sullen populace to the trilogy. But Hollywood's infatuation with the glamour of gangsterland is matched by the nostalgic, whimsical appeal of such films as *Cinema*

Paradiso and *Il Postino*. Giuseppe Tornatore is the best-known Sicilian director, thanks to the Oscar-winning *Cinema Paradiso* (1988). This nostalgic slice of history, which shows the arrival of the Talkies in a benighted backwater, celebrates Sicilian exuberance with a bitter-sweet humour that mocks the grinding poverty. In the United States, the film broke box-office records for a foreign film.

In Naples, director Francesco Rosi's gritty film, *La Sfida* (The Challenge, 1957), tackles the Camorra's corrupt control of the city markets. The story is revisited in Matteo Garrone's *Gomorrah* (2008), which is a far more brutal exposé of the same Neapolitan Mafia today.

theme in his films. Antonioni's exploration of existential angst and individual crises reached a climax with *Blow Up* (1967). Another Antonioni masterpiece, *Identification of a Woman* (1982) shows Venice as a magical yet murky world. However, the undisputed Venetian masterpiece is Visconti's *Death in Venice* (1970), based on Thomas Mann's classic novella. Visconti wanted "the light of the sirocco, the pale, still pearl light" and, with his artistic decision to use dawn and night shoots, forced his stars into sleeplessness.

The incomparable Fellini, arguably the greatest Italian director of all time, produced a string

he held a distorting mirror to Roman reality. *La Dolce Vita* (1960) was the first time Fellini worked with his male muse, Marcello Mastroianni, who was chosen for his simplicity and "normal face, a face with no personality". The filmic frolicking in Rome's Trevi Fountain turned Anita Ekberg into

> The acclaimed 2016 TV series The Young Pope by Italian director Paolo Sorrentino and starring Jude Law and Diane Keaton, shows Rome in all its splendour and intrigue.

Anita Ekberg and Marcello Mastroianni in Fellini's La Dolce Vita (1960).

of classics. His characters are torn between self-realisation and conformity. Fellini said that his films were a "marriage of innocence and experience", but they were also about fantasy and loss, tinged with irony, fun and sadness. In *Amarcord* (1975), Fellini's surreal flights of fancy turned Rimini, his home town, into a virtual-reality world. It was sweet revenge on the "inert, provincial, opaque, dull" Adriatic seaside resort he left for Roman chic. In his 1954 masterpiece *La Strada*, he based the central character on the lost innocence of his actress wife, Giulietta Masina, who starred in the film.

Fellini, who had a virtual monopoly on Roman sensibility, loved to satirise his fellow citizens on film. In *La Dolce Vita* (1960) and *Roma* (1972),

an international sex symbol.

In 1967, with *A Fistful of Dollars* and *The Good, the Bad and the Ugly*, Sergio Leone gave world cinema a new genre: the Spaghetti Western. These witty and stylised films, made on surprisingly low budgets, became the Italian movie industry's most successful exports since Sophia Loren, Gina Lollobrigida and Claudia Cardinale, sirens matched by Monica Bellucci today.

In the 1980s the generation of angry young Marxists and Sixties radicals gave way to commercial producers eager to create pale imitations of Hollywood action pictures. Bernardo Bertolucci is an exception in his ability to command Hollywood budgets for international blockbusters or to concentrate on more low-key work. Although best-known for *The Last Emperor* (1987), Bertolucci returned to Tuscany to shoot *Stealing Beauty* (1996), set in a rustic villa and idyllic wine estates.

The next generation

A new wave of actors and directors are slowly putting Italian cinema back on the world map. Italian cinema needed a boost. Competition from Italian television networks has had a detrimental effect on feature films, as did the privatisation of Cinecittà, the Roman film studios and former hothouse for Italian directors. Yet, after years in the wilderness, Cinecittà is mak-

Regional film commissions, including those in Campania, Ischia and Tuscany, are instrumental in attracting foreign filmmakers and fostering new movie-making, particularly in southern Italy, which has long been a source of inspiration for filmmakers, with turbulent settings galore.

It is invidious to single out stars, but Roberto Benigni is arguably the most popular comic actor since the legendary Totò. Benigni shot to fame with his Oscar-winning performance in *La Vita è Bella* (*Life is Beautiful*, 1997). Italy's most consistently acclaimed director is witty maverick Nanni Moretti, Rome's left-wing Woody Allen.

Oscar-winner La Grande Bellezza.

ing a comeback. Although the main focus is television, rather than feature films, the state-of-the-art studios are attracting foreign producers. In 2002, Martin Scorsese reconstructed blocks of New York slums in the studios for *Gangs of New York* – but the extras were all Romans. The array of international productions includes Mel Gibson's *The Passion of the Christ* (2004), Steven Soderbergh's *Ocean's Twelve* (2004) and the BBC television epic, *Rome* (2005). More recently, the musical *Nine* (2010), starring Daniel Day Lewis, was filmed in Cinecittà and is a tribute to the studios as well as to Fellini's *Eight and a Half*. In 2013, Paul Harris directed his latest romantic drama film *The Third Person*, starring Kim Basinger and Liam Neeson at Cinecittà.

The capital's changing moods are confronted by Moretti in his magical comedy *Caro Diario* (*Dear Diary*, 1994). Another film, *The Son's Room*, was awarded the Palme d'Or at Cannes in 2001. More recently, Paolo Sorrentino gained international fame and an Oscar with his Rome-based 2013 film *La Grande Bellezza* (The Great Beauty). He directed Michael Caine and Harvey Keitel in *Youth* (2015) and his *The Young Pope* TV series first aired in 2016 to much acclaim.

As for putting on the glitz, Venice Film Festival never fails. Whatever the failings of the films, the city shines. The Lido is awash with sleek movie stars scurrying from screenings to private yachts. Stephen Spielberg laps it up: "More than anything, we are in show-business – this is the show."

MUSIC AND OPERA

Italy's contribution to music is unparalleled.
And where better to enjoy the art of opera
than where it began and flourished?

Bewildering plots, exotic locations, spectacular music and temperamental singers
and conductors: this is the world of opera,"
claims Antonio Pappano, director of London's
Royal Opera. Italy is rightly known as the home
of music, and Milan's image is inextricably
bound up with La Scala, Italy's principal opera
house and a symphony of red, cream and gold.
When opera houses burn down, people cry in
public and the country grieves. Fortunately, the
country still has an abundance of major opera
houses. However, Italy's contribution to Western
music goes beyond operatic rococo interiors
and impassioned outpourings of Verdi.

It was an Italian monk, Guido d'Arezzo, who
devised the musical scale, while a Venetian
printer, Ottavino Petrucci, invented a method
of printing music with movable type. The
language of music remains resolutely Italian,
including such terms as *soprano, drammatico*
and *soprano lirico*.

Italy also gave us the piano, the accordion and
the fabulous Stradivarius and Guarneri violins
and cellos. Cremona has been the capital of violin
masters since the 16th century. Indeed, it is not
too fanciful to see the curves of violins echoed in
the elaborate spiral cornices of city palaces.

The food of love

Without the Italian sensibility, the world of
music would be without the nobility and intensity of Verdi or the seductive strains of Vivaldi.
The lush strings of Albinoni perfectly chime
with the public's taste for haunting Baroque
music, while opera-lovers are rewarded with
Rossini's *Il Barbiere di Siviglia (The Barber of
Seville)*, a comic masterpiece, Bellini's ravishing
melodies, and the dramatic flow of Puccini's
Tosca and *Turandot*. Other musical keynotes are

Opera at the Teatro Massimo in Palermo.

THE LEGEND OF "BIG LUCY"

In his lifetime, Luciano Pavarotti (1935–2007) was
the world's most recognised tenor. "Big Lucy"
began singing for sweets aged five, and his career
was launched when he won a Welsh choral competition. Throughout his long career, he was as happy
singing Neapolitan love duets and Puccini arias as
crooning with international rock stars such as Sting
and U2. He achieved legendary status in the 1990s
singing with Carreras and Domingo as the "Three
Tenors". His last performance was in 2006 at Turin's
Winter Olympics opening ceremony. Pavarotti, who
died at home in Modena, is remembered as one of
the 20th century's greatest tenors.

bel canto, the traditional Italian art of singing, and Neapolitan love songs, as much part of the passionate city as pizza and Mount Vesuvius.

Opera was Italy's greatest musical achievement, a rousing art form which came into being in 14th-century Florence and was perfected by Monteverdi. In his opera *Orfeo*, the title role was taken by a *castrato*, a male soprano or contralto with an unbroken voice. *Castrati* were in great demand during the 17th and 18th centuries, thanks to their strong, flexible yet voluptuous voices. Farinelli (1705–82) was the most famous, a soprano whose singing and stage presence

film and theatre director Giorgio Ferrara. As for conductors, this has been an Italian forte since Toscanini, whose first public performance at the age of 19 was *Aida*, conducted from memory after stepping in at short notice. After Toscanini, Claudio Abbado was arguably the greatest Italian conductor of the 20th century. Joint artistic director at La Scala from 1976, he then succeeded Herbert von Karajan at the helm of the Berlin Philharmonic in 1989. Before his death in 2014, he was musical director of the Mozart Orchestra of Bologna and the Lucerne Festival Orchestra. Riccardo Muti is currently music director at

Greek theatre in Taormina, Sicily.

caused women to faint with excitement. Italian divas have also graced the stages of the great *teatri lirici* (opera houses), including Cecilia Bartoli in the present day, the mezzo-soprano acclaimed for her interpretations of Mozart. Italy, which gave the world Enrico Caruso and Beniamino Gigli, has also boasted a clutch of talented tenors, from Luciano Pavarotti to Andrea Bocelli, as well as the romantic Roberto d'Alagna, raised in Paris by Sicilian parents.

Notable names

Gian Carlo Menotti (1911–2007) was acclaimed as the founder of the Spoleto Festival in Umbria, which continues to be a highbrow celebration of music, theatre and ballet. It is currently led by

both the Chicago Symphony Orchestra and the Orchestra Giovanile Luigi Cherubini in Ravenna. He is also involved in the Ravenna Music Festival, run by his wife Maria Cristina Mazzavilani, close to his home. Conductors Daniele Gatti, currently a chief conductor at Amsterdam' Royal Concertgebouw Orchestra, Riccardo Chailly, conductor at Filiarmonica della Scala, and the late Giuseppe Sinopoli have also found fame abroad.

Conductors working abroad are probably relieved to escape their knowledgeable but critical audiences back home. Italian audiences are hard taskmasters, with applause led by the official clapping societies that are present in the major houses. Yet if the opera falls short of perfection, the *loggionisti*, those in the gods, are ready to rain down abuse on fallen divas, with booing and hissing commonplace. Ultimately, as long as the opera provides a spectacle, of people-watching or, perish the thought, of mellifluous music, then an Italian audience usually goes home happy, whether the fat lady sings or not.

Opera's golden age

Giacomo Puccini once said of himself, "I have more heart than mind." In these characteristics lies the key to Italian opera. It is essentially sensual and lush, appealing more to the emotions than the intellect.

Verdi, great opera composer and Italian patriot.

Brave visitors who wish to show their appreciation at the end of an operatic performance can shout bravo for tenors, brava for sopranos and bravi for all.

The bookends of Italian opera's golden age stand clear: on the one side, the 1815 production of Rossini's classic *opera buffa* (comic opera), *Il Barbiere di Siviglia*; on the other, the posthumous 1926 opening of Puccini's last and unfinished opus, *Turandot*. Between the two lies more than a century of operatic triumphs.

During the 19th century, when Giocchino Rossini, Gaetano Donizetti and Vincenzo Bellini dominated the scene, Italian opera became infused with vitality, and Europe once again looked towards Italy for operatic innovation. All three composers, born within a decade of one another, shared much in style, and their careers followed similar paths and detours.

Rossini is probably most celebrated for his productions of *Il Barbiere di Siviglia* and *Guillaume Tell*, while Donizetti's masterpieces are *Lucia di Lammermoor* and *La Fille du Régiment*. Bellini is celebrated for his *semi seria* works, *La Sonnambula, Norma* and *I Puritani*. These operas are part of standard repertoires which are performed throughout the world.

The three composers shared a small-town background, and all enjoyed great success at an early age, although Bellini was already 22 years old when he made his operatic debut. Not surprisingly, there was a fierce and jealous rivalry between them. Upon hearing that Rossini had

TOP FESTIVALS

The best-known opera festival is the Arena di Verona, with operas performed outdoors, in Verona's magnificent Roman amphitheatre. Florence's Maggio Musicale, the oldest music festival in Italy, is matched by Umbria's Festival dei Due Mondi in Spoleto, which embraces classical, jazz and world music. The Stresa Festival, centred on Lake Maggiore, combines world-famous orchestras with smaller concerts in churches around the lake. On the Adriatic, the Ravenna Festival focuses on Italian opera. Parma, forever associated with Verdi, has an annual festival in his honour, with a similar festival dedicated to Rossini in Pesaro. Loveliest of all, Torre del Lago in Tuscany celebrates its illustrious son,

Puccini, every summer with opera by the lake.

Other spellbinding festival settings range from Ravello, overlooking the Amalfi Coast, to Sicily, where Taormina's summer showcase presents theatre, ballet, rock and opera in its Greek theatre. The Roma Opera Festival benefits from its setting in the ancient Baths of Caracalla. Summer in the Dolomites ushers in music festivals in the South Tyrol (Alto Adige) and Trentino. South Tyrol's concert cycle, The Sound of Music, means that, even without Julie Andrews, the hills are alive with concerts. Equally magical is Trentino's Sounds of the Dolomites, when summer concerts are staged in glorious scenery, often reached by cable car.

composed *Il Barbiere di Siviglia* in 13 days, Donizetti shrugged proudly and concluded, "No wonder – he is so lazy."

They acquired gold and glory all over Europe, but, tragically, all three burnt themselves out. Bellini and Donizetti died young, the latter a crazed syphilitic, and Rossini's last triumph was achieved before he reached 40. They were followed by the brightest light in Italian opera.

The brightest star

Giuseppe Verdi was born in 1813 (the same year as Richard Wagner) in Le Roncole, a small village near Parma. Verdi came from a poor, unmusical background but young Giuseppe made a mark as the local church organist. In 1832, he was denied admission to the prestigious Milan Conservatory. But the young Verdi was persistent, and, although his first two productions, *Oberto* (1839) and *Un Giorno di Regno* (1840), met with lacklustre receptions at La Scala premières, rave notices for the epic *Nabucco* (1842) marked the beginning of a long and distinguished career. From then on, Verdi saw success after success, highlighted by *Rigoletto* (1851), *Il Trovatore* (1853), *La Traviata* (1853),

The gilt and red velvet interior of Palermo's Teatro Massimo.

ITALY'S OPERA HOUSES

Beyond their gilt-and-stucco interiors, Italy's glittering opera houses *(teatri lirici)* are mostly neoclassical affairs. Historically, the rivalry of noble courts gave birth to private opera houses, which gradually opened their doors to the public – beginning with Venice in 1637. The fashion for opera spread, and by the 18th century there were 20 in Venice alone. Most opera houses are in Lombardy and Emilia-Romagna, linked to great courts such as Cremona, Parma and Mantua. Milan's La Scala is the premier opera house. Opened in 1778, it has been radically refurbished. All the great Italian composers have written for La Scala, notably Rossini, Donizetti, Bellini, Puccini and Verdi. Its heyday coincided with Verdi's patriotic works, but glory returned under Toscanini's direction in the early 20th century. Naples's Teatro San Carlo, rebuilt in 1816, enjoys a reputation second only to La Scala, followed by Venice, Florence and Rome. Venice's La Fenice (The Phoenix) was devastated by fires in 1836 and 1996 but rose from the ashes in 2003, a red-and-gold rococo confection rebuilt exactly as before. Other theatres include Parma, Genoa, Bergamo, Modena and Turin. Palermo's Teatro Massimo reopened in 1998 with a glittering production of Verdi's *Aida*, after a scandalous 25-year closure, during which it had opened its doors only once – to allow the filming of *The Godfather: Part III*.

La Forza del Destino (1862), *Don Carlo* (1867), *Aida* (1871) and *Otello* (1887). With premières in London, Paris, St Petersburg and Cairo, along with those in the theatres of Italy, Verdi was a composer of true international stature.

Verdi's sharp, almost brutal dynamism freed Italian opera from the lingering vestiges of empty convention. Verdi also refused to tailor his works to the whims of individual singers, something that no composer had dared do in the past. His independence extended to his personal life. In a very conservative and religious society, he openly lived with his mistress, the soprano

death in 1901, Verdi was mourned not only as a composer but also as a patriot.

The best-loved tunes

Although operas of fine quality continue to be composed today, the golden age of Italian opera drew to a close with the career of Giacomo Puccini, who was inspired by Verdi's *Aida* to become an operatic composer. Others contended for the mantle of Verdi, but Puccini had the advantage of the blessing of the old man himself. "Now there are dynasties, also in art," lamented rival Alfredo Catalani, "and I know that Puccini 'has

Opera in Rome.

Giuseppina Strepponi, for more than a decade before taking her to the altar in 1859.

If Verdi was permitted artistic and personal freedom, he was still constrained by the political realities of his day. Censorship was a constant impediment in an Italy dominated by foreign powers. Verdi was himself an ardent nationalist. His historical works were charged with analogies of the Italians' plight not lost upon native audiences. From 1848, his name became a rallying cry for his countrymen in the fight for freedom from Austrian rule. The acronym V(ittorio) E(manuele) R(e) D'I(talia) was used as a reference to the first king of Italy, eventually crowned in 1861. A dear friend of Count Cavour, Verdi briefly served in the new chamber of deputies after unification. On his

> *Before the fire which destroyed Venice's La Fenice, diva Joan Sutherland dubbed it "the most beautiful opera house in the world, like being inside a diamond". Critics complain that the "reborn" theatre is too brash.*

to be' the successor of Verdi... who, like a good king, often invites the 'crown prince' to dinner!" A dynasty it may have been, but one clearly based on merit. Puccini's success lay as much in his great gift for melody as in his unerring sense of theatre. *La Bohème* (1896), *Tosca* (1900) and *Madama Butterfly* (1904) are today among the best-loved works of opera.

Sounds of Success

In the last 60 years Italy has developed a successful homegrown music scene to compete with British and American pop imports.

Italy's pop singers have sometimes found success beyond national boundaries. This was particularly true in the 1950s when Italian-American singers like Sinatra, Perry Como and Tony Bennett were defining the easy-listening sound. Dean Martin crooned Domenico Modugno's *Volare* to international fame, and his version of *Arriverderci Roma* was a nostalgic hit for people remembering their Italian holidays.

During the 1960s, a group of young pop stars emerged to dominate the domestic market. These included Mina, Rita Pavone, Adriano Celentano, Lucio Battisti and Gianni Morandi. In his 40-year career Celentano sold 70 million records, while Battisti's classics, such as *La Canzone del Sole*, *Mare Nero* and *Aqua Azzurra Acqua Chiara* were the soundtrack for a generation of 1970s adolescents.

As the political dissent and liberation movement of the late 1960s took hold, a group of engaged singer-songwriters emerged. Known as *cantautori*, they created some of the most innovative Italian contemporary music, though their lyric-rich compositions were never going to translate abroad.

Italy's Bob Dylan is considered to be the late Fabrizio De Andre, with compositions such as *La Canzone di Marinella* and *La Guerra di Piero*. Singer-songwriter Francesco De Gregori's album Rimmel is vintage 1970s, while Ivano Fossati peerlessly mined Italy's melancholic soul with compositions like *I Treni a Vapore*. His *La Canzone Popolare* remains an election anthem for the centre-left. Also well-known abroad is jazz singer, composer and pianist Paolo Conte.

Rome's local cantautore Antonello Venditti immortalised his city in *Roma Capoccia*, and his albums of well-crafted, if sometimes disposable, pop still chart. Neapolitan musical tradition continues with Eduardo Bennato's politically tinged rock. But the city's musical statesman was Pino Daniele. Singing in his local dialect, Daniele fused rock, blues and jazz. His hometown anthem, *Napule E'*, encapsulates the city's melancholic spirit.

Bolognese songwriter Lucio Dalla emerged in the 1970s with a lyrical blend of humour, politics and profanity. From the satirical peace anthem *Se Io Fossi* *Angelo* to the domestic reality of *Anna e Marco, Dalla* chronicled all aspects of Italian life.

Italian rock music has flourished in recent decades, even if it is often mocked abroad, with the most dated aspects showcased in the annual San Remo song contest, which is still considered the country's major musical event.

Although the English-speaking world has been more resistant to Italian pop, the rest of the world has embraced two of the nation's singers. Laura Pausini has racked up global sales of 28 million records, and in 2006 she became the first Italian female to win a Grammy, taking Best Latin Pop Album with *Escucha*.

Pop concert in Taormina's Teatro Greco.

Roman-born popster Eros Ramazzotti has found fame beyond Italian shores, with his catchy singer-songwriting talents. Megastar Zucchero scored a rare success in the British market when he re-versioned the classic hit *Senza una Donna*, duetting with Paul Young.

One Italian singer who has become a household name at home and abroad is Andrea Bocelli, who offers a mellifluous blend of classical music, traditional song and pop. He has performed on international opera stages and even sang at the White House. The legacy of popular legends from Caruso to Pavarotti would weigh heavy on any tenor, but Bocelli, it seems, is more than capable of picking up the baton.

In recent years though Italy has come to the world stage with a plethora of international DJs and hit producers.

Positano, the pearl of the
Amalfi Coast.

Classic Val d'Orcia landscape, Tuscany.

Piazza San Marco in Venice.

INTRODUCTION

A detailed guide to the entire country, with principal sights cross-referenced by number to the maps.

A snapshot of Sardinia's Costa Smeralda.

Negotiating the tangle of one-way streets in an Italian city takes years of experience. Often a helpful native will point the way, or even take you there personally. But if no one materialises, simply follow the signs for *Centro Storico* (historic centre) and *Duomo* (cathedral), and remember that *senso unico* means "one way". Then find the first *parcheggio* (car park), for most Italian cities are best explored on foot and increasingly pedestrianised. If you arrive by train, the station will invariably be in the seedier part of town, so leave it behind for the better-preserved *Centro Storico*.

Modern life has stamped even small villages with a bar and a large population of moped-riding youths. Every town has its Duomo, but how different is the austere Romanesque cathedral of Puglia from the lavish Baroque one in Turin. Every town has at least one piazza: in the south they might be crowded with men smoking and playing cards; in the north, the men are still there, but so are the women and the tourists.

Our favourite places in Italy include many spots less frequented than the tried and true trio of Rome, Florence and Venice. We suggest that, after visiting Rome, you take an excursion east into Abruzzo or Molise, those hitherto remote regions whose architecture, parks, mountains and beaches rank among the most refreshing vacation spots in the country. Or, if you happen to be exploring the Bay of Naples, rent a car and continue down to Italy's heel and toe – Puglia, Basilicata and Calabria – even tak-

The winged Lion of St Mark is the symbol of Venice.

ing the ferry across to Sicily. Puglia (also known as Apulia) is increasingly popular, while Basilicata is an emerging destination.

The north has Venice, of course, but also Milan and Turin, two utterly contemporary cities packed with art and history. You could follow the path of generations of travellers who, with Dante and Ariosto in hand, toured the cities of Lombardy, the Veneto, Emilia-Romagna and Tuscany. If you want to catch your breath and relax, retreat into the green hills of Umbria, home of Italy's beloved St Francis of Assisi.

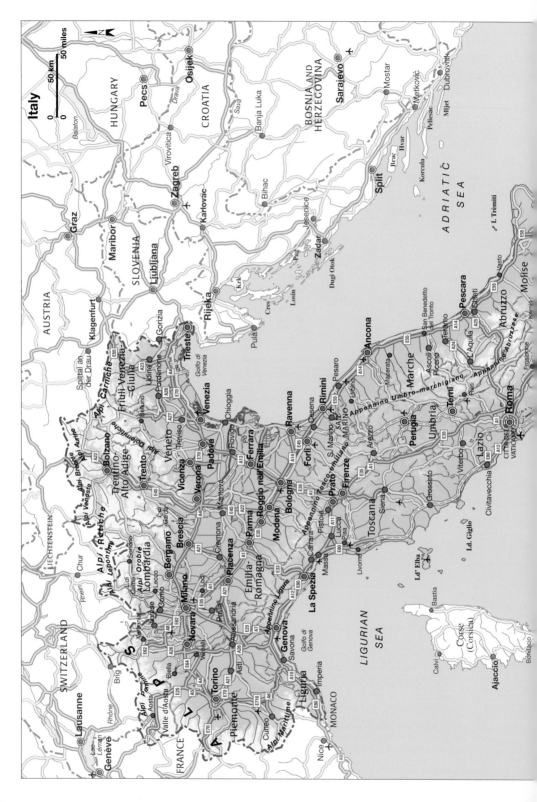

Italy

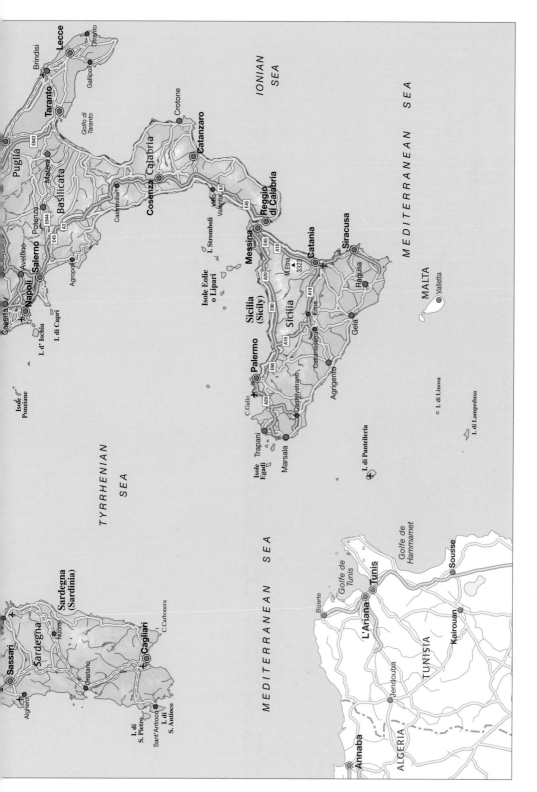

IONIAN SEA

MEDITERRANEAN SEA

TYRRHENIAN SEA

MEDITERRANEAN SEA

MEDITERRANEAN SEA

Otranto
Lecce
Brindisi
Gallipoli
Taranto
Golfo di Taranto
Crotone
Puglia
E843
Matera
Basilicata
Potenza
Avellino
E844
Salerno
Napoli
Caserta
Agropoli
Castrovillari
Cosenza
Calabria
Catanzaro
Catanzaro
I. Stromboli
Isole Eolie o Lipari
Valletta
A3
Reggio di Calabria
Messina
E45
A20
M.Etna 3323
A18
Catania
Siracusa
Ragusa
Enna
A19
Gela
Sicilia (Sicily)
Sicilia
E90
A19
Palermo
E90
Caltanissetta
Agrigento
A29
Castelvetrano
C.Gallo
Trapani
Isole Egadi
Marsala
I. di Pantelleria
MALTA
Valletta
I. di Linosa
I. di Lampedusa

I. d'Ischia
I. di Capri
Isole Ponziane

Sardegna (Sardinia)
Sassari
Sardegna
Nuoro
Oristano
Alghero
Cagliari
C.Carbonara
I. di S. Pietro
Sant'Antioco
I. di S. Antioco

Golfe de Hammamet
Sousse
Golfe de Tunis
Bizerte
Tunis
L'Ariana
Jendouba
TUNISIA
Kairouan
ALGERIA
Annaba

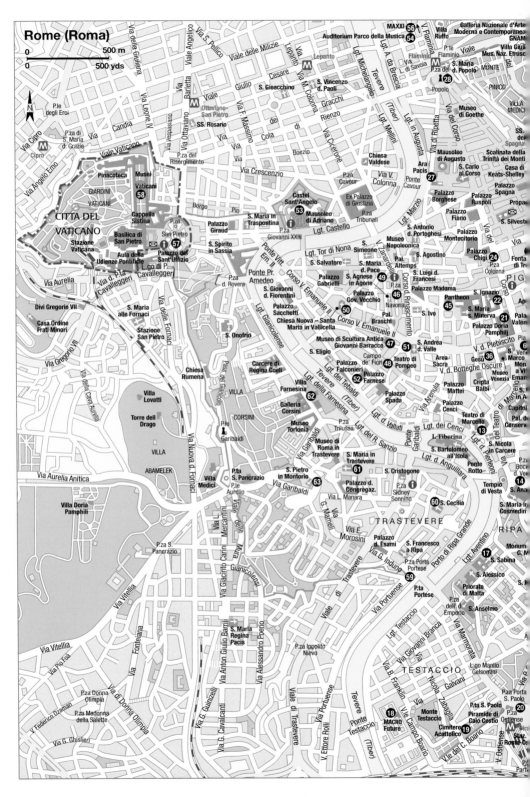

Rome (Roma)

0   500 m
0   500 yds

MAXXI **56**
Auditorium Parco della Musica **54**
Galleria Nazionale d'Arte
Moderna e Contemporanea
GNAM
Villa
Ruffo
Villa Giulia
Mus. Naz. Etrusc.
Flaminio
P.le
Flaminio
Viale
S. Maria
d. Popolo
P.za del
Popolo **28**
MONTE
PINCIO
VILLA
MEDICI
Museo
di Goethe
SS.
Spagna
Scalinata della
Trinità dei Monti
Casa di
Keats-Shelley

Via delle Giuliana
Via delle Milizie
Viale delle Milizie
Viale Angelico
Via S. Pellico
Via Lepanto
Via
Lepanto
Via Michelangelo
Tevere
Lgt. A. da Brescia
Via
di Savoia
Lgt. del Corso
Via del Corso
Via di Ripetta

Viale Giulio Cesare
Barletta
Giulio
Viale
S. Vincenzo
d. Paoli
Gracchi
Via M. Colonna
Mausoleo
di Augusto
Via in Augusta
Palazzo
Borghese
Palazzo
Ruspoli
Palazzo
Spagna
Propa

Via Candia
Via Leone IV
Via Ottaviano
Via Vespasiano
S. Gioacchino
Ottaviano-
San Pietro
SS. Rosario
Via F. Massimo
Via
Cola
Via Cicerone
Via del
Via
Via V.
Colonna
Ponte
Cavour
Palazzo
Fiano
Palazzo
Montecitorio
S. Carlo
al Corso
S. Silve

P.le
degli Eroi
Via Cipro
Cipro
P.za di
S. Maria
d. Grazie
Via
P.za del
Risorgimento
Viale Vaticano
Via Crescenzio
Rienzo
Boezio
Via V.
Colonna
P.za
Cavour
Chiesa
Valdese
Via V.
Colonna
Ara
Pacis **27**
Mausoleo
di Augusto
Casa di
Keats-Shelley
Palazzo
Borghese
S. Antonio
d. Portoghesi

Pinacoteca
Musei
Vaticani **58**
GIARDINI
VATICANI
Borgo
Castel
Sant'Angelo **53**
Mausoleo
di Adriano
Ex Palazzo
di Giustizia
P.za
Tribunali
Lgt. Marzio
Via
Lgt. Castello
Palazzo
Fiano
Palazzo
Chigi **24**
Fonta
di Tre
P.za
Colonna

CITTÀ DEL
VATICANO
Cappella
Sistina
Basilica di
San Pietro
Stazione
Vaticana
Aula delle
Udienze Pontificie
Palazzo del
Sant'Uffizio **57**
San Pietro
Palazzo
Giraud
S. Maria in
Traspontina
Pio
Palazzo
Gov. Vecchio
S. Maria in
S. Spirito
in Sassia
Via della Conciliazione
Ponte Vitt.
Em. II
Via Banco di S. Spirito
S.
Simeone
S. Salvatore
S. Maria
d. Pace
S. Agnese
in Agone **49**
Navona
Pal.
Braschi
Pal.
Altemps
Corso del Rinascimento
S. Agostino
S. Luigi dei
Francesi
Palazzo Madama
S. Ivo
Pantheon
S. Maria
s. Minerva
Palazzo
Valen
PIG
Museo
Napoleonica
Pal.
Madama **46**
S. Ignazio **22**
45
21

Divi Gregorio VII
S. Maria
alle Fornaci
S. Onofrio
P.za
d. Rovere
Ponte Pr.
Amedeo
S. Giovanni
d. Fiorentini
Palazzo
Sacchetti
Chiesa Nuova – Santa
Maria in Vallicella
Museo di Scultura Antica
Giovanni Barracco **47**
S. Eligio
Corso V. Emanuele II
Campo
de' Fiori
Palazzo
Falconieri
Via Gianicolense
Lgt. Tor di Nona
Lgt. dei Tebaldi
S. Andrea
d. Valle **51**
Teatro di
Pompeo **48**
Palazzo
Farnese
Area
Sacra
V. d. Plebiscito
Gesù **36**
V. d. Botteghe Oscure
Museo
Venezia
S. Marco
Mon
a Vi
Cripta
Balbi
Eman
Palazzo
Spada
Palazzo
Mattei
Palazzo
Cenci

Casa Ordine
Frati Minori
Stazione
San Pietro
Carcere di
Regina Coeli
VILLA
Villa
Farnesina
Galleria
Corsini **62**
Lgt. della Farnesina (Tiber)
Lgt. dei Vallati
Lgt. dei Cenci
Teatro di
Marcello **13**
Palazzo
Cenci
Pal. d.
Conserv
Capitol
L'Isola Tiberina

Via Aurelia
Via Gregorio VII
Via della Cava Aurelia
Chiesa
Rumena
Villa
Lovatti
Torre dell
Drago
P.le
Garibaldi
CORSINI
Museo
Torlonia
Museo di
Roma in
Trastevere
Via Garibaldi
S. Maria in
Trastevere **61**
S. Cristogono
P.za
Sidney
Sonnino
S. Bartolomeo
all'Isola
Ponte
Rotto
S. Nicola
in Carcere
Tempio
di Vesta
S. Ana

Via Aurelia Antica
VILLA
ABAMELEK
Villa
Medici
P.ta
S. Pancrazio
P.le
Aurelio
S. Pietro
in Montorio **63**
Via Garibaldi
Via L. Manara
Palazzo d.
Congregaz.
60 S. Cecilia
S. Maria in
Cosmedin
RIPA

Villa Doria
Pamphili
Via G.
Mameli
Via E.
Morosini
TRASTEVERE
Palazzo
d. Esami
S. Francesco
a Ripa
Via G. Induno
Porto di Ripa Grande
Monum
G. M
S. Sabina **17**
Lgt. Aventino
Via Aventino

P.za S.
Pancrazio
Via Giacinto Carini
Viale delle Mura
Via G. Mameli
P.ta
Portese **59**
P.ta
Portese
Via Porta
Portese
Via Portuense
S. Alessio
Priorato
di Malta
S. Anselmo
S. Ana

Villa Doria
Pamphili
Via Vitellia
Via Anton Giulio Barrilli
S. Maria
Regina
Pacis
P.za Ippolito
Nievo
Via Portuense
Tevere
P.za
dell'
Emporio
Via Marmorata
TESTACCIO
Lgt. Testaccio

Via Vitellia
Via Pio-Foa
V. Federico Ozanam
P.za Donna
Olimpia
P.za Madonna
della Salette
Via G. Cavalcanti
Via G. Guinzelli
Via Alessandro Poerio
Viale di Trastevere
Via B. Franklin
Via C. Balbo
Nicola
Galvani
Lgo Manlio
Gelsomini
Via Giovanni Branca
P.za Porta
S. Paolo
S. **20**

Via Fonteiana
Via di Donna Olimpia
Via G. Ghislieri
Ponte
Testaccio
MACRO
Future **18**
Monte
Testaccio
Cimitero
Acattolico **19**
Piramide di
Caio Cestio
P.ta S. Paolo
Via Ostiense
Vle di C. Baro
Stazione
Roma-Os
Parti

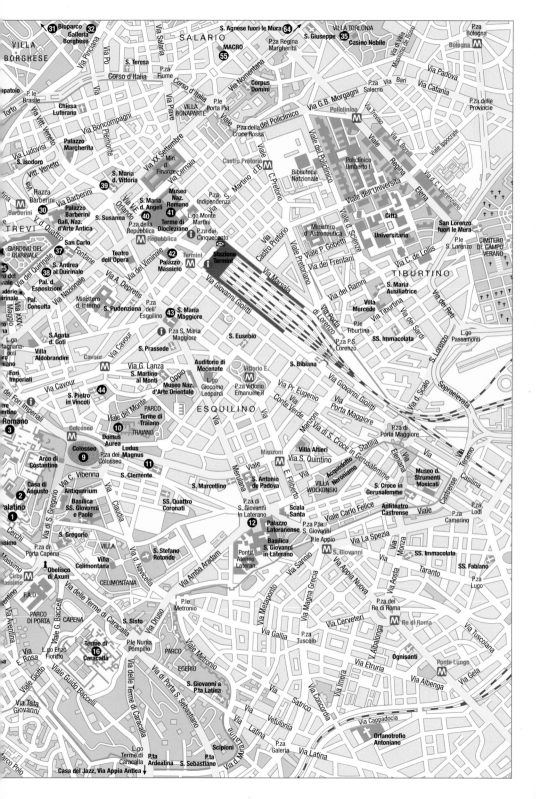

ROME

Follow in the footsteps of emperors and saints, discovering the monuments and churches that define Rome as the capital of Italy and the ancient world.

R ome really does have it all. This is a city of contrasts, bathed in sunlight at any time of year. History is on every corner and you can glory in the sights of Ancient Rome, on the Palatine Hill and at the Colosseum, the Forum, the Pantheon and in the Capitoline Museums. First-class art collections can be found in beautiful buildings such as the Villa Borghese, and you can people-watch in stunning squares such as Piazza Navona, which have long attracted the crowds. But Rome has its modern side, too, with gritty neighbourhoods like Testaccio, home to contemporary art galleries and a funky club scene.

Since its millennial revamp for Holy Year, Rome has rarely looked lovelier. The Eternal City has shaken off its dusty toga and slipped into contemporary clothes. And ever since, its most important tourist attractions have been given a new lease of life thanks to joint public and private partnerships. The recent revamp of the Spanish Steps was sponsored by the luxury brand Bulgari, the Trevi Fountain looks glorious once again thanks to the fashion house of Fendi and the restoration of the Colosseum comes courtesy of another luxury goods brand, Tod's. The facelift to its ancient sites has been matched by subtle plastic surgery to its arts scene. Revamped galleries, new contemporary art museums and the creation of

a superb music complex have helped turn the city's face towards the future.

The Palatine Hill

The best introduction to Rome is not Piazza Venezia, the terrifying roundabout at the centre of the modern city, but the more pastoral **Palatino** ❶ (Palatine Hill; www.coopculture.it; daily 8.30am–7.15pm Apr–Aug, Sept until 7pm, Oct until 6.30pm, Nov–mid-Feb until 4.30pm, mid-Feb–mid-Mar until 5pm, mid-Mar–end Mar until 5.30pm, last entry one hour before closing;

Main Attractions
Palatine Hill
Roman Forum
Capitoline Museums
The Colosseum
San Giovanni in Laterano
Trevi Fountain
Palazzo Barberini
Galleria Borghese
The Pantheon
Piazza Navona

The panoramic view from the Pincian Hill.

combined ticket with Foro Romano; free first Sun of the month). The Palatine is traditionally associated with Romulus, the legendary founder of Rome. Remarkably, his presumed cave dwelling has recently been identified. Decorated with seashells, mosaics and pumice stones, the grotto was discovered near the ruins of the palace of Emperor Augustus.

Nearby are the remains of the **Tempio di Cibele**, picturesquely planted with an ilex grove. The cult of the Eastern goddess of fertility was introduced to Italy during the Second Punic War (218–201 BC). Though its mystical rites – involving throngs of frenzied female worshippers, priests committing self-mutilation, and bull sacrifices – were distasteful to old-fashioned Romans, the cult spread widely during the imperial era.

In Roman times the Palatine Hill was celebrated for the splendour of its palatial dwellings, the preferred home of the emperors. The earliest was the Domus Augustana. A portion of it, known as the **Casa di Livia** (Livia was Augustus' second wife), is renowned

for its wall paintings and floor mosaics. Best of all is the section known as the **Casa di Augusto** ❷ (www.coop culture.it; Mon–Fri 9am–1pm, 2–5pm, Sat 9am–2pm; guided tours only, two-day ticket also valid for the Forum and Colosseum; free first Sun of the month; to book tel: 06-3996 7700). The emblematic ruins reveal colonnaded gardens and the emperor's frescoed quarters, including his study.

To the north, alongside the Palazzo di Tiberio (now mostly covered by the Farnese Gardens) runs the **Criptoporticus**, a vaulted underground passage built by Nero to connect the palaces of Augustus, Tiberius and Caligula to his own sumptuous Golden House (Domus Aurea) on the Esquiline Hill. To the southeast of this passage extend the remains of the **Domus Flavia**, built at the end of the 1st century AD by the Emperor Domitian. An infamous sadist who took pleasure in torturing everything from flies to senators, Domitian suffered from an obsessive fear of assassination. According to the ancient historian Suetonius, author of *Lives of the Caesars*, an

Friendly Roman welcome.

entertaining if not entirely trustworthy source, the emperor covered the walls of the peristyle (the section with an octagonal maze) with reflective moonstone so that no assassin could creep up on him unobserved. Next to the peristyle lie the remains of a splendid banqueting hall.

Following the fortunes of the city, the imperial palaces fell into disuse during the Middle Ages, when monks made their home among the ruins. During the Renaissance building boom, Cardinal Alessandro Farnese bought a large part of the Palatine and in 1625 laid out the world's first botanical gardens on the slope overlooking the Forum. The lush **Orti Farnesiani** are delightful, with their formal landscaping, the sounds of fountains and birds, and views over Rome.

For lovers of the picturesque, the ruins of the Palatine are hard to beat. It is the last place in Rome where you can find a pastoral scene as it might have been drawn by Piranesi or Claude Lorraine. Roses, moss and poppies growing amid the crumbling bricks and shattered marble give it a romantic rather than an imperial splendour. It is the perfect place in which to wander, dream, sketch or picnic.

The Roman Forum

The Clivus Palatinus leads from the domestic extravagances of the emperors down into the **Foro Romano** ❸ (Roman Forum; http://archeoroma.beni culturali.it or www.coopculture.it; same opening times as Palatino), the civic centre of Ancient Rome. This area, once a swamp between the Capitoline and Palatine hills, used as a burial ground by the original inhabitants of the surrounding hills, was drained by an Etruscan king in the 6th century BC. Until excavations began in the 19th century, the Forum – buried under 8 metres (25ft) of debris – was known as the *"Campo Vaccino"* (Cow Field) because smallholders tended their herds among the ruins. Today it reveals a stupendous array of ruined temples, public buildings, arches and shops.

At the bottom of the Clivus Palatinus, the **Arco di Tito** (Arch of Titus) commemorates that emperor's destruction of Jerusalem and its

The Arch of Titus.

View over the Forum.

sacred Temple in AD 70. Until Israel was founded in 1948 and the return to Palestine became possible, pious Jews refused to walk under this arch.

The Via Sacra leads past the three remaining arches of the **Basilica di Costantino**, a source of inspiration for Renaissance architects. Bramante said of his design for St Peter's: "I shall place the Pantheon on top of the Basilica of Constantine." The **Tempio di Antonino e Faustina**, also known as San Lorenzo in Miranda, is a superb example of Rome's architectural layering. Originally a temple erected in AD 141 by the Emperor Antoninus Pius, it was converted into a church in the Middle Ages. During the 17th century a Baroque facade was added, as was the case with so many Roman churches.

Across the Via Sacra is the lovely, round **Tempio di Vesta** (Vesta was the goddess of the hearth), where the six Vestal Virgins took turns tending the sacred fire. The punishment for allowing the fire to die down was a whipping by the priest. Service was for 30 years and chastity was the rule. Few patricians were eager to offer their

The much-derided Vittoriano monument.

daughters, and the Emperor Augustus had to pick girls by lot. Laxity about vows was common, and the Emperor Domitian resorted to the traditional punishment of burying errant virgins alive and stoning their lovers to death. Living in the lovely **Casa delle Vestali** was some compensation for this demanding life. The ruins remain a rose-scented haven.

The ancient Romans were keen litigants. Walk past the three elegant columns of the Temple of Castor and Pollux to the **Basilica Julia** (on the left of the Via Sacra), where trials were held, as many as four at a time. The Senate met across the way in the Curia, the best-preserved building in the Forum. Its sombre, solid appearance befits the seriousness of its purpose.

At the western end of the Forum rises the famed **Rostra**, where the orator Cicero declaimed to the Roman masses. After his death, during the second Triumvirate's anti-Republican edicts, Cicero's hands and head were displayed here. Opposite the Rostra is the single **Colonna di Foca** (Column of Phocas). For centuries the symbol

of the Forum, it was described by Byron as the "eloquent and nameless column with the buried base". Unburied and named, it is still, as the Italians say, *suggestivo* (atmospheric). To the right is the **Arco di Settimio Severo**.

At the end of the Via Sacra, in the shadow of the Capitoline Hill, rise the eight Ionic columns of the **Tempio di Saturno**. Saturn's festival, the Saturnalia, marked the merriest occasion in the Roman calendar, when gifts were exchanged and distinctions between master and slave reversed. Occurring in the middle of winter, this was the feast that Christians later transformed into Christmas. Behind the temple are, from left to right, the Temple of Vespasian and Titus, and the Temple of the Concordia.

Outside the Forum excavations, across from Pietro da Cortona's Chiesa di Santi Luca e Martina, is the **Carcere Mamertino** ❹ (Mamertine Prison; www.operaromanapellegrinaggi.org; Sat–Sun, Tue and Thu 9am–noon, 2–4pm; 15 people allowed at a time every 30 minutes; guided tours only), home to some famous prisoners. According to

legend, this dank, gloomy dungeon was where St Peter converted his pagan guards. Miraculously, a fountain sprang up so that he could baptise the new Christians.

The Capitoline Hill

From the **Capitolino** ❺ (Capitoline Hill) the Temple of Jupiter Capitolinus (509 BC) watched over the city. It was here also that modern Italians raised their tribute to Italy's unification. The **Vittoriano** (Victor Emmanuel Monument; www.polomusealelazio. beniculturali.it; daily 9.30am–7.30pm; free), completed in 1911 and dedicated to Italy's first king, captures the neoclassical bad taste of the 19th century. The monument is famously despised by locals, who call it the "typewriter" or "wedding cake".

Throughout Rome's history hopes for Italy's future have centred on this hill. In 1300, the poet Petrarch was crowned laureate here; in 1347 Cola di Rienzo roused the Roman populace to support his short-lived attempt to revive the Roman Republic; in the 16th century Michelangelo planned

The monumental statue of Marcus Aurelius inside the Musei Capitolini.

The 'Marforio' statue graces the courtyard of the Palazzo dei Conservatori.

the elegant Campidoglio, thus restoring the Capitoline's status as the architectural focal point of the city.

If you are feeling energetic, climb the 124 steps to the 7th-century **Santa Maria in Aracoeli** (if you happen to be here at Christmas, come for the Midnight Mass). The weak-kneed will probably prefer Michelangelo's regal staircase (known as the *cordonata*), flanked at the top by monumental statues of Castor and Pollux. In the back of the Campidoglio, Palazzo Senatorio (closed to the public) surmounts the ancient Tabularium, dating from Republican times. On the right of Palazzo Senatorio rises **Palazzo dei Conservatori,** and on the left, the **Palazzo Nuovo**. Together they make up the revamped **Capitoline Museums** (entry is via the Palazzo dei Conservatori; www.museicapitolini.org; daily 9.30am–7.30pm), an imposing collection of classical art and statuary. Highlights include the Etruscan bronze she-wolf nursing Romulus and Remus and, in the new wing, a bronze of Hercules and a monumental statue of Marcus Aurelius. Escape to the café-terrace (www.terrazzacaffarelli.it) for panoramic views and time to ponder on the world-weary physiognomies of the later Roman emperors.

Mussolini's remodelling of Ancient Rome

Piazza Venezia ❻, at the foot of the Vittoriano, marks the centre of modern-day Rome. Brave the traffic to reach the Palazzo di Venezia. Rome's first great Renaissance palace (built in 1455), dominates one side. This was Mussolini's headquarters from 1929, and his most famous speeches were delivered from the balcony. The light burning in his bedroom at all hours reassured the Italians that the "sleepless one" was busy solving the nation's problems (though according to Luigi Barzini the light was often left on when Mussolini was not there). Now the palace contains the **Museo di Palazzo Venezia** (www.museopalazzo venezia.beniculturali.it; Tue–Sun 8.30am–7.30pm), with a collection of medieval and Renaissance paintings, sculptures and tapestries.

"Ten years from now, comrades, no one will recognise Italy," proclaimed *Il Duce* in 1926. One of the most dramatic changes the Fascists wrought on Rome was the Via dei Fori Imperiali. Mussolini demolished old neighbourhoods (reminders of Rome's decadent period) in order to excavate the fora and build the road. Such brutal means were intended to create a symbolic connection between Rome's glorious past and his own regime.

The Forum and Colosseum

North of the Imperial Fora is **Foro Traiano** ❼ (Trajan's Forum), dominated by the famous **Trajan's Column**, sculpted with his victories over the Dacians. Behind are the **Mercati di Traiano** (Trajan's Markets; www.mercatidi traiano.it; daily 9.30am–7.30pm; charge), host to the Museo dei Fori Imperiali. This engaging, well-conceived museum complex aims to explain the function and design of all the main Roman fora,

Palazzo di Venezia.

as well as putting the impressive five-storey market into context.

Adjoining the Forum but reached along Via IV Novembre is **Palazzo Valentini** ❽, the seat of the provincial and prefectural administration of Rome. It houses **Le Domus Romane** (www.palazzovalentini.it; access from the Foro Traiano; Wed–Mon 9.30am–6.30pm; advance booking advisable; guided tours in English at 1pm, 2pm and 2.30pm), a wonderful new Roman site beneath the palace. The unearthing of several patrician villas prompted the restoration project of 2nd–4th-century mosaics which were discovered amid the debris of a World War II air-raid shelter. The site is illuminated by a virtual reality presentation by Piero Angelo, Italy's finest popular historian. The palazzo, and the remains of these senatorial villas, connect with the majestic open-air museum in the heart of Ancient Rome, which remains the haunt of the city's ubiquitous *gatti* (cats).

At the end of all this ruined splendour rises the **Colosseo** ❾ (**Colosseum**; http://archeoroma.beniculturali.it or www.coopculture.it; daily Apr–Aug 8.30am–7.15pm, Sept until 7pm, Oct until 6.30pm, Nov–mid-Feb until 4.30pm, mid-Feb–mid-Mar until 5pm, mid-Mar–end Mar until 5.30pm, night tours Apr–Oct Mon and Thu–Sat 8.10pm–midnight; free first Sun of the month; ticket also valid for the Palatine and Forum). Stripped of its picturesque wild flowers and weeds and encircled by a swirling moat of traffic, for years the site looked rather forlorn. In 2016 this symbol of the Eternal City was spruced up following a €25-million makeover. It has partially reopened to visitors, who can now explore the third tier as well as the hypogeum (underground chamber), which gives you a behind-the-scenes glimpse into the preparation of gladiatorial combat with various machinery, tools and trap doors (guided tour only at 1.40pm; booking recommended).

The Colosseum was begun in AD 79 when the Emperor Vespasian drained the lake of Emperor Nero's **Domus Aurea** ❿ (Golden House; http://archeoroma.beniculturali.it/cantieredomusaurea/en and www.coopculture.it; closed for

The Colosseum at night.

Mosaic fragments in the Baths of Caracalla.

Piazza del Quirinale.

restoration; limited access to the work-site Mon–Fri 9am–1pm, 2–5pm, Sat 9am–2pm, tel: 06-3996 7700 for information). The message was clear: where Nero had been profligate, emptying the imperial coffers to construct his own pleasure palace, the Colosseum's creator built a public monument. Also nearby is the **Arco di Costantino** (Arch of Constantine).

From the Colosseum, Via di San Giovanni in Laterano leads to **San Clemente** ⓫ (www.basilicasanclemente. com; Mon–Sat 9am–12.30pm and 3–6pm, Sun noon–6pm), an intriguing puzzle of a church. A 12th-century basilica descends to a 4th-century basilica, which, in turn, leads to a 1st-century Roman apartment building containing, in its courtyard, a Mithraic temple honouring the most popular cult of imperial Rome.

Further along, Via di San Giovanni opens up into **Piazza di San Giovanni in Laterano** ⓬, containing some of the most important buildings in Christendom. The **Obelisk** is the tallest and oldest in Rome and a suitable marker for the Church of Rome, **San Giovanni**

in Laterano (daily 7am–6.30pm; free), founded by Constantine the Great. The **Palazzo del Laterano** was the home of the popes until the Avignon exile in 1309. The beautifully decorated Papal Apartments can be visited on the first floor (access via the Vatican Historical Museum, tours Mon–Sat at 9am, 10am, 11am and noon). The pious may want to ascend the 28 steps (on their knees of course) of the nearby **Scala Santa** (www.scala-santa.com; Mon–Sat 6.30am–7pm, until 6.30pm in winter, Sun from 7am), said to be the "holy steps" Christ descended after being condemned by Pontius Pilate. Constantine's mother, St Helena, retrieved them from Jerusalem.

The Ghetto

Rome's former Ghetto lies on the western side of the Capitoline Hill, near the ruins of the **Teatro di Marcello** ⓭, an ancient theatre. The city has had a substantial Jewish community since the Republican era, but its isolation dates from the Counter-Reformation and the papacy of Paul IV (1555–9). From then on, the gates to the Ghetto were locked from sunset to sunrise, Jewish men had to wear a yellow hat, the women a yellow scarf, and most professions were closed to Jews.

A plaque on Via Portico d'Ottavia is a reminder that more than 2,000 Roman Jews were deported to a Nazi concentration camp. Next to the synagogue on Lungotevere Cenci, the **Museo Ebraico** (Jewish Museum; www.museoebraico.roma.it; Sun–Thu 10am–7pm, until 5pm in winter, Fri 10am–4pm, until 2pm in winter) sensitively documents the history of Rome's Jewish population. To lift your spirits, taste Jewish Rome in **Da Giggetto** (Via del Portico d'Ottavia; www. giggetto.it), including fried artichokes and salted cod.

The Via del Teatro di Marcello leads south to **Piazza Bocca della Verità** ⓮, which yokes together two Roman temples, a Baroque fountain and the medieval church of Santa Maria in Cosmedin. In the portico of this

church is the **Bocca della Verità** (daily 9.30am–5pm, until 6pm in summer), a marble slab resembling a human face and considered to be one of the world's oldest lie detectors. If a perjurer puts his hand in the mouth, so the legend goes, it will be bitten off. In fact, the slab's origin is sadly prosaic: it once covered a drain.

The oldest and largest of the famed Roman racetracks, the **Circo Massimo** ⓕ (Circus Maximus) is nestled between the Aventine and the Palatine hills. It once seated 250,000 people. In addition to the main event, vendors, fortune tellers and prostitutes plied their trades beneath the arcades.

The ancient Romans are probably best known for their love of bathing, and their public baths inspired great praise. In addition to three pools (hot, warm and cold), the **Terme di Caracalla** ⓖ (Baths of Caracalla, http://archeoroma.beniculturali.it or www.coopculture.it; Apr–Aug 9am–7pm, Sept until 7.15pm, Oct until 6.30pm, Nov–mid-Feb until 4.30pm, mid-Feb–mid-Mar until 5pm, mid-Mar–end Mar 5.30pm; free first Sun of the month)

offered gyms, libraries and lecture halls, for the improvement of mind and body – along with less salubrious activities, especially when mixed bathing was permitted. But essentially the baths represent a triumph of the Roman public spirit, demonstrating that cleanliness was a right, not a privilege for the rich. The new museum in the basement beautifully displays local archaeological finds. At night, the baths are illuminated and become a stage-set for opera in summer.

The Aventine and Testaccio

Escape the dusty ruins by visiting the Aventine, one of modern Rome's most desirable residential neighbourhoods. As you climb the Clivo dei Pubblici, the smell of roses wafts down from the pretty garden at the top of the hill. Via Santa Sabina leads to **Santa Sabina** ⓗ, a perfectly preserved 5th-century basilica. Inside, shafts of sunlight illuminate the antique columns of the nave. Outside, in the portico, are some of the oldest wooden doors in existence (5th century).

TIP

The so-called Protestant Cemetery covers all religions except Catholicism and is divided into two parts: the older section, containing the tomb of Keats, lies to the left of the entrance. Keats fans can also visit the poet's home in Rome (see page 145).

The nave of Santa Sabina is lined with antique columns.

Bordered by Via Marmorata to the east is **Testaccio**, the former meatpacking district centred on an artificial mound – essentially an ancient landfill site formed by shards of amphorae. Testaccio retains its gritty neighbourhood charge despite pockets of gentrification and its notoriety as the pulsating heart of clubland. A reliable food market on Piazza Testaccio is now complemented by trendy boutiques and bars fanning out from its new cultural hub: the cutting-edge contemporary art museum known as the **MACRO Future** (Piazza Orazio Giustiniani 4; www.museomacro.org; Tue–Sun 10.30am–7pm). Set in the Mattatoio complex, formerly Rome's slaughterhouse, it accommodates large-scale exhibitions that wouldn't work in the MACRO, its sister museum (see page 153).

South of Testaccio, in the shadow of the Piramide Cestio, lies the **Cimitero Acattolico** ⑲ (Protestant Cemetery; www.cemeteryrome.it; Mon–Sat 9am–5pm, Sun 9am–1pm; donation), one of the most picturesque spots in Rome. Scores of unfortunate travellers who

Piazza del Popolo.

fell fatally ill on a Grand Tour are buried here. In the old section lies Keats's tomb, graced by the epitaph: "Here lies one whose name was writ in water." In accordance with the poet's wishes, the tombstone does not mention Keats by name. The modern part of the cemetery contains Shelley's heart – his body was burnt on the shore near Pisa. As Keats's close friend Lord Byron put it: "All of Shelley was consumed, except his heart, which could not take the flame and is now preserved in spirits of wine."

Outside the **Porta San Paolo** ⑳ is the basilica of **San Paolo fuori le Mura** (www.basilicasanpaolo.org; daily 7am–6.30pm; cloister from 8.30am; free), one of the major basilicas of Rome, which is built on the supposed site of St Paul's tomb. A fire in 1823 means that much of what you see now dates from the 19th century, but it is impressive nonetheless. The bronze aisle doors are original, dating from 1070, as is the cloister.

The Corso

Back in the city centre, **Via del Corso** ("the Corso") provides a delightful amble through Roman history, taking in Baroque churches and fountains, patrician palaces, classical remains, and the ancient gateway to the city. The Corso stretches from Piazza Venezia to **Piazza del Popolo** (see page 144). Lined with elegant *palazzi*, this bustling shopping street has always been a place for taking the pulse of the city.

At the Piazza Venezia end of the Corso is **Palazzo Doria Pamphilj** ㉑ (www.doriapamphilj.it; daily 9am–7pm), home of the Galleria Doria Pamphilj. The collection is superb and a rarity, housed in a palace inhabited by the same family for centuries. The grand apartments and ornate galleries make an atmospheric backdrop to paintings by Titian, Caravaggio and Raphael. The star of the collection is Velázquez's portrait of Pope Innocent X. Concerts of Baroque music with a guided tour in English are held every Saturday at 11am.

Further along stands the Jesuit church of **Sant'Ignazio** ㉒ (http://santignazio.gesuiti.it; Mon–Sat 7.30am–7pm, Sun from 9am) with a ceiling by Andrea dal Pozzo. To appreciate its fantastic Baroque perspectives, stand in the middle of the nave and look heavenwards: the vault seems to disappear as an ecstatic St Ignatius receives the light he will disperse to the four corners of the earth. Pozzo also painted a fake dome, since the Jesuit fathers were unable to afford a real one.

Via delle Muratte, to the right off the Corso, leads to the most grandiose of Rome's Baroque fountains: the newly spruced-up **Fontana di Trevi** ㉓ (Trevi Fountain), where the voluptuous Anita Ekberg frolicked in Fellini's film *La Dolce Vita* (1960). Tossing a coin into the pool is supposed to ensure your return to Rome.

But the ancient city rears its head even in a seemingly contemporary shopping district. **Piazza Colonna** ㉔, about halfway down the Corso, displays the Column of Marcus Aurelius (AD 180–93). Sixtus V (1585–90) crowned this column with a statue of St Paul and Trajan's Column with one of St Peter. (Sixtus was always eager to appropriate Roman triumphal symbols for Christianity: he placed many fallen, forgotten obelisks in front of churches.)

From the Trevi Fountain, consider strolling to the **Piazza del Quirinale,** dominated by colossal statues of Castor and Pollux, originally from Constantine's Baths, complemented by the obelisk taken from the Mausoleum of Augustus. Facing the square is the imposing **Palazzo del Quirinale** ㉕, once the summer palace of the popes but now the residence of the Italian president (http://palazzo.quirinale.it). On the far side are the former papal stables, **Le Scuderie del Quirinale** ㉖ (www.scuderiequirinale.it; Sun–Fri noon–8pm, Sat noon-11pm). The monumental Quirinale Stables, constructed over the remains of a Roman temple and baths, represent a dramatic space for major art exhibitions. The Quirinale is also a convenient stepping stone to Rome's greatest Baroque churches (see page 144).

The controversial glass, steel and travertine Ara Pacis.

The ever-popular Spanish Steps.

Detail from Pietro da Cortona's The Triumph of Divine Providence, a highlight from the Galleria Nazionale d'Arte Antica.

Galleria Borghese is one of Italy's best small museums.

Off the northern end of the Corso lie impressive relics of the Augustan era, restored and reassembled during the Fascist era: the **Mausoleo di Augusto** and the **Ara Pacis Augustae** ㉗ (www.arapacis.it; daily 9.30am–7.30pm; free first Sun of the month).

For centuries the Ara Pacis, built from 13–8 BC to celebrate peace throughout the empire, was in pieces. Fragments were found in the Louvre in Paris and the Uffizi in Florence. Finally, in 1983, the Ara Pacis altar was reconstructed but remains the most controversial of revitalised Roman sites, especially in a city where novelty is often conceived as an affront to the natural order. This steel, glass and travertine structure was designed to house a 2,000 year-old Altar of Peace that, ironically, was used for sacrifices. Created by Richard Meier, this is the first new public monument erected in the historic centre since Mussolini's day. Art critic Vittorio Sgarbi called it "an indecent cesspit", while others have praised it as an airy, accessible building that lets citizens see into the mindset of Emperor Augustus and Ancient Rome.

Marking the end of the Corso, the **Piazza del Popolo** ㉘ remains one of Rome's loveliest squares, with views southwards into the city's heart. Everyone – from triumphant emperors to footsore pilgrims – has entered Rome through the **Porta del Popolo** (Porta Flaminia). To the east rises the lush green of the Pincian Hill, reputedly haunted by Emperor Nero's ghost. **Santa Maria del Popolo**, the landmark church on the square, contains splendidly decorated chapels adorned with art by Pinturicchio, Raphael (the Chigi Chapel) and Caravaggio, notably his masterly *Conversion of St Paul* and *The Crucifixion of St Peter*. The church was allegedly erected over the burial place of Nero in an attempt to sanctify the site.

Rome's drawing room

From Piazza del Popolo, take Via del Babuino to **Piazza di Spagna**, named after the seat of the Spanish embassy to the Vatican. Essentially Rome's drawing room, the square's daily parade revolves around the famous Spanish Steps, the **Scalinata della Trinità dei Monti** ㉙, renovated in

BAROQUE ROME

The Baroque art movement (1600–1750), characterised by bold, curving forms, elaborate ornamentation, and a sense of balance in design, was born in Rome and was nurtured by a papal campaign to make the city one of unparalleled beauty "for the greater glory of God and the Church".

One of the first artists to answer the call was Michelangelo Merisi da Caravaggio (1573–1610), whose early secular portraits of sybaritic youths revealed him to be a painfully realistic artist. His later monumental religious painting entitled *The Calling of St Matthew*, in San Luigi dei Francesi, shocked the city by setting a holy act in a contemporary tavern.

The decoration of St Peter's by Gianlorenzo Bernini (1598–1680) was more acceptable to the Romans: a bronze tabernacle with spiralling columns at the main altar, a magnificent throne with angels clustered around a burst of sacred light at the end of the church and, for the exterior, the classically simple colonnade embracing the piazza (1657).

Bernini's rival was Francesco Borromini (1599–1667), whose eccentric designs were the opposite of Bernini's classics. Many of Borromini's most famous designs hinge on a complex interplay of concave and convex surfaces, which can be seen in the undulating facades of San Carlo alle Quattro Fontane, Sant'Ivo and Sant'Agnese in Piazza Navona (1653–63).

2015. Caricaturists sketch tourists; old crones sell roasted chestnuts; sightseers rinse their hands in Bernini's fountain; students sunbathe on the steps; buskers strum guitars, and the moneyed set joins Roman matrons in ogling the elegant shop-windows. The Romans are divided as to whether the steps should be fenced off, at least at nighttime – as proposed by the sponsor of the renovation, Paolo Bulgari – to protect them from modern vandals. Off this piazza stretch the most fashionable shopping streets in Rome: Via dei Condotti, Via Frattina and Via Borgognona with all the Italian design giants – Armani, Bulgari, Gucci, Prada, Valentino et al. Underneath the Pincian Hill, the quiet Via Margutta is the place to buy art.

Since the Romantic era, this quarter has been the haunt of British and American expatriates. John Keats died in the house overlooking the steps, which now contains literary memorabilia. The **Keats-Shelley House** (tel: 06-678 4235; www.keats-shelley-house.org; Mon–Sat 10am–1pm and 2–6pm) is essential viewing for romantic

ghost-seekers. Muse some more over high tea in **Babingtons** (Piazza di Spagna; www.babingtons.com), where expat writers and Roman high society have taken tea since 1893.

The street between Trinità dei Monti and Santa Maria Maggiore was carved out by Sixtus V, a pope bent on improving Rome and glorifying his own name. The view down the length of the road is dramatic – culminating in the obelisk which Sixtus raised in front of Santa Maria Maggiore. Once called Strada Felice, the road now changes name three times as it cuts through the tangled streets.

The first leg, Via Sistina, leads down to **Piazza Barberini** ③⓪, in the centre of which is Bernini's sensual **Fontana del Tritone**, featuring a sea deity blowing fiercely on a conch shell. In the base is the unmistakable coat of arms of the Barberini family: three bees. Designed by Bernini and Borromini, the neighbouring **Palazzo Barberini** houses the **Galleria Nazionale d'Arte Antica** (http://galleriabarberini.beniculturali.it; Tue–Sun 8.30am–7pm). Don't miss Pietro da

Feeding the ducks in Villa Borghese park.

Mosaic depicting the four seasons, Palazzo Massimo.

The gilt and marble interior of Sant'Andrea al Quirinale church.

Cortona's *The Triumph of Divine Providence*, a celebration of the Barberini Pope Urban VIII – a pope who quarried the ruins of Ancient Rome so extensively that he inspired the witticism: "What the barbarians didn't do, the Barberini did."

Via Veneto swoops off the Piazza Barberini. Before strolling along its wide streets or retiring to one of its cafés, stop at the **Chiesa dei Cappuccini**, also known as Santa Maria Concezione (www.cappucciniviaveneto. it; church Mon–Sat 7am–1pm and 3–6pm, Sun 9.30am–noon, 3.30–6pm; free; museum and crypt daily 9am–7pm) to see its macabre crypt. According to legend, a group of artistically and ghoulishly inclined friars decided to put the dead brothers' bones (4,000 monks in all) to a cautionary use. Four rooms of rococo sculptures contain a playful filigree of hip bones, a garland of spines and an array of skulls stacked as neatly as oranges and apples on a fruit vendor's stall.

The **Via Veneto** became famous after World War II as the centre of Rome's *dolce vita*. Although no longer the hub of glamorous Roman nightlife, Via Veneto is still an excuse for donning your shades and sipping a glass of Frascati at an outdoor café before going for a stroll in the gorgeous Villa Borghese gardens to the north.

Villa Borgese and gardens

The **Villa Borghese**, which encompasses the 17th-century grounds of Cardinal Scipione Borghese's fabulous villa, serves as a repository for some of Rome's finest treasures. Paradoxically, it is also the city's loveliest park and a bucolic retreat when the weight of history proves overwhelming. Children might be tempted by the **Bioparco** ㉛ (www.bioparco.it; Apr–Sept Mon–Fri 9.30am–6pm, Sat–Sun 9.30am–7pm, Oct daily 9.30am–6pm, Nov–Mar 9.30am–5pm), the small-scale zoo, but the park itself has infinite family appeal, whether for picnicking, boating or kite-flying. For adults, the Villa Borghese's Orangery now houses the **Carlo Bilotti Museum** (www.museocarlobilotti. it; June–Sept Tue–Fri 1–7pm, Sat–Sun from 10am, Oct–May Tue–Fri

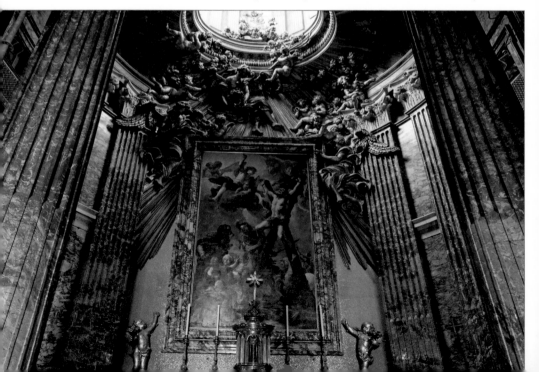

10am–4pm, Sat–Sun until 7pm; free), a quirky collection including works by de Chirico and Warhol.

Close to the Via Veneto entrance awaits one of Rome's heart-stopping collections, the **Galleria Borghese** ㉜ (tel: 06-32810; http://galleriaborghese.beniculturali.it; Tue–Sun 9am–7pm; admission every two hours, last one at 5pm, visits by reservation only; free first Sun of the month). Created by the cultured Cardinal Borghese, the world-class collection is housed in the cardinal's palatial summer residence, a frescoed affair studded with masterpieces by Bernini, Caravaggio, Raphael, Titian, Rubens and Canova.

Instead, if drawn by Italy's more recent artistic achievements, visit the **Galleria Nazionale d'Arte Moderna e Contemporanea** (GNAM) ㉝ (http://lagallerianazionale.com; Tue–Sun 8.30am–7.30pm; free first Sun of the month). Although Italian artists feature prominently, so too do international artists of the stature of Henry Moore, Pollock, Cézanne and Kandinsky, and many more dating from the 1800s to the present.

To the northwest of the Villa Borghese is another aristocratic palace, built for Julius III. The **Villa Giulia** ㉞ has a beautiful Renaissance garden and, inside, the fascinating **Museo Nazionale Etrusco di Villa Giulia** (www.villagiulia.beniculturali.it; Tue–Sun 8.30am–7.30pm; free first Sun of the month) full of pre-Roman art. The Etruscan terracotta sculptures are masterly, as is a statue of Apollo and a touching, Volterra-style sarcophagus of a husband and wife with enigmatic smiles.

East of Villa Borghese lies **Villa Torlonia** ㉟, another patrician park dotted with intriguing villas and follies. The centrepiece is the **Casino Nobile** (www.museivillatorlonia.it; summer Tue–Sun 9am–7pm), the last grand villa to grace Rome's skyline. Now a museum, the neoclassical affair was Mussolini's ostentatious residence between 1925 until 1943 and is linked to his stark bunker. Less overweaning is the neighbouring **Casina delle Civette** (times as above), a patrician folly built for Prince Torlonia which combines a Swiss chalet-style facade with a faux-medieval interior.

The much-photographed Trevi Fountain.

MUSEO NAZIONALE ROMANO

The Museo Nazionale Romano (www.archeorm.arti.beniculturali.it/en/node/482) is one of the most important archaeological collections in the world. It is split up into four main sites. The vast **Terme di Diocleziano** (Baths of Diocletian; Via Enrico de Nicola 78 (see page 149) was the original home of the museum. The Aula Ottagona (Octagonal Hall, Via Romita 8), an integral part of the baths, still contains some important sculptures. But the bulk of the collection is at the **Palazzo Massimo alle Terme** (Largo di Villa Peretti 1). Highlights include splendid floor mosaics and wall paintings from the villas of wealthy Romans, seen at their best in the delicate frescoes from Villa Livia. The **Palazzo Altemps** (Piazza Sant'Apollinare 44) is a Renaissance palace off Piazza Navona, with a beautiful courtyard which houses a fine collection of ancient sculptures. The **Crypta Balbi** (Via delle Botteghe Oscure 31) – the remains of the theatre built by Balbus in 13 BC – traces the city's development from the pre-imperial era to early Christian and medieval times.

All sites are open Tue–Sun 9am–7.30/7.45pm, June–Sept also Fri 8–11pm. A ticket is valid for all the sites of the museums for a period of three days (free access on the first Sun of the month). An Archeologia Card includes the four museum sites, the Colosseum, the Palatine, the Baths of Caracalla, the Tomb of Cecilia Metella and the Villa of the Quintili. Book online at www.coopculture.it or tel: 06-3996 7700.

The Baroque:
Bernini and Borromini

Baroque is a Roman art form par excellence. Exuberant, awe-inspiring and outrageous, Baroque architecture offers such a profusion of decorative detail, gilt and marble statuary that it often overwhelms. But what pleasure there is in discovering a particularly winning putto winking at you from an architrave, in craning to see a fantastic ceiling by Pietro da Cortona or Andrea dal Pozzo, and in seeing saints and biblical figures made flesh by Bernini. In terms of art, the most prodigious talent was Caravaggio, whose works adorn the city churches. Rome's Baroque churches are also the setting for classical recitals.

Roman Baroque can best be grasped in the **Gesù ③⑥** (www.chiesadelgesu.org; daily 7am–12.30, 4–7.45pm), near Piazza Venezia on the Via del Plebiscito. This was the headquarters of the Jesuit Order, champions of the Counter-Reformation. The Council of Trent (1545–63) laid down the rigorous principles for strengthening the Catholic Church against the Protestant heretics. Originally, the Gesù was meant to be austere; its Baroque makeover took place in the late 17th century when the Counter-Reformers used the art to illuminate the biblical message and impress their fervent flock with the immense power of the Church. Andrea dal Pozzo's altar to St Ignatius is particularly sumptuous. But the glory is the ceiling, with Il Baciccia's painting *The Triumph of the Name of Jesus*. Statues cling to the gilded vaults, some supporting the central painting which spills out of its frame.

In Via Botteghe Oscure, near the Gesù, make time for the **Crypta Balbi** (see box), which is a key to understanding Roman history long before Baroque existed.

From here head east towards the Palazzo del Quirinale (see page 143). The route then fans east to the Esquilino district, and takes in some of the wonders of both Baroque and Ancient Rome in the area around the railway station.

From the intersection of **Via delle Quattro Fontane** and Via XX Settembre admire the drama of Roman urban planning, where obelisks scrape the sky in three directions. The Via XX Settembre contains several splendid Baroque churches, notably **San Carlo alle Quattro Fontane ③⑦**. Also known as San Carlino, this tiny church was designed by Francesco Borromini (1599–1667). The undulating facade is a hallmark of this eccentric architect's style, as is the fantastic game of ovals inside. The astute monks who commissioned the church were impressed by Borromini's ability to economise – by using delicate stucco-work rather than marble or gilding – but without detracting from the beauty of the interior.

Along Via del Quirinale, off the other side of Via delle Quattro Fontane, is another oval gem by Borromini's arch rival, Gianlorenzo Bernini (1598–1680). **Sant'Andrea al Quirinale ③⑧** offers quite a contrast to its neighbour. Every inch of this church is covered with gilt and marble. Putti ascend the wall as if in a cloud of smoke. Yet the architect's masterful,

Admiring the statuary in the Palazzo Massimo.

classical handling of space creates a marvellous sense of simplicity.

For another masterpiece, head to **Santa Maria della Vittoria 39**, in Largo Santa Susanna (off Via XX Settembre), home to Bernini's sculpture of the 17th-century Spanish mystic St Teresa of Avila. The artist captures her at the moment when she was being struck by the arrow of divine love.

Return to Ancient Rome

Amid all the Baroque, Ancient Rome still rears its head again. Across Via XX Settembre, on the north side of Piazza della Repubblica, is **Santa Maria degli Angeli 40**, a church Michelangelo created from the tepidarium of the **Terme di Diocleziano** (Baths of Diocletian; see box), the most extensive baths in Rome, built between AD 298 and 306. The *esedra*, the open space surrounded by porticoes and seats where the Romans would chat, gave its form to Piazza della Repubblica. The **Fontana delle Naiadi** (Fountain of the Naiads) in the centre of the square, dating from around 1900, caused a scandal when it was unveiled, because of the "obscene" postures of the

nymphs. The baths were also once the principal venue of the **Museo Nazionale Romano 41**, but this great collection of ancient art is now dotted among four significant sites, notably in the neighbouring **Palazzo Massimo 42**, just across from Santa Maria degli Angeli. This is undoubtedly the most impressive section of the Museo Nazionale Romano, with its superb collection of statuary, frescoes and mosaics (see box page 147).

Rome has more churches dedicated to the Virgin Mary than to any other saint. The largest and most splendid is **Santa Maria Maggiore 43** (www.vatican.va; daily 7am–7pm), one of the four patriarchal churches of Rome. Here the mixture of architectural styles is surprisingly harmonious: early Christianity is represented in the basilican form and in the 5th-century mosaics in the nave. Medieval remodelling includes the campanile (the largest in Rome), the Cosmati floor and the mosaics in the apse. The coffered ceiling was supposedly gilded with gold Columbus brought from America. But the overwhelming effect is Baroque, so the

A lively market is held in Campo de' Fiori.

Rome is eminently strollable.

The battered statue on Piazza di Pasquino.

Inside the Pantheon dome.

church represents a fitting resting place for Bernini, the master of the genre.

If your head is spinning with a surfeit of gilt and marble, head down the Via Cavour to **San Pietro in Vincoli** 🅐 (daily 8am–12.30pm and 3–7pm, until 6pm in winter) to discover Michelangelo's massive and dignified *Moses*, the incarnation of the powerful law-giver. The statue was intended to form part of an enormous freestanding tomb for Pope Julius II. Giorgio Vasari, the first historian of art, waxed lyrical over the work: "No modern work will ever approach it in beauty." The church also displays the chains that bound St Peter in his prison cells in Rome and Judaea, hence the name of the church (St Peter in Chains).

For a dramatic shift eastwards in global terms, visit Palazzo Brancaccio, near Santa Maria Maggiore, to see the most important collection of oriental art in Italy, the **Museo Nazionale d'Arte Orientale** (Via Merulana 248, on the Esquiline Hill; www.museorientale.beniculturali.it; Tue, Wed, Fri 9am–2pm, Thu, Sat, Sun 9am–7.30pm; free first Sun of the month).

Around the Pantheon

During the Middle Ages, most of Rome's population was concentrated between Via del Corso and the Tiber (Campus Martius to the ancients) or crowded into **Trastevere** (see page 161) across the river. Trastevere is best reached on a walk across the charming island the **Isola Tiberina**. Now, the Pantheon quarter, sandwiched between the Corso and the Tiber, remains one of the most engaging districts and, despite the hordes of tourists, offers a flavour of real Roman life. While buzzing at night, early morning holds its own appeal, when you can admire palatial facades in peace, enter churches with only the faithful as companions, and watch the Romans starting their day.

Have a *cornetto* (an Italian croissant) and a cappuccino in **Piazza della Rotonda** and admire the exterior of the **Pantheon** 🅑 (www.polomusealelazio.beniculturali.it; Mon–Sat 9am–7.30pm, Sun and holidays 9am–6pm; free) – the best preserved of all ancient Roman buildings. For those who question the greatness of Roman architecture and dismiss it as inferior to Greek, the Pantheon is

---

CAMPO DE' FIORI

South of Piazza Navona is the equally vibrant Campo de' Fiori. It has been the site of a raffish market for centuries, and was one of the liveliest areas of medieval and Renaissance Rome, when cardinals and pilgrims would rub shoulders with fishmongers, vegetable sellers and prostitutes. The Campo de' Fiori is the most secular of Roman squares, for although it is as old as Rome itself, it has never been dedicated to any cult, and to this day is free of churches. Its present aspect dates from the end of the 15th century, when the whole area was reshaped. It was surrounded by inns for pilgrims and travellers. In the Renaissance, some of these hotels were the homes of successful courtesans, Vannozza Catanei, mistress of the Borgia Pope Alexander VI, among them. On the corner of the square and Via del Pellegrino you can see her shield, which she had decorated with her own coat of arms and those of her husband and lover. With its reputation for being a carnal, pagan place, the square must have seemed a natural spot to hold executions. Of all the unfortunate victims, Giordano Bruno was the most important figure to be burnt at the stake here, in 1600. A priest and philosopher, he was accused of heresy and found guilty of freethinking. The dominant statue of Bruno in the middle of the piazza was erected in 1887, marking the exact spot of his death.

an eloquent answer. This perfectly proportioned round temple proves how adept the Romans were in shaping interior space. Rebuilt by the Emperor Hadrian, its architectural antecedents are not the Republican round temples – such as the one in the Forum Boarium – but the round chambers used in the baths.

Western architecture owes the Romans an enormous debt for their skilful work with vaults and domes. The only light is provided by a large hole set in the centre of the dome – the *oculus* – and this means that the building has been open to the elements for nearly 2,000 years.

Facing the Pantheon is the **Caffè San Eustachio** (http://santeustachioilcaffe.it), which supposedly serves the best coffee in town, with *gran caffè*, a sweet, frothy double espresso, its signature drink.

Near the Pantheon, in front of **Santa Maria Sopra Minerva** (Mon–Fri 7.30am–7pm, Sat 7.30am–12.30pm, 3.30–7pm, Sun 8am–noon, 2–7pm), Bernini's much-loved elephant carries the smallest of Rome's obelisks. Inside the church, the only Gothic church in Rome, are a chapel decorated by Fra Filippo Lippi and Michelangelo's statue of *Christ Bearing the Cross*. Caravaggio masterpieces adorn neighbouring churches. **San Luigi dei Francesi** (daily 10am–12.30pm and 4–7pm, closed Thu pm) features *The Calling of St Matthew*, *St Matthew and the Angel* and *The Martyrdom of St Matthew*. Another Caravaggio work, *The Madonna of the Pilgrims*, is displayed in Sant'Agostino. Borromini's **Sant'Ivo**, tucked into the courtyard of Palazzo Sapienza, boasts a dazzling interior and a spiralling campanile.

Around Piazza Navona

Although the chariot races are no more, nothing can mask the vibrancy of **Piazza Navona** ⓐ, from the milling crowds of mime artists, caricaturists and ice-cream eaters to the preening girls and patrolling Roman youths. This space was once the Stadium of Domitian, parts of which can still be seen off the northern end. On Piazza

Sant'Apollinare, just across the street, stands the **Palazzo Altemps** (see page 147), a Renaissance palace housing a fine collection of classical statuary.

Between Piazza Navona and the Campo de' Fiori is the **Museo di Scultura Antica Giovanni Barracco** ⓐ (www.museobarracco.it; June–Sept Tue–Sun 1–7pm, Oct–May 10am–4pm; free), which showcases Egyptian, Etruscan and Roman sculpture in an intimate setting. At any time of day, the neighbouring **Campo de' Fiori** ⓑ makes a perfect stop for the footsore.

Nearby, the church of **Sant'Agnese in Agone** (closed Mon) boasts a curvaceous Borromini facade. In one version of the saint's martyrdom, Agnes, who had vowed to be a virgin bride of Christ, was banished to a brothel where her chastity was miraculously preserved; a subsequent attempt to burn her was also unsuccessful; finally, she was beheaded.

Borromini's rival Bernini designed the **Fontana dei Quattro Fiumi** (Fountain of the Four Rivers) in the centre of the piazza. A popular tale claims that the statue of the Nile facing Sant'Agnese is covering its eyes for fear it will collapse.

Shopping for prints on Piazza Navona.

Large-scale installation at MACRO.

Exhibition at MAXXI.

However, the fountain was completed in 1651, before Borromini had even started work on the church.

Close by, **Piazza di Pasquino** contains a battered statue that once functioned as the underground newspaper of Rome. The papal censors allowed so little criticism that irrepressible commentators attached their writings to statues in the city. The most famous satirist was Pasquino.

Near the piazza is the elegant church of **Santa Maria della Pace** ④ (Mon, Wed, Sat 9am–noon). Inside are frescoes by Raphael and beautiful cloisters by Bramante, which are often the setting for displays of contemporary art. If the front door is locked, enter through the Bramante cloister (www.chiostrodelbramante.it; Mon–Fri 10am–8pm, Sat–Sun until 9pm; free). To the north, Via dei Coronari is lit with torches every night.

At the end of Via dei Cornari, turn left to reach the **Chiesa Nuova** – **Santa Maria in Vallicella** ⑤ (www.vallicella.org; daily 7.30am–noon and 4.30–7.30pm), dedicated to St Filippo Neri, one of Rome's patron saints, who lies buried here. The apse contains three fine works

by Rubens, who lived in Rome from 1606 to 1608. The Oratorio dei Filippini was built between 1637 and 1662 by Borromini as a place of worship for the fraternity of St Philip Neri, who instituted the musical gatherings that later became known as oratorios.

But the district's show-stopping Baroque church is the ornate **Sant'-Andrea della Valle** ⑤, which Puccini chose as a setting for the opening act of *Tosca*. Act II takes place at the nearby **Palazzo Farnese** ⑤, the most splendid of Renaissance palaces and suitably intimidating as headquarters for the villainous Scarpia. The palace is now the French embassy so, in order to see Annibale Carracci's *frescoes*, you need to book a guided tour (www.inventerrome.com for bookings, Mon and Fri at 5pm, Wed at 3pm and 4pm).

Act III of Puccini's *Tosca* takes place on the west bank of the Tiber, in the notorious **Castel Sant'Angelo** ⑤ prison (http://castelsantangelo.beniculturali.it; or www.polomusealelazio.beniculturali.it; daily 9am–7.30pm; free first Sun of the month). Visiting this fortress takes us from Rome into the **Vatican City**, the world's smallest state, see page 157.

Roman resurgence

For all its history, Rome is no longer mired in the past: its reputation for partying is slowly being matched by a new contemporary art, music and theatre scene that is dragging the city into the 21st century. This being Rome, there is often a retro touch or some tacit recycling involved.

In the Villa Borghese gardens, **Globe Theatre Roma** (www.globetheatreroma.com; June–Sept) is a case in point. This replica of London's Elizabethan theatre of the same name stages Shakespearean and contemporary drama. The open-air theatre is a reminder that summer is when Rome comes alive, with a riot of outdoor events held in villas, gardens and squares, from open-air concerts to parties in the park.

The music scene has been revitalised by the Renzo Piano-designed

Auditorium Parco della Musica ❺❹ (tel: 06-80241281; www.auditorium.com). Set north of the Borghese gardens, this is Rome's pre-eminent music venue. Beetle-like pods create perfect acoustics in settings just right for recitals, rock and Latin music, from symphonies to soul, or from Rachmaninov to Tony Bennett. The Academy of Santa Cecilia, one of the oldest musical institutions in the world, founded in 1585, is now based here. The orchestra is led by Antonio Pappano, the Italian, London-born but American-educated conductor.

The **Casa del Jazz** (www.casajazz.it; tel: 06-704731), set in the gardens of Villa Osio, a property confiscated from a Mafia boss, has grown into the city's major dedicated jazz venue, although the biggest names tend to perform at the Auditorium. The arts scene has been revitalised with bold showcases for contemporary art, a sign that the city has regained its radicalism. Not far from the Auditorium is the **MACRO** ❺❺, the Museo d'Arte Contemporanea Roma (www.museomacro.org; Tue–Sun 10.30am–7pm). Set in a converted brewery on Via Reggio Emilia, Rome's primary contemporary art museum has been remodelled by French architect Odile Decq, with a new gallery and rooftop restaurant. The permanent collection explores trend-setting Italian artwork since the 1960s that has represented cutting-edge approaches to contemporary art. The museum is complemented by **MACRO Future** in Testaccio (see page 142).

Architecturally, the most radical arts museum is the **MAXXI** ❺❻ (www.fondazionemaxxi.it; Tue–Fri, Sun 11am–7pm, Sat 11am–10pm). Set on Via Guido Reni, this grand project sees a former army barracks reborn as the Museum of 21st-Century Arts. Designed by the late Zaha Hadid, the gallery, ribboned with walkways and a curving staircase, eclipses the work but is gradually acquiring worthy collections of art and photography. Pippo Ciorra, MAXXI'S senior curator, heralds the project as a breakthrough in a city where young Romans are crying out for modernity: "The city has been a battleground for modern architecture," he laments. But given the glories of Ancient Rome, few visitors care too deeply.

Palazzo Farnese now houses the French embassy.

THE COLOSSEUM: BREAD AND CIRCUSES

"While the Colosseum stands, Rome shall stand; when the Colosseum falls, Rome shall fall; when Rome falls, the world shall fall".

The Venerable Bede's 8th-century prophecy has been taken to heart and the Colosseum shored up ever since. The ancient amphitheatre is a stirring sight, a place of stupendous size and spatial harmony. Begun by Vespasian, it was inaugurated by his son Titus in AD 80, and completed by Domitian (AD 81–96). Titus used Jewish captives as masons. The Colosseum had 80 entrances, allowing over 50,000 spectators to be seated. "Bread and circuses" was how Juvenal, the 2nd-century satirist, mocked the Romans who sold their souls for free food and entertainment.

Fall and ruin

With the fall of the empire, the Colosseum fell into disuse. During the Renaissance, the ruins were plundered to create churches and palaces, including the Palazzo Farnese, now the French embassy. The Colosseum was still neglected on the German writer Goethe's visit in 1787, with a hermit and beggars "at home in the crumbling vaults". In 1817 Lord Byron was enthralled by this "noble wreck in ruinous perfection", while Edgar Allan Poe celebrated its "grandeur, gloom and glory".

Mussolini, attracted to the power that the Colosseum represented, demolished a line of buildings to create a clear view of it from his balcony on the Palazzo di Venezia.

The Colosseum is undergoing a multi-million-euro renovation sponsored by the luxury fashion brand Tod's. The first phase of the restoration was completed in 2016, when the façade's new facelift was unveiled and the top tier and hypogeum (underground chamber and tunnels) reopened to the public.

The Colosseum all spruced up after its multi-million restoration.

The underground chambers and tunnels are also being renovated as part of a major renovation programme.

This 18th-century view by Giovanni Volpato reflects the nostalgic sensibility of the Romantic era. Visitors on the Grand Tour were beguiled by the ruins bathed in moonlight or haunted by the sense of a lost civilisation.

Gladiatorial combat was a favourite form of entertainment for all strata of society.

ENTERTAINMENT FOR THE MASSES

The Roman appetite for bloodshed was legendary, with barbaric blood sports introduced as a corrupt version of Greek games. The animals, mostly imported from Africa, included lions, elephants, giraffes, hyenas, hippos and zebras. The contests also served to eliminate slaves and proscribed sects, Christians and criminals, political agitators and prisoners of war. Variants included battles involving mock hunts and freak shows with panthers pulling chariots or cripples pitted against clowns. Seneca, Nero's tutor, came expecting "fun, wit and some relaxation", but was dumbfounded by the butchery and cries of "Kill him! Lash him! Why does he meet the sword so timidly?"

In AD 248, the millennium of the founding of Rome was celebrated by contests involving 2,000 gladiators and the slaying of giraffes and hippos as well as big cats. Although convicted criminals were fed to the lions, Christian martyrdom here is less well documented. St Ignatius of Antioch, who described himself as "the wheat of Christ", was dutifully devoured by lions in AD 107. Gladiatorial combat was banned in 404, while animal fights ended in the following century.

A movable wooden floor covered in sand (to soak up the blood) concealed the animal cages and sophisticated technical apparatus, from winches and mechanical lifts to ramps and trapdoors.

Renaissance historians believed that Roman arenas were sometimes flooded to stage mock naval battles, but there is scant evidence to suggest such a display ever took place in the Colosseum.

Gladiator's helmet.

St Peter's magnificent dome.

THE VATICAN AND TRASTEVERE

From the spirituality of St Peter's, with its extensive museums and magnificent art treasures to the earthiness of Rome's medieval quarter.

The west bank of the Tiber offers contrasting experiences. Cheek by jowl with the Vatican, with all its papal pomp, is the intimate district of Trastevere, with its narrow streets and lively nightlife. The sheer size of St Peter's, the world's most important church set in the equally impressive St Peter's Square, can't fail to leave you unmoved even if you inevitably have to jostle with the crowds. The sight of Michelangelo's ceiling in the Sistine Chapel is awe-inspiring and the works of art in the Vatican Museums sublime. For a complete change come down to earth in engaging Trastevere. From here you can visit the catacombs and stroll along the Via Appia Antica.

As you cross the Tiber using Ponte Sant'Angelo, it is not the domed heart of the Vatican you see first, but the almost windowless walls of the medieval citadel, the **Castel Sant'Angelo** (http://castelsantangelo. beniculturali.it or www.polomusealelazio. beniculturali.it; daily 9am–7.30pm; free first Sun of the month).

Back in AD 139, this was the site of the mausoleum of the Emperor Hadrian. Later it became a fortress and prison, then a residence to which the popes could flee in times of turbulence. Today it reveals intriguing shifts between the Roman mausoleum, cisterns and oil stores to the medieval prisons, princely fortress and frescoed papal apartments. The night tours take in the prisons, as well as Clement VII's frescoed bathroom, complete with underfloor heating.

Puccini's heroine, Tosca, plunged to her death from the parapet where visitors now come to admire the views across Rome. Towering over the battlements is a gigantic statue of St Michael, the warlike archangel after whom the castle is named.

Main Attractions

Piazza San Pietro
Basilica di San Pietro
  (St Peter's)
Vatican Museums
Sistine Chapel
Trastevere
Via Appia Antica
Catacombs

Castel Sant'Angelo.

Vatican City

For centuries the Vatican was the unchallenged centre of the Western world. Its symbolic significance and its enduring international role, as both a religious and a diplomatic force, have put this tiny city-state on the map.

Covering a total area of slightly more than 40 hectares (100 acres), the Vatican City is by far the world's smallest independent sovereign entity, crossed at a leisurely pace in under half an hour. Yet the Vatican serves as an exception to the rule that tiny nations are famous for little more than their postage stamps.

In imperial Roman days, the lower part of what is now the Vatican City was an unhealthy bog, known for its snakes and diseases. In the 1st century AD, the dowager empress Agrippina had the Vatican Valley drained and planted with imperial gardens. Under Caligula and Nero, chariot racing and executions – including that of St Peter – were regular events on what was to become St Peter's Square.

Aside from an impressive array of palaces and office buildings, there is also a Vatican prison, a supermarket and a printing press, which publishes the daily *L'Osservatore Romano* and scripts in a wide range of languages, from Coptic to Ecclesiastical Georgian to Tamil.

Novelist Alberto Moravia used to say: "Rome is an administrative city dominated by two institutions: the State and the Church." While an over-simplification, Rome *is* the meeting place of temporal and spiritual powers and, as the capital, lives and breathes politics. As for piety, the Vatican has traditionally been treated as a temporal power, as the corporate arm of the papacy. "Faith is made here but believed elsewhere," is the local dictum. Essentially, the Romans are more ritualistic than religious, even if the death of John Paul II saw an outpouring of emotion that surprised cynical Rome-watchers.

Piazza San Pietro

From Castel Sant'Angelo, Via della Conciliazione leads to St Peter's, at the heart of the Vatican City. Bernini's spectacular, colonnaded **Piazza**

The bronze statue of St Peter's, much-loved by pilgrims.

A ROMAN EASTER

Easter is the most heartfelt Roman festival, when history and tradition merge with common piety and cheerful consumerism. At Easter, the Eternal City is at ease with its Roman and Christian heritage, from St Peter's relics to the Scala Santa, the marble staircase that Christ supposedly ascended to meet Pontius Pilate. In San Giovanni in Laterano, the faithful climb to the top on their knees. On Good Friday, the Pope retraces Christ's Via Crucis on a moving candlelit procession, ending in a huge open-air Mass on St Peter's Square on Easter Sunday.

On becoming pope, Benedict XVI opened up the Porta Santa Rosa entrance to the Vatican, as a gesture of openness. The Easter procession winds from the Colosseum to Monte Palatino, re-enacting the 14 Stations of the Cross, from Christ's death sentence to his entombment, with the Pope uttering prayers at each station. Pilgrims gather with torches to follow this solemn procession, which coincides with concerts in city churches. Rome's pastry shops display Easter eggs stuffed with tiny silver picture frames or costume jewellery. Wealthier Romans even instruct their chocolatiers to encase treasured gifts in the eggs, ranging from engagement rings to symbolic crosses. Despite their sophistication, Romans love the chocolate-wrapped trappings of piety, and tangible symbols of truth, a reminder that even Christian Rome was founded on relics.

San Pietro ⑤ is, according to one's viewpoint, either the welcoming embrace of the Mother Church or her grasping claws.

The Via della Conciliazione, constructed in 1937 to commemorate the reconciliation between Mussolini and Pope Pius XI, changed the original impact of the space. Before this thoroughfare provided a monumental approach to St Peter's, the entrance was by way of smaller streets, winding through the old Borgo and arriving, finally, in the enclosed open space, with the biggest church in the world at one end and an enormous Egyptian obelisk in the centre.

Church, museum, mausoleum: the Basilica di San Pietro, **St Peter's** (daily 7am–7pm, until 6.30pm in winter; dome 8am–6pm, until 5pm in winter; modest dress code; free except for visits to the dome) is all three. No other temple surpasses it in terms of historical significance or architectural splendour. The immensity of the interior might seem at odds with the intimate act of prayer, but the architects and patrons of St Peter's intended the building to symbolise worldly power as much as spiritual piety. Just about every important Renaissance and Baroque architect from Bramante onwards had a hand in the design of St Peter's. The idea for rebuilding the original 4th-century basilica only became a reality when Julius II became pope. Bramante was succeeded by Raphael, Michelangelo and Bernini, to name but three masters.

The interior is vast – 186 metres (610ft) long, with a capacity for around 60,000 people. On the right, as you walk in, is Michelangelo's *Pietà*, an inspiration to beholders ever since the sculptor finished it in 1500, at the age of 25. At the end of the nave is the bronze statue of *St Peter*, its toe worn away by the kisses of pilgrims.

Over the high altar, which is directly above the tomb of St Peter, rises Bernini's garish bronze baldachin, resembling the canopy of an imperial bed; Pope Urban VIII stripped the bronze from the Pantheon. But Bernini outdid himself in the design for the Cathedra Petri (the Chair of St Peter) in the apse. Four gilt bronze figures of the Church Fathers hold up the chair. Above, light streams through the golden glass of a window crowned by a dove (symbol of the Holy Ghost). The chair bears a relief of Christ's command to Peter to "charge his sheep". Thus the position of the Pope is explained and bolstered by Christ's words and the teachings of the Church Fathers, and blessed by the Holy Ghost.

Further confirmation of the Pope's sacred trust is found in Christ's words inscribed on the dome: "You are Peter and on this rock I will build my Church and I will give you the keys to the kingdom of heaven."

The Vatican Museums

The **Musei Vaticani ⑤** (www.museivaticani.va; Mon–Sat 9am–6pm, last Sun of the month 9am–2pm, last entry two hours before closing, free Sun; to avoid

Inside the Vatican's Galleria delle carte geografiche (Gallery of Maps).

View over the Vatican from St Peter's dome.

Subjects of the Holy See

The papal ranks have included patrons of the arts, great persuaders and profligate princes, not to mention numerous political players.

To be one of the 1,000 or so citizens with a Vatican passport is to belong to one of the world's most exclusive clubs – the privilege of citizenship hinges on a direct and continuous relationship with the Holy See. The Pope himself carries passport No. 1, and he rules absolutely over the Vatican City.

The word "pope" comes from the Greek *pappas*, meaning "father". Despite two millennia having passed since St Peter first assumed the mantle, the Pope's role remains paternal, alternating between concern for humanity and stern warnings against theological or spiritual deviation. John Paul II (1978–2005) asserted his moral authority vigorously. His 1993 encyclical denounced contraception, homosexuality and other infringements of the faith as "intrinsically evil". His successor, Benedict XVI, was cast in the same ethical mould. He took the personal decision to renounce the papacy in 2013.

Swiss Guard at the Vatican.

His successor, Pope Francis, is the first Pope to come from Latin America and the first Jesuit to hold the position. Noted for his humility he has shunned pomp and lives a life of simplicity. His is a less formal approach to the papacy, and whilst retaining its core values, is prepared to listen to minority groups, although this may prove to be controversial at times.

A global leader

There have been 263 popes. While the great majority have been of either Roman or Italian extraction, Spain, Greece, Syria, France and Germany have all been represented, and there has been at least one of African birth (Miltiades, 311–14), and one from England (Hadrian IV, 1154–9). John Paul II was the first Pole to lead the Catholic Church. At least 14 popes abdicated or were deposed. Ten popes met violent deaths, including a record three in a row in the 10th century.

The shortest reign of a pope was that of Stephen II, who died four days after his election in March 752. At the other extreme, the 19th century's Pius IX, famous for his practical jokes and his love of billiards, headed the Holy See for 32 years. The youngest pope on record, John XI, was just 16 when he took the helm in 931; the oldest, Gregory IX, managed to survive 14 years after his election in 1227 at the age of 86.

Choosing the pope

The process of electing a new pope is necessarily unique, as the papacy is the world's only elective monarchy. Members of the Sacred College of Cardinals, a largely titular body of 120 bishops and archbishops, are sealed into the Sistine Chapel soon after the death knell tolls in the Vatican Palace. They cannot leave until a new successor has been chosen. Voting can proceed by acclamation, whereby the cardinals all shout the same name at the same time; by scrutiny, in which four ballots are cast daily until one candidate has captured a two-thirds majority plus one; or, as a last resort, by compromise.

All modern popes have been selected by the second method. Paper ballots are burnt after each tally, and onlookers watch the chapel's chimney for dark smoke, which indicates an inconclusive vote, or white plumes, which denote a winner (electors are provided with special chemicals so that there can be no mistake). Finally the cardinal dean announces "Habemus Papam" (We have a pope) to the faithful, and the chosen cardinal appears in one of three robes (sized small, medium and large) kept on hand for the occasion. The coronation takes place on the following day. In the words of the Medici Pope Leo X: "God has given us the papacy – let us enjoy it.").

queues book online at https://biglietteriamusei.vatican.va) merit a lifetime's study. But for those who have only a few hours, some sights should not be missed. If you have time, select the additional gardens or the necropolis tours (email: visiteguidatesingoli.musei@scv.va). If hurried, head for the **Museo Pio-Clementino**, which contains the Pope's collection of antiquities.

Be sure to visit the Belvedere Courtyard, home of the cerebral *Apollo Belvedere* and the contrasting muscle-bound, sensual *Laocoön*. The Gabinetto delle Maschere (Mask Room) displays mosaics of theatrical masks from Hadrian's Villa in Tivoli. The Vatican **Pinacoteca** contains superb paintings, including Raphael's *Madonna of Foligno* and *Transfiguration*. The **Raphael Rooms** (the Stanze di Raffaello) comprise four rooms painted by Raphael. Downstairs, colourful frescoes by Pinturicchio decorate the Borgia Apartments.

But the world's most sublime frescoes await in the **Cappella Sistina** (**Sistine Chapel**). The chapel has always served as both the Pope's private chapel and the setting for the conclaves by which new popes are elected (see page 160). The walls are covered in paintings by the Renaissance masters Botticelli, Pinturicchio and Ghirlandaio, but the star of the show is Michelangelo's ceiling, begun in 1508 and completed by 1512. The shallow barrel vault is divided into panels tracing the story of the Creation.

No reproduction can ever do justice to the interplay of painting and architecture, to the drama of the whole chapel, alive with colour and human emotion.

Trastevere

The heart of medieval Trastevere, literally "across the Tiber", is southeast of the Vatican City. This is home to a popular restaurant and nightlife district as well as to a sprawling Sunday flea market, the **Porta Portese** 59 (8am–2pm). Once fiercely working-class, Trastevere is now largely gentrified but retains its engagingly bohemian air, despite the touristy restaurants and boisterous wine bars. The winding streets are the perfect

Bramante's Tempietto, the first monument in High Renaissance style.

Giuseppe Momo's helicoidal staircase.

place to seek out an original gift from the area's many artisanal workshops.

South of Viale di Trastevere are two churches worth visiting. **Santa Cecilia** ⑥⓪ (daily 10am–1pm and 4–7pm; charge for crypt and frescoes) was built on top of the house of a Christian martyr whom the Roman authorities attempted to scald to death in her own *caldarium* (hot bath). When this failed, she was sentenced to decapitation, but three blows failed to sever her head and she lived for a further three days (enough time to consecrate her house as a church). Carlo Maderno's touching statue of the saint curled in a foetal position was inspired by his observations when her tomb was opened in 1599. Also of note are the beautiful medieval frescoes by Cavallini (Mon–Fri 10am–12.30pm), especially his *Last Judgement*, which is considered his masterpiece.

A contrastingly sublime statue of a woman in her death throes is Bernini's *Blessed Luisa Albertoni* in nearby **San Francesco a Ripa** (www.sanfrancescoaripa.com). This late work

of the master captures even more powerfully than his St Teresa the conflict between joy and sorrow felt by a woman who is between this world and the next.

In the piazza of the same name, **Santa Maria in Trastevere** ⑥① (daily 7.30am–9pm) is one of the oldest churches in Rome, built on a site where a fountain of oil is said to have sprung on the day of Christ's birth. Most of the structure you see today dates from 1140. The church has some beautiful Byzantine mosaics, and it is worth taking a pair of binoculars to enjoy their details. *The Life of the Virgin* series is by Cavallini (1291).

After these sobering places of worship, preoccupied with the horrors of this world and the glories of the next, it is a relief to come to the **Villa Farnesina** ⑥② (www.villafarnesina.it; Mon–Sat 9am–2pm, second Sun of the month 9am–5pm; guided tours in English Sat at 10am), a jewel of the Renaissance, worldly and pagan. A ceiling fresco by Raphael details the love of Cupid and Psyche. In the next room, Raphael's *Galatea* captures the moment when

Admiring Raphael's 'Madonna of Foligno' and 'Transfiguration' in the Pinacoteca.

the nymph, safe from the clutches of the cyclops, looks round. Upstairs, Baldassare Peruzzi, who designed the villa, devised a fantastic *trompe l'œil* of bucolic life. In the bedroom is Sodoma's erotic painting *The Wedding of Alexander and Roxanne*.

To reach another important Renaissance monument, climb the steps up the Gianicolo to the church of **San Pietro in Montorio** ⑥ (daily 8.30am–noon Mon–Fri 3–4pm; free). In the courtyard is Bramante's **Tempietto** (Tue–Sun 10am–6pm, free), a circular church that marks what was once mistakenly believed to be the site of St Peter's martyrdom. It is a homage to antiquity and the first monument in High Renaissance style.

Climb a little further to the Fontana Paola, and the shady **Passeggiata del Gianicolo** (meaning "a stroll up Janiculum Hill") leads to panoramic views over the city. The flat dome of the Pantheon, the twin domes of Santa Maria Maggiore and the Victor Emmanuel Monument are all easy to spot from up here.

Into the bowels of the earth

Do make time for the basilicas and catacombs from the early Christian era. The secretive beginnings of Christianity are recalled in **Sant'Agnese fuori le Mura** ⑥ (Mon–Sat 9am–noon and 3–6pm, Sun only pm) beyond Michelangelo's Porta Pia on the Via Nomentana. Beneath the church run extensive catacombs (daily 9am–noon and 5–7pm; Sun only pm), where the martyred Roman maiden St Agnes was buried.

Also in the complex is the incomparable **Santa Costanza**, the mausoleum of Constantine's daughter, which is encrusted with some of Rome's most beautiful mosaics. For those not averse to tortuous tunnels winding endlessly past burial niches, there are countless catacombs outside the walls of Rome, along the picturesque **Via Appia Antica** (Appian Way; visit

on the handy Archeobus or by bike, especially on Sunday when it's closed to cars; www.parcoappiaantica.it). You can picnic amid the remains of the **Villa of the Quintili** (http://archeoroma.beniculturali.it or www.coopculture.it; Apr–Aug Tue–Sun 9am–7.15pm, Sept until 7pm, Oct until 6.30pm, Nov–mid-Feb until 4.30pm, mid-Feb–mid-Mar until 5pm, mid-Mar–end Mar until 5.30pm; free first Sun of the month), an area overrun with wild flowers and lizards. Above ground sits what Byron called the "stern round tower" of the **Tomba di Cecilia Metella** (times as above). Below spread the **Catacombs of St Callixtus** (San Callisto), the most famous in Rome (www.catacombe.roma.it; Thu–Tue 9am–noon and 2–5pm, closed Feb) and those of saints Sebastian and Domitilla.

Return to **Trastevere** for some light relief. Clubland is centred on Testaccio and Via Ostiense, but Trastevere's arty ambience is more low-key and mellow, offering an evening spent listening to the blues, followed by an *affogato* ice cream, drenched in liqueur. Roman life is too Latin for a Protestant work ethic.

Equestrian statue of Garibaldi in Piazza Garibaldi.

ROME'S ENVIRONS

Escape to the Castelli Romani, Rome's hills, villas and gardens, a playground first popularised by the Roman emperors, before visiting Etruscan settlements for an insight into a vanished world.

During the sweltering summers, Romans head for the hills, the lakes and the beach. Away from the city's bustle the gentle, wine-growing Castelli Romani hills provide a pleasant respite. Tivoli has long been a country retreat and one of the most popular day trips from Rome, featuring gorgeous villas, ancient woods and scenic waterfalls. Villa d'Este, with its pleasure palace and water gardens, has been a favoured spot since Roman times, while Ostia Antica draws romantics to its ruined amphitheatre. For lovers of all things ancient an escape from the city reveals the important Etruscan sites of Cerveteri and Tarquinia.

Curiously, Ancient Rome and Fascism are inextricably entwined in **Lazio** (former Latium). The Fascists boasted that they represented the continuation of Ancient Rome; the official art of the regime appropriated forms of Roman grandeur. Mosaics inspired by ancient Roman floors decorate the walls of the **Foro Italico ❶**, the ambitious sports centre created in 1931 northwest of the capital. Sixty colossal statues of athletes set the scene, even if the sheer scale of the modern Olympic Stadium (www. coni.it) overpowers Mussolini's legacy.

There is similar bombastic homage in **EUR ❷** (Esposizione Universale di Roma), the city's strangest suburb, and Mussolini's attempt to showcase imperial Rome and Fascist achievements. In

1938 Mussolini aspired to build a magnificent Third Rome, the natural successor to imperial Rome and the Rome of the Renaissance. Plans for an exhibition in 1942 to commemorate 20 years of Fascism were overtaken by World War II, and the overall design was left uncompleted. In the 1950s, expansion saw government offices and museums move here, and EUR evolved into a sought-after residential quarter.

Among the showpieces is the **Palazzo della Civiltà del Lavoro** – commonly called the "Square Colosseum" – now

Main Attractions

Ostia Antica
Castelli Romani
Villa Adriana
Villa d'Este
Villa Gregoriana
Cerveteri
Tarquinia

Rustic sign in Tarquinia.

the headquarters of fashion house Fendi; there are plans to transform the ground floor into the Made in Italy and Design Museum. Also compelling is the **Museo della Civiltà Romana** (www.museocivilta romana.it; closed for renovation, see website for details), devoted to the history of Ancient Rome. The museum contains bizarre scale models of Roman sites, as well as a cast of Trajan's Column and a model of the city under Constantine.

Ancient harbour city

Ostia Antica ❸ (www.ostiaantica.benicul turali.it or www.ostiaantica.info; Apr–Aug Tue–Sun 8.30am–7.15pm, Sept until 7pm, Oct until 6.30pm, Nov–mid-Feb until 4.30pm, mid-Feb–mid Mar until 5pm, mid-Mar–end Mar until 5.30pm) was founded around the end of the 4th century BC as a fortified city to guard the mouth of the Tiber. Later it developed into the commercial port of Rome as well as its naval base.

It was from here that the Romans set out to establish their empire. By the time of Constantine, Ostia had turned into a residential town for middle- and lower-class Romans. The legacy is a city whose ruins are second only to Pompeii in their legibility: the stratified nature of an ancient Italian city is laid bare. Ostia's innovations included social housing and a surprisingly modern resort-style complex with communal gardens. In the case of the early apartment block, the inner courtyard has remained a feature of Italian housing ever since. The *domus*, the typical Pompeiian residence built for the very rich, and restricted to one floor, was very rare in Ostia.

The **Piazzale delle Corporazioni** merchant quarter includes mosaics that denote the traders' wares, from the sign of a flotilla, indicating shipping services, to an elephant used to signify the importation of exotic circus animals. Flanking one side of the square, the **Teatro** was enlarged by Septimius Severus at the end of the 2nd century to seat 4,000 spectators. Today, this theatre is used as a summer venue for concerts, drama, dance and cabaret.

Tours of the complex's main buildings, such as the House of Diana and the Insula of Jupiter, are by appointment only Sundays at 10.30am (email ss-col.domusostia@beniculturali.it to book).

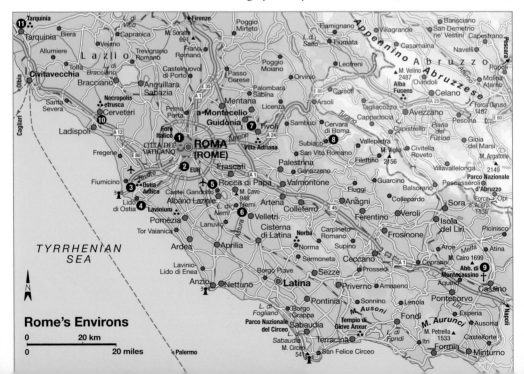

Rome's Environs

0   20 km

0   20 miles

If heading to the beach, spurn the overcrowded **Lido di Ostia** ❹ in favour of **Fregene**, a northern resort with pine groves and cachet, or, to the south, choose charming Sperlonga, Gaeta, and the island of Ponza.

The Castelli Romani

The Alban hills, clustered around the capital, have long represented a summer retreat for Romans. Known as the **Castelli Romani**, in ancient times these hills were scattered with villas and pleasure gardens, a tradition followed by the Renaissance popes. **Castel Gandolfo** ❺, overlooking Lake Albano, is the retreat of the papacy. When in residence, the Pope would address the crowds from the balcony of the papal palace. But things changed when Pope Francis was given the keys to the palace: a modest man, he shunned its luxury and decided to open it up to the public, who can now stroll through the beautiful Barberini Gardens overlooking the lake and visit the Gallery of the Pontiffs and papal apartments (pre-booked guided tours only; https://biglietteriamusei.vatican.va for bookings; www.museivaticani.va).

On summer weekends, this cluster of hill towns is still a popular pretext for Roman recreation, with the appeal lying in hilltop views and gentle walks, especially if linked to lunch in a local inn, or wine-tasting around **Frascati**, famed for its villas and crisp white wine.

Volcanic **Nemi** ❻, 10 miles (6km) southeast, is another popular weekend excursion, with its early medieval castle and compelling views over the dark-blue waters of Lake Nemi.

Tivoli

At the height of the Roman Empire, **Tibur** ❼ (**Tivoli**), on the lower slopes of the Sabine hills, was a retreat for the ruling elite, and eulogised by Roman poets. The lavish villas scattered around sacred woods and scenic waterfalls entertained visitors of the stature of Horace, Catullus and the Emperor Trajan. In AD 117 the Emperor Hadrian commissioned his luxurious retirement

home on the gently sloping plain below Tivoli. **Villa Adriana** (Hadrian's Villa; www.coopculture.it; daily May–Aug 9am–7.30pm, Apr and Sept until 7pm, Mar and Oct until 6.30pm, Feb until 6pm, Nov–Jan until 5.30pm; museum closed 1.15–2.15pm and 30 minutes before vila closing time; free first Sun of the month) was the largest and richest residence in the Roman Empire, inspired by the monuments which had most impressed Hadrian on his extensive travels. Yet these soothing, romantic ruins go beyond mere imitation. The succession of terraces, water basins and baths seems a joyful reaction against functionality, but the design doesn't resort to extravagant artifice. Instead, it is a rigorous, geometrical, classical controlling of nature.

By contrast, a spirit of glorious frivolity pervades Tivoli's **Villa d'Este** (www.villadestetivoli.info; Tue–Sun 8.30am–one hour before sunset, July–mid-Sept also 8.30pm–midnight; free first Sun of the month), the sumptuous residence commissioned by Cardinal Ippolito d'Este, son of Lucrezia Borgia. The frescoed Renaissance mansion has a

The Roman Temple of Vesta at the Villa Gregoriana.

Fountains at the Villa d'Este.

faded grandeur, but the glory lies in the water gardens, steeply raked on terraces. Pools and elegiac cypresses extend into the distance; water spouts from obelisks, gurgles from the mouths of mythological monsters, springs from the nipples of a sphinx or from the multiple-breasted Artemis of Ephesus. Dedicated purely to pleasure, the gardens display triumphant theatricality, signalling the beginnings of Baroque.

Nearby, **Villa Gregoriana** (www. visitfai.it/parcovillagregoriana; Tue–Sun Apr–Oct 10am–6.30pm, Mar, Nov and Dec until 4pm), an oasis of waterfalls, ravines and grottoes, is wilder than Villa d'Este. The park has been revitalised, with walks from the main waterfall, which plunges into a rocky gorge, to the Temple of Vesta, an elegant structure dating back to the 1st century BC.

Monastic foundations

Picturesque **Subiaco** ❽, a summer playground in Emperor Nero's day, is better known as the birthplace of Western monasticism. The future St Benedict spent several years here as a hermit in a rock-hewn cave. His legacy remains in several surviving monasteries. The **Abbazia di Santa Scolastica** has three delightful cloisters and pillars recycled from Nero's villa. The **Abbazia di San Benedetto**, however, perched on a craggy peak, displays Perugian and Sienese frescoes and, in the depths, Benedict's original grotto, hewn out of the mountainside. A staircase leads to a portrait of St Francis, believed to have been painted from life.

Around AD 529 Benedict and his faithful monks moved to **Montecassino** ❾ and founded a monastery which followed the Benedictine Rule, thereby setting the model for monastic orders ever since. By St Benedict's death in AD 547, the abbey (www.abbaziamontecassino. org; Mon–Sat mid Mar–Oct 8.45am–7pm Nov–mid-Mar 9am–4.45pm, Sun 8.45–5.15pm) was one of the richest in the world. The illuminated manuscripts, frescoes and mosaics were so skilfully executed that they became the inspiration for others throughout medieval Europe.

During World War II, Montecassino rose to prominence once more. After US forces entered Naples, Montecassino became the Germans' front line (the so-called Gustav Line), designed to defend Rome. When repeated attacks by the Allies failed to penetrate the powerfully strengthened bulwark, a decision was made to bomb. It resulted in the total destruction of Montecassino. The ancient abbey was swept away. What one sees today is a faithful reconstruction of what existed before the catastrophe.

Etruscan Cerveteri

Before Rome ruled supreme, central Italy had a highly refined civilisation: that of the Etruscans (see page 35). Their zest for life and emphasis on physical vitality has fascinated many, including D.H. Lawrence, who saw them as a happy contrast to the puritanical Romans. Although Tuscany considers itself the soul of the Etruscan civilisation and has fine Etruscan museums, Lazio boasts the best-preserved Etruscan tombs.

The small medieval town of **Cerveteri** ❿, north of Rome on the Via Aurelia, was built on the site of the Etruscan town

Part of the Etruscan necropolis at Cerveteri.

of Caere. In the 6th and 5th centuries BC, Caere was one of the most populated towns of the Mediterranean. Artistic and trading links with Greece made Caere a sophisticated cultural centre. Its decline began in AD 384, when Pyrgi harbour, its main port, was devastated by a Greek incursion. Eventually the barbaric strength of Rome wiped away what had been a refined and joyous civilisation. Nothing remains today of the ancient town of Caere, bar a few walls.

Caere's necropolis occupies a hill outside the city proper, the **Necropoli della Banditaccia** (www.cerveteri.beniculturali. it; Tue–Sun 8.30am–one hour before sunset). From here it could be seen from the ramparts of the city, gay with painted houses and temples. The oldest tombs (8th century BC) have a small circular well carved into the stone, where the urns containing the ashes of the dead were placed. (Two modes of burial, cremation and inhumation, continued side by side for centuries.) The first chamber tombs, also cut into the stone and covered with rocky blocks and mounds *(tumuli)*, appeared as early as the beginning of the 7th century BC. The noble Etruscans were either enclosed in great sarcophagi with their effigies on top, or laid out on stone beds in their chamber tombs.

Excavations of the tombs not already rifled – the Romans were the first collectors of Etruscan antiquities – revealed goods of gold, silver, ivory, bronze and ceramic. The vases show strong Greek influence as well as superb Etruscan craftmanship. Much is now on display in the **Museo Nazionale Archeologico di Cerveteri** (www.tarquinia-cerveteri.it; Tue–Sun 8.30am–7.30pm), housed here, in the medieval Castello di Ruspoli, as well as in Rome's Museo di Villa Giulia and in the Vatican Museums (see page 159).

Etruscan Tarquinia

The Etruscan town of **Tarquinia** ⓫ stood on a hill northwest of the picturesque medieval town bearing the same name. The town existed as early as the 9th century BC, and two centuries later was at its height. The **Museo Nazionale Tarquiniense** (www.tarquinia-cerveteri.it; Tue–Sun 8.30am–7.30pm), set in a 15th-century *palazzo*, displays Etruscan treasures, including the famous 4th-century BC terracotta winged horses.

The **Necropolis of Tarquinia** (www. tarquinia-cerveteri.it; Tue–Sun 8.30am–one hour before sunset), together with that of Caere, is the most important Etruscan necropolis. It stands on a hill south of the original town, occupying an area 5km (3 miles) long by 1km (0.5 mile) wide. The frescoed tombs needed to be bright in order to stand out in the shadowy setting, lit only by faint oil lamps. Ribbons of colours frame the animated scenes below: the feasting in the Tomba dei Leopardi; the hunters in the Tomba del Cacciatore; the erotic scenes in the Tomba dei Tori; the prancing dancers, diving dolphins and soaring birds of the Tomba della Leonessa. Many of the scenes depict the distress of departing the earthly world, but there are also sombre scenes and glimpses of demonic dancing, reflecting the decline of Etruscan civilisation. Yet overwhelmingly, visitors leave these dusty houses of death full of renewed faith in life and its many mysteries.

Etruscan sculpture at Tarquinia.

The island of San Giorgio Maggiore, dominated by the monastic church of the same name.

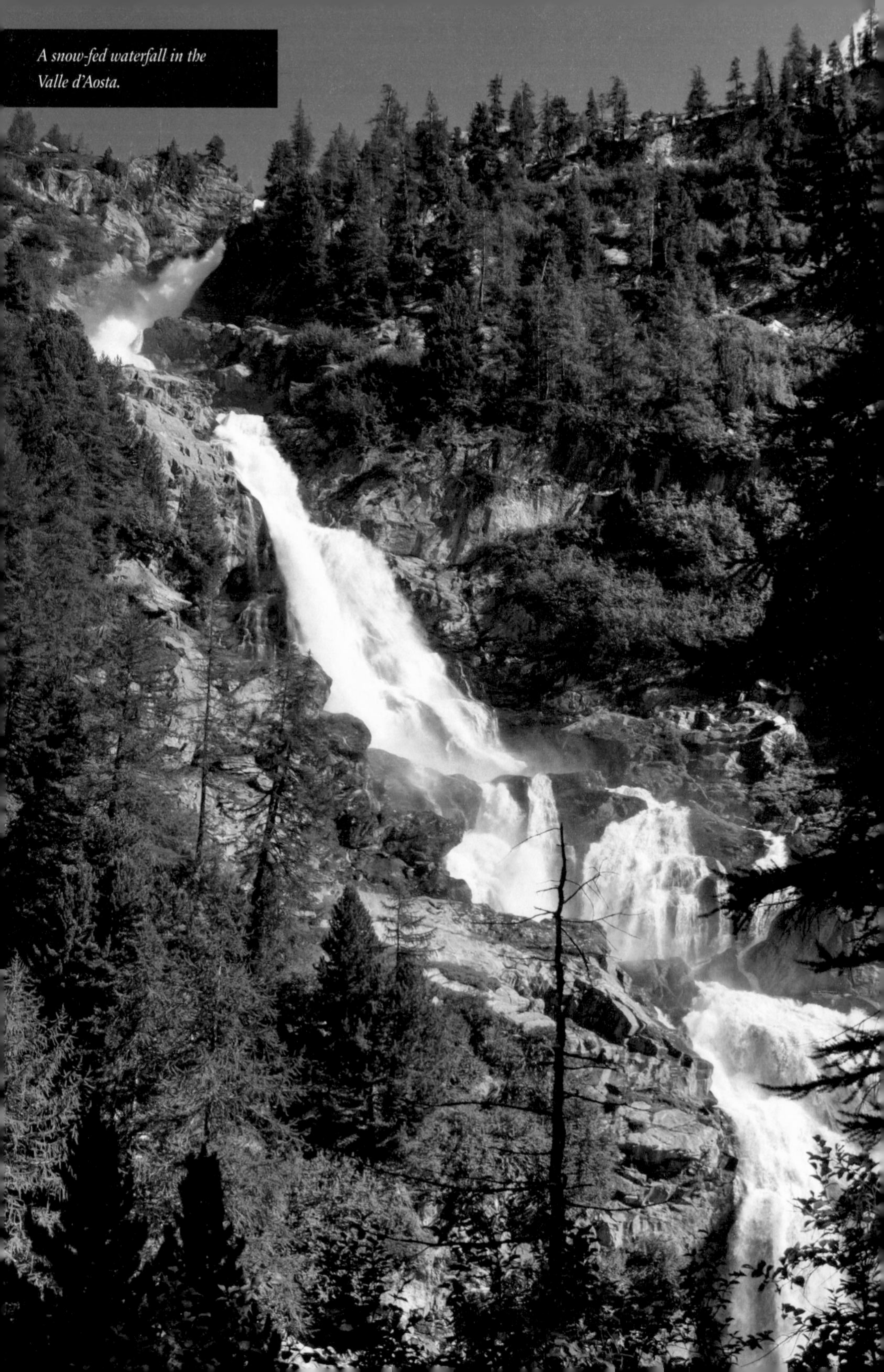

A snow-fed waterfall in the Valle d'Aosta.

THE NORTH

Explore magnificent mountains, shimmering lakes and gentle plains, interspersed with romantic and sophisticated cities, whose culture and cuisine has been influenced by countries to the north and the east.

Juliet's balcony in Verona, where Shakespeare set Romeo and Juliet.

For centuries, most travellers arrived in Italy from the north. They crossed the mountains from Switzerland or France, and often, if physically fit and romantically minded – as was the young Henry James – made part of the journey on foot. This way Italy came into focus gradually, as they left the cold north behind and made their way south from the lakes to Milan, and the cities of the Po Valley.

This is still the best way to approach northern Italy. Rather than rush through, with your eyes on the train timetables and your mind checking off the cities, see fewer places, but see them well. Each one is awash with artistic and literary associations. After all, this is the Italy of Shakespeare – *Romeo and Juliet* (Verona), *The Taming of the Shrew* (Padua) – and of medieval city-states and Renaissance princes. The great families – the Visconti in Milan, the Gonzaga in Mantua, the della Scala in Verona – are still remembered for their artistic triumphs, as well as for the political scandals of their courts.

We pass from Byzantine Venice to the great cities of the Veneto – Padua, Verona and Vicenza – magnets for university students since the Middle Ages. From Venice to the Brenta Canal and Treviso, this is Palladio country, studded with Palladian villas designed in a harmonious architectural style that has conquered the world.

Riva del Garda on Lake Garda.

We then move to Milan, the style and shopping capital of Italy, via the magnificent glaciated landscapes of the Alps to the villas, lakes and gorgeous romantic gardens of the Italian lake district.

Northern Italians, although more aloof and self-contained than the gregarious southerners, are always pleased to share a little-known fact about their hometown with a stranger. The locals might well bear more than a fleeting resemblance to the figures in the 15th-century frescoes of the local Duomo – in these regions, the past is always present.

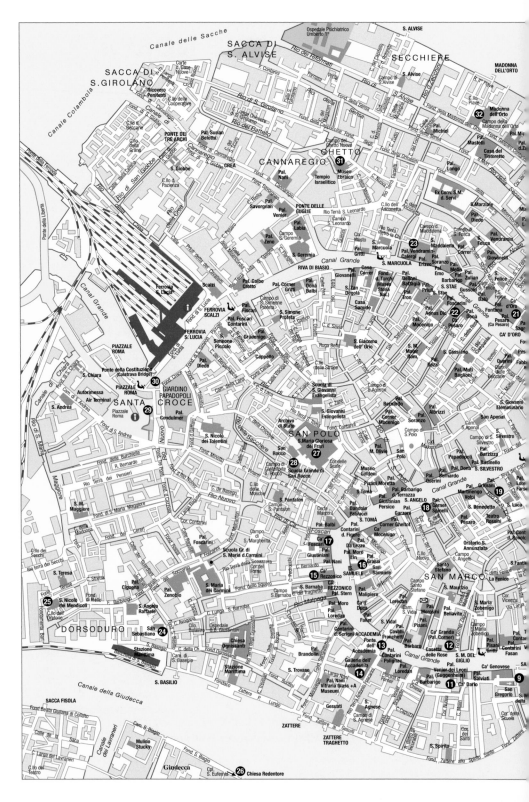

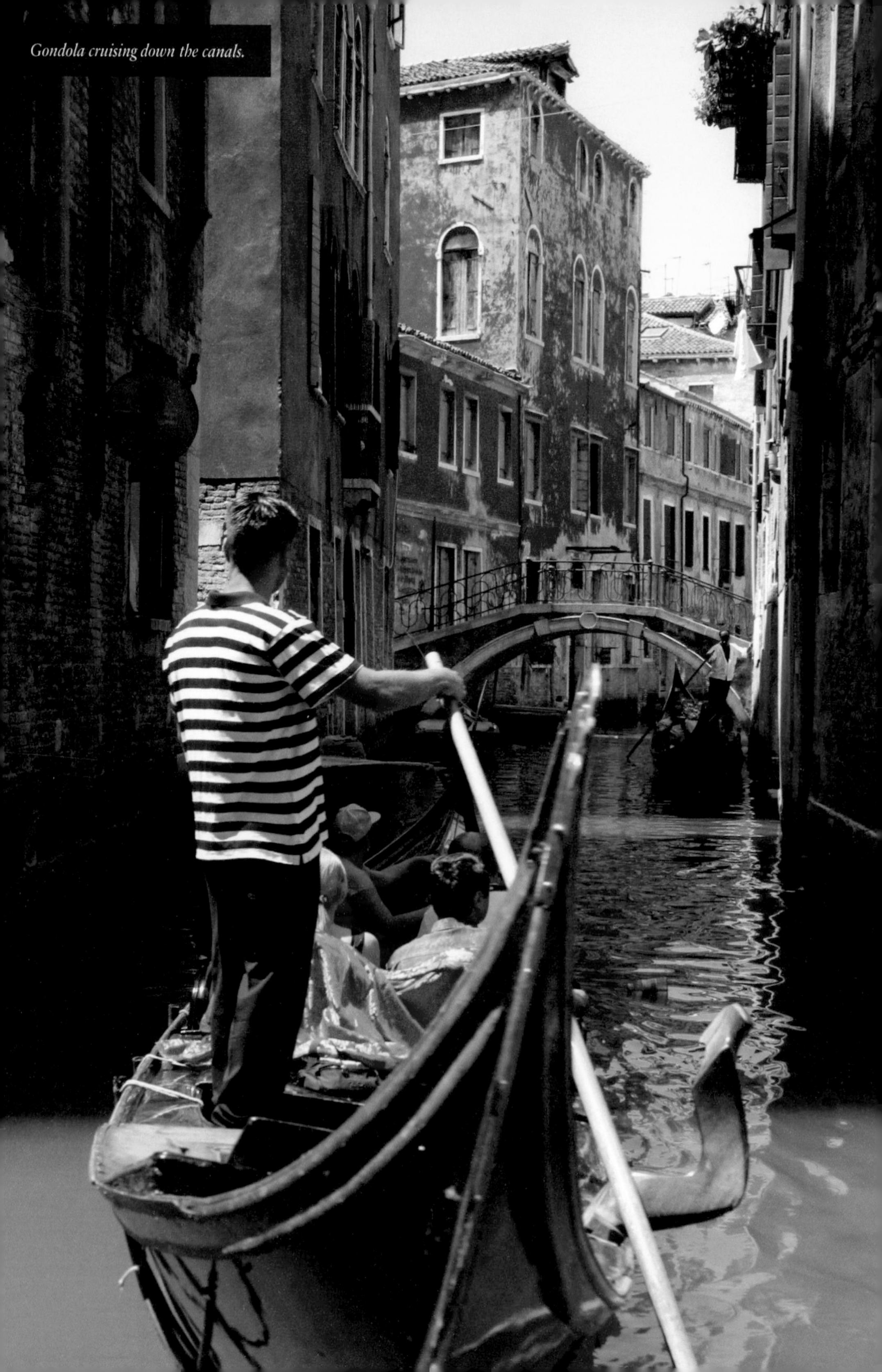
Gondola cruising down the canals.

VENICE

Venice charms, captivates and seduces with its
dazzling and unique beauty, encapsulated in its
enchanting buildings and picturesque waterways.

Main Attractions
Basilica di San Marco
San Giorgio Maggiore
Palazzo Ducale (Doge's
  Palace)
Canal Grande (Grand Canal)
Guggenheim
Accademia
Ca' Rezzonico
Ca d'Oro
Santa Maria Gloriosa dei
  Frari
Burano

There is nowhere in the world quite like Venice. Despite problems with too many tourists, threat of flooding and crumbling buildings, it is a magical place. First on the itinerary is surely St Mark's Square, the iconic Basilica and the grandiose Doges' Palace. Cruise down the Grand Canal to take in sights such as the Guggenheim gallery and the Gallerie dell'Accademia, both with world-class art collections. Along the banks is a procession of stunning palaces, including the Ca' d'Oro. Back on dry land visit the six different districts, including laid back Dorsoduro, bustling San Polo and unspoilt Santa Croce. And there's nothing like an island trip to Murano, Burano or Torcello.

When Lord Byron arrived in Venice in 1810, the "Queen of the Adriatic" had been in decline for many years. Though nonetheless enchanted by the beauty of the city, the poet describes her palaces as "crumbling to the shore".

But even if Venice was crumbling for years, it continued to captivate visitors. For centuries the city has inspired poets, painters and writers, including Proust, Hemingway and Henry James. Few other cities in the world have produced a more talented school of painters, from Bellini and Giorgione to Titian, Tintoretto and Tiepolo.

Built on over 100 islets, supported by millions of wooden piles and linked by 400 bridges, Venice is the only city in the world which is built entirely on water. The sense of precariousness, associated with the city for centuries, inevitably adds to the fascination.

In January 1996 La Fenice, Venice's historic opera house – where Verdi's *La Traviata* and *Rigoletto* were first performed – was razed to the ground. La Fenice finally rose from the ashes in 2003 after a fire which was started by disgruntled electricians. The plush, gilt-encrusted interior has been faithfully recreated, but the city faces far greater challenges today.

St Mark's Square.

MOSE, the controversial mobile flood barriers designed to protect the city from major inundation, was at the heart of a huge corruption scandal involving dozens of officials including former city major Giorgio Orsoni. The project suffered many delays and is now scheduled to be fully completed by 2018–2020. However, according to Venice in Peril, water levels are still chronically high and damaging the building fabric. Further controversy surrounds the cruise ship terminal and the impact these huge ships have on the city and the vast passenger numbers disgorged into the city every day. Continuing protests in 2013 highlighted the effect of vibration from the ships on the buildings, the pollution from the engines and the concern for safety of the smaller boats on the water. Suggestions to have the terminal located to a newly-dredged site on the lagoon have met with opposition, in particular from environmentalists concerned for the delicate ecosystem. A series of bans on large cruisers entering the city through St Mark's basin and the Guidecca Canal were introduced only

The Rio Canonica and Bridge of Sighs.

to be lifted by the regional court. In 2016, the UN threatened to put Venice on the list of endangered heritage sites if the city authorities fail to impose a ban on giant cruise ships entering the lagoon by 2017.

Yet even if the physical threats come from the sea, the social challenges are no less serious. Venice may be mired in its glorious past, with Gothic palaces galore, but it needs to retain its population if it is to stave off its fate as a theme park. Since the population has fallen to below 60,000, the city has had a rude wake-up call. A simmering rebellion against exorbitant property prices and the creeping colonisation of mask shops and hotels reflects a local backlash against mass tourism. There is concern over the mass production of imported "Venetian" products endangering the survival of traditional crafts, not just in maskmaking but also ceramics, jewellery, bookbinding and handmade paper goods. There is no magical solution, but pressure groups are calling for investment in culture and crafts, and a revitalised contemporary arts and

NAVIGATING VENICE

Venice is Italy's most expensive, confusing and popular city. To keep costs down, and to avoid queuing at major attractions, it's worth pre-booking from among the myriad city museum, church and transport passes. The sites with the longest queues are St Mark's Basilica, the Doge's Palace and the Accademia. The attractions that must be pre-booked are the Clock Tower and the Secret Itineraries tour of the Doge's Palace.

Venice Museum (www.venice-museum.com) sells museum passes and tickets as well as guided tours (including Secret Itineraries).

Venezia Unica (www.veneziaunica.it; tel: 041-2424) is most useful as a transport- and/or museum-booking system and sells the Venezia UnicaCard, which covers 13 museums and the 16 Chorus churches (see page 178), and offers the full range of integrated transport passes for different times.

Vivaticket (www.vivaticket.it; tel: 892 234) is a booking service for opera, concerts, ballet and blockbuster exhibitions, as well as major attractions and unusual guided tours, notably the Secret Itineraries tour and the Clock Tower, both around St Mark's.

The Chorus Pass (www.chorusvenezia.org; tel: 041-275 0462) allows access to 18 Venetian churches (including the Frari), with charges going towards local church restoration projects.

events scene, to prevent *La Serenissima* from sinking into museum-dom.

St Mark's Square

The heart of Venice is the vast **Piazza di San Marco ❶**. Described by Napoleon as the most elegant drawing room in Europe, this is the great architectural showpiece of Venice. With its café bands and exotic shops under the arcades, it is also the hub of tourist Venice; only late at night does it revert to a semblance of solitude. At one end of the piazza, crouching like an enormous, amphibious reptile, the great Basilica di San Marco (St Mark's Basilica) invites visitors to explore its mysterious depths.

Basilica di San Marco

The **Basilica di San Marco ❷** (www.basilicasanmarco.it; Mon–Sat 9.45am–5pm, Sun 2–4pm, until 5pm in summer, daily from 7am for worshippers; free; online booking to avoid queues; charge to Sanctuary, Pala d'Oro and Treasury; all bags need to be left in the Ateneo San Basso on Piazzetta dei Leoncini – a free left-luggage service) is named after the Evangelist St Mark, whose remains were recovered (or stolen, depending on your viewpoint) by the Venetians from Alexandria in the 9th century.

If fully visible, the square reveals its lovely Clock Tower at the landward end of the piazza, and the Basilica itself, with its sumptuous portals decorated with shimmering mosaics. The only original mosaic – in the doorway to the far left – gives a good idea of the appearance of the basilica in the 13th century. Above the main portal are replicas of the famous bronze horses, thought to be Roman or Hellenistic works of the 3rd or 4th century AD and looted by the Venetians from Constantinople in 1204. They were taken to Paris by Napoleon in 1797 and returned in 1815, and are now kept inside the Basilica, protected from pigeons and pollution.

The Basilica's interior, in the shape of a Greek cross, is thought to have been inspired by the Church of the Apostles in Constantinople. Above the columns of the minor naves, lining the arms of the cross, are the women's galleries or *matronei*, designed in accordance with Greek Orthodox custom, which separates the sexes. The luxurious

St Mark's Basilica.

Mosaic of Christ in St Mark's.

atmosphere of the interior is enhanced by the decoration of the walls: marble slabs cover the lower part, while golden mosaics adorn the vaults, arches and domes. Following a complex iconographic plan, the mosaics cover 4,000 sq metres (43,000 sq ft), which is why St Mark's is sometimes called the Basilica d'Oro (Church of Gold).

Among the many gems housed in the church are the **Pala d'Oro**, a jewel-studded gold-and-enamel altarpiece dating from the 10th century. The **Treasury** also houses a priceless collection of gold and silver from Byzantium. The **Museo Marciano** (daily 10am–5pm), reached by steep steps from the entrance narthex, affords fine views of the interior as a whole, while the open-air terrace beyond the museum gives a bird's-eye view of Piazza di San Marco. It was here that the doge and other dignitaries gathered to watch celebrations taking place below. The museum holds the original bronze horses (see above) and Paolo Veneziano's exquisite *Pala Feriale*, a painted panel that was used to cover the Pala d'Oro on weekdays.

Doge's Palace.

A panoramic view

A striking feature of the square is the soaring **Campanile** ❸ (daily mid-June–Sept 9am–9pm, Apr–mid-June and Oct 9am–7pm, Nov–Mar 9.30am–3.45pm), a faithful replica of the original tower that collapsed in 1902. Inside, a lift – or, for the energetic, a stairway – climbs 100 metres (330ft) to the top for a sweeping panorama of the city and lagoon. The piazza's other tower is Coducci's intricate **Torre dell'Orologio** ❹, the Clock Tower, designed in 1496 (English-language tours Mon–Wed 10 and 11am, Thu–Sun 2 and 3pm; for booking, tel: 848 082 000; http://torreorologio.visitmuve.it). Adjoining the piazza and extending to the waterfront is the **Piazzetta San Marco**. On the right as you face the lagoon stands the 16th-century **Biblioteca Nazionale Marciana**, which is home to the **Libreria Sansoviniana** ❺ (guided visits only Mon–Fri and Sun at set times, book at 041 2407 238; http://marciana.venezia.sbn.it, also combined ticket and access via Museo Correr tel: 041-240 5211), where classical concerts are occasionally staged. Palladio, Italy's

greatest 16th-century architect, considered this structure one of the most beautiful buildings ever constructed. Today it houses the **Museo Archeologico** (daily 10am–5pm, until 7pm in summer; www.polomuseale.venezia.beniculturali.it, combined ticket and access via Museo Correr; free first Sun of the month), the National Library of St Mark and the Venetian Old Library – with a collection of treasures from the city's golden years.

At the lagoon end of the Piazzetta stand two large 12th-century columns, one crowned with a winged lion, the symbol of Venice, the other with a statue of St Theodore, the original patron saint of the city. The square has served as a marketplace, meeting place and execution site, with public executions once staged between the two columns.

Across the water lies one of Venice's great landmarks – the majestic church of **San Giorgio Maggiore** ➏ (daily Apr–Oct 9am–7pm, Nov–Mar 8.30–6pm, no visits during Mass Sun 10.40am–noon; charge for Campanile). This classical masterpiece by Andrea Palladio, the finest monastic church

in the lagoon, displays works of art by Tintoretto; and the views from the Campanile extend, on a clear day, as far as the Alps.

The Doge's Palace

The **Palazzo Ducale** ➐ (daily Apr–Oct 8.30am–7pm, Nov–Mar 8.30am–5.30pm, mid-June–mid-Oct Fri–Sun until 11pm; http://palazzoducale.visitmuve.it) flanks the eastern side of the Piazzetta. This "vast and sumptuous pile", as Byron described it, is the grandest and most conspicuous example of Venetian Gothic in the city. The official residence of the doge and the seat of government during the republic, it stands today as eloquent evidence of the power and pomp of Venice in its heyday.

Inside, the three wings of the palace reveal a seemingly endless series of grandiose rooms and halls. The art collection here gives a foretaste of the countless artistic treasures scattered throughout the city, and includes works by the two Venetian giants – Tintoretto and Veronese. Tintoretto's *Paradise* (1588–92) was for many years the largest painting in the world (7 metres by

TIP

The *Itinerari Segreti* (Secret Itineraries) are fascinating guided tours of lesser-known parts of the Doge's Palace and prison cells (tel: 041-4273 0892 or, in Italy, tel: 84 808 2000; www.palazzoducale.visitmuve.it; tours in English run daily 9.55am, 10.45am and 11.35am; booking essential).

Carnival costume – the disconcertingly blank mask (called a bauta), complete with bold tricorne hat and full-length black cloak, will lend any carnival-goer an undeniably cruel charisma.

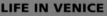

LIFE IN VENICE

Venice is being bold again, with a sleek bridge over the Grand Canal, a nearly completed mobile flood barrier, a revamped Art Biennale, designer B&Bs, and a cutting-edge contemporary art museum facing St Mark's. But it's a delicate balancing act: visitors also come for the gondolas, the Gothic palaces and the sense of being marooned in a gorgeous Disneyland for grown-ups. The sleepy Castello district is redrawing its image to attract modern art merchants of Venice. During the Biennale jamboree, an arty crowd heads to the pavilions in the Giardini gardens and to the exhibition spaces in the historic Arsenale. Over the water, bohemian Dorsoduro is becoming less maiden aunt and more arty trustafarian. Few would complain if they had an aunt as eclectic as Peggy Guggenheim, whose legacy lingers on in the eponymous modern art collection. But the latest flagship lies a short stroll along the waterfront. **Punta della Dogana** showcases a superb collection of contemporary art belonging to French fashion tycoon François Pinault. Around the corner, **Lineadombra** (Ponte dell'Umilta; www.ristorantelineadombra.com) is one of many design-conscious restaurants that are challenging Venetian stereotypes. It is matched by design B&Bs, such as **DD694** (www.thecharminghouse.com). As for chic bars, on Giudecca, **Skyline** (www.skylinebarvenice.com), in Molino Stucky, is a cool rooftop haunt, suspended over the lagoon, where Japanese raspberry-vodka cocktails are de rigueur. Quintessential "new Venice".

22 metres/23ft by 72ft). In the same room, Veronese's *Apotheosis of Venice* is another compelling masterpiece, though his finest work in the palace is *The Rape of Europa* in the Anticollegio.

Adjoining the palace is the former prison. Once tried and convicted in the palace, prisoners were led across the slender covered bridge to their cell. Since the windowed bridge offered the captive his last glimpse of freedom, it was called **Il Ponte dei Sospiri** ❽ (the Bridge of Sighs). However grim its original purpose, it has a romantic air, and is favoured today by young lovers who believe that if they kiss under the bridge (presumably in a gondola) their love will last.

A tour of the Ducal Palace is best rounded off with a coffee break in the piazza. The most famous café is **Florian** (www.caffeflorian.com), once a fashionable high-society haunt. Henry James conjures up the atmosphere in *The Aspern Papers* (1888): "I sat in front of Florian's café, eating ices, listening to music, talking with acquaintances: the traveller will remember how the immense cluster of tables and little chairs stretches like a promontory into the smooth lake of the Piazza."

The Grand Canal

The **Canal Grande** winds for 3.5km (2 miles) through the city. This splendid shimmering thoroughfare is flanked by pastel-coloured palaces in a mixture of Byzantine, Gothic, Renaissance and Baroque styles, built mostly between the 13th and the 18th centuries.

The best way to see the canal is from a boat. If you are feeling flush, hire a gondola from the San Marco waterfront. Thomas Mann, who commented that the gondolas of Venice were "black as nothing else on earth except a coffin", nonetheless found their seats "the softest, most luxurious, most relaxing in the world". Far cheaper, but equally engaging, is the No. 1 waterbus (*vaporetto*), which plies the length of the canal at frequent intervals. Alternatively, try the faster No. 2 service, which makes fewer stops.

Starting from San Marco, the canal is overshadowed by the great Baroque church of **Santa Maria della Salute** ❾, designed by the 17th-century architect

A boat ride down the Grand Canal affords unparalleled views.

Baldassare Longhena, and erected in thanks for the city's deliverance from the plague of 1630.

Beside it, commanding the point, is the **Punta della Dogana** ❿ (Wed–Mon, 10am–7pm; www.palazzograssi.it), the former Customs House, now a showcase for contemporary art. Restored by the Japanese architect Tadao Ando, the airy mezzanine space allows for a lovely interplay between the interior and the exterior (see page 181).

The Guggenheim

On the same side is **Palazzo Venier dei Leoni** ⓫, better known as the **Guggenheim** (www.guggenheim-venice. it; Wed–Mon 10am–6pm), the famous residence-museum of the late American patron of the arts, Peggy Guggenheim (1898–1979).

This is Venice's leading contemporary art museum, with a superb, eclectic collection of works representing the major avant-garde movements of the last century. Paintings by legendary names including Picasso, Braque, Kandinsky and Bacon are all on display alongside a large representation of Surrealist art, which was close to Guggenheim's heart – she was briefly married to Max Ernst, one of the movement's founders. His works, along with those of Dalí, Magritte, Jackson Pollock and de Kooning, are all here. It is a splendidly eccentric setting for the collection, with a lovely garden, chic café and courtyard, where chained lions were once kept, earning it the sobriquet "dei Leoni".

The Accademia

On the right bank opposite is **Ca' Granda** ⓬, a Renaissance residence by Sansovino, now the office of the city magistrate. The first bridge that spans the canal is the wooden **Ponte dell'Accademia** ⓭, built in 1932 as a temporary structure but retained through popular demand. It is named after the nearby **Gallerie dell'Accademia** ⓮ (www.gallerie accademia.org; Tue–Sun 8.15am–7.15pm, Fri until 10.15pm, Mon 8.15am–2pm;

booking online and tel: 041-520 0345) housed in the former Scuola della Carità. This contains the world's finest collection of Venetian paintings, with works by Mantegna, Bellini, Giorgione (*The Tempest*), Carpaccio, Titian, Tintoretto, Veronese, Tiepolo, Guardi and Canaletto, mostly arranged in chronological order.

Baroque palace

Further down the canal on the same side stands the imposing Baroque palace of **Ca' Rezzonico** ⓯ (www.carezz onico.visitmuve.it; Wed–Mon Apr–Oct 10am–6pm, Nov–Mar 10am–5pm), housing a superb museum of 18th-century Venice, dedicated to the swansong of the Serene Republic – La Serenissima. The stately rooms are richly decorated with period paintings, furniture and frescoes. It was here that the poet Robert Browning died in 1889.

Palazzo Grassi ⓰ (www.palazzo grassi.it; Wed–Mon, 10am–7pm), on the opposite bank, is an imposing patrician palace and model of neoclassical restraint. Now linked to the **Punta della Dogana**, Tadao Ando's

Admiring Francis Bacon's 'Study for Chimpanzee' at the Guggenheim.

The Rialto, built in the late 16th century, is the oldest bridge across the Grand Canal.

Fishmonger at the arcaded Pescheria, Venice's main fish market.

conversion has turned the palace into another slick showcase for exhibitions based on the collections of the owner, French magnate François Pinault.

Back on the left bank, **Palazzi Giustiniani** was where Richard Wagner composed the second act of *Tristan and Isolde* in 1858–9. Next door, **Ca' Foscari** ⓱ is the ancestral home of the 15th-century doge who masterminded Venetian conquests on the Italian mainland.

Beyond the Sant'Angelo landing stage, on the Ωright bank, **Palazzo Corner Spinelli** ⓲ was designed during the early Venetian Renaissance in the Lombardic style by Coducci. Beyond the next side canal, the **Palazzo Grimani** ⓳ (www.palazzogrimani.org; Tue–Sun 8.15am–7.15pm) is a museum housing a wonderful painting collection including Venetian as well as foreign masters such as Bosch, Memling or Dürer. In front of you, Venice's most famous bridge, **Ponte di Rialto** ⓴, arches over the canal. The former wooden drawbridges built across the canal at this point all collapsed, necessitating the erection of a more weighty stone structure. Antonio da Ponte beat the

greatest architects of the day, including Michaelangelo and Palladio, to secure the commission, and supervised its construction between 1588 and 1592. The single-span, balustraded bridge has two parallel rows of tightly packed shops selling jewellery, leather, masks, silk and souvenirs. Past the bridge, on the right side of the canal, is the former seat of the **Fondaco dei Tedeschi**, now the luxury T Galleria department store (www.dfs.com) offering the best Italian produce and fashion.

Ca' d'Oro

The most beautiful Gothic palace in Venice, the **Ca' d'Oro** ㉑ (www.cadoro. org; Tue–Sun 8.15am–7.15pm, Mon 8.15am–2pm) appears on the right at the first landing stage beyond the bridge. When built in 1420 by the wealthy patrician Marino Contarini, it was covered in gold leaf, hence the name "House of Gold". Inside, the Giorgio Franchetti art gallery displays paintings, frescoes and sculpture.

Further along, on the left bank, the enormous Baroque **Ca' Pesaro** ㉒ is another masterpiece by Longhena; this one houses the Galleria d'Arte Moderna and the Museo Orientale (www. capesaro.visitmuve.it; Tue–Sun, Apr–Oct 10am–6pm, Nov–Mar 10am–5pm). The last building of note before the railway station is **Palazzo Vendramin-Calergi** ㉓, one of the finest Renaissance palaces by Mauro Coducci (1440–1504), now housing the elegant city casino (tel: 041-529 7111; www.casinovenezia.it). This is also where Wagner died in 1883 and there is a small Wagner Museum (Tue and Sat am, Thu pm, booking essential, tel: 041 276 0407).

The six districts of Venice

The greatest experience the city can offer to the inquisitive visitor is the maze of tiny alleys, the narrow silent canals and the pretty squares and courtyards only minutes away from **San Marco**, the most central of the six districts (*sestieri*) of Venice. Leading north from the Piazza San Marco, starting at the Clock Tower, is the **Merceria dell'Orologia**. This ancient maze of alleys is still devoted to commerce, and is awash with small shops and boutiques.

Dorsoduro is the most southerly section of historic Venice – an excellent area to stay if you are looking for a sought-after small hotel within easy access of St Mark's. To the south, the area is bounded by the **Zattere**, a long, broad and peaceful quayside whose cafés and restaurants afford splendid views across the water to the island of Giudecca. East of the Accademia, the Dorsoduro is quiet and intimate, characterised by pretty canals, chic residences, galleries and the excellent Vitraria Glass A + Museum (Palazzo Nani, Dorsoduro 960, Tue–Sun 10.30am–6.30pm; www.vitraria.com) that celebrates glass as both an item of everyday use and an object of artistic creation. .

Northwest of the Accademia, the area around San Barnaba was traditionally the quarter for impoverished Venetian nobility. Today it is the scene of cafés, artisans and one of the last surviving vegetable barges. Further west, the 16th-century church of **San Sebastiano** ㉔

(Mon–Sat 10.30am–4pm; book through Chorus, see page 178) was the parish church of Veronese and provided a classical canvas for his opulent masterpieces, painted between 1555 and 1565.

The area becomes picturesquely shabby and appealing towards San Nicolò dei Mendicoli, erstwhile home of sailors and fishermen. The charming Romanesque church of **San Nicolò dei Mendicoli** ㉕ (Mon–Sat 10am–noon and 3–5.30pm, Sun 9am–noon) was expertly restored by the British Venice in Peril Fund in the 1970s.

The island of **Giudecca**, across the Giudecca Canal, is Venice's most diverse neighbourhood, a mixture of earthy working-class, funky designer and palatial grandeur. The main landmark on its waterfront is Andrea Palladio's **Redentore** church ㉖ (Mon 10.30am–4pm, Tue–Sat 10.30am–4.30pm), built in gratitude for the city's deliverance from plague in 1576. On the third Sunday in July, the city commemorates this event by building a bridge of boats from the Zattere to the Redentore, where a special Mass is held. That night, a firework display lights up the sky.

Venetian barman.

A VENETIAN BAR CRAWL

The Rialto market marks the start of a Venetian bar crawl, a *giro di ombre*, in the backstreet wine and tapas bars known as *bacari*. On offer are an array of exotic Venetian snacks *(cichetti)* and glasses of wine *(ombre)* in snug, rough-and-ready bars, often dating back to the 15th century. All'Arco, in Calle Arco, serves titbits such as calamari or prawns on bread, while Bancogiro, on Campo San Giacometto, brings the *bacaro* concept up to date. On Calle delle Veste, near the Fenice opera house, Vino Vino is the place to rub shoulders with gondoliers over tasty tapas, from sweet-and-sour sardines to salt cod and polenta. Good food, gruff service and gondoliers generally go together. In Canareggio, Alla Vedova is another delightful den for gorging on meatballs and guzzling a Veneto house red.

On a wine crawl, don't forget to sample the local aperitif, *spritz* (pronounced "spriss" in dialect). The lurid-looking drink was introduced under Austrian rule (named after the introduction of selzer, tonic water) and soon became a firm favourite. It consists of roughly equal parts of dry white wine, tonic and an aperitif, usually Campari or Aperol. Ask for a *spritz al bitter* for a stronger, less cloying taste. The spritz may be an acquired taste, but once acquired, it's the clearest sign that you've fallen for Venice.

The view from Piazzale Roma.

San Polo

The *sestiere* of **San Polo** lies within the large bend of the Grand Canal, northwest of San Marco. The quarter around the **Rialto**, the oldest inhabited part of mainland Venice, became the gathering place of merchants from the East and thence the commercial hub of the city. It is still a bustling area, with shops and market stalls. Fruit and vegetables are laid out under the arcades of the Fabbriche Vecchie, while the mock-Gothic stone loggia of the **Pescheria** marks the site of the morning fish market. Arrive early, as the market begins to close by noon.

The Frari

The major church of San Polo is the majestic brick Gothic **Santa Maria Gloriosa dei Frari** ㉗ (Mon–Sat 9am–6pm, Sun 1–6pm; www.chorusvenezia.org), usually referred to as the Frari. The interior houses some of Venice's finest masterpieces, including an exquisite *Madonna and Child* by Bellini, Titian's celebrated *Assumption* (crowning the main altar) and his *Madonna di Ca' Pesaro*. Buried in the Frari are the composer Claudio Monteverdi, the sculptor Canova (who lies in a pyramidal tomb he designed as a monument to Titian) and several doges.

Nearby, the **Scuola Grande di San Rocco** ㉘ (www.scuolagrandesanrocco.org; daily 9.30am–5.30pm) is celebrated for its series of religious works by Tintoretto, painted on the walls and ceilings in 1564–87. The scenes from *The Life of Christ* culminate in *The Crucifixion*, of which Henry James wrote: "Surely no single picture in the world contains more human life; there is everything in it, including the most exquisite beauty."

Santa Croce ㉙, lying north and west of San Polo, is a relatively unexplored district. Its core is a maze of covered alleyways lined by peeling facades and criss-crossed by canals barely wide enough for the passage of a barge. Its squares are pleasingly shabby, bustling with local life. The only real concession to tourism is the **Piazzale Roma**, the arrival point for those coming by road. The area is enlivened by the strikingly contemporary **Ponte della Costituzione** ㉚, the

fourth bridge over the Grand Canal, and the only one to be illuminated at night. Designed by Santiago Calatrava, the acclaimed Spanish architect and bridge fanatic, this elegant, understated sliver of a structure connects the station with the road terminal.

The origins of the Ghetto

Cannaregio is the quietest and most remote district in Venice. Its name derives from *canne* (reeds), for this area was once marshland. The *sestiere* forms the northern arc of the city, stretching from the railway station to the Rio dei Mendicanti in the east. At its heart lies the **Ghetto ③**. Its name originated from an iron foundry *(getto)* which once stood here. This was Europe's first ghetto, an area for the exclusive but confined occupation of Jews. Built in the early 16th century, it gave its name to isolated Jewish communities throughout the world. It remained a ghetto until Napoleonic times. Though very few Jews live here, the synagogues, tenements and kosher restaurants lend a distinctive Jewish air, and the area's history is well documented in the **Museo Ebraico** (tel: 041-715 359; www.museoebraico.it; Sun–Fri 10am–7pm, Oct–May until 5.30pm, and earlier closing on Fri; closed Jewish holidays; no luggage allowed), a museum on the main square, and the starting point for guided walks round the Ghetto.

In the northern part of Cannaregio is the lovely Gothic church of the **Madonna dell'Orto ③** (Mon–Sat 10am–5pm). Tintoretto was born round here and lived at No. 3399, near the Campo dei Mori. Forming the northern border of Cannaregio, the **Fondamente Nuove** are the main departure point for ferries to the northern islands. Across the water you can see the walled cemetery on the island of San Michele. Back from the quayside, the Baroque church of the **Gesuiti ③** (daily 10am–noon and 4–6pm; free) has an outrageously extravagant green-and-white marble

interior, and contains Titian's dramatic *Martyrdom of St Lawrence*.

It is worth exploring the warren of alleys and canals to the east of Cannaregio. With luck, you will stumble upon the church of **Santa Maria dei Miracoli ③** (Mon 10.30am–4pm, Tue–Sat 10.30am–4.30pm). Designed in the 1480s by Pietro Lombardo and his workshop, it is one of the loveliest Renaissance churches in the city. Decorated inside and out with marble, it is often likened to a jewel-box.

Castello

The city's eastern section, **Castello**, varies in character from the busy southern waterfront near San Marco to the humble cheek-by-jowl residences of the north. The area behind Riva degli Schiavoni is worth exploring for its pretty canals, quaysides and elegant faded palaces. Essential viewing for those interested in art is the frieze by Carpaccio in the **Scuola di San Giorgio degli Schiavoni ③** (Mon 2.45–6pm, Tue–Sat 9.15am–1pm and 2.45–6pm, Sun 9.15am–1pm) and Coducci's 16th-century

Cannaregio at dusk.

The church of Santa Maria Assunta in Torcello.

Renaissance gateway to the Arsenale, built in 1460 by Antonio Gambello.

church of **San Zaccaria** ㊱ (Mon–Sat 10am-noon, 4–6pm).

The **Campo Santa Maria Formosa** ㊲ (church: Mon 10.30am–4pm, until 4.30pm Tue–Sat) is a pleasant market square with a fine Renaissance church, which is home to Palma il Vecchio's splendid *St Barbara and Saints* of 1510. The spiritual heart of Castello is **Campo Santi Giovanni e Paolo** ㊳, better known in Venetian dialect as San Zanipolo. The square is dominated by Andrea del Verrocchio's masterly bronze equestrian statue of the mercenary Bartolomeo Colleoni. Presiding over the square is the majestic Gothic church of **Santi Giovanni e Paolo** ㊴ (daily 9am–6pm, Sun and holidays noon–6pm), where 46 doges are buried. Many of their tomb monuments are magnificent, as is Paolo Veronese's *Adoration of the Shepherds* in the Cappella del Rosario.

Part of eastern Castello is occupied by the **Arsenale** ㊵, the great shipyard of the republic where Venice's galleys were built and refurbished. It is now largely abandoned and inaccessible to the public, but you can explore parts

of it during the Art Biennale, and there is the excellent **Museo Storico Navale** (Naval Museum; Mon–Fri 8.45am–1.30pm, Sat until 1pm;) alongside the main entrance gate.The nearby Ships Pavillion (daily 10am–5pm) is a branch of the museum housing historic vessels. To the east of the public gardens is the site of the **Art Biennale** ㊶, an international exhibition of modern art (held in odd-numbered years).

Island excursions

Beyond "central Venice", yet reached on regular ferries, the scattered lagoon islands make a refreshing retreat from hardcore culture and the summer crowds. The island of **San Michele**, just north of Venice, is occupied by the cemetery (summer 7.30am–6pm, until 4pm in winter) and the early Renaissance church of San Michele in Isola, designed by Coducci. As the first church faced in white Istrian stone, San Michele was the model for similar churches throughout the Veneto. Napoleon, who forbade burials in the historic centre, established

the cemetery. Ezra Pound and Igor Stravinsky were two of the eminent visitors to Venice who are buried here. As the island closest to Venice, it is served by ferries from the Fondamente Nuove.

Further north, the island of **Murano**, which resembles a smaller-scale Venice, has been the centre of the city's glass-blowing industry since the 13th century, when factories were moved from the centre for fear of fire. The **Museo del Vetro** (www.museovetro.visit muve.it; daily 10am– 6pm, until 5pm in winter) is housed in the Fondamenta Giustinian, originally the seat of the bishop of Torcello, which was transferred here after the earlier settlement was abandoned. The museum has exquisite examples of glasswork.

Venice's tiny lace industry is based in **Burano**, northeast of Venice. This is a colourful island where canals are lined by brightly painted fishermen's cottages, unpretentious seafood restaurants and stalls selling lace. For a flavour of rural Venice, cross the footbridge to the island of **Mazzorbo** and visit **Venissa** (tel: 041-527 2281; http:// venissa.it), rescued as Venice's sole vineyard by the Bisol company. The Veneto wines can be sampled over dinner with bed an option if you overindulge on Bisol Prosecco.

Torcello, the most remote of these islands (an hour by ferry), is the least populated and, for many, the most interesting. This rural, marshy island was the site of the original settlement in the Venetian lagoon. Still standing is the magnificent Byzantine cathedral. A large striking mosaic of the Virgin, standing above a frieze of Apostles, decorates the chancel apse of the church, while the entire western wall is covered by a huge and elaborate mosaic depicting *The Last Judgement*.

To the south of Venice, on a different route, lies the **Lido**, where Thomas Mann's unhappy Aschenbach loitered too long, feasting his tired eyes on the unattainable boy Tadzio, and died of cholera. The Lido is no longer the fashionable resort depicted in *Death in Venice*, but in the hot summer months, when the city and its sights can be overwhelming, the sands and sea air provide a welcome break.

Colourful houses in Torcello.

LIFE AS A MASQUERADE

Carnival in Venice is supreme self-indulgence, a giddy round of masked balls and private parties suggesting mystery and promising romance.

In Venice, Carnival is a 10-day pre-Lenten extravaganza, culminating in the burning of the effigy of Carnival on Shrove Tuesday. Carnival represents rebellion without the risk of ridicule. The essence of the "feast of fools" lies in the unfolding Venetian vistas: processions of plague doctors, doges, nuns and Casanovas swan past shimmering palaces, passing surreal masqueraders tumbling out of gondolas. As the revellers flock to café Florian or pose by the waterfront, the air is sickly sweet with the scent of fritters and the sound of lush Baroque music. Carnival capers include costumed balls, bands, firework displays and historical parades. In an attempt to reclaim Carnival, the Venetians are shifting celebrations to the neighbourhoods, but the set-pieces and the crowds still congregate on St Mark's Square.

Spirit of resistance

Carnival is often dismissed as crassly commercialised, but Venetian traditionalists view it differently. The leader of a venerable Carnival company sees the event as saving his city: "Life in Venice is inconvenient and costly. With the Carnival, we give a positive picture and show the pleasure of living here. Carnival is a form of resistance. By resisting the temptation to leave, we are saving the spirit of the city for future generations."

A mask makes everyone equal. Masqueraders are addressed as "sior maschera" (masked gentleman) regardless of age, rank or even gender.

Masks originally allowed the nobility to mingle incognito with the common people in casini (private clubs), but are now an excuse for all-purpose revelry.

The painted white mask is a popular disguise. It is a modern variant on the slightly sinister volto, the traditional Venetian mask.

The most common disguises; including the sinister black-caped plague-doctor on the right.

MASTERS OF DISGUISE

Mask-makers had their own guild in medieval times, when a *mascheraio* (mask-maker) helped a secretive, stratified society run smoothly. Venetians wore masks for about six months a year, with the *bauta*, the expressionless white mask, the most common disguise. Masks were a ploy for protecting the identity of pleasure-seeking Venetians, from secret gamblers to lascivious priests and un-virginal nuns.

Modern masqueraders can follow suit, choosing between the deathly-white *volto* mask, the gaudy harlequin, the Rococo courtesan, or the sinister black-caped plague-doctor, with his white-beaked mask. *Columbina* (Columbine) is the elegant domino mask; more catlike and seductive is the *civetta* (flirt).

Traditional masks are made of leather or papier-mâché, but contemporary creations can be ceramic or silk. If seeking inspiration, study Pietro Longhi's exquisite Carnival paintings, which hang in Ca' Rezzonico. To don a stunning disguise, visit Atelier Nicolao, the most authentic costumier's (tel: 041-520 7051; www.nicolao.com). Choose a cloak and handcrafted mask or rent a full costume and slip back into Casanova's era. Nicolao designed the costumes for Casanova and can turn anyone into a convincing Latin lover or Venetian courtesan.

Costumes can be historical, traditional or simply surreal. You can hire out noble Renaissance and rococo costumes in all their finery.

The classic Venetian disguise of the 17th and 18th centuries was known as the maschera nobile, the patrician mask, and you will see many varieties of this in the city.

You will see amazing fantasy masks on display in shop windows; they are creative rather than authentic, and appeal to individual tastes.

THE VENETO

Although Venice reigns supreme, the Veneto also embraces romantic Verona, Palladian Vicenza, Giotto's Padua – and a countryside dotted with wine trails.

Basilica di Sant'Antonio, Padua.

Veneto's civilised cities and landscaped countryside have left a legacy of impressive merchant palaces and Palladian villas. Many of the magnificent buildings were built on the wealth from trade with nearby **Venice ❶**; others by fashionable Venetian patricians. In this region you can take a journey to Padua, with its Roman origins and old university, discover the lesser known Treviso, and marvel at the wonders of the great architect Palladio's Vicenza. For romantics there is Verona, full of history but touched by modern sophistication. Orchards, river valleys and vineyards dot the area, which is noted for sparkling Prosecco, Valpolicella and Merlot.

The Veneto stretches up into the apricot-tinged Dolomites and Cortina d'Ampezzo, but is bordered by the Adriatic in the east, Lake Garda in the west (see page 235), and the River Po to the south. From Venice and Padua, the bucolic **Brenta Canal** (see page 196) winds languidly through the noble countryside, with Palladian villas, formal gardens and farms lining the banks.

Shakespeare called **Padua ❷** (Padova) "Fair Padua, nursery of Arts", and described it as a place where Renaissance Englishmen came to "suck the sweets of sweet philosophy". Dante and Galileo both lectured here, and in the mid-17th century a learned woman earned a doctorate here, the first woman in Europe to do so. (Padua's most famous daughter is, without doubt, Katherina, Shakespeare's tameable shrew.)

Padua is Italy's second-oldest university city (after Bologna), but long before the university was established in 1222, Padua was an important Roman town, and the birthplace of the Roman historian Livy. Padua is also a magnet for the faithful. Every June, pilgrims come from all over the world to honour St Anthony of Padua, a 13th-century itinerant

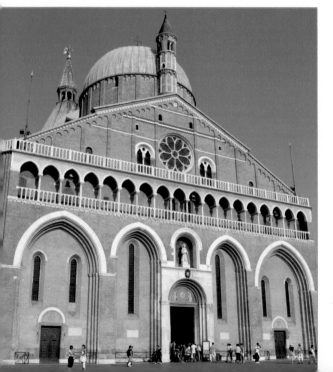

preacher whose spellbinding sermons packed churches.

The **Basilica di Sant'Antonio** (www.santantonio.org; daily 6.20am–6.45pm, until 7.45pm in summer), built over his remains between 1232 and 1307, celebrates his sanctity handsomely, notably with works by Donatello (who lived in Padua 1443–53). Venice is, of course, very close to Padua, and Venetian influence is evident in the church's design. Byzantine domes, an ornate facade and two slender bell-towers give the exterior an oriental appearance.

Padua's piazzas

In **Piazza del Santo**, to one side of the basilica, stands Donatello's famous equestrian statue *Gattamelata*. This sculpture of the great Venetian *condottiere* (mercenary) is believed to be the first great bronze cast in Italy during the Renaissance. Also in the piazza is the **Oratorio di San Giorgio** (9am–12.30pm and 2.30–7pm, closes at 5pm in winter), originally a private mausoleum but best known for an oratory decorated with Giotto-esque frescoes.

On the square is the **Scuola del Santo** (daily 10am–12pm and 3–5pm), with paintings by Bellini, Titian and Giorgione.

Via Belludi leads to another notable piazza, the **Prato della Valle**, centred on a small park bounded by four stone bridges and a circular moat. In the park, a circle of statues represents famous past citizens of Padua.

The lively **Piazza delle Erbe** is home to the **Palazzo della Ragione**, known as **Il Salone** (Tue–Sun 9am–7pm, Nov–Jan until 6pm). Designed as law courts in 1218, this is the largest undivided medieval hall in Europe.

Behind Il Salone is **Caffè Pedrocchi** (www.caffepedrocchi.it), famous as a gathering place for intellectuals during the Risorgimento (see page 61), and today still a popular meeting place for conversation or jazz sessions.

A short walk through **Piazza dei Signori** leads to Padua's **Duomo**. Although the cathedral was designed by Michelangelo, subsequent rebuilding and alterations make for a rather disappointing result, unlike the

TIP

The Padova Card (www.padovacard.it) is a museum and transport pass for Padua and its province. The pass grants free entrance to historic sites, including key museums, as well as offering discounted fares on the Riviera del Brenta boats. It is valid for either 48 or 72 hours (€16 and €21 respectively).

Giotto's fresco cycle in the Cappella degli Scrovegni.

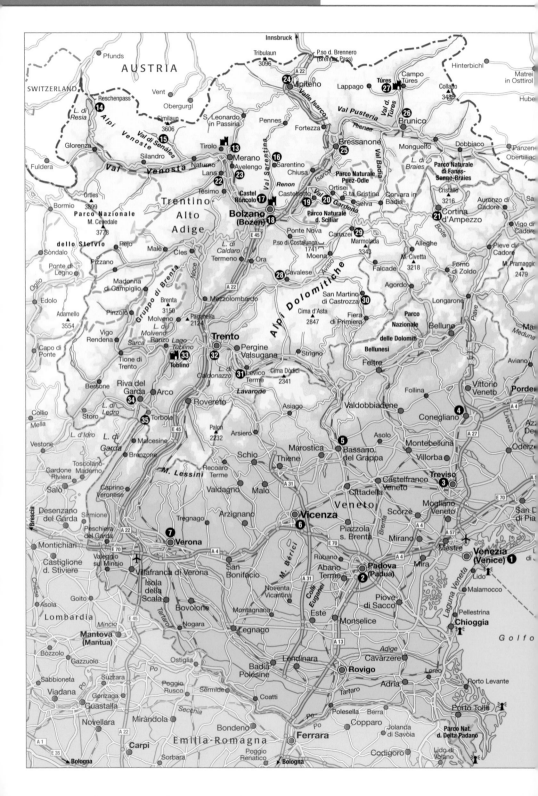

magnificent frescoed baptistery (Mon–Fri 7.30am–noon and 3.30–7.30pm, Sat–Sun 8am–1pm and 3.30–8.45pm; baptistery daily 10am–6pm).

Cappella degli Scrovegni

To the north of the university lies the **Cappella degli Scrovegni** (tel: 049-201 0020; www.cappelladegliscrovegni.it; daily 9am–7pm and often until 10pm; by appointment only and book well in advance, every 20 minutes). Enrico Scrovegni commissioned this richly decorated chapel in 1303 to atone for his father's miserliness and usury. Inside is Giotto's masterpiece, a fresco cycle dedicated to the Virgin, the Life of Christ and the Last Judgement. The solidity and emotional depth of the figures marked a turning point in Western painting.

Thankfully, the chapel escaped the fate of the nearby **Eremitani** church whose apse, covered with precious Mantegna frescoes, was bombed during World War II – Italy's greatest art loss of the war.

This bare church stands in poignant contrast to the rich collection of paintings, frescoes, bronzes and mosaics in the **Musei Civici**, now part of the **Complesso Eremitani** (Tue–Sun 9am–7pm; combined ticket for all museums), a complex which also comprises the **Museo d'Arte Medioevale e Moderna** (holder of Bellini's *Portrait of a Young Suitor* and Tintoretto's *The Crucifixion*), the **Museo Archeologico**, the **Cappella degli Scrovegni** and **Palazzo Zuckermann**.

Garden of Venice

Underrated **Treviso** ❸, often dubbed "the garden of Venice", makes a tranquil base from which to explore Venice and the Palladian countryside, with the lagoon city a mere 30 minutes away by train. Treviso is more a living city than a museum city so its charms are subtle, centred on picturesque canals and a self-consciously slow pace of life. The prettiest spot is the **Buranelli Canal**, which reveals pastel palaces, quaint bridges and tiny inns tucked into the backstreets – in contrast to the designer boutiques and hip bars elsewhere in town.

Cruising the Brenta Canal

Inspired by Palladian masterpieces around Padua, Vicenza and Treviso, the villas along the Brenta Canal reflect gracious country living.

The Brenta Canal (36km/22 miles) is a placid showcase for Venice's rural treasures, sumptuous villas which are regularly open to visitors. This limpid area linking Venice and Padua is known as the Riviera del Brenta, reflecting its role as a summer retreat for the Venetian nobility. In echoes of the Grand Tour, visitors can take a canal-boat along the Brenta to Padua, passing more than 50 sumptuous villas. The route involves nine swing-bridges and five locks, a reminder that there is a 10-metre (33ft) difference in water level between Venice and Padua.

Palladian style

The Veneto possesses the blueprint for the patrician villa, a harmonious rural retreat framed by waterside formal gardens and a working farm estate. Characterised by a classical portico, and modelled on a Graeco-Roman temple, these Palladian gems have

The palatial Villa Pisani.

influenced architectural styles the world over. From Renaissance times, the Venetian nobility commissioned these residences as retreats from the summer heat. The villa also represented the glorification of the dynasty and a practical investment of profits earned from maritime trade. In summer, the villa became a society haunt, originally a focus for humanist gatherings, but later a setting for lavish festivities, notably gambling, a Venetian vice. To this end, most villas have a *barchessa*, a colonnaded wing used as a summer house, banqueting hall or gambling pavilion.

Standout villas

From Venice, the first masterpiece is Villa Foscari, better known as La Malcontenta (www.lamalcontenta.com) because of its troubled romantic past. This distinctive villa was designed for the Foscari family, and is still owned by their descendants. Raised on an elevated pedestal to protect it from floods, it has a temple-like facade mirrored in the Brenta and a vaulted piano nobile modelled on the interiors of Roman baths.

Further along, set on a scenic bend in the canal, is Villa Widmann, decorated in fanciful French Rococo style. The grounds are lined with cypresses, horse-chestnut and limes, and dotted with neoclassical statuary, centred on an ornamental lake. Barchessa Valmarana, which faces Villa Widmann across the water, is all that remains of a villa destroyed in the early 20th century to avoid death duties. Although reduced to its colonnaded guest wings, this glorious relic has been restored and contains frescoes rivalling its more famous neighbours.

Closer to Padua is Villa Pisani (www.villapisani.beniculturali.it), a palatial masterpiece which owes much to French classicism. A ballroom frescoed by Tiepolo is matched by grandiose grounds dotted with follies, an appropriate setting for Mussolini and Hitler's first meeting in 1934. At Stra, just beyond Villa Pisani, looms Villa Foscarini Rossi (www.villafoscarini.it), a testament to the ambitions of the Foscarini dynasty. The Palladian-inspired villa contains Baroque trompe l'œil frescoes depicting allegories of war and peace, science and the arts. The heroic adventurer Lord Byron, a previous resident, must have felt at home.

Getting there

The best way to explore the Brenta Canal is on a cruise from Venice or Padua, with a bus making the return trip. Several companies offer Brenta boat trips between March and October, including visits to several villas and an optional lunch included. Il Burchiello (www.ilburchiello.it; tel: 049-876 0233) is a recommended tour company.

North of Treviso, Prosecco country beckons. **Conegliano ❹** boasts Europe's oldest wine school, while neighbouring Valdobbiadene is awash with tastings in wine bars. Prosecco can be downed with *cicchetti*, Venetian tapas, such as marinated artichokes, meatballs in deep-fried breadcrumbs, or polenta topped with creamy salt cod. But for a serious tasting in a Palladian-style ambience, Villa Barbaro (see page 199) is an atmospheric villa-estate. Any sparkling Prosecco trail around Treviso swiftly turns into a Palladian parade.

Towards Vicenza, **Bassano del Grappa ❺** is a delightful old town noted for **Palladio's Bridge**, dating from 1569, but faithfully rebuilt after war damage. The bridge, supported by four trapezoidal piers and topped by a trussed roof, was designed in wood to offer more flexibility and resistance to the fast-flowing river. At the western end lies **Grapperia Nardini** (tel: 0424-227 741; www.nardini.it), the Veneto's oldest grappa distillery, and an intriguing port of call, not just for those looking for something stronger than Prosecco.

Palladio's Vicenza

In **Vicenza ❻** Andrea Palladio remodelled the city, focusing on private palaces and public buildings, matched by princely villas around Vicenza and Treviso. As the most prominent architect of the Italian High Renaissance, Palladio (1508–80) was given free rein by the Vicenza gentry. As a result, there is hardly a street in central Vicenza not graced by a Palladian mansion, despite the destruction of 14 of Palladio's buildings in World War II. Palladio's glorious architecture led Unesco to declare the city a World Heritage site.

In **Piazza dei Signori**, at the city's heart, stand two of Palladio's masterpieces. The now restored **Basilica**, his first major work, is not a church but a remodelling of a Gothic courthouse (called *basilica* in the Roman sense – a place where justice is administered). Palladio's elegant design features two open galleries, the lower one with Tuscan Doric columns and the upper one with Ionic columns. Facing the Basilica is the **Loggia del Capitaniato**, a later Palladian work commissioned in

TIP

To find out about unusual tours around Treviso, from wine-tasting to villas, contact Guide Veneto (www.guideveneto.com; tel: 0422-56470) and the helpful tourist office Marca Treviso (www.marcatreviso.it; tel: 0422-541 052).

Romeo's Juliet immortalised in bronze.

PERFECT PALLADIANISM

Andrea Palladio (1508–80) was the first modern architect, a stone-cutter who changed the way we see the world. If these symmetrical, ghostly villas seem familiar, maybe they've flitted across your screen in *Casanova* or *The Merchant of Venice*. More likely they're simply part of your birthright, an imprint of an ideal home that's both familiar but timeless. The 500th anniversary of the West's most influential architect was celebrated worldwide in 2008.

From the White House to plantation piles in Southern Carolina, Palladianism proffers dignity and status – to connoisseurs or charlatans. We have Palladio to thank for the "classical homes" on executive estates and for footballers' wives' pillared and porticoed mansions. But between Venice and Vicenza, the original Palladian villas wipe the floor.

The Palladian rural retreat represented a perfect "machine for living": although a place for contemplation and noble pursuits, it was also the hub of a prosperous farm estate. In the 16th century, the craze for country living allowed the Venetian nobility to turn to their lands. They could easily believe that the ennoblement of agriculture validated the glorification of the dynasty. Palladio had even grander aspirations. Behind his blueprint for living was a desire to create harmony and set standards for civilised behaviour, values that went well beyond porticoes and pediments.

1571 to honour the victory over the Turks at Lepanto.

The rebuilt city's Gothic-style **Duomo** stands just behind the Basilica and is crowned by a Palladian cupola. North of the Duomo is **Corso Palladio**, the city's main street, lined with fine residences. Number 163 is the so-called **Casa del Palladio,** distinguished by its classic lines and precise geometric proportions. But the embodiment of the Palladian urban style is **Palazzo Chiericati**, in Piazza Matteotti, at the end of Corso Palladio. This harmonious mansion houses the **Pinacoteca di Palazzo Chiericati** (www.museicivicivicenza.it; Tue–Sun 9am–5pm, until 6pm in summer), a gallery with works including Tintoretto's *Miracle of St Augustine* and works by Flemish artists.

The **Teatro Olimpico** (www.teatr olimpicovicenza.it; Tue–Sun 9am–5pm, until 6pm in summer) is the city's greatest sight, a perfect example of Renaissance architecture. The still functioning theatre is a wood-and-stucco structure with a permanent stage-set of a piazza and streets in perfect perspective. Built between 1580–82, the world's oldest surviving indoor theatre was Palladio's theatrical last gasp.

To learn more of the great man visit the **Palladio Museum** (Palazzo Barabarano, Contra' Porti 11; www.palla diomuseum.org; Tue–Sun 10am–6pm) where the emphasis is on accessibility to all to the often dry subject of architecture. Here multimedia displays and superb models make it all seem more fun than it sounds.

The Palladian trail

A new Veneto-wide project to promote tourism has seen Palladio-inspired villas and gardens being gradually restored and opened to the public. Others are being turned into model estates, boutique hotels and wineries. The following are just a few of the delightful villas that can be visited from Vicenza and Treviso. Set on a low hill outside Vicenza, Villa Capra is better known as **La Rotonda** (www.villalarotonda.it: grounds: Tue–Sun mid-Mar–Oct 10am–noon and 3–6pm, Nov–mid-Mar 10am–noon

Palladio's Villa Capa (La Rotonda), outside Vicenza.

and 2.30–5pm; interior: Wed and Sat, same hours; exterior: Sun, Tue, Thu, Fri). La Rotonda is an architectural set-piece, a stage for admiring the undulating view. Inspired by the Pantheon in Rome, the cube-shaped villa is topped by a shallow dome.

At Maser, near Treviso, **Villa Barbaro** (Villa di Maser; tel: 042-392 3004; www.villadimaser.it; Apr–June, Sept–Oct Tue–Sat 10am–6pm and Sun 11am–6pm, Nov–Feb Sat–Sun 11am–5pm) is an iconic Palladian villa which still doubles as a wine estate. Often described as the "perfect house" the villa combines grandeur with intimacy and an emotional charge.

At Fanzolo, just west of Treviso, **Villa Emo** (www.villaemo.org; May–Oct Mon–Fri 10.30am–12.30pm and 2–6pm, Sat–Sun 10.30am–18.30pm, Nov–Apr Mon–Fri 9.30am–12.30pm and 2–5pm, Sat–Sun 10.30am–6.30pm) resembles a shimmering Greek temple but is as functional as it is decorative. In typical Palladian style, the adjoining farm outbuildings taper into dovecotes. (The carrier pigeons carried messages to Venice in under an hour.)

Inside the villa proper, the "noble floor" is sumptuously frescoed living space, with the kitchens and cellars on the floor below, and the granaries consigned to the roof space.

Between Vicenza and Bassano del Grappa, **Villa Godi Malinverni** (www.villagodi.com; May–Sept Tue 3–7pm, Sat 9am–2pm and Sun 10am–7pm, Mar–Apr, Oct–Nov Tue 2–6pm, Sat 9am–2pm, Sun 2–6pm) is a Palladian pile which, heretically, puts fine dining before an architectural feast. The villa's **Il Torchio Antico** (www.iltorchio antico.it; tel: 0445-860 358; closed Mon–Tue) serves dishes dating from Palladio's day, such as zabaglione with pine nuts, spices and candied peel. You can even rent **Villa Saraceno**, south of Vicenza (www.landmarktrust. org.uk, visit by appointment Apr-Oct Wed only 2–4pm). Palladio's layout has been respected, from the granary to the theatrical grand sala, flanked by

frescoed apartments and a loggia. The villa is set in gentle countryside, in a setting of plains, poplars and canals unchanged since Palladio's day.

Verona

Built in the distinctive local pink marble, **Verona ❼** has a rosy hue, as if the sun were constantly setting. What was once a thriving Roman settlement is today one of the most prosperous and elegant cities in Italy. Shakespeare's setting for *Romeo and Juliet* appeals to lovers of all ages. You can now even get married on "Juliet's Balcony". The celebrated Arena di Verona opera season attracts opera buffs to the Roman amphitheatre. The sophisticated centre remains a people-watching parade, from café-studded Piazza Brà to Piazza delle Erbe, once the site of the Roman forum. Verona is also a citadel of consumerism, awash with sunglasses, shoes and jewellery.

The **Piazza Brà Ⓐ** is where the Veronese gather day and night to talk, shop and drink together. They sit or stroll in the shadow of the glorious 1st-century AD Roman **Arena Ⓑ** (www.

The winged lion of St Mark in Piazza delle Erbe, Verona.

Piazza Brà, Verona.

arena.it; tel: 045-800 5151; Tue–Sun 8.30am–7.30pm, Mon 1.30–7.30pm, last entry one hour before closure), the third-largest structure of its kind in existence. The highest fragment, called the Ala, reveals the Arena's original height. It is often used for city fairs and, in summer, up to 25,000 people at a time fill it to attend performances of popular Italian opera – notably Verdi's *Aida* (if you are fortunate enough to get tickets, take a cushion and do not drink for several hours beforehand – the toilets are virtually impossible to reach).

The Roman Forum was located in what is now **Piazza delle Erbe** ⓒ, off the **Via Mazzini**. This large open space has a quirky beauty, due to the variety of *palazzi* and towers that line its sides. Among the most impressive is the Baroque **Palazzo Maffei**, next to the **Torre del Gardello**, the tallest Gothic structure in the square. The palace with the attractive double-arched windows on the corner of Via Palladio is the medieval guildhouse – the **Casa dei Mercanti**.

The adjoining **Piazza dei Signori** ⓓ is more formal than its neighbour.

The **Palazzo della Ragione**, the Gothic law courts, borders the two squares. The inner courtyard has a delicate Gothic stairway. Opposite rises the **Loggia del Consiglio**, considered the finest Renaissance building in the city. Nearby are the tombs of the della Scala family (the Scaligeri), one-time rulers of Verona. The elaborately sculpted monuments stand outside the tiny church of Santa Maria Antica, surrounded by a wrought-iron fence featuring the family's staircase motif (della Scala means "of the stairs").

Verona is, of course, the city of *Romeo and Juliet*. Though the Capulet and Montague families immortalised by Shakespeare did exist, the story of the star-crossed lovers was entirely fictional. However, what is now a dilapidated private home on the Via delle Arche Scaligeri was allegedly the **Casa di Romeo** ⓔ. Rather better maintained is **Juliet's House** ⓕ (Tue–Sun 8.30am–7.30pm, Mon 1.30–7.30pm) at No. 23 Via Cappello, a medieval townhouse complete with balcony, where lovers can now exchange their vows. It is also possible to visit a slightly tacky

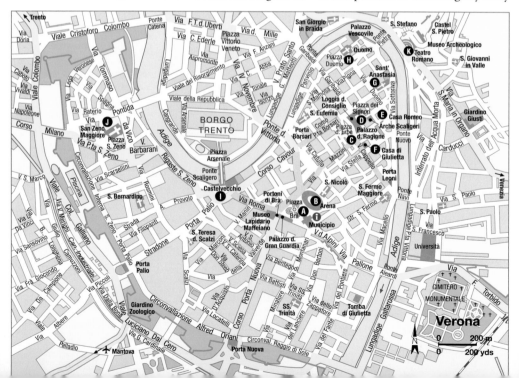

Verona

0 ___ 200 m
0 ___ 200 yds

Juliet shrine. The "tomb" (Tue–Sun 8.30am–7.30pm, Mon 1.30–7.30pm) is several miles out of the centre on Via del Pontiere, along the Lungoadige Capuleti.

If your taste runs to the Gothic, head for **Sant'Anastasia** , which houses a magnificent painting by Pisanello of St George, and frescoes by Altichiero and Turone. Verona's **Duomo** (Mar–Oct Mon–Sat 10am–5.30pm, Sun 1.30–5.30pm, Nov–Feb Tue–Sat 10am–5pm, Sun 1.30pm–5pm) is nearby. Inside is Titian's *Assumption of the Virgin*.

The **Castelvecchio** (Tue–Sun 8.30am–7.30pm, Mon 1.30–7.30pm) on the River Adige is a reminder of one of the grimmer chapters in the history of "fair Verona". The castle was first built in 1354 by the hated tyrant Cangrande II Scaliger for protection if a rebellion occurred. But he met his end not at the hands of the mob but through the treachery and ambition of his own brother, who stabbed him. As elsewhere in Italy, this fortress is now an excellent museum (museodicastelvecchio.comune.verona.it; same hours as the castle), with works by Veronese and Tiepolo.

A saint and a prophet

Little is known about St Zeno, Verona's patron saint, but his basilica is one of the finest Romanesque monuments in Italy. St Zeno's most famous miracle is depicted by Nicola Pisano on the porch of the **Basilica di San Zeno Maggiore** (Mar–Oct Mon–Sat 8.30am–6pm, Sun 12.30–6pm, Nov–Feb Tue–Sat 10am–5pm, Sun 12.30–5pm). According to the story, the saint was out fishing when he saw a man being dragged into the Adige by crazed oxen. St Zeno made the sign of the cross and exorcised the devils. The bronze doors of the church are of splendid workmanship.

Most people are drawn to Verona because of *Romeo and Juliet* and other Shakespeare plays which are frequently performed in the **Teatro Romano** , the perfectly proportioned Roman theatre dating from the 1st century BC. The theatre (Mon 1.30am–7.30pm, Tue–Sun 8.30am–7.30pm) is carved into the hillside in a strategic spot overlooking a bend in the river.

Fresco in Verona's cathedral.

Boats line the Grand Canal, Trieste.

FRIULI-VENEZIA GIULIA

The influence of successive invaders has given Italy's northeastern corner a cosmopolitan feel, combining flavours of Italy, Austria and Slovenia.

Rome

Main Attractions
Trieste
Castello di Miramare
Castello di Duino
Grotta Gigante
Aquileia
Udine

The Friuli-Venezia Giulia region belongs to everyone and no one. If Trieste feels marooned in Mitteleuropa, Aquileia feels resolutely Roman, Udine feels resolutely Venetian, while the slumbering lagoon resort of Grado feels Byzantine. Since the 2nd century BC – when the Romans took over this corner of the Italian peninsula – Friuli-Venezia Giulia has been a victim of invasions. Attila the Hun earned his nickname "the Scourge of God" here in 452, and in 489 came Theodoric and the Ostrogoths. Today you can pay homage to this history reflected in the towns, and also visit some magical castles, including the Castello di Miramare and the Castello di Duino.

Many of today's gracious modern towns began as barbarian outposts, such as **Cividale del Friuli**, which as a result has an outstanding collection of sculpture, jewellery and weapons from this period, displayed in the **Museo Archeologico** (Tue–Sun 8.30am–7.30pm, Mon 9am–2pm; www.museoarcheologicocividale.benicul turali.it; free for EU citizens under 18) and the **Museo Cristiano** in the cathedral (www.turismofvg.it; Wed–Sun 10am–1pm and 3–6pm). A short walk away is the **Tempietto Longobardo** (www.tempiettolongobardo.it; Apr–Sept Mon–Fri 10am–1pm and 3–6pm, Sat–Sun 10am–6pm, Oct–Mar Mon–Fri 10am–1pm and 2–5pm, Sat–Sun 10am–5pm). This prestigious monument is an 8th-century Lombardic relic with fine 14th-century frescoes.

The border runs through the bilingual city of **Gorizia**, which has a fascinating castle (www.turismofvg.it; Mon 9.30–11.30am, Tue–Sun 10am–7pm) and several museums, including a World War I museum. On the coast, the spa town of **Grado**, which was founded by the Habsburgs, is today a seaside resort somewhat stuck out on a limb.

Palazzo del Governo, Trieste.

Fairytale Castello di Miramare.

Trieste

Of all Friuli's foreign "invaders", perhaps the best known is James Joyce, who arrived in **Trieste ❽** in 1905 and made the city his home for the next 10 years.

Today the city has an air of faded elegance. Once Venice's rival for trade on the Adriatic, later the maritime gateway for the Austro-Hungarian Empire, Trieste is now a port without a hinterland, a city that history left behind. In the Città Nuova, long, straight avenues flank a Grand Canal where tall ships once anchored. Southwest of the canal is the café-filled **Piazza dell'Unità d'Italia** – the largest sea-facing piazza in Italy, and a favourite promenade area. On the east side of the piazza stands the ornate **Municipio** (town hall), of 19th-century Austrian inspiration. At its foot, across the railroad tracks, stretches the long quay with its **Acquario Marino** (www.aquariomarinotrieste.it; Thu–Tue 9am–5pm) exhibiting Adriatic and tropical fish. Also of note is a restored **Centrale Idrodinamica** (www.centraleidrodinamica.it; Tue–Thu 4–8pm, Fri–Sun 11am–8pm) an old hydrodynamic plant which once operated all cranes in the Trieste harbour.

The Old City

Behind the Municipio are the narrow, winding streets of the **Città Vecchia**. Stairs by the **Teatro Romano** (open daily) ascend steeply to the 6th-century **Duomo di San Giusto**. Two 5th-century basilicas were here combined into a single four-aisled structure in the 14th century. The hill is surmounted by the 15th-century Venetian **Castello di San Giusto** (Piazza Cattedrale 3; Tue–Sun 10am–7pm), with a sweeping view of the city and harbour. The **Museo del Castello di San Giusto** (Tue–Sun 10am–7pm) displays a collection of art and weaponry. On your way back down, consider stopping at the **Civico Museo di Storia ed Arte** (www.museostoriaeartetrieste.it; Apr–Oct Tue–Sat 10am–1pm and 4–7pm, Sun 10am–7pm, Nov–Mar Tue–Sun 10am–5pm), which features relics from the invaders and inhabitants of Friuli-Venezia Giulia. Also worth a visit is the 12th-century **Basilica of San Silvestro** on the hillside. Overlooking Piazza Venezia is the **Museo Revoltella** (www.museorevoltella.it; Via Diaz 27; Wed–Mon 10am–7pm). This was once the grand residence of Trieste's most important merchant, but now showcases modern art.

Before leaving Trieste, embark on a café crawl; the cosmopolitan port is home to historic, literary cafés that make it the capital of Italian coffee culture. Caffè degli Specchi and Caffè Pasticceria Pirona are just two of the Viennese-style literary cafés, with original decor and rich Mitteleuropean cakes.

Fairytale castles

Ten kilometres (6 miles) west of Trieste, set in lush green gardens, is the fairytale **Castello di Miramare ❾**, near the seaside town of **Barcola**. A mock medieval fortress, it was the summer home of Archduke Maximilian. This was his dream palace, built with his wife Charlotte, daughter of Leopold I of Belgium, between 1856 and 1860. Set on a promontory overlooking the sea, with rooms resembling the interiors of ships, this is Italy's best relic of the Austro-Hungarian Empire. A museum (www.castello-miramare.it; daily 9am–7pm, garden hours vary) honours the ill-fated archduke, who later became Emperor of Mexico and died in front of a revolutionary firing squad. The surrounding Miramare Park is also worth a stroll.

Castello di Duino ❿ (www.castellodi-duino.it; Apr–Sept Wed–Mon 9.30am–5.30pm, in winter Sat–Sun and holidays 9.30am–4pm), just along the coast, is an equally splendid castle, a medieval affair with delightful grounds, sweeping seascapes and a romantic cliffside walk.

Only 15km (9 miles) from Trieste is the **Grotta Gigante** (Giant Cave; www.grottagigante.it; tel: 040-327 312; guided tours Tue–Sun in summer every hour 10am–6pm, in winter every hour 10am–4pm), a vast cavern which is part of an underground river system.

South of the city centre but easily reached by bus from Trieste is the solemn **Risiera San Sabba** (www.risierasansabba.it; daily 9am–7pm; free), a former rice-husking plant turned detention centre and concentration camp during World War II (the only one on Italian soil). From here prisoners were sent to Auschwitz or German death camps. The fleeing Germans destroyed almost everything, but prison cells and the remains of a crematory are poignant reminders of the atrocities committed here

Roman and Venetian towns

The Romans based their Northern Adriatic fleet at **Aquileia** ⓫, which now lies several miles inland. Here is the ruin of a once-vast harbour, dating from the 1st century AD. Best of all is the **Basilica** (www.basilicadiaquileia.it; daily, summer 9am–7pm, winter 10am–4pm), begun in AD 313. The stunning Roman mosaic floor depicts biblical tales and mythological scenes. Stretching the entire length of the nave, it was laid down in 314, but the current building was consecrated in 1031 under Patriarch Poppo, who had the mosaics covered. They did not see daylight again until 1909, and in 2000 a major restoration took place.

Udine ⓬ has an appealing style all its own. Echoes of Venetian rule are everywhere: the 16th-century **Castello** that towers over the city was built as the residence for Udine's Venetian governors and now houses the city's art and archaeology museums (May–Sept Tue–Sun 10.30am–7pm, Oct–Apr 10.30am–5pm). At the foot of the castle hill, the graceful Piazza della Libertà boasts a Gothic, Venetian-style loggia and graceful Renaissance porticoes. The **Museo di Arte Moderna e Contemporanea di Udine** (GAMUD, www.udinecultura.it; Tue–Sun 10.30am–7pm, until 5pm Oct–Apr) in Casa Cavazzini showcases both Italian and foreign 20th-century art. Tiepolo, the greatest Venetian Rococo painter, painted three gold-and-pink chapels in the city's **Duomo**.

Northwest of Udine, the hillside town of **San Daniele del Friuli** produces raw *prosciutto*, and has done since the time of the Celts. Some people consider San Daniele ham to be superior even to Parma ham. San Daniele pigs are kept outside so their flesh is leaner, and their diet of acorns gives it a distinctive flavour. Produced in much smaller quantities than Parma ham, it is even more expensive.

Loggia di San Giovanni, Udine.

South Tyrol landscape.

Rome

TRENTINO-ALTO ADIGE

The limestone peaks of the Dolomites frame an area of castles, lakes and Mitteleuropean-style spas, with its own distinctive mix of Italian and Germanic culture.

The mountainous region of Trentino-Alto Adige stretches north to the Italian-Austrian border. It is a popular holiday retreat for hikers, skiers and watersports enthusiasts, stretching from Lake Garda to the Dolomites, from charming Riva to the spa town of Merano and to medieval Brunico. Here, it is possible to hike around a secluded Alpine lake in the morning, sample wine in an Italian vineyard at noon, stroll along the palm-lined promenade of a Continental spa in the afternoon and then slip into bed in a medieval castle at the end of the day. It is the mix of cultures, as well as the rugged scenery, that make this region so intriguing.

The region first came to the attention of tourists in the English-speaking world in 1837 when John Murray, the London publisher, brought out a handbook for travellers. The book's description of the Dolomites sparked interest particularly among mountaineers who had conquered the Swiss Alps and were looking for new challenges: "They are unlike any other mountains, and are to be seen nowhere else among the Alps. They arrest the attention by the singularity and picturesqueness of their forms, by their sharp peaks or horns, sometimes rising up in pinnacles and obelisks, at others extending in serrated ridges, teethed like the jaw of an alligator."

Germanic traditions are still flourishing in this region.

Two provinces: two cultures

Yet Trentino-Alto Adige is an anomaly, reflecting the region's chequered ethnic divide. Each is a province with the mentality of a region. Trentino is resolutely Italian, with a Latin soul, while Alto Adige is decidedly Teutonic and German-speaking, though officially bilingual. Alto Adige also prefers to be known as the Sudtirol (South Tyrol). It belonged to Austria until the end of World War I so still resembles the Austrian Tyrol and feels Tyrolean. In contrast, Trentino, the southern province,

Main Attractions

Bolzano's "Ice Man"
Alpe di Siusi
The Dolomites
Ski resorts
Bressanone
Hiking in Trentino
Castello Del Buonconsiglio
Riva Del Garda

prides itself on looking (and sounding) more Italian, though the subtle distinction is often lost on visitors.

The Germanic traditions, culture and language colour the South Tyrol, despite post-World War I efforts by Mussolini to stamp them out. In a subtle form of ethnic cleansing, the dictator Italianised the names of the towns, mountains and rivers and forbade schools to teach in German. Today the two autonomous provinces tolerate one another but cherish their separate cultural identities and go their own way.

The South Tyrol

In terms of scenery and culture, the South Tyrol resembles the Austrian Tyrol. Here, signs are bilingual, with place names written in both Italian and German, as in Bolzano (Bozen) or Merano (Meran), but German is preferred. The sleepy spa town of **Merano** ⓭ (Meran), with its palm-lined promenades, exclusive shops, fine restaurants and Belle Epoque cafés, offers the visitor a taste of Old Europe. Merano has played host to the great and the gracious for well over a century. Those who can

afford it come to relax and take the cure in a Mediterranean-like climate. The city owes its famously mild climate to its position in a deep basin, protected to the north by the massive Alpine peaks and opening to the Etsch Valley in the south. Merano flourished between the late 13th and early 15th centuries, when it was the capital of the Tyrol. Thereafter, it passed into relative insignificance until its value as a spa town was discovered. Merano hosts one of the biggest wine festivals in Italy in the first weekend of November (www.meranowinefestival.com). It also offers "grape cures", which involve a copious diet of grapes for the duration of the regime.

A short distance north of Merano is the romantic **Castel Tirolo** (Schloss Tirol), the ancestral home of the counts of Tyrol, and now an imaginative museum of Tyrolean history (www.schlosstirol.it; mid-Mar–mid-Dec Tue–Sun 10am–5pm, Aug until 6pm). Just down the hill is **Castel Brunnenburg**, (www.brunnenburg.net), where Ezra Pound (1885–1972) spent the last years of his life.

To the west of Merano, the **Venosta**

Mountainbiking with Mount Ortler in the background.

TRENTINO ON A PLATE

When eating out, expect homely charm and Slow Food in cosy inns and *rifugi*, rustic Alpine lodges which often double as ski huts. The hearty yet refined local cuisine blends Italian and Austrian traditions. Peasant-style dishes with a Tyrolean twist include dumplings *(canederli)*, gnocchi, smoked meats and venison, *finferli* mushroom risotto, and steaming polenta oozing with cheese. The region also produces around a third of Italian sparkling wines, which rival even Champagne. Other major wines include Marzemino, Mozart's favourite tipple, as well as purplish Teroldego and elegant Pinot Grigio. Look out for the Osteria Tipica Trentina logo, which denotes a convivial atmosphere, rustic charm and regional produce, including local wine and juniper-flavoured grappa.

(Vinschgau) Valley extends all the way to the Swiss–Austrian–Italian border. The route leading over the **Reschen Pass** ⓮ was first constructed during Roman times as an important link between Augsburg and the Po Valley. Vinschgauer bread, a speciality of the region baked in small flat loaves and flavoured with aniseed, is worth sampling.

The **Val di Senales** ⓯ (Schnals Valley), which branches to the north, just past Naturno, passes through the region of the Similaun glacier. It was here that the 5,000-year-old "Ice Man" was found in 1991. This frozen corpse is now on view in Bolzano.

In the heart of Alto Adige lies the **Val Sarentina** (Sarn Valley), a place where time seems to have stood still. Old farms perch precariously on the mountainsides, rushing brooks carve deep gorges through the mountain walls, and the people themselves, celebrating traditional festivals dressed in colourful costumes, add to the feeling of yesteryear. In **Sarentino** ⓰ (Sarnthein) you can watch the craftsmen at work embroidering leather shoes, braces, handbags and book covers.

The road leading out of the valley towards the provincial capital of Bolzano winds through numerous tunnels before emerging at **Castel Roncolo** ⓱ (Schloss Runkelstein; www.runkelstein.info), built on a towering cliff in 1250 and today housing a museum enlivened by Gothic frescoes (mid-Mar–Oct Tue–Sun 10am–6pm; until 5pm in winter).

Bolzano

Bolzano ⓲ (Bozen) is a testament to the coexistence of Italian and Germanic cultures in one city. The vibrant old part of the city, centred on Piazza Walther and the arcades of the Via dei Portici, is marked by patrician houses and German Gothic architecture. Adjacent to Piazza Walther is the impressive Gothic **Duomo**, and reputedly the oldest hall church in Alto Adige.

The **Museo Archeologico dell'Alto Adige** (www.iceman.it; Tue–Sun 10am–6pm, daily July–Aug, Dec) has a fascinating collection including, famously, the mummified body of "Ötzi", the Ice Man. Found by hikers in the Ötzaler Alps in 1991, the extraordinarily

The improbably perched Castel Roncolo.

Paraglider in the Dolomites.

well-preserved remains, including his clothing and copper axe, are estimated to be over 5,000 years old.

Mountains and pasture

From Bolzano a cable car (see www. ritten.com for timetable) takes visitors on a scenic journey up to the **Renón** (Ritten) **Plateau**, a popular resort area. On a clear day, the views of the Dolomite formations are spectacular.

South of the city, **Schloss Sigmundskron** (www.messner-mountain-museum. it; mid-Mar–mid-Nov Fri–Wed 10am–6pm) is a medieval castle that houses MMM Firnian, the centrepiece of Reinhold Messner's mountain project, spread over five castles and one underground structure. The Dolomites have inspired the Dalai Lama, Pope John Paul II and, of course, Reinhold Messner, the charismatic South Tyrolean mountaineer. This particular castle is dedicated to the inspiration behind mountaineering, and to the South Tyrol in particular.

Just east of Bolzano is the **Sciliar** (Schlern) massif, towering like a great stone fortress above the surrounding

Bolzano market.

area. At its base is the **Alpe di Siusi** (Seiser Alm), Europe's largest expanse of mountain pastureland, comprising almost 50 sq km (20 sq miles) and offering an abundance of hiking and ski trails. Following the road from Sciliar to **Castelrotto** ⓲, one emerges in the **Val Gardena** (Grödner Valley) ⓳, with the popular ski resorts of **Ortisei** (St-Ulrich), **Santa Cristina** and **Selva.**

Ortisei is famed for its woodcarving, but many other villages have maintained their craft traditions. Linger over handcrafted lace, embroidered leather – or even a *loden*, that typical Tyrolean coat.

From **Selva**, the Sella Joch Pass winds its way between the jagged peaks of Mount Langkofel and the majestic Sella massif. Travellers through this pass enjoy a panoramic view of the Marmolada, the region's highest mountain, standing at 3,343 metres (10,965ft). This route connects with the Great Dolomite Road which leads east to **Cortina d'Ampezzo** ⓴, in the Veneto, a chic winter resort, and west over the **Costalunga** (Karer Pass) to Bolzano. The road from Bolzano passes the **Catinaccio** (Rosengarten) massif. At twilight, the rose-coloured rays of the setting sun bathe the cliffs of the Rosengarten (literally "rose garden") in red, which is known as the *enrosadira*.

Lana ㉒, located between Bolzano and Merano, is the centre of the apple-growing region. The parish church in **Niederlana** contains Alto Adige's largest late Gothic altarpiece, over 14 metres (46ft) in height. Across the valley is **Avelengo** ㉓ (Hafling), home of the famous Hafling breed of horses.

In central Alto Adige, the **Isarco** (Eisach) **Valley** has, for the past 2,000 years, served as the major route connecting the German north to the Latin south via the Brenner Pass. The former commercial importance of **Vipiteno** ㉔ (Sterzing), the northernmost town on this route, is still evident today in its patrician houses.

Bressanone

Bressanone ㉕ (Brixen), the region's oldest settlement, was a bishopric from 990 until 1964, when the bishop moved to Bolzano. Interesting sights include the prince-bishop's palace and the Baroque Duomo, which features impressive marble work and fine ceiling frescoes. A stroll through the Gothic cloisters adjacent to the Duomo is worthwhile. The frescoes here, dating from 1390 to 1509, are among the best examples of Gothic painting in the Alto Adige. The Romanesque chapel of St John at the southern end of the cloisters was built as a baptismal church.

Just north of Bressanone, stretching to the east, is the **Pusteria Valley**. The valley's chief town is **Brunico** ㉖ (Bruneck), its main street lined with medieval houses overshadowed by the castle. **Schloss Bruneck**, the site for Messner's fifth castle museum, MMM Ripa. From Brunico, the **Túres Valley** leads north to **Castèl di Túres** ㉗ (Schloss Taufers). This frescoed and fully furnished castle is one of the finest in the South Tyrol (www.burgen institut.com; May–Oct daily 10am–noon, 2–5pm; guided tours by prior arrangement all year round). The Pusteria Valley is the gateway to the Sexten Dolomites, where the majestic Three Pinnacles and the Sexten

Skiing in the Dolomites.

Walking the Sentiero sul Catinaccio.

Sundial formations are located. The latter was used by early astronomers as a point of orientation.

Trentino and the Dolomites

Trentino is an inspirational lakes and mountains destination, with almost 300 lakes and a foothold on Lake Garda. The majestic Dolomites tower over forests, pastures and vineyards – or the ski slopes (see page 210). Whether grey and windswept or bathed sunset-pink, the peaks are inspirational enough to persuade mere mortals to pick up their hiking boots. In 2009 the Dolomites were added to Unesco's list of World Heritage sites.

Southeast of Bolzano awaits the rugged landscape around **Cavalese** ㉘, the chief resort for the Val di Fiemme. Both a ski resort and a delightful summer retreat, Cavalese has a sumptuously frescoed medieval town hall.

Further north is **Canazei** ㉙, the centre of the Val di Fassa, and another popular ski and summer destination. Spectacular views of the Dolomites, including the Marmolada, lie in wait at Belvedere, reached by cableway.

Legendary trails

In the Trentino Dolomites, the scenery may be Tyrolean but the welcome is Italian. The "Legendary Trails" cover the majestic mountains in eastern Trentino and are classic high trails with superb vantage points. This 200km (125-mile) circuit covers the Val di Fiemme, Val di Fassa and Pale di San Martino peaks. South of Canazei, **San Martino di Castrozza** ㉚ basks in typical Dolomites landscape, lying at the foot of the pinnacle-crowned mountains. The **Pale di San Martino** form the main mountain group in the southern Dolomites and are a springboard for hiking excursions. Chair lifts give access to stunning views over glaciers and craggy peaks soaring over meadows and woodland. These mountains also shelter Paneveggio, the magical forest where Antonio Stradivari selected the finest spruce to make his legendary violins.

Here, and in the vertiginous canyons of the Fassa and Fiemme valleys, walkers enjoy stunning views over glaciers and visions of craggy peaks

soaring over meadows, forests and Alpine lakes. The scenery spans the lunar landscape of Sass Pordoi, the screes of Catinaccio and dramatic mountain passes. One trail connects San Martino di Castrozza, the Colbricon lakes and Mount Cauriol.

There are hikes to suit walkers of all abilities, with most allowing for easy access back to the valleys, either by cable car, bus, or by pre-arranged pick-up. This allows hikers to stay in cosy, walker-friendly hotels rather than in basic Alpine huts. The Peace Path, in southern Trentino, hugs the former front line in the Great War and is an intriguing trail, running from Austro-Hungarian military fortifications to Roman ruins and vineyards (www.trentinograndeguerra.it; see page 24).

A long winding route leads south to **Levico Terme** ❸, a dignified spa resort dotted with Art Nouveau villas. Nearby, **Lago di Caldonazzo** offers swimming, sailing and canoeing.

Trento to Lake Garda

Just west is **Trento** ❷, the provincial capital and site of the Council of Trent (1545–63). It was during these sessions, called by the Catholic Church to discuss the rising threat of Lutheranism, that the seeds of the Counter-Reformation were sown. Noteworthy sights include streets lined with frescoed facades, the Romanesque-Gothic **Duomo**, and the **Castello del Buonconsiglio**, one of Italy's grandest castles and the residence of the prince-bishops who ruled the city for centuries. The bastion contains exquisite Gothic frescoes contrasting the noble high life with peasant labours in a cycle of the months (www.buonconsiglio.it; Tue–Sun 10am–6pm in summer, 9.30am–5pm in winter; free first Sun of the month). Modern art lovers can make a little detour to **Rovereto** to see the **Museo di Arte Moderna e Contemporanea di Trento e Rovereto** or **MART** (www.mart.trento. it; Tue–Sun 10am–6pm, Fri until 9pm) for its collection of modern art

as well as to admire architect Mario Botta's building.

Castel Toblino ❸, west of Trento, is a romantic lakeside castle, sensitively converted into a restaurant (www.casteltoblino.com; tel: 0461-864 036) and marks the start of a short walking trail.

Further south, **Riva del Garda** ❹ lies on the rugged northern tip of Lake Garda. Riva is charmingly sedate, blessed with a castle, compact medieval quarter and lush Mediterranean vegetation. As the most popular resort in the region, it makes a natural base for exploring the lake. Trentino also lays claim to being Italy's most environmentally aware region, with pristine lakes, and a ban on motor boats on its stretch of the sea-like Lake Garda.

Torbole ❺, Riva's sister resort, is a watersports mecca, where windsurfers race in the afternoon breeze, turning the lake into a flurry of pastel-coloured sails. Yet just beyond the lake loom the jagged pinkish peaks of the ever-present Dolomites, creating the illusion of the Mediterranean meeting the mountains.

Vineyards in the Alto Adige.

Galleria Vittorio Emanuele.

MILAN

Sassy, confident Milan is often overlooked by tourists heading for the hot-spot cities of Italy, but it has history, cutting-edge style and some first-class restaurants.

Milan (Milano) is one of the world's fashion capitals, and home to both Leonardo's *Last Supper* and the world's premier opera house, La Scala. Above all, Milan is the centre of business in Italy, a hub for media and advertising companies, and a magnet for design and fashion. The prosperous Milanese are courteous, but reserved towards visitors. This is a city of contrasts, with its highly elaborate cathedral and medieval churches on the one hand and sleek minimalist lines of the PAC art gallery and the futuristic EXPO 2015 buildings on the other. Bohemian Navigli adds another dimension to the mix.

There is no better place to begin a tour of Milan than at its spiritual hub, the **Duomo** Ⓐ (www.duomo milano.it; daily 8am–7pm), described by Mark Twain as "a poem in marble". The gargantuan Gothic cathedral (the third-largest church in Europe after St Peter's in Rome and Seville's cathedral) was begun in 1386 but not finished until 1813. Decorating the exterior are 135 pinnacles and over 3,400 marble statues from all periods. The "Madonnina", a beautiful 4-metre (13ft) gilded statue, graces the top of the Duomo's highest pinnacle, soaring 109 metres (358ft) above ground. The building requires continuous restoration and can be treated as a work in progress.

Inside the Duomo

The English novelist D.H. Lawrence called the Duomo "an imitation hedgehog of a cathedral", because of its pointy intricate exterior. But inside the church is simple, majestic and vast. Five great aisles stretch from the entrance to the altar. Enormous stone pillars dominate the nave, which is big enough to accommodate some 40,000 worshippers. In the apse, three large and intricate stained-glass windows attributed to Nicolas de Bonaventura shed a soft half-light over the area behind the altar.

View from the roof of the Duomo.

FACT

The Museo del Novecento (Museum of the 20th century) located in the Palazzo Arengario in Via Marconi, directly opposite the Duomo, is proving very popular since its opening in 2010. The collection of Italian modern art is well displayed in cool, peaceful surroundings and the temporary exhibitions draw the crowds. For information check www.museodelnove cento.org.

Buon appetito!

The central window features the shield of the Visconti, Milan's ruling family during the 13th and 14th centuries. It was Duke Gian Galeazzo Visconti, the most powerful member of the family, who commissioned the Duomo.

A gruesome statue of the flayed St Bartholomew, carrying his skin, stands in the left transept. In the right transept is an imposing 16th-century Michelangelo-esque marble tomb made for Giacomo di Medici.

Outside, a lift – or you can go up by foot – goes up to the **Duomo rooftops** (tel: 02-7202 2656; daily 9am–7pm, summer Thu–Sun until 9pm) among the pinnacles and carved rosettes. The view is spectacular: on a clear day it stretches as far as the Alps.

Of interest too are the crypt of St Charles, the museum in San Gottardo church and the archaeological area, which all require a separate ticket so you are better off buying the Duomo pass granting access to all of them.

Piazza del Duomo

Come down into the well-restored **Piazza del Duomo B**, where Milan's

many worlds converge. The large equestrian statue standing at one end of the square honours Italy's first king, Victor Emmanuel (after whom major boulevards in cities throughout Italy are named). The piazza is lined on two sides with porticoes, where Milanese of all ages and styles love to gather. To the north is the entrance to the **Galleria Vittorio Emanuele C**, Italy's oldest and most elegant shopping mall. Its four-storey arcade is full of boutiques, bookshops, bars and restaurants. But, before you sit down to watch the world go by, be forewarned: the cafés here are pricey. Among the Galleria's best cafés and restaurants are the Art Nouveau Camparino at No. 78, a classic spot for an *aperitivo*, especially a Campari – Davide Campari, the inventor of the drink, was born here on the first floor. Another perfect people-watching spot is the Gucci café.

La Scala

At the other side of the Galleria is **Piazza della Scala D**, site of the famed **La Scala** opera house, which has now been opulently restored. It was built between 1776 and 1778 by Giuseppe Piermarini, and it was here that Verdi's *Otello* and Puccini's *Madama Butterfly* were first performed. The **Museo Teatrale alla Scala E** (Opera House Museum; www.teatroallascala.org; daily 9am–5.30pm) displays a rich collection of memorabilia, including original scores by Verdi, Liszt's piano and other objects connected to great musicians and composers. The visit includes a look into the theatre itself from one of the boxes – as long as there are no rehearsals under way.

Follow the Via Verdi from La Scala to the **Pinacoteca di Brera F** (Tue–Sun 8.30am–7.15pm, Thu until 10.15pm; for bookings tel: 02-9280 0361), home of one of Italy's finest art collections. Paintings of the 15th to the 18th century are especially well represented. Famous works included in the collection are Mantegna's *The Dead Christ* (viewed from the pierced soles of his

feet), Caravaggio's *Supper at Emmaus*, and the restored 15th-century *Madonna and Saints* by Piero della Francesca. Raphael's beautiful *Betrothal of the Virgin (Lo Sposalizio)*, a masterpiece of his Umbrian period, was his first painting to show powers of composition and draughtsmanship far in advance of his biggest stylistic influence, Perugino.

Castello Sforzesco

Off the Piazza del Duomo is Via Mercanto. From there, Via Dante leads to the **Castello Sforzesco** Ⓖ (www.milanocastello.it; daily 7am–7pm, until 6pm in winter; museums Tue–Sun 9am–5.30pm; free Tue from 2pm and one hour before closing Wed–Sun), stronghold and residence of the Sforza family, the despotic rulers of Milan in the 15th century (*forza* means strength in Italian). The greatest was Francesco, a mercenary general who became the fourth duke of Milan, and commissioned this Sforza castle.

Inside the castle's Spanish Hospital section is the new **Pietà Rondanini Museum** (http://rondanini.milanocastello. it), solely dedicated to Michelangelo's last masterpiece – *Rondanini Pietà* (1554–64), an almost abstract work charged with emotion. Michelangelo worked on this *pietà* until within a few days of his death in 1564.

West of the castle stands the church of **Santa Maria delle Grazie** Ⓗ (daily 7.30am–noon and 3–7.15pm), begun in 1466 but expanded in 1492 by Bramante, who also built the exquisite cloisters.

The Last Supper

Next door, the **Cenacolo Vinciano** Ⓘ (tel: 02-9280 0360; www.cenacolo. it; Tue–Sun 8.15am–7pm; booking essential, visit restricted to 15 minutes), once a refectory for Dominican friars, is home to Leonardo's iconic *The Last Supper* (1495–7). Leonardo painted on dry plaster, which would allow him more time to retouch the work, using an experimental mix of tempera and oil. However, excessive humidity combined with the faulty mixture used for binding the paint caused the fresco to deteriorate even during Leonardo's lifetime. Restoration of the work began in 1977 and took 22 years to complete.

Pinacoteca di Brera.

Milan

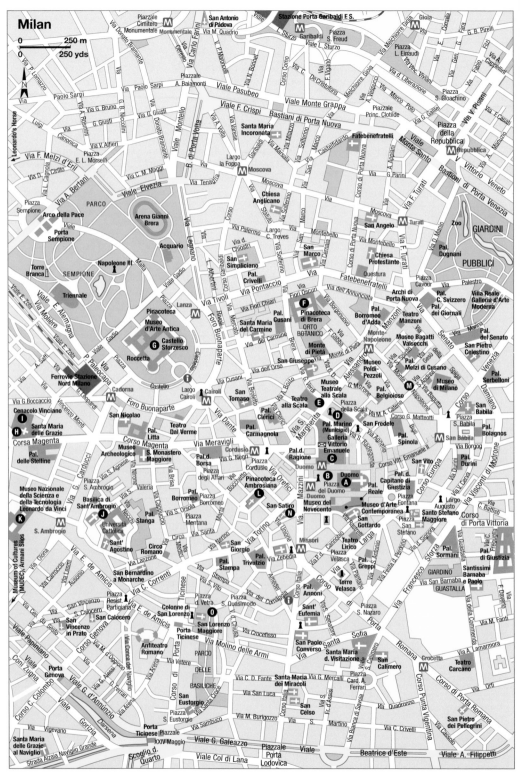

0   250 m
0   250 yds

Leonardo's Horse

Stazione Porta Garibaldi F.S.
Piazzale Cimitero Monumentale
San Antonio di Pádova
Garibaldi
S. Freud
Piazza L. Einaudi
Gioia
G. B. Pirelli

Viale Pasubeo
Viale Monte Grappa
Viale F. Crispi
Bastioni di Porta Nuova
Santa Maria Incoronata
Piazzale Princ. Clotilde
Piazza S. Gioachino
Paolo Sarpi
Piazza A. Baiamonti
Largo la Foppa
Moscova
Piazza della Repubblica
Vittorio Veneto

Viale Elvezia
PARCO
Chiesa Anglicano
Moscova
San Angelo
Turati
Zoo
GIARDINI

Arco della Pace
Arena Gianni Brera
Porta Sempione
Acquario
San Marco
Chiesa Protestante
PUBBLICI
Pal. Dugnani

Torre Branca
SEMPIONE
Napoleone III
San Simpliciano
Pal. Crivelli
Questura
Piazza Cavour
Archi di Porta Nuova
Pal. C. Svizzero
Pal. dei Giornali
Villa Reale Galleria d'Arte Moderna

Triennale
Via Pontaccio
Pal. Cusani
Pinacoteca di Brera
ORTO BOTANICO
Pal. Borromeo d'Adda
Monte-Napoleone
Museo Bagatti Valsecchi
Pal. del Senato

Pinacoteca Museo d'Arte Antica
Santa Maria del Carmine
Monte di Pietà
San Giuseppe
Museo Poldi-Pezzoli
San Pietro Celestino
Melzi di Cusano
Pal. Serbelloni

Castello Sforzesco
Roccetta
San Giorgio dell'Orso
Museo Teatrale alla Scala
Pal. Belgioioso
Museo di Milano

Ferrovie Stazione Nord Milano
Cadorna
Largo Cairoli
San Tomaso
San Briletto
Teatro alla Scala
Piazza della Scala
Corso G. Matteotti
San Babila
Pal. Bolagnos

Cenacolo Vinciano
Santa Maria delle Grazie
Corsa Magenta
San Nicolao
Teatro Dal Verme
Pal. Clérici
Pal. Marino (Municipio)
San Fredele
S. Babila
Pal. Durini

Pal. delle Stelline
Pal. Litta
Corso Magenta
Pal. Carmagnola
Galleria Vittorio Emanuele
Pal. Spinola
San Babila

Museo Archeologico
S. Monastero Maggiore
Via Meravigli
Pal.d. Borsa
Pal.d. Ragione
Duomo
San Vito
Pal. Durini

Museo Nazionale della Scienza e della Tecnologia Leonardo da Vinci
Basilica di Sant'Ambrogio
Università Cattolica
Pal. Stanga
Pinacoteca Ambrosiana
Duomo
Pal. Reale
Museo del Novecento
Pal. d. Capitano di Giustizia
Santo Stefano Maggiore

Museum of Cultures (MUDEC; Armani Silos)
S. Ambrogio
Sant' Agostino
Circo Romano
Pal. Borromeo
San Satiro
San Gottardo
Museo d'Arte Contemporanea
Largo Augusto

San Bernardino a Monache
San Giorgio
Pal. Trivulzio
Teatro Lirico
Pal. Greppi
Pal. Sormani
Pal. di Giustizia

Colonne di San Lorenzo
Porta Ticinese
San Lorenzo Maggiore
Torre Velasca
Pal. Annoni
GIARDINO
GUASTALLA
Santissimi Barnaba e Paolo

San Vincenzo in Prato
San Calocero
Anfiteatro Romano
Sant' Eufemia
San Paolo Converso
Santa Maria d. Visitazione
San Calimero
Teatro Carcano

Porta Genova
Porta Ticinese
San Eustorgio
Santa Maria dei Miracoli
San Celso
San Pietro dei Pellegrini

Santa Maria delle Grazie al Naviglio
Porta Ticinese
XXIV Maggio
Piazzale Porta Lodovica
Viale G. Galeazzo
Beatrice d'Este
Viale A. Filippetti

Whatever your view of its controversial restoration, *The Last Supper* remains a powerful and moving work. It is far larger than expected – some 9 metres (30ft) wide and 4.5 metres (15ft) high. It vividly captures the moment when Jesus announces that one of the disciples is about to betray him. This painting was seminal to the perception of the artist as a creative thinker rather than just an artisan. The painting's popularity has been even further enhanced by the huge success of Dan Brown's thriller *The Da Vinci Code*, in which it played a significant role. Do not leave before seeing the equally thrilling **Sacrestia Bramante** (Bramante's Sacristy; Tue–Sun 10am–6pm; www.leonardo-ambrosiana.it).

From Santa Maria delle Grazie, proceed to the **Basilica di Sant'Ambrogio** ❶ (Via Carducci; 10am–noon and 2.30–5.30pm). Milan's best-loved and most beguiling church is dedicated to the city's patron saint, St Ambrose.

The church is dark and low, but compelling in its antiquity. Founded between 379 and 386 by St Ambrose, then Bishop of Milan – it was he who converted St Augustine – the basilica was enlarged first in the 9th century and again in the 11th. The brick-ribbed square vaults that support the galleries are typical of Lombardic Romanesque architecture. Church, crypt and cloisters are free; there is a small charge to see additional chapel areas. Don't miss the splendid gold altar by Volvinio.

Leonardo in Milan

Down Via San Vittore is the **Museo della Scienza e della Tecnologia Leonardo da Vinci** ❷ (www.museo scienza.org; Tue–Fri 9.30am–5pm, Sat–Sun until 6.30pm). The highlight is the huge gallery filled with wooden models of Leonardo da Vinci's most ingenious inventions. It remains one of the most important science and technology museums in the world. Don't miss the reconstruction of his famous flying machine.

Return in the direction of the Duomo to the **Pinacoteca Ambrosiana** ❸, an art gallery founded by Cardinal Federico Borromeo in 1618, along with a frescoed library that also displays designs by Leonardo da Vinci

Leonardo da Vinci's masterpiece, "The Last Supper".

(for bookings tel: 02-806 921; www.ambrosiana.eu; Tue–Sun 10am–6pm). The restored gallery (same times) houses an art collection dating from the 15th to the 17th century. Most notable among the works are Leonardo's *Portrait of a Musician*, Titian's *Adoration of the Magi* and Caravaggio's *Basket of Fruit*.

Leonardo da Vinci is inextricably linked to Milan, even if Milan is rarely linked to the Renaissance. Apart from his celebrated *Last Supper* and the ingenious inventions on display in the Museum of Science, Leonardo, with his passion for hydraulic engineering, also designed the complex locks in Milan's Navigli canals. Leonardo was the complete Renaissance Man, at home with art, astronomy, mechanics and warfare. Nowhere is this revealed better than in the Sacrestia Bramante, Bramante's Renaissance sacristy, and the Biblioteca Ambrosiana, a 17th-century frescoed library, sites chosen to display the polymath's complete Codex Atlanticus folios. The Codex, the largest extant collection of Leonardo drawings and designs, has been in the Ambrosiana since 1637, but can only be displayed properly now.

Fashion avenue

For a break from culture and sightseeing, stroll down **Via Monte Napoleone** , which extends off Corso Vittorio Emanuele between the Duomo and Piazza Santa Babila. The "Vie" Montenapoleone, Sant'Andrea, della Spiga and Manzoni are home to great designer shops.

Also within Milan's designer area is the eccentric **Museo Bagatti Valsecchi** (Via Gesù; www.museobagatti valsecchi.org; Tue–Sun 1–5.45pm). The Bagatti Valsecchi brothers were avid collectors, and commissioned period-style furnishings from skilled Lombard craftsmen in order to recreate an authentic Renaissance atmosphere in their own home. The resulting museum, housed in a delightful neo-Renaissance *palazzo*, is a collector's paradise, where it is fun to try to distinguish authentic 16th-century pieces from the reproductions.

In this cutting-edge city, cutting-edge art is showcased at the **Padiglione**

Scooting around the city in style.

FASHION FOR FOODIES

Visitors come to Milan as much to shop and dine as to take in Leonardo's *Last Supper*. As with the fresco, you will need to book in advance if you plan to eat at a top establishment. For exclusivity try the two Michelin-starred **Cracco**, at Via Victor Hugo 4, where you can enjoy gourmet creative cuisine, including asparagus ravioli with black truffles (tel: 02-876 774; www.ristorantecracco.it). **Sadler** in the Navigli district (Via Asciano Sforza 77; tel: 02-5810 4451; www.sadler.it) is another 2-star Michelin-studded temple to gastronomy, but for exceptionally good value try its stylish offshoot, **Chic' n Quick** (tel: 02-8950 3222; same address). You'll find a modern take on Milanese cuisine at another Michelin-starred restaurant, **Vun** (Via Silvio Pellico 3; tel: 02-8821 1234; www.ristorante-vun.it) located in the Park Hyatt hotel. Choose from à la carte menu or tasting menus such as "Land and Sea in Nine Courses". If your budget doesn't allow for the full gastronomic blow-out, you can always shop for picnic ingredients at **Gastronomia Peck**, Via Spadari 9 (tel: 02-802 3161; www.peck.it), choosing from the enticing selection of top-quality gourmet cheeses, meats and pastries on display. When in the Quadrilatero, at the junction of Montenapoleone and Sant'Andrea, seek refuge from the haughty sales staff in the **Caffè Cova** (http://cova.com.hk/aboutcova/milan).

d'Arte Contemporanea (PAC) (Via Palestro 14; www.pacmilano.it; Tue–Sun 9.30am–7.30pm, Fri until 10.30pm). Large, experimental works of contemporary art in all its forms feature in this museum.

The **Museo Poldi-Pezzoli** (Via Alessandro Manzoni 12; www.museopoldipezzoli.it; Wed–Mon 10am–6pm) is a treasure trove amassed by the wealthy Giacomo Poldi-Pezzoli in 1881. The interior is a testament to 19th-century patrician tastes, filled with paintings (by Botticelli, Bellini, Piero della Francesca and Mantegna), jewellery, porcelain, timepieces and sundials, tapestries, ancient armaments and period furniture.

If you have time, two more churches are worth seeking out. In the Via Torino, near the Piazza del Duomo, stands **San Satiro** Ⓝ, built by Bramante in 1478–80. Inside, the architect cleverly used stucco to give the impression that the church is far larger than it actually is. **San Lorenzo Maggiore** Ⓞ, nearby on Corso di Porta Ticinese, attests to Milan's antiquity. The basilica was founded in the 4th century and rebuilt in 1103. Martino Bassi restored it in 1574–88, but its octagonal shape and many beautiful 5th-century mosaics are original. The vast dome creates an awe-inspiring interior.

Milan's expansion

Much like the Duomo, Milan is a work in progress, building with more panache than anywhere else in Italy, for good or ill. Milan is slowly doubling the reach of its metro system and upgrading its railways. In 2012 a city congestion charge system was implemented, known as Area C. Dilapidated industrial areas are being transformed, and Futurist-style districts being created, including "Vertical Forest", skyscrapers covered in greenery to curb pollution in the city.

But the major redevelopment project, comparable with London's 2012 Olympic site, has been EXPO 2015: *Feeding the Planet, Energy for Life,* designed to relaunch Milan as a model of urban renewal. Elsewhere, historical districts, such as the Navigli canal quarter, the bohemian entertainment centre (see margin), have also been given a facelift. The area is now home to a range of excellent new cultural institutions including the **Museum of Cultures** (MUDEC; Mon 2.30–7.30pm, Tue–Sun 9.30am–7.30pm, Thu and Sun until 10.30pm; www.mudec.it), opened in 2015 and housed in a splendid building designed by architect David Chipperfield on the site of the former Ansaldo factory. Besides ethnographic collections, this interdisciplinary centre offers cultural activities, workshops and temporary exhibitions. There are also restaurants, a library, an auditorium, lecture rooms and the Mudec Junior area where children aged 4–11 can learn in an innovative and engaging way about world cultures. And of course there is the **Triennale** design centre (www.triennale.org; 10.30am–8.30pm; see page 223).One would expect nothing less revolutionary from a city where Leonardo da Vinci made such a mark.

see page 223

The renovated Navigli quarter.

Planet Fashion

Milan has become a brand, Planet Fashion, a glitzy galaxy where you can live by fashion alone – but the designers also give something back.

After waking up in Frette sheets in the Bulgari design hotel (Via Privata Fratelli Gabba), you can have breakfast in the glass-domed Gucci café, trim your designer stubble at the Dolce & Gabbana barber and take a dip in Giorgio Armani's spa retreat. That's before sipping cocktails in Just Cavalli, attending the opera at La Scala and/or dining nearby in the fashion designers' Trussardi alla Scala (Piazza della Scala 5; tel: 02-8068 8201). Afterwards, rub shoulders with the glitterati and dance the night away at the Hollywood night club on Corso Como.

Not that the Milanese designers are all vapid airheads. A Milanese tradition of patronage of the arts means that many major designers boast lofty cultural foundations. Fondazione Prada (Via Fogazzaro 36) favours contemporary art exhibitions, as does Trussardi (as above).

A Prada shop window with the inevitable tempting display.

Quadrilatero d'Oro

Piazza Duomo is as good a spot as any to plan a shopping campaign. Overlooking the cathedral is Rinascente (www.rinascente.it), the city's slick department store, where Giorgio Armani started his career as a window-dresser. From here, fashionistas will be drawn to the designer honey-pots of the Golden Triangle. Known as the Quadrilatero d'Oro, this chic (but physically square) fashion district is bounded by Via della Spiga, Via Manzoni, Via Montenapoleone, Via Sant'Andrea and Corso Venezia.

In this partly pedestrianised district, discreet courtyards and classical palaces conceal the most ostentatious of international brands. Via Montenapoleone takes in Emilio Pucci, a Prada flagship store, an Armani boutique, Versace glitz, Gucci glamour, luxury accessories from Bulgari, sumptuous cashmere from Loro Piana and Alberta Ferretti. Other designers include Salvatore Ferragamo, Fratelli Rossetti, Agnona – the womenswear arm of Ermenegildo Zegna, Bottega Veneta, Valentino, Cartier, Sergio Rossi, Etro and Louis Vuitton. Ultra-chic Via della Spiga is home to Dolce & Gabbana, Roberto Cavalli, as well as Krizia and Tod's.

Designer lifestyle

All the designers are getting in on the lifestyle act, adding spas or bars with gay abandon. Dolce & Gabbana menswear emporium (Corso Venezia 15) has a grooming salon and Martini bar. Roberto Cavalli (Via della Spiga), where more is always more, responds with a goldfish bowl, a fashionable bar framed by an aquarium with models parading around in the latest tactile collection. Less theatrically, Emporio Armani (Via Manzoni 31) pays homage to the master of minimalism and showcases his main collections, as well as a more recent hotel and spa. Diehard fans will salivate over Armani books, cutlery and designer chocolate in the store's Armani Café and swanky Nobu restaurant partly owned by actor Robert de Niro (tel: 02-7231 8645; armanirestaurants.com).

Fashionistas are easily satisfied, but the city also caters to a more conservative set. For dapper Italian politicians, the king of ties is Angelo Fusco Cravatte Sette Pieghe (Via Montenapoleone 25). Created as an amusing sideline by Angelo, a practising cosmetic surgeon, the firm produces intricate designer ties made of seven-times-folded jacquard silk, hand-stitched and presented in a wax-sealed box.

For couples with a wedding list, Italy between the sheets is best represented by Frette (Via Montenapoleone 21). The firm is the leading creator of desirable bed linen, embracing linen sheets, baby blankets, cashmere throws and silk cushions, tempting lovers of luxury.

For those on a non-designer budget, salvation lies in the form of Il Salvagente (Via Fratelli Bronzetti 16), one of Milan's most reliable discount outlets for designer clothes.

At the other end of the spectrum, the most beguiling shopping experience in Milan remains the stylish 10 Corso Como (Corso Como 10; tel: 02-2900 2674; www.10corsocomo.com), Milan's sexiest concept store. Designed by a former fashion editor, this bazaar-like emporium, café and restaurant is the haunt of style gurus and supermodels.

After celebrity-spotting over handbags or home furnishings, slip away from the designer clothes to the store's stylish design gallery or the café in the conservatory (where low-carb menus attract the waif-like models).

Design capital

Milan is as much a design mecca as it is a fashion capital. For inspiration and design history, visit the Triennale (Via Alemagna; www.triennale.org; Tue–Sun 10.30am–8.30pm), Italy's major design museum.

For cutting-edge furniture and lighting, make tracks for Via Durini. Dominating "Design Street" are the rival showrooms of B&B Italia, Cassina and Meritalia. High Tech (Piazza XXV Aprile 12) is an eclectic homeware store housed in a former ink factory. Stylish Armani Casa can be found at Via Sant' Andrea 19. For seductive design icons, Alessi (Via Manzoni 14–16) is a style guru who specialises in corkscrews and coffee pots, cutlery and kitchenware. Also consider attending the world's finest Furniture Fair, Salone del Mobile, which coincides with arty spring events.

Not far from fashion central is the elegant Brera district, centred on Via Solferino, and home to upmarket yet bohemian boutiques. The funky Navigli canal district is a cool quarter, boasting hip shops and vibrant nightlife. Via Tortona is the design centre, with a Design Week in April. Fashion buffs should not miss the **Armani Silos** exhibition centre (Wed–Sun 11am–7pm, Thu and Sat until 9pm; www.armanisilos.com). Inaugurated in 2015 to mark the designer's forty years in business, it displays his most emblematic creations including Richard Gere's suit in the film *American Gigolo*.

Antonioli (Via Pasquale Paoli 1) sells cutting-edge fashion labels in a former cinema, while Kitchen (Via E. De Amicis 45) is packed with cooking utensils and cookbooks. On the rise is the Garibaldi station district: its funky design outlets are no longer the wrong side of the tracks but in an old steam factory known as the Fabbrica del Vapore.

Como silk

A short train ride from Milan, Como is to silk what Milan is to fashion and Venice is to glassware. The city remains the country's leading centre for luxurious silk creations, with Mantero and Seteria Bianchi the leading manufacturers. The silk was imported from China for economic reasons but the Lakes region has reopened silk factories in recent years. Design and production continues as ever and there is even a silk museum. There are plenty of shops to satisfy designer tastes along Via Vittorio Emanuele. The company Tessabit, founded in 1953, has 11 individual shops devoted to luxury fashion spread about the town. Como is a delightful interlude, but Milan's masters of merchandising will soon tempt you back to Planet Fashion.

Window-cleaning in style.

Limone sul Garda.

LOMBARDY

With a deep sense of the past and passionate individuality, Lombardy looks more to its northern European neighbours than its southern cousins.

From the heights of the central Alps to Lake Como and the low-lying plains of the Po Valley, the province of Lombardy is remarkably diverse. With its capital Milan, these cities of art – Pavia, Cremona, Mantua and Bergamo – flourished in medieval and Renaissance times and still maintain their distinct identities. In fact, the land was named after the Lombards, one of the barbarian tribes who invaded Italy in the 6th century. A strong sense of a Lombard identity is still felt locally, including support for separatism in an area that is the stronghold of the Northern League's separatist movement.

Certosa di Pavia

An easy day trip from **Milan ❶**, or a stopover on a journey south, is the **Certosa di Pavia ❷** (Charterhouse of Pavia; Tue–Sat 9.30am–noon, 3.30–5.15pm, Sun pm only). This world-famous church, mausoleum and monastery complex, founded in 1396, is a masterpiece of Lombardic Renaissance architecture, complete with relief sculpture and inlaid marble. The interior of the church is Gothic in plan, but highly embellished with Renaissance and Baroque details. Inside stand the tombs of Ludovico Visconti and his child-bride, Beatrice d'Este.

Behind the Certosa is the magnificent Great Cloister where Carthusian monks, who had taken vows of silence,

Cloister at Certosa di Pavia.

lived in individual dwellings and collected meals through a hatch beside the doorway.

Nowadays, Pavia is a backwater, but between the 6th and 8th centuries it was the capital city of the Lombards. Pavia's fame was augmented in 1361 when the university was founded, and to this day it remains a prestigious centre of learning.

Other sights in Pavia

On the Via Diacono, in the old centre of town, is the church of **San Michele**

Main Attractions
Certosa di Pavia
Mantua
Palazzo Ducale
Accademia Carrara
Bergamo Alta
Colleoni Chapel

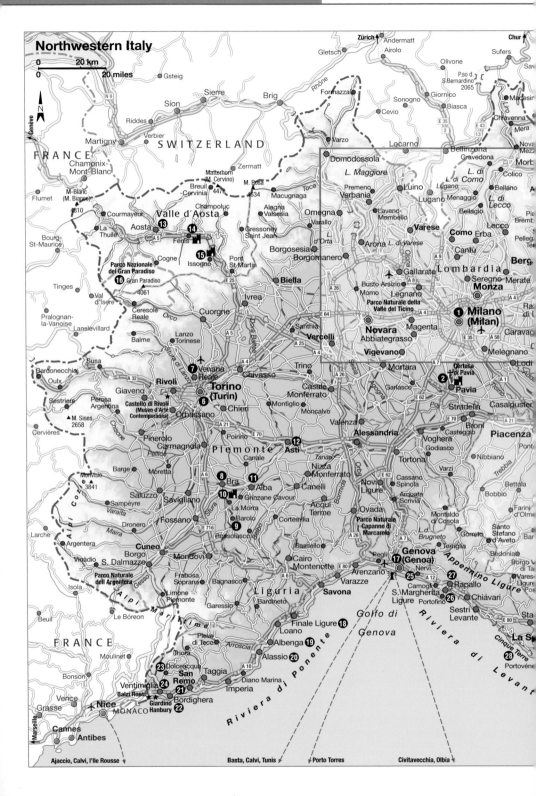

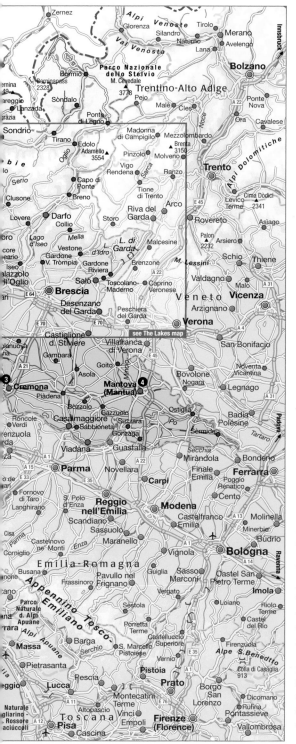

(www.sanmichelepavia.it), consecrated in 1155. Here the great medieval Lombard leader, Frederick Barbarossa, was crowned King of Italy. Look for the carefully sculpted scenes of the battle between good and evil above the three doorways.

To reach the **Duomo**, follow the Strada Nuova from San Michele. This cathedral is an eclectic mixture of four centuries of architectural styles. The basic design is Renaissance (Bramante and Leonardo worked on it), but the immense dome, the third-largest in Italy, is a late 19th-century touch, and the facade was added in 1933.

If you continue on the Strada Nuova you will arrive at the **Università**, (www.unipv.eu), where some 23,000 students currently attend classes. One of Pavia's most famous past graduates was Alessandro Volta, the physicist who discovered and gave his name to electrical volts. His statue stands in the left-hand court of the university complex.

At the end of the Strada Nuova stands the **Castello Visconteo**, an imposing square fortress built in 1360–65. Today, the castle is the home of the **Museo Civico** (www.museicivici.pavia.it; Tue–Sun 10am–5.50pm, July–Aug, Dec–Jan 9am–1.30pm). Included in the museum's collection are many fine Lombardic Romanesque sculptures and remnants of Roman Pavia, including inscriptions, glass and pottery.

Go west from the castle to reach **San Pietro in Ciel d'Oro**, a fine Lombardic Romanesque church, smaller than San Michele, but quite similar. A richly decorated Gothic arch at the high altar is said to contain the relics of St Augustine.

Cremona

About two hours' drive from Pavia lies the city of **Cremona** ❸, a world-famous centre of violin-making set on the banks of the River Po. The greatest of Cremonese violin-makers was Antonio Stradivari (1644–1737), whose secret formula for varnish may partly account for the beautiful sound of a Stradivarius violin. The **Museo del Violino** (www.museodelviolino.org; Tue–Sun 10am–6pm), located in the Palazzo dell'Arte, a utility building completed in 1947, has displays relating to the origins of the violin and superb Stradivarius artefacts including drawings, models and original tools. The museum also houses a 450-seat auditorium, specifically designed with perfect acoustics for the violin. The modern **International School of Violin-Making** (www.scuoladiliuteria.it) is located in Corso Garibaldi.

The pink marble **Duomo** was built in the Lombardic Romanesque style. Although consecrated in 1190, it was not completed until much later. Inside are 17th-century tapestries representing the *Life of Samson*.

Mantua

Because **Mantua** ❹ (Mantova) lies on a peninsula in the River Mincio, surrounded by a lagoon on three sides, it is known as *Piccola Venezia* (Little Venice). But history has given the city a more resonant name: "Ducal Mantua", because from 1328–1707 the enlightened but despotic Gonzaga family ruled the city-state from their sombre fortress.

During the Renaissance, the Gonzaga court was one of the bright lights of Italian culture, especially under the influence of Isabella d'Este (1474–1539), who modelled her life on *Il Cortegione*, a textbook for courtiers and ladies written by Castiglione. She also hired Raphael, Mantegna and Giulio Romano to decorate the **Palazzo Ducale** (Reggia dei Gonzaga), once the largest palace in Europe. A selection of the palace's 450 or so rooms can be visited (www.mantovaducale.beniculturali.it; Tue–Sun 8.30am–7.15pm; free first Sun of the month). Particularly worth seeing are the tapestries in the Appartamento degli Arazzi that were made in Flanders from drawings by Raphael. The Camera degli Sposi (the Matrimonial Suite) is decorated with frescoes by Mantegna depicting scenes from the lives of Ludovico Gonzaga and his wife, Barbara of Brandenburg.

Across town is the **Palazzo del Te** (www.palazzote.it), the supremely elegant Gonzaga summer retreat which doubled as a boudoir for Gonzaga mistresses. Designed by Giulio Romano in 1525, this Renaissance palace is delicate and pleasing, featuring rooms frescoed with summery scenes, and complemented by a lovely garden. It is home to the **Civic Museum** (www.museicivici.mn.it; Mon 1–7.30pm, Tue–Sun 9am–7.30pm) with a permanent exhibition of Egyptian art and a collection of 250 Mesopotamian artefacts brought back from Bagdad by Italian archaeologist Ugo Sissa.

Mantua's **Duomo**, located near the Reggia, has a Baroque facade and a Renaissance interior, with stuccowork by Giulio Romano. Also worth a visit is the **Basilica di Sant'Andrea** in Piazza Mantegna. The Florentine architect Alberti designed most of Sant'Andrea, starting in 1472, but the dome was added in the 18th century. Inside, the celebrated frescoes that adorn the walls were designed by the great painter Andrea Mantegna, who died in 1506, and executed by his pupils, among them Correggio.

Café break in Cremona.

Bergamo

If you want to escape from the hot stillness of "the waveless plain of Lombardy", **Bergamo ❺** makes a refreshing diversion. The combination of cobbled streets, cypress-clad hills and mountain air adds to its appeal. Curiously, Bergamo is, in fact, two cities: Bergamo Bassa and Bergamo Alta.

Though pleasant and spacious, the modern **Bergamo Bassa** lacks the appeal of Bergamo Alta, perched on a rough-hewn crag above. The main reason for visiting this area is the newly refurbished **Accademia Carrara** (www.lacarrara.it; Wed–Mon 10am–7pm), holding works by Pisanello, Botticelli, Bellini, Carpaccio, Mantegna, Tiepolo and Canaletto. Where else but in Italy can you find, in a small city, a collection of paintings that the grandest metropolis would be proud to have? In this case, it is thanks to the good taste of the 18th-century Count Giacomo Carrara.

Opposite the Carrara, the **Galleria d'Arte Moderna e Contemporanea GAMeC** (www.gamec.it; collection Tue–Sun 9am–1pm and 3–6pm; free, exhibitions Wed–Mon 10am–7pm, Thu until 10pm) hosts a permanent collection featuring such artists as Sutherland and Kandinsky, as well as exhibitions by contemporary artists and sculptors.

A creaking funicular will transport you to **Bergamo Alta**, a medieval town built in warm brown stone. The best spot in which to sit and admire it is the central **Piazza Vecchia** – a good place to find the local speciality *polenta con gli uccelli* (polenta with quail). The piazza is flanked by the 17th-century Palazzo Nuovo and the 12th-century Palazzo della Ragione. Beyond the medieval building's arcade is the small Piazza del Duomo, packed with ecclesiastical treasures: the Romanesque **Santa Maria Maggiore** and the Renaissance **Colleoni Chapel** (Mar–Oct daily 9am–12.30pm and 2–6.30pm, Nov–Feb Tue–Sun until 4.30pm),

designed by Amadeo who contributed to the Certosa di Pavia, and with an 18th-century ceiling by Tiepolo. The chapel is dedicated to the Bergamesque *condottiere* Bartolomeo Colleoni. The mercenary fought so well for the Venetians that he was rewarded with an estate in his native province, which was then under Venetian rule.

Opera composer Gaetano Donizetti, the city's most famous son, is buried here. He died here in 1848, quite insane, having composed 75 operas, of which the best known today is *Lucia di Lammermoor*. Just behind the Citadella is the **Museo Donizettiano** (http://fondazione.bergamoestoria.it; Donizetti Birthplace Museum; June–Sept Tue–Sun 9.30am–1pm and 2.30–6pm, Oct–May Tue–Fri 9.30–1pm, Sat–Sun 9.30am–1pm and 2.30–6pm). Within are several of the composer's artefacts, such as his piano and portraits.

Ongoing excavations in Bergamo have unearthed traces of an Early Christian basilica below the Duomo, and part of the Roman forum near the Palazzo del Podesta.

Basilica di Santa Maria Maggiore in Bergamo.

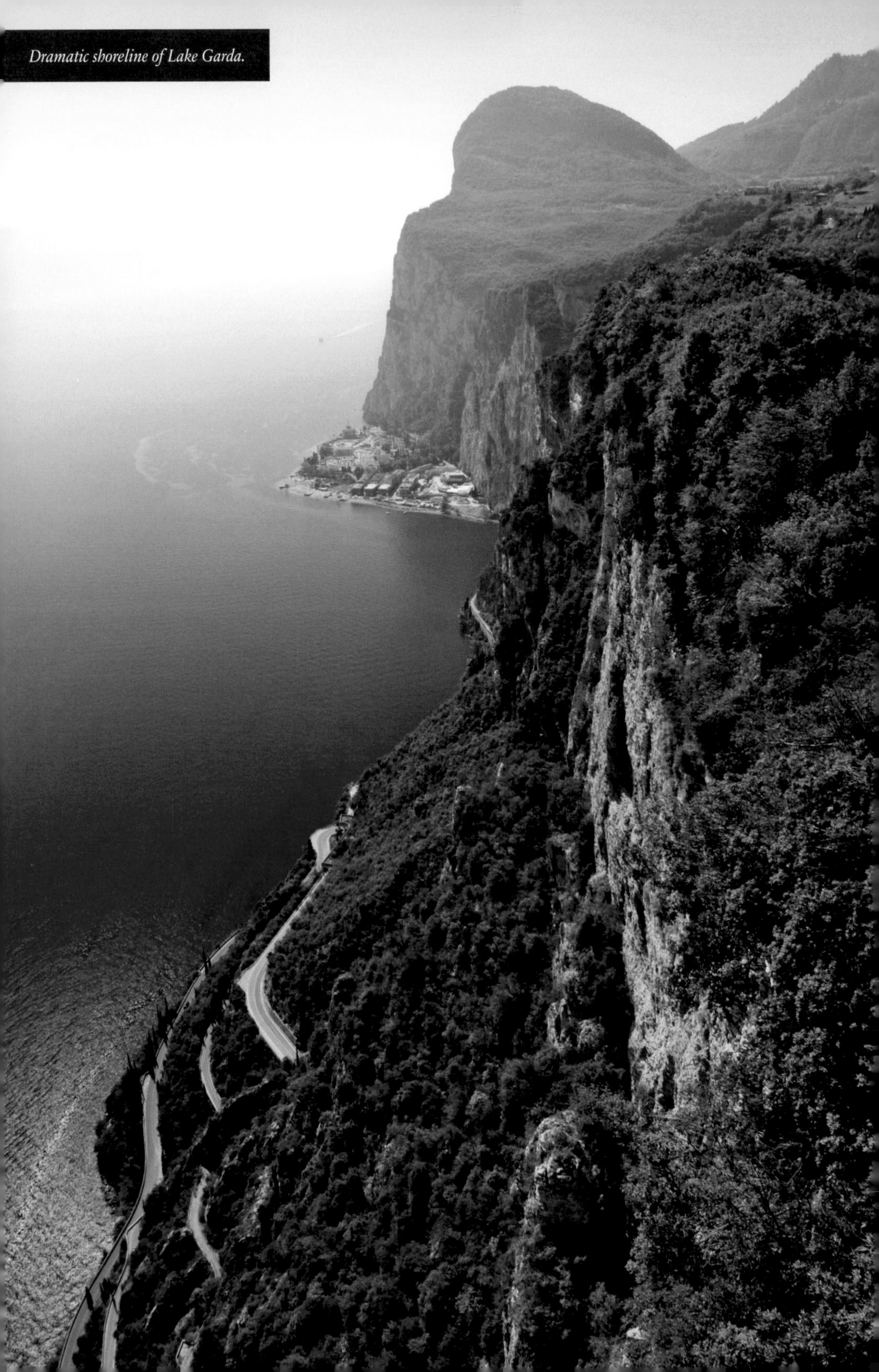
Dramatic shoreline of Lake Garda.

THE LAKES

Sheltered by the Alps, most Italian Lakes benefit from a superb microclimate, allowing for that perfect combination – a Mediterranean lifestyle in a mountainous landscape.

The Italian Lakes have long been a retreat for romantics. Writers drawn to their shores include Pliny the Younger, Shelley, Stendhal and D.H. Lawrence, all entranced by the beauty of the region. There are five major lakes in the Italian lake district; from west to east: lakes Maggiore (with its stunning Borromean Islands), Lugano, Como, Iseo and Garda, and each has its own character. Most of the lakes enjoy sheltered microclimates that make them warm and mild in winter, with the southern shores benefiting from winter sunshine – while the northern shores tend to be overshadowed by Alpine peaks.

The lakes were formed during the last Ice Age, which ended around 11,000 years ago, and are the result of glaciers thrusting down from the Alps and gouging out deep valleys wherever softer rock created an easy pathway for the ice. Later, as the ice melted, the lakes were formed in the valley bottoms.

Lake Maggiore

The westernmost lake, **Lago Maggiore** ❶, has a special attraction: the **Isole Borromee** ❷ (**Borromean Islands**), named after their owners, a Milanese family whose members included a cardinal, a bishop and a saint. **Isola Bella**, the most romantic of the three islands, was a desolate rock with just a few cottages until the 16th century,

when Count Charles Borromeo III decided to civilise the island in honour of his wife, Isabella. With the help of the architect Angelo Crivelli, Charles designed the splendid palace and gardens (www.isoleborromee.it; mid-Mar–mid Oct daily 9am–5.30pm).

Isola dei Pescatori is, as the name suggests, a fishing village. Another Borromean palace and elaborate botanical gardens decorate **Isola Madre** (same opening times as Isola Bella). All three are served by ferries (www.navigazion elaghi.it) from the main lakeside towns.

Main Attractions

Borromean Islands
Lake Como by boat
Bellagio
Monte Isola, Lake Iseo
Val Camonica rock carvings
Santa Giulia Museum
Sirmione
Lake Garda by boat

Sun and sport at Torbole, Lake Garda.

The most celebrated settlement on the shores of Lake Maggiore is **Stresa** ❸ (put on the literary map by Hemingway's *A Farewell to Arms*), with its many beautiful Belle Epoque villas. Two famous villas adjoining the landing stage are the **Villa Ducale**, residence of the philosopher Antonio Rosmini (1797–1855), and the **Villa Pallavicino** (www.parcozoopallavicino.it; daily mid-Mar–Oct 9am–6pm) just outside town on the road to Arona, remarkable for its fine gardens. From Stresa, it's a short drive or 20-minute cable-car ride (www.stresa-mottarone.it) from Stresa Lido to the summit of **Monte Mottarone** and a stunning view of the Alps, the lake and the town below.

Baveno ❹, northwest of Stresa, is noted for its villas, among them the **Castello Branca** where Queen Victoria spent the spring of 1879. The drive south from Stresa to **Arona** ❺ along the Lungolago is especially pretty: the road is tree-lined, the views of the lakes and islands spectacular. Arona itself is a rather unremarkable resort town, but it does contain a number of attractive 15th-century buildings.

Lake Lugano

Much of **Lago di Lugano** ❻ lies within Swiss territory; only the very eastern tip is Italian, plus the enclave of Campione d'Italia, a little lakeside town that remains proudly and typically Italian, whilst being entirely surrounded by Swiss territory (and using Swiss currency and postage stamps). Visitors come to Campione for the casino (www.casinocampione.it) and its nightlife.

Lake Como

Lago di Como ❼, known locally as "Lario", is the most dramatic of the lakes. It is almost 50km (30 miles) long and up to 5km (3 miles) across; at 410 metres (1,345ft), it is the deepest inland lake in Europe. At many points the shore is a sheer cliff, and the Alps (providing year-round skiing on the glaciers, although they are receding) loom like a wall at the northern end of the lake.

Como ❽ itself is a historic yet thriving town. Silk-weaving, a traditional craft, is still significant, with Como supplying 70 percent of Europe's silk, including to most of the big fashion

Postcard-pretty Como tumbles down to the shoreline.

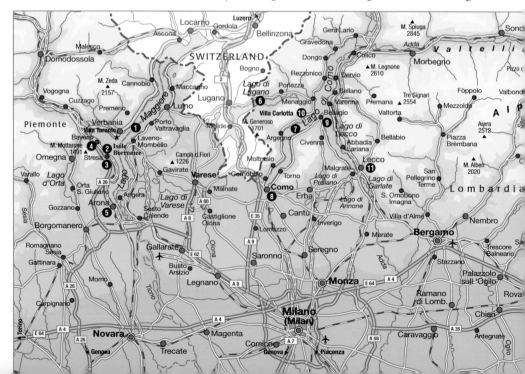

designers. The silk itself may now come from China but it is "finished" in Como, with the creation of sheens, pleating and veining. (That said, in recent years the region has opened up silk factories so the trend of importing the raw material is slowly shifting back to Italy.)

Como's peaceful gardens, the **Giardini Pubblici,** are home to the Tempio Voltiano (Tue–Sun 10am–6pm; free first Sun of the month), a classic rotunda dedicated to Alessandro Volta, who gave his name to the volt. Many of the instruments he used in his electrical experiments are on display.

It's an easy walk across the town to **Santa Maria Maggiore** (www.cattedraledicomo.it; Mon–Sat 7.30–7.30, Sun until 7.30pm, museum Mon–Sat 9.30am–5.30pm, Sun 1–4.30pm), Como's 14th-century marble cathedral. The intricately carved portal is flanked by a statue of the two Plinys, who were among the earliest admirers of Lake Como. "Are you given to studying, or do you prefer fishing or hunting, or do you go in for all three?" the younger Pliny asked a friend, and

boasted that all three activities were possible at Lake Como.

The 11th-century church of **Sant'-Abbondio** (daily 8am–6pm, until 4.30 in winter) on the outskirts of Como will transport you back to Como's pre-resort days, when it was a pious and prosperous medieval village. The chances are that you will have this solemn Lombardic church to yourself, including the 14th-century frescoes of the *Life of Jesus* in the apse.

It can take an hour of driving on narrow, twisting roads to reach **Bellagio** ❾, "the jewel of the lake", from Como. Going by public boat from Como's pier is a more pleasant way of getting there. Bellagio sits on the point of land that divides Lake Como into three parts, revealing a spectacular view of the Alps. "Sublimity and grace here combine to a degree which is equalled but not surpassed by the most famous site in the world, the Bay of Naples," wrote Stendhal in *The Charterhouse of Parma*. The Frenchman set part of his novel in the **Villa Carlotta** ❿ (across the lake from Bellagio) after staying here as a guest. Today the villa (www.villacarlotta.it; Apr–mid-Oct daily

Santa Maria delle Neve, Iseo.

9am–6pm, Mar and mid-Oct 10am–5pm, Nov until 4pm), originally built by a Prussian princess for her daughter, and its idyllic gardens, provide the perfect setting for a picnic lunch.

On the way to Lecco, in Mandello del Lario, motoring fans will want to drop into the **Moto Guzzi Museum** (www.motoguzzi.com; Mon–Fri 3–4pm, Jul 2.30–4.30pm; free admission and guided tour), one of the oldest motorcycle manufacturers in the world still operating, to see its spectacular collection and learn about the company's long history.

Lecco ⓫, at the southeastern end of Lake Como, is famous as the setting of Alessandro Manzoni's novel *The Betrothed*, a classic which most Italians study at school. The author, Italy's greatest 19th-century novelist, was a native of Lecco and a political activist instrumental in bringing about Italian unification. Visitors can explore his childhood home, the **Villa Manzoni** (Tue–Fri 9.30am–6pm, Sat–Sun from 10am).

Although Lecco's scenery is more inspiring than the sights, spare a moment for the **Basilica**, with its medieval frescoes depicting *The Annunciation*,

Lake Garda ferry.

The Deposition and *The Life of St Anthony*. Lecco's pride and joy is the Ponte Vecchio, the reconstructed 14th-century bridge spanning the River Adda.

Lake Iseo

Lago d'Iseo ⓬ is sweeter, quieter and less self-consciously quaint than its rival lakes. Measuring 24km (15 miles) long by 5km (3 miles), the lake is dominated by the bulky form of **Monte Isola** which, at a height of 600 metres (1,970ft), makes it the highest lake island in Europe. The charm of Lake Iseo embraces the lakeside port of **Iseo**, as well as the peaceful island itself, whose shores are lined with reliable fish restaurants. A day out in the neighbouring vineyards of **Franciacorta** is a way to combine prestigious wine estates with castles and gastro inns.

To the northeast, **Capo di Ponte** is the springboard for exploring the unpolished Val Camonica (www.vallecamonicaunesco.it), renowned for its prehistoric rock carvings. In Italy's first designated Unesco World Heritage site, over 300,000 rock carvings have been found, dating as far back as 8,000 years ago. The carvings, etched into glacier-seared sandstone, are a record of the hunting, farming, social and religious rituals of the local Camuni tribes. The sites are scattered over a wide area, but the most convenient site is the **Parco Nazionale delle Incisioni Rupestri di Naquane** (National Rock Engravings Park; www.parcoincisioni.capodiponte.beniculturali.it; Tue–Sun 8.30am–7pm, Mon–Sat until 4.30pm and Sun until 1.30pm in winter). Given the bewildering array, focus on the impressive boulders nearest the entrance.

Brescia

Southeast of the lake is Lombardy's prosperous but vastly underrated second city, **Brescia** ⓭, which has a world-class museum. Indeed, **Santa Giulia Museo della Città** (www.bresciamusei.com; Tue–Sun mid-June–Sept 10.30am–4pm, Oct–mid-June 11am–5pm) is arguably the best historical and

archaeological museum complex in Italy and part of the Unesco "Lombards in Italy" sites. Santa Giulia showcases Brescia's past in monuments from the Bronze Age to Roman times and the present day. The beguiling complex incorporates an 8th-century nunnery, the Renaissance church and cloisters of Santa Giulia, the Romanesque oratory of Santa Maria, and the Lombard basilica of San Salvatore. The church alone is a major monument, with Byzantine, Lombard and Roman remains.

Also in Brescia is the Capitolium and Teatro Romano, a reminder of the city's rich Roman heritage. Surmounting the hill, a medieval castle houses the **Museo delle Armi**, Italy's finest collection of ancient weaponry (www.bresciamusei.com; June–Sept Fri–Sun 11am–7pm, Oct–Mar Thu–Fri 9am–4pm, Sat–Sun 10am–5pm).

Lake Garda

Lago di Garda ⓮ is the cleanest and largest of the Italian lakes. It is especially popular with northern European tourists, who come to sail, windsurf and water-ski. Its equable climate is responsible for Soave and Valpolicella wines, as well as for producing the most northerly olives in Europe, close to Riva del Garda. Lemons, grown in Limone del Garda for centuries, also add to the lakes' Mediterranean air.

On the shores of this lake is a garish remnant of the Fascist era – **Il Vittoriale** ⓯ – the home of the flamboyant Italian poet and patriot Gabriele d'Annunzio, which was given to him by his greatest admirer, Benito Mussolini (www.vittoriale.it; grounds and museum daily Apr–Oct 9am–8pm, Mon from 10am, Nov–Mar Tue–Sun 9am–4pm, last entry one hour before closing; house which must be seen on a guided tour). Located in **Gardone Riviera**, once Lake Garda's most fashionable resort, Il Vittoriale is more than a house, it is a shrine to d'Annunzio's dreams of Italian imperialism. Included in the estate is the prow of the warship *Puglia*, built into the hillside. In the auditorium, the

plane d'Annunzio flew during World War I is suspended from the ceiling. The house itself is a monument to megalomania but still remains one of the most memorable sights in Italy.

From Salò and Gardone Riviera it takes no more than an hour to reach **Sirmione** ⓰, a medieval town built on a spit of land extending into the lake. The picturesque castle and self-conscious charm of the resort means that it is besieged on summer weekends.

The **Rocca Scaligera** (www.roccascaligerasirmione.beniculturali.it; Tue–Sat 8.30am–7.30pm), a fairytale castle, dominates the town's entrance. It was originally the fortress of the Scaligeri family, rulers of Garda in the 13th century, and it is said that they entertained the poet Dante here. An enjoyable hour or two can be spent exploring the local shops, dipping into churches and following the footpath that leads to the tip of the peninsula, with its extensive ruins of a Roman spa, the **Grotte di Catullo** (www.grottedicatullo.beniculturali.it; Tue–Sat 8.30am–7.30pm, Sun until 6.30pm, in winter until 4.30pm and the museum until 7.30pm).

Villa Fiordaliso on Lake Garda.

PIEDMONT, VALLE D'AOSTA AND LIGURIA

From high Alpine pastures to the sparkling Ligurian Sea, the northwestern corner of Italy has a magic all of its own.

Main Attractions
Turin
Venaria Reale
Le Langhe
Alba
Aosta
Genoa
Portofino
Le Cinque Terre

The Alps form a dramatic backdrop to Turin.

The bordering nations of France and Switzerland have greatly influenced the cultural life of this northwestern region, as have the unforgiving Alpine landscapes. Turin, the capital of the Piedmont region, has reinvented itself as a city of the arts, design and gastronomy. Travel outside the city and you will find fairytale castles and ancient vineyards. The alpine valleys of the Valle d'Aosta, dotted with castles, entice hikers in summer and skiers in winter. Coming down to the coast, Genoa is at the centre of the Ligurian region, with its museums and traditional cafés. Here you are far from the mountains and can sun yourself on the stylish Italian Riviera.

Piedmont (Piemonte) may strike today's visitors as not very Italian but the particularly sensible Piedmontese twist on Italian life is not unappealing. No wonder that it was a Piedmontese king, Victor Emmanuel, and his Piedmontese adviser, Count Camillo di Cavour, who guided Italy to independence.

Yet sensible **Turin ❻** (Torino) is also a seductive city, with its gilt-encrusted cafés designed for dangerous liaisons, and its Baroque squares built for grand gestures. Curiously, this former industrial powerhouse, first capital of a unified Italy and historic home to the Savoy kings, has always been ambivalent about its heritage. The Piedmontese are diffident and undemonstrative by nature; they would rather let the city do the talking. Of course, it helps if the menu includes Italy's most aristocratic cuisine and finest wines – served in the capital of Slow Food. As the cradle of Italian café culture, the city also abounds in opulent coffee houses and chocolate shops.

But Turin now prefers to cast itself as a vibrant, visionary city, proud of its contemporary arts scene, its cinematic heritage and its cutting-edge design. Turin was made World Design Capital in 2008, which confirmed its status as Italy's leading city for contemporary

art and design. The city has built on its industrial car design heritage to become a creative place for all designers and architects. This creative confidence is demonstrated in the glut of cool city art galleries and the stylish Luci d'Artista festival, which celebrates contemporary art installations in public spaces. Turin's innate conservatism is being challenged by the city's burgeoning new districts and by the success of Lingotto, an exhibition centre born out of the former Fiat factory, which was the epicentre of the 2006 Winter Olympic Games (www. lingottofiere.it).

Historic town centre

The hub of civic life in Turin is the fashionable **Via Roma**, an arcaded shopping street that connects the **Stazione Porta Nuova** Ⓐ with **Piazza Castello** Ⓑ, a huge rectangular Renaissance square planned in 1584. In the centre stands **Palazzo Madama**, a 15th-century castle that houses the **Museo Civico di Arte Antica** (Museum of Ancient Art; www.palazzomadamatorino.it, Wed–Mon 10am–6pm). Included in this museum's collections is a copy of part of the famous *Book of Hours* of the Duc de Berry, illustrated by Jan van Eyck.

Here, too, is the Baroque church of **San Lorenzo**, once the royal chapel (http://eng.sanlorenzo.torino.it). The royal residence was the 17th-century **Palazzo Reale** Ⓒ (www.museireali.beniculturali. it; Tue–Sun 8.30am–7.30pm; guided tours; combined ticket for all museums; free first Sun of the month; garden open daily). From its balcony, Prince Carlo Alberto declared war on Austria in March 1848. The palace is now home to the **Galleria Sabauda** (details as for palace). Made up of the main art collection of the House of Savoy, this is a treasure trove of Italian Masters, Dutch and Flemish artists and French landscape artists. Also open to the public are the Royal Armoury and Museum of Antiquities (times as above).

Behind the Palazzo Reale, in **Piazza San Giovanni**, are the Renaissance **Duomo** Ⓓ (Mon–Sat 7am–12.30pm

and 3–7pm, Sun 8am–12.30pm and 3–7pm) and Baroque **Campanile**. The Duomo was damaged by fire in 1997, but fortunately the flames did not consume the **Cappella della Sacra Sindone** (Chapel of the Holy Shroud). The chapel contains the Turin Shroud, for centuries believed to be the shroud in which Christ was wrapped after the Crucifixion. The cloth is imprinted with the image of a bearded man crowned with thorns. Although controversy reigns about the authenticity of the shroud, thousands of fervent believers flock to see it on the rare occasions it is on public display (check www.sindone.org; daily 8am–7pm; booking necessary).

On Via San Domenico, the **MAO (Museo d'Arte Orientale)** Ⓔ is Turin's impressive Museum of Oriental Art (tel: 011-443 6927; www.maotorino.it; Tue–Fri 10am–6pm, Sat–Sun 11am–7pm). The eclectic collection is divided according to theme, but highlights include: the Japanese meditative rock gardens; the Chinese ceremonial bronzes and lacquer-ware; Buddhist statuary from Southeast Asia; and Islamic ceramics from Turkey, Iran and Iraq.

TIP

The superb Torino+Piemonte Card (www.turismotorino.org) allows free entry to over 180 museums, monuments, exhibitions, fortresses, castles and royal residences in Turin and Piedmont, along with free public transport, including on the Po river boats.

Turin tram.

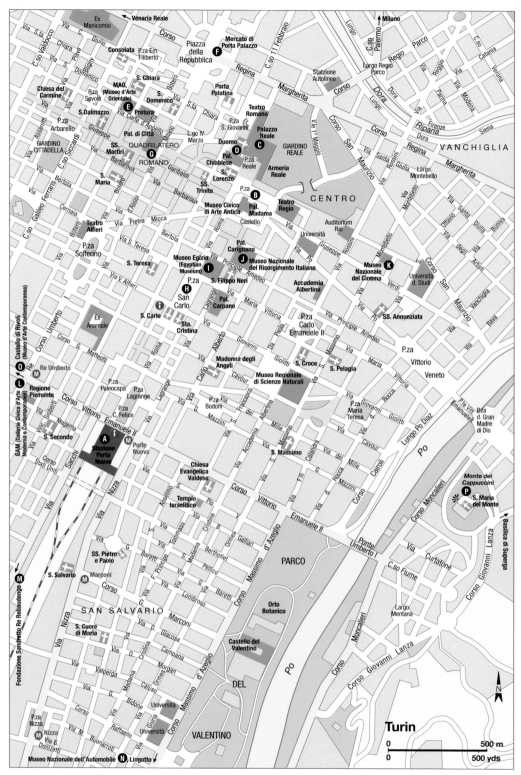

Turin

0   500 m
0   500 yds

Nearby is the **Porta Palazzo market** **F** (Mon–Fri 7am–2pm, some parts 8.30am–1.30pm, Sat 7am–7.30pm), which sprawls around Piazza della Repubblica. The market attracts a cosmopolitan crowd and sells everything from flowers to hams, cheeses and squid. The market adjoins the intriguing **Quadrilatero Romano** **G** district, the so-called Roman Quarter west of Piazza Castello. Clustered around the ruins of a Roman theatre and gate, this peaceful pedestrianised area livens up at night. Nearby, sedate **Piazza San Carlo** **H** is dubbed Turin's drawing room, and is a place of Baroque facades and Belle Epoque coffee houses.

Around the corner is the **Museo Egizio** **I**, the revamped Egyptian Museum (www.museoegizio.it; Mon 9am–2pm, Tue–Sun 9am–6.30pm) housed in the Palazzo dell'Accademia delle Scienze, off Via Roma. As the greatest assemblage Egyptian treasures outside Cairo, the newly revamped collection is unmissable. Its centrepiece is a statue of Rameses II, one of the masterpieces of Egyptian sculpture.

Across the road in the Palazzo Carignano is the **Museo Nazionale del Risorgimento Italiano** **J** (www.museo risorgimentotorino.it; Tue–Sun 10am–6pm) reopened in 2011 after renovation to coincide with the 150th anniversary of Italian Unification. Its 30 rooms display Italian nationalism through the eyes of not only Turin, Piedmont and Italy but the whole of Europe, too.

Cine scene

For sheer theatricality, the Egyptian Museum is surpassed by the star-studded **Museo Nazionale del Cinema** **K** (Cinema Museum; www.museocinema. it; Wed–Fri and Sun–Mon 9am–8pm, until 11pm on Sat), set in a show-stopping, cavernous, former synagogue, dissected by a panoramic, glass-walled lift. This is the iconic **Mole Antonelliana**, a local landmark. From 1906 to 1916 Turin was the world film-production capital, until overtaken by Hollywood. The story of cinema is told through myriad means, from film clips to costumes ranging from Marilyn Monroe's bodice to Fellini's scarf, coat and hat. The ride in the lift to the top (times as above) leads to spectacular views over the city and the Alps; or you can also take the stairs up to the cupola (guided tours Sat–Sun noon–4.30pm).

Modern art-lovers will be tempted by the **GAM** **L** (Galleria Civica d'Arte Moderna e Contemporanea; www.gamtorino.it; Tue–Sun 10am–6pm; free first Tue of the month). The museum has excellent visiting exhibitions and an illustrious permanent collection featuring works by such luminaries as Picasso, Modigliani, Chagall, Renoir and Klee.

For more contemporary art, visit the **Fondazione Sandretto Re Rebaudengo** **M** (www.fsrr.org, Thu 8am–11pm, Fri–Sun noon–7pm; free Thu), where cutting-edge art is showcased in a minimalist gallery in the gritty San Paolo district. There's also the **Merz Fondazione** (www.fondazionemerz.org) and the **Parco Arte Vivente PAV** (http://parco artevivente.it), a landscaped open-air exhibition space with an ecological theme.

TIP

Juventus fans – and football fans in general – will want to visit the team's state-of-the-art stadium, which also includes a museum (the J-Museum). Even better: take a match-day special tour (information and booking at www.juventus.com).

Inside the Museo Nazionale del Cinema.

FACT

The Slow Food Movement was born in Piedmont and urges us to "rediscover the flavours and savours of regional cooking and banish the degrading effects of fast food". Sample the delights at the October Salone del Gusto (www.salonedelgusto. it), staged in Turin's Lingotto complex.

Lingotto, car capital

It is no surprise that the car capital of Italy has a fine car museum. It can take hours to explore the **Museo Nazionale dell'Automobile** (www.museoauto. it; Fri–Sat 10am–9pm, Wed–Thu and Sun 10am–7pm, Mon 10am–2pm, Tue 2–7pm). The revamped and expanded museum has a first-class library and documentation centre, a bookshop and auditorium. Exhibits include the earliest Fiat, the Itala that won the world's longest automobile race (between Peking and Paris in 1907) and an elegant Rolls-Royce Silver Ghost. This area south of the city centre was the heart of Turin's car industry. The Fiat company, founded in 1899, made Turin the city of cars. The areas of Lingotto, Italia 61, Mirafiori and Millefonti, once the powerhouse of the industry, have been transformed into a multi-million-euro "suburbs project", with many sports and leisure facilities, which were constructed for the 2006 Winter Olympics.

Under the skilful eye of architect Renzo Piano, the area was transformed into a multi-purpose exhibition centre.

Today, it is the setting for cultural events and fairs, such as the Salone del Gusto, the showcase of the international Slow Food Movement (www.salonedelgusto. com). Lingotto also encompasses an auditorium, shopping mall, hotels and a racing track.

Turin still represents Italian passion for design and speed. In the revitalised Lingotto district, Turin's former car factory is gorgeous enough to welcome the suitably high-tech NH Lingotto Tech (www.nh-hotels.it), an Art Deco hotel with a racing track on the roof – and emblem of Turin's prestigious design heritage. This spectacular rooftop test track was the setting for a Mini Cooper car chase in the iconic *Italian Job* but is now the preserve of hotel guests with a head for heights and a passion for jogging.

Also on the Lingotto rooftop is the **Pinacoteca Giovanni e Marella Agnelli** (www.pinacoteca-agnelli.it; Tue–Sun 10am–7pm). Designed by Renzo Piano and known as "Lo Scrigno" (the jewellery box), it showcases treasures from the art collection of the Agnelli family, the owners of Fiat, including works by Picasso and Renoir.

Eataly

Lingotto's final surprise is reserved for foodies. **Eataly** (www.eataly.net; Via Nizza 230/14; tel: 011-1950 6801; Sat–Sun 10am–10.30pm) claims to be the world's largest food and wine centre. Appropriately for Turin, it has a history: the factory that originally produced Vermouth has become a gastrodome in the fullest sense of the word. The aperitif was first invented here in 1786, when Carpano produced Vermouth by means of a secret blend of white wine and an infusion of herbs.

Today, reborn as a food laboratory, Eataly is dedicated to the tastes of Italy. As well as meals, curious visitors can do cookery courses, wine-tastings, ice cream-making or quiz top food producers and well-known chefs. Naturally, Eataly works with Slow Food because, in Turin, eating is always about food culture as well as flavour.

Gran Paradiso National Park, south of Aosta.

To the west of the city, at the gateway to the Valle di Susa, lies the eye-catching **Castello di Rivoli**, which houses the **Museo d'Arte Contemporanea ⊙** (www.castellodirivoli.org; Tue–Fri 10am–5pm, Sat–Sun 10am–7pm). The imposing Baroque building, designed by Juvarra, contrasts with cutting-edge installations. Works by avant-garde artists such as Jeff Koons contrast dramatically with the stuccoed interior. There are around 400 pieces in the permanent collection, and major temporary exhibitions are also staged. There is a good museum café and a famous gastro-haunt, the Combal.Zero.

Cross the Po to visit the **Monte dei Cappuccini ℗**, a small hill crowned by a Capuchin convent. From here, take a bus to the **Basilica di Superga** (www.basilicadisuperga.com; Mar–Oct Thu–Tue Mon–Fri 10am–7pm, Nov–Feb Sat–Sun 10am–6pm). This basilica sits on a hill overlooking the natural amphitheatre of the Alps and the view is stunning. The circular church is dominated by its 75-metre (246ft) dome, flanked by twin 60-metre (196-ft) -high bell towers. It can be reached by car, on foot or by the Superga Rack Tramway (www.gtt.to.it/cms/en/touristfacilities#tramway).

After hurtling through museums and palaces all day, you can sink into cafés all night. Piedmontese cuisine, from creamy risotto to pungent white truffles, is among the finest in Italy. Despite all its transformations, Turin stays faithful to its café culture; you'll find sophisticated *Torinesi* in the chocolate-box interior of Caffe Baratti & Milan (www.barattiemilano.it) for example, where *cioccolato Baratti* is a deliciously dark drink. Taking place between 6 and 8pm, the ritual of the *aperitivi* remains an excuse to sample Turin's aperitifs and tapas in beguiling old-world bars.

Outside Turin

Just 10km (6 miles) to the north of the city is the stunningly restored **Venaria Reale ❼** (www.lavenaria.it; castle: Tue–Fri 9am–5pm, Sat–Sun 9am–6.30pm, gardens: Jul–Sep Tue–Fri 10am–6pm, Sat–Sun until 7.30pm, Apr–Jun Tue–Sun 9am–6.30, Mar and Oct Tue–Fri 9am–5pm, Sat–Sun until 6.30pm, Nov–Jan 9am–4pm, closed Feb; fountain water show summer Tue–Fri at noon, Sat–Sun at 7.30pm). Often called the Italian Versailles, this was a royal hunting lodge that became a royal palace, complete with frescoed interiors, chapels, stables, parkland and a model town.

Southeast of Turin, Piedmont turns into a region of rolling hills, faintly reminiscent of Tuscany. Like Tuscany it is an excellent wine-growing area, with the most prestigious estates in **Le Langhe,** the area around Alba. The hills are cloaked with vineyards and crowned with medieval fortresses.

From Turin head towards Alba along the *autostrada*. If you have time, make a stop at **Bra ❽**, birthplace of the Slow Food Movement (see page 101), to see a fine Baroque church, **Sant' Andrea**. The slopes surrounding the small town of La Morra, 10km (6 miles) from Bra, represent red wine country. In particular, the charming village of **Barolo ❾** boasts a medieval castle, wine-tasting centre and vineyards that produce the

Some of Italy's finest wines come from Le Langhe, the hilly region south of Turin.

Castello di Aymavilles in the Valle d'Aosta.

"king" of Italian red wines. In neighbouring **Grinzane Cavour** ❿ looms the Castello Cavour, an imposing medieval castle, the feudal home of Count Cavour, which also houses a wine and food museum (www.castellogrinzane.com; Apr–Aug Wed–Mon 9.30am–7pm, Feb–Mar and Nov–Dec until 6pm, Sep–Nov daily 9.30am–6pm).

As the centre of the white truffle district, prosperous **Alba** ⓫ has long been a favourite with gourmets. Truffles can be sniffed at the autumnal truffle fairs or sampled in the city's reliable restaurants during the October–January truffle season. At other times, you will have to content yourself with culture, and the late Gothic cathedral, with its noted Renaissance choir.

For more tickling of the tastebuds, head to **Asti** ⓬, famous for its production of sparkling Asti Spumante, even if Piedmontese reds, notably Barolo and Barbaresco, are vastly superior.

Valle d'Aosta

The beautiful Alpine valleys around Piedmont have much to offer. The region is noted for its glaciers, hilltop castles,

Genoa's historic streets.

clear mountain lakes and streams, pine forests and green meadows. The most striking area is the Valle d'Aosta. Here rise Europe's highest mountains: Mont Blanc, Monte Rosa and the Cervino (Matterhorn). The capital, **Aosta** ⓭, was an important city in Roman times and has many interesting Roman ruins. Roman walls surround the city, and the ruins of the **Roman Theatre** (Mar–Sep daily 9am–7pm, Oct–Dec daily 10am–1pm, 2–5pm), in the northwest corner of Aosta, include the well-preserved backdrop of the stage.

Dating from Aosta's medieval period are the cathedral and several smaller churches. Among the latter group, the **Church of Sant'Orso** (daily 9am–5.30pm; to see Ottonian frescoes and priory chapel call local tourist office tel. 0165 236627; free) is the most striking, a blend of Gothic and Romanesque. St Orso – who converted the first Christians in the Valle d'Aosta – is buried beneath the altar. Be sure to visit the Romanesque cloisters, noted for their sculpted pillars.

The valley southeast of Aosta abounds in fine castles, notably the

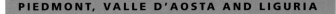

fairy-tale fortress at **Fénis** ⓮ (Apr–Sept daily 9am–7pm, Oct–Mar Wed–Mon 10am–1pm and 2–5pm), which bristles with towers, turrets and crenellations, and **Issogne** ⓯ (daily 9am–7pm in summer, 10am–1pm, 2–5pm in winter), which is more a chateau than a fortress.

Centred on **Cogne**, just to the west, the **Gran Paradiso park** ⓰, (www. pngp.it) at 4,061 metres (13,321ft), was the royal hunting reserve of the House of Savoy but is now a paradise for ibex, chamois, marmots and ermines. Set in a landscape of meadows, valleys, glaciers, waterfalls and high Alpine beauty, the park is criss-crossed with mule-tracks and marked trails. The *rifugi* (mountain huts) welcome summer hikers.

The region of Liguria

Liguria is still an underrated destination. Centred on regenerated Genoa, this rugged region celebrates the outdoors lifestyle, with picturesque fishing villages, hidden coves and an authentic hinterland. Protected by the Alps, and perched on a crescent-shaped sliver of coast, Ligurian resorts enjoy balmy weather, with the Riviera di Levante the wilder stretch, especially around the Cinque Terre coastal reserve. Portofino is perfection, an idealised fishing village that put the Italian Riviera on the map.

Sandwiched between the mountains and the sea, **Genoa** ⓱ is a concertina of a city, with slate-topped palaces and squat skyscrapers bearing down on the old port. By turns sleekly streamlined and self-consciously restored, the ancient port is the glittering symbol of regenerated Genoa. Above is a dramatic natural amphitheatre ringed by ridge-top forts. In between are alleys burrowing under medieval palaces, funiculars reaching dizzying heights, and tunnels emerging where least expected.

Genoa is a complex yet conspiratorial city. Walk everywhere in this pedestrianised maze, stopping for coffee in time-warp cafés; stroll with your gaze focused upwards: virtually every alleyway has striking architectural details, from friezes to *trompe l'œil* frescoes.

Immediately behind the docks, the lower city begins. The ancient, winding alleys – called *carrugi* – are lined with exotic shops. The late afternoon *passeggiata* takes place on the elegant **Via Luccoli Ⓐ**.

Not far from the docks stands the **Stazione Principe Ⓑ**, with a striking statue of Christopher Columbus facing the station. From here, Via Balbi leads past sombre Renaissance palaces to the centre. Stop at the 17th-century **Palazzo Reale Ⓒ**, famous for the Galleria degli Specchi (Hall of Mirrors) and its art collection (www.palazzorealegenova. beniculturali.it; Tue–Sat 9am–7pm, Sun 1.30–7pm; free first Sun of the month).

Continue along Via Balbi until it becomes the patrician **Via Garibaldi Ⓓ**. Once the heart of aristocratic and mercantile Genoa, this is now the museum district, with late Renaissance palaces sprouting grandiose courtyards, hanging gardens, the odd waterfall and Baroque grotto, as well as major art collections. These Unesco-listed homes of the richest families were designated ambassadorial residences, "Palazzi dei Rolli", fit for visiting kings or courtiers.

Inside Genoa's Palazzo Ducale.

Stylish San Remo.

Palazzo Bianco ❺ (Tue–Fri 9am–7pm, Sat–Sun 10am–7.30pm in summer, Tue–Fri 9am–6.30pm, Sat–Sat 9.30am–6.30pm in winter) is one of the most magnificent palaces and boasts a collection of Flemish masters. Across the street is **Palazzo Rosso ❻** (same times as Palazzo Bianco), where great art by Veronese and Guercino is outdone by the frescoed and stuccoed interior and lovely courtyard.

Nearby, on Piazza Pelliceria, **Palazzo Spinola ❼** (www.palazzospinola.beni culturali.it; Mon 8.30am–1.30pm, Tue–Sat 8.30am–7.30pm, Sun 1.30–7.30pm) is a gilded tribute to its ancestral owners. When the Spinola line died out in 1958, the palace was preserved in aspic, with its frescoed family chapel and gallery of mirrors, modelled on Versailles. It now houses the National Gallery.

Further south, the Romanesque-Gothic **Duomo ❽** is dedicated to St Lawrence, and a Gothic portal depicts the Roman saint's gruesome martyrdom. While being burnt alive, St Lawrence said to his tormentors: "One side has been roasted, turn me over and eat it."

The Doria family, who ruled Genoa in the Middle Ages, built their residences and a private church around the **Piazza San Matteo ❾**, lying just behind the cathedral. Each of the buildings on this small, elegant piazza has a black-and-white facade. Between San Matteo and the port lies the most beguiling part of Old Genoa. Also near the cathedral is the 16th-century **Palazzo Ducale ❿**, (www.palazzoducale.genova.it) once the seat of government but now a cool cultural centre, which stages concerts, theatre and art exhibitions.

Towards the medieval city's eastern limits is the **Porta Soprana**, the twin-towered gateway and the **Casa Colombo de Cristoforo** (www.coop culture.it; June–Aug Tue–Sun 11am–6pm, Apr–May and Sep–Oct Tue–Sun 11am–5pm, Nov–Mar Tue–Thu 11am–3pm, Fri–Sun 10am–4pm). This is the reconstructed boyhood home of Genoa's most famous son, Christopher Columbus (1451–1506).

Genoa's port

The aromas of pesto, pasta and grilled fish mingle in the labyrinthine alleys behind the glittering waterfront and the **Porto Antico ⓚ** (www.portoantico. it). As a medieval trading empire, Genoa fought with Venice and Pisa for mastery over the Mediterranean shipping channels and trade with the Orient. Today, the city is Italy's most important port, with one of the most densely packed historical centres in Europe.

Genoa's second-most famous son is the architect Renzo Piano, whose work has helped transform the city. The transformation began with the Columbus celebrations in 1992, which marked the 500th anniversary of the discovery of the Americas. Building upon Piano's work on the harbour, the Porto Antico was given a facelift for the city's celebrations as European City of Culture in 2004. In this model urban regeneration project, which covered the whole city, the port area retained its raffish charm, with rough and ready dockside cafés, at one with the sensitive conversion of

Camogli.

shipyards and customs houses.

Styled on an ocean-going cargo ship docked in the harbour, Renzo Piano's **Acquario** (Aquarium; www.acquariodigenova.it; daily 8.30am–9pm, last entrance 2 hours before closing) is the biggest in Europe, and is one of Italy's most visited attractions. The Aquarium houses spectacular shark and dolphin tanks, and plays a vital role in monitoring the coast and rescuing beached dolphins.

Next door, Renzo Piano's **La Biosfera**, also called **La Bolla**, (www.biosferagenova.it; daily Apr–Sep 10am–7pm, Mar and Oct until 6pm, Nov–Feb until 5pm) is a futuristic glass-and-steel bubble containing tropical plants and a collection of rare ferns, among which butterflies flit around freely. Inspired by sails, **Il Bigo** ❶ (same times as Aquarium; times usually reduced in winter) is an enormous crane, visible for miles, which whisks passengers 40 metres (130ft) high in a cylindrical lift for panoramic views over the city and waterfront.

The dockyards (Darsena) have also been regenerated, creating new entertainment and cultural centres. Maritime culture is showcased in the **Galata**

Museo del Mare (Museum of the Sea; www.galatamuseodelmare.it; daily Mar–Oct 10am–7.30pm, Nov–Feb Tue–Fri 10am–6pm, Sat–Sun 10am–7.30pm, last entry 1 hour before closing). The highlight is a faithful reconstruction of a 17th-century Genoese galley, a design that conquered the world.

With the redesigned waterfront, Genoa now has a port worthy of a maritime republic. As well as welcoming new museums, Porto Antico functions as the new city piazza: it has a swimming pool that transforms into an open-air theatre in summer; and an ice rink that turns into a summer concert venue. All done with great taste and no hint of a theme park.

The Italian Rivieras

Flanking Genoa are two distinctive coasts and different moods. The western **Riviera di Ponente**, stretching from Genoa to the French border, is generally home to the larger, long-established resorts. In contrast, the eastern **Riviera di Levante** is characterised by rocky cliffs and promontories, as well as by smaller, more romantic resorts, which

San Remo's Russian Orthodox church.

In Genoa's aquarium.

GENOA CAFÉ LIFE

Sweet-toothed Genoa is serious about its pastry shops and traditional tea-rooms, where you can tuck into cakes and coffee at most times of day. Caffè Klainguti (Via di Soziglia 100) is a marble-and-gilt tearooms, bar and pastry shop in business since 1829. The Art Nouveau tearooms, complete with chandeliers, are a classic haunt for shoppers. Romanengo (Piazza di Soziglia 74) is the most celebrated *pasticceria* in town, a frescoed, mirrored and chandeliered setting for pyramids of cakes, chocolate and candied fruit, with secret family recipes dating back to 1780, including the delicate rose products, There is another branch at Via Roma 51. Pasticceria Villa (Via del Portello 2, www.villa1827.it) is noted for *pandolce*, a rich cake studded with candied fruit.

are mostly overgrown fishing villages.

Heading towards France from Genoa, miss the industrial port of **Savona** in favour of **Finale Ligure** ⓲, where the church of **San Biagio** is graced by an octagonal Gothic bell tower.

Albenga ⓳, the most appealing town on the Riviera di Ponente, is a Roman town with well-preserved medieval walls, 17th-century gates and a cathedral dating from the 5th century. Even older are the Roman aqueduct and the ruins of a Roman amphitheatre. In addition to the historic monuments are opportunities for swimming and boating. The neighbouring resort of **Alassio** ⓴ has long been popular with celebrities, who are drawn to the pretty bay and long sandy beach.

The resort of **San Remo** ㉑ was once a watering hole of the European aristocracy and retains an air of sophistication, accentuated by its palm-lined promenade and popular casino. The **Chiesa Russa**, an authentic Russian Orthodox church (1913) reflects San Remo's heyday as a haunt of the Russian nobility (daily 9.30am–12.30pm and 3–6.30pm). Another landmark is the Art Nouveau

Villa Nobel, erstwhile home of philanthropist Alfred Nobel (1833–96). But the biggest boost to tourism is the exciting new coastal cycle-pedestrian path, which follows a disused railway line and revels in stunning sea and mountain views (see box).

Further along the coast is the more charming **Bordighera** ㉒, where the medieval Old Town is complemented by a palm-lined promenade, which makes a delightful evening *passeggiata*, with artisanal ice cream the usual pretext. Just inland lies a rugged, more authentic Liguria, where picturesque **Dolceacqua** ㉓ surveys a ruined castle, humpbacked stone bridge and vineyards beyond.

The gateway to France is via rundown **Ventimiglia** ㉔, a centre of flower cultivation, with an excellent Friday market and a dilapidated medieval quarter. Set on the Cape about 6km (4 miles) away is the **Giardini Hanbury** (www.giardini-hanbury.com; mid-June–mid-Sept daily 9.30am–7pm, Mar–mid June and mid-Sep–mid Oct until 6pm, mid Oct–Feb until 5pm). Here, Sir Thomas Hanbury, an English botanist and Victorian merchant, created an atmospheric botanical

Portovenere.

THE RIVIERA ROUTE

A spectacular new cycle and pedestrian path hugs the picturesque Ligurian coast en route to the French Riviera. It is the perfect way to explore quaint fishing villages and the glamorous resort of San Remo.

The first 24km (15 miles) from Ospedaletti to San Lorenzo al Mare offer an exhilarating Riviera break for cycling fans, families or walkers. When finished this will be Europe's longest coastal cycle path, part of a regenerated coastal park. The 74km (46-mile) -long path will extend to Finale Ligure but already has magnificent coastal views in abundance, as well as links to food trails in the hills. The current path provides access to 5km (3 miles) of previously unreachable beaches and a vast marine park, which acts as a whale sanctuary.

paradise, widely regarded as the most evocative gardens in Liguria.

West of Ventimiglia, virtually on the French frontier, are the prehistoric caves, **Balzi Rossi** (Tue–Sun 8.30am–7.30pm). In addition to skeletons dating from over 100,000 years ago, there are fossils, fertility figures, weapons and tools.

Riviera di Levante

Among the eastern suburbs of Genoa is **Quarto dei Mille**, famous as the starting point of Garibaldi's valiant 1,000-man expedition that liberated Sicily and led to the unification of Italy. Nearby **Nervi** ㉕, reached by train or on a boat trip from Porto Antico, is dotted with lavish villas, including several turned into art museums. Come for the combination of low-key art in intimate villas, cliff-top strolls, swimming off the rocks, or grilled fish and a crisp white Cinque Terre wine.

After the beguiling former fishing village of **Camogli**, drive or take a boat to picture-postcard **Portofino** ㉖, the Riviera's calling card. Once, only fishing boats docked in the narrow, deep-green inlet, edged by high cliffs, but it is now a berth for luxury yachts.

Part of Portofino's attraction is its size. There are no beaches, and little to do except lap up the views, especially from the quaint Castello Browne at the top of the village. The pleasures of the port are visual – the watery reflection of painted facades, the ragged edges of stone heights set against the brilliant blue sky. Far more down to earth is **Rapallo** ㉗, a sedate resort, with a large beach, unpretentious hotels and a welcoming atmosphere.

"Paradise on earth" is how Lord Byron described the cluster of five little fishing villages that make up **Le Cinque Terre** ㉘ (www.lecinqueterre.org). Monterosso al Mare, Vernazza, Corniglia, Manarola and Riomaggiore cling perilously to the steep rocky coast north of La Spezia, and are best reached by train (www.parconazionale5terre.it). This 16km (10-mile) stretch of protected parkland is laced with cliffside walking trails which offer

vertiginous views over terraced olive groves and jaunty villages. Hikes usually end over a plate of pesto-scented pasta and aromatic white wine. Rumours have been circulating about limiting the number of annual visitors to Le Cinque Terre in order to preserve the site, however there are no restrictions as yet.

From Dante to Shelley, the Gulf of La Spezia has been praised so often by poets that it is also known as the Golfo dei Poeti. On its western point the elongated orange-and-yellow houses of **Portovenere** ㉙ stretch up the precipitous mountain.

Anglophiles and romantics should make a pilgrimage to the grotto from where the virile Lord Byron began his famous swim across the Gulf to visit Shelley in **Casa Magni**. If you take the 20-minute boat ride to **Lerici** ㉚ you will appreciate what a powerful swimmer the poet must have been.

Shelley had less luck against the waves when his ship sank off the coast. A plaque on Casa Magni commemorates the tragedy: "Sailing on a fragile bark he was landed, by an unforeseen chance, in the silence of the Elysian Fields."

Church above Portovenere.

La dolce vita: enjoying the nightlife.

CENTRAL ITALY

Subtle differences in art, cooking, architecture and attitude to life – even between neighbouring towns – help to form a destination that appeals to both the heart and the head.

Pisa's Leaning Tower.

To many travellers, central Italy is the true Italy – that is, the Italy they know from Merchant-Ivory films of E.M. Forster novels, or from the pictures that adorn all the tour brochures. Ironically, the people of this region are reluctant to admit to being Italian at all. They are Tuscan, Florentine, Sienese, Bolognese or Perugian – not a semantic distinction, but a deeply held conviction based on history, culture, and even tribal and genetic differences from the pre-Roman era. And this is an area where history is not the dry stuff of academic books, but a living part of the culture – for anthropologists, central Italy has long been fertile ground for testing the belief that competition for resources leads people to emphasise their differences. If you want to see this process in action, visit any Umbrian or Tuscan town during its annual festivities – not to mention Siena during Palio, or Florence during Calcio Storico (Football in Costume) – and feel the intense and elemental atmosphere of inter-parish rivalry.

Such rivalries are reflected in myriad ways that make exploring the region a delight for the sensitive and enquiring traveller. Food is an obvious indicator, whether it be the subtle differences between sheep's-milk cheeses, the more emphatic distinctions between a crisp Orvieto wine and a soft, fruity Chianti, or whether it be the view firmly held by every seafront restaurant along the Tuscan Riviera that theirs is the only authentic fish soup (*cacciucco*), and that it is far superior to anything the French produce.

Sixth-century mosaics in San Vitale Basilica, Ravenna, of Christ the Redeemer.

Art and architecture is another indicator: labels, such as Florentine, Lombardic or Pisan Romanesque, at first seem designed to confuse the uninitiated, until continued exposure to some of the world's finest artistic creations helps you distinguish between the light-filled limpidity of the School of Perugino and the crisply delineated and boldly coloured frescoes of Benozzo Gozzoli – unmistakably Florentine even when encountered in the tiny Umbrian hill town of Montefalco.

EMILIA-ROMAGNA

Italy's gastronomic heartland is also noted for its cities of art, smart beach resorts and the late Roman mosaics of Ravenna – these are beguiling cities, built on a human scale.

The reddish hues of Bologna.

Emilia-Romagna is the land of plenty, arguably the most civilised region in Italy. Fertile plains and centuries of agricultural wealth have helped foster a well-managed economy, typified by the citizens' love of good food. It is no accident that Bologna is the country's gastronomic capital and that the region is home to Parma ham and Parmesan cheese. The region is also home to some of Italy's greatest cities of art, including the Unesco World Heritage sites of Ferrara, Ravenna and Modena. Then there is the Riviera dominated by the revitalised Rimini, which now draws a crowd of more stylish Italians in summer.

Bologna

The capital of Emilia-Romagna, **Bologna ❶** mastered the art of living in medieval times when a pink-brick town grew up around Europe's oldest university. The city is also celebrated for its cuisine, its traditional left-wing stance and its beautifully preserved medieval heart. Built in a soft reddish brick, the city is lined with handsome porticoes, designed to shelter the population from inclement weather. The porticoes, Bologna's trademark, also add an air of conviviality to every-day life.

The Old City evolved around two adjoining squares, **Piazza Maggiore ❹** and **Piazza del Nettuno ❺**. Together these squares form the symbolic heart of the city, showcasing the political and religious institutions that define independent-minded Bologna. The space also forms a stage set for Bolognese life, from Prada-clad beauties to protesting students and pot-bellied sausage-makers.

On the south side of Piazza Maggiore stands **San Petronio ❻**, the largest church in Bologna. Originally, the Bolognese had hoped to outdo St Peter's in Rome, but Church authorities decreed that some funds be set aside for the construction of nearby Archiginnasio. San Petronio's barn-like design is by Antonio di Vincenzo, and although

construction began in 1390, the facade is still unfinished. The completed sections are of red-and-white marble and decorated with reliefs of biblical scenes. The interior is simple but elegant. Most of the bare brick walls remain unadorned. In the fifth chapel on the left is a spectacular 15th-century altarpiece of the *Martyrdom of St Sebastian* by Lorenzo Costa. A recent restoration has seen the addition of a new terrace (daily 10am–1pm, 3–6pm) offering a panoramic view over the town.

Behind San Petronio is the **Palazzo Archiginnasio ⓓ**, former seat of Europe's most ancient university. It now houses the municipal library and the 17th-century **Sala Anatomica** (www.archiginnasio.it; Mon–Fri 10am–6pm, Sat 10am–7pm, Sun 10am–2pm), where some of the first dissections in Europe were performed.

Stroll back to Piazza del Nettuno to appreciate the **Fontana di Nettuno ⓔ**, a 16th-century fountain with bronze sculptures by Giambologna of a muscle-bound Neptune surrounded by cherubs and mermaids. A puritanical papal edict once decreed that Neptune should be robed, but the priapic sea god is now free to frolic. (The locals take great delight in pointing out the best vantage point for viewing the god's impressive manhood.). On its west side is the majestic **Palazzo Comunale ⓕ**, the medieval town hall remodelled in the Renaissance. The bronze statue above the gateway is of Pope Gregory XIII, a native of Bologna. To the left is a beautiful terracotta Madonna by Niccolò dell'Arca. Inside are grand public rooms – part of the Collezioni Comunali d'Arte, they are lavishly decorated with furniture and paintings from the 15th–18th centuries (Tue–Fri 9am–6.30pm, Sat–Sun 10am–6.30pm; free first Sun of the month).

Foodie heaven

From here, plunge into the maze of alleys known as the **Mercato di Mezzo ⓖ** (daily 8.30am–midnight). Here, the mood is as boisterously authentic as it was in its medieval heyday. **Via Pescherie Vecchie** even conceals Bologna's oldest "inn", Osteria del Sole, a wine shop since 1486. This market area promises a true taste of Emilia, with open-air stalls, food shops and a covered market selling the finest regional produce, from parmesan to *charcuterie*, olive oil, pasta and wine. Gaze and graze is the mantra as eyes are drawn to: juicy peaches; sculpted pastries; belly-button shaped pasta; slivers of pink Parma ham; succulent Bolognese mortadella; Modena artisanal balsamic vinegar; single-estate virgin olive oil; jiggling, jelly-like ricotta; still-flapping fish; and wedges of superior "black rind" parmesan. Few can resist a pasta-based lunch on meaty ravioli or tortellini at **Tamburini** (www.tamburini.com; Via Drapperie/Via Caprarie 1), a legendary gourmet delicatessen and self-service.

Piazza del Nettuno acts as a familiar magnet, now sending you to Bologna's leaning towers. Simply follow **Via Rizzoli**, a picturesque street lined with cafés, down to **Piazza di Porta Ravegnana ⓗ**, at the foot of the **Due Torri**, the "leaning towers" of Bologna.

Shopping arcade, Bologna.

In medieval days, 180 of these towers were built by the city's leading families; now only a dozen remain. Legend has it that the two richest families in Bologna – the Asinelli and the Garisenda – competed to build the tallest and most beautiful tower in the city. However, the Torre Garisenda was built on weak foundations and was never finished. For safety's sake it was shortened between 1351 and 1360, and is now only 48 metres (157ft) high and leans more than 3 metres (10ft) to one side. The **Torre degli Asinelli** (Apr–Sep daily 9am–7pm, Oct until 6pm and until 5pm in winter) is still standing at its original height of 97 metres (318ft), but it too leans more than 1 metre (3ft) out of the perpendicular. It's a stiff climb to the top up 498 steps, but worth the effort for the wonderful views.

The **Strada Maggiore** leads east from the two towers along the original line of the Via Aemilia Roman road to the **Basilica di San Bartolomeo** ❶. Inside, look for the *Annunciation* by Albani in the fourth chapel of the south aisle, and a beautiful Madonna by Guido Reni in the north transept.

Further down the porticoed, patrician Strada Maggiore (at No. 34) is the **Museo Internazionale e Biblioteca della Musica** ❶ (www.museibologna.it/musica; Tue–Fri 9.30am–4pm, Sat–Sun 10am–6.30pm, end Jul–mid-Sep Tue also 4–9pm; free first Sun of the month). Portraits of musicians and instruments are displayed in a palatial setting. Even non-classical music fans will be entranced by the *trompe l'œil* courtyard and the frescoed interiors – a rare chance to see how the Bolognese nobility lived. Beyond is **Santa Maria dei Servi** ❶, a well-preserved Gothic church.

The **Abbazia di Santo Stefano** ❶ (daily 8am–7pm; voluntary donation) – a complex of churches all dedicated to St Stephen – is further down Via Santo Stefano, just south of the Casa Isolani, a medieval warren of palaces converted into chic galleries and pleasant cafés.

Santo Stefano is seven churches in one, like a nest of Chinese boxes. Dating back to AD 392, the complex became a Lombard basilica, then a Benedictine sanctuary in the 10th century. A harmonious ensemble is created by the

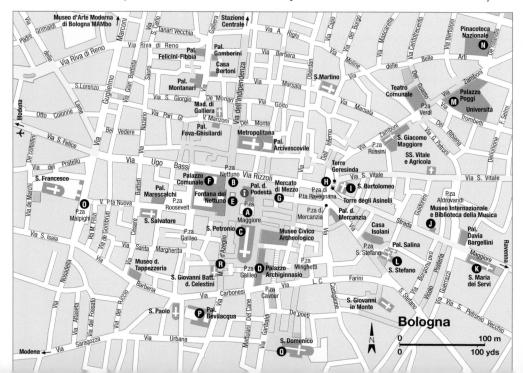

Bologna

interlocking churches and courtyards, including the Benedictine cloisters, graced by an elegant well-head. Bathed in mystical light, Santi Vitale e Agricola feels the most compelling church, while Santo Sepolcro houses the tomb of St Petronius, the city patron.

Ancient university

Bologna's **University**, located on **Via Zamboni**, is the oldest in Italy and indeed Europe; it was founded in the 11th century and was famous in its early days for reviving the study of Roman law. Petrarch attended classes here, as did Copernicus, and the late Umberto Eco, author of *The Name of Rose*, *Foucault's Pendulum* and *Prague Cemetery* was a professor of semiology and semiotics here. Today, although faculties are spread throughout the city, the official seat is the 16th-century **Palazzo Poggi** Ⓜ (www.museopalazzo poggi.unibo.it), which holds a rich collection of instruments for astronomical studies such as medieval astrolabes and celestial and terrestrial globes.

Past the university, on the left, is the **Pinacoteca Nazionale** Ⓝ (National Gallery; www.pinacotecabologna.benicultur ali.it; Tue–Wed 9am–1.30pm, Thu–Sun 2–7pm; other site at via Castiglione, 7, Tue–Wed 2–7pm, Thu–Sun 9am– 1.30pm), which showcases Bolognese and Emilian art from the Middle Ages to the 1700s, including works by Vitale da Bologna (especially the painting of *St George and the Dragon*) and Guido Reni. Other highlights are Raphael's *Ecstasy of St Cecilia* (1515) and Perugino's *Madonna in Glory* (1491).

South and west of the Piazza Maggiore, Bologna has more architectural treasures. Follow the Via Ugo Bassi west to **Piazza Malpighi** Ⓞ. On the west side of this piazza rises **San Francesco**, a church constructed between 1236 and 1263, with a design of French Gothic inspiration. From San Francesco walk southeast until you reach **Palazzo Bevilacqua** Ⓟ, a medieval Tuscan-style palace where the Council of Trent met for two sessions after fleeing an epidemic in Trent. It is the boldest of Bologna's senatorial palaces and has a sandstone facade, wrought-iron balconies and a courtyard surrounded by a loggia.

Old-fashioned pasticceria in Modena.

FACT

Fast-car enthusiasts will enjoy a visit to the Museo Enzo Ferrari (http://museo modena.ferrari.com) at Via Paolo Ferrari 85 in Modena, where Ferraris and Maseratis are displayed in a gigantic showroom and Enzo Ferrari's fascinating life story is related in the converted workshop of his father. A regular shuttle bus connect the museum with Maranello, 20km (12.5 miles) south of Modena, where the Museo Ferrari (www.museo maranello.ferrari.com) showcases the world's largest collection of Ferraris, with models through the ages – and a simulator where visitors can experience driving a Ferrari single-seater on the Monza track.

Nearby, **San Domenico** Ⓠ (www. conventosandomenico.org) dominates Piazza San Domenico. Dating from 1228, it was remodelled in Baroque style but incorporates Romanesque walls. The interior displays the tomb of St Dominic, founder of the Dominican Order, decorated with sculptures by Nicola Pisano and Arnolfo di Cambio of the Pisan School, as well as two by the young Michelangelo.

Return to Piazza Maggiore along **Via d'Azeglio** Ⓡ. This forms part of the city's *passeggiata*, or ritual evening stroll, and is a chance to see the city at its most sociable. This pedestrianised street is known as *"il salotto"*, the open-air drawing room, the place for chatting over cocktails and designer shopping.

On the northwestern edge of the centre, transformed from a former municipal bakery, is the **Museo d'Arte Moderna di Bologna MAMbo** (www. mambo-bologna.org; check times online as these vary but usually Tue–Sun 10am–7pm) with a permanent collection tracing the history of Italian art from World War II to the present day. It is also temporary home to the **Museo Morandi**, a

fine collection of works by Bolognese artist Giorgio Morandi (1890–1964), one of the great still-life painters of modern times. The museum forms part of the new **Manifattura delle Arti** (www.manifatturadellearti.org) complex, transformed from the old harbour and industrial area of the city by architect Aldo Rossi. Bologna has earned a number of epithets: *"La Dotta"* (The Learned One), *"La Turritta"* (The Turreted One), *"La Rossa"* (The Red One, as much for its reddish buildings as for its politics) and finally *"La Grassa"* (The Fat One) for its rich cooking. Consider dining on mortadella (salami), tortellini or tagliatelle, said to have been invented for the marriage feast of Lucrezia Borgia and the Duke of Ferrara.

Modena

Prosperous **Modena** ❷ is associated with fat tenors and sleek cars. The late Pavarotti came from Modena, as do Maserati and Ferrari. But the city is a Unesco World Heritage site in its own right. If Modena remains underrated it is partly because the smug locals have done little to attract visitors. Since the

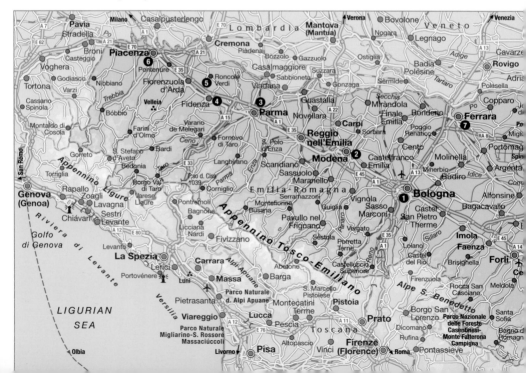

Romans conquered Modena in the 2nd century BC, the city has thrived. The success of the food, Ferrari and ceramics industries has been instrumental in making tourism a mere afterthought in this cosseted land of plenty.

Modena's massive and magnificent Romanesque **Duomo** was founded in the late 11th century by Countess Matilda of Tuscany, who engaged Lanfranco, the greatest architect of the time, to mastermind the project. The pink Verona marble structure is a mirror of the medieval mind, with friezes of saints and monsters, pilgrims and knights, griffins and doves, dragons and deer. The **Museo del Duomo** (Tue–Sun 9.30am–12.30pm and 3.30–6.30pm) contains impressive 12th-century metopes, low reliefs which once surmounted the flying buttresses.

The partly Gothic, partly Romanesque bell tower that stands to one side is the famous **Torre Ghirlandina**. It contains a bucket whose theft from Bologna in 1325 sparked off a war between the two cities.

Frequently seen strolling around Modena are the smartly dressed students of the **Accademia Militare**, Italy's military academy, housed in a 17th-century palace in the centre of Modena.

The major Modenese cultural hub, **Palazzo dei Musei**, contains several galleries, including the impressive art collection in the **Galleria Estense** (Mon 2–7.30pm, Tue–Sat 8.30am–7.30pm, the first Sun of the month 2–7.30pm; free Sun), and the **Biblioteca Estense** (Mon–Thu 8.30am–17pm, Fri 8.30am–3.30pm, Sat until 1.30pm; exhibitions: Tue–Thu 9am–1.30pm, 2.30–6pm, Mon, Fri and Sat am only), the library of the d'Este family, dukes of Modena as well as Ferrara. On permanent display in the library is a collection of illuminated manuscripts, a 1481 copy of Dante's *Divine Comedy*, and the stunning Borso d'Este Bible, which contains 1,200 miniatures.

Parma

Parma ❸ is a byword for fine living, from Parmesan and Parma ham to music and Mannerist art. There is no better place to become a connoisseur

Parma ham (prosciutto di Parma) has a slightly nutty flavour, which comes from the fact that Parmesan whey is sometimes added to the pigs' diet.

Modena's Romanesque Duomo.

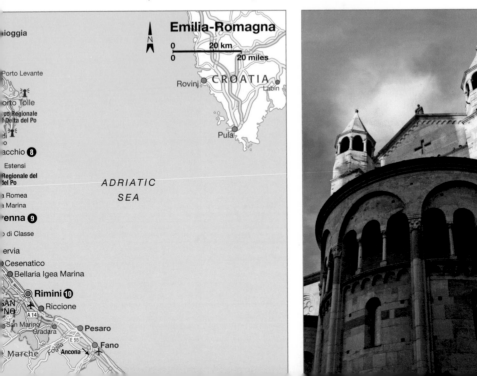

Emilia-Romagna

0   20 km
0   20 miles

ADRIATIC
SEA

CROATIA

Rovinj   Labin

Pula

ioggia
Porto Levante
orto Tolle
co Regionale
Delta del Po
di
o
acchio ❽
Estensi
Regionale del
del Po
a Romea
a Marina
enna ❾
di Classe
ervia
Cesenatico
Bellaria Igea Marina
Rimini ❿
AN
NO   Riccione
A14
San Marino   Pesaro
Gradara
E55   Fano
Marche   Ancona

of *parmigiano* (Parmesan) than in Parma, where the cheese is made.

Napoleon's widow, Marie Louise, was ceded this city after her husband's death. Apart from building roads and founding public institutions, she also created the superb **Galleria Nazionale** (www.parmabeniartistici.beniculturali.it; Tue–Sat 8.30am–7pm, Sun until 2pm; free first Sun of the month 1.30–7pm). It is set in the 16th-century **Palazzo della Pilotta**, a palace which also contains the **Teatro Farnese**, a Palladian theatre with Italy's first revolving stage. Italy's noble courts gave birth to countless such theatres, but this one was the largest of its day.

However, the main attraction in Parma is the **Duomo** (www.piazzaduomoparma.com; daily 10am–7pm) and adjoining Baptistery. Its nave and cupola are decorated with splendid frescoes by Correggio. Contemporaries gushed over them: Titian said that if the dome of the cathedral were turned upside down and filled with gold it would not be as valuable as Correggio's frescoes. Vasari wrote of the *Assumption*: "It seems impossible

Parmesan, the king of Italian cheeses.

that a man could have conceived such a work as this is, and more impossible still, that he should have done it with human hands."

The brilliantly restored **Baptistery** (Mar–Oct daily 10am–6.30pm, Nov–Feb 10m–4pm) is the work of Benedetto Antelami, who built this octagonal building in rich rose-pink Verona marble and then sculpted the reliefs that adorn both the interior and the exterior. Inside is a superb cycle of frescoes. Antelami's earliest known work, the *Deposizione* (1178), can be seen in the Duomo. This deeply moving sculpture was hewn from a single piece of marble.

In the dome of **San Giovanni Evangelista** (www.parmabeniartistici.beniculturali.it, Fri–Wed 9am–noon, 3–6pm, Sun pm only) another splendidly sensuous Correggio fresco (*c.*1520) can be seen. It depicts St John gazing up at heaven where the Apostles are gathered, and is matched by frescoes by Parmigiano. Nearby are Renaissance cloisters, a refectory and a Benedictine library. Of particular interest is the Antica Spezieria (pharmacy; Tue–Sun

PARMA HAM AND PARMESAN

Parma ham and Parmesan cheese *(Parmigiano)* are intricately linked, because it is the whey – the waste-product from Parmesan production – that is used to feed the pigs that used to make Parma ham. True Parma ham is branded with the five-pointed crown of the medieval dukes of Parma, and is produced in the hills south of the city. Here the raw hind thighs are hung in drying sheds for up to 10 months. The air that blows through the sheds is said to impart a sweet flavour to the meat – unlike cheap, mass-produced *prosciutto crudo*, which is injected with brine and artificially dried to speed up the curing process.

Try Parma ham as a starter *(antipasto)*, sliced into wafer-thin slivers for eating with bread, melon or figs; and end your meal, perhaps, with slivers of superior Parmigiano-Reggiano, partnered with apples, pears or a just a good red wine.

Another regional speciality is *aceto balsamico* (balsamic vinegar), which, in its prized (and pricey) artisanal version, bears no resemblance to the industrial slime often found in supermarkets. It is made from sweet grape juice, boiled slowly and reduced to a syrup, mixed with vinegar and then aged in wooden casks for many years. A few drops transform a salad, but it can even be drizzled over fresh berries or ice cream.

8.30am–2pm), complete with 16th-century apothecary's jars.

Beyond Parma

If driving northwest on the Via Aemilia towards Piacenza, consider making a quick stop in **Fidenza** ❹ to see another glorious Romanesque cathedral. Just beyond Fidenza is the turn-off for the little town of **Roncole Verdi** ❺, where you can visit the humble cottage in which Giuseppe Verdi (1813–1901) was born (www.casanataleverdi.it; Apr–Oct Tue–Sun 9.30am–12.10pm and 2.30–5.10pm, Mar until 4.10pm, Jan–Feb Sat–Sun 10.30am–12.30pm, 2–3.30pm; visits every 40 min.).

Situated at the point where the Via Aemilia meets the Po, **Piacenza** ❻ has been a lively trading post since 218 BC. Nothing remains of the Roman period, though there are many fine medieval and Renaissance buildings. At the centre of the city is the massive **Palazzo del Comune** (not open to the public), called "Il Gotico". Begun in 1280, it is a well-preserved building of brick, marble and terracotta.

In front of it loom two massive Baroque equestrian statues of Piacenza's 16th-century rulers, the Farnese dukes. At the end of Via Venti Settembre stands Piacenza's Romanesque **Duomo** (www.duomopiacenza.it; daily 9am–noon and 4–7pm). Although gloomy inside, the cathedral is worth a visit for the frescoes on the columns near the entrance, and there is also a small museum.

Ferrara

Set on the banks of the misty River Po, **Ferrara** ❼ is both a one-dynasty town and one of most beguiling cities in the region. Its Unesco World Heritage status springs from its artistic self-sufficiency and the jewel-like appeal of its frescoed, Renaissance palaces. The mist lends an air of mystery, as do the secret gardens and city walls.

The d'Este family ruled Ferrara from the late 13th century until 1598, a time of prosperity when their court attracted poets, scholars and artists. The Renaissance, the city's golden age, is reflected in all the major monuments.

Dominating Ferrara's skyline is the restored medieval **Castello Estense** (www.castelloestense.it; June daily and Jul–Aug Tue–Sun 9.30am–1.30pm and 3–7pm, Mar–May, Oct daily and Nov–Feb Tue–Sun 9.30am–5.30pm; café and bookshop inside), complete with moats, drawbridges and towers. Just behind the castle is Ferrara's 12th-century **Duomo**. Among the noteworthy paintings here and in the adjoining museum (Museo della Cattedrale; Tue–Sun 9.30am–1pm and 3–6pm) are Cosimo Tura's *St George* and his *Annunciation*, and Jacopo della Quercia's *Madonna della Melagrana* (1408).

Across from the Duomo is the **Palazzo Municipale** (Mon–Fri 9am–1pm, Tue and Thu also 3–5pm; free), a medieval building with a beautiful Renaissance staircase. The piazza in front of this town hall is the hub of life in modern Ferrara, and teeming with bicycles, the number-one method of transport in this very flat region of the Po Valley.

Inside Ferrara's cathedral.

Medieval city

Many of the medieval streets south of the cathedral are lined with fortified mansions, and, stretching across the **Via delle Volte**, a narrow street near the Po, there are a number of elegant arches. At the beautiful **Palazzo Schifanoia** (Tue–Sun 9.30am–6pm; limited access to some rooms due to 2012 earthquake), one of the d'Este family's summer residences, you can climb the steep stairs to the Salone dei Mesi, a large, high room decorated with colourful frescoes of the months. However, most have deteriorated and their colours dulled. These were executed for the duke of Borgo d'Este by masters of the Ferrarese School, including Ercole de' Roberti.

Just around the corner is another d'Este palace, the **Palazzo Costabili di Ludovico il Moro**, designed by the famous Ferrarese Renaissance architect Biagio Rossetti. This houses the **Museo Archeologico Nazionale** (Via XX Settembre 124; Tue–Sun 9.30am–5pm), which has a fine collection of Etruscan artefacts.

North of the Duomo, Ferrara is a city of broad avenues. Along one of the prettiest streets, Corso Ercole d'Este, is Rossetti's **Palazzo dei Diamanti**, a late Renaissance structure, characterised by a bizarre facade studded with diamond shapes created in honour of the d'Este family, whose emblem it was. The first floor is home to the **Pinacoteca Nazionale** (daily 9am–2pm, Thu 9am–7pm), a permanent collection of masterpieces from the Veneto and Venice. The Galleria d'Arte Moderna on the ground floor is dedicated to temporary blockbuster exhibitions of modern or contemporary art (www.palazzodiamanti.it).

The Po Delta

From Ferrara you can explore the **Po Delta wetlands** by car, with lunch in **Comacchio ⑧**, a miniature Venice, and a visit to **Abbazia di Pomposa** (**Pomposa Abbey**), a Romanesque Benedictine foundation with fine frescoes.

The drive through Italy's Camargue, between Ferrara and Comacchio, passes nature reserves, water defences and drainage schemes, from locks and flood plains to the raised canal banks, which now serve as scenic roads and cycle tracks. A summer trip could end at a discreet beach. **Lido degli Estensi** is a sought-after resort set among pine groves, while the sand dunes at Lido di Pomposa are conveniently close to Pomposa Abbey.

Ravenna

When the unstoppable barbarians overran Rome in the 5th century AD, **Ravenna ⑨** benefited, gaining the honourable rank of capital of the Western Empire. This Adriatic port town continued as capital under the Ostrogoths, and the barbarian leaders Odoacer and Theodoric also ruled their vast dominions from here. Later, when the Byzantine emperor Justinian reconquered part of Italy, he too made Ravenna its capital, liking it for its imperial tradition under the barbarians and – perhaps more importantly – for its direct sea links to Byzantium.

Interior of Sant'Apollinaire in Classe, Ravenna.

Under Justinian's rule the Ravenna we know today began to take shape. New buildings arose all over the city, including a handful of churches that are among the wonders of Italian art and architecture. There is no preparation in their simple brick exteriors for the brilliant mosaics within. It is these mosaics that make modern Ravenna, if no longer capital of the Western world, at least a capital of the Western art world.

Amazing mosaics

Start with **San Vitale** (www.ravenna mosaici.it; Apr–Sep daily 9am–7pm, Mar and Oct until 5.30pm, Nov–Feb 9.30am–5pm), the city's great 6th-century octagonal basilica, famous for the mosaics in its choir and apse. These "monuments of unageing intellect", as the Irish poet W.B. Yeats called them, immediately draw the eye with their marvellous colours and intricate detail. Bright ducks, bulls, lions, dolphins and a phoenix intertwine with flowers and corners of buildings to frame Old Testament scenes and portraits of Byzantine rulers with humour and exactitude.

In the dome of the apse a purple-clad and beardless Christ sits on a blue globe flanked by archangels and, at the far sides, St Vitalis and Bishop Ecclesius. Christ hands the saint (Ravenna's patron) a triumphal crown, while the bishop (who founded the church in 521) carries a model of the building as it finally appeared many years after his death. Below stretch imperial scenes of Justinian with his courtiers and Theodora, his beloved wife, with hers.

San Vitale is not the only place to see mosaics in Ravenna. Nearly every church contains a pristine example of the art. Just north, another set may be seen at the **Mausoleo di Galla Placidia** (times as above). This interesting lady was born a Roman princess, sister to Emperor Honorius, but after she was captured by the Goths, she married their leader, Athaulf, and ruled with him. He, however, soon died, and she next married a Roman general to whom she bore a son. This son became Emperor Valentinian III. As Valentinian's regent, and a woman with connections in the highest barbarian circles, Galla Placidia played a powerful role in

Mosaics at the Mausoleo di Galla Placidia.

the world of "the decline". The building that houses her tomb has a simple exterior, but inside the walls, floors and ceiling are covered with glorious mosaics, the oldest in Ravenna. Built between 425 and 450, it is bathed in green light which becomes aquamarine higher up the walls. The mystical atmosphere is intensified by the strikingly simple style of the mosaics, including the cobalt-blue sky sprinkled with gold stars. Despite the simple Christian iconography, the realism of the figures reflects the naturalistic Roman style as much as a nascent Christian one.

Through the gate that lies between San Vitale and Galla Placidia are two Renaissance cloisters that now house the **Museo Nazionale** (Tue–Sun 8.30am–7.30pm). The museum includes, as one might expect, many mosaics, as well as other relics from Ravenna's past. There is glass from San Vitale and also fabrics from the tomb of St Julian at Rimini.

The Baroque Duomo

A pleasant walk along Via Fanni, Via Barbiani and left onto Via d'Azeglio

leads to Ravenna's **Duomo** – originally constructed in the 5th century but redone in Baroque style in the 1730s. Far more attractive than the cathedral itself is the adjoining **Battistero Neoniano** (www.ravennamosaici.it; Apr–Sep daily 9am–7pm, Mar and Oct 9.30–5.30pm, Nov–Feb 10am–5pm), a 5th-century octagonal baptistery that was once a Roman bathhouse. The interior combines spectacular Byzantine mosaics with marble inlay from the original.

Across Piazza Caduti from the cathedral complex is **San Francesco**, another 5th-century church almost completely redone in the Baroque style. To the left stands the **Tomba di Dante** (daily Mar–Oct 10am–8pm, Nov–Feb until 4pm; free), not a remarkable building architecturally, but significant historically. Dante, the author of *The Divine Comedy*, was exiled from his home in Florence for his political outspokenness and found refuge in Ravenna in 1317. He spent the remaining four years of his life here, putting the finishing touches to his great work

Down the Via di Roma is another church full of mosaics, **Sant'Apollinare**

Mosaic of the three Magi in Sant'Apollinare Nuovo in Ravenna.

+SCS BALTHASSAR +SCS MELCHIOR +SCS GASPAR .

Nuovo (www.ravennamosaici.it; Apr–Sep daily 9am–7pm, Mar and Oct 9.30–5.30pm, Nov–Feb 10am–5pm). Flanked by a cylindrical bell tower, it was built between 493 and 496. The scenes are of processions, one of virgins and the other of martyrs who appear to be moving towards the altar between rows of palms. Above, the decorations depict episodes from the *Life of Christ*. Opposite stands the basilica of **San Giovanni Evangelista** (daily 8am–noon, 2.30–7pm; free), with a sculpted marble portal. Dating from the 5th century but much altered, it was built by Galla Placidia. Legend has it that she had vowed to build the church in return for surviving a shipwreck on a voyage from Constantinople.

Rimini

As the capital of the Riviera, **Rimini ➓** is a year-round destination, although regularly dismissed as a lacklustre beach resort. The coastal strip may be dominated by bland hotels, but the San Giuliano fishing district is quaint and the historic centre charming.

Begin in its heart, in Piazza Cavour, and admire the **Vecchia Peschiera**, the former fish market, just off the square. This area is part of Rimini's revival, confirmed by a clutch of boutique hotels, bars and design stores which are drawing more sophisticated visitors. But this is no mere makeover: the resort has been revitalised by the opening of a major new Roman site, complemented by an intriguing archaeological museum, and the transformation of the dynastic Malatesta castle into a cultural centre (with outdoor market Wed and Sat; www.castelsismondoestate.com). Rimini's seaside sauciness remains, but the resort's reputation as a graveyard for pensioners on package tours is being put to rest.

Roman remains

From Piazza Cavour the bustling Corso leads to **Piazza Ferrari**, home to the **Rimini Domus** archaeological site, the adjoining Roman **Surgeon's House** (**Domus del Chirugo**; www.domusrimini.com; Jun–Aug Tue–Sat 2–11pm, Tue and Thu also

Fishermen in Cattolica, a town in the province of Rimini.

POETIC LICENCE

After the death of Dante, Italy's greatest poet, the repentant Florentines wished to honour their famous son with a splendid tomb, but proud Ravenna refused to give up the poet's remains. The battle over the bones continued for hundreds of years.

In 1519, the rich and powerful Medici of Florence sent their representatives to Ravenna with a papal injunction demanding the relics. The sarcophagus was duly opened, but the bones were not inside. Someone had been warned of the Florentine scheme and had removed the bones to a secret hiding place. They were not found again until 1865, and now rest within Dante's sarcophagus in Ravenna. To this day, the city of Florence provides the oil for the lamp which burns on his tomb.

10am–12.30pm, Sun 5–11pm, Sep–May Tue–Sat 8.30am–1pm, 4–7pm, Sun 10am–12.30, 3–7pm, Sep–Oct until 8pm) and the archaeological wing of the **Museo della Citta** (www.museicomunalirimini.it; Tue–Sat 9.30am–1pm and 4–7pm, Sun 10am–7pm). The interlinked complex contains fine Roman mosaics and frescoes, which date back to the 2nd century AD. This grand home belonged to an army surgeon, whose medical instruments are on display, including mortars, scalpels and a gruesome gadget designed to extract arrowheads. The area was then abandoned until the early 5th century, with the transfer of the imperial capital to Ravenna. The new archaeological section charts the region's history from pre-Roman to Celtic times.

A stroll along the Corso leads to **Piazza Tre Martiri**, named in honour of three Italian partisans hanged here by the Nazis in 1944. Yet the square is also the site of the Roman forum, whose columns now support the porticoes of the two eastern buildings.

Around the corner is the **Tempio Malatestiano** (Mon–Fri 8.30am–noon, 3.30–6.30pm, Sat 8.30am–12.30pm, 3.30–7pm, Sun 9am–12.30, 3.30–6.30pm) a tribute to the dynastic ruler Sigismondo Malatesta, who transformed a Gothic Franciscan church into a Renaissance gem fit for his mistress Isotta. Pope Pius II threatened to excommunicate the debauched Sigismondo, calling the site "a temple of devil-worshippers".

Sigismondo had better luck with women and artists. He was patron of such luminaries as Leon Battista Alberti, who designed this temple, inspired by the Roman Arch of Augustus which still stands at the gates of Rimini. Inside the temple, on the right, is Sigismondo's tomb, decorated with his initials intertwined with Isotta's. Note the fresco of Sigismondo praying at the feet of St Sigismond, by Piero della Francesca.

For a Roman farewell to Rimini, walk along **Corso di Augusto** to the **Arco di Augusto**, dating from 27 BC. This Arch of Augustus marked the junction of the Via Aemilia and Via Flaminia, the route from Rome to the Adriatic.

Arco di Augusto, Rimini.

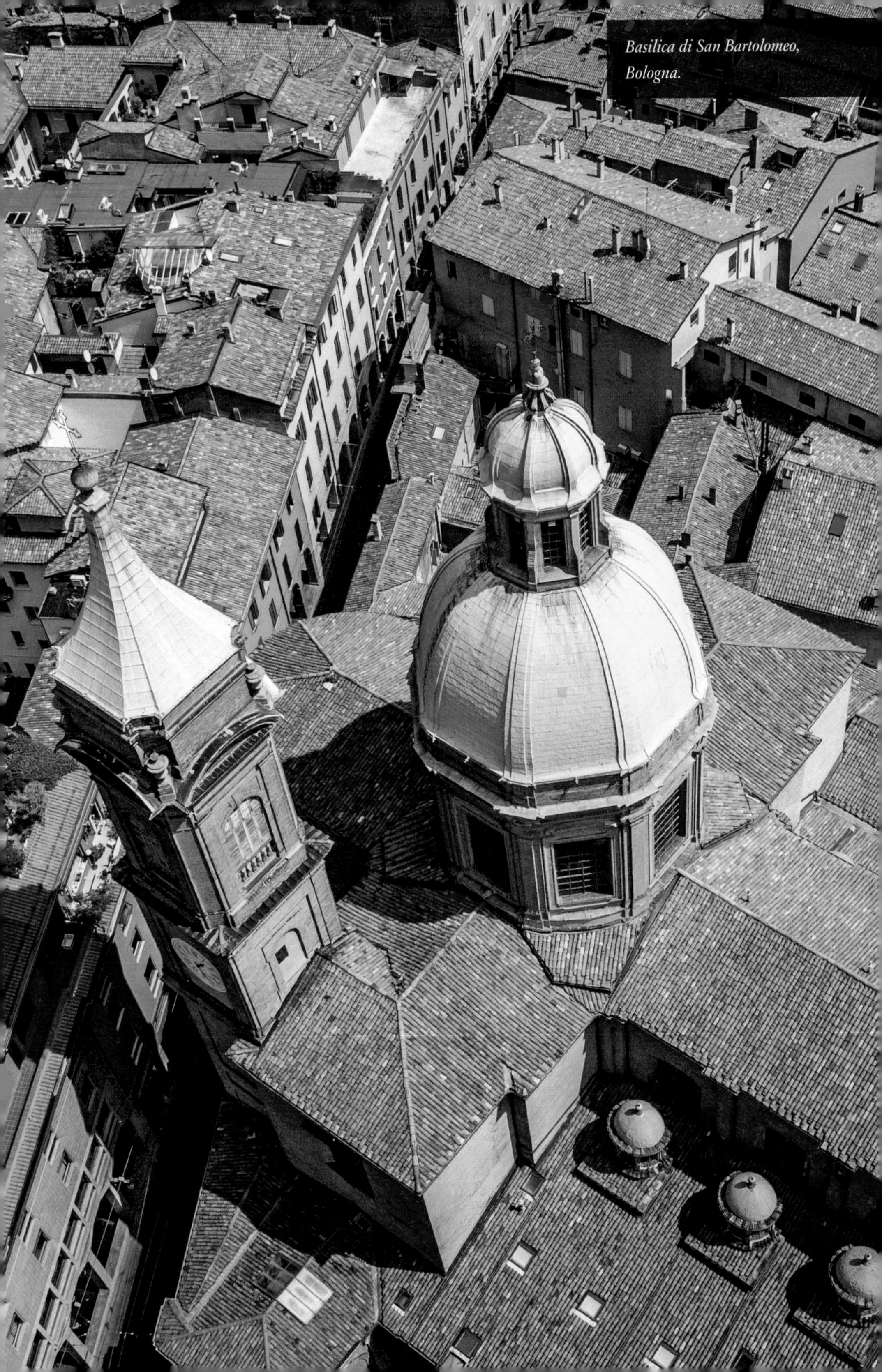

Basilica di San Bartolomeo, Bologna.

FLORENCE

One of the world's great historic cities, packed with architectural masterpieces, palaces and art galleries, Florence is an essential destination in its own right.

lorence, the Cradle of Renaissance has been the focal point of creative activity for some of the world's greatest artistic talents. The city's major churches, such as Santa Croce, and world-renowned museums and galleries like the Uffizi Gallery and Academia proudly watch over their prized masterpieces. The narrow streets and spacious piazzas are lined with elegant shops, traditional cafés and opulent palaces – none more magnificent than the Palazzo Pitti, across the Ponte Vecchio in Oltrarno. But if you want to see where the Renaissance began, the sublime Duomo and its surrounding complex is the perfect place to begin exploring this artistic shrine.

In 1743 Anna Maria Lodovica, the last of the Medici line, bequeathed her property to Florence, ensuring that the Medici collections remained intact for ever. As a result, Florence is still awash with many of the treasures that Vasari, the first art historian, mentions in his *Lives of the Artists* (1550). Although these Renaissance glories have given way to insatiable art tourism, the city remains the most harmonious in Italy.

Where the Renaissance started

Approaching **Piazza del Duomo**, you file through sober streets lined with buildings presenting a stern defensive face. Suddenly the **Duomo** ❶

On the steps of the Duomo.

(www.operaduomo.firenze.it; Cathedral; Mon–Wed, Fri 10am–5pm, Thu 10am–4.45pm, Sat 10am–4.45pm, Sun 1.30–4.45pm, closed first Tue of each month; free) is revealed, all festive in its polychrome marble – green from Prato, white from Carrara and red from the Maremma. The design echoes that of Giotto's slender **Campanile** (daily 8.15am–6.50pm; charge), arguably Italy's loveliest bell tower. You can climb the 414 steps of the bell tower for intimate views of the cathedral dome and roofscape, or simply contemplate the

TIP

To counter the crowds, visit out of season, combine major and minor attractions, and book a private guide to see a secret side of Florence reflecting your own interests (Link; tel: 055-218 191; www.linkfirenze.it).

bold cathedral facades from one of the cafés on the south side of the square.

The octagonal **Battistero** (Baptistery; Mon–Wed and Fri 8.15–10.15am and 11.15am–6.30pm, Thu and Sat 8.15am–6.30pm, Sun 8.15am–1.30pm; charge), to the west of the cathedral, dates from the 6th century, though the interior was redesigned and given its ceiling mosaics of the *Creation* and *Last Judgement* in 1300. The Baptistery has several sets of bronze doors, and those to the north play a seminal role in art history, often seen as marking the start of the Renaissance. In 1401 Ghiberti and Brunelleschi were adjudged joint winners of a competition to design the doors, but Brunelleschi, a fiery-tempered genius, refused to work with Ghiberti, who completed the doors in 1424. The doors show the hallmarks of Renaissance art: realism, a sense of perspective, and narrative clarity combined with dramatic tension. Ghiberti's following set of doors, for the east portal (1452), are known as the Paradise Doors after Michelangelo hailed them as fit to serve as the "gates of Paradise".

The originals are on view in the Opera del Duomo museum.

Biggest dome in the world

Brunelleschi (1377–1446) returned from studying ancient Roman architecture in Rome, confident that he could complete the cathedral by erecting the vast **dome**. In typically Florentine fashion, the city had decided to build the biggest dome in the world without knowing how to achieve it. If you enter the cathedral and climb the 436 steps to the top (Mon–Fri 8.30am–6.20pm, Sat until 5pm, Sun 1–4pm; charge) you can study how the problem was solved.

Brunelleschi's stroke of genius was to devise a cunning system of an inner shell and outer dome to distribute the weight of the cupola, with thick walls negating the need for further buttressing. Brunelleschi went on to create some of the purest Renaissance architecture in the city, buildings which are striking in their simplicity and pared-down loveliness. Using rigorous geometry based on classical forms, the buildings are the perfect expression of a rational use of space. Out of respect

The Uffizi at night.

for Brunelleschi's achievement, the city forbade the construction of any building taller than the Duomo; to this day, the massive dome dominates the red rooftops, rising almost higher than the surrounding hills. Brunelleschi was also buried in the cathedral – an honour granted to him alone – and his tomb can be seen in the **Crypt of Santa Reparata** (Mon–Sat 10am–4.30pm; charge), among the excavated ruins of Santa Reparata, the city's first (4th-century) cathedral.

The cathedral's stark interior features a fine fresco on the north aisle wall, painted by Paolo Uccello in 1436, depicting Sir John Hawkwood, the English mercenary who served as captain of the Florentine army from 1377 to 1394. Otherwise, to see the cathedral treasures you must visit the revamped **Museo dell'Opera del Duomo** ❷ (Mon and Fri–Sat 9am–9pm, Tue–Thu and Sun 9am–7pm; www.museumflorence.com) on the east side of Piazza del Duomo. On display are outstanding sculptures, from Donatello's haggard *Mary Magdalene*, carved in wood in the 1460s, to the same artist's superb *cantoria* (choir gallery), decorated with angels and cherubs engaged in frenzied music and song. One of the star exhibits here is Michelangelo's *Pietà*, begun around 1550. Michelangelo intended this for his own tomb, but left it unfinished. Its magnetic hold over visitors derives from the fact that the tall hooded figure of Nicodemus is Michelangelo's self-portrait. All 10 of the original Gates of Paradise from the Baptistery were finally reunited in the museum in 2012 after 27 years of restoration and are now beautifully displayed in their own space, 'Paradise Hall'.

Showpiece of the guilds

From the cathedral square, **Via dei Calzaiuoli** leads south. This was the principal street of Roman and medieval Florence, and is lined with interesting shops. Partway down, on the right, is the church of **Orsanmichele** ❸ (church: Tue–Sun 10am–5pm,

museum: Mon 10am–5pm; free), a former granary and church. The exterior niches are filled with Renaissance statues sponsored by the guilds. The finest, Donatello's *St George*, made for the Guild of Armourers, has been moved to the Bargello museum (see page 274) and replaced by a copy.

The same fate befell Michelangelo's *David*, which once stood in **Piazza della Signoria** ❹, just to the south. The original was moved to the Accademia (see page 276) in 1873, but the copy that now stands in front of the Palazzo Vecchio is faithful to the original. David's companions are *Hercules* (1534, by Bandinelli), the mythical founder of Florence, and Ammannati's licentious *Neptune Fountain* (1575). Nearby, the **Loggia dei Lanzi** ❺ (1382) shelters Cellini's *Perseus* (1554) and Giambologna's *Rape of the Sabine Women* (1583), alongside ancient Roman statues.

These statues are highly symbolic, not least *David* himself, carved by Michelangelo to represent Florentine independence. Yet Goliath, in the form of Cosimo de' Medici, triumphed, crushing republicanism and

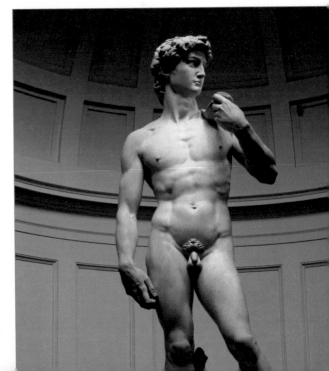

Michelangelo's masterpiece, David.

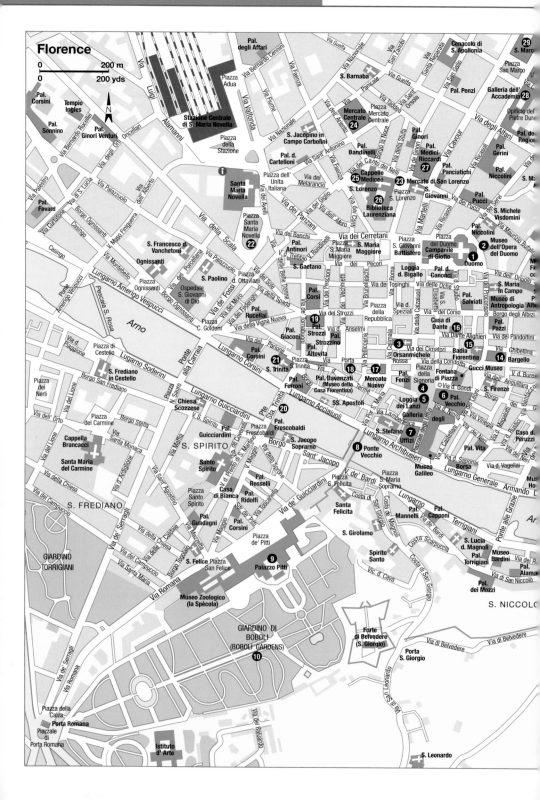

Florence

0 _____ 200 m
0 _____ 200 yds

N

Pal. Corsini

Tempio Ingles

Pal. Sonnino

Pal. Ginori Venturi

Pal. Favard

Pal. degli Affari

Piazza Adua

Via Guelfa

Via Nazionale

Via Santa Reparata

Via San Zanobi

Cenacolo di S. Apollonia

29 S. Marc

Piazza San Marco

S. Barnaba

Via Guelfa

Pal. Penzi

Galleria dell' Accademia 28

Opificio di Pietre Dure

Stazione Centrale di S. Maria Novella

Piazza della Stazione

Via Nazionale

Via dell' Alberto

Mercato Centrale 24

Piazza Mercato Centrale

Via Cavour

Via degli Alfani

Pal. del Region

S. Jacopino in Campo Corbolini

Pal. d. Cartelloni

Via Sant' Antonino

Pal. Bandinelli

Pal. Ginori

Pal. Medici Riccardi 27

Pal. Gerini

Santa Maria Novella

Piazza dell' Unita Italiana

Via del Melarancio

Cappelle Medicee 25

23 Mercato di San Lorenzo

S. Giovanni

Pal. Panciatichi

Pal. Niccolini

S. M

S. Lorenzo

26

Piazza S. Lorenzo

Pal. Pucci

Piazza Santa Maria Novella 22

Biblioteca Laurenziana

Via dei Banchi

Via dei Cerretani

Piazza S. Giovanni Battistero

Piazza del Duomo Campanile di Giotto

Duomo 1

S. Michele Visdomini

Pal. Niccolini 2 Museo dell' Opera del Duomo

Pal. Antinori

S. Maria Maggiore

S. Maria Maggiore

S. Maria Maggiore

715 Maria Maggiore

S. Gaetano

Via dei Pecori

Loggia d. Bigallo

Pal. d. Canonici

Via dell' Oriuolo

Via degli Speziali

Via dei Calzaiuoli

Pal. Salviati

S. Maria in Campo

Museo di Antropologia e

Pal. Corsi

S. Francesco d. Vanchetoni

Ognissanti

Via Palazzuolo

S. Paolino

Piazza Ognissanti

Via della Spada

Pal. Strozzi 19

Pal. Strozzino

Via d. Anselmi

Orsanmichele

Rossa

Casa di Dante

Via Dante Alighieri 15

Pal. Pazzi

16

14 Bargello

Ospedale S. Giovanni di Dio

Via de' Fossi

Pal. Rucellai

Piazza C. Goldoni

Via della Vigna Nuova

Pal. Giaconi

Piazza della Repubblica

Pal. Altovita

Pal. Davanzati (Museo della Casa Fiorentina)

Badia Fiorentina

Gucci Museo

V. d. Burei

Arno

Lungarno Amerigo Vespucci

Ponte alla Carraia

Lungarno Corsini

Pal. Corsini 21

Pal. Ferroni

S. Trinita

Piazza S. Trinita

Mercato Nuovo

Pal. Fenzi

18

17

Piazza della Signoria

Fontana di Piazza

S. Firenze

V. d. Gondi

Borgo

Piazza di Cestello

Lungarno Soderini

S. Frediano in Cestello

Piazza dei Nerli

N. Chiesa Scozzese

Lungarno Guicciardini

SS. Apostoli

Ponte S. Trinita 20

Pal. Frescobaldi

S. Jacopo Soprarno

Pal. Fenzi

Loggia dei Lanzi 5

Galleria degli

Pal. Vecchio 6

Casa dei Peruzzi

Via dell' Orto

Cappella Brancacci

Santa Maria del Carmine

Via della Chiesa

Piazza del Carmine

S. SPIRITO

Pal. Guicciardini

Santo Spirito

Casa di Bianca

Pal. Ridolfi

Pal. Rosselli

Borgo Sant' Jacopo

8 Ponte Vecchio

S. Stefano 7 Uffizi

Museo Galileo

Borsa

Mus Ho

S. FREDIANO

Piazza Santo Spirito

Pal. Guadagni

Pal. Corsini

S. Felice Piazza San Felice

9 Palazzo Pitti

Piazza de' Pitti

Costa de Magnoli

Piazza S. Felicita

Santa Felicita

S. Girolamo

Pal. Mannelli

Pal. Capponi

Lungarno Generale Armando

Ar

Pal. Vita

Lungarno Archibusieri

GIARDINO TORRIGIANI

Via Romana

Museo Zoologico (la Spècola)

Spirito Santo

Vic. di Cava

S. Lucia d. Magnoli

Pal. Torrigiani

Museo Bardini

Pal. Alama

Pal. dei Mozzi

S. NICCOLÒ

GIARDINO DI BOBOLI (BOBOLI GARDENS)

10

Forte di Belvedere (S. Giorgio)

Porta S. Giorgio

Via di Belvedere

Via di Belvedere

Piazza della Calza

Porta Romana

Piazzale di Porta Romana

Istituto d' Arte

Via del Ballardo

S. Leonardo

S. Leonardo

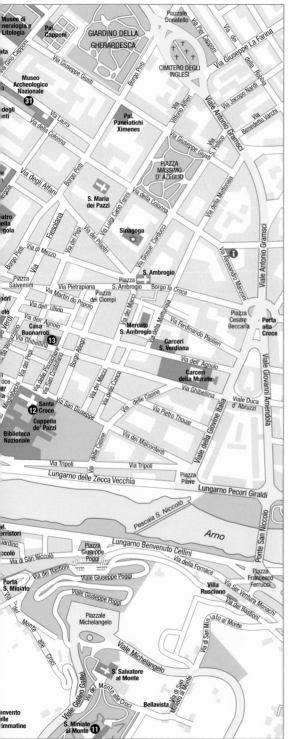

entrenching Medici power through a duke-dom which remained in place until Tuscany joined the united Kingdom of Italy in 1861. The Medici administration was based in the **Palazzo Vecchio** ❻ (http://musefirenze.it; Apr–Sept daily 9am–11pm, Thu until 2pm; Oct–Mar daily 9am–7pm, Thu until 2pm), which remains the town hall of Florence, and which was comprehensively redesigned during the reign of Cosimo I.

The Palazzo Vecchio, with its bold swal-lowtail crenellations and asymmetrical bell tower, is the most evocative of city symbols. The palace, under different guises, has been the emblem of Florentine power since the 14th century. Vasari's monumental staircase leads to the frescoed **Salone dei Cinque-cento**, the Hall of the Five Hundred, where members of the Great Council held their meetings. Cosimo I set his stamp on the chamber by commissioning a series of vast frescoes, painted by Vasari, which glorified his military triumphs. Beyond the art and the style, the palace is revealing of everyday Medici court life. It is also one of the few museums in conservative Florence to have moved into the 21st century in terms of pres-entation. The use of multimedia, "secret itin-eraries" and a children's perspective on great artworks has proved a resounding success.

The Uffizi

Under Cosimo I, Tuscan bureaucracy grew to the point where new offices were required to house the burgeoning army of lawyers and notaries, the guilds and the judiciary. Thus it was that the **Uffizi** ❼ (www.uffizi.beniculturali. it; Tue–Sun 8.15am–6.50pm, last entry 45 mins before closing) came to be built along-side the Palazzo Vecchio – now a world-famous art gallery but originally intended to serve as utilitarian offices.

Vasari built a well-lit upper storey, using iron reinforcement to create an almost con-tinuous wall of glass running round the long inner courtyard, a novel idea. (It was this glass wall that caused so much damage when a terrorist bomb exploded near the west wing of the Uffizi in May 1993.) Cosimo's heirs decided that the airy upper corridor would make a perfect exhibition space for the family statues, carpets and paintings, and Italy's first public gallery was born. As the world's greatest collection of Italian art, the Uffizi is both a feast for the senses and an indigestible banquet. What you choose to be moved by will depend on your mood. Expect crowds in the Leonardo da Vinci room, which pays tribute to the greatest genius of the age, the master of the High Renaissance style. Contemplation of great works of art is still possible, at least away from the Leonardo da Vinci line, the Botticelli bottleneck and the Giotto genuflection. Fra Angelico, Perugino, Pollaiuolo and Mantegna, to name but a few of their Renaissance peers, are often left to sleepy custodians and connoisseurs.

The Uffizi corridors are lined with ancient Roman and Greek statues, but the collection's star attractions include Botticelli's *Primavera* (1480) and the *Birth of Venus* (1485). As part of an ongoing project that aims to double the exhibition space currently available at the Uffizi a series of new rooms have opened in the last decade. The eight new "Blue Rooms" feature non-Italian art from the 17th and 18th centuries as well as portraits and self-portraits by Rembrandt. The new nine "Red

Rooms" display the great Medici family portraits by Bronzino, including his *Portrait of Bia*, illegitimate daughter of Cosimo I (1542). The octagonal Tribune is now closed off to the public; you can still have a look inside but you can no longer enter the room. The masterpieces it contained have moved, including Michelangelo's influential *Holy Family (Doni Tondo*, 1506–8) which is now found in the Michelangelo hall. In the Raphael hall, the highlight is his tender *Madonna of the Goldfinch* (1506) and in the Titian rooms, his erotic *Venus of Urbino* (1538) is a must-see. Adjacent to the Michelangelo hall are two new "green rooms", featuring classical works which influenced the great artist.

En route to the Pitti Palace, the corridor passes over the **Ponte Vecchio** ❽, with its medieval workshops used by butchers and tanners until these noxious trades were banned by ducal ordinance in 1593. Today, the bridge has been taken over by jewellers, buskers and streams of tourists shopping for trinkets. It was the only Florentine bridge to be spared by the Germans in World War II.

The Ponte Vecchio, built in 1345.

Eclectic craft shops await in the Oltrarno district south of the bridge, as do the churches of **Santo Spirito**, an architectural masterpiece by Brunelleschi, and **Santa Maria del Carmine** (Wed–Sat and Mon 10am–5pm, Sun 1–5pm), where the **Cappella Brancacci** contains Masaccio's moving fresco cycle, one of the great works of the early Renaissance. The Brancacci Chapel is tiny, with room for only 30 people, so expect queues and a visit limited to 20 minutes (tel: 055-276 8224 to book).

Residence of the Medici Grand Dukes

Space is not a problem at the fortress-like **Palazzo Pitti ❾** (Pitti Palace), the "new" residence of the Medici Grand Dukes. Brunelleschi produced bold plans for the palace shortly before his death. Set on a slope to create more impact, and built on solid rock to support the weighty foundations, the Pitti was the first private palace to be built commanding its own *piazza*. The Medici swiftly shaped the palace in their own image, establishing summer and winter apartments, private picture galleries and libraries.

The most rewarding collection is the **Galleria Palatina** (Palatine Gallery; www.uffizi.beniculturali.it; Tue–Sun 8.15am–6.50pm, ticket office closes 45 mins earlier, booking online suggested), especially the richly decorated ceiling frescoes by Pietro da Cortona. These illustrate the education of a prince under the tutorship of the gods. In Room 1, the prince is torn from the arms of Venus (love) by Minerva (knowledge), and later learns about science from Apollo, war from Mars and leadership from Jupiter. Finally the prince takes his place alongside Saturn, who, in mythology, presided over the Golden Age.

Among the paintings displayed are wonderful portraits by Titian, who turns the reformed prostitute, Mary Magdalene, into a delectable study of the delights of the female form. More disturbing is Rubens's celebrated masterpiece *The Consequences of War* (1638),

an allegory of the Thirty Years War.

Behind the Palazzo Pitti lies the **Giardino di Boboli ❿** (daily 8.15am–4.30pm, Mar and Oct until 5.30pm, Apr–May and Sept until 6.30pm, June–Aug until 7.30pm; closed first and last Mon of month; summer concerts). The landscaping of the Boboli Gardens, following the natural slope of the hill, perfectly complements the sumptuous palace, and became the model for Italianate gardens for centuries to come. As Florence's most beguiling late Renaissance garden, the Boboli reveal statues, fountains, ornamental pools, grottoes and even an Egyptian obelisk. At every turn, classical and Renaissance statuary gives way to whimsical Mannerist grottoes dotted with grotesque sculpture.

San Miniato al Monte

On one of the hills above Florence sits **San Miniato al Monte ⓫** (www.sanminiatoalmonte.it; Sun 8.15am–7pm, Mon–Sat 9.30am–1pm and 3–7pm, until 8pm in summer; free), a jewel-like Romanesque church. Catch the No. 13 bus up, and meander down on foot via **Piazzale Michelangelo** for a

To the south of the Mercato Nuovo is Il Porcellino (the piglet), a 17th-century bronze statue of a boar; copied from a Roman marble original now in the Uffizi. Legend has it that if you stroke his nose you will return to the city.

Palazzo Pitti.

A copy of Michelangelo's David in Piazza della Signoria.

The sweeping view from Piazzale Michelangelo.

classic Florentine vista. Set high above the city, the terrace is adorned by copies of Michelangelo's famous works, and overlooks the River Arno and the full sweep of the city below.

Prominent in the view, to the east of the city, is the massive Gothic church of **Santa Croce** ⓬, which features in E.M. Forster's novel (and the Merchant-Ivory film) *A Room with a View* (www.santacroceopera.it; Mon–Sat 9.30am–5.30pm, Sun 2–5.30pm; ticket includes Capella de' Pazzi, cloisters and museum). Here you will find frescoes by Giotto and his pupils, and the tombs and monuments of famous Florentines, including Michelangelo, Machiavelli and Galileo (who was protected by the Medici after his excommunication for holding the heretical view that the earth goes round the sun, rather than the reverse).

Weaving your way back through the Santa Croce district, you pass the **Casa Buonarroti** ⓭ (Wed–Mon 10am–4pm, until 5pm in summer; www.casabuonarroti.it). Michelangelo's former home contains a juvenile work, the *Madonna della Scala*.

Sustained by an ice cream at **Bar Vivoli Gelateria** (Via Isole delle Stinche 7; http://vivoli.it), continue along the art trail to the **Bargello** ⓮ (www.uffizi.com; Mon–Sat and 2nd and 4th Sun of the month 8.15am–1.50pm, closed 2nd and 4th Mon). Once a prison, the Bargello is now a museum devoted to sculpture by Donatello, Michelangelo, Cellini and Giambologna. The Bargello's tantalising calling card is Donatello's coquettish *David*, a rival to Michelangelo's more virile version in the Accademia.

Dante was born in this district in 1265, and opposite the Bargello you can see the abbey church, the **Badia Fiorentina** ⓯ (Mon 3–5pm; free), where the poet watched his beloved Beatrice attending Mass. Round the corner is the **Casa di Dante** ⓰ (daily 10am–6pm, Tue–Sun until 5pm in winter), the poet's presumed birthplace.

Further west stands the **Mercato Nuovo** ⓱ (www.mercatodelporcellino.it; daily 9am–6.30pm), a "New Market" that has been here since 1551. Few can resist touching the talismanic bronze boar, **Il Porcellino**, whose shiny nose attests to the good fortune bestowed on countless visitors.

From here, Via Porta Rossa leads to the now restored **Palazzo Davanzati** ⓲, a delightful townhouse and museum (daily 8.15am–2pm; free first Sun of the month). A vivid picture of domestic life in late medieval Florence unfolds in the vaulted entrance hall and the staircase supported by flying buttresses. The great Gothic halls on the second and third floors (group visits only by appointment) are frescoed to give the semblance of fabrics and drapery. The lofty, galleried palace bridges the medieval and Renaissance eras, making Palazzo Davanzati the most authentic surviving example of a merchant dwelling from the period.

Far grander is **Palazzo Strozzi** ⓳ (tel: 055-264 5155; www.palazzostrozzi.org; daily 10am–8pm, Thu until 11pm; charge for exhibitions),

a neighbouring cultural centre and the setting for blockbuster art exhibitions. This bombastic building is a testament to the overweening pride of the powerful merchant banker Filippo Strozzi, who dared to build a bigger palace than the Medici's. The monumental nature of the rusticated facade is echoed by the inner courtyard. As the quintessential 15th-century Florentine princely palace, Palazzo Strozzi was a model for centuries to come.

Straddling the **River Arno** is the **Ponte Santa Trinità** ⑳, a bridge blown up by the retreating Nazis in 1944 but dredged up from the river bed and fully restored. Beside it stands **Santa Trinità** ㉑ (Mon–Sat 8am–noon and 4–6pm, Sun 8–10.45am and 4–6pm; free), a church frescoed by Ghirlandaio.

Beyond is escapism in **Via de' Tornabuoni,** lined with chic boutiques showcasing such Florentine designers as Ferragamo and Cavalli, not to mention Gucci, who began as a humble saddle-maker in the city and now has a dedicated museum (www.guccimuseo. com; daily 10am–8pm, Fri until 11pm) located in Piazza della Signoria. Call into the aristocratic **Palazzo Antinori** to sample Tuscan wines (www.antinori. it) or try a Negroni cocktail in **Caffè Giacosa** (www.caffegiacosa.com), which is where it was invented. Now owned by Roberto Cavalli, who lives in the Florentine hills, the chic café is both a celebrity haunt and a place to try the designer's estate wine and chocolates.

Piazza Santa Maria Novella ㉒ is dominated by the **Basilica di Santa Maria Novella.** The Dominican complex features in Boccaccio's *Decameron*, and contains vivid frescoes by Ghirlandaio and Masaccio. In the adjoining **cloisters** (Mon–Thu and Sat 9am–5.30pm, Fri 11am–5.30pm, Sun 1am–5pm) you can see what remains of Paolo Uccello's masterpiece, the *Universal Deluge*, a depiction of the flood that drowned all but Noah and his entourage, and a fresco that was, ironically, badly damaged by the Florentine floods of 1966.

Around San Lorenzo

Heading back to the heart of town, browse in the market maze of **San Lorenzo** ㉓, which sells bags, belts and shoes (Tue–Sat 9am–7pm). On the adjoining square awaits the more rewarding covered food market, **San Lorenzo Mercato Centrale** ㉔ (www. mercatocentrale.it; daily 10am–midnight) which has been revamped into a gastronomic and cultural centre. There are cooking classes where you can now learn how to make real pasta (www.cucinaldm.com) and a food court on the first floor. Although increasingly touristy, it still is a reliable place for Tuscan specialities. Some, such as offal, are not for the faint-hearted, but the intrepid will try a hot tripe sandwich (*lampredotto*) at Nerbone. The squeamish might prefer the myriad oils, cheeses, mushrooms, salami, cantuccini biscuits and even truffles. The kinder stallholders will let you try before buying, or you can stay for a tripe-free picnic lunch.

At the back of San Lorenzo is the entrance to the **Cappelle Medicee** ㉕ (www.cappellemedicee.it; daily

Santa Maria Novella.

8.15am–6pm, closed 2nd and 4th Sun and 1st, 2nd and 3rd Mon of the month), the mausoleum of the Medici family, for which Michelangelo carved two splendid tombs featuring the allegorical figures of *Night* and *Day*, *Dusk* and *Dawn*. The church itself represents Renaissance rationalism, all cool whites and greys and restrained classical decoration. By contrast, the two huge pulpits carved by Donatello with scenes from the *Life of Christ* are full of impassioned emotion, and Michelangelo's staircase leading to the **Biblioteca Medicea Laurenziana** ㉖ (Laurentian Library; Mon–Fri 9.30am–1.30pm; www.bmlonline.it), off the cloisters, is even more exuberant.

Just off Piazza di San Lorenzo is the **Palazzo Medici-Riccardi** ㉗ (www.palazzomedici.it; Thu–Tue 9am–7pm; entrance limited to 10 visitors every 7 mins), the first Medici seat, containing a frescoed chapel, state rooms and library. The palace's masterpiece is the Cappella dei Magi, frescoed by Benozzo Gozzoli (1420–97). The *Procession of the Magi*, painted in 1459, fuses worldliness and piety in a gorgeous cavalcade. Yet if visitors smile involuntarily upon entering the room, it is because the work represents Renaissance art on an intimate, human scale.

There is no escaping Michelangelo's most famous work, *David*, in the **Galleria dell'Accademia** ㉘ (www.galleria accademiafirenze.beniculturali.it; Tue–Sun 8.15am–6.50pm; free first Sun of the month) close by, in Via Ricasoli. Other highlights include Michelangelo's unfinished *Four Slaves*, the plaster cast of Giambologna's *Rape of the Sabines* (on display in the Loggia dei Lanzi) and Filippino Lippi's striking *Deposition from the Cross*.

The nearby monastery of **San Marco** ㉙ (church: Mon–Sat 8.30am–noon; museum: Mon–Fri 8.15am–1.50pm, Sat–Sun until 4.30pm; closed 1st, 3rd, 5th Sun and 2nd and 4th Mon every month) contains virtually every painting and fresco produced by the saintly artist Fra Angelico.

Return home via the **Piazza della Santissima Annunziata** ㉚, with its delicate Renaissance colonnade adorning the **Spedale degli Innocenti** orphanage, the work of Brunelleschi, and the **Museo Archeologico Nazionale** ㉛ (Mon 8.30am–2pm, Tue–Fri 8.30am–7pm, Sat–Sun 8.30am–2pm; free first Sun of the month), with its ancient Etruscan and Egyptian treasures.

If the glory of Florence is that it contains the world's greatest concentration of Renaissance art and architecture, the price is responsibility. The American critic Mary McCarthy put the dilemma forcefully: "Historic Florence is an incubus on its present population. It is like a vast piece of family property whose upkeep is too much for the heirs, who nevertheless find themselves criticised by strangers for letting the old place go to rack and ruin."

Thankfully, the Florentines are respecting the trust put in them by the last of the Medici. Rack and ruin look a long way off.

The grand Piazza della Repubblica.

Florentine Firsts

From street paving and glasses to capitalism and the theory of the universe – Florence's contributions to the modern world are amazing.

Old records show that street paving began in Florence in the year 1235, and by 1339 the city had paved all its streets – the first in Europe to do so. And while Florentines had little to do with the discovery of the New World, Amerigo Vespucci provided the word "America", and Leonardo da Vinci created the first world maps showing America. A tablet in Santa Maria Maggiore church documents another first: "Here Lies Salvino d'Amato degli Armata of Florence, the Inventor of Eyeglasses, May God Forgive His Sins, Year 1317."

Two developments in music are among the most solidly documented Florentine firsts. The pianoforte was invented in Florence in 1711 by Cristofori, and the origins of opera are traced to the performance, in 1600, of Euridice, a new form of musical drama written by Iacopo Peri in honour of the marriage in Florence of Maria de' Medici to Henry IV of France.

Science, architecture and etiquette

An earlier marriage was the impetus for modern table manners. When Catherine de' Medici wed the future Henry II and moved to France, she was apparently appalled at the French court's table manners; in contrast to Florence, no one used a fork. Before long, all of Paris society was imitating her. It is also possible that Catherine, equally appalled at French food, sent for her own chefs, and was responsible for the birth of French haute cuisine.

In the field of science, Galileo, the first astronomer to make full use of the telescope, is often called the father of modern astronomy. Not that Florentine prophets were universally lauded: Galileo was jailed by the Inquisition, while Dante was exiled. Many firsts, of course, are related to the arts. Florentine-based artists produced the first Renaissance masterpieces. Donatello's David (1430) is regarded as the first freestanding nude statue of the Renaissance. Donatello is also credited with the first freestanding equestrian statue of the Renaissance.

The grandiose claim that Brunelleschi is the father of modern architecture is one of the least contested. He was the first Renaissance architect to evolve the rules of linear perspective, and he developed a new approach, detailing specifications in advance and separating design from construction.

Science and finance

Machiavelli, through The Prince and other works, is credited with inventing modern political science. Another literary great was Dante, whose Florentine language became the basis for modern Italian. Also in the literary field, Petrarch can be considered the father of vernacular Italian poetry and Boccaccio the father of modern Italian prose. Guicciardini is sometimes heralded as the father of modern history.

In the financial world, it is arguable that the 13th-century Florentine banks were responsible for modern capitalism, and that the city's medieval merchants were the first of a new, and eventually dominant, social class.

But there is less doubt that those early Florentine financiers originated credit banking and double-entry bookkeeping, both of which contributed to the success of capitalism. Finally, it is well documented that in 1252 Florence became the first city to mint its own gold coin, the florin, which was widely used throughout Europe.

Dante sketched by A. Bronzino.

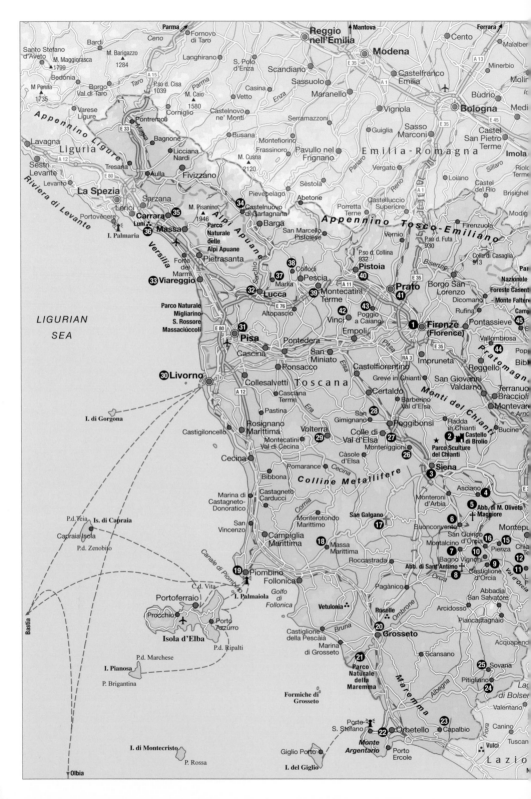

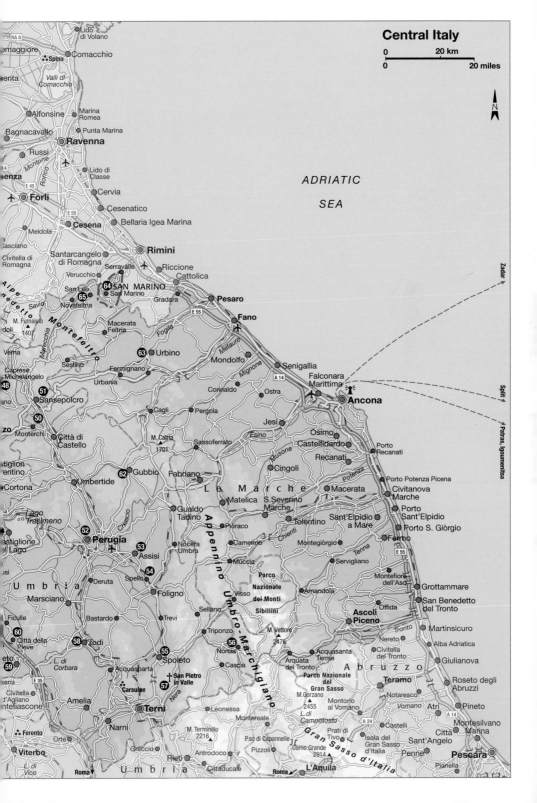

Central Italy

0   20 km
0   20 miles

N

ADRIATIC

SEA

Zadar

Split

Patras, Igoumenitsa

RA 8

Lido
di Volano

omaggio   Spina   Comacchio

Valli di
Comacchio

renta

Alfonsine   Marina
Romea

Bagnacavallo   Punta Marina

Russi   Ravenna

enza   Montone   Lido di
Classe

Forlì   Cervia

Cesenatico

Meldola   Bellaria Igea Marina

asciano   Cesena

Civitella di   Santarcangelo   Rimini
Romagna   di Romagna   Riccione
Verucchio   Serravalle   Cattolica
San Leo   64 SAN MARINO
65   San Marino   Gradara   Pesaro
Novafeltria   E 55
Savio   Fano
M. Fumaiolo   Macerata
doli   1407   Feltria   Foglia
Verna   63 Urbino   Metauro
Caprese   Fermignano   Mondolfo
Michelangelo   Urbania   Mignone   Senigallia
48   no   Corinaldo   Ostra   Falconara
51 Sansepolcro   Cagli   Pergola   Marittima
50   Ancona
Monterchi   Sassoferrato   Jesi
zo   Città di   M. Catria   Esino   Osimo
Castello   1701   Castelfidardo   Porto
iglion   62 Gubbio   Fabriano   Cingoli   Recanati
entino   Umbertide   Recanati
Cortona   Matelica   S.Severino   Porto Potenza Picena
Lago   La   M a r c h e   Marche   Macerata   Civitanova
Trasimeno   Gualdo   Marche
astiglione   52 Perugia   Tadino   Pioraco   Sant'Elpidio   Porto
el Lago   53   Nocera   Camerino   a Mare   Sant'Elpidio
Umbria   Assisi   Umbra   Chienti   Porto S. Giòrgio
usi   54   Muccia   Montegiòrgio   Fermo
U m b r i a   Deruta   Spello   E 55
Marsciano   Foligno   Parco   Servigliano
Ficulle   Bastardo   Visso   Nazionale   Montefiore
Trevi   Sellano   dei Monti   dell'Aso   Grottammare
60   Sibillini   Amandola   San Benedetto
Città della   58 Todi   Triponzo   M. Vettore   Offida   del Tronto
Pieve   55   2476   Ascoli   Martinsicuro
eto   59   Spoleto   Norcia   56   Piceno   Nereto   Alba Adriatica
sena   L. di   Acquasparta   Cascia   Arquata   Acquasanta   Civitella   Giulianova
Corbara   San Pietro   del Tronto   Terme   del Tronto   A b r u z z o
E 35   Carsulae   57 in Valle   Parco Nazionale   Teramo   Roseto degli
Civitella   del   Notaresco   Abruzzi
d'Agliano   Amelia   Leonessa   Gran Sasso   Vomano   Atri   Pineto
ntefiascone   Terni   M.Gorzano   Montorio   A 14
Narni   Montereale   2455   al Vomano   Castelli   Città   Montesilvano
Ferento   M. Terminillo   L.di   Sant'Angelo   Marina
Orte   2216   Campotosto   Castelli   Penne   Pescara
Greccio   Prati di   Isola del   Pianella
Viterbo   Antrodoco   Pizzoli   Tivo   Gran Sasso   Pescara
L. di   Rieti   P.so di Capannelle   Corno Grande   d'Italia
Vico   Roma   Cittaducale   Roma   L'Aquila   G r a n   S a s s o   d' I t a l i a   2914
U m b r i a

A4

E 45

E 55

A 14

A 24

Marecchia   Montefeltro   A l p e   B e n e d e t t o

Savio

Chiascio

Nera

Topino

Tenna

Tronto

Potenza

Musone

A p p e n n i n o   U m b r o - M a r c h i g i a n o

A typical Tuscan landscape of rolling hills, olive groves and cypress trees.

TUSCANY

Compelling architecture, seductive cities of art, evocative landscapes, spas and soft red wine form an essential part of Tuscany's appeal.

Rome

With its rolling hills, vines, olives and cypresses Tuscany's soothing scenery, dotted with stunning hill towns like San Gimignano and Montepulciano, inspired the Renaissance masters. The art and architecture of medieval Siena and Renaissance Florence may be unmissable, but spare time for compelling but less well-known cities, such as Lucca, Pienza and Pisa. Also lap up the Unesco-protected Val d'Orcia countryside south of Siena, mountainous Garfagnana, and the wild coastal area of the Maremma. If you still have any energy left explore the Chianti region and its plethora of vineyards and the Etruscan sites around Volterra.

It's a travesty to equate Tuscany with "Chiantishire", a parody of English country-house party transposed to Italy. It is also misleading to reduce the region to Renaissance art, as the landscape is as beautiful as the art.

The Tuscan lifestyle is also one of its greatest draws, with villa rentals or farm stays the ideal way of appreciating the landscape. The Tuscans seem to have found a perfect balance between country and city living. As well as pampering in olive oil treatments and wallowing in hot springs, you can enjoy pasta feasts and gorgeous views.

On the Chianti wine trail

For those not fascinated by frescoes, the delights of **Florence** ❶ can quickly fade, and the desire to escape the cauldron-like atmosphere of the city in summer can prove overwhelming, as it did in the case of the English writer Laurie Lee: "I'd had my fill of Florence, lovely but indigestible city. My eyes were choked with pictures and frescoes… I began to long for the cool uplands, the country air, the dateless wild olive and the uncatalogued cuckoo."

Pisa's Leaning Tower and Duomo.

Lee escaped to the **Chianti**, walking south along the Chiantigiana, the Chianti Way (the N222 (SR222) road), which takes you to Siena via pretty towns in the Chianti Classico wine-growing region. If you are driving, the journey takes around an hour from Florence, unless you succumb to the scores of *fattorie* (wine estates) offering tastings and wine sales (*vendita diretta*).

Florence's **Greve in Chianti** might be quintessential Chiantishire, but the Sienese Chianti is quieter, yet just as charming. A meander between wine estates acts as an introduction to the region's famous red wines.

A charming variant is to leave the N222 (SR222) at **Castellina in Chianti** and drive east, stopping for a walk round the pretty town of **Radda in Chianti** before rejoining the N429 (SS429) to the **Badia a Coltibuono** (Apr–Oct daily 2.30–6.30pm, guided tours only), a 12th-century abbey estate set among pines, oaks, chestnuts and vines. Below the abbey are cellars filled with Chianti Classico, the abbey's traditional living. Wine,

together with locally produced olive oil and chestnut honey, can be bought on the premises or savoured in the excellent abbey restaurant (tel: 0577-749 031; www.coltibuono.com). The erstwhile monastic cells (now a farm stay) await those who overindulge.

South of Gaiole in Chianti is **Castello di Brolio ❷** (tel: 0577-7301; www.ricasoli.it), the birthplace of the modern Chianti industry. It was in this castle in 1870 that Barone Bettino Ricasoli established the formula for making Chianti wines that has been used ever since, requiring a precise blend of white and red grape juice and the addition of dried grapes to the vat to give the wine its softness and fruit-filled flavour. This large estate is still run by the noble Ricasoli family: Tuscan aristocrats, including the Antinori and Frescobaldi families, have often been making wine since Renaissance times.

Civilised Siena

Siena ❸ is the counterpoint to Florence and is as medieval as its ancient rival is Renaissance. This compact,

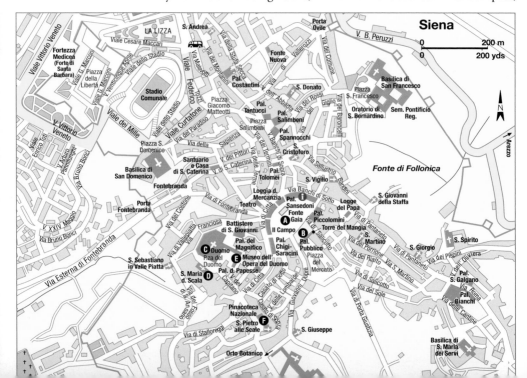

pink-tinged city is a delight to explore, from the shell-shaped Campo to the galleries full of soft-eyed Sienese Madonnas. Given its narrow alleys threading between tall rose-brick palaces, Siena is mostly pedestrianised. There are parkings outside the city walls; visitors with hotel reservations are generally allowed to drive in to drop off their luggage.

All roads eventually lead to the **Piazza del Campo Ⓐ**, the huge amphitheatre of a space – the Sienese liken it to the enveloping cloak of the Madonna, who, with St Catherine of Siena, is the city's patron saint.

From the comfort of a café on the curved side of the Campo, note the division of the paved surface into nine segments, commemorating the beneficent rule of the Council of Nine Good Men which governed Siena from the mid-13th century to the early 14th, a period of stability and prosperity when most of the city's main public monuments were built. Twice a year, on 2 July and 16 August, the Sienese recreate their medieval heritage in the Palio, a sumptuous pageant-cum-horserace around the Campo. The Palio has raced through war, famine and plague: the residents of the city's 17 *contrade*, or districts, pack the square as their representative horses and riders career around the Campo, and the rider who wins the race and the Palio, a heraldic banner, becomes an instant local hero.

At the bottom of the square stands the **Palazzo Pubblico Ⓑ**, with its crenellated facade and waving banners. Erected in the 14th century, it housed the offices of the city government and is framed by a slender bell tower, the **Torre del Mangia** (daily Mar–Oct 10am–7pm, Nov–Feb 10am–4pm). Climb more than 500 steps for a panorama of the city.

Although bureaucrats still toil in parts of the *palazzo*, as they have for some seven centuries, much of the complex is now devoted to the **Museo Civico** (www.comune.siena.it; daily 10am–7pm in summer, until 6pm in winter; combined ticket tower/museum valid for two days), which houses some of the city's

Medieval Siena.

TIP

To save up to 50 percent on entry fees to the excellent Siena museums purchase the Opa Si Pass. For details see www.operaduomo.siena.it.

greatest treasures. Siena's city council once met in the vast **Sala del Mappamondo**, although the huge globe that then graced the walls has disappeared. What remains are two frescoes attributed to the medieval master Simone Martini: the majestic mounted figure of Guidoriccio da Fogliano and, opposite, the *Maestà*. The *Maestà* is signed in Simone Martini's own hand, but in recent years doubts have been cast on the authenticity of the Guidoriccio. A smaller fresco recently uncovered below the huge panel may be Simone Martini's original, and the Guidoriccio may have been executed long after the artist's death.

In the Sala della Pace is Ambrogio Lorenzetti's *Allegory of Good and Bad Government*. Intended as a constant moral reminder to the city fathers, it depicts the entire sweep of medieval society, from the king and his court down to the peasants working the terraced hillsides outside the city walls.

Just up the hill is the **Duomo** **C**, a vast striped cathedral (www. operaduomo.siena.it; Mar–Oct 10.30am–7pm, Nov–Feb 10.30am–5.30pm). The facade is a riot of green, pink and white marble, a prelude to the bold black-and-white geometric patterns of the interior. The Duomo is at its best in August and October when the intricate marble inlaid paving is on display.

Duccio's masterpiece, the *Maestà*, the Virgin enthroned, painted for the altar, is now in the Museo dell'Opera del Duomo. The **crypt** is an extraordinary discovery, with recently revealed frescoes attributed to Duccio or his school. Because the frescoes were perfectly concealed for so long, the intensity of the colours shines through in a vivid array of blue, gold and red. Given that the frescoes date from 1280, the "modern" expressiveness is all the more remarkable.

Opposite the cathedral, **Santa Maria della Scala** **D** (www.santamaria dellascala.com; daily 10.30am–6.30pm) is often described as a city within a city. The far-sighted foundation functioned as a hospital and pilgrims' hostel for nearly 1,000 years, but is now a magnificent museum complex,

The Palio race in Siena's Piazza del Campo.

embracing frescoed churches, granaries and an archaeological museum.
The Pilgrims' Hall, depicting care for
the sick, is frescoed by Siena's finest
15th-century artists.

Siena has two other important
museums: the **Museo dell'Opera
del Duomo ❸** (Cathedral Museum;
www.museumflorence.com; Mon, Fri–
Sat 9am–9pm, Tue–Thu and Sun
9am–7pm), to the right (south) of the
cathedral, and the **Pinacoteca Nazionale ❺** (National Gallery; http://
pinacotecanazionale.siena.it; Tue–Sat
8.15am–7.15pm, Sun and Mon 9am–
1pm), in the Palazzo Buonsignori on
the Via San Pietro, just south of the
Campo. If the Pinacoteca is full of
luminous Madonnas, the Cathedral
Museum's main attraction is Duccio
di Buoninsegna, especially his moving
Maestà (1308).

The Crete region

All routes from Siena are lovely, especially the route southwest along the
N438 to the dramatic Crete region.
The N438 leads to unpromising
Asciano ❹, passing through postcard Tuscany. The Crete is a moon-
scape of pale clay hummocks and
treeless gullies, with sightings of
stately avenues of cypresses, winding
across the landscape to an isolated
farm, Romanesque church or *borgo*, a
fortified village.

Asciano's main street, Corso Giacomo Matteotti, is lined with stately
palazzi and home to the Romanesque
Collegiata and the **Museo Civico
Archeologico e d'Arte Sacra** (www.
museisenesi.org; Nov–Mar Sat–Sun
10am–1pm and 3–6pm, Apr–Oct
daily 10am–1pm and 3–7pm, Jul–Aug
5–10pm), an illuminating collection
of Sienese Gothic art, as well as minor
archaeological finds.

Beyond lies the spiritual remoteness of the Benedictine **Abbazia di
Monte Oliveto Maggiore ❺** (www.
monteolivetomaggiore.it; daily 9.15am–
noon and 3.15–5pm, until 6pm in
winter; free). Set among cypress

groves, Tuscany's most atmospheric
monastery exudes an air of aloof-
ness. The Great Cloister is covered in
quirky, memorable frescoes ostensibly
depicting the *Life of St Benedict*, begun
by Luca Signorelli in 1495 and completed by Sodoma from 1505. In one
scene Sodoma portrays himself with
his pet badgers (one wearing a scar-
let collar) looking like a pair of well-
trained dogs.

Bound by massive medieval walls,
Buonconvento ❻ links the moody
Crete area with the domesticated Tuscany of vineyards surveyed by hilltop
towns. From a distance, **Montalcino
❼** even looks like a *Trecento* Sienese
painting. The streets are narrow and
steep, and from the airy heights of
the walls there are entrancing views.
The highest point is the **Fortezza**
(Fortress), housing a respected wine
centre or *enoteca* (www.enotecalafortezza.
com; daily 9am–8pm), where regional
vintages can be sampled and the
ramparts explored. Few need much
prompting to indulge in a leisurely
lunch, washed down by full-bodied
Brunello di Montalcino.

*Terme San Filippo,
Val d'Orcia.*

Further south is another postcard sight that is ravishingly beautiful in the flesh. The ancient abbey church of **Sant'Antimo** ❽ (www.antimo.it), built of creamy travertine and set against tree-clad hills, has inspired poets and painters for years. The Romanesque church reveals capitals carved with biblical scenes, and recorded plainsong echoes around the walls as you explore. The small community of Augustinian monks who tend the church sing the Gregorian chant at Mass every Sunday afternoon throughout the year.

Val d'Orcia

A tortuous route leads through the **Val d'Orcia**, a Unesco World Heritage landscape. This part of Tuscany has been landscaped since time immemorial, with the Val d'Orcia, south of Siena, representing quintessential Tuscany: clusters of cypresses, ribbons of plane trees, vineyards on the slopes and farms perched on limestone ridges.

At its heart are **Castiglione d'Orcia** ❾ and **Rocca d'Orcia**. Both

In Siena, the Enoteca Medicea (tel: 0577-228 811; Mon–Tue noon– 7.30pm, Wed–Sat noon–midnight), the wine centre in the old Medici fortress, is the place to study and savour Sienese wines, from Chianti Classico to Vino Nobile di Montepulciano, Brunello di Montalcino and Vernaccia di San Gimignano.

hilltop villages boast medieval castles built to watch over the valley of the River Orcia, and down to the tiny spa town of **Bagno Vignoni** ❿. Where the village square ought to be, there is a large stone-lined pool: sulphurous vapours rise above the hot, bubbling waters which well up from volcanic rocks deep under the earth. Some famous bodies have bathed in this pool in times past, including St Catherine of Siena. Bathing is now forbidden, but on the main square you can sample the spa and Tuscan trattoria at Albergo Le Terme (tel: 0577-887 150).

Just north of Bagno Vignoni, a minor road leads up to **Castellúccio** and **La Foce** ⓫, from where there are spectacular views of a cypress-lined Etruscan road zigzagging up the hill. The next town is **Chianciano Terme** ⓬, a popular spa resort with the pampering **Terme Sensoriali** (www.termesensoriali.it; tel: 848 800 243) making a delightful day spa. Although better-known for its spas, historic centre (currently undergoing renovation and regeneration), and tiny Etruscan museum, Chianciano

TUSCAN SPAS

Tuscan spas are arguably the most beguiling in Italy. Landscape as seductive as the history plays a part: you can wallow in sybaritic spas that have been around since Etruscan or Roman times. In the 1st century AD, Emperor Augustus' physician issued a prescription to the poet Horace to visit the Tuscan spas, which is one of the first medical prescriptions on record. Lorenzo the Magnificent, ruler of Florence, who suffered from arthritis, was a notable spa enthusiast. Near Pisa, spas such as **Bagni di Pisa** and **Grotta Giusti** combine gracious 19th-century living with thermal pools and steamy grottoes dubbed "the eighth wonder of the world" by Giuseppe Verdi.

Fonteverde is a true destination spa and a favoured hideaway for anyone wishing to lap up laidback luxury among Siena's remote, rolling hills. **Saturnia**, set in the Maremma, and fed by historic springs, is a sophisticated resort at odds with the rugged Etruscan countryside beyond. In Chianciano, the **Terme Sensoriali** are both exhilarating and pampering. In Rapolano, the stylishness of **Terme di San Giovanni** contrasts with the unpretentiousness of its friendly rival, the Antica Querciolaia baths. The old-school spa, **Bagni San Filippo**, floats along on faded charm and a Fellini-esque blend of a surreal setting, cheerful improvisation and larger-than-life characters.

is now on the art map. The **Museum of Art of Chianciano** (280 Viale della Liberta; tel: 0578-60732; www.museodarte.org; Wed–Sun 10am–1pm, 4–7.30pm) boasts a fine collection of works by the Realists, Surrealists and Post-Impressionists.

Chiusi ⓭, one of the most powerful cities in the ancient Etruscan League, is more compelling for Etruscan history. Chiusi's pride is the **Museo Archeologico Nazionale** (daily 9am–8pm; free first Sun of the month), which has one of the finest collections in Italy – a thoughtfully arranged display of Etruscan funerary urns, canopic jars, sculptures and Greek-style vases excavated from local tombs. Arrangements can be made at the museum for a guided visit to one of the tombs in the vicinity.

The town's Romanesque church is a delight, built from recycled Roman pillars and capitals, while the **Museo della Cattedrale** (www.prolocochiusi.it; Feb–Mar Tue, Thu and Sat 9.45am–12.45pm, Sun also 3–5.15pm; Apr–May daily 9.45am–12.45pm, Sun 4–6.30pm; June–Oct daily 9.45am–12.45pm and 4–6.30pm; Oct–Jan daily 9.45am–12.45pm, Sun also 4–6.30pm) displays a collection of Roman and Lombardic sculpture. It is also the place to book a fascinating guided visit of an underground network of galleries, the Labyrinth of Porsenna, dug by the Etruscans and reused as Christian catacombs. The tour passes a giant Roman cistern and ends under the bell tower, which you can climb for views of Monte Amiata and the Val d'Orcia.

Chiusi stands almost on the border with Umbria, but our Tuscany tour continues north, up the fertile Val di Chiana, where cattle supply the raw ingredients of *bistecca alla fiorentina* (steak Florentine), then west to **Montepulciano ⓮**. This splendid hilltop town deserves leisurely exploration, with stops to sample the local Vino Nobile wines, either in rock-hewn cellars or in the elegant Caffè Poliziano (Via del Corso Voltaia 27/29). As the stand-in for Volterra in a popular vampire series, Montepulciano's main square now draws teenagers looking for bloodsucking romance.

Some of the best producers of Vino Nobile di Montepulciano are Avignonesi, Le Casalte and Poliziano.

Highly perched Montalcino.

The **Piazza Grande** sits at the town's highest point. On one side is the 15th-century **Palazzo Comunale** (Town Hall), a miniature version of the Palazzo Vecchio in Florence. On the other side, Sangallo's intriguing 16th-century **Palazzo Contucci** houses apartments for rent. The Contucci family has lived in Montepulciano since the 11th century and has been making wine since the Renaissance. Between the two palaces stands the gloomy **Duomo** (daily 9am–12.30pm and 3–6pm), which contains an altarpiece from the Siena School, the huge *Assumption* triptych (1401) by Taddeo di Bartolo. The revamped local museum complex, the **Musei di Montepulciano** (www.museocivico montepulciano.it; Tue–Sun 10am–1pm and 3–6pm, until 7pm in summer, Nov–Feb only Sat–Sun), features Gothic art in a Gothic palace.

When leaving Montepulciano for Pienza, do not resist the **Madonna di San Biagio**, perched on a platform below the city walls. This domed church of honey-and-cream-coloured stone, a Renaissance gem begun in 1518, is an Antonio da Sangallo masterpiece.

Model Renaissance city, built for a pope

Pienza ⓯ is an exquisite Renaissance construct, a city inspired by one vision. It is also famous for its Pecorino cheese, and for the fact that the future Pope Pius II was born here in 1405. He commissioned Bernardo Rossellino to rebuild the village of his birth as a model Renaissance city. Only the papal palace and the cathedral were completed and both are now suffering from subsidence.

Despite the cracks, the listing cathedral is uplifting, flooded with light from the great windows that the Pope requested – he wanted a *domus vitrea*, a house of glass, to symbolise the enlightenment of the Humanist Age. The **Palazzo Piccolomini** (www.palazzopiccolominipienza.it; Tue–Sun 10am–4.30pm, until 6.30pm in summer) is filled with the Pope's possessions, while the loggia was designed to frame views of Monte Amiata, the distant, cone-shaped peak of an

The stone-lined pool at Bagno Vignoni.

extinct volcano. In summer, the palace opens its courtyard to classical concerts.

To complete a tour around Val d'Orcia, visit **San Quirico d'Orcia** ⑯, with its splendid Collegiata (parish church), including a Romanesque west portal carved with dragons and mermaids.

Back in Siena, the N73 winds southwest through the sparsely populated foothills of the Colline Metalliferre, the Metal-Bearing Hills, which have been mined for iron, copper, silver and lead ores since Etruscan times.

Some 20km (12 miles) out of Siena, make time for the ruined Cistercian abbey of **San Galgano** ⑰, with its huge and roofless abbey church, where swallows skim in and out of the glassless Gothic windows and sunlight plays on the richly carved capitals of the nave. On a hill above the church is the beehive-shaped oratory built in 1182 on the site of San Galgano's hermitage. Look out for the sword in the stone, thrust there by the saint when he renounced his military career to become a hermit.

The Maremma

The Maremma is an evocative term but confusingly embraces the hilltop villages of the Alta Maremma, such as Massa Marittima, as well as the inland Etruscan settlements, such as Pitigliano. That's in addition to the unspoilt coastline, centred on the chic Monte Argentario peninsula and the simpler Castiglione della Pescaia. The landscape ranges from metal-bearing hills to lagoons, dunes and drained marshland.

Massa Marittima ⑱ is the ancient mining capital, but there are no ugly industrial scars, just two museums (www.museidimaremma.it) devoted to the history of mining (which flourished in the 13th century) and an impressive Romanesque church, decorated with sculptures. Massa Marittima is the gateway to the south coast's sandy beaches. These enjoy a sunnier reputation, notably different from the harsher climate to the north.

From **Piombino** ⑲, ferries take visitors to the island of **Elba**, either on day trips to see the villa where Napoleon was exiled, or for a relaxing

Montepulciano's Madonna di San Biagio, a Renaissance gem.

week of *cacciucco* fish soups at family-friendly resorts.

Further south along the coastal Via Aurelia, the city of **Grosseto** ⓴ is only worth visiting for its **Museo Archeologico** (www.museidimaremma. it; June–Sept Tue–Fri 10am–6pm, Sat–Sun 10am–1pm and 5–8pm, Oct–Mar Tue–Fri 9am–2pm, Sat–Sun 10am–1pm and 4–7pm, Apr–May Tue–Fri 9.30am–4pm, Sat–Sun 10am–1pm and 4–7pm). The collection sheds light on the otherwise indecipherable Etruscan ruins at **Vetulonia** (22km/13 miles northwest of Grosseto) and **Roselle** (7km/4 miles north).

Just south of Grosseto lie the drained marshes of the **Maremma**, including an unspoilt coastal park with deep Etruscan roots, and white cattle watched over by the *butteri*, Tuscan cowboys. The **Parco della Maremma** ㉑ (www.parco-maremma. it), also known as the Uccellina, is a protected traffic-free nature reserve, rich in wildlife, with a long stretch of unspoilt beaches. The visitor centre in **Alberese** (daily 8.30am–6pm) supplies information on walking trails.

The **Monte Argentario** peninsula presents a different face of the Maremma, from the chic resort of **Porto Ercole** to the wildlife haven in the lagoon north of Orbetello, an important wintering spot for birds. **Orbetello** ㉒ was a Spanish garrison town, and the Baroque architecture reflects this, with the sea lapping the stout city walls.

Inland, tiny villages like **Capalbio** ㉓ specialise in robust Tuscan dishes, such as wild boar and even baked porcupine (both are hunted locally). For a sybaritic experience, swim beneath the stars in the hot falls just south of **Saturnia** or opt for a Roman treatment in the luxury spa of the same name. The other villages in this forgotten corner of Tuscany are situated above dramatic tufa-stone cliffs. These are spectacular at **Pitigliano** ㉔, where the locals have long excavated caves in the rock for storing wine and olive oil, and at **Sovana** ㉕, where the Etruscans excavated tombs in the soft rock below the town. The tiny one-street village has two outstanding proto-Romanesque churches.

San Gimignano to Pisa

More spectacular sights await to the west of Siena. The N2 (SR2) passes **Monteriggioni** ㉖, a hilltop town built in 1213 to guard the northern borders of Sienese territory, encircled by walls and 14 towers.

Next, drive through the lower, modern town of **Colle di Val d'Elsa** ㉗ and, taking the Volterra road, head for the more ancient upper town. Here the main street is lined with severe 16th-century *palazzi*, only broken by a viaduct from which there are splendid views of the surrounding landscape. The shops here are filled with fine glassware made in the factories down in the valley.

Perhaps the most spectacular sight anywhere in Tuscany is **San Gimignano** ㉘, bristling with ancient towers (see page 299). This "medieval Manhattan" has scarcely changed in

The roofless abbey of San Galgano.

appearance since the Middle Ages and remains richly rewarding – despite the huge number of visitors. (It is best to stay overnight here, in one of the characteristic hotels, to savour the atmosphere after the day-trippers have gone). The bustling main street is lined with speciality food shops, with the best buys being Vernaccia wines and wild-boar ham.

The tall defensive towers that dominate the two squares at the highest point of the town were built as status symbols rather than for defensive purposes. Other highlights are the *Wedding Scene* frescoes in the **Museo Civico** (www.sangimignano.com; daily Apr–Oct 9.30am–6.30pm, Nov–Mar 11am–5pm), showing the newly-weds taking a bath together and climbing into bed. Equally engrossing are the frescoes that cover every inch of wall space in the **Collegio**, the collegiate church, depicting the *Last Judgement* and stories from the Old and New Testaments.

Volterra ㉙ is another rewarding place, sited high on a plateau with distant views to the sea. The entrance to the city is dominated by a Medicean castle, now used as a prison, and if you wander through the park that lies beneath its walls you will come to the **Museo Etrusco Guarnacci** (daily mid-Mar–Oct 9am–7pm, Nov–mid-Mar 8.30am–4.30pm) in Via Don Minzoni. This is packed with Etruscan urns excavated from cemeteries. *The Married Couple* urn is a masterpiece of realistic portraiture, and even more stunning is the bronze statuette known as *L'Ombra della Sera* (The Shadow of the Night), resembling a Giacometti sculpture but cast in the 5th century BC.

The Piazza dei Priori, the present-day town hall, was designed by Maestro Riccardo of Como in 1208. Younger fans are flocking to it as the "true" setting for the vampires' home in *Twilight*, even if the film preferred Montepulciano as a more luminous location. Volterra's handsome main square has some of the oldest civic buildings in Tuscany, and provides a showroom for the local alabaster-carving industry; galleries selling alabaster are located all over the town.

Pitigliano sits on top of a tufa-stone cliff.

The iconic Leaning Tower of Pisa.

The cathedral has a wealth of carvings from an earlier age, including a balletic *Deposition*, sculpted in wood in the 13th century.

West or north of Volterra, the landscape changes rapidly from hilly terrain to marshy coastline. You could be forgiven for missing out **Livorno** ㉚, for, although it has a gritty harbour area and a famous Renaissance statue (the *Four Moors* monument), World War II bombing and modern industry have stripped the city of its character.

Pisa ㉛, by contrast, is a must. All the main attractions lie around the well-named **Campo dei Miracoli** (the Field of Miracles). The Cathedral and Baptistery owe much to the influence of Islamic architecture, which Pisan merchants and scholars experienced through trading with Moorish Spain and North Africa. The gleaming marble facades are covered in arabesques and other ornamentation, as densely patterned as an oriental carpet.

Piazza del Duomo, San Gimignano.

The **Duomo** (Cathedral; 10am–7pm), built between 1068 and 1118,

is one of Italy's major monuments and contains one of its greatest sculptures, the magnificent pulpit by Giovanni Pisano. At the time of writing, the Opera del Duomo Museum was closed; see www.opapisa.it for up-to-date information.

The **Battistero** (Baptistery; 9am–7pm), built in the same Pisan Romanesque style as the cathedral, has another fine pulpit, sculpted in 1260 by Giovanni's father, Nicola. Also see the related sculpture museums and the cloisters (same times as Battistero), a lovely spot for summer concerts.

In 2001, after a decade under wraps to halt the dramatic tilt, the iconic **Leaning Tower** reopened (Torre Pendente; www.opapisa.it; daily Apr–Sept 8.30am–8.30pm, Mar and Oct 9am–7pm, Nov–Feb 9am–6pm; no entry to children under eight years; no bags). Visits are restricted to 40 people at a time, so aim to arrive for opening time if you can, or book in advance through the website. It may be possible to buy tickets on the day from the Campo dei Miracoli information office to the right of the Tower, open

daily 8.30am–8pm, shorter hours in winter. In summer, lucky visitors can attend a classical concert in the cloisters off the Field of Miracles. Equally atmospheric is **Bagni di Pisa**, just outside town: the romantic 18th-century spa resort even enjoys a view of the Leaning Tower.

Lucca, Garfagnana and the Tuscan Riviera

Lucca ㉜, a short way north, is a city of seductive charms, not least the ramparts encircling the city, which were transformed into a tree-lined promenade in the 19th century. The city has more than its fair share of splendid Pisan-Romanesque churches, with ornate facades of green, grey and white marble. The best include **San Michele** (daily 7.40am–noon and 3–6pm), with its tiers of arcading and hunting scenes, **San Frediano** (daily 9am–6pm), with its massive Romanesque font, and the splendid **Duomo di San Martino** (Mon–Fri 9.30am–5pm, Sat until 6pm, Sun 11.30am–5pm).The Duomo contains one of the most famous relics of medieval

Europe, the *Volto Santo* (Holy Face), conceivably carved by Nicodemus, who witnessed the Crucifixion – hence it was believed to be a true portrait of Christ (in fact, the highly stylised figure is probably a 13th-century copy of an 11th-century copy of an 8th-century "original"). Each year on 13 September, this revered relic is paraded through the candlelit streets in a huge procession that captivates the whole population.

Lucca is a classic Tuscan city on a human scale, with just enough cultural attractions to beguile but not bewilder. In summer, outdoor concerts add to Lucca's appeal, as do the discreet wine bars and cosy inns. Before leaving, browse the city's delightfully old-fashioned yet upmarket shops, including L'Erbario Toscano (www.erbariotoscano.it), which sells Tuscan beauty products and local crafts, from silk scarves to embroidery.

Lucca is the gateway to domesticated villa country as well as to mountainous Garfagnana, and to the **Tuscan Riviera**, a string of coastal towns known as **Versilia**. The

FACT

Villa Bernardini (tel: 0583-1646057; www.villa bernardini.it; pre-booking essential via website), outside Lucca, is one of the most engaging villas, gardens and wine estates. It is also a stunning location for events and weddings to be held.

Volterra's roman theatre.

FACT

Torre del Lago, 5km (3 miles) from Viareggio, has been staging the Puccini Festival, created by Giacomo Puccini (1858–1924), every summer since 1930. The Maestro's villa, mausoleum and outdoor theatre wallow in a suitably operatic lakeside location (www.puccinifestival.it).

Sculpture from the Eremo di Camaldoli, a small monastery near Arezzo which, unlike some monasteries, can be visited by both men and women (tel: 0575-556 021; www.camaldoli.it).

beaches have a regimented feel (you pay for access but get facilities such as sun-loungers, showers, beach cabins and a bar or restaurant). **Viareggio** ❸ is most interesting for its Art Nouveau architecture, its plentiful fish restaurants specialising in *cacciucco* (a hearty fish soup) and its atmospheric harbour area. It is the oldest of the coastal towns in Versilia and is famous for its February Carnival. Themed floats are usually spiced up with political satire and irony. Slightly further up the coast is **Forte dei Marmi**, *the* resort for socialising and being seen, while the Maremma beaches are for low-key nature-lovers.

To the north, towards the Emilian border, Tuscany becomes more rugged, dramatised by deep forests, Michelangelo's marble quarries and the Apuan Alps around the **Garfagnana**. This is a wild area of high mountains, seemingly perpetually covered in snow because the peaks are made of marble. Designated a nature reserve, the Garfagnana is not just a hiking paradise but a citadel of Slow Food. Information on waymarked trails is available from the main town, **Castelnuovo di Garfagnana** ❸ or to meet the cheesemakers and craftsmen, weavers and wine makers, book a day's tour with Sapori + Saperi (tel: 339-763 6321; www.sapori-e-saperi.com) who specialise in Slow Travel and Slow Food in northern Tuscany.

Further west, in the Apuan Alps awaits the marble town of **Carrara** ❸, with several quarries offering guided tours and workshops. Just outside Carrara is **Luni** ❸, the site of well-preserved Roman ruins.

Towards Lucca, numerous ornate villas and gardens are open to the public, including the **Villa Reale** (www.parcovillareale.it), at **Marlia** ❸. The villa itself is being renovated prior to be sold off as a hotel but its sumptuous gardens and Teatro Verde (Green Theatre), surrounded by clipped yew hedges, are open to visitors (daily 8am–6pm; pre-booked visits only: tel. 0583 30108 or email info@ parcovillareale.it).

Another splendid villa, with theatrical gardens spilling down the steep

COOKERY COURSES

Across the country Italy has seen a big growth in cookery courses, but this is particularly evident in Tuscany and Emilia Romagna. Ranging from those that take place in simple farm stays to those that are conducted by celebrity chefs, there is a huge selection to suit all tastes and some excellent options.

Cooking courses are a splendid chance to immerse oneself in the unique Italian lifestyle and hospitality while savouring the fantastic tastes and sights that these beautiful regions have to offer. Italian regionalism makes these courses all very different, and they can be combined with visits to markets, vineyards and food and wine matching.

One of the first cooking schools of its kind, founded by famous author and cookbook writer Lorenza de Medici over 20 years ago, is the Badia a Coltibuono cooking school (tel: 0577 74481; www.coltibuono.com). This is just one of many in idyllic settings where guests can learn the secrets of authentic regional Italian cuisine. Lessons here are taught by the Florentine Chef Benedetta Vitali, author of many cookbooks published in Italy and the US: with a natural, easy going style and a hand's on approach, Benedetta ensures that guests are guaranteed to bring back great authentic Italian recipes and menus to be used year round for all occasions.

hillside, is the **Villa Garzoni** (garden daily 8.30am–sunset, Nov–Feb Sat and Sun only) at **Collodi** ㊳. Collodi was also the pen name of Carlo Lenzini, the author of *The Adventures of Pinocchio* (1881), who spent his childhood here. The Pinocchio theme park in the village (www.pinocchio.it; daily 10am–sunset, Nov–Feb Sat–Sun only) is a welcome distraction for children and is dotted with sculptures based on episodes from the book.

Montecatini Terme ㊴ is the most elegant spa town in Tuscany, with ornate buildings surrounded by flower beds and manicured lawns. Day tickets allow you to sample the waters and admire the delightful marble-lined pools, splashing fountains and Art Nouveau tiles depicting nymphs at the **Terme Tettuccio** (www.termemontecatini.it).

Pistoia, Prato and Arezzo

Pistoia ㊵ and its neighbour Prato are both industrial towns specialising in textiles and metalworking, but with attractive historical centres. Both towns share an enthusiasm for contemporary art lacking in much of Tuscany. Pistoia's Piazza del Duomo is graced with the Romanesque **Cattedrale di San Zeno** and Baptistery. The town's churches contain a remarkable number of carved fonts and pulpits from the pre-Renaissance period; they include Giovanni Pisano's pulpit of 1301 in **Sant'Andrea church**, his masterpiece, more accomplished even than the pulpit he made for Pisa Cathedral in 1302. Instead, the Church of Tau displays work by a prominent modern sculptor, Marino Marini (1901–80), now part of the **Museo Marino Marini** (www.fondazionemarinomarini.it; Apr–Sept Mon–Sat 10am–6pm, until 5pm in winter), on Corso Silvano Fedi.

Prato ㊶ is a complex city, at once an ancient textile town and a city open to contemporary art and foreign immigration. The **Duomo** displays superb newly restored frescoes by Fra Filippo Lippi and Agnolo Gaddi. More bizarrely, on the facade, Donatello's outside pulpit also displays the Virgin's Girdle four times a year. (A local merchant had married

Piazza dell'Anfiteatro, Lucca.

a Palestinian woman in 1180 and discovered that her dowry included this unique relic.)

Instead, Prato's textile heritage can be seen in the excellent **Museo del Tessuto** (www.museodeltessuto.it; Tue–Thu 10am–3pm, Fri–Sat 10am–7pm, Sun 3–7pm). Also worth visiting is the 13th-century **Castello dell'Imperatore** (Wed–Mon 10am–1pm and 4–8pm), the only one of its kind in Italy, built for the Holy Roman Emperor Frederick II of Swabia. Set in a Tuscan rationalist building, the recently extended **Luigi Pecci Centro per Arte Contemporanea** (www.centropecci.it; Tue–Sun 11am–11pm) includes a sculpture park as part of this dynamic contemporary art complex.

On the Leonardo and Piero della Francesca trails

Beyond Pistoia is the tiny hilltop village of **Vinci** ㊷, birthplace of Leonardo da Vinci, where the castle has been turned into an entertaining **museum** (www.museoleonardiano.it; daily 9.30am–6/7pm) dedicated to the great man and his inventions.

The displays consist of wooden models of a bicycle, a submarine, a tank, a helicopter – all beautifully crafted and based on Leonardo's notebooks.

From Vinci, take a winding rural road into Florence, stopping at **Poggio a Caiano** ㊸ (daily June–Aug 8.15am–7.30pm, Apr–May and Sept–Oct until 6.30pm, Mar until 5.30pm, Nov–Feb until 4.30pm; closed 2nd and 3rd Mon each month; guided tour only).

Built for Lorenzo de' Medici, the villa became the archetype for the grand Tuscan summer residence. Skirting Florence, you can speed south to Arezzo on the A1 *autostrada*, or break the journey by leaving at the Incisa intersection and following signs for **Vallombrosa** ㊹. The reward is the surrounding beech wood; the poet John Milton, visiting in 1638, was inspired enough to write a description of Vallombrosa's autumnal leaves in *Paradise Lost*.

More delights await if you take the N70 (SP70) to **Stia** ㊺. From here, you can visit two sacred sites set high in spectacular woodland, cut by mountain streams and waterfalls. One is

Filippo Lippi's 'Scenes from the Life of St John the Baptist' in Prato Cathedral.

the hermitage at **Camaldoli** ㊻ (open only to male visitors), 17km (10 miles) east of Stia; the other is the monastery at **La Verna** ㊼, further south, best reached by driving east from Bibbiena. It was here that the hands and feet of St Francis were miraculously marked with the stigmata in 1224. The monastery commands panoramic views.

On the way south from here to Arezzo, seek out **Caprese Michelangelo** ㊽, which has a sculpture park in the grounds of the castle where Michelangelo was born. The views over Alpine countryside explain why Michelangelo attributed his good brains to the mountain air he breathed as a child.

Arezzo ㊾ has an **archaeological museum** in a monastery occupying the site of the Roman amphitheatre (www.museistataliarezzo.it; daily 8.30am–7.30pm; free first Sun of the month). It is full of Arretine tableware, fashionable during the Roman period. For most visitors, though, the highlight will be Piero della Francesca's painstakingly restored fresco cycle in the church of **San Francesco** (tel: 0575-352727; www.pierodellafrancesca.it; Mon–Fri 9am–6pm, Sat 9am–5.30pm, Sun 1–5.30pm; essential to pre-book). The frescoes illustrate the *Legend of the True Cross*, a complex story presented in the artist's compelling, beguiling style. Fans of his work will be tempted to follow the Piero della Francesca trail, like the heroine of *A Summer's Lease*, a novel by the English writer John Mortimer. If so, the trail proceeds to **Monterchi** ㊿, 25km (15 miles) west along the N73 (SS73), where a former schoolhouse displays his striking *Madonna del Parto*, the Pregnant Madonna.

From there, you should continue 12km (7 miles) north to **Sansepolcro** (51), where the **Museo Civico** (www.museocivicosansepolcro.it; daily 10am–1pm and 2.30–6pm, until 7pm in summer) has Piero della Francesca's 1463 masterpiece, *The Resurrection*, hailed by Aldous Huxley as "the best picture in the world". To complete the trail, spend time in **Urbino**, in the Marches, to see *The Flagellation of Christ* and other works in the Ducal Palace (see page 309).

Antique stall on Arezzo's main square.

ROLLING HILLS AND CYPRESS TREES

The harmonious, cultivated Tuscan countryside has for centuries been a favourite haunt of travellers looking to escape the madding crowds.

As glorious as its historic cities and artistic treasures may be, Tuscany's timeless landscape has long been a draw to visitors. After a hectic, sticky visit to Florence, Siena, Pisa or any of the other major towns, the relative coolness and freshness of a rural escape is a welcome treat. Small medieval hilltop towns overlook a rolling landscape which embraces both orderly agriculture and nature at its wildest. Terraces of vines and silvery groves of olives vie for attention with Tuscany's own peculiar landmark – tall, slender cypresses, often planted in rows as windbreaks. These elegant trees have studded the skyline here for centuries, prompting the writer D.H. Lawrence to accuse them of hiding the secrets of the Etruscans, the early settlers of these parts. He described them as "the sinuous, flame-tall cypresses/That swayed their length of darkness all around/ Etruscan-dusky, wavering men of old Etruria". These and other images of the Tuscan countryside feature strongly in the background of some of the greatest works of Renaissance art.

The hills around San Gimignano are dominated by rows of vines growing predominantly Vernaccia grapes, which are pressed to make Vernaccia, a fine white wine.

Some wine estates now produce very high-quality olive oils. Badia a Coltibuono also offers cookery courses to help you appreciate its wines and oils.

Cypress trees are planted in tight rows to serve as windbreaks.

The San Gimignano skyline.

TOWERS OF POWER AND PRESTIGE

In the Middle Ages, towers protected the wealthiest families in times of internal and external strife; today, they mark out some of Tuscany's oldest towns, catching the traveller's eye from afar. No better example exists of this distinctive skyscape than San Gimignano, which has 13 towers – although at one time it had more than 70.

San Gimignano's many towers date from the 12th and 13th centuries, and are mostly windowless, possibly to afford further protection; families could retreat into the many rooms inside for months at a time. Defence was not the only purpose of these lofty extensions, however: they were also status symbols. Building a tall, imperious tower was a way of flaunting your wealth and social standing.

Another theory about the towers concerns the textile trade for which San Gimignano was noted. Towers may have been built to house and protect valuable dyed fabrics, as there was little room to spread them out at ground level.

As many of Tuscany's medieval towns were built on hilltops, a climb to the top of a tower is usually rewarded with magnificent views over the town and the beautiful surrounding countryside.

Volterra church.

The hills around Siena are known for their reddish-brown clay, used in the construction of most of the city's buildings. The distinctive pigment in the clay is known as burnt sienna.

Chianina cattle, native to the region, provide the meat for bistecca alla fiorentina, the classic Florentine steak dish. Tuscan farmers also cultivate olives, fruit, barley, maize and tobacco.

UMBRIA AND THE MARCHES

Castles cling to ravines and woodland cloaks the wild mountains in the green heart of Italy, home to one of Christianity's best-loved saints.

Umbria, the birthplace of St Benedict and Francis of Assisi, seems bathed in a mystical glow. The magical undulating landscape encapsulates medieval hill towns such as Todi, the ancient yet cosmopolitan city of Perugia, and a medley of lakes north of Orvieto with its strong Etruscan presence. **The Marches** (Le Marche) are a place apart with their low-key churches counterpointed by the grandeur of the Sibillini mountainscape. The university town of Urbino has some of the most stunning Renaissance palaces in Italy while equally as fascinating is the microstate of San Marino.

Perugia

Perugia ➒ is the sun around which the other towns of Umbria orbit. In Perugia's **Piazza IV Novembre** spouts the splendid **Fontana Maggiore**, a Romanesque masterpiece created by the Pisan sculptors Nicola and Giovanni Pisano. On the far side of the fountain rise the steps to the austere Gothic cathedral, where people and pigeons gather to preen and flirt. Inside, the mystic *Deposition*, painted by Barocci while under the influence of poison proffered by a rival, inspired the Rubens masterpiece known as *The Antwerp Descent*.

Sweeping down from the piazza is the bustling **Corso Vannucci**. On the

right bristle the Gothic crenellations of the **Palazzo dei Priori** (Town Hall), one of the grandest public palaces in Italy. Fan-shaped steps lead to the **Sala dei Notari**, the lawyers' meeting hall, painted at the end of the 13th century.

The complex houses the **Galleria Nazionale dell'Umbria** (Tue–Sun 8.30am–7.30pm), a repository of Umbrian art, displaying works by Perugino and Pinturicchio, as well as Tuscan masterpieces by Piero della Francesca and Fra Angelico. Next door is the 15th-century **Collegio del**

Main Attractions

Perugia
Assisi
Spoleto
Monti Sibillini
Todi
Orvieto
Urbino
San Marino

Madonna in the Palazzo dei Priori, Galleria Nazionale dell'Umbria.

Assisi.

Cambio (www.collegiodelcambio.it; Mon–Sat 9am–12.30pm and 2.30–5.30pm, Sun 9am–1pm, closed Mon pm in winter). This medieval money exchange is graced by Perugino's frescoes, which fuse classical and Christian themes.

Corso Vannucci, and its early evening *passeggiata*, can best be appreciated from a café terrace, and includes a parade of locals dressed up to the nines as well as foreign students. Strolls often end in the **Giardini Carducci** and the second-best view in Perugia: the hills twinkling under the stars. No wonder Henry James called Perugia the "little city of infinite views".

South of the town is the eclectic **San Pietro**, with its superb 16th-century choir stalls, carved with a medieval bestiary featuring ducks, crocodiles and elephants. Closer is the barn-like **San Domenico**, with a melancholy interior redeemed by the striking tomb of Pope Benedict XI, who died in Perugia in 1304 after eating poisoned figs.

The adjacent cloisters are home to the **Museo Archeologico Nazionale dell'Umbria** (daily 8.30am–7.30pm) and a collection of Etruscan pottery

and metalwork, including a bronze chariot. West of the centre stands **San Bernardino**, its facade decorated with angels and musicians in diaphanous robes, much like figures in Mucha's *Art Nouveau* posters, except that these date back to 1451, not to the 1890s.

Assisi and the Vale of Spoleto

There is no place quite like **Assisi** ㊿. Despite the crowds, and despite the damage caused by the 1997 earthquakes, it remains an inspiring and spiritual city. The sight, as you approach Assisi, of the mighty arches supporting the Basilica di San Francesco, rising above the perpetual Umbrian haze, and of Monte Subasio, the great peak towering behind, is sufficient to make the rest of the world seem blissfully far away. The streets are almost too postcard-perfect: flower-bedecked balconies give way to secret gardens, and the smell of roses and wood smoke permeates the air.

The **Basilica di San Francesco** (www.sanfrancescoassisi.org; daily, Lower Church 6am–6.50pm in summer,

until 6pm in winter; Upper Church from 8.30am–6.50pm, until 6pm in winter; closed Sun am for services; audioguides available) is perfectly situated for sunsets. The facade, designed by a military architect, is like the saint it commemorates, beautiful in its austerity. The main doors lead into the Upper Basilica, decorated with Giotto's famous fresco cycle on the *Life of St Francis*. The frescoes have been restored following the 1997 earthquake: several saints have been reinstated, though the cycle will never look like it used to; the restoration is fragmentary yet faithful. With this cycle, Giotto revived the art of fresco painting in Italy, and this is his most accomplished work (though it is now believed that at least three other artists contributed to the cycle, including Pietro Cavallini), admired by all the great artists of the Renaissance for the degree to which it introduced realism into Western art.

The walls of the **Basilica Inferiore** (Lower Basilica) are a jigsaw puzzle of frescoes by many hands, all inspired by the life of St Francis. They vary between scenes of uplifting sweetness by Simone Martini, where even the horses seem to smile, to the sternly didactic vault frescoes depicting the monastic virtues of Chastity, Poverty and Obedience. Equally stern is the crypt where St Francis is buried, but the face of the little monk, painted in the transept by Cimabue and said to be a faithful portrait, tells a very different story.

Chronologically, a tour of the rest of Assisi begins with the **Roman Forum** beneath the **Piazza del Comune**. The forum's above-ground vestige is the **Tempio di Minerva** (Minerva's Temple), whose interior has been revamped in an unfortunately gaudy manner. In the northeast sector of town, the **Anfiteatro Romano** (Roman Amphitheatre), where live naval battles were staged, has been topped by homes that follow its original oval structure.

The forbidding **Rocca Maggiore**, looming above the town, was part of a string of towers guarding Assisi.

The Romanesque **Duomo di San Rufino** (7am–noon and 2pm–sunset) is best appreciated for the its three-tiered facade and sculpted central portal, decorated with lions and griffons. Below the Duomo stands **Santa Chiara** (same times as the cathedral), dedicated to the founder of the Order of the Poor Clares, the female wing of the Franciscans. The pink-and-white exterior is supported by buttresses that are decidedly feminine in their generous curves. The tomb of Santa Chiara, containing the saint's preserved body, can be seen in the crypt.

For a sense of the solitude and spirituality that suffused the lives of St Francis and St Clare, visit a couple of evocative retreats on the outskirts of Assisi. **San Damiano**, just south of town, is the convent where St Clare spent most of her reclusive life, and it retains the air of a simple religious retreat. More remote still is the Franciscan hermitage of the **Eremo delle Carceri** (daily 8.30am–sunset), a tranquil spot on the wooded slopes of Monte Subasio, 3km (2 miles) east of the town.

Assisi's Basilica di San Francesco.

Unrivalled views stretch from the summit of **Monte Subasio** (1,290 metres/4,230ft). For centuries the mountain was quarried for its pink stone, from which so many of the local buildings are made. The road through the Parco Regionale del Monte Subasio begins at the hermitage car park (closed at 6pm).

The town of Assisi sits on the rim of a dried-up lake bed called the Vale of Spoleto, which was drained in the 16th century. Several other towns of great character line the eastern shore, including **Spello** ㉞, which boasts Umbrian-style frescoes by Pinturicchio. **Spoleto** ㉟, which sits at the southernmost point of the former lake, is renowned for its summer arts jamboree, the Festival dei Due Mondi, a highbrow summer arts festival. The Upper Town has a monopoly on charm, even if the Lower Town is home to several Romanesque churches and Roman ruins.

The town's dominant building, the **Rocca Albornoziana** (Tue–Sun 9.30am–7.30pm, Mon 9.30am–2pm; tel: 0743-224 952) was built as a papal stronghold and became the home of Lucrezia Borgia. It served as a prison until 1983, including incarcerating members of the Red Brigades, but now the well-restored castle contains the Museo del Ducato (Duchy Museum), dedicated to local archaeology, art and history, including the spread of monasticism. Alongside is the striking **Ponte delle Torri**, spanning the gorge that yawns between the castle and the opposite hill. The medieval bridge was built as an aqueduct in the 13th century, and you can walk across the top of the (now dry) water channel.

Spoleto's outstanding treasure is the harmonious Romanesque **Duomo**, or **Cattedrale di Santa Maria Assunta**, (daily 8.30am–6pm). Its medieval porch is surmounted by a rose window, while the bell tower incorporates recycled Roman stone. The cathedral floor has an intricate herringbone and spiral Romanesque design. The chapel to the right was decorated by Pinturicchio, while the apse is ablaze with Filippo Lippi's final work, an exquisite Madonna surrounded by a rainbow and an arc of angels.

A selection of salami for sale, including coglioni de mulo ("mule's balls"), a speciality of the region – made from pork, not donkey.

UMBRIA'S GREEN HEART

Umbria's arty hill towns are often surpassed by the wild scenery to the east of the region, close to the borders with Le Marche. The rural area bounded by Spoleto, Terni and Norcia offers stunning landscapes and food trails. These wild hilltop hamlets are places to try peasant cheeses, salami and lentils, as well as local olive oil and princely black truffles.

The Nera Valley (Valnerina) is often called "the soul of Umbria" for its entrancing blend of narrow river gorges, fast-flowing waters and wooded slopes dotted with hermitages and fortified hamlets. The Marmore waterfall (www.marmorefalls.it), created by the Romans, remains a magnificent sight. The Nera River Park (tel: 0744- 0744-629 82; www. marmorefalls.it) appeals to outdoor enthusiasts who can indulge in canoeing and rafting on the river. The valley flows into the far larger Sibillini park (tel: 0737-972 711; www.sibillini.net). Spoleto is a stepping stone to the mountainous east of Umbria, where winding narrow roads climb past beech forests to the snowy peaks of the Monti Sibillini range, arguably the loveliest section of the Apennines. Norcia, with its tempting truffles and salami feasts, makes a good base. From Norcia, roads climb ever higher to the spectacular Piano Grande, a vast open plain that is carpeted in rare Alpine plants in summer. High pastureland and seemingly impenetrable forests make this area a hikers' paradise and the home of wolves and wild cats, peregrine falcons and golden eagles.

On the north side of the stairs leading to the Piazza del Duomo is the solemn Romanesque **Basilica di Sant'Eufemia** (Thu–Fri 11am–1.30, Sat–Sun 11.30am–4.30pm); its chaste perfection contrasts with the cathedral's grandeur. Note Sant'Eufemia's massive and ancient stone throne behind the altar. Next to the church in the Archbishop's Palace is the **Diocesan Museum** (same times as above), with a fine collection of paintings from the 13th and 18th centuries including works by Filippino Lippi and Domenico Beccafumi.

Spoleto makes a good base for exploring the **Monti Sibillini** range in the east of Umbria. An appealing drive leads, via Triponzo, to **Norcia** ⑤⑥, the birthplace of St Benedict and a major centre of the truffle and salami industries. On the return journey you can take in the pleasing 8th-century monastery at **San Pietro in Valle** ⑤⑦ (www.sanpietroinvalle.com). The monastic complex is now a hotel, but the church, with its Lombardic sculpture and 12th-century frescoes can still be visited (Mar Sat–Sun 10am–12.30pm and 2.30–4pm; Apr–Sept daily 10am–1pm and 3–6pm; other times by reservation: tel. 335 6543 008).

Todi

West of Spoleto is the hilltop town of **Todi** ⑤⑧, a beguiling medieval city of Etruscan and Roman origins. The town transcends its quiet charms, from labyrinthine alleyways to film-set main square. Unsurprisingly, Todi has become the haunt of history of art scholars and a smugly knowing expat set.

The lovely view from the **Piazza Garibaldi** is enhanced by scents from the gardens below. Nearby is the mesmerising **Piazza del Popolo**, seat of the civic and religious powers, and widely regarded as one of Italy's most magical medieval squares. Symbolically surrounding the Duomo are the three medieval civic powers, represented by the Gothic **Palazzo dei Priori, Palazzo del Capitano** and **Palazzo del Popolo**. The well-restored Palazzo dei Priori (1293–1337), today's town hall, commands most attention with its crenellations, battlements and mullioned windows. The grand staircase leads to

Ponte delle Torri, Spoleto.

a **Museo Civico** (Civic Museum; currently closed for renovation, check reopening at www.sistemamuseo.it), which retraces the city's history with a collection of paintings, coins and artefacts.

The **Duomo** (daily 8.30am–1pm and 3pm–6pm, no visits during Mass) dates from the early 12th century and stands on the site of a Roman Temple to Apollo. The three-tiered facade and bold rose window reveal a dusky interior, fine choir and stained-glass windows. The Gothic campanile, built 100 years later, strays from the fine Romanesque style.

The area is just as exciting underground. Indeed under the Duomo and neighbouring piazzas unravels a 5km- (3 mile-) network of tunnels dotted with pre-Roman, Roman and medieval wells and cisterns, some of which are open to visitors (Apr–Oct Tue–Sun 10am–1.30pm and 3–6pm, Nov–Mar Sat–Sun 10.30am–1pm and 2.30–5pm).

A brisk walk around the hill will bring you to the church of **San Fortunato**. The seemingly squat structure was begun in 1292 but only finished in 1462. In keeping with Umbrian tradition, it is a large vaulted church, a variant on simpler, low-pitched Tuscan "barn" churches. The sculpted central portal reveals whimsical Gothic depictions of humans and beasts. The interior is light and airy, with the eggshell whiteness of the stone enhanced by the deep sable colour of the finely carved choir.

After enjoying the view from San Fortunato's bell tower, head through **Parco della Rocca** for more sweeping views, and on down the mountain to the Renaissance church of **Santa Maria della Consolazione** and the shady gardens nearby. The church, based on a Greek cross design, has mistakenly been attributed to Bramante because of the similarities with St Peter's in Rome. The stark, if airy, interior comes as a slight let down after the harmonious exterior but remains one of Todi's rare disappointments.

Vine-growing Orvieto

Looming on a sheer ledge of lavastone, **Orvieto** ❺❾ is a brooding Etruscan presence hewn out of dark volcanic rock. As such, the hill is porous and in danger of bringing the city down as it crumbles. More positively, the fertile volcanic slopes are covered in the vineyards that produce Orvieto's famously crisp white wines.

A climb up serpentine curves, past scaffolding-clad streets, is rewarded with the startling expanse of the **Piazza del Duomo**. With any luck, the late-afternoon sun will be glittering off the mosaics of the 14th-century cathedral's astonishing facade. The Romanesque-Gothic **Duomo** (Apr–Sept daily 7.30am–7.30pm, Mar and Oct 7.30am–6.30pm, Nov–Feb 7.30am–1pm, crypt Mon–Fri only; free) was commissioned in 1290 but was only completed four centuries later. The massive undertaking required the input of legions of architects, sculptors, painters and mosaicists. The facade is bolstered by striped horizontals of basalt and travertine.

Inside the cathedral, the black-and-white stripes point up the curvilinear

St Patrick's Well in Orvieto, which dates back to 1527.

arches. The apse is decorated with scenes from the *Life of the Virgin*, completed by Pinturicchio. On the left-hand side of the altar is the **Cappella del Corporale**, painted by Ugolino and his assistants and depicting *The Miracle of Bolsena*. To the right of the altar is the boldly frescoed **Cappella Nuova**, whose decoration was begun by Fra Angelico in 1447 and completed by Luca Signorelli at the turn of the next century.

Also on Piazza del Duomo, opposite the cathedral, is the **Museo Claudio Faina** (Tue–Sun Apr–Sept 9.30am–6pm, Oct–Mar 10am–5pm). This is home to an important archaeological collection of Etruscan and Hellenistic works. The highlights include Etruscan black *bucchero* ware, Attic vases and 4th-century pots depicting Vanth, the Etruscan winged goddess of the underworld, who has snakes wrapped around her arms.

Via Duomo and **Corso Cavour** are lined with elegant restaurants, boutiques and craft shops selling Orvietan ceramics, including reproduction Etruscan ware or carved wooden sculptures. To the right, off Corso Cavour, is

the striking 12th-century **Palazzo del Popolo**, made of basalt and tufa-stone.

Straight ahead are the **Palazzo Comunale** and the church of **Sant'Andrea** in the **Piazza della Repubblica**. The dark volcanic stone lends a slightly gloomy air to the city, but the **medieval quarter** remains an engaging part of the town, tucked into ancient walls hung with pots of tumbling geraniums, and tiny cave-like workrooms of Orvietan artisans.

A fascinating **underground tour** (www.orvietounderground.it; daily at 11am, 12.15am, 4pm, 5.15pm; in summer every 15 minutes) visits the hidden city that winds its way underneath the main monuments, and reveals secret Etruscan tunnels. You can even get married in one of the Etruscan chambers.

Also of interest is the 6th-century BC **Crocifisso del Tufo** necropolis (daily 8.30am–7pm, until 5pm in winter), located on the north side of Orvieto's cliff. The ancient Etruscan tombs made from tufa blocks are lined up in such a regular pattern which betrays an early interest concern in urban planning. The combined ticket also

Orvieto cathedral.

Detail of a 13th-century mosaic in the dome of Orvieto Cathedral.

allows entry to the **National Archeological Museum** (daily 8.30am–7.30pm) in the Papal Palace, with its fine collection of Etruscan pottery.

Lake Trasimeno

The road north from Orvieto will take you to **Città della Pieve** 60, birthplace of Perugino, father of the Umbrian School of painting. The town has several of his works, including *The Adoration of the Magi*, which features Lake Trasimeno in the background.

Today **Lake Trasimeno** (Lago di Trasimeno) is Umbria's summer playground, ringed by campsites and with opportunities for tennis, riding, swimming, sailing, boat trips and wine-tasting. **Castiglione del Lago** 61, strung out along a charming promontory, is the lake's engagingly touristy capital, offering splendid views from the ramparts of the 14th-century castle.

North of the lake, the road through Umbertide takes you to **Gubbio** 62, which lays claim to being one of the most intact medieval towns in Italy. Once known as the "city of silence" because of its desolate position in the

The beautifully preserved hill town of Urbino.

Umbrian backwoods, today it is within easy reach of those who love good food and architecture. Gubbio clings to the side of Monte Ingino, and its major buildings are stacked on steep terraces.

At the top of Monte Ingino (take the funicular railway from the station in Via San Geraloma to the top, then walk back down) rises the **Basilica di Sant'Ubaldo**. The remains of the saint are kept here in a crystal urn above the altar. The basilica also displays the three immense candles with which the sturdy men of Gubbio race up the hill in a celebration of the saint's day every 15 May.

Returning to the town, your path should take you to the fine **cathedral** to see the great Gothic rib-vaulting and the medieval stained glass. Across a small passage from the cathedral is the **Palazzo Ducale** (Tue–Sun 8.30am–7.30pm), begun in 1476 by Federico da Montefeltro, Duke of Urbino.

Gubbio's skyline is dominated by the bell tower of the restored 14th-century **Palazzo dei Consoli**, which is home to the **Museo Civico** (daily Apr–Oct 10am–1pm and 3–6pm, until 5.30pm in winter). Its Great Hall

houses a quixotic collection of medieval paraphernalia, including examples of medieval plumbing. A side room contains the **Tavole Eugubine**: seven bronze plates upon which a precise hand has translated the ancient Umbrian language into Latin.

The Marches (Le Marche)

After the stunning hill towns of Umbria, the neighbouring region of the Marches holds very few sights that can compete, with the singular exception of **Urbino** ❸, the stronghold of the wise old warrior Duke Federico da Montefeltro. Here he constructed one of the loveliest Renaissance palaces in Italy. Urbino is an eyrie whose golden buildings are set high amid spectacular mountains. Urbino remains one of the few hill towns left in Italy not ringed by the unsavoury intrusions of modernity. The original Old City remains almost completely "unimproved", perched at the top of its two peaks.

The **Piazza del Popolo** is a tourist centre by day. By night, groups of university students recline here on the steps or in the cafés, or stand in the street and discuss politics, the latest foreign film, or last night's poetry reading. The facades are old; the faces are generally young. The contrast exemplifies the relaxed symbiosis that exists between Urbino's walls and the lives they enclose.

The duke and his humanist contemporaries felt man was the centre of the universe – a significant break with Christian philosophy. The courtyard of his **Palazzo Ducale** is paved with a hub, with radiating spokes of marble to symbolise man's central position. The building itself is part palace and part fortress: a graceful, secure nest in the rarefied mountain air for the duke to feather with marvellous works of art. The **Galleria Nazionale delle Marche** (www.palazzoducaleurbino.it; Tue–Sun 8.30am–7.15pm, Mon 8.30am–2pm, last entry 75 mins before closing; tours available), now housed in the palace, has several fine works by Piero della Francesca, including his enigmatic and disturbing *Flagellation of Christ*, and by the town's most famous artist, Raphael. Also remarkable is the *trompe l'œil* inlay work in the duke's study.

Pottery for sale in Orvieto.

Down the street from the ducal palace is **Casa di Raffaello** (www.palazzo ducaleurbino.it; times vary, check website for details) where Raphael spent his childhood. In the courtyard is the stone upon which Raphael and his father, Giovanni, also an artist, ground their pigments.

San Marino

Nearby awaits the **Republic of San Marino** ⑥, a toy-town state which nevertheless commands territory larger than Monaco. The appeal of this pocket principality lies in its anomalous status: self-governing San Marino produces its own stamps and arms, allowing its 32,000-strong population to live on tourism supported by tax-haven revenues. The foundation of the republic is celebrated every 3 September with a crossbow competition and a game of bingo. Tax-free crossbows aside, the citadel also offers magnificent fortifications and breathtaking hilltop views.

Park by the cable-car entrance and ride up to the **Rocca**, a citadel bound by 16th-century walls and studded with touristy shops selling everything from bejewelled daggers to full body armour. A steep stairway affords views of massive 16th-century walls and medieval towers. San Marino's other vocation is much in evidence on the main square, with a duty-free shop proclaiming: "Booze at the right price." Surveying the scene from above is Torre di Gualta, the Citadel's boldest castle.

Just west of San Marino stands Federico da Montefeltro's hilltop fortress of **San Leo** ⑥, a perfectly preserved citadel perched on a cliff. Resembling an aloof hermitage, San Leo commands a bold panorama stretching from the Adriatic to the Apennines. Before heading to the castle, collect your thoughts in the Romanesque **Duomo**, as well as in the parish church where St Francis preached. Known as the **Rocca** (www.san-leo.it; Mon–Fri 10.30am–4.20pm, Sat–Sun 9am–6pm), the castle offers vertiginous views over a rocky spur towards San Marino. Inside there is a fine collection of firearms old and new. San Leo is infinitely more seductive than San Marino, with an other-worldly air that survives the patina of tourism.

The citadel of San Marino.

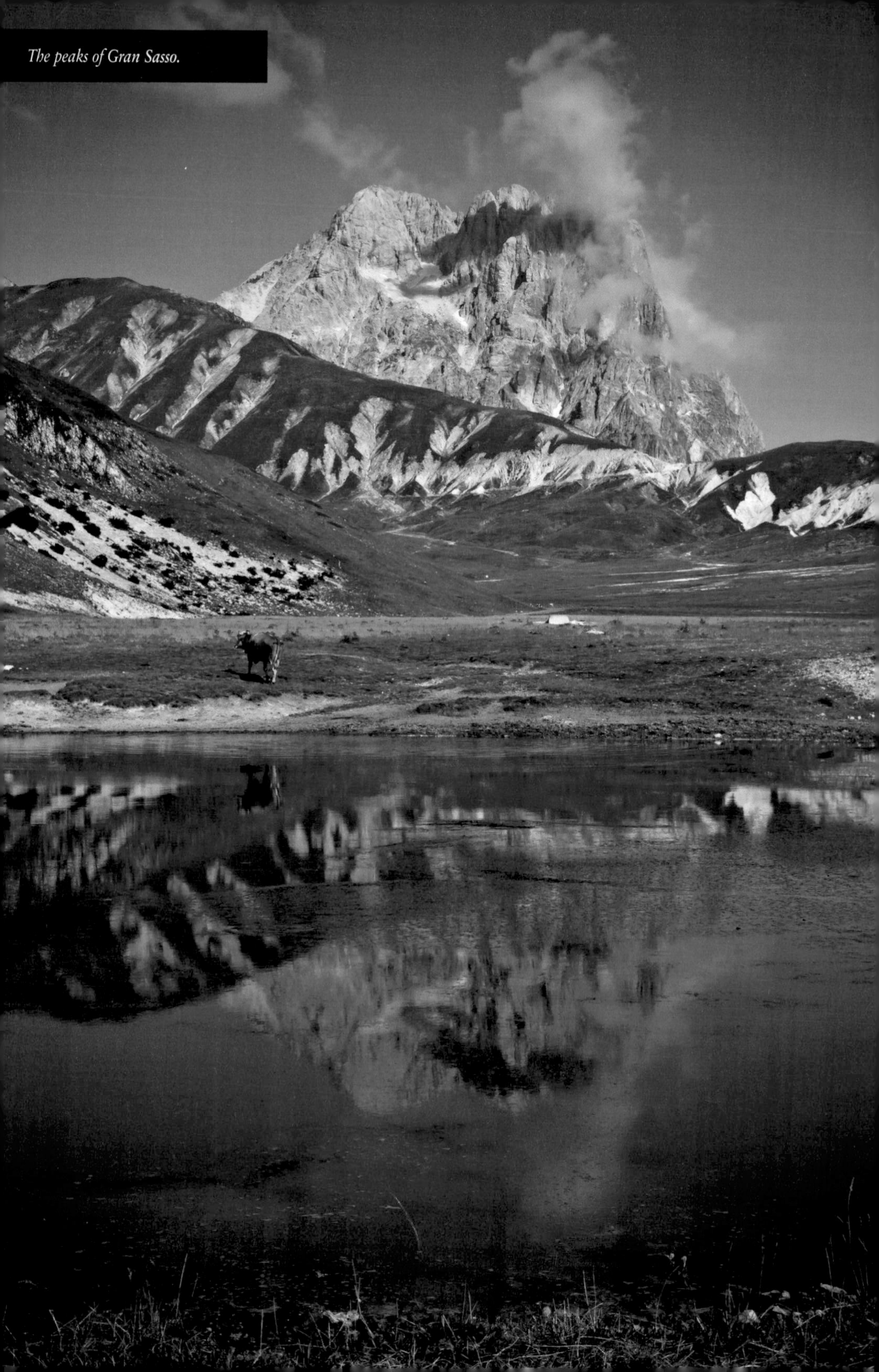

The peaks of Gran Sasso.

ABRUZZO AND MOLISE

Two huge national parks, Abruzzo and Gran
Sasso, make this a region where the
wonders of nature rule supreme.

From rugged mountainous scenery and craggy medieval hill towns to the sandy Adriatic coastline, Abruzzo offers everything an Italophile could wish for. Abruzzo is best known for its superb Parco Nazionale dell'Abruzzo, Italy's third-largest park. The Gran Sasso massif is a magnet for outdoor enthusiasts and wilderness lovers, while L'Aquila is the region's bustling and prosperous capital. Sleepy Molise, Abruzzo's smaller undiscovered neighbour, offers more remote rolling hill country and attractive unspoilt beach resorts such as Termoli.

For years the region's wild beauty was hidden from the world by the Apennines. Then, helped by regular flights to Pescara, the growth of eco-tourism and Slow Food, this once hidden corner began to emerge from the shadows. The region received a major blow when its capital, L'Aquila, was struck by an earthquake in 2009 (see page 319). And in 2016, another devastating earthquake truck Amatrice, 50km (31 miles) north of L'Aquila. The rest of the region remains unscathed, although desperately dependent on tourism to relaunch the shaken local economy. But at heart, Abruzzo remains as robust as its ruby-red signature wine, Montepulciano d'Abruzzo, and as earthy as Abruzzese cuisine.

Sunflowers abound in summer.

Pescara

The energetic city of **Pescara** ❶ has been a stepping stone to the Adriatic since Roman times. The modern-day communication links have turned the city into a bustling commercial capital. Even so, Pescara, which was heavily bombed in World War II, would win few beauty contests. Much of the local building may be mundane but, with an eye to becoming an Adriatic Riviera hotspot, Pescara is changing. The centre has smartened itself up, with much of the action gravitating around

Main Attractions

La Civitella
Vasto
Adriatic beaches
Parco Nazionale
  dell'Abruzzo
Sulmona
Santo Stefano
L'Aquila
Saepinum

Piazza della Rinascita. By day, stroll the pedestrianised streets with their Art Nouveau-style facades, including the birthplace of Italy's bold but bombastic poet, d'Annunzio (www.casad annunzio.beniculturali.it; Corso Man-thonè 116; daily 9am–2pm).

In the hinterland, the hilltop towns of **Loreto Aprutino** ② and Penne are a short drive away, but a world away in atmosphere. Loreto Aprutino is a medieval settlement clustered around a castle with a distinctive restaurant (Il Celliere) and views to match. Here, as elsewhere in Abruzzo, there is a passion for Slow Food, which can be experienced on market day (Thursday). Simple dishes include chargrilled meats, fish stews, ribbon pasta dishes, salami, wild

saffron and Pecorino cheese. **Penne** ③, another quaint village, is the province's oldest settlement, and a place for pottering from the cathedral to Corso Alessandrini, which is lined with noble facades.

Chieti to the coast

Half an hour inland from Pescara is the ancient town of **Chieti** ④, spread over a ridge. Known since antiquity for its views across mainland Abruzzo and the sea, it is home to the region's finest archaeological museum, **La Civitella** (www. archeoabruzzo.beniculturali.it; Tue–Sat 8.30am–7.30pm, Sun until 1.30pm; free first Sun of the month), which itself occupies the site of the Roman amphitheatre. The highlights include

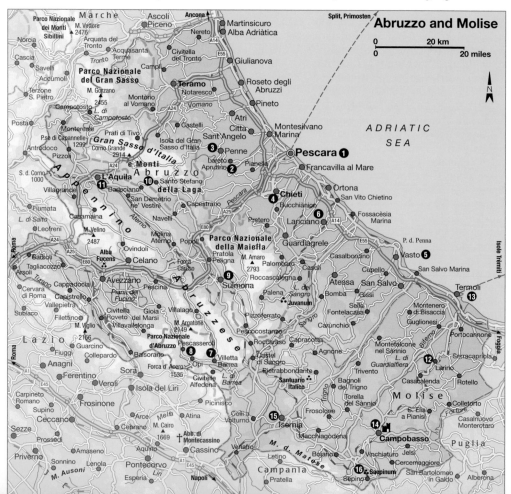

temple friezes, imperial busts and the symbol of Abruzzo, the serene, 6th-century BC Capestrano Warrior, who embodies the Zen-like fighting spirit of the region.

As you travel south down the coast from Pescara on the coast road towards **Vasto ⑤**, the natural beauty of Abruzzo reveals itself. Beach umbrellas disappear as you reach the coast of the *trabocchi*. Fishermen weave tales of these fantastical stilt-like fishing platforms, supposedly created by local farmers too timid to take a fishing boat out to sea. Vasto's resort, the **Marina di Vasto**, embraces both sand dunes and rocky inlets, while Vasto itself, perched above the coast, indulges its foodie spirit and sense of fun. Summer visitors can combine castle-visiting with a two-month Slow Food festival dedicated to fish stew, known as Il Brodetto. Traditionally a poor fisherman's stew, made from leftover fish, the feast involves infinite variety and is as big a draw as the summer music festival, charming main square and 15th-century castle.

The rugged interior

Inland from the coast runs the Sangro Valley, which leads to **Lanciano ⑥**, and possibly a truffle lunch when in season. Lanciano also boasts a fine cathedral and an imposing clock tower built on brick bridges which may date back to Roman times.

After World War II many farmers left to look for work, and the hill towns were often ringed with ugly apartment blocks to accommodate them. A notable exception is **Roccascalegna**, where St Peter's Church and Castle is a beacon for conservation, balancing on top of a limestone bluff. The **Castle** (Mar–June and Sept–Dec Sat–Sun 10am–1pm and 3–6pm, Jan until 5pm, Jul–Aug daily 10am–1pm, 3–7pm; closed Feb) is home to the legend of a wicked baron who was murdered when he made a local girl submit to the *droit de seigneur*.

As the River Sangro forges down the valley towards the majestic Maiella mountain, it pauses to form the lake at **Bomba**. You can go canoeing or cruise the lake and spot leaping fish and diving herons. Or

The dramatic landscape of the national park of Gran Sasso.

Trabocchi are traditional wooden fishing platforms.

PARK LIFE

Known as the "region of parks", a third of Abruzzo's territory is protected – including in the Abruzzo, Maiella and Gran Sasso-Laga (www.gransassolagapark.it) national parks. The most diverse landscape is the Abruzzo national park, home to a surviving 40 or so Marsican bears. Rangers escort the public on bear-watching trips, where visitors have a reasonable chance of viewing the 227kg (500lb) Marsicans. The park is also home to around 50 Apennine wolves, as well as lynxes, chamois, roe deer, wild boar, eagles and griffons. Although no longer endangered, the wolves are elusive but can be spotted on a wildlife tour. Ecotur (tel: 0863-912 760; www.ecotur.org), based in Pescasseroli in the heart of the park, leads groups on wolf-howling sessions, with the wild wolves responding to a soundtrack of howling.

Santo Stefano, an example of sustainable tourism.

you can simply sit by the shore and watch the sun go down to the sound of a frog chorus. Hikers can head up into Monte Palano, with its oak and chestnut-tree woods underscored by a seasonal explosion of cyclamen, wild roses, broom and rare orchids.

The nearby ruins of **Juvanum** are a reminder of ancient times, including the remains of Samnite temples and a Roman theatre. Walk in the footsteps of legionaries at this Roman settlement sitting among farmers' fields against the backdrop of the Maiella peaks (www.parcomajella.it; park open until dusk, museum: mid-Jul–Aug daily, Jul and Sept Sat–Sun 10.30am–1pm and 4.30–7pm).

From Lanciano, either head to Vasto and the coast or explore the rugged hinterland. The Sangro Valley opens onto Abruzzo's treasured **Parco Nazionale** (www.parcoabruzzo.it). Founded in 1923, the park is home to some of Europe's rarest animals (see page 315). Medieval **Barrea** ❼ makes an inviting gateway, with its terracotta rooftops and stone-clad Old Town sitting above a deep blue lake.

Across the valley from Barrea is the hillside town **Civitella Alfedena**, known as the "village of the wolves". Sightings of wolves and lynxes living in semi-captivity are frequent. From Alfedena it's a short drive down to **Pescasseroli** ❽, a curious mixture of Alpine architecture and traditional *centro storico*. As well as being an engaging ski resort, in summer it becomes a base camp for nature-lovers. This is hiking country, with sightings of eagles, falcons and hawks, and conceivably even wolves. The rugged terrain and dense forests give way to fields of wheat, vineyards and olive groves closer to the coast.

Heading away from the national park towards L'Aquila, you reach the appealing town of **Sulmona** ❾. "*Sulmo mihi patria est*" (Sulmona is my homeland) proclaimed its most famous son, the Roman poet Ovid, whose statue takes pride of place in Piazza Settembre. Sulmona is also noted for its religiosity and heartfelt Easter festivities, which end with the flight of doves, from which the local people claim to predict the bountifulness of

the harvest. Visitors with a sweet tooth will not miss a chance to sample the local speciality of sugared almonds.

Sulmona's pride is the **Palazzo della Santissima Annunziata**, once a combination of hospital, church (Wed–Fri and Mon 9am–1pm and 3–6pm, Sat–Sun 9am–6pm) and granary. It wears its four centuries of architecture in style: with a Gothic portal on the left, a Renaissance doorway, and a flamboyant Baroque church next door. On the first floor of the Annunziata is a museum of local archaeology (Tues–Sun 9am–1pm and 3.30–6.30pm).

The road between Sulmona and L'Aquila (Route 261) offers one of the most spectacular drives in Abruzzo, following the Aterno River Valley past medieval villages, each with its ruined castle and church. Expect the Gran Sasso mountain to dominate: this is the high point of the Apennines in every sense – 2,912 metres (9,560ft) of majestic rock, reminiscent of the limestone peaks in the Tyrol.

Santo Stefano

Just inside the Gran Sasso Park lies the delightful village of **Santo Stefano** ⑩, once an unknown *borgo* but now a model of rural living (see box). Peering down on Santo Stefano is **Rocca Calascio**, a picturesque stony hamlet. Beyond stretch the plains of **Campo Imperatore**, a low-key winter sports resort and summer outdoor playground. This Alpine highland resonates to a soundtrack of cowbells and bleating sheep. Known as "little Tibet", in summer its dried ravines and riverbeds contrast with vivid green pastures – an ideal place for hiking and cycling.

L'Aquila's earthquake zone

Dominated by the Gran Sasso, the highest mountain in the Apennines, **L'Aquila** ⑪ was Abruzzo's loveliest city until struck by a major earthquake in April 2009 (see page 319). If some suburbs have been restored, only voyeurs will find any solace in the

scene of devastation that awaits – still today – in the historic centre, so the city is best avoided for the foreseeable future. After the capital of Abruzzo is restored, and the city centre reopened, come back to see whether this masterpiece of medieval town planning is a shadow of its former self.

Molise

Molise broke away from Abruzzo in 1963, and has been a separate entity ever since; it enjoys the lowest profile of any Italian region. Although clinging onto Abruzzo's coat-tails, Molise shares a similarly wild spirit. Molise is a place for lapping up the rural, sleepy lifestyle, rather than the sites. Foodies will appreciate the robust red wines and ricotta-filled ravioli, as well as the fish soup, truffles, mushrooms and Caciocavallo cheese. Families will head to the wild coastline and the sandy beaches on the Adriatic. The cities are often disappointing but beyond those, Molise is frontier country: catch it while it lasts.

If you take the train from Termoli to Campobasso between 24 and 27

EAT

Molise is rural rather than backward, with tasty produce ranging from olive oil to truffles, mushrooms and Caciocavallo cheese. Sample Brodetto fish soup from Termoli and Calcioni ravioli filled with ricotta, pork and Provolone cheese. The full-bodied red wines include Montepulciano di Molise and Aglianico.

VILLAGE PEOPLE

A decade or so ago the medieval hamlet of Santo Stefano (www.sextantio.it) was crumbling into the hills of Abruzzo, and fast becoming a ghost town. Then Daniele Kihlgren, an idealistic Milanese-Swedish entrepreneur, rode by on his motorbike. Smitten by a vista unchanged for 500 years, he bought up the abandoned buildings and hatched an idea, an "extended hotel" *(albergo diffuso)*. The idea was to build nothing new but simply make use of existing rooms located in different houses dotted throughout the village. Despite designer quirks, each bedroom is faithful to its medieval origins; ancient 15cm (6-inch) long iron keys open timeless doors; traditional bed covers are hand-woven and dyed in Santo Stefano's own craft workshop.

Santo Stefano is the flagship for Kihlgren's mission to awaken Abruzzo and draw attention to the region's neglected heritage. Given the exodus from the countryside and Italy's overabundance of ancient villages, scant attention has sometimes been paid to the importance of conserving "everyday" buildings. The rejuvenated Santo Stefano has drawn praise from its politician and writer guests, including Romano Prodi and the late Umberto Eco. Kihlgren, who is working on further ruined villages in Abruzzo, continues to campaign for sustainable tourism and planning regulations which will preserve the region's character.

May, stop at the medieval village of **Larino** ⓬. The Sagra di San Pardo festival takes place at this time, when ox-carts are paraded through the streets. While there, visit the old cathedral, with its beautiful facade, and climb up the monumental staircase of the Palazzo Reale: Larino is little known yet deeply rewarding.

Termoli ⓭, on the Adriatic, is a popular fishing port and beach resort which boasts a lovely Blue Flag beach at Rio Vivo and a bay which is popular with yachties. The Old Town, set on a promontory, offers appealing views. Well garrisoned behind a small castle built by Frederick II are labyrinthine streets and a fine cathedral.

The gulf between old and new Molise is revealed in **Campobasso** ⓮, the dispiriting capital. Presided over by the medieval Castello Monforte, from which tumble the steeply stepped streets of the Old Town, Campobasso's modern quarters spread out to the station below.

Ninety minutes away by train is **Isernia** ⓯, a springboard to the remote hill towns. In 1979, an ancient settlement was discovered on the out-skirts, with evidence that man lived there a million years before the birth of Christ. Bones of elephants, rhinoceroses, hippos, bison and bear were also discovered, some now displayed in the **Museo Nazionale del Paleolitico** (www.museopaleois.it, Tue–Sun 9am–7pm). There is also an archaeological museum, the **Museo Santa Maria delle Monache** (www.archeologicamolise.beniculturali.it; closed for refurbishment at the time of writing, check website for update).

A far more worthwhile sight awaits at **Sepino**, where the rugged medieval town in the foothills of the Matese mountains is the base for exploring the Roman ruins of **Saepinum** ⓰. The site reveals the model for a surprisingly well-preserved Roman provincial town. The charm lies in the rural setting, with the mountains beyond, and the complexity of the site, complete with public baths, basilicas, battlements and a small museum (www.archeologicamolise.beniculturali.it; daily 8.30am–2pm, 2.30–5pm).

The fishing port of Termoli.

L'Aquila Earthquake

Italians live with the fact that most of the country is seismically active – Abruzzo, on geological fault lines, was simply the latest casualty.

On 6 April 2009 in the early hours of the morning a magnitude-6.3 earthquake struck L'Aquila, Abruzzo's handsome capital. Dawn revealed 308 dead, 1,500 injured, around 65,000 citizens made homeless and 10,000 buildings in the city and surrounding areas damaged.

Government action

Initially the government was credited with providing fast emergency relief and re-housing 17,000 people before the first winter after the tragedy. Since then, however, a string of sleaze scandals have tainted what was seen as an act of huge generosity by the government. During the first two years after the disaster, the town and the surrounding areas were placed under emergency rule by the Berlusconi-led government. While hardly any of the promised restoration work was carried out on L'Aquila's ravaged centre, controversially expensive "new towns" were built on the outskirts for the 73,000 homeless residents, sparking allegations of corruption.

Forgotten city

Leading the fight to return this town to its former glory, Mayor Massimo Cialente has accused the government of forgetting about L'Aquila. More than six years on, L'Aquila city centre still lies in ruins. The 13th-century town centre remains crippled, guarded by the military who only allow those with authorisation to enter; street after street, the buildings are derelict, only standing because steel beams and wooden timbers are propping them up. Many homeless are still unable to return to their houses and are living in the rapidly built blocks of flats on the outskirts, but only some 70 percent of the reconstruction needed on the outskirts has been completed.

Living in hope

L'Aquila's fate finally seems to be improving. Minister for Regional Development, Carlo Trigilia, acknowledges problems with the fraudulent use of funds and maintains that L'Aquila is now a priority for the government. Trigilia has pledged 1bn euros a year over eight years and claims that the government is keeping a close eye on where the money is going. The first round of restoration projects is now under way: an initial €14m to restore the 15th-century Spanish castle, which houses the Museo Nazionale d'Abruzzo, and €10m will be spent on the 18th-century Duomo. The future might look brighter for L'Aquila but the amount of damage to the town's historic centre and the surrounding area is so vast that works are expected to carry on at least until 2021. Given the complexities of rebuilding and the economic situation in Italy, not everyone is convinced that the flow of money will be sufficient to restore the soul of this medieval city.

2016: Amatrice's turn

In August 2016, only 50km (3 miles) north of L'Aquila, disaster struck again. A 6.2 earthquake killed nearly 300 people and annihilated half the town of Amatrice. It appears that some of the buildings destroyed, including an elementary school renovated as recently as 2013, didn't meet the required antiseismic standards. It is alleged that contractors with mafia connections obtained several building permits for work that was never carried out.

The aftermath of the earthquake that struck Amatrice in August 2016.

Taormina's Piazza IX Aprile, Sicily.

THE SOUTH

To discover one of Europe's most seductive regions, venture beyond Naples and Sicily into the Mezzogiorno.

Catania's fish market, Sicily.

When foreign travellers visit the remote parts of Basilicata and Calabria, they are sometimes greeted by stares. So few foreigners visit these sun-baked regions that anybody who does is looked upon as a bit of a maverick. The growing number of travellers who do come, follow the footsteps of the Greeks and Romans to Naples, Pompeii, the Amalfi Coast and Capri. They flock to Sicily and its temples or Sardinia's glitzy Costa Smeralda but skim over the rest.

Then there is northern prejudice. Northerners see themselves as enlightened, industrious and entrepreneurial. Southerners are dismissed as superstitious, fatalistic and backward. But get beyond the stereotypes and you will find that southern hospitality and hidden treasures more than compensate for poor public transport and itineraries which don't go according to plan – but are better.

Southern Italy is utterly bewitching. It is a romantic land of castles, churches and classical ruins, endless plains, and misty mountains where shepherds roam. It is increasingly a place for contemporary retreats, whether in Sicilian villas, cool cave dwellings, Positano palaces, or Puglian manor-houses *(masserie)*. Culturally, Naples, the Bay of Naples and Sicily are the richest regions, from the classical sites to museum collections and even cuisine. In Sicily, the Hellenistic temples are matched by Arab-Norman cathedrals and a cultural resurgence in key cities. Sardinia is increasingly popular, as much for its rural lifestyle as its beaches, now rivalled by resorts on the Aeolian Islands.

Temple at Selinunte, Sicily.

Puglia is firmly on the map, helped by its Romanesque and Baroque architecture, crusader castles and conical beehive dwellings known as *trulli*. Basilicata is an emerging destination, partly thanks to its "deep south" spirit. In Calabria, rediscover the Greeks – in particular, the Greek bronzes of Riace and landscapes first described by Homer.

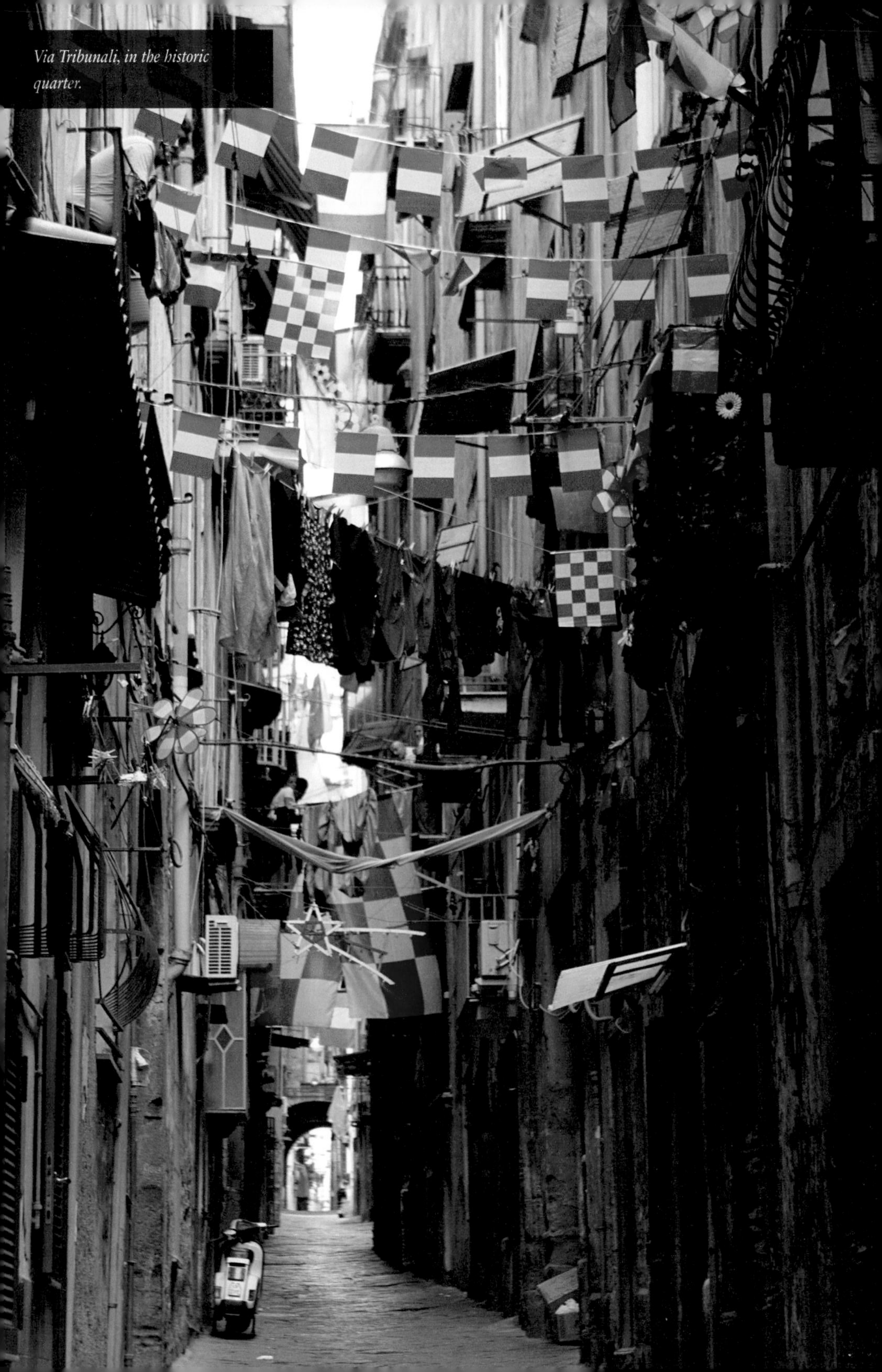

Via Tribunali, in the historic quarter.

NAPLES

Noisy but thrilling, Naples has it all – Baroque churches, buzzing street life, world-class museums and cosmopolitan verve.

Life in southern Italy's great city is almost theatrical, full of wonderful architecture and museums, and flanked by an idyllic bay. The grid plan of medieval streets that make up the *centro storico* conceal such delights as the fascinating Museo Archeologico Nazionale, Naples' great Franciscan church Santa Chiara, and the magnificent Gothic Duomo. To the north, on a hilltop, stands Museo Nazionale di Capodimonte, containing one of Italy's richest museums, while further south on the waterfront rises the Castel Nuovo, a huge castle erected in 1282. The shoreline then curves away west, passing the delightful Villa Comunale with its famous aquarium.

Naples (Napoli) remains a glorious assault on your senses, as explosive as Vesuvius, its local volcano. Naples has always been the black sheep of Italian cities, the misfit, the outcast, the messy brother that nobody knew quite what to do with. It is burdened by poverty, unemployment, bureaucratic inefficiency and organised crime, but remains, nonetheless, a triumph of the human spirit. Fortunately, Naples is one of the most beautiful Italian cities, with a friendly population and beguiling cultural heritage. Like all black sheep, troubled Naples is simply the most interesting member of its family.

The name Naples derives from Neapolis, the New City founded by settlers from Cumae in the 6th century BC. Romans flocked there, drawn by the golden climate, the sparkling bay and the political freedom which retention of the Greek constitution allowed. Virgil wrote the *Aeneid* here; emperors built gardens and bathed in this *Campania felix*, or "happy land".

Since then, the Neapolitans have survived Norman, Spanish and Bourbon rule, as well as infamous Camorra (the local crime syndicate; see page 72) control to remain an irrepressible force – and a thorn in the side of modern Italy.

Main Attractions

Castel Nuovo
Palazzo Reale
Museo Archeologico
  Nazionale
Santa Chiara
Duomo
Cappella di Sansevero
Palazzo Reale di
  Capodimonte
Chiaia

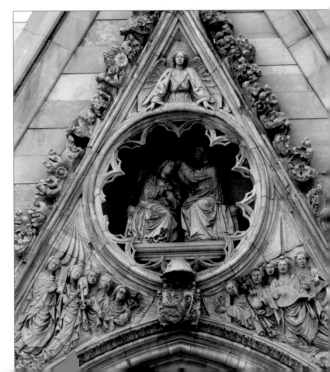
Elaborate Gothic sculpture on Naples's Duomo.

Orientation

Naples is a fabulous but frenetic city, so take more care than you would elsewhere in Italy. The only way to get a feel for the city is to walk its different quarters and ride the **funiculars** up the Vomero hill. Also try the glossy **metro line** from Piazza Dante to Vomero, even if you don't need to travel by train. Each station is adorned with bold contemporary artworks.

Make easy forays to **Pompeii, Herculaneum** and the **islands** (see page 335) but avoid the crime-infested city suburbs – unless you want to play-act being in *Gomorrah*, a brutal Neapolitan version of *The Godfather*.

From **Piazza Garibaldi** ❶, the long **Corso Umberto I** juts down to the southwest to **Piazza Bovio** ❷, and extends to **Piazza Municipio** ❸. The thoroughfare was carved through the narrow, crowded streets in 1888, in an effort to improve air circulation following a cholera epidemic. The rather drab **Università** ❹ looms halfway down. From **Piazza del Plebiscito** ❺ the city fans out. After its restoration, this is the heart of town, and home to the Palazzo Reale, the Royal Palace.

Castles, coffee and music

When Charles I of Anjou built the **Castel Nuovo** ❻ (Museo Civico; Mon–Sat 9am–7pm) in 1282, he could not have known that seven centuries later it would still serve as the political hub of the city. The City Council meets in the huge **Sala dei Baroni**, where Charles is said to have performed some of his bloodiest executions. The finest architectural element in this imposing fortress is the Triumphal Arch, built from 1454–67 to commemorate Alfonso I's defeat of the French. It is the only Renaissance arch ever to have been built at the entrance to a castle.

A short walk up Via San Carlo brings you swiftly to the **Teatro di San Carlo** ❼ (www.teatrosancarlo.it), the largest opera house in Italy and one of the finest in the world. It is all red velvet and gold trim, with six tiers of boxes rising from the stage. Constructed in 1737, under the direction of Charles III of Bourbon, the theatre retains its perfect acoustics.

Across the street is the **Galleria Umberto I** ❽, erected in 1887 on a neoclassical design

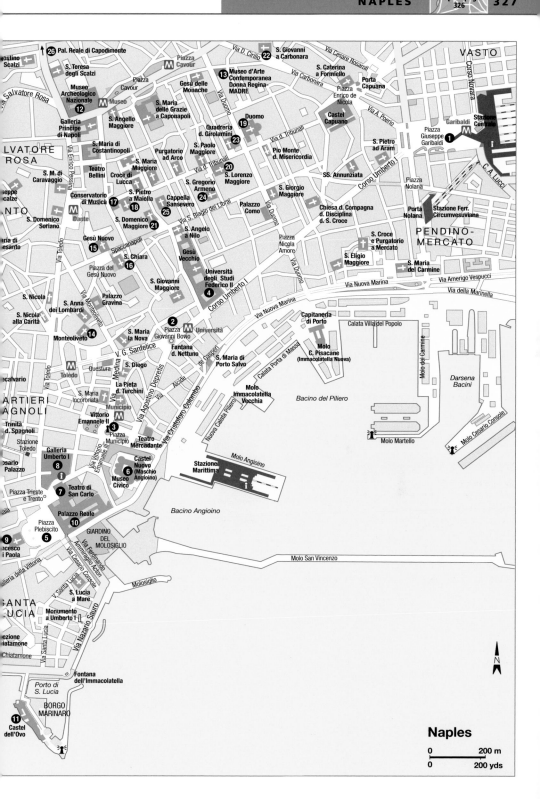

26 Pal. Reale di Capodimonte

Agostino
Scalzi

S. Teresa
degli Scalzi

Museo
Archeologico
Nazionale
12

Galleria
Principe
di Napoli

S. Angello
Maggiore

Piazza
Cavour

Piazza
Cavour

Gesù delle
Monache

Museo

S. Maria
delle Grazie
a Caponapoli

13 Museo d'Arte
Contemporanea
Donna Regina-
MADRE

Via D. Cirillo

22 S. Giovanni
a Carbonara

Via Cesare Rosaroll

VASTO

S. Caterina
a Formiello

Via Carbonara

Porta
Capuana

Piazza
Enrico de
Nicola

Corso Novara

Via A. Poerio

Duomo

19

Quadreria
d. Girolamini

23

Castel
Capuano

Garibaldi
Piazza
Giuseppe
Garibaldi
1

Stazione
Centrale

S. Pietro
ad Aram

SALVATORE
ROSA

Via Salvatore Rosa

Via Enrico Pessina

S. M. di
Caravaggio

S. Maria di
Costantinopoli

Teatro
Bellini

Croce di
Lucca

S. Maria
Maggiore

S. Paolo
Maggiore

Purgatorio
ad Arco

S. Gregorio
Armeno

S. Pietro
a Maiella

Cappella
Sansevero

24

Conservatorio
di Musica 17

18

giuseppe
calze

S. Domenico
Soriano

Dante

25

S. Domenico
Maggiore 21

Gesù Nuovo
15

S. Pietro
Maggiore

Via d. Tribunali

20 S. Lorenzo
Maggiore

Via d. Tribunali

S. Giorgio
Maggiore

Via S. Biagio dei Librai

Pio Monte
d. Misericordia

SS. Annunziata

Corso Umberto I

Piazza
Nolana

Porta
Nolana

Stazione Ferr.
Circumvesuviana

Chiesa d. Compagna
d. Disciplina
d. S. Croce

PENDINO-
MERCATO

aria di
esanto

S. Chiara
16

Spaccanapoli

Gesù
Vecchio

Palazzo
Como

S. Angelo
a Nilo

Piazza
Nicola
Amore

S. Croce
e Purgatorio
a Mercato

S. Maria
del Carmine

S. Nicola

Piazza
del
Gesù Nuovo

S. Giovanni
Maggiore

Università
degli Studi
Federico II
4

Corso Umberto I

S. Eligio
Maggiore

Via Nuova Marina

Via Amerigo Vespucci

Via della Marinella

S. Anna
dei Lombardi

Palazzo
Gravina

Via Monteoliveto

S. Nicola
alla Carità

Monteoliveto
14

Via Toledo

S. Maria
la Nova

V. G. Sanfelice

Medina

Piazza
Giovanni Bovio

Università

2

Fontana
d. Nettuno

Via de Gasperi

Via Nuova Marina

Capitaneria
di Porto

Calata Villa del Popolo

Molo del Carmine

Darsena
Bacini

QUARTIERI
SPAGNOLI

S. Diego

Questura

Toledo

La Pietà
d. Turchini

S. Maria
Incoronata

Via Toledo

Via Agostino Depretis

Alcide

Via Cristoforo Colombo

Nuova Calata Piliero

Calata Porta di Massa

S. Maria di
Porto Salvo

Molo
Immacolatella
Vecchia

Molo
C. Pisacane
(Immacolatella Nuova)

Bacino del Piliero

Vittorio
Emanuele II

Municipio

3

Piazza
Municipio

Teatro
Mercadante

Castel
Nuovo
(Maschio
Angioino)

Museo
Civico

Stazione
Marittima

Molo Angioino

Molo Martello

Molo Cesario Console

Trinità
d. Spagnoli

Stazione
Toledo

Galleria
Umberto I
8

Teatro di
San Carlo
7

6

osario
Palazzo

Piazza Trieste
e Trento

Palazzo Reale

Piazza
Plebiscito
5

10

9

ncesco
i Paola

GIARDINO
DEL
MOLOSIGLIO

Bacino Angioino

Molo San Vincenzo

Galleria della Vittoria

Via Ferdinando
Ammiraglio Acton

Via Cesario Console

Molosiglio

SANTA
LUCIA

V. Santa Lucia

S. Lucia
a Mare

Via Nazario Sauro

Via Santa Lucia

ezione
hiatamone

Monumento
a Umberto I

Chiatamone

Fontana
dell'Immacolatella

Porto di
S. Lucia

BORGO
MARINARO

11

Castel
dell'Ovo

N

Naples

0   200 m

0   200 yds

similar to that of its older brother in Milan. Its glass ceiling, 56 metres (184ft) high, and its mosaic-covered floor were reconstructed after bomb damage in World War II. Just west, beyond the other side of **Via Toledo**, lies the **Quartieri Spagnoli** (Spanish Quarter), a kasbah where little sunlight penetrates a grid-like maze built to garrison Spanish troops in the 17th century. With its low-slung, windowless houses, washing strewn across alleys, and urchins and hawkers in full flow, this is the picturesque Neapolitan slum of legend.

The **Piazza Plebiscito** around the corner is embraced by the twin arcades of the **Chiesa di San Francesco di Paola** ❾ (1817–32), modelled on the Pantheon in Rome. Considered the heart of a revitalised Naples, the pedestrianised square is popular with buskers and artists as well as being the setting for art installations and open-air concerts. On the corner stands **Caffè Gambrinus**, the city's sleekest old-world café (http://grancaffegambrinus. com), a place to try Neapolitan coffee, arguably the best in Italy because of the city's distinctive water.

A professional at work.

The sprawling red facade of the **Palazzo Reale** ❿ (Royal Apartments; Thu–Tue 9am–8pm) looms across the street with its eight statues illustrating the eight Neapolitan dynasties. At the foot of its monumental marble staircase stand the original bronze doors from the Castel Nuovo. The cannonball lodged in the left door is a reminder of an early siege. Upstairs are a throne room and a small but lavish theatre. Further rooms stretch off in a seemingly endless series of period furniture and Dresden china.

Another famous castle, the **Castel dell'Ovo** ⓫ (www.castel-dell-ovo. com; Mon–Sat 9am–7.30pm, winter until 6.30pm, Sun 9am–2pm; free) on the waterfront, is used for hosting exhibitions and cultural events. Its oval shape (hence the name) is the product of its evolution from Roman villa to Norman bulwark to Spanish fortress. Beneath the ramparts, appealing restaurants line the shore; children belly-flop from the causeway, and the speedboats of the Guardia di Finanza (Fraud Squad) lurk just along the quay.

HOME OF THE PIZZA

Pizza was born in Naples, and genuine Neapolitan pizza is unbeatable. Its secret, apart from the fresh mozzarella – another regional speciality – lies in the baking. It is cooked quickly, at a high temperature, in a dome-shaped, wood-fired brick oven. The classic Neapolitan pizza is the Margherita, topped by tomatoes and mozzarella, and supposedly invented in 1889 to welcome Queen Margherita on her visit to Naples. Its rival is the marinara, made with tomatoes and oregano. Authentic pizzerias, which are often cramped and crowded, with marble-top tables, include Di Matteo (Via Tribunali 94; www.pizzeriadimatteo.com; tel: 081-455 262) and Da Michele (Via Sersale 1; http://damichele.net; tel: 081-553 9204). The Piazza Sannazzaro, at the heart of the Mergellina district, also has a reputation for excellent pizza.

National Archaeology Museum

Directly north, up Via Toledo, also known as Via Roma, is the **Museo Archeologico Nazionale di Napoli** ⑫ (Wed–Mon 9am–7.30pm), one of the great museums of the world, housing the most spectacular finds from Pompeii and Herculaneum and fine examples of Greek sculpture. A trip to the museum will take an entire morning. The highlights include the so-called "Secret Cabinet" (Gabinetto Segreto), a collection of erotic images which lift the lid on the racy ancient world. Graphic sex scenes are depicted on Greek vases, Roman terracottas and Etruscan mirrors. In the steam room, for instance, scenes show nymphs and satyrs disporting themselves, or an over-endowed Priapus simultaneously impaling several victims on his many-pronged member.

The ground floor is devoted to classical sculpture and Egyptian art. In the main entrance hall, a monolithic sarcophagus depicts Prometheus creating man out of clay. Another sarcophagus presents a raucous Bacchanalian celebration. Through a doorway to the right, a pair of statues of Harmodius and Aristogeiton, who killed the tyrant Hipparchus, fairly leap out at you as you enter the room. These are actually Roman copies of originals once installed in the Agora in Athens.

In a further room stands a Roman copy of the famous statue of Doryphorus by Polycleitus (440 BC), considered the "canon of perfection" of manly proportions. This statue, found at Pompeii, is evidence of the refined tastes of early Greek settlers. The Farnese Collection includes a Hercules and the *Farnese Bull* (the largest piece of antique sculpture ever found) from Rome's Baths of Caracalla.

The rich collection of mosaics on the mezzanine floor comes from houses unearthed at Pompeii. The freshness and colour of these works after centuries buried in ash are an amazing tribute to the craftsmanship of their ancient makers.

The Nile scenes in Room LX, from a later period, feature ducks, crocodiles, hippopotami and snakes. These mosaics originally framed the *Battle of Issus*, in Room LXI. In this scene, Alexander the Great is presented in his victorious battle against the Persian emperor Darius III in 333 BC. The thicket of spears creates the illusion of an army far larger than that actually shown.

Rooms on the first floor show paintings of Pompeii and a reconstruction of the Villa of the Papyri in Herculaneum, including an extraordinary collection of marble and bronze sculptures.

Through the large Salone dell'Atlante at the top of the stairs is a series of rooms containing wall paintings from various Campanian cities. Especially startling is the 6th-century BC *Sacrifice of Iphigenia*, the Greek equivalent of the biblical sacrifice of Isaac. The deer borne by Artemis in the top of the picture replaced Iphigenia at the last minute, just as Isaac was replaced by a ram. Far happier is *The Rustic Concert*, in which Pan and nymphs tune up for a Roman celebration.

Castel Nuovo, built by Charles I in 1282.

Inside the Archaeological Museum, Naples.

San Lorenzo Maggiore, which was built on top of the ancient Greek high street.

Majolica-tiled walls in the cloisters of Santa Chiara.

Set on Via Settembrini just east, **MADRE** , the Museo d'Arte Contemporanea Donna Regina (www.madrenapoli.it; Wed–Mon 10am–7.30pm; free Mon) is a celebration of contemporary art in all its forms, with works by Jeff Koons, Richard Serra and Anish Kapoor. The bookshop-café and library are also worth a pit stop.

Neapolitan churches

The churches of Naples, like the churches of any Italian city, offer glimpses into Italian life. In the south, a visit to a church, a quick confession, a genuflection in front of an altar are still a daily ritual for some people. Because of this, churches open every day (but many close 1–4.30pm).

The church of **Monteoliveto** ⓮, halfway up Via Roma, contains a wealth of Renaissance monuments hidden away in surprising corners. Far in the back of this aisle-less basilica, begun in 1411, stands a bizarre group of terracotta figures by the artist Guido Mazzoni. The eight statues, looking almost alive in the dim light that filters into the chapel, represent the *Pietà*, and are said to be portraits of Mazzoni's 15th-century friends. Further back, down a side passage, is the Old Sacristy, containing frescoes by Vasari and wooden stalls inlaid with biblical scenes. Another passage leads to the Piccolomini Chapel, where a relief of a Nativity scene by the Florentine Antonio Rossellino (1475) is a delight to behold.

Unlike in Rome, which is heavily Baroque, no single architectural style predominates in Naples. The Gothic, the Renaissance and the Baroque are all represented. The **Gesù Nuovo** ⓯ (Mon–Sat 6.30am–12.45pm and 4.15pm–7.30pm, Sun 6.30am–1.30pm) on **Trinità Maggiore** presents perhaps the most harmonious example of Neapolitan Baroque. The embossed stone facade originally formed the wall of a Renaissance palace. At noon on Saturdays, when weddings take place here, the massive front doors are thrown open to give a splendid view of fully lit Baroque at its best. The coloured marble and bright frescoes seem to spiral up into the dome. Directly above the main portal, just inside the church, stretches a wide fresco by Francesco

Solimena (1725) depicting Heliodorus driven from the temple. The ubiquitous Solimena dominated Neapolitan painting in the first half of the 18th century.

At the other end of the scale, the Provençale Gothic church of **Santa Chiara** ⑯ (daily 7am–12.30pm and 4.30–6.30pm, Sun 10am–2.30pm) maintains an austere beauty, and houses the medieval tombs of the Angevin kings. This church became the favourite place of worship of the Neapolitan nobility. But the showpiece is the stunning decoration in the cloisters (Mon–Sat 9.30am–1pm and 2.30–5.30pm, Sun 9am–1pm), a testament to the Neapolitans' love of colour and exoticism. Majolica-tiled pathways meander through a half-tamed garden of roses and fruit trees, the same species grown here in Bourbon times. Restoration has revealed medieval frescoes under the arcades and newly unearthed mosaics.

The steep **Via Santa Maria di Costantinopoli** climbs up to the **Conservatorio di Musica** ⑰, founded in 1537, and the oldest *conservatoire* in Europe. It has an important library and museum (www.sanpietroamajella. it; tel: 081-564 4411), but it is also enjoyable to wander through its courtyard listening to the music of violins, organs, harps and pianos spilling down from upper storeys. Further along, the Gothic church of **San Pietro a Maiella** ⑱ is a masterpiece by the 17th-century Calabrian painter Mattia Preti.

The Duomo

The Naples **Duomo** ⑲ (daily 9am–noon and 4.30–6.30pm) is a magnificent Gothic reliquary from every period of the city's history. In a chapel off the right aisle are the head of San Gennaro, the patron saint of the city, and two phials of his blood. The mysterious powers of the congealed blood are the subject of what Mark Twain called "one of the wretchedest of all the religious impostures in Italy – the miraculous liquefaction of the blood". The miracle has been taking place

every year on the first Saturday in May, 19 September and 16 December since the saint's body was brought to Naples from Pozzuoli, the place of his martyrdom, by Bishop Severus in the time of Constantine. It is said that if the blood fails to liquefy a disaster is in store for the city. The last great eruption of Vesuvius in 1944 and the earthquake northeast of Naples in 1980 occurred in years that the blood did not liquefy.

Another notable church in the historic heart is **San Lorenzo Maggiore** ⑳, where archaeological excavations have revealed the old *Decumano* (main street) running through the cloisters, and the Roman forum built over the Greek agora. Also significant are the Gothic **San Domenico Maggiore** ㉑, the 14th-century **San Giovanni a Carbonara** ㉒, **Girolamini** ㉓, Pio Monte della Misericordia (which displays Caravaggio's masterpiece Seven Acts of Mercy) and **Santa Patrizia**, with its monastery of **San Gregorio Armeno** ㉔. The adjoining street, **Via San Gregoria Armeno**, set on the main artery of the Roman city, is famous for its workshops producing *presepi* (Christmas cribs), an

Inside Naples's Duomo.

The sweet lemon liqueur known as Limoncello.

Palazzo Reale di Capodimonte.

important Neapolitan tradition. This "street of superstitions" also sells bizarre talismans that ward off the "evil eye".

The **Cappella di Sansevero** ㉕ (www. museosansevero.it; Wed–Mon 9.30am–6.30pm), a small deconsecrated church near the church of San Domenico Maggiore, should not be missed. It contains a moving and remarkably realistic sculpture known as the *Cristo Velato* (Veiled Christ) carved out of a single piece of marble by Giuseppe Sammartino. The chapel was once the workshop of Prince Raimondo, a well-known 18th-century alchemist who was excommunicated by the Pope for dabbling in the occult. In the crypt are the gruesome results of some of his experiments.

Subterranean Naples

One of the most fascinating aspects of Naples history is its labyrinth of caves, tunnels and passageways running 40 metres (130ft) below street level. The passages were originally hewn by the Greeks to extract tufa stone used in construction and to channel water from Mount Vesuvius. Conducted tours of these chambers are led by Napolisotterranea at Piazza San Gaetano (www.napolisotterranea.org).

Top Neapolitan museums

Two of the greatest museums in Naples stand high on bluffs overlooking the city. The **Museo Nazionale di Capodimonte** occupies the **Palazzo Reale di Capodimonte** ㉖ (Thu–Tue 8.30am–7.30pm). Set in a shady park, this 18th-century Bourbon palace can also be admired for its grand public apartments. The museum contains some of the best paintings in southern Italy. At its heart is the important Farnese collection, which by the late 18th century numbered over 1,700 paintings. Among the high points are Bellini's *Transfiguration*, various works of Titian, Caravaggio's *Flagellation* and Andy Warhol's *Vesuvius* (1985). The Salottina di Porcellano is lined throughout with magnificent Capodimonte porcelain tiles which were made in King Charles III's factory in 1757. These originally adorned the queen's parlour in the royal palace at Portici.

A trip up the Montesanto funicular brings the visitor to the top of the

Vomero hill, home of the **Certosa e Museo di San Martino** ㉗ (Thu–Tue 8.30am–7.30pm), located in the well-restored 14th-century Carthusian monastery of the same name. Like so many buildings in Naples, the Certosa has been given a Baroque make-over. Some of the foremost painters of the Neapolitan Baroque are represented here, including Salvator Rosa, Francesco Solimena and the prolific Luca Giordano. Belvederes give access to the best views in town – the wide sweep of the Bay of Naples.

Good views can also be had from the **Castel Sant'Elmo** ㉘ (Wed–Mon 8.30am–7.30pm) next door, a 14th-century fortress long used as a prison for political troublemakers. Also on the Vomero, the stately gardens of the **Villa Floridiana** ㉙ (daily 8.30am to 1 hour before sunset; free) house the **Museo Duca di Martina** ㉚ (Wed–Mon 9.30am–2pm) home to an extensive collection of decorative arts.

On the bay

When the appeal of the chaotic city centre palls, succumb to the allure of **waterfront strolls** punctuated by leisurely stops for seafood, ice cream or café life. To appreciate the splendour of the bay, walk through the **Villa Comunale gardens** ㉛ west towards **Mergellina** ㉜, the departure point for ferries to the islands of Capri and Ischia (see page 338). Both Mergellina and **Posillipo,** the chic, villa-studded district further west, represent enticing summer escapes, with the neighbouring fishing village of **Marechiaro** particularly appealing to seafood-lovers. Mergellina also makes a delightful early evening stroll along the Via Caracciolo waterfront. From Mergellina, views stretch back over the entire city, with Mount Vesuvius looming in the background haze.

Naples renaissance

Alternatively, head to the hilly **Vomero** residential district, or to elegant **Chiaia.** If you take a funicular, such as the Funicolare di Chaia from Piazza Amedeo, the teeming masses are swiftly left behind. The chic Chiaia quarter exudes a sense of ease and elegance otherwise lacking in Naples. While the smug atmosphere, cutting-edge art galleries and stylish boutiques characterise the lower part, the upper part is more maze-like and evocative. Bustling Piazza dei Martiri is the place for *aperitivi*, while the **PAN** ㉝ (Palazzo delle Arti Napoli; www.comune.napoli.it; Wed–Sat 9.30am–7.30pm and Sun 9.30am–2.30pm), with its excellent temporary exhibitions, is spearheading Naples's commitment to contemporary art, architecture and photography. Chiaia is at the heart of a Neapolitan resurgence, with stylish B&Bs and boutique hotels. But Neapolitan creativity even goes underground: 14 metro stations have been turned into temples of modern art.

In unruly Naples, the joke is that the red traffic light is only kept "to brighten the place up". But this subversive spirit also bubbles over into artistic creativity, summer street theatre and music in city squares. As always, any Neapolitan cultural resurgence will follow its own wayward path.

Display in the aquarium.

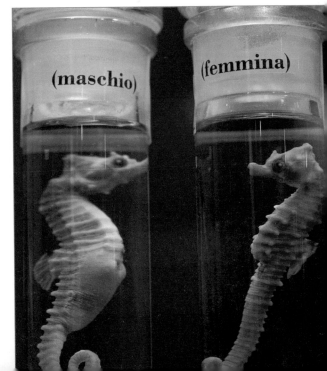

CAMPANIA

An endless succession of jewel-like coves ripples down the Naples Coast, with Pompeii and Herculaneum just inland.

Fresco at Villa dei Misteri.

I t will be the breathtakingly beautiful Amalfi Coast that most visitors remember about Campania. Every twist and turn produces yet another spectacular vista: the truly charming town of Sorrento, the first glance of colourful Positano tumbling down the cliff side, and lovely Ravello that unveils perhaps the finest views of the coast. But there are so many other highlights in this region to capture the imagination: you won't want to miss the classical sites of Pompeii and Herculaneum, with Mount Vesuvius looming in the background, or the magical island of Capri and its larger neighbour Ischia.

In classical times, Naples was a mere stripling overshadowed by its powerful parent **Cumae ❶** (Cuma), 30km (19 miles) to the west, the first Greek colony on the Italian mainland and a beacon of Hellenistic culture.

Here Aeneas came to consult the Sybil before his descent into the Underworld. The famous **Antro della Sibilla Cumana** (Cave of the Cumaean Sybil) consists of a trapezoidal *dromos* (corridor), 44 metres (144ft) long, punctuated by six airshafts. At the far end is a rectangular chamber cut with niches where the Sybil apparently sat and uttered her prophecies. Virgil described it as "a cavern perforated a hundred times, having a hundred mouths with rushing voices carrying the responses of the Sybil". Unfortunately, the cave has been closed to the public since 2014, and you can only peer into the shaft. From the cave's mouth it is possible to climb up to the acropolis, whose ruined, lizard-haunted temples offer fine views of the coastline and the sea.

The geologically unstable region between Cumae and Naples is known as the **Campi Flegrei** (Phlegrean Fields). These "fiery fields" were mythologised by Homer as the entrance to Hades, the mythical Greek Underworld, hellishly conjured up in a succession of rumblings and gaseous exhalations. The **Lago di Averno**, a once gloomy lake in the crater of an extinct volcano, is the legendary "dark pool" from which Aeneas began his descent into Hades. No bird was said to be able to fly across this lake and live, due to the poisonous gases.

This theory was cruelly tested at the **Grotta del Cane** on the nearby Lago d'Agnano. Dogs were subjected to the carbon dioxide that issued from the floor of the cave until they expired. "The dog dies in a minute and a half – a chicken instantly," reported Mark Twain. The experiment was repeated nine or 10 times a day for the benefit of tourists.

Volcanic crater

Pozzuoli ❷, a wealthy trading centre in Greek and Roman times but later devastated by wars and malaria, is now famous for its **Solfatara** (www.vulcano solfatara.it; daily 8.30am–7pm, until 4.30pm in winter), a volcanic crater releasing jets of sulphurous gases. The Solfatara is thought to have inspired Milton's description of Hell in *Paradise Lost*. Pozzuoli also boasts a well-restored amphitheatre, the third-largest in Italy (Wed–Mon 9am–6pm) and used for summer concerts. Pozzuoli is also the birthplace of fiery actress Sophia Loren. On the waterfront, enclosed in a small park, lies a rectangular structure formerly known as the **Serapeo** (Temple of Serapis), but now thought to have been a market hall.

Baia ❸ derives its name from Baios, Odysseus' navigator. Here Roman society came to swim. The modern town, with its view across the Gulf of Pozzuoli, contains extensive ruins of Roman palaces enclosed in a picturesque **Parco Archeologico** (Tue–Sun 9am–1 hour before sunset) on the hillside. At the lowest level of the park is a rectangular *piscina* (bathing pool) and a domed bathhouse, a circular structure identified as the model for the Pantheon in Rome.

Pompeii and Herculaneum

The region's most popular sight is the Roman city of **Pompeii ❹** (tel: 081-857 5111/347; www.pompeiisites.org; Apr–Oct daily 9am–7.30pm, Nov–Mar daily 8.30am–5.30pm, last entry 90 mins before closure).

TIP

From Naples, the best way to reach Pompeii and Herculaneum is to take the Circumvesuviana railway (www.eavsrl.it) to either destination. For Pompeii get off at the Pompeii-Scavi Villa dei Misteri stop and for Herculaneum get off at Ercolano Scavi. To reach the top of Vesuvius, take the same train to Ercolano Scavi from where regular buses leave and drop passengers at the road. It is then a 20-minute climb up a well-beaten track.

Capri colour and style.

POMPEII REVISITED

Pompeii is Italy's most contentious major attraction. The site had been suffering from galloping decay, caused by neglect but exacerbated by the sheer number of visitors (2.5 million every year), when in November 2010, the 2,000-year-old House of Gladiators collapsed, leading to calls for the city to be privatised. Institutional apathy, incompetence and lack of funding meant that swathes of the site were often closed and only a handful of houses attested to the full glory that was Pompeii. Things began to change in 2012 when Pompeii received €100 million from the EU and the Italian government. But the real turnaround came when the Great Pompeii Project was put in charge of the renovations. Since then, some parts of the sites have been successfully restored and have reopened to the public.

Pompeii and Herculaneum, buried by the eruption of Mount Vesuvius in AD 79, have solved what the archaeologist Amedeo Maiuri has called "the essential problem in the history of civilisation: the origin and development of the house". Pompeii, earlier ruled by the Greeks, was a Roman playground and commercial centre at the time of its sudden immersion in pumice stone and ash. It was a city of shops, markets and merchant houses, with paved streets, a stadium, two theatres, temples, baths and brothels. Its chance rediscovery in the 16th century, and subsequent years of excavation, have revealed an intimate picture of life in a 1st-century Roman city.

The Pompeian house is thought to have evolved from the relatively simple design of the Etruscan farmhouse. The structure was built around a central courtyard (*atrium*) whose roof sloped inwards on all four sides to a rectangular opening in the centre known as the *compluvium*. Through the *compluvium*, rainwater fell into a corresponding rectangular tank called the *impluvium*. Around the *atrium* itself were the various family quarters, including the bedrooms (*cubicula*), the dining rooms (*triclinia*) and, directly opposite the narrow entranceway (*vestibule*), the living room (*tablinum*).

As the plan developed, a further peristyle courtyard was added, often containing a fountain. Shops were built into the front of the house; sections of the house were subdivided and let, with separate entranceways, to strangers (for example, the **Villa di Julia Felix**); another storey was added up top, until the Etruscan prototype had metamorphosed into the palatial townhouses typified by the **Casa dei Vettii** and the **Casa del Fauno**.

Frescoes and detail

A striking feature of the Pompeian house was the colourful and often highly refined frescoes, many of which have been taken to the Museo Archeologico in Naples (see page 329). But many are still in situ, including at the **Villa dei Misteri**, just outside Porto Ercolano, where a series of 10 scenes depict the sometimes alarming initiation of brides into the Dionysiac mysteries.

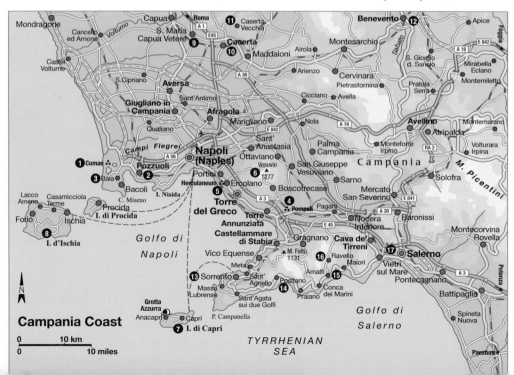

Campania Coast

The meaning of these paintings, which feature, among other things, the whipping of a young bride, is still far from clear, although it is generally agreed that the woman in the final scene is probably a portrait of the mistress of the house, who may have been a Dionysiac priestess.

The most remarkable thing about Pompeii is the mass of detail, including images of phalluses, carved into paving stones. In Roman times, signs displaying phalluses were considered symbols of good luck, as well as of virility and fertility, and it was believed they would ward off evil spirits. A sign of a phallus outside a bakery might also indicate a plentiful supply of fresh loaves.

Walls are covered with inscriptions, from lists of upcoming plays to the scribbled accounts of shopkeepers, from election notices to billets-doux. "It is a wonder, O Wall," wrote one cynic on the wall of the basilica, "that thou hast not yet crumbled under the weight of so much written nonsense."

Herculaneum and Mount Vesuvius

Herculaneum ❺ (Ercolano; tel: 081-857 5347; www.pompeiisites.org; Apr–Oct daily 9am–7.30pm, Nov–Mar daily 8.30am–5.30pm, last admission 90 mins before closure) was built for the enjoyment of sea breezes and views across the Bay of Naples. Instead of the compact townhouses of Pompeian businessmen, there are sprawling villas of wealthy patricians. There is a free, spontaneous form of architecture, and the houses, freed of the mud in which they were encased for so long, are generally in a better state of preservation than those of Pompeii.

One of the pleasures of Herculaneum (aside from the fact that it is less crowded than Pompeii) is the carbonised pieces of wooden furniture, door mouldings and screens still inside the houses. Fine frescoes, such as *The Rape of Europa* in the **Casa Sannitica**, adorn the walls, and mosaics carpet the floors. Particularly striking are the black-and-white mosaics on the floor of the **Casa dell'Atrio a Mosaico** and the frescoes and statuary in the **Casa dei Cervi** (House of the Stags). The newest discovery on view is the **Barca Romana** (Roman Boat), which has been painstakingly restored. The **Villa dei Papiri**, believed to contain the "lost library" of Latin and Greek literary masterpieces, is closed for long-term restoration, but a number of the papyrus scrolls have gone to Naples Archaeological Museum.

Herculaneum is the best starting point for an afternoon ascent of **Mount Vesuvius ❻**, which looms over the modern city of **Ercolano**.

Just before the fateful eruption of AD 79, trees and olive groves covered Vesuvius up to its very peak. In the 20th century, a constant plume of smoke billowed from a cone inside the crater until 1944, when, during the volcano's last major eruption, the cone was destroyed. Aware that 1 million people are sitting on a time bomb and that a major eruption is overdue, the Italian authorities offered to help

The view down to the bay from the Giardini di Augusto, Capri.

re-house local families, but the take-up from Neapolitans has been minimal.

Island playgrounds

Of the three islands just outside the Gulf of Naples, **Capri** ❼ is the star. This is Italy's St Tropez, where the mild climate, lush vegetation and sybaritic lifestyle have captivated writers, artists and Roman emperors. Emperor Tiberius retired here in AD 27, reportedly to indulge in the secret orgies which the historians Tacitus and Suetonius claim characterised the closing years of his reign. While on Capri, writes Suetonius, the emperor "devised little nooks of lechery in the woods and glades… and had boys and girls dressed up as Pans and nymphs posted in front of caverns or grottoes; so that the island was now openly and generally called 'Caprineum' because of his goatish antics." The writer Norman Douglas, who also lived on Capri, attributed such legends to the idle exaggerations of resentful peasants.

Today's traveller, arriving by ferry or hydrofoil from Naples or Sorrento, can reach the remains of **Tiberius' Villa** (Villa Jovis; www.capri.net; Tue–Sun May 10am–6pm, June–Aug until 7pm, Sept–Oct until 6pm, Nov–Apr until 4pm) by bus from the town of Capri. A boat trip will whisk the weary to the celebrated cavern of the **Grotta Azzurra** (Blue Grotto), supposedly Tiberius' private bathing pool.

From **Anacapri**, on the far side of the island, a chair lift climbs up **Monte Solaro** (from Piazza Vittoria; www.capriseggiovia.it). Its 360-degree view encompasses the southern Apeninnes, Naples, Vesuvius, Sorrento and Ischia. In Anacapri itself, the church of **San Michele** (www.chiesa-san-michele. com; daily Apr–Sept 9am–7pm, Oct–Mar 9am–3pm) is worth a visit for its majolica-tiled pavement. In Capri town, stroll through the lush **Giardini di Augusto**, created over a Roman settlement, before taking the winding Via Krupp down to the sea. **Marina Piccola** is a beguiling spot for walks and a seafood lunch by the bay. Limoncello di Capri, the lemon-infused liqueur, enhances any melodramatic view. Contrary to its reputation, Capri's sultry lifestyle and cliffside trails are far

Ischia stands proud.

more enticing than the celebrity antics and designer shopping.

Ischia ❽ is less enchanting than Capri, but this verdant volcanic outcrop delights in rejuvenating thermal springs, delicious cuisine and the loveliest garden in southern Italy. Compared with Capri, Ischia is larger, wilder and decidedly less manicured than its chic but more sought-after neighbour. Bustling **Ischia Porto** is close to **Ischia Ponte**, a causeway leading to the **Castello Aragonese** (daily 9am–sunset), a moody castle and monastery built by Alfonso I of Naples in 1450. (After wandering the ruined castle, you might be tempted by the terraces of the decidedly un-monastic hotel café.)

Lacco Ameno, on the north coast, is synonymous with its mud baths, which contain the most radioactive waters in Italy, perfect for a winter break. More appealing are the **Giardini di Poseidon** thermal baths (www.giardiniposeidonterme.com) on the south coast, which can be treated as a day spa. Nearby, **Sant'Angelo**, a prettified fishing village, has some of the best beaches on the island. But Ischia's star attraction is the garden of **La Mortella** (tel: 081-986 220; www.lamortella. org; Apr–Oct Tue, Thu, and Sat–Sun 9am–7pm) created by the English composer William Walton (1902–83) and his late wife, Susana. The Mediterranean and tropical gardens still provide a magnificent setting for chamber music and orchestral performances, including in the open-air Greek Theatre.

Procida, the smallest of the three islands, has good beaches and a thriving fishing industry. Unlike its bigger sisters, it remains refreshingly demure, old-fashioned and immune to mass tourism.

Old Campania

Inland from Naples, at **Santa Maria Capua Vetere** ❾, are the remains of Italy's second-largest amphitheatre after the Colosseum (Tue–Sun 9am–until 1 hour before sunset, museum 9am–1.30pm). This magnificent crumbling structure reveals the subterranean passages where wild beasts once roamed.

Caserta ❿ has been referred to as the Versailles of Naples for its lavish **Reggia** (www.reggiadicaserta.beniculturali.it; Royal Palace; Wed–Mon 8.30am–7.30pm, gardens opening times vary so check website), designed by Luigi Vanvitelli in 1752 for the Bourbon king Charles III. But the future of this great palace is uncertain as it shows signs of neglect amid government funding cuts. Its statues may be mildewed, its marble floors disfigured and plaster tumbles from the facade, but the fine collection of artwork inside and the 120 hectares (300 acres) of parkland at the back is still worth the trip.

Caserta Vecchia ⓫, set on a hilltop 10km (6 miles) northeast, is an engaging medieval town with a Romanesque cathedral. In the mountains, further east, the former Roman colony of **Benevento** ⓬ suffered from bombing raids in World War II but several

Local pastime in Sorrento.

TIP

The scenic route from Naples to Ravello is to leave the motorway at Vietri Sul Mare and follow signs to the Costiera Amalfitana (Amalfi Coast), taking in the villages of Cetara, Maiori and Minori. (It's a popular route, so best avoided at weekends).

Roman sites survived. On the ancient **Via Appia** stands the **Arch of Trajan**, decorated with magnificently bombastic reliefs depicting Trajan's military triumphs. Antiquities are also on display in the Unesco-listed **Museo del Sannio** (www.museodelsannio.it; Tue–Sun 9am–7pm), but the abbey complex, and its delightful cloisters, are just as appealing.

Sorrento

The visitor to **Sorrento** ⓭, whether arriving from the noisy streets of Naples or from the scorched ruins of Pompeii, will find a peaceful retreat and a sedate resort that, unlike much of the south, caters supremely well to tourists. There's not much more to Sorrento than sniffing lemon groves and quaffing Limoncello from cafés with cliffside views – but that is exactly what Sorrento has been doing beautifully for centuries. Charming, slightly faded hotels and gracious service compensate for the tiny beaches. Above all, Sorrento makes a serene base from which to sally forth to Capri and the Amalfi Coast, as well as

to make more energy-sapping sorties to Naples and Pompeii.

The dramatic **Amalfi Coast** stretches from **Positano** to **Salerno** and has some of the most spectacular scenery in Italy. The thrilling **Amalfi Drive** doggedly follows each frightening twist of the shoreline, with fabulous views at every turn. Pastel-painted houses cling to the slopes, and gardens descend in tiers to the sea.

Positano and Amalfi

Positano ⓮, with its cute cottages clustered on a steeply shelving slope, enjoys a mystique at odds with its self-conscious simplicity. Although beloved by the *dolce vita* crowd, picturesque Positano is best appreciated out of season or reached on a summer boat trip from another Amalfi Coast resort.

The precipitous Positano–Amalfi road passes through several tunnels before reaching the **Grotta di Smeraldo**, a cavern bathed in emerald-green light. (The cavern can also be reached on a boat trip from Amalfi.) Through yet more tunnels (watch out for cyclists) lies **Amalfi** ⓯, a major trading centre in Byzantine times but now visited for its cathedral, picturesque alleys and engaging seafront. From the main piazza, adorned by a fountain, a flight of steps ascends to the 11th-century bronze door of Amalfi's **Duomo** (7.30–10am and 5.30–7pm). The cathedral is a Romanesque affair complemented by Saracen-influenced cloisters. In the crypt lies the body of St Andrew the Apostle, delivered from Constantinople in 1208. Before leaving, linger over a Limoncello or window-shop for Vietri ceramics and Amalfi handmade paper.

Ravello

The loveliest town on the Amalfi Coast is **Ravello** ⓰, which luxuriates in lush gardens and vertiginous views, the best on the coast. Ravello's **Duomo** is celebrated for its Romanesque bronze doors and fine marble

The pastel-hued houses of Positano.

pulpit, held aloft by six roaring lions. The pulpit was presented to the church in 1272 by the Rufolo dynasty, who built the splendid **Villa Rufolo** (www.villarufolo.it; daily 9am–7pm) opposite. The villa's romantic gardens and Moorish cloister overlook the sea and are the setting for the Ravello Festival, a highbrow summer music celebration (www.ravellofestival.com; tel: 089-858 422).

But the most memorable views are from the extensive gardens at the **Villa Cimbrone** (www.villacimbrone.com; gardens: daily 9am–dusk), built at the end of the 19th century by a wealthy Englishman, Ernest William Beckett. The villa, once a haunt of the Bloomsbury Group, is now an exquisite hotel with a Michelin-star restaurant.

Salerno

It was just south of **Salerno** ⑰ that the Allies began their assault on Italy on 9 September 1943. A belated restoration of the historic centre has been helped by the successful revival of the medieval Fiera Vecchia, a large food and handicrafts fair held in May. The city, strung out along the shore, has a good beach and one of the loveliest cathedrals in southern Italy, which is reached through an atrium incorporating 28 columns from Paestum. Inside, the removal of 18th-century plaster has revealed a number of medieval frescoes.

Paestum and the Cilento

The English novelist George Eliot regarded the **Temple of Neptune** at **Paestum** (www.infopaestum.it; daily 8.30am–7pm) as "the finest thing, I verily believe, we have seen in Italy". Her words echo the sentiments of many 19th-century travellers, for whom this Greek city was the final stop on the Grand Tour.

There are few sights so arresting as Paestum's three well-preserved Doric temples standing empty on the grassy plain that surrounds them. The Temple of Neptune, the most majestic of

these, was built in the 5th century BC of a reddish travertine whose warmth, as Eliot wrote, "seems to glow and deepen under one's eyes".

The so-called **basilica** beside the Temple of Neptune dates from the 6th century BC. The third temple, the **Temple of Ceres**, is separated from the other two by the **Roman forum** and **baths**, and a **Greek theatre**. Across the street, in the **Paestum Archeological Museum** (daily 8.30am–7.30pm; closed 1st and 3rd Mon of the month) are famous mural paintings from the **Tomb of the Diver** (480 BC).

Paestum is the gateway to the **Cilento**, one of the most engaging national parks in the south, and where the locals holiday near quiet coves, clean beaches and authentic mountain villages. Celebrated by Homer and Virgil, the dramatic shoreline rivals the Amalfi Coast. Atmospheric **Castellabate** makes a good base for exploring a rugged coastline riddled with caverns and dotted with watchtowers, as at Punta Licosa. Tuck into picnics of mozzarella and tomato in the confidence that both are sourced locally.

The spectacular coastline near Positano.

Temple of Neptune at Paestum.

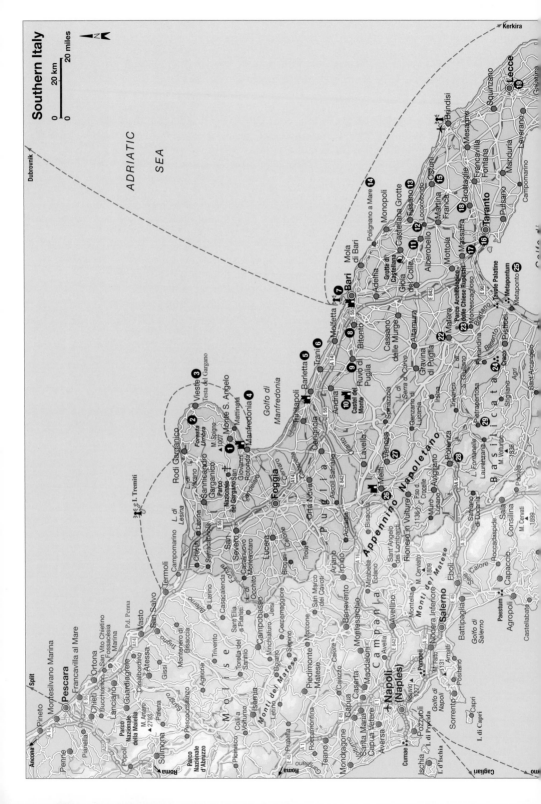

Southern Italy

ADRIATIC

SEA

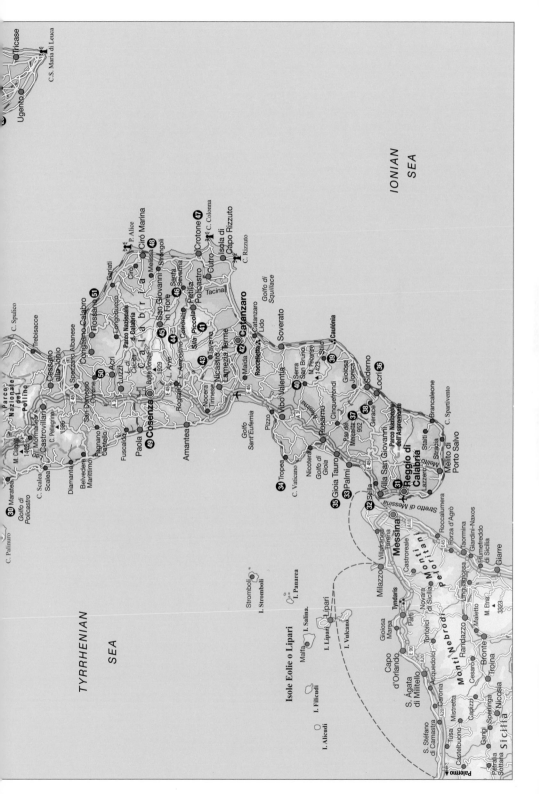

PUGLIA

Forming the heel and spur of Italy's boot, Puglia abounds in glorious churches, castles, fortified farmhouses and sun-drenched beaches.

A s a fertile land of plenty, Puglia possesses more olive trees than people. The area is dotted with unique towns like Lecce, fancifully ornamented with its own style of Baroque, and Alberobello, noted for its strange-looking whitewashed houses known as *trulli*. Ancient Bari, with its Arabic echoes, is Puglia's rival to Naples, where a delightfully confusing warren of narrow streets conceal fine Romanesque churches. Not that Puglia can be reduced to its exotic architecture. Puglia promises a sun-bleached Mediterranean laid-back lifestyle. Visitors are drawn to the untouched coastline and the Gargano promontory that strikes a happy balance between rural charm and good facilities.

Everyone with a fleet has invaded Puglia, from the Greeks and Romans to the Byzantines, Saracens and Normans. Most invaders have left a mark, but none more so than Frederick II of Hohenstaufen, Holy Roman Emperor, King of Germany and King of Sicily. Known to his 13th-century contemporaries as *stupor mundi et immutator mirabilis* – wonder of the world and extraordinary innovator – Frederick built most of the castles that define the region. He also founded splendid churches, carrying on the tradition of Puglian Romanesque begun by his Norman predecessors a century before.

Verdant orchard.

If Frederick II is the predominant figure in Puglia's history, then Puglian Romanesque is its architectural legacy. The style, fusing Byzantine, Saracenic and Italian decorative techniques with the French-Norman forms, first appeared in the church of San Nicola at Bari in 1087.

The Gargano promontory

The landscape of northern Puglia is dominated by endless wheatfields, hence the region's fame as a pasta producer. The only real mountains are

Main Attractions

Gargano promontory
Bari
Alberobello
Masserie (fortified farmhouses)
Taranto Archaeological Museum
Lecce

TIP

From Vieste you can catch a ferry to the Tremiti Islands, 40km (25 miles) offshore, which are sparsely populated but offer good beaches and clear water (www.collegamentiisole tremiti.com).

clustered on the **Gargano promontory**, now part of the Parco Nazionale del Gargano (www.parcogargano.gov.it), a thickly forested peninsula that juts out into the Adriatic to form the "spur" of the boot of Italy. The landscape ranges from a wooded interior to a rocky eastern coast with lagoons and sandy beaches in the north.

The oldest settlement here is **Monte Sant'Angelo ❶**, home to the **Santuario di San Michele** (www.santuario sanmichele.it; daily July–Sept 7.30am–7.30pm, Apr–June and Oct Mon–Fri 7.30am–12.30pm and 2.30–7pm, Sun 7am–1pm and 2.30–8pm (until 7pm in winter), Nov–Mar 7.30am–12.30pm and 2.30–5pm), now a Unesco World Heritage site. This cave is reputed to be where the Archangel Michael revealed himself to local bishops at the end of the 5th century. The cave is entered through a pair of bronze doors forged in Constantinople in 1076 and adorned with brass rings that were supposed to be knocked loudly to wake the Archangel within.

Monte Sant'Angelo is a good place to buy a picnic lunch to eat in the **Foresta**

Umbra ❷, where ancient beech, oak and chestnut trees shade winding trails. From here, you can drive along the coastline to **Vieste ❸**, a bright town on the tip of the promontory containing a castle built by Frederick II.

The road continues west along a serpentine coastline studded with beaches and grottoes, passing an impressive rock formation known as *Pizzomuno*, referred to by locals as "the top of the world".

Catholics will be drawn to a neighbouring pilgrimage shrine, **San Giovanni Rotondo**, dedicated to Padre Pio (1887–1968). Canonised in 2002, Padre Pio was, according to Pope John Paul II, the personification of simplicity, charity and prayer. Padre Pio made lesser claims: "I am a poor brother who prays." Millions of faithful fans have already visited the friar's beloved monastic church, where the latter-day saint worshipped for half a century. However, Padre Pio's fame prompted the resident friars to commission an immense domed church, designed by Renzo Piano and consecrated in 2004.

Manfredonia ❹ is a port and beach

Castel del Monte, built by Frederick II.

FREDERICK II

Some people visit Puglia for its architecture, some for its landscape and some for its food, but all go away haunted by memories of a single man: Frederick II of Hohenstaufen.

Holy Roman Emperor and King of Germany and Sicily, Frederick was an enlightened ruler who waged a bitter and ultimately unsuccessful feud with the popes in Rome. He was also an avid sportsman whose brilliant treatise on falconry still ranks among the most accurate descriptions of the subject. His just laws and tolerance of the Islamic beliefs of the Saracens are legendary. Frederick's death in 1250 and the tragic defeat of his illegitimate son, Manfred, at the battle of Benevento in 1266, ushered in a period of economic and spiritual decline that is only now being reversed.

resort with a pretty historic centre including a castle, begun by Manfred (son of Frederick II) in 1256 but extended by the Angevins and Spanish. Near Manfredonia are the beautiful medieval churches of **Santa Maria di Siponto**, with a 5th-century crypt and an altar made from an early Christian sarcophagus, and **San Leonardo**, with a facade guarded by two stone lions. Adjacent to Santa Maria di Siponto is Edoardo Tresoldi's amazing wire-mesh recreation of the original 12th-century basilica which once stood here before being destroyed by earthquakes and abandoned in the 13th century. It took the young Italian artist 4,500 square metres (48,500 sq ft) of wire mesh to recreate the volume of the original church. The installation really comes into its own when lit up at night as it could be mistaken for a hologram.

Siponto, once a thriving medieval port, also has good, though crowded, sandy beaches.

Coastal route to Bari

The coastal route to Bari is lined with seaport towns, all doing a brisk trade in vegetables, fruit and wine. The oldest, most important and, today, least attractive of these is **Barletta** ❺, where Manfred established his court in 1259.

Here, at the junction of the corsos Garibaldi and Vittorio Emanuele, stands the intriguing **Colosso**, a 4th-century Byzantine statue thought to represent the Emperor Valentinian I (364–75). Only the head and torso are original; the rest was recast in the 15th century. Behind rises the **Basilica di San Sepolcro** (open for Mass only: Mon–Fri 9.30am and 7.30pm and Sat–Sun 8.30am and 10am, noon and 7pm), with a nice Gothic portal and an octagonal cupola reminiscent of Byzantine designs. Barletta's **Duomo** (9am–noon and 4.30–7.30pm) is a confusing edifice built on a Romanesque plan, with five radiating apses in French Gothic style and a Renaissance main portal. By the sea lies Manfred's 13th-century castle, much expanded in later centuries.

A far more picturesque port, 13km (8 miles) south of Barletta, is **Trani** ❻, the cosmopolitan centre of the local wine trade. Its Romanesque **Cathedral**

The Gargano peninsula.

(www.cattedraletrani.it; Mon–Sat 8.30am–12.30pm and 3.30–6.30pm, Sun 9am–12.30pm and 4–8.30pm, reduced hours in winter), founded in 1097 but not completed until the middle of the 13th century, is perhaps the most beautiful church in Puglia.

Beneath its richly carved rose window is a smaller window flanked by pillars resting on the backs of elephants. The wonderful bronze doors are the work of the local artist Barisano da Trani, who is also responsible for the celebrated doors on the cathedral at Ravello.

The interior of the church, bright and austere, has the usual three apses and three naves, with triforium arcades above the side-aisles supported, here, by six pairs of columns on either side. Steps descend to the underground church of **Santa Maria della Scala** and the crypt. Even further down is the underground **Ipogeo di San Leucio**, 1.5 metres (5ft) below sea level, containing two primitive but delightful frescoes.

Bewildering Bari

Ancient **Bari** ❼, founded by the Greeks and developed by the Romans

Festive Bari.

as an important trading centre, was destroyed by William the Bad in 1156 and restored by William the Good in 1169. Today it is the largest and most important commercial centre in Puglia. The city is divided into two distinct parts: the kasbah-like Città Vecchia, at the end of Corso Cavour, with its tight tangle of medieval streets and dazzling white houses, and the Città Nuova, the modern city, with wide, grid-like boulevards. The tortuous alleyways of the Moorish-style Old City protected the inhabitants from the wind and from invaders. Although intriguing and generally safe, this maze of alleys can be bewildering, so visitors are advised to keep their wits about them.

The basilica of **San Nicola** (www.basilicasannicola.it; Mon–Sat 7am–8.30pm, Sun until 10pm) was founded in 1087 to house the relics of St Nicholas, patron saint of Russia – stolen from Myra in Asia Minor by 47 sailors from Bari. Most Puglian Romanesque churches were inspired by this seminal basilica, with its austere facade, fortress-like towers, tall gabled section and lavish portals carved with animals, flowers and biblical scenes. Its facade echoes that of the cathedral at Trani, though is even plainer. The interior is best visited in the early evening, when the dying sun illuminates the three great transverse arches. Beyond the choir screen is the 12th-century *ciborium* (freestanding canopy) over the high altar and, behind it, an 11th-century episcopal throne supported by three grotesque telamones. To the left is a Renaissance altarpiece, *Madonna and Four Saints*, by the Venetian Bartolomeo Vivarini. The crypt contains the precious relics of St Nicholas, visited by pilgrims for centuries. There is also a **Museo Nicolaiano** (daily 10.30am–6pm) featuring a collection of enamels, coats of arms, reliquaries, chalices and ancient coins.

Bari's Puglian-Romanesque **Duomo**, west of San Nicola, was erected between 1170 and 1178 over the remains of a Byzantine church destroyed by William the Bad during his rampage through the city in 1156. Basilican in plan, the church follows San Nicola in most details of its design, with deep arcades along both flanks and a false wall at the rear that masks the protrusions of the three semicircular apses. A particularly fine window adorns the rear facade.

Nearby, off the Piazza Federico II di Svevia, is the **Castello** (daily 8.30am– 7.30pm), built in Norman times, refurbished by Frederick II, and enlarged by Isabella of Aragon in the 16th century.

Bari's **Pinacoteca Provinciale** (www. pinacotecabari.it; Tue–Sat 9am–7pm, Sun 9am–1pm), containing paintings from the 11th century to the present, is in the less appealing part of town, the Città Nuova, along the Lungomare Nazario Sauro. The best painting is undoubtedly Bartolomeo Vivarini's *Annunciation* in Room II. Further rooms contain Giambellino's startling *San Pietro Martire* and works by Neapolitan Baroque painters, including Antonio Vaccaro and the prolific Luca Giordano. Francesco Netti, the Italian Impressionist, a native son of Bari, is also represented, and there is in addition a collection of contemporary art.

Heading inland

A day-long excursion into Puglia's architectural past begins 18km (11 miles) west of Bari in the olive-oil-producing centre of **Bitonto** ❽. The city's **Cathedral** (www.vieniabitonto. it; 9.30am–noon and 4–7pm), built between 1175 and 1200, is perhaps the fullest expression of Puglian Romanesque. The beautiful facade boasts a rose window and richly carved main portal, flanked by the familiar lions. The pelican above the doorway is a symbol of Christ – in medieval times, the pelican was thought to peck at its own flesh to feed its young, bleeding as Christ did on the cross for humanity.

The town of **Ruvo di Puglia** ❾, 18km (11 miles) further west, was known as Rubi in Roman times, when it was famous for its ceramics. The 13th-century **Duomo** (www.ruvosistemamuseale.it) was widened in the 17th century to provide room for Baroque side-chapels, and, though restorations have shrunk the interior's width back to its original Romanesque proportions, the wide facade retains its Baroque girth, giving the church a somewhat squat

The tower of Fiera del Levante in Bari.

TRULLI EXTRAORDINARY

With their grey conical roofs, whitewashed walls and mystical graffiti, Puglia's *trulli* are Italy's most curious houses. These twee homes originally served as storehouses or as overnight lodgings for farmers, but a 15th-century tax dodge led to a whole town of *trulli* springing up at Alberobello. The Count of Conversano enjoyed feudal rights over Alberobello, but did not enjoy paying his masters for the privilege. The emperor taxed every home in the count's domain – but not farmers' lodgings. So the crafty count ordered that the only buildings in Alberobello would be *trulli*. The Albererobelesi became people of the *trulli* There are 1,500 of them, and even a double-topped *trullo*, once home to two brothers who fell in love with the same woman. The girl was promised to the elder, but fell for the younger, and the brothers fought until the only solution was to divide the house.

The *trulli* roofs are painted with primitive symbols: hearts and crosses blending Christian and erotic love; icons to Saturn, Jupiter and Mercury; to the pagan powers of the earth, sun and sky. Designed to be easy to dismantle, these hobbit houses are only too permanent today, and are sought-after as shops or quaint holiday homes. Long Travel (www.long-travel.co.uk; tel: +44-01694-722 193) is a UK-based tour operator specialising in *trulli* holidays, including trulli with pools and vineyards.

appearance. Fortunately, the medieval sculpture on the facade largely remains; the seated figure at the top is thought to represent the ubiquitous Frederick II. Beneath the nearby **Chiesa del Purgatorio** lie some Roman remains. Ruvo's excellent **Museo Archeologico Jatta** (tel: 080-361 2848; Mon–Wed, Fri and Sun 8.30am–1.30pm, Sat and Thu 8.30am–9.30pm; free) is devoted to Rubian ceramics excavated from nearby necropolises and dating from the 5th to the 3rd century BC.

On a hilltop 30km (19 miles) west of Ruvo stands the **Castel del Monte** ❿ (daily 10.15am–7.45pm in summer, 9am–6.30pm in winter), Frederick II's architectural wonder. The eight-sided building has two storeys and eight Gothic towers; curiously enough, the main entrance is adorned with a Roman triumphal arch. Historians disagree as to whether Frederick II erected the small fortress as a hunting lodge or as a military outpost, but all agree that he married his daughter, Violanta, to the Count of Caserta here in 1249. The castle was later abandoned, becoming a hideout for brigands and political exiles. The eerie emptiness is accentuated by its isolated position on a hilltop perch that's visible for miles around. Much speculation also hinges on the arcane symbolism of the number eight, as the number is an integral part of the castle's architectural design.

Trulli country

Alberobello ⓫, southeast of Bari, is celebrated for its conical (and somewhat comical) peasant dwellings known as *trulli*. Nobody knows the exact origins of these whitewashed houses, but they did allow for easy home-extension through the addition of another unit, and modern building in the area is often based on the *trulli* shape. Many have been turned into B&Bs or eclectic gift shops awash with local liqueurs, fabrics and sculpture. This area has witnessed the greatest increase in visitors staying in *masserie*, the traditional Puglian farmsteads.

South of Alberobello, less touristy **Locorotondo** ⓬ is another place to find *trulli*. This fortified hilltop outpost is a member of the *Borghi più belli*

Trulli in Alberobello.

MAGNIFICENT MASSERIE

Puglia's *masserie* (fortified farmhouses) are all the rage: family-run Moorish, white-washed retreats surrounded by olive, almond or lemon groves, their former estates. Romantic yet remote, these are not simply chic retreats but authentic farmsteads that could withstand a siege. While some remain working farms, others have been reborn as delightful boutique hotels. In Savelletri di Fasano, Masseria Torre Coccaro is a fascinating 16th-century retreat set between olive and almond groves and the sea. The chic spa and pool occupy former stables carved into a grotto (www.masseriatorrecoccaro.com; tel: 080-482 9310). Its sister hotel is the Torre Maizza, which aspires to boutique hotel chic yet still overlooks olive groves and the sea from its tower (www.masseriatorre maizza.com; tel: 080-482 7838). Close by, Borgo Egnazia is a chic *masseria*-style resort, with luxury villas and a spa harking back to Roman baths (www.borgoegnazia.com; tel: 080-225 5000). The renowned Masseria San Domenico is a more formal, luxurious affair, a 15th-century mansion and thalassotherapy centre surrounded by olive groves (www.masseriasandomenico.com; tel: 080-482 7769). Near the port of Monopoli, Il Melograno tucks a discreet spa into this 16th-century limestone-hewn farmhouse (www.melograno.com; tel: 080-6909030). Closer to Lecce, Ruri Pulcra is a guesthouse in a charmingly converted *masseria* (www.masseriaruripulcra.it; tel: 0833-752813).

d'Italia, the most beautiful villages in Italy. The circular streets all seem to lead back to the Rococo Palazzo Morelli, generally via shops selling local wines.

The rural route between neighbouring **Fasano** ⑬ and Ostuni is lined with cypresses and *masserie*, working farms offering cheese, olive oil, jam and Locorotondo wine. The flat coast is given over to gnarled olive trees, but becomes more undulating above Fasano, with limestone escarpments, compact walled towns, and hairpin bends shooting down to the coast.

Perched on top of limestone cliffs, **Polignano a Mare** ⑭, just north of Monopoli, is an appealingly scruffy port with a low-key charm and whitewashed medieval centre. Few visitors can resist dining at the foot of the cliffs in the Grotta Palazzese (www.grottapalazzese.it; tel: 080-424 0677). This romantic seafood restaurant occupies a sea-washed grotto that was created as a banqueting hall in the 18th century.

The **Grotte di Castellana** (www.grottedicastellana.it; guided tours daily, check online for times; charge) is another of the region's great attractions. The 20km (12-mile) network of caves contains pools, grottoes and ceilings that drip with stalactites. You can opt for a one- or two-hour trip; the latter takes in the spectacular Grotta Bianca (White Cave).

To the east, beyond the olive groves, is the whitewashed hill town of **Ostuni** ⑮, a kasbah of a place, with its 15th-century cathedral and labyrinthine alleys that are a delight to wander around. As elsewhere in Puglia, the town is both deeply authentic and surprisingly contemporary, typified by Caffè Cavour (http://ristorantecaffecavour.com; tel: 0831-301 709), a cool cave-bar converted from a 12th-century olive mill. The success of the local *masserie* hotels (see box) means that the designer boutiques are doing as well as the shops selling ceramics, leather sandals, and baskets woven from olive branches.

Spartan Taranto

Taranto ⑯, the ancient Taras founded by Spartan navigators in 706 BC, was in the 4th century BC the largest city in *Magna Graecia*, boasting a population of 300,000 and a city wall 15km (9 miles) in circumference. It was, like many towns on this coast, a centre of Pythagorean philosophy and visited by such luminaries as Plato and Aristoxenus (author of the first treatise on music). Today, little remains from the Spartan period; the city was also severely damaged in World War II and is girdled by heavy industry. The engaging Old Town, once a Roman citadel, is effectively an island separated from the modern and industrial quarters by canals. Taranto is still worth visiting for its superb archaeological museum.

In the modern town, Taranto's **MARTA, Museo Nazionale d'Archeologia** (www.museotaranto.org; daily 8.30am–7.30pm), is the second-most important archaeological museum in southern Italy. The collection is rivalled only by its equivalent in Naples for the splendour of its antiquities. Set in

Fisherman.

a monastery, the displays recall Taras' importance as a centre of *Magna Graecia*. The collection includes Greek and Roman sculpture, Roman floor mosaics and a superb collection of ancient ceramics. The highlights include Doric friezes, Greek funerary monuments, Hellenistic busts, ancient jewellery crafted in Taras, and Roman mosaics depicting griffons.

In Taranto's Old City is the church of **San Domenico Maggiore**, founded by Frederick II in 1223, rebuilt in 1302 by Giovanni Taurisano, but heavily altered in Baroque times. Nearby, on the Via Cariati, is a lively fish market. Here, too, is the **Duomo** (www.cattedral etaranto.it), which contains a catacomb-like crypt, Byzantine mosaic floors and antique columns from pagan temples.

A fascinating side-trip (21km/13 miles) can be made from Taranto to the nearby town of **Massafra** ⑰, known for its early Christian cave churches hewn into the sides of a deep ravine that snakes through the centre of the town. The Santuario della Madonna della Scala contains a 12th-century *Madonna and Child* fresco, reached via a Baroque staircase from the town centre. At the bottom of the ravine is the Farmacia del Mago Gregorio – a maze of caves and tunnels once used by monks as a herb store (tel: 099-8804695 to enquire about access to the cave churches).

From Massafra by back roads (37km/23 miles), or from Taranto by *superstrada* (22km/14 miles), you can reach **Grottaglie** ⑱, a hilltop town where you can watch Puglian potters make the ceramic pitchers, plates, bowls and cups available across the region. The decorative spaghetti plates produced here are known throughout Italy.

Baroque Lecce

Southern Italians have long known about **Lecce** ⑲ and its glorious profusion of Baroque mansions and churches. But foreign tourism has only recently discovered the city. Unlike many southern cities, Lecce is enjoying something of a renaissance, with renovation matched by renewed confidence.

Lecce owes its appearance to the malleable characteristics of the local sandstone, which is easy to carve when it comes out of the ground but hardens with time. The growth of religious orders, particularly the Franciscans, Jesuits and Theatines, in the 17th and 18th centuries led to intensive building which created an architectural uniformity unique in southern Italy. Churches drip with ornate altars and swirling columns. Outside, shadeless streets meander past curving yellow palaces bright with bursts of bougainvillea.

The heart of Lecce is the cobblestoned **Piazza Sant'Oronzo**. At its centre stands a single Roman column which marked the southern terminus of the Appian Way (Via Appia) from Rome. A bronze statue of St Orontius, patron saint of the city, stands on top of the column. The southern half of the square is dominated by excavations of part of a well-preserved **Roman amphitheatre**

Baroque cathedral at Lecce.

(daily 10.15am–12.15pm and 5.15–7.15pm) dating from the 2nd century AD. Discovered in the 1930s, it was reopened in the year 2000 as a concert venue. A small museum on the site displays some fine frescoes and mosaics. The unusual Renaissance pavilion facing onto the piazza used to be the town hall.

Lecce's harmonious **Piazza del Duomo**, just off the **Corso Vittorio Emanuele**, is framed by the facades of the **Duomo**, the **Palazzo Vescovile** and the **Seminario**, all built or reworked in the 17th century. The Duomo actually has two facades: the lavish one facing the Corso, with its statue of St Orontius, and the more austere one facing the Palazzo Vescovile. The altars inside the Duomo, carved with flowers, fruit and human figures, are typical of the ornate local style.

The most complete and impressive expression of Leccese Baroque is the **Basilica di Santa Croce** (daily 9am–noon and 5–8pm), built in 1549–1679. Its exuberant facade sports a balcony supported by eight grotesque caryatids. The bright interior has an overall restraint that unifies the different designs of its chapels. A chapel in the left transept contains a series of 12 *bas-reliefs* showing the life of St Francis of Paola.

Lecce's **Museo Provinciale** (Viale Gallipoli 28; Mon–Sat 9am–1.30pm and 2.30–7.30pm, Sun 9am–1pm; free), just outside the Old City, is built around a spiral ramp reminiscent of the Guggenheim Museum in New York.

Best beaches

The rewards of travelling in Puglia, as in neighbouring Basilicata and Calabria, include the pleasure of ending the day on a beach. Puglia has the longest coastline in Italy, a fact which has made it peculiarly attractive to foreign invaders, from the ancient worshippers of Zeus to the sun-worshipping visitors of today. Lecce is within easy reach of beaches at **Gallipoli** ⑳ on the Ionian Sea and **Otranto** ㉑ on the Adriatic. Otranto has the added attraction of a Romanesque cathedral (daily 7am–noon and 3–7pm in summer, until 5pm in winter) with an impressive mosaic floor.

The Moorish-style Villa Sticchi, built in the late 19th century, is in Santa Cesarea Terme, a seaside resort south of Otranto.

The beach at Vieste.

Matera.

BASILICATA

With its primeval forests, sandy coves, chic cave dwellings, castles and ancient rock-hewn churches, Basilicata is both a timeless biblical land and a beguiling new destination for visitors.

Main Attractions
Matera
Rock churches
Tavole Palatine
Melfi
Venosa
Maratea

Basilicata may be of the beaten track but, nonetheless, it is an emerging tourist destination that has become surprisingly accessible. Crusader castles, the ravishing coast, eclectic archaeological parks, and cool cave-hotels are inspiring even the most jaded visitors. At pretty Maratea, majestic mountains provide the backdrop for lovely coves, a sharp contrast to the flat lands along the Ionian Sea to the east. The alluring interior offers great hiking country and the Parco Nazionale del Pollino, is a big draw, as is Unesco World Heritage Site Matera, noted for its rock-cut cave dwellings.

Matera and the Sassi

The region's most beguiling city is **Matera** ㉒, a fabulous troglodyte town of prehistoric grottoes, cave tabernacles, abandoned hovels and Renaissance houses – all excavated into the luminous limestone tufa.

The rock-cut cave dwellings – known as the Sassi – date back to Byzantine times. Up until the 1950s the caves were home to peasants who lived alongside their donkeys in dark hovels. Then the Italian government, embarrassed by the poverty, re-housed the entire population.

By the 1980s a number of intrepid Materani started to return, and now

the Sassi are the region's main attraction – recognised by Unesco as the finest example of "cave architecture" in the Mediterranean.

A hill splits the Sassi into two areas: Sasso Caveoso and Sasso Barisano. The only way to penetrate this mysterious world is on foot, exploring galleries and shops to see the inventive use of cave interiors. The caves may look crumbling but many are now cool B&Bs or bars, which have burgeoned ever since Mel Gibson's epic *Passion of the Christ* put Matera on the

The Sanctuary of Santa Maria di Anglona in Tursi, a town in the province of Matera.

map. You can pick up maps from the tourist office (Via de Viti de Marco 9; tel: 0835-331 983) and book tours at the **MUSMA, Museo della Scultura Contemporanea** (www.musma.it; Apr–Sept Tue–Sun 10am–2pm and 4–8pm, Oct–Mar 10am–2pm only), the refurbished sculpture museum, set in moodily lit caves.

Across the canyon from the Caveoso and Barisano are the original cave dwellings, dating back to 6 BC. This Stone Age history is documented in the **Museo Ridola** (Via Ridola 24; daily 2–8pm).

The great legacy of Byzantine civilisation in Basilicata are the so-called *chiese rupestri*: 9th–15th-century rock-hewn churches with built-in altars, pilasters, domes and frescoes. Over 150 survive, with some 48 in the Sassi themselves. Among the most important and best preserved are Santa Barbara, Santa Maria de Idris, Santa Lucia alle Malve, San Nicola dei Greci and Santa Maria della Valle. They are not easy to find, so go with a guide, who will often have keys to unguarded churches.

In the Sassi, many of Matera's homes are hewn out of the rocks.

Other attractions include the Baroque **Palazzo Lanfranchi** (Piazza Giovanni Pascoli; Thu–Tue 9am–8pm), which houses the Museum of Medieval Art.

The Baroque **Chiesa del Purgatorio**, dedicated to the medieval cult of the Holy Souls of Purgatory, features a curvaceous facade and gruesome Halloween-style decorations carved into the main doorway.

At the junction of Via Ridola and Via del Corso is the 17th-century Chiesa di San Francesco, home to painting by the early Renaissance master Bartolomeo Vivarini.

The nearby Piazza del Sedile, dominated by the local *conservatoire*, leads into Via Duomo, with its Romanesque cathedral. Dedicated to Matera's patron saint, the Madonna della Bruna, she is depicted in the Byzantine-style fresco above the first altar to the left. Of the rock churches, **Santa Lucia** contains the two most famous medieval frescoes in Matera, the *Madonna del Latte* and *San Michele Arcangelo e San Gregorio*.

More rock churches

In the **Murgia** area, around 14km (9 miles) from Matera, lies the fascinating Unesco-listed **Parco Archeologico delle Chiese Rupestri ㉓** (tel: 0835-336 166; www.parcomurgia. it), studded with over 100 rock churches (*chiese rupestri*). Many date back to the days when Matera was part of the Byzantine Empire. The most spectacular is the **Cripta del Peccato Originale**, the Crypt of Original Sin (tel: 320-334 5323; www. criptadelpeccatooriginale.it; reservations required; Apr–Sept 9am–6pm, until 3pm in winter). Its bold 9th-century frescoes depict Adam and Eve and God the Creator.

If travelling between Matera and the Parco Pollino, stop at **Craco ㉔**, a bewitching ghost town abandoned after a landslide, which is now used as a film set.

Ancient sights

It's an easy day trip from Matera to Basilicata's Ionian Coast, which is dotted with ancient ruins. Just north of **Lido di Metaponto** ㉕ – a traditional seaside resort with a family focus –are the remains of the Greek colony of Metapontum. This is the only ancient Mediterranean colony where archaeologists have completely mapped the urban layout. Even more evocative are the **Tavole Palatine** (daily 9am until 1 hour before sunset; tel: 0835-745 327), the remains of 15 standing columns from the 6th-century BC Doric Temple of Hera.

At **Policoro** excavations are still in progress at the **Parco Archeologico di Policoro** (daily 9am until 1 hour before sunset), where the remains of the 5th-century BC Acropolis of Heraclea are on view. The **Museo della Siritide** (Wed–Mon 9am–8pm, Tue 2–8pm; combined ticket for museum/archaeological area) displays bronzes and statuettes.

Melfi ㉖, between Foggia and Potenza, was once the stronghold of Holy Roman Emperor Frederick Barbarossa's Swabian dynasty, and houses an archaeological museum in a **crusader castle** where the First Crusade was launched by Pope Urban II (Tue–Sun 9am–8pm, Mon 2–8pm).

The Melfi area is dominated by the Vulture mountain range, with its extinct volcanic craters filled by two lakes, the Laghi di Monticchio. From the Lago Grande (Big Lake) and Lago Piccolo (Small Lake) there are amazing views up to Monte Vulture (1,326 metres/4,350ft). Another splendid view is from the heavily restored Norman Abbazia di San Michele, located on the wooded slopes of the Lago Piccolo crater.

Roman Venusia

Less than an hour away from Melfi is **Venosa** ㉗. Originally the prosperous Roman city of Venusia, it has survived thanks to its dominant position. For centuries it was a centre of learning, and was also the birthplace of the Latin poet Horace (65–8 BC). According to legend, he lived in Vico Orazio, where the remains of a Roman structure known as the

The castle at Venosa, where you'll find the Archaeological Museum.

The bewitching ghost town of Craco.

COOL CAVES

Matera has undergone a style makeover, with intriguing cafés, inns, hotels and galleries opening in the Sassi, the caverns gouged out of the side of a canyon by cavemen 9,000 years ago. **Le Grotte della Civita** (tel: 0835-332 744; http://legrottedellacivita.sextantio.it) is the most magical of the cave-hotels. The owners wanted to maintain the caves' integrity, "without turning the hotel into a peasant theme park" – and succeeded. The beds are raised on metal trusses, echoing the ancient technique for discouraging domestic animals from hopping into bed too. The **Locanda di San Martino** (Via Fiorentini; tel: 0835-256 600; www.locandadisanmartino.it) is a romantic honeycomb of a cave-hotel incorporating a deconsecrated church and a cave spa. **Baccanti** (Via Sant'Angelo 58; tel: 0835-333 704; www.baccantiristorante.com) is a creative cave-restaurant serving local pasta and full-bodied Aglianico del Vulture red wine. More bizarre is **19A Buca** (Via Lombardi 3; tel: 0835-333 592; www.diciannovesimabuca.com), an eclectic restaurant and wine bar that also slots a virtual golf course into an ancient underground cistern. Set on a rocky spur dividing Matera, the **Palazzo Gattini** (Piazza Duomo; tel: 0835-334 358; www.palazzogattini.it) is a luxurious designer retreat overlooking the Sassi. Naturally, the chic spa is set in a cave complex.

FACT

Archaeologists have unearthed in recent years the remains of a 6th-century BC Hellenistic temple, complete with detailed assembly instructions likened to an Ikea do-it-yourself furniture pack. The site is at Torre Satriano near Potenza, an area once part of Magna Graecia.

Casa di Orazio are visible. The castle is home to the **Museo Archeologico** (Wed–Mon 9am–8pm, Tue 2–8pm).

Take the Via Frusci which leads out of the town centre to the fascinating ruins in the **Parco Archeologico di Venosa** (Wed–Mon 9am–1.30pm). Centred on the Abbazia della Trinità, the site includes Roman and Palaeo-Christian remains, Jewish and Christian catacombs, thermal baths and a 10,000-seat amphitheatre.

The **Abbazia della Trinità** (tel: 0972-34211; call for details of opening) is one of the most intriguing abbeys in the south, and the largest monastic complex in Basilicata. It is made up of the chiesa vecchia (the old Norman church), and the roofless chiesa nuova, a later Benedictine foundation. Built of stones recycled from a Roman temple on the site, the abbey is a treasure trove of inscriptions, crusader tombs and frescoes emerging from the small olive grove. The local castle, Castello Ducale del Balzo (daily 9am–8pm), and the Jewish-Christian catacombs are also worth a look.

The jagged coastline at Maratea.

Potenza and the Apennine Dolomites

Built on a spur of rock between two valleys, the historic centre of **Potenza** ㉘ looks down on modern suburbs scattered at its feet. The capital of Basilicata has been battered by earthquakes: since the last big tremor in 1980, reconstruction has not exactly been miraculous. The highlight is the **Museo Archeologico Provinciale** (Via Ciccotti; Tue 8am–1pm, Wed–Sat 9am–1pm and 4am–7pm), as well as the attractive churches along Via Pretoria.

South of Potenza stretch the **Lucano Apennines**, the Apennine Dolomites. Along the River Basento these bare, pointed peaks have been beaten into bizarre forms by the elements. The best-known attraction is **Pietrapertosa** ㉙ (southeast of Potenza, off the SS407). The lofty village is dominated by a rugged fortress and encircled by anthropomorphic spires. From here, the foolhardy can take the exhilarating **Volo dell'Angelo Zipway** and, strapped into a safety harness, "fly like angels" between

A WALK ON THE WILD SIDE

Maratea is sandwiched between two competing national parks. Bordering the Calabrian side is the Parco Nazionale del Pollino (www.parcopollino.it) – a great place for walking and wildlife. The enormous park stretches across 200,000 hectares (500,000 acres) of wilderness which host many protected species, including a colony of wolves, black squirrels, golden eagles, vultures, falcons, buzzards and otters. The park's symbol is the rare loricate pine. It has declined since the last Ice Age as the climate has warmed, and is only found here and in the Balkans. There are underground caves with bat colonies and craft workshops. The park is also home to ethnic Albanians who tenaciously preserve their Arbëreshe (Italian-Albanian).

To the north, the sprawling Parco del Cilento (www.cilentoediano.it) in Campania stretches from the Tyrrhenian Coast to the foot of the Apennines in Basilicata, and includes the peaks of the Alburni Mountains, a wild mountain chain with caves, large beech forests and stark rocks. An endangered population of wolves and wild cats survive in a few remote corners of the park, as well as over 1,800 species of plants. Instead, closer to Matera, the Unesco-listed Murgia Park (www.parcomurgia.it) is fascinating, as are the flinty granite outcrops around Pietrapertosa. (For information on all Italian parks, visit www.parks.it.)

Pietrapertosa and Castelmuzzo (www. volodellangelo.com).

The Portofino of the South

Maratea ③⓪ looks down on a cluster of coastal villages strung out along a spectacular, jagged coastline, and also on the **Porto di Maratea** yachting marina. The hillsides are covered with pines, carobs and oak trees sweeping down to the Gulf of Policastro and sightings of ruined watchtowers.

Maratea's unmistakable landmark is a statue of Christ the Redeemer – designed to ward off misfortune. The Redeemer's charms worked during the 1960s when Maratea was dubbed "the Portofino of the South". Its status was underscored by a visitor list featuring Frank Sinatra, Richard Burton and Princess Diana.

Maratea's faded charm is back in fashion. The town's revival was spearheaded by the local bigshot behind the Mediterranean-style Santavenere resort (tel: 09738-76910; www.santavenere.it). It was Pietro Carnivale who wanted to give Maratea "the joys of the Amalfi coastline, without the permanent traffic jam and the vulgar chaos".

The result is laidback southern style without the bling, but with just enough trendy bars, pavement cafés and hotels to suffice a more sophisticated tourism. Not that the growing number of luxury yachts and beautiful people are absent from Porto di Maratea; they are just not so prevalent. On the shore, the stalactite-encrusted **La Grotta delle Meraviglia** is a rare sea-cave accessible on foot.

Up on the hill, Maratea's **Old Town** is picturesquely distressed, at one with the limestone cliffs and dolce vita lifestyle. Lolling along the side of Monte San Biagio, medieval houses and myriad churches bear the cracks of an earthquake which struck in the 1980s. The unpolished Old Town looks down on Santavenere's ritzy resort with insouciance. Any trip to Maratea should end in a romantic inn with a promise to return.

The vast Parco Nazionale del Pollino.

The spectacularly perched village of Roghudi in the Reggia Calabria region.

CALABRIA

When Rome was still a village of shepherds, Pythagoras was teaching philosophy here. But today, behind miles of shoreline, Calabria conceals some of the remotest spots in Italy.

Main Attractions
Bronzes of Riace
Museo della Magna Graecia
Tropea promontory
The Tyrrhenian Coast
Scilla
Albanian Villages
Rossano

This is the Italian deep-south – small untouched towns and villages, rugged mountain ranges and national parks sandwiched between the Ionian and Tyrrhenian seas. The coast north from Reggio di Calabria is a string of small villages popular with Italian tourists. Perched above a golden beach, Tropea is by far the prettiest and tucked beneath the dramatic coastline is the fishing port of Scilla. The northern end is dominated by Cosenza, a modern city blessed with a stunning Gothic cathedral. Isolated on the east coast, Crotone is the gateway to Sila national park where flora and fauna flourish among upland meadows and forests reminiscent of northern Italy landscapes.

Calabria is closer in spirit than any other region to the Italy of Byron and Shelley – the land of crumbling ruins that inspired the romantic thoughts of 19th-century travellers. Apart from pockets such as Tropea, tourism often feels like an afterthought. Compared with Puglia, there are few distinctive hotels, despite delightful restaurants and romantic scenery.

The rugged landscape is dominated by a backbone of mountains that descend in a series of fantastic foothills to the sea. Not surprisingly, it was from the sea that Calabria's first invaders, the Greeks, came in the 8th century BC, crossing the Straits of Messina from Sicily.

Spectacular treasure trove

Also from the sea are the **Riace Bronzes** – Calabria's most celebrated reminder of those early settlers. Discovered by a snorkeller off Riace in 1972, these two colossal Greek statues – thought to have been lost overboard from a ship sailing between Calabria and Greece 2,000 years ago – are the star attractions in the newly renovated **Museo Archeologico Reggio**

The charming fishing port of Scilla.

Calabria (Tue–Sun 9am–7.30pm) in **Reggio di Calabria** ㉛.

Along the Tyrrhenian coast

The coastline just north of Reggio was first described by Homer in Book XII of the *Odyssey*, the earliest navigational guide to the Tyrrhenian Sea. Here lurked the infamous monster Scylla, whose "six heads like nightmares of ferocity, with triple serried rows of fangs and deep gullets of black death" did away with six of Odysseus' best men. **Scilla** ㉜ itself is a charming fishing port whose spirit, dialect and traditions feel more Sicilian than Calabrian. The view over the Strait of Messina at sunset is stunning. Stroll down to Chianalea and explore the picturesque fishermen's quarters. The houses are built on the water, so each one has two entrances – one facing the sea and the other facing the street. Further north, **Palmi** ㉝ is worth visiting for its **Ethnographic Museum** just outside town (Mon–Fri 8am–2pm), which has an extensive collection of ceramic masks

designed to ward off the evil eye, and collections of agricultural and maritime life.

Rising dramatically from sea level at Reggio is the Parco Nazionale dell'Aspromonte (www.parco aspromonte.gov.it), a craggy wilderness, and a tempting area for walking and mountain-biking, despite the presence of clan villages. Its highest point is Montalto at 1,955 metres (6,410ft), dominated by an immense statue of Christ.

Tropea ㉞, suspended from a cliff over one of the many fine beaches that line the shore, is the most picturesque town on the Tyrrhenian Coast, a welcome change from the bleaker Ionian Coast, which is best visited for its archaeological sites. Tropea is infinitely more appealing and deservedly the most popular destination in Calabria for discerning visitors. The Tyrrhenian Coast is a place for savouring the laidback Calabrian lifestyle over long, languorous meals. The Old Town boasts a beautiful **Norman cathedral** and, behind the high altar, the *Madonna di Romania*, a portrait supposedly painted by St Luke.

Crossing the toe

Highway SS111 is the loneliest road in Calabria. It twists across the central mountain chain following an ancient trade route connecting **Gioia Tauro** ㉟ on the Tyrrhenian Sea with **Locri** ㊱ on the Ionian Sea. Fierce brigands once ruled this wooded terrain. From the **Passo del Mercante** ㊲, the road's highest and loneliest point, both seas are visible. From here the road descends to the beautiful town of **Gerace** ㊳, situated on a seemingly inaccessible crag. It is best to visit Gerace in the evening on foot, to appreciate the romantic sunset views from the grassy ruins of its castle. Before the 10th century, a miracle-working saint – San Antonio del Castello – conjured up a spring of pure water in a cave in the cliff that surrounds the castle. Multi-layered

The stunning Calabrian coast.

Gerace justifies the phrase, "If you know Gerace, you know Calabria." The cathedral, Calabria's largest, was begun in 1045 on top of an older church – now in the crypt. Both cathedral and crypt contain columns from the Greek settlement at Locri. Some parts of this 7th-century BC town, including walls and temples, can still be seen.

The **Cattolica** at **Stilo** ⊛, one of the best-preserved Byzantine churches, is a reminder that in medieval times Calabria's rugged interior was a vibrant religious centre. The tiny 9th-century church, built on a square floor plan with five cylindrical cupolas, clings to the flank of Monte Consolino, just above Stilo, like a miniature castle overlooking its town. Its bright interior is adorned with fragments of frescoes. The four columns supporting the vault are from a pre-Christian temple, but were placed upside down to symbolise the Church's victory over paganism.

Another important religious centre further inland is the Carthusian monastery at **Serra San Bruno** ⊛,

where you can visit the **Museo della Certosa** (www.museocertosa.org; Apr–Oct daily 10am–1pm and 3–6/8pm, Nov–Mar Tue–Sun daily 10am–1pm and 3–5pm, times vary so check the website).

Calabria's mountains

Of Calabria's four great mountain clusters – the Aspromonte, the Sila Piccola, the Sila Grande and the Sila Greca – the **Sila Piccola** ⊛, in the middle, has most to offer. (The Apromonte, in all its scorched beauty, is a base for the Calabrian Mafia.) Sila revels in its dense pine groves and cool meadows, where shepherd boys still wander with their flocks. The climate up here is refreshing after the dry heat of the coast.

The twisting road up to **Catanzaro** ⊛ climbs first to **Taverna** ⊛, the home town of Calabria's foremost painter, Mattia Preti, who made his name in Naples. The church of **San Domenico**, just off the main square, contains the best of Preti's Baroque art, with more in Santa Barbara and San Martino.

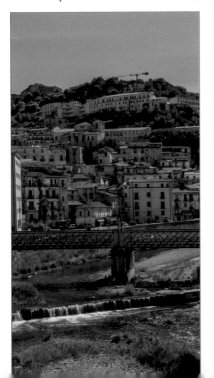

The Old Town of Cosenza.

THE RIACE BRONZES

In 1972 a holidaymaker saw a bronze arm emerge from the Riace Marina. Fate decreed that it appear at exactly the same spot where the locals immersed the reliquary of the Saints Cosma and Damiano to summon rain. For the faithful, there was no doubt that this was the divine intervention of the two miraculous martyrs. The so-called Bronzes of Riace have brought great fame to the Ionian coastal town. After restoration in Florence, and display in Rome, these two Greek bronzes returned "home" to the then-called Museo Nazionale della Magna (now the **Museo Archeologico Reggio Calabria**) in Reggio Calabria and were greeted with the veneration normally attached to saints. Many Calabresi tried to caress the statues and lifted babies to touch them. The atmosphere was similar to that of a southern Italian religious festival.

These glorious, virile 2-metre (7.5-ft) warriors are a patriotic reminder for the Calabresi that their remote toe of the Italian boot was once home to some of the Western world's most important cities in a land of philosophers and artists. Created in the 5th century BC, these bronzes were commemorative offerings presented to the winners of races carried out in full armour. The museum is being refurbished, but in the meantime the star exhibits, including the bronzes, are on view in the seat of Reggio's Regional Council (Sala Monteleone, Palazzo Campanella, Via Cardinale Portanova).

A few resorts dot the vast pine groves of the **Sila Grande**, including ski resorts and fishing centres, reached by long winding roads, but the overwhelming sense of isolation remains. Nature rules even around **Lago Ampollino** , an appealing man-made lake and reservoir.

San Giovanni in Fiore , the biggest town in the Sila, is noted for the black-and-purple costumes of its womenfolk. More compelling is the lovely hilltop town of **Santa Severina** , famed for its medieval scholastic tradition and castle. Attached to the cathedral is an 8th–9th-century Byzantine baptistery built originally as a *martyrium* (a shrine for the sacred relics of honoured members of the local Christian community) when it stood alone. At the entrance to the town, the Byzantine church of **San Filomena** has a cylindrical dome of Armenian inspiration, and three tiny apses that seem to anticipate Romanesque design.

The coastal town of **Crotone** , also a gateway to the Sila, was founded by Greeks in 710 BC. Here the mystical mathematician Pythagoras came up with his theorem on right-angled triangles and taught the doctrine of metempsychosis, in which the soul is conceived as a free agent which, as John Donne later imagined, can as easily attach itself to an elephant as to a mouse before briefly inhabiting the head of a man. Other than scholarly associations, the modern town on its crowded promontory has little to offer apart from a national **Archaeological Museum** (Tue–Sat 9am–7.30pm) which in 2010 saw the return of the Askos, a Greek bronze Siren which had been illegally sold to the Getty Museum. Find time to try wine made since antiquity in the nearby village of **Melissa** .

Northern Calabria

The Old Town of **Cosenza** stands on a hilltop surrounded by the featureless, sprawling modern city. In the heart of the *centro storico* stands a beautiful Gothic cathedral, consecrated in the presence of Frederick II in 1222. In the **Tesoro**

Medieval rooftops of Gerace.

dell'Archivescovado behind the cathedral is a Byzantine reliquary cross that Frederick II donated to the church at the time of its consecration. The partially ruined **Castello** at the top of the Old Town has excellent views.

When the travel writer Norman Douglas visited the Albanian village of **San Demetrio Corone** ⑤⓪ in 1911, he was told by the amazed inhabitants that he was the first Englishman ever to have set foot in the town. Although visitors are no longer a rarity in these parts, be prepared for the curious stares of barbers, policemen, shopkeepers and women in bright Albanian dresses.

The Albanians first fled to Calabria in 1448 to escape persecution by the Arabs. Today they form the largest ethnic minority in the region. They have their own language, literature and dress, and their own Greek Orthodox bishop. As isolated as San Demetrio is in the backhills of the Sila Greca, this was once one of the most important centres of learning in Calabria, the site of the famous Albanian College where the revolutionary poet Girolamo de Rada taught for many years. Inside the college, the little church of Sant'Adriano contains a Norman font and a wonderful mosaic pavement.

On the Ionian Coast, overlooking the sea, stands lonely **Rossano** ⑤①, a major centre in the south between the 8th and 11th centuries. It is home to the famous **Codex Purpureus**, a rare 6th-century Greek manuscript adorned with 16 colourful miniatures drawn from the Gospels and the Old Testament. This extraordinary book can be seen in the **Museo Diocesano** (mid-Sept–June Tue–Sat 9.30am–12.30pm and 3–6pm, July–mid-Sept Tue–Sat 9.30am–12.30pm and 4.30–8.30pm, Sun 10am–noon and 4–6pm; tel: 0983-525 263) beside the cathedral. At the top of the grey-stone town, the five-domed Byzantine church of **San Marco** offers views across the valley. Below the Old Town lies the bustling resort of Rossano Scalo, somewhat at odds with the ethos of Calabria, which is dedicated to life in the slow lane.

Deer in the Sila national park.

CALABRIAN FOOD

You will not be disappointed by the food in Calabria. A true Calabrese breakfast, typical of Reggio and the Ionian Coast up to Crotone, features several round brioches soaked in a glass of iced almond milk. For lunch, you can enjoy the Greek influence which is still present in the local cuisine, in the form of aubergines, olives, swordfish and plenty of sweet-toothed treats such as figs, honey and almonds. Peppers, chillies and ginger are used more liberally than in other regions.

Also popular are porcini mushrooms, which grow in the forests of the Sila and the Serre. And in this land of shepherds and their flocks, a variety of succulent cheeses are abundant wherever you go. Try ricotta, Pecorino or Caciocavallo washed down with Calabrian red wine.

Ballaro market, Palermo.

SICILY

The island of Sicily, set in the middle of the Mediterranean and once the centre of the known world, has the finest array of classical and Moorish sites in Italy.

Rome

S icily's history spans 5,000 years and this beautiful island, home over the centuries to Greeks, Romans, Arabs and Normans, has everything from classical sites and cities, such as Palermo and Syracuse, to *high* inland mountains, woodlands, a dramatic coastline and rich agricultural land producing olives, vines and citrus fruits. The eastern half is dominated by Mount Etna, Europe's largest volcano, while the interior pushes north to the coast in the shape of the Monti Madonie. Good beaches are plentiful, washed by some of the clearest waters in the Mediterranean. On the east coast is the Sicily's most attractive holiday resort, Taormina.

Sicily may be Italian, but the islanders are Latin only by adoption. They may look back at Magna Graecia or Moorish Sicily but mostly sleepwalk their way through history. Set against Sicilian fatalism is a kaleidoscope of swirling foreignness, the legacy of a land whose heyday was over 700 years ago. It is most visible in the diversity of architectural styles, from Roman and Hellenistic to Arab-Norman and Spanish Baroque. Sicily's great epochs were Greek colonisation (8th–3rd century BC), the Arab invasions (9th–10th century) and Norman domination (11th–12th century). Sicily is intoxicating, from the Classical temples and Etna's eruptions to the volcanic nature of the Sicilians.

Temple in Selinunte.

The Ionian coastline

A ferry crosses between Villa San Giovanni in Calabria and **Messina** ❶ in half an hour. Cradled by the Peloritani mountains, Messina swiftly reveals itself as a grid-like city with low-rise buildings and wide avenues.

Although founded in the Classical Age by Greek settlers and flourishing between the 15th and 17th centuries, Messina has little to show for its ancient origins. On a fateful morning in 1908, terrifying earthquake jolts, followed by a violent seaquake, shook

Main Attractions
Taormina
Mount Etna
Syracuse
Villa Romana del Casale
Selinunte
Palermo
Cefalù
Isole Eolie (Aeolian Islands)

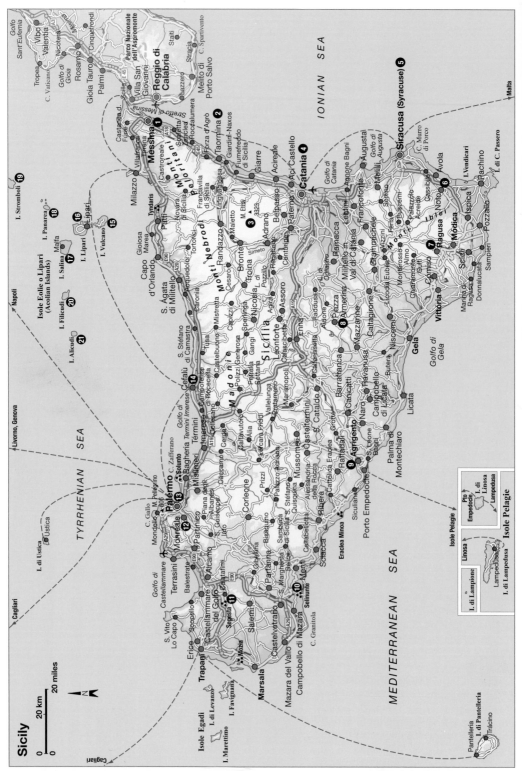

the city and razed it to the ground. Despite this disaster, several churches survived, including the **Duomo** (daily 7.30am–12.30pm and 4–8pm), as well as the Orion fountain, designed by a pupil of Michelangelo. At midday, the astronomical clock on the cathedral bell tower puts on a bold show, mixing mythological and religious figures with sound effects, such as a crowing cock and lion's roar.

In the shadow of Etna

After 45km (28 miles), the road from Messina winds up to a town that is the essence of Sicily. "It is the greatest work of art and nature!" exclaimed Goethe in *Italian Journey*. **Taormina** ❷ is Sicily's most dramatic resort, a stirring place celebrated since classical times. Its beauty is made up of light, colour and sea. It slopes down a cliff "as if", wrote Guy de Maupassant, "it had rolled down there from the peak". Its shoulders are embraced by the looming Mount Etna.

Climb the hill to the **Greek Theatre** (daily 9am–7pm in summer, until 4pm in winter; also open for summer concerts, film festival, opera and drama July–Sept, tickets and information from tel: 0942-628 730; www. teatrogrecotaormina.com), Taormina's most famous monument. Built in the 3rd century BC, but completely remodelled by the Romans in the 2nd century AD, it illustrates the Greeks' knack of choosing settings where nature enhances art. The jagged coastline of Taormina is dramatic: outcrops of rocks are intercut by narrow creeks, ravines and inlets.

Corso Umberto, which cuts through the old centre, is the place for browsing, grazing and people-watching. Despite the cosmopolitan crowd and designer nonchalance, the atmosphere somehow remains villagey. You can see this village in its churches or in the grand *palazzi* with their mullioned windows, marble tracery, scrolls and billowing balconies. Taormina is often likened to a Sicilian St Tropez, stylish but slightly unreal. Cynics insist the city is uncontaminated by corruption because even the Mafia likes a crime-free holiday haunt.

Sicily's smokestack

The landscape south of Taormina is dominated by **Mount Etna** ❸, the majestic volcano (3,323 metres/ 10,959ft) with its snow-capped peak (added to the list of Unesco World Heritage Sites in 2013). It is one of only a few active volcanoes in Europe; its surface is punctuated by about 200 cones, smaller craters, accumulated layers of lava, gashes and valleys. Etna's history is one of semi-ruinous eruptions, from the one in 396 BC, which halted the Carthaginians, to one in 1981, which destroyed part of the cableway. Even a smaller eruption in 1992 required help from the US marines to staunch the lava flow. The volcano has been in eruptive mode for over a decade but a massive eruption in 2013 forced authorities to shut down Catania airport. There are increasing concerns about the levels of activity from the volcano; in spring

TIP

To appreciate Etna's grandeur, drive around the base or follow a similar route on the Circumetnea railway from Catania (www.circumetnea. it), past almond groves, interspersed with barren black lava-stone.

The lively Piazza IX Aprile in Taormina.

2016 it started spewing ash clouds and lava again. Etna can be a damp squib smelling of rotten eggs or prove the most dramatic memory of your stay. To discuss options of getting close to Mount Etna, book one of the various tours through Taormina or Catania tourist offices. For advice on conditions and hiking routes, visit the Etna Park in Nicolosi (www.parcoetna.ct.it; tel: 095-821 111).

Catania ❹, set in a fertile plain at the southern foot of Mount Etna, was an important Greek colony, and still sees itself as more Greek, compared with the Moorish spirit prevalent in Palermo. If Palermo is perceived as being fatalistic, Catania is seen as more entrepreneurial. Destroyed twice by violent earthquakes (in 1169 and 1693), the city was covered in 1669 by lava which even advanced into the sea for about 700 metres (2,300ft).

Catania is the hub of the richest area of Sicily and has a modern feel, with an urban plan characterised by wide avenues and dark lava-stone palaces. Its main axis is the elegant, austere **Via Etnea**, where people gather for the *passeggiata* and window-shopping. But Catania's Baroque soul is better tasted in the smaller **Via Crociferi**, in which churches and monastic buildings open like wings of a theatre, including **San Benedetto**, a vast, unfinished Benedictine monastery (www.monastero-deibenedettini.it) that is now part of the University of Catania. No visit would be complete without seeing the well-restored **Castello Ursino** (Mon–Fri 9am–7pm, Sat–Sun until 8.30pm), erected by Emperor Frederick II (1239–50). The Swabian castle contains an art museum. You can then rest in the landscaped gardens of **Villa Bellini**.

Syracuse

From Catania head for **Syracuse** ❺ (Siracusa) through landscapes of classical beauty, counterpointed by archaeological remains. Built in 734 BC by a group of Corinthian farmers who settled on the small isle of **Ortigia**, Syracuse became one of the most important centres of the Mediterranean. After a dalliance with democracy, Syracuse flourished under despotism, and Dionysius.

Newly revitalised Syracuse is Sicily's most charming large city, especially in Ortigia, the island at the heart of the Greek city. This quietly cultured backwater is a place for aimless wandering between bold churches, Baroque curlicues and windswept views. The most compelling sight is the **Tempio di Atena** (5th century BC), a Greek temple that later became the **Duomo** (daily 8am–7pm).

Leave Ortigia across the **Ponte Nuovo** and head north to **Neapolis** (daily 9am–5.30pm), the sprawling archaeological park home to the **Teatro Greco**, one of the greatest theatres in the Greek world, which accommodated 15,000 spectators. Here, in summer, a series of high-quality classical performances allow lucky visitors to end up in the very spot where Plato or Archimedes sat for their night on the town. (For details, tel: 0931-487 211; www.indafondazione.org.)

Catania's fish market.

Nearby lie the **Latomie**, ancient honeycombed quarries which were used as prisons for Athenians sentenced to hard labour. In the **Latomia del Paradiso**, a man-made cave known as Dionysius' Ear has an amazing echo. A whisper amplified by the walls permitted the tyrant Dionysius to eavesdrop on prisoners. If you relish ancient legends, stop at the lively bars by the **Arethusa Fountain** back in Ortigia. According to local lore, the beautiful nymph jumped into the sea in order to escape from the river god Alfeus and was transformed into this spring.

From Syracuse, an excursion through the parched interior visits the theatrically Baroque town of **Noto** ❻. It stands on a ridge of the **Iblei Mountains**, furrowed by a long and straight road, which widens out into wonderful inclined squares. Here Spanish Baroque architecture triumphs in churches, palaces and monasteries, all cast in golden-coloured stone. Piazza Municipio encompasses a riot of pilasters, adorned windows, loggias, terraces and bell towers. Another highlight is **Palazzo Villa-Dorata**: a facade incorporating Ionic columns and balconies awash with lions, cherubs, gorgons and monsters.

From Noto, either visit the clean **beaches** to the south, or head west to **Ragusa** ❼, a city divided into two distinct entities, with Ragusa Ibla the star, and undergoing a revival. As a Baroque city recreated on a medieval street plan, an old-world intimacy prevails. Ibla is a place of moods rather than sights, graced by secret shrines, tawny-coloured mansions, filigree balconies and friendly bars. **Piazza Duomo** is lined by palm trees and mansions but the centrepiece is San Giorgio, a masterpiece of Sicilian Baroque.

Sicily's harsh and imposing heart

From the coast, an excursion leads through the bare interior, with its reddish sulphur mines. This landscape, established as a Geopark (**Rocca di Cerere**) in 2001, was an important extraction site from prehistoric times. Sicily became the first producer of sulphur minerals in the world but with the collapse of the Sicilian sulphur

The superb Cattedrale di San Niccolo in Noto.

market, mining complexes were abandoned. The park, which manages these important sites, is formed by nine towns and contains four natural reserves.

A visit to the hilltop town of **Aidone**, must include the Museo Archeologico Regionale (daily 9am–7pm), where you can admire the "looted" goddess of Morgantina statue, repatriated here in 2011 from the Getty Museum.

Outside the hilltop town of **Piazza Armerina** ❽ is the **Villa Romana del Casale** (daily Apr–Oct 9am–6pm, Nov–Mar 9am–until 4pm; free first Sun of the month), an imperial mansion or grand hunting lodge. The 3rd- and 4th-century villa was classified as a Unesco World Heritage site because "as the mainstay of the rural economy of the Western Roman Empire, the villa symbolises the Roman exploitation of the countryside and is one of the most sumptuous examples of its type". Indeed, the villa's splendid mosaics triumph as "the last pagan achievement in Sicily executed under the old dispensation". The villa's magic lies in the 50 rooms covered in

Roman-African mosaics. Their vitality set them apart from models in Tunisia or Antioch. The stylisation of these mosaics is undercut by humour, realism, sensuality and subtlety. In 2012, the site reopened following the completion of an ongoing EU-funded restoration project. Aside from the mosaics, which needed major conservation, the project involved replacing the transparent cover with a solid roof, and maintaining the elevated walkways, providing an above-ground view of the mosaics over the original villa walls.

Agrigento

Luminous **Agrigento** ❾, described by the Greek poet Pindar as "the most beautiful city of mortals", is a magnificent sight linked to a disappointing city. Syracuse may have been the most powerful city in Greek Sicily but Agrigento (Akragas) was the most hedonistic. The origins of Agrigento date from 581 BC. The Valley of the Temples forms a natural amphitheatre, with a string of Doric temples straddling a ridge south of the city. Ideally, glimpse it first at night, when the temples glow in the black countryside, radiating a sense of serenity.

The classical city, **Valle dei Templi** (Valley of the Temples; www.valleyofthe-temples.com; main zone daily 8.30am–7pm) comprises magnificent temples and tombs. The finest are: Tempio di Giove (Olympian Zeus), the largest Doric temple ever known; Tempio di Giunone (Juno/Hera), which commands a view of the valley; and Tempio della Concordia, one of the best-preserved temples in the world.

The splendid temples of **Selinunte** ❿ (daily 9am–7pm, until 5pm in winter) can be seen from afar, on a promontory between a river and a plain in the middle of a gulf with no name. Selinunte looks like a puzzle made of stone pieces: divided columns, chipped capitals, and white-and-grey cubes are all heaped together, as if a giant hand had mixed the pieces to

Doric temple at Segesta.

---

make the reassembling of the original image more difficult. However, the stones speak volumes, revealing libraries, warehouses, courthouses, temples – all testifying to a prosperous ancient town in the middle of fertile lands. Amid the stones grows *selinon*, the wild parsley which gave its name to the powerful Greek colony.

Selinunte was destroyed in its attempt to expand at the expense of Segesta: in 409 BC, 16,000 citizens of Selinunte were slain by their Carthaginian rivals. To complete the plunge into the past, go to the rival **Segesta** ⑪ (www.segestawelcome.com; daily 9am–7.30pm in summer, 9am–5pm in winter). In spite of the frequent devastations of wars between the Greeks and the Carthaginians, an imposing Doric **temple** has survived. It stands on the side of an arid, wind-beaten hill, and is propped up by 36 columns. Further up is the **Theatre** (Teatro), constructed in the 3rd century AD over the top of Mount Barbaro and from which stretches a splendid view over the **Gulf of Castellammare**; in summer there are open-air performances.

The Conca d'Oro

Enclosed by a chain of mountains, the Conca d'Oro is a valley of citrus groves, fast succumbing to ribbon development. The valley is dominated by **Monreale** ⑫, which was founded in the 11th century around a famous Benedictine abbey. The **Duomo** (www.cattedralemonreale.it; daily 8.30am–12.30pm and 2.30–5pm; chapel and terraces closed noon–3.30pm) is a masterpiece of 12th-century Arab-Norman architecture, and a Unesco World Heritage Site since 2015 along with the cathedral of Cefalù and Palermo's Arab-Norman heart. The church owes its fame to the mosaics, made by Byzantine and Venetian artists and craftsmen. The mosaics illustrate biblical scenes, from the Creation to the Apostles, in a golden splendour which fades away into grey, giving a tone of "sad brightness" summed up by the glance of the huge Pantocrator (Almighty). The **cloisters** (Mon–Sat 9am–7.30pm, Sun 9am–1.30pm) are the most sumptuous Romanesque cloisters in the world. The sophistication of these columns suggests a Provençal influence,

Soaking up the serenity inside the cloisters of Monreale's stunning 12th-century cathedral.

while the Moorish mood, evoked by mosaic inlays or arabesque carvings, conjures up the Alhambra.

After admiring the view of the Conca d'Oro from the church's terraces (180 steps), proceed to **Palermo** ⓭, the island capital. Lying at the bottom of a wide bay enclosed by Capo Zafferano and Mount Pellegrino, Goethe described it as "the most beautiful promontory in the world".

Discovering Palermo

Sicily's capital is a synthesis of sumptuous Arab-Norman and Baroque splendour interspersed with an intriguing Moorish muddle. It was only with Arab colonisation that Palermo prospered as the most multiracial city in Europe. The city was home to Jewish merchants, Greek craftsmen, Persian artists and Berber slaves. Palermo remains an exotic jumble of periods and styles.

Begin in the **Palazzo dei Normanni** Ⓐ, the splendid Norman palace (www.federicosecondo.org; Mon–Sat 8.15am–5.40pm, Sun 8.15am–1pm) and seat of the Sicilian parliament (also known as the Palazzo Reale).

The puppet theatre (Museo delle Marionette; Piazzetta Pasqualino; Mon–Sat 9am–1pm and 2.30–7pm, in summer 10am–7pm) is one of the best of its kind in the world. In their shiny armour and with their stern expressions, these marionettes remain as an evocation of Norman Sicily. All the puppets are handmade, some of them centuries old.

Inside are the **Cappella Palatina** (same times as the palace) and the **Sala di Re Ruggero**, featuring glittering chambers enlivened with mosaics. The Cappella's ceiling is unique in a Christian church, a composition of ineffable oriental splendour. The Normans asked Arab craftsmen to portray paradise and they maliciously obliged with naked maidens which the Normans prudishly clothed and crowned with haloes. The site became a Unesco World Heritage list in 2015.

From there, follow the **Via Vittorio Emanuele** Ⓑ to the **Quattro Canti** Ⓒ, adorned by Baroque fountains and statues. You will unexpectedly run into the majestic **Duomo** (www.cattedrale.palermo.it; Mon–Sat 7am–7pm, Sun 8am–1pm and 4–7pm) rising among the narrow streets, with its spire towers, double lancet windows, and intertwined and pointed arches.

Another beautiful 16th-century fountain stands in **Piazza Pretoria** Ⓓ, once nicknamed the Piazza Vergogna (Square of Shame), due to the saucy nudes cavorting in its fountain. Near the Vucciria market

are elaborately decorated **Oratorio di Santa Cita** and the **Oratorio del Rosario di San Domenico**.

A few more steps lead back to the Arab-Norman age, when Palermo was defined by the geographer Idrisi as the "town which turns the head of those who look at it". Here are two churches: **La Martorana** Ⓔ (9.45am–1pm and 3.30–5.30pm, Sun 9–10.30 and 11.45am–1pm), decorated with Byzantine mosaics, and **San Cataldo** Ⓕ (Mon–Sat 9am–1pm and 3.30–6.30, in winter daily 9am–1pm), which preserves three red Moorish domes. The nuns of La Martorana are famous for inventing *pasta reale*, the popular marzipan fruit-shaped sweets.

Between Via Maqueda and the Palazzo dei Normanni extends the **Albergheria Quarter**. In spite of the architectural chaos, **Ballarò market** (http://palermo.com; daily 8am–2pm) is a triumphant spectacle. Palermo's markets serve up gastro-porn at its most deadly: writhing octopus, slithery eels and bloody swordfish glisten on ice blocks; beyond are cartloads of lemons, barrels of olives, bunches of mint, trays of saccharine pastries and sacks of spices.

Isolated by an oasis of green is the small church of **San Giovanni degli Eremiti** Ⓖ (Mon–Sat 9am–7pm, Sun 9am–1.30pm), a masterpiece of medieval architecture and now a Unesco site. Its five Moorish domes recall the 500 mosques that once dotted the town, as described by the traveller Ibn Hawqal in the 10th century.

FACT

Palermo's Museo Archeologico Regionale Antonio Salinas (www.regione.sicilia.it/bbccaa/salinas; ground floor: Tue–Sat 9.30–1.30 and 2.3–5.30, Sat–Sun 9.30am–1.30pm) is undergoing restoration but has reopened its ground floor to visitors. In the inner courtyard amidst lush vegetation, you can see fine examples of Egyptian and Greek statuary.

Palermo

Urban regeneration has brought new life back to the **Kalsa**, the south-eastern quarter, with **Piazza Marina** the liveliest area. A witness to its turbulent history is the splendid 14th-century **Palazzo Chiaramonte**, a Catalan Gothic fortress (Tue–Sat 9am–1pm and 2.30–6.30pm, Sun 10am–2pm) which became the headquarters of the Inquisition in the 17th century. To the west of the square, the **Galleria d'Arte Moderna** ❶ (GAM; www.gampalermo.it; Via Sant'Anna; Tue–Sun 9.30am–6.30pm; free first Sun of the month) concentrates on Sicilian works, particularly those of Palermitano artists, and takes visitors on a tour from the late 1800s to the mid-20th century. The museum makes perfect use of its beautiful setting in a converted convent, with its courtyard and spacious rooms.

For more modern art in Palermo check out the **Museo d'Arte Contemporanea RISO** (Corso Vittorio Emanuele 365; Tue, Wed, Sun 10am–7.30pm, Thu–Sat 10am–11.30pm; www.palazzoriso.it), housed in the beautifully renovated neoclassical Palazzo Belmonte Riso, with its collection of works by Sicilian, Italian and international contemporary artists who spent time in the island.

In the ancient harbour, the church of **Santa Maria della Catena** ❶ is a synthesis of Gothic and Renaissance art. Via Alloro, the hub of the quarter, contains Sicily's most important art gallery in the imposing **Palazzo Abatellis** ❶ (Tue-Fri 9am–6.30, Sat–Sun 9am–1pm). The **Galleria Regionale della Sicilia** has a collection of medieval paintings.

Stroll in **Villa Giulia** ❶, 18th-century Italianate gardens (7am–8pm), before visiting the **Orto Botanico** ❶ (www.ortobotanico.unipa.it; daily 9am–5pm in winter, until 8pm in summer), among whose exotic plants and rare trees Goethe loved to rest. Beyond lies the **Foro Italico**, an esplanade leading to the **Cala** ❶, the old port. Although it no longer functions as a port, the Cala remains a picturesque shelter for gaily coloured fishing boats.

The rather characterless commercial city centre embraces **Via Ruggero Settimo** and **Viale della Libertà** ❶,

Triumph of Death fresco at Palazzo Abatellis, Palermo.

BEST BEACHES

Any trip to Sicily should include a day or two at the beach. There are numerous clean beaches and miles of coastline.

Calamosche (Noto) doesn't offer anything other than its simple beauty. A mile-long walk delivers soft white sand and transparent waters that are second to none.

Lungomare di Cefalù is the golden-coloured main beach of Cefalù. Just a few steps from the historic centre, this lovely beach offers views of the colourful fishing village and the mountains.

Rabbit Beach (Isole di Lampedusa) has been called "the best beach in the world", and it's easy to see why when you first catch a glimpse of the incredible turquoise water and white sand. This is one of the few places in the Mediterranean where loggerhead sea turtles lay their eggs, and can only be accessed by boat.

San Vito Lo Capo (Reserva della Zingaro), with its white sand and clear water, lies on a lovely bay between spectacular mountains.

Scala dei Turchi (Realmonte) is not your archetypal beach. Breathtaking white cliffs carved out by the sea fluently descend into the pure waters. Climb the white giants and then relax on the peaceful beaches below.

Spiaggia Vendicari (Noto) is one of Sicily's last undiscovered paradises in the heart of the Vendicari Nature Reserve. The golden sand dunes, backed by lagoons and scrub, provide a peaceful refuge.

an area redeemed by elegant shops and cafés. Palermo's picturesque side is more visible in such food markets as the **Vucciria** and in the **Castello della Zisa** in the suburbs (daily 9am–6.30pm), built in 1160 by William I, where significant Islamic artefacts that come from the Mediterranean basin are displayed.

Along the Tyrrhenian Coast

Sitting snugly below a headland, **Cefalù** ⓮ is Taormina's west coast rival. Taormina has better hotels, nightlife and atmosphere, but Cefalù is more compact, peaceful and family-oriented. Cefalù's fame lies in its medieval charm and great Arab-Norman cathedral. These luminous Byzantine mosaics are among the earliest created by the Normans yet are also praised as the purest extant depiction of Christ. Along with Monreale Cathedral and Palermo's Arab-Norman district, **Cefalù Cathedral** became a Unesco World Heritage Site in 2015. A highlight is the charming medieval wash basins (Lavatoio Medioevale) spurting out freezing water from the Cefalino river.

Aeolian Islands (Isole Eolie)

Situated off the north coast of Sicily, the **Aeolian Islands**, steeped in mythology, were named after Aeolus, the Greek god of the winds. This is Sicily's most enchanting archipelago, with the best beaches and most exotic experiences. **Vulcano** ⓯, the first ferry stop, offers yellow sulphurous baths and volcanic craters. **Lípari** ⓰, the largest and most populated island, is the richest historically and, on its pumice beach, offers the only white sand in the archipelago. **Salina** ⓱, the highest and greenest island, is topped by two symmetrical volcanoes.

Panarea ⓲, the most exclusive summer retreat, is a picturesque anchorage for yachties and celebrities. **Stromboli** ⓳, the "black giant", boasts two villages, separated by burning lava flows. Like Etna, it is constantly active, and regular rumblings can be heard. At night you get the best view of the orange lava.

The quietest, most eco-friendly islands are **Filicudi** ⓴ and **Alicudi** ㉑, refuges not only for divers and marine-life enthusiasts but for lovers of peace and solitude.

The view of the islands from Vulcano.

THE LIVING EARTH: ITALY'S VOLCANOES

Bubbling, seething and angry, or silent, solemn and threatening, Italy's volcanoes dictate the way of life of those in their shadow.

The area from the island of Sicily north to Campania on the Italian mainland is notoriously unstable geologically. Here, the earth's crust continues to suffer earthquakes, changes in land levels and volcanic activity. From Vesuvius brooding over the Bay of Naples to imperious, seething Etna on Sicily, Italian volcanoes have shaped the way of life of local people for centuries. The destruction and devastation that has followed major eruptions has on the one hand caused trepidation and exodus but, on the other, has offered long-term compensation in the legacy of fertile soil enriched with volcanic extract.

Spreading the word

The fame of Italy's volcanoes owes much to its classical writers. Virgil and Pliny the Younger both described the might of volcanic activity in the region. Pliny, in particular, left us a detailed account of the eruption of Vesuvius in AD 79 which saw the death of his uncle, Pliny the Elder, and destroyed the towns of Herculaneum and Pompeii. In turn, Vesuvian mud and ash has preserved for us a unique picture of life in Roman times (see page 335).

Etna remains a constant threat. A massive eruption in 2013 forced authorities to shut down Catania airport and in 2016 the mighty volcano began to spew ashes again.

Vesuvius is actually a volcano within another, much larger volcano.

The seas around the Aeolian Islands can be radioactive and in places are warmed by underwater jets of steam. Sulphurous mud pools are sought out for the treatment of rheumatism.

'Vesuvius from Portici' by Joseph Wright of Derby, 18th century.

THE MIGHT AND POWER OF THE GODS

The power of Italy's active volcanoes is a phenomenon that defied explanation in ancient times. The Romans attributed the fiery convulsions to Vulcan, the god of fire and metalworking, whom they believed lived deep beneath the Aeolian island of Vulcano. In addition, the poet Virgil told of the giant Enceladus who, he declared, was interred below Mount Etna, his groanings and rumblings accounting for the earth-shaking, violent eruptions.

Early Christians, too, saw divine activity in volcanic outbursts. In the year 253, the mere production of the veil covering the tomb of the recently martyred St Agatha was said to have staunched the lava flow from Etna that threatened to envelop Catania and its people. Even in relatively modern times, the citizens of Naples have been quick to turn to their patron saint, Januarius (San Gennaro), for help whenever Vesuvius belches smoke.

However, some observers over the centuries have been more pragmatic about the causes of volcanic activity. One anonymous Roman poet suggested that the phenomenon was wind-induced: "It is the winds which arouse all these forces of havoc: the rocks which they have massed thickly together they whirl in eddying storm…"

Volcano tourism really began in the 19th century when Vesuvius, then Etna (below) became part of the traveller's itinerary. Sedan chairs or donkeys were used to convey lazy visitors to the top.

Etna is Europe's largest active volcano and Italy's highest mountain outside the Alps. Though it is prone to eruption, and the area around the main crater is now out of bounds, it is possible to climb – provided common sense and local advice are heeded. Wear warm clothing, even in the height of summer, and strong shoes.

The village of Regalbuto and its imposing cathedral, with Mount Etna looming large in the background.

Crystal-clear waters at Villasimius.

SARDINIA

Seven thousand prehistoric stone towers, countless beaches and more sheep than people make Sardinia the perfect place to get away from it all.

Rome

Sardinia has many unique charms but its main attraction is its stunning bays lapped by turquoise crystal clear water, which attracts the rich and famous from all over Europe. The biggest magnets may be the internationally renowned ritzy resorts of the Costa Smeralda, but the more down-to-earth Cagliari and Catalan-infused Alghero are also popular holiday spots. Most holiday-makers come for the beaches but there is more to Sardinia than that, including the intriguing remnants of the prehistoric Nuraghic civilisation, most evident at Su Nuraxi. The Gennargentu Mountains lie at the heart of the island's rugged interior, preserved within a huge national park.

Sardinia has little in common with the rest of Italy. The Mediterranean's second-largest island offers a restricted diet of art and architecture; rather, its appeal lies in its beaches, rocky coastline, rugged landscape and rural hotels. Much of its 1,600km (1,000-mile) coastline is given over to duney sands and romantic coves nestling in pine and juniper woods. The interior, where sheep outnumber humans, is wild and mountainous, and covered in a knotty carpet of herby, shrubby *macchia*. Even the island's cuisine is different from the mainland's. Here, the robust, meat-based cuisine comes

in the form of roast lamb and suckling pig, as well as Pecorino cheese made from ewe's milk, *seadas* or cheese pastries served with honey, and *carta da musica* – crisp, wafer-thin bread said to resemble sheets of music.

Lying within Gallura, the sparsely inhabited northeastern region of Sardinia where pinky, granite rocks tower like castles over swathes of *macchia* and juniper, cork and oak woods, is the **Costa Smeralda** ❶, or Emerald Coast. In the early 1960s, the Aga Khan and associates bought up this

Playing the local instrument, launedda, at a festival.

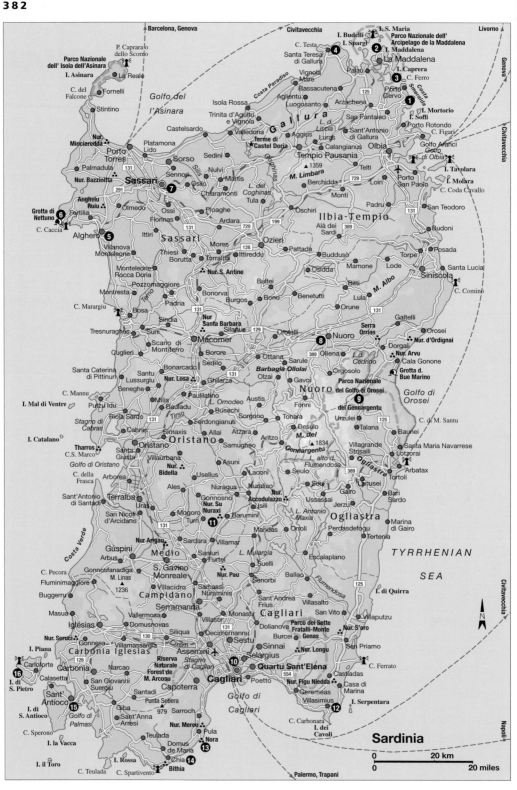

Civitavecchia

Livorno

I. S. Maria
I. Budelli
Parco Nazionale dell'
I. Spargi
Arcipelago de la Maddalena
C. Testa
I. Maddalena
Santa Teresa
di Gallura
La Maddalena
P. Caprara lo
dello Scorno
Vignola
Mare
Palau
C. Ferro
Parco Nazionale
dell' Isola dell'Asinara
Porto
Cervo
Costa Smeralda
I. Asinara
La Reale
Bassacutena
Arzachena
Costa Paradiso
Aglientu
I. Mortorio
C. del
Falcone
Fornelli
Isola Rossa
Luogosanto
I. Soffi
Stintino
Trinità d'Agultu
e Vignola
San Pantaleo
Porto Rotondo
C. Figari
Golfo del
l'Asinara
Valledoria
Sant'Antonio
di Gallura
Golfo Aranci
Golfo
di Olbia
Castelsardo
Gallura
L. d.
Liscia
Aggius
Calangianus
Olbia
Nur.
Minciaredda
Platamona
Lido
Terme di
Castel Doria
Luras
Tempio Pausania
I. Tavolara
Porto
Torres
Sorso
Sedini
Coghinas
M. Limbara
1359
Telti
Porto
San Paolo
I. Molara
Palmadula
131
Sennori
Nulvi
Martis
Berchidda
729
C. Coda Cavallo
Nur. Bazzinitta
Sassari
Osilo
Chiaramonti
Tula
L. del
Coghinas
Monti
Loiri
Padru
291
7
Ploaghe
Oschiri
San Teodoro
Anghelu
Ruiu
Olmedo
Ossi
Florinas
Ardara
Alà dei
Sardi
Ilbia-Tempio
131
Grotta di
Nettuno
6
Fertilia
131
199
Budoni
C. Caccia
Alghero
5
Ittiri
Sassari
Mores
Ozieri
128
389
Posada
Vilanova
Monteleone
Thiesi
Borutta
Ittireddu
Pattada
Buddusò
Santa Lucia
Monteleone
Rocca Doria
Torralba
Osidda
Mamone
Lode
Siniscola
Pozzomaggiore
Nur. S. Antine
Bultei
Bitti
M. Albo
C. Comino
Montresta
Padria
Bonorva
Burgos
Benetutti
Lula
C. Marargiu
Bosa
Sindia
Nur
Santa Barbara
Silanus
129
Bono
Orune
131
Galtelli
Tresnuraghes
Suni
Scano di
Montiferro
Macomer
Orotelli
8
Nuoro
Serra
Orries
Orosei
Nur. d'Ordingai
Cuglieri
Borore
Sedilo
Ottana
Sarule
Oliena
L.d.
Cedrino
Dorgali
Nur. Arvu
Cala Gonone
Santa Caterina
di Pittinuri
Santu
Lussurgiu
Bonarcado
Nur. Losa
Ghilarza
Olzai
Gavoi
Orgosolo
Grotta d.
Bue Marino
Seneghe
Paulilatino
Austis
Parco Nazionale
del Golfo di Orosei
Golfo
di
Orosei
C. Mannu
Milis
L. Omodeo
Busachi
Sorgono
Fonni
Nuoro
9
I. Mal di Ventre
Putzu Idu
Riola Sardo
Tirso
Fordongianus
del Gennargentu
Urzulei
C. di M. Santu
Stagno di
Cabras
Cabras
131
Samugheo
Aritzo
Atzara
Desulo
Talana
Baunei
I. Catalano
Simaxis
Allai
M. del
Gennargentu
Villagrande
Strisaili
Santa Maria Navarrese
Tharros
Oristano
1834
Lotzorai
C.S. Marco
Santa
Giusta
Villaurbana
Asuni
L. alto d.
Flumendosa
Tortolì
Golfo di Oristano
Nur.
Bidella
Ales
Usellus
Laconi
Seulo
389
Arbatax
C. della
Frasca
Arborea
Nuragus
Nur.
Accodalazzo
Sadali
Lanusei
Bari
Sardo
Sant'Antonio
di Santadi
Terralba
Uras
Gonnosno
Nur. Su
Nuraxi
Isili
Jerzu
Ogliastra
San Nicolò
d'Arcidano
Mogoro
Turri
Barumini
L. Antonio
Maxia
Marina
di Gairo
131
11
Mandas
Ortoli
Perdasdefogu
Tertenia
Nur Arixau
Sardara
Villamar
Sanluri
Escalaplano
TYRRHENIAN
Guspini
Medio
Furtei
L. Mulargia
Arbus
S. Gavino
Monreale
Suelli
125
SEA
C. Pecora
Gonnosfanadiga
M. Linas
Villacidro
Nur. Pau
Senorbi
Ballao
Flumendosa
I. di Quirra
Fluminimaggiore
1236
Sanassi
Nuraminis
Campidano
Sant'Andrea
Frius
Villasalto
Buggerru
Serramanna
Villasor
Monastir
Cagliari
San Vito
Villaputzu
Masua
Vallermosa
Domusnovas
Siliqua
Dolianova
Burcei
Nur. S'oro
Iglesias
130
Decimomannu
Sestu
Sinnai
San Priamo
Parco dei Sette
Fratalli-Monte
Genas
Nur. Seruci
Gonnesa
Villamassargia
Oxerri
Selargius
Nur. Longu
C. Ferrato
I. Piana
Assemini
Quartu Sant'Elena
Carbonia Iglesias
126
Riserva
Naturale
Forest de
M. Arcosu
Cagliari
Casteliadas
Carloforte
Carbonia
Narcao
Capoterra
554
Poetto
Nur. Figu Niedda
Casa di
Marina
I. di
S. Pietro
Calasetta
San Giovanni
Suergiu
Santadi
Golfo di
Cagliari
Geremeas
Sant'
Antioco
Giba
Punta Sebera
979
Sant'Anna
Arresi
Sarroch
Villasimius
I. Serpentara
I. di
S. Antioco
Golfo di
Palmas
Nur. Mereu
Pula
12
C. Carbonara
I. dei
Cavoli
C. Sperone
Teulada
Nora
Domus
de Maria
13
I. la Vacca
Chia
14
I. il Toro
I. Rossa
Bithia
C. Teulada
C. Spartivento
Sardinia

0   20 km
0   20 miles

Palermo, Trapani

Napoli

Genova
Civitavecchia
Civitavecchia

impossibly picturesque little piece of coastline – a mere 10km (6 miles) end to end by road – and turned it into a hedonistic bolt-hole, now the flagship of the island's tourism. Development is rigorously controlled. Virtually every hotel and apartment complex comes in regulation "Mediterranean" style, with pantiled roofs and pink-and-russet walls.

Even if you can't afford to partake in the jet-set lifestyle, it makes a great spectator sport. Head for millionaires playground, **Porto Cervo**, the only resort where Armani and Versace boutiques compete for attention with extravagant yachts, and **Cala di Volpe** (www.caladivolpe.com), half Moorish castle, half rustic homestead and the most stylish of the hotels. Many of the gorgeous coves are inaccessible, but you can wander through groves to those on the Cappriccioli peninsula. Impressive **Cala Liscia Ruja**, just south, is the area's biggest beach, but **Spiaggia del Principe** is dreamier, as are the twin beaches of overpopular **Cappriccioli**. The resort of **Baia Sardinia**, just north of the Costa Smeralda proper, is equally contrived, but far less pretentious and more affordable.

Much of the rest of the Galluran coastline is being spoilt by overdevelopment. This is true of **Palau**, the departure point for ferries to **La Maddalena ❷**, part of the Maddalena archipelago (declared a national park). Formerly a NATO military zone and US submarine base, the island now has a restored Arsenal, marina, naval museum, new exhibition centres, as well as good beaches, and a bridge to **Caprera ❸**, where you can visit the house in which Garibaldi spent his last years. Back on the mainland, **Santa Teresa di Gallura ❹** is a study in pink, and there are a couple of great sandy beaches at nearby **Capo Testa**, fringed by bizarre rocks the size of houses.

Alghero

Northwestern Sardinia is a more benign, softer region than the northeast, with sandy strands cupped in pine woods. Its big draw is **Alghero ❺**, the resort with the most genuine character and history: in the 14th

EAT

Alghero is arguably the best place on the island for fresh seafood. Stop at the market in Via Sassari for lobster, sea urchins and squid, or try the local restaurants.

Inland, sheep outnumber Sardinians.

century, the port was occupied by Catalans, and street names are still written in that language. Alghero's charm lies in its Catalan atmosphere, breezy bastions and sea views. Today, Alghero manages to combine its role of tourist city with that of a thriving marina. Its old traffic-free walled town on the sea front is a labyrinth of narrow lanes. After admiring the Romanesque cloisters in **San Francesco**, succumb to coffee and cake at an old-world café on Piazza Civica. The best beach is **Spiaggia di Maria Pia**, matched by a boat trip across the bay to the **Grotta di Nettuno** ❻, a cave system at the foot of a towering, tilted cliff. Nearby, the Capo Caccio headland has exhilarating views over the city and is also home to peregrine falcons and griffon vultures.

Un-touristy **Sassari** ❼, a 45-minute drive inland, has enjoyably earthy backstreets between the overblown, neo-Gothic **Piazza d'Italia** and the Baroque-fronted cathedral, and the **National Museum G.A Sanna** (Tue–Sun 9am–2pm; charge), with its fine collection of archaeological and ethnographic finds – after Cagliari's museum, it is the best place to immerse yourself in the nuraghic culture.

Sardinia's dramatic interior – with imposing tablelands, pine woods, massive walls and granite amphitheatres – is the historic, cultural and geographic heart of the island. Here, safely sheltered from foreign invaders, a population of shepherds developed a fierce and isolated society. The growth of delightful rural hotels now makes this a much more authentic way of exploring the whole island.

Nuoro ❽ is only worth visiting for its folk museum, the **Museo della Vita e delle Tradizioni Sarde** (Tue–Sun Oct–mid-June 9am–1pm and 3–5pm, daily mid-Jun–Sept 9am–8pm). Immediately south is the most accessible part of the region, where vineyards and olive groves are intensively cultivated on the hillsides. From here you can easily reach the huge **Parco Nazionale del Gennargentu** (www.parcogennargentu. it) ❾, which offers excellent hiking and is home to such wildlife as wild boar, griffon vultures and eagles. The long, lonely drive south on the SS125, which clings unnervingly to mountainsides from Dorgali to Arbatax and beyond, is the island's most exhilarating.

The south

Cagliari ❿, the island's hectic capital, is rewarding if you ignore the traffic-ridden port and climb up into **Castello**, the medieval centre where steep, atmospheric streets lie within 13th-century walls and towers. The cathedral (www.duomodicagliari.it), a hotchpotch of styles, and a Roman amphitheatre are outshone by the **Museo Archeologico Nazionale** (Tue–Sun 9am–8pm), famous for exquisite bronze statuettes and votive boats from the nuraghic culture. There is also the **Cittadella dei Musei** (Citadel of Museums), a modern complex converted from an

---

BEST BEACHES

The waters around Sardinia are among the clearest and cleanest in the Mediterranean and the beaches range from tiny hidden coves to glorious stretches of golden sands.

Baia Chia, with its white sand dunes and turquoise water, is reminiscent of a Caribbean beach. Inland the Spartivento and Chia lagoons are important flamingo breeding grounds. Less than an hour from Cagliari, it can get busy on summer weekends with surfers here to catch a wave.

Cala Goloritzé is a Unesco World Heritage site on the Golfo di Orosei, very secluded and out of reach from any road. Get there via an amazing path descending between canyons; as soon as you see the deep blue sea you realise it was worth the long trek. For a more leisurely approach, board a boat at Cala Gonone or Santa Maria Navarrese.

Cala Mariolu also opens into the Golfo di Orosei and is stunning but its enchanting beauty and natural scenery draws a crowd. It also is accessed by boat from the ports of Cala Gonone and Arbatax.

Spiaggia di Porto Giunco, near Villasimius, is one of Sardinia's most beautiful beaches. Its crystal-clear water and gleaming white sand make it a rare find, even on an island so replete with natural wonders.

Spiaggia del Principe, a Costa Smeralda hidden gem untouched by crowds, forms a perfect crescent of fine sand enclosing a blue-green bay excellent for snorkelling.

old arsenal, which houses a group of important museums.

If the beach is more your thing, hop on a public bus to the beautiful Poetto beach, a 15km- (9.3-mile) stretch of fine sand and clear waters dotted with restaurants and snack bars.

An hour's drive north, skirting the fertile **Campidano** plain, brings you to the island's most impressive *nuraghe*, **Su Nuraxi** ⓫ (www.fondazione barumini.it; daily May–Sept 9am–7pm; Oct–Apr until 4pm) at Barumini. Dating from the 13th–16th century BC, the colossal fortification is made up of beautifully formed, beehive-shaped rooms; the maze of low stone walls at its base was once a dependent village.

The coastal road east from Cagliari leads to enormous tranches of the finest sand in the island's isolated southeastern corner. However, **Villasimius** ⓬ and the **Costa Rei**, the un-fancy resorts that have grown up around them, are rather characterless, comprising mainly campsites and self-catering complexes.

The gentle, pine-clad coastline southwest from Cagliari, scattered with holiday homes and a few smart hotels, is more interesting. Punic and Roman **Nora** ⓭ (daily 9am–8pm, winter until 5.30pm) is Sardinia's most extensive classical site, with clearly defined houses, as well as a temple, theatre and mosaics. Equally rewarding is the waterside location, on a little peninsula next to a long curve of sand. Many finds from Nora are housed in the **Museo Archeologico** (Tue–Sun 9am–8pm, winter until 5.30pm) in nearby **Pula**.

Just south lies the **Forte Village**, a famous resort which adjoins a good beach, though the area's best is at **Chia** ⓮, backed by hillock-high dunes. The drive beyond along the **Costa del Sud** passes craggy headlands and azure waters in deep inlets on its way to **Sant'Antíoco** ⓯. Linked to the mainland by an ancient causeway, the island's eponymous town has Christian catacombs under its main church.

Ferries run to **San Pietro** ⓰, known for the bloody *mattanza*, when schools of tuna were slaughtered en masse until overfishing recently led to the curtailment of this barbaric pursuit.

Traditional folk costume.

Cagliari's medieval centre is up a steep hill.

Busy street in Catania, Sicily.

TRAVEL TIPS
ITALY

TRANSPORT

GETTING THERE AND GETTING AROUND

Airports

Rome

Leonardo da Vinci/Fiumicino
Rome's main airport (www.adr.it) is 35.5 km (22.5 miles) southwest of central Rome.

A direct train, the Leonardo Express, runs every 15-30 mins (daily 6.23am–11.23pm, from Rome 5.35am–10.35pm) between Fiumicino airport and Termini station in central Rome. Tickets cost €14, or €15 if bought on the platform at Termini (accompanied children aged under 12 travel free). They can be bought in advance online and at the airport from station counters, vending machines and newsstands. Tickets not bought online must be validated (stamped) in machines by the platform before you board the train. The journey takes 32 mins.

A cheaper and slower local train (FL1 line, around €8) runs roughly every 15 mins (daily 5.57am–11.27pm, from Rome around 5am–11.30pm) and stops at Trastevere, Tiburtina, Ostiense and several other suburban stations across Rome, connecting with the Rome metro; the journey to Trastevere takes about 40 mins. Information and bookings are available through www.trenitalia.com. Shuttle bus services and private transfers are also available, notably with Sitbus Shuttle (www.sitbusshuttle.it). Cotral (www.cotralspa.it) bus links airport with Rome Tiburtina railway station, Cornelia station (metro Line A) and Eur-Magliana Station (metro Line B).

Catching a white taxi with a meter (unofficial taxis can charge extortionate fares and even be dangerous) from the airport can be a good alternative. Fixed rates (including luggage and up to 4 people) are as follows: €45 to Ostiense station, €48 to Aurelian Walls, €50 to Ciampino airport.

Roma Ciampino
Rome's second airport (www.adr.it) is only 12km (7.5 miles) southeast of the city centre, and used especially by low-cost airlines such as easyJet and Ryanair. There is no rail link, but several bus services. The efficient Terravision bus shuttle runs to Via Marsala, near Termini station (daily roughly 9am–midnight, from Rome 4.30am–9.20pm; single tickets €4 online, €6 in airport or at stop; www.terravision.eu), and the Sit-Bus Shuttle, which works in association with easyJet, operates on the same route, usually 7.15am–10.10pm, from Via Marsala 4.30am–9.30pm, and offers a range of fair deals.

Alternatively, the Cotral airport bus runs roughly every 30 mins, 6am–10.40pm, from the airport to Anagnina metro station at the end of Linea A, for just €1.20. From there, it's 30 mins to Termini and the centre of town. The cost of a taxi between Ciampino and central Rome should be €30/40.

Northern Italy

Bergamo (Orio al Serio)
A local airport (www.orioaeroporto. it) "discovered" by low-cost airlines, especially Ryanair, which refers to it as "Milan-Bergamo" and has services to it from across Europe. It is 45km (28 miles) east of Milan; a Terravision

If you're in Rome for a few days, the Roma Pass, a three-day tourist card, can be a worthwhile investment. The €38,50 pass (or €28 for two days) includes unlimited travel on the entire transport network, free entrance to the first two museums or archaeological sites you visit, plus further discounts on entrance to museums, concerts and events. A map and events guide are included. Roma Pass can be bought from the sites themselves, from tourist offices or in advance through www.romapass.it.

bus runs to the city (www.terravision. eu) every 30 minutes, and there are buses to Bergamo train station (10 mins). The airport is also convenient for exploring the Lakes and Lombardy.

Genoa
Useful for Genoa itself and the Ligurian Coast, and served by Ryanair from London Stansted and BA from Gatwick. For details, see www.airport.genova.it.

Milan
Milano Malpensa, Milan's intercontinental airport (www.milano malpensa-airport.com), is 40km (25 miles) from the centre of Milan

The *Malpensa Express* **train** (www.malpensaexpress.it) runs from the airport's Terminal 1 to the centre of Milan (Cadorna station, which is on the metro M1 and M2 lines, and to Stazione Centrale, Milan's main railway station). The train takes about 40 mins and operates daily 5.43am–1ampm; single fare is €13. A free shuttle bus runs to the airport station from Terminal 2.

Alternatively, *Malpensa Shuttle* **buses** (www.malpensashuttle.it) ferry passengers between the airport and Stazione Centrale train station. Buses run almost round the clock (more frequently during the day) and take around 50 mins; single fare is around €10.

A **taxi** to the centre will take 45 mins–1 hour and cost around €90.

Milano Linate, Milan's second airport (www.milanolinate-airport. com), is only 8km (5 miles) from the centre, and has European and Italian domestic flights, with Air France, Iberia, Alitalia and British Airways and easyJet from the UK. The **ATM bus 73** and a faster **X73** run regularly (approximately 5.35am–12.35pm, every 10 mins) from the airport to Piazza San Babila in the city, and the **Starfly** airport bus (www.starfly.net) runs to Stazione Termini (daily 6am–11.45pm, every 30 mins). There is also a shuttle bus connection to Malpensa.

Turin
Small but handy for Piedmont, its vineyards, the Italian Alps and the Valle d'Aosta. Ryanair flies here from London Stansted. For details, check www.aeroportoditorino.it.

Venice
Marco Polo airport is at Tessera on the mainland 8km (5 miles) north of Venice. To reach Venice there are **buses** (lines 5 or 35) to Piazzale Roma station (30 mins), a private **land taxi** (20–25 mins) or the hourly **Alilaguna waterbus** (www.alilaguna. it), which crosses the lagoon to various destinations in Venice, and takes about 75 mins, depending on your stop. Tickets cost €15 one way. The luxury option is a private **water-taxi**, which costs from about €100 (depending where you staying) for up to four people with luggage. Buses also run to Mestre train station, on the mainland, which is the best place to get trains to areas around Venice.

Venice/Treviso
Treviso, 20km (12.5 miles) north of Venice, is used as an alternative Venice airport (www.trevisoairport.it) by low-cost airlines, especially Ryanair, which calls it "Venice-Treviso". It also has rapid access to the Veneto and northeast Italy. ATVO buses run to Venice Piazzale Roma, Mestre railway station, Venice railway station as well as seaside resorts including Jesolo, Cavallino, Bibione, Eraclea and Lignano.

Verona
Verona airport (www.aeroportoverona. it), 5km (3 miles) west of the city,

not to be confused with Verona Brescia, is convenient for the Lakes or the Veneto. EasyJet flies here from London Gatwick and Ryanair from Birmingham and London Stansted.

Central Italy

Ancona
Convenient for the Marche region, parts of Tuscany, Emilia and Umbria, and used by Ryanair and Italian domestic airlines. For details see www.aeroportomarche.it.

Bologna
One of Italy's larger regional airports and well placed for Emilia-Romagna, Rimini or north and east Tuscany. It has flights from a great many European and North African destinations, including Ryanair. The **Aerobus-BLQ** shuttle bus (www.tper.it) runs to the city every 30 mins (single fare €6), and there are also direct buses to Modena and Siena. A **taxi** takes 15 mins, and costs around €15. For details, see www.bologna-airport.it.

Florence
Florence's **Peretola** airport (www. aeroporto.firenze.it) is only 4km (2.5 miles) northwest of the city, but is very small, and used by only a few airlines. Far more Tuscany flights use Pisa.

Parma
A smaller alternative to Bologna; Ryanair flies from Stansted, and has connections to Sicily and Sardinia. For details, see www.parma-airport.it.

Pescara
Abruzzo airport is a good destination for exploring the Adriatic Coast, the Abruzzo and Molise. It has flights from Europe with low-cost airlines, including Ryanair. For details, see www.abruzzoairport.com.

Pisa
Galileo Galilei is the principal airport for Tuscany and so the most usual entry point for international visitors to Florence. Pisa is served by many airlines, and in summer there are direct Delta flights from New York. The airport (www.pisa-airport.com) has its own **train station**, with a 5-minute shuttle service to Pisa Centrale station in the city, from where there are frequent connections to Florence (about one hour).

Rimini
Naturally handy for the Adriatic, **Federico Fellini airport** (http://rimini airport.com) is another small one used by smaller operators.

Southern Italy

Bari and Brindisi
Both city airports are useful for exploring Italy's heel – Puglia and Basilicata. Bari (www.bari-airport. com) is the busiest, with services with British Airways, Ryanair, EasyJet and many Italian domestic flights, while Brindisi (www.brindisiairport.net) is mainly used by Ryanair and Alitalia.

Calabria ✓
Calabria's **Lamezia-Terme** airport (www.lameziaairport.it) was created in the middle of nowhere, between the region's three main cities (Catanzaro, Cosenza and Reggio Calabria).

Naples
The largest airport in the south, Naples (www.aeroportodinapoli.it) is served by major carriers and low-cost operators. Airport **buses** (local lines or Alibus) run every 30 mins to central Naples and Piazza Garibaldi (the main train station); the Alibus also stops at the quays for boat services to Capri and other islands. A **taxi** should cost about €15–25.

Sardinia
Cagliari-Elmas is best for the southern end of the island. More convenient for northern Sardinia are **Olbia**, on the Costa Smeralda, and **Alghero**.

Sicily
Palermo's Falcone e Borselino airport (www.gesap.it) is 32km (20 miles) west of the city, but there is a frequent train link, which takes about 45 mins. There is also a bus shuttle to the city centre. Some low-cost airlines prefer to use **Trapani** airport (www.aeroportotrapani.com), 98km (60 miles) west of Palermo. A Segesta bus (www.interbus.it) offers a direct service to/from Palermo airport.

Catania-Fontanarossa, the airport for eastern Sicily, is 7km (4 miles) southwest of Catania and has many Italian domestic and European flights.

By car
When calculating the cost of driving to Italy, if you intend to travel quickly, allow for the price of motorway tolls in France, Switzerland and Italy (those in Germany are toll-free) as well as accommodation en route and fuel. The busiest road routes into Italy are, from France, the Mont Blanc Tunnel from Chamonix and the Tunnel du Fréjus between Grenoble and Turin, and, from Switzerland, the Grand St-Bernard Tunnel between Sion

and Aosta. If you avoid tunnels, be aware that many of the Alpine passes are seasonal, so check on current conditions before setting off.

To take your car into Italy, you will need a valid driving licence (with an Italian translation if it's not a standard EU licence), the vehicle registration document and insurance documents. You must carry a warning triangle and a yellow reflective waistcoat for use in case of breakdown; if you have to pull over by the roadside, you must put on the reflective jacket, and place the warning triangle 100 metres/yards behind the car. To drive in Italy you must have your headlights duly adjusted.

By rail

Compared with flying, travelling to Italy by rail is naturally slower and, depending on when you go, more expensive. However, it can be a very attractive way to travel, especially if you stop off en route. From the UK, for example, one route to Rome is on a daytime Eurostar to Paris, where you change from Gare du Nord to the Gare de Lyon, from where a Thello sleeper train leaves daily at 7.11pm for Venice, arriving at Milan's central railway station at 5.55am the next day. From there you can catch a high-speed Frecciarossa (www.trenitalia.com) train to Rome at 7am. It arrives in Rome's Stazione Termini T at 9.59am.

Information and bookings can be obtained through **Rail Europe**, tel: (UK) 0844-848 4064, (US) 1-800-622 8600, (Canada) 1-800-361 7245; www.raileurope.com, and all kinds of information can be found on www.seat61.com.

GETTING AROUND

By air

State-owned Alitalia continues to serve the whole country, but is increasingly challenged by low-cost operators such as Meridiana Fly (www.meridiana.it) and Blu-express (www.blu-express.com), with frequent fare offers.

By rail

In general the cheapest, fastest and most convenient way to travel around Italy is by train. Most rail lines are operated by **Trenitalia** (www.trenitalia.com). There are several types of train: the figureheads of the network are the Frecce group of trains: the *Frecciarossa*, the high-speed only train, the *Frecciargento* long-distance tilting train, which goes on high-

speed and conventional track, and the *Frecciabianca* which travels on traditional track only. All have a high standard of comfort. There is also the *InterCity* which is air-conditioned, comfortable and the cheaper option, but stops rather more frequently. Supplements *(supplementi)* are charged for these trains, and it is also obligatory to reserve a seat, although this can be done up to a few minutes before the train departs. On long-distance routes overnight sleeper trains are also available.

More local trains may be called *Regionale, Diretto, Interregionale* or, rather inappropriately, *Espresso*. They are much slower, since they generally stop at a great many stations. No reservations are necessary.

Some local lines are operated by regional companies, notably **Ferrovie Emilia-Romagna** (FER; www.fer.it) around Bologna, **Ferrovie Nord Milano** (www.ferrovienord.it) from Milan, **SAD** (www.sad.it) in the Dolomites and **Arst Sardegna** (www.arst.sardegna.it) in Sardinia, which in summer runs *Trenino Verde* sightseeing trains on a spectacular line through the centre of the island (which also has Trenitalia lines). All these companies have their own fare systems. In the south and Sicily, buses can be a better option because some areas are poorly served by rail. Exceptions to this are the fascinating *Circumetnea* line (www.circumetnea.it) around Etna and the Naples *Circumvesuviana* (www.eavsrl.it), which is the best way of seeing Pompeii, Herculaneum and other classical sites.

Train tickets

Tickets for nearly all Trenitalia trains can be bought online through www.trenitalia.com (in English) and at stations, which have self-service ticket machines that accept cash and credit cards. If you book online or by phone you will be given or emailed a booking code; when you get on the train, you show this to the ticket collector, who will issue your ticket. If you have a conventional paper ticket from a counter or a machine you must validate it by stamping it in one of the yellow machines on station platforms just before you board the train; otherwise you can be fined.

The Trenitalia website sometimes rejects non-Italian credit and debit cards, so you may still have to go to a station. Some suggestions on how to get around this are on www.seat61.com. Mainline trains can also be booked through Rail Europe, but a booking fee will be added. Substantial

Train Information

Train information is available from *Uffici Informazioni* at major stations, and all stations have lists of all arrivals *(arrivi)* and departures *(partenze)* from that station.

Information and bookings for all Trenitalia services: tel: 892 021 (from outside Italy, 0039-06-6847 5475); www.trenitalia.it

From outside Italy you can also check www.raileurope.com.

discounts are also offered if you book in advance.

Rail passes

Because of the generally low level of Italian rail fares, and the discounts available, rail passes such as InterRail (for European residents) and Eurail (for the rest of the world) are of limited benefit in Italy. For long-distance Italian trains passholders still have to pay a supplement, and must reserve a seat. See www.raileurope.com.

By bus

Each province in Italy has its own regional bus company. This can lead to confusion since, particularly in Sicily, rival firms do not provide information about one another and connections are not always co-ordinated. However, in some areas such as the south, and in mountains, buses are the best method of travel. The journey from Siena to Florence is also faster by bus than by train. **BusItalia** (www.fsbusitalia.it) is a large company that runs long-distance services, and regional services across Italy. Some other major regional companies are listed below.

Rome

COTRAL, tel: 800-174 471; www.cotralspa.it; covers Lazio.

Milan

Autostradale, tel: 02-3008 9000; www.autostradale.it. Services across Lombardy and the Lakes, and sightseeing tours.

Trentino

Trentino Trasporti, tel: 0461-821 000; www.ttesercizio.it; runs bus services throughout the Trentino area.

Alto Adige

SAD, Bolzano, tel: 0471 450 111; www.sad.it. Bus services throughout the Alto Adige (South Tyrol), and rail lines along the Val Venosta, Val Pusteria and to the Brenner Pass.

Florence

BusItalia, Viale dei Cadorna 105, tel: 055 478 21 , www.fsbusitalia.it. Services throughout Tuscany.

Ferries and hydrofoils

Frequent car and passenger ferries run between mainland ports and Italy's islands. For **Sardinia**, there are ferries to Cagliari from Civitavecchia, Naples, Palermo and Trapani, to Olbia from Civitavecchia, Livorno and Genoa, to Porto Torres from Genoa and Civitavecchia, and to smaller ports. There are also regular ferries to Corsica and mainland France. For **Sicily** the fastest route is Caronte Lines (www. carontetourist.it), 20-minute shuttle between Villa San Giovanni, near Reggio di Calabria, and Messina, but there also ferries to Palermo, Catania and Trapani from Genoa, Livorno, Civitavecchia, Naples, Salerno and Cagliari.

The Sicilian Liberty Lines (www.liberty lines.it) also operates boat connections to the **Aeolian Islands**, **Pantelleria** and other small islands around Sicily, while ferries to **Elba** are operated by Moby Lines (www.mobylines.com) from Piombino. Frequent fast hydrofoils and car ferries run from Naples to **Capri**, **Ischia** and other islands in the bay, mainly with Caremar (www.caremar.it) and SNAV (www.snav.it), which also has services to the Aeolian Islands.

Ferries and hydrofoils also operate on the northern **lakes** of Como, Garda, Iseo and Maggiore, and some lake towns are linked by car ferry. Information and timetables are available from tourist offices and, for smaller ferries, at the jetties *(imbarc-aderi)*. See www.ferriesonline.com.

By car

Italian motorways *(autostrade)* are generally fast and uncongested, except in midsummer and on key holidays, such as Easter. Tolls are charged for virtually all *autostrade*; an *autostrade* website (in English, www.autostrade. it/en) allows you to check current tolls for any journey, and provides extensive further information. Tolls can be paid in cash or by credit card, and for convenience you can also buy a Viacard at various outlets, prepaid with *autostrada* credits for €25, €50 or €75. Regular users can register for a Telepass subscription, but this is of little use for visitors. Do not drive through Telepass lanes at toll stations (signed in yellow) if you are not registered.

Dipped headlights must be turned on during the day in poor visibility, on motorways and in tunnels. In mountain areas in winter, it is often compulsory to fit snow chains, and they must be carried in the car even when not needed; check on current conditions with the nearest tourist office.

Having a car in Italy is naturally excellent for exploring the countryside, but generally of little use in cities, due to the often impenetrable traffic. For outsiders, city driving is especially to be avoided in Rome and above all Naples, where local drivers customarily do not stop at red lights (this is true, not a stereotype). Also, be aware that in many Italian towns the old centre *(centro storico)* is closed to all drivers except residents, as a *Zona a Traffico Limitato* (ZTL). A sign with a red circle on white and *traffico limitato* indicates when this is so. If you are staying at a hotel in the historic centre of any town, ask the hotel beforehand what to do with your car.

Car rentals

Hiring a car is relatively expensive in Italy. International agencies such as Avis, Hertz and Europcar have offices at airports and in main towns, and in tourist areas there are local agencies. Nowadays, to get the best rates it's advisable to book ahead through major travel websites or specialists such as www.auto-europe.co.uk. Collision damage waiver is nearly always included in the price, and additional insurance cover is available for an extra cost. The renter must be over 21 and have a valid driver's licence and a credit card, for a deposit.

Parking

Parking space is also at a premium in towns, so again, it is best to leave your car in a hotel car park. Pay attention to street "no parking" signs, as illegally parked vehicles may be towed away. In a city, if you cannot use a hotel car park, find a pay car park, and leave the car for the day; charges are generally reasonable. Never leave valuables inside.

Speed limits

Urban areas: 50km/h (31mph)
Roads outside urban areas: 90km/h (55mph)
Dual carriageways: 110km/h (70mph)
Motorways *(autostrade)*: 130km/h (80mph)

Inner-city travel

Rome

Most visitors rely on public transport, taxis or their feet to access the centre of Rome, as only residents' cars are allowed there. If you drive into Rome for the day, there are large car parks around the central area (see www.parkingrome.it), the biggest of them **Parcheggio Borghese** near Villa Borghese, where you can leave a car for the day for around €18.

The Roman metro covers a limited area but is efficient, and there are several suburban rail lines. There are also night buses and tourist bus routes. Rome also now has cycle routes and a rather unsuccessful "bike-sharing" scheme. Tourist offices have more information; cycling in Rome is daunting during the week, but more enjoyable on Sundays.

Buses

Rome's city buses and metro are run by the transport authority **Atac** (www.atac.roma.it), while buses around Lazio are operated by **Cotral**. The great hub of the transport system is Stazione Termini. ATAC information and route maps are available from the kiosk in Piazza dei Cinquecento in front of Termini, main metro stations and tourist offices. City bus routes cover every part of the city and run 5.30am–midnight, after which time there are night services. A range of Atac *Metrebus* tickets is available from metro stations, tobacco shops, newsstands, some bars and tourist offices. All are equally valid for city buses, the metro and rail lines within the city. A single BIT ticket (€1.50) is valid for one bus journey of up to 75 mins, or one metro or train trip; a *Roma 24h ticket costs* €7, 48h: €12,50 and 72h: €18. A Roma pass (www.roma pass.it) will prove a more economical option as it combines unlimited travel with free entry to the best museums and/or substantial discounts.

Among the most useful city bus routes are the 40 and 64, which connect Termini with Piazza Venezia, the Centro Storico and the Vatican (the 64 stops more often). The city also has small electric buses which cope with the narrow alleys of the historic centre: line 116 passes through or close to Piazza Navona, Campo de' Fiori and St Peter's.

If you prefer the ease of an hop-on hop-off tourist bus, **City Sightseeing Bus** (www.roma.city-sightseeing. it) covers all the main sites from Termini station to Piazza Barberini. Buses run from 9am to 5pm (until 7pm Apr–Oct) every 10-20 minutes. Tickets are valid for 24h (€25) or 48h (€28). Children aged 5–15 pay half price. Other companies offering a similar experience are **Big Bus Rome** (http://eng.bigbustours.com),

I love Rome Bus (www.grayline.com), the **Roma Cristiana Open Bus** (www.operaromanapellegrinaggi.org), **Rome Open Tour** (www.romeopentour.com), **Green Line Tour Bus** (www.greenlinetours.com) and **Hop On Hop Off Bus & Attraction** (www.hop-on-hop-off-bus.com).

Metro

Rome's metro system *(Metropolitana)* has two main lines, A, and B, forming a cross and meeting at Stazione Termini. A new line, C, opened in 2014/15 running from Monte Compatri, about 20km (12 miles) southeast of the city, to Lodi, on the city outskirts, is currently of little use to tourists. It is to be extended to the Colosseum and Piazza Venezia by 2020. The metro runs daily 5.30am–11.30pm (until 12.30am on Sat) every few minutes, and is most useful for getting to areas outside the centre. Suburban rail lines connect with the metro particularly at Termini, Tiburtina, Tuscolana and Ostiense.

Milan

Milan has a highly efficient integrated transport system, operated by the ATM (www.atm-mi.it). The **Metropolitana Milanese** (MM) is the best underground railway in Italy, with four lines (M1, M2, M3, M5). All stations on the new M5 line are now opened. However, work on the new M4 line has been delayed and won't be completed before 2022.There's also a comprehensive bus and tram network and local rail lines. Tickets valid for all systems are bought from the usual outlets (*tabacchi* shops, news kiosks, metro stations). A single ticket costs €1.50 and once stamped is valid for 90 mins' travel on any system within the urban area. Useful for visitors can be a weekly 2x6 pass (10€), which includes two daily standard tickets for a period of six days, or unlimited travel passes for one or two days or a week (€4.50–€8.25–€11.30). Separate passes cover travel in "Greater Milan" and Lombardy.

For **taxis**, which are all white, go to one of the many ranks (such as San Babila or Stazione Centrale). Milan also has a bike-sharing scheme, which functions more effectively than the one in Rome (www.bikemi.com).

Florence

The main **bus** company is ATAF (www.ataf.net); and its kiosk in Piazza Stazione has free bus maps. Tickets are sold at the usual outlets (with an ATAF sticker) and at machines by bus stops, and once stamped a single

ticket (€1.20) is valid for 90 mins. One-day tickets (€5), 4-ticket carnets and longer-term passes (3 days, €12, 7 days, €18) are available. Unusually, single tickets can be bought on board, but they are more expensive.

Most of central Florence is closed to non-resident vehicles, but large car parks are provided on the edge of town (eg Piazza Independenza), linked by public transport. Really, the simplest way of getting around is on foot, but Florence also has a cycle route network, and the tourist office provides information on bike-hire shops. In the centre, you can also get around by horse-drawn carriage or rickshaw, and taxi ranks are easy to find.

Venice

Venice's transport system, coordinated by the **ACTV**, is naturally unique. The city is small enough to be covered on foot, but a good map is essential for exploring the maze of alleys and squares. For longer or faster trips, the main form of transport is the *vaporetto* (water-bus). Route information is available at the Venezia Unica ticket office on Piazzale Roma or on http://actv.avmspa.it. Tickets can be bought online through the ACTV or Venezia Unica offices (www.veneziaunica.it) or from authorised outlets in Venice. A single ticket costs €1.50 (land network only) and once stamped is valid for 75 mins, but several other options are available, such as a 24-hour card for €20, or a 3-day travelcard for €40. Children aged under 5 travel free.

The most scenic, but slowest, line is the No. 1 *Accelerato*, down the Grand Canal. Line 82 provides a faster service on the same route. *Vaporetti* also run to the Lido and the outer islands of Murano, Burano and Torchello. **Water-taxis** take up to four people and, like regular taxis, display meters. There are water-taxi "ranks" at main points in the city. Charges are high, and often complicated; two of the main services are Consorzio Motoscafi Venezia,

tel: 041-2406 712 (weekdays), www.motoscafivenezia.it, and Venice Link, tel: 041-240 1715, www.venice link.com, which also offers tours.

The official rate for hiring a **gondola** during the day is around €80 for 40 mins and another €40 for each 20 mins thereafter, and after 7pm it's €100, though it is advisable to haggle. A singing gondolier costs extra. A maximum of six people are accepted, and gondolas booked as a group tour may be cheaper. Very much cheaper are *traghetto* gondolas, which cross the Grand Canal where there are no bridges.

Naples

The hub of Naples's transport is Piazza Garibaldi, by the main train station, where most bus routes originate. Due to the city's chaotic traffic, buses often move very slowly, so it can be easier just to walk. Naples's **metro** lines (www.metro.na.it), the *Metropolitana FS* (which mostly run above ground), are elderly but naturally faster, and Line 2 is especially useful for getting from Piazza Garibaldi through the centre to Mergellina, for Capri and Ischia ferries. The same *Unico Nápoli* tickets are used on metro and buses, and the famous funiculars that help get up the city's steep hills; single tickets are €1.50 (for 90-min travel) or €1 for a single ride, or a day pass costs around €3.50.

Taxis can obviously be as traffic-snarled as buses. Naples taxis have a bad reputation for scams, so use only licensed taxis (with a city crest on the door and a number) from a rank, and check the meter is turned on (at zero) when you get in.

Ferries to the islands in the Bay of Naples leave from Molo Beverello, in the centre, and the more attractive Mergellina. Two enjoyable **local railways** are the *Circumvesuviana*, which goes from Piazza Garibaldi to Pompeii, Herculaneum and Sorrento, and the *Circumflegrea*, which runs around the west side of the Bay of Naples.

Useful Contacts: Rome, Milan, Naples and Florence

Rome: ATAC, tel: 335 199 0679; www.atac.roma.it; in English, but less user-friendly than the city tourism site, www.turismoroma.it. Taxis: 06-3570, 06-4157 or 06-6645.
Milan: ATM: tel: 0248 607 607; www.atm.it. Taxis: tel: 02-4040 or 02-8585.
Naples: ANM, tel: 081 7631 111;

www.anm.it.
Linea Circumvesuviana: tel: 800-211 388; www.eavsrl.it.
Linea Cumana-Circumflegrea: tel: 800-181-313; www.eavsrl.it. Taxis: use an official rank or call: 081-556 0202 or 081-202 020.
Florence: ATAF, tel: 800-424 500; www.ataf.net. Taxis: use a rank, or call: 055-4390 or 055-4499.

TRANSPORT

A – Z

A HANDY SUMMARY
OF PRACTICAL INFORMATION

A-Z

A

Accommodation

Italy has a great variety of accommodation in all categories, from luxury villa hotels and palatial apartments to small family-run hotels, rustic retreats and B&Bs. You are unlikely to find many real bargains but standards are reasonably good and accommodation is strictly regulated.
Hotels Every hotel, called *hotel* or *albergo*, is classified in categories by stars from one (basic) to five (luxury). Hotels can be grand guesthouses, chic chalets, hip boutique hotels converted fortresses, Zen-like spa-hotels or ecohotels. Breakfast is usually included in the price. During high season, some resort hotels require guests to stay a minimum of three nights on half-board *(mezza pensione)*.
B&Bs Italy has seen a boom in B&Bs, both in cities and regions. The quality of accommodation is variable but places are generally clean, simple and welcoming. In the main cities, chic guesthouses have replaced the outdated *pensione*, a category that no longer officially exists. For full up-to-date listings visit www.bbitalia.it or www.caffe lletto.it.
Spiritual Retreats Italy abounds in religious retreats that have been transformed into leading luxury hotels, but you can also find monasteries run by religious organisations that provide rooms and meals for guests at reasonable rates. Visit www.monasterystays. com for convents and monasteries throughout the country.

Self-catering Apartments, villas, houses and other self-catering accommodation provide a cost-effective alternative to hotels, and can sometimes be rented for as little as a couple of nights. Villas are quite pricey but standards are high and many enjoy superb locations. For a variety of options see www.rentvillas.com, or www.luxuryretreats.com.
Agriturismo If you have a car, consider staying on a **farm**, in a cottage, a modernised farmhouse, or a 17th-century castle, and enjoy such activities as grape-harvesting, mushroom-gathering, fishing, horse riding or golf. For details contact Agriturist, the National Association for Rural Tourism at www.agriturist.it or www.agriturismoinitalia.com.
Mountain Huts The Italian Alpine Club (CAI) owns around 500 hundred *rifugi* or **mountain refuges** and detailed information can be found on their website (www.cai.it).
See the Walking Eye app for full accommodation listings.

Admission charges

The price of admission for an adult to major museums such as the Capitolini in Rome or the Uffizi in Florence, and major monuments such as the Colosseum or the ruins of Pompeii, is generally around €11–16, while for smaller museums it's usually around €5–10. Admission is free (or in a few cases only discounted) to all public museums and monuments for European Union citizens aged under 18 or over 65. Private museums such as the Venice Guggenheim have their own charges (around €8–15) and discounts for older and younger visitors, as do the Vatican Museums, which are

free to under-6s and to everyone on the last Sunday of each month. Nearly all the major museums now have websites that allow you to book tickets online. This is highly advisable for big attractions such as the Uffizi, especially in peak seasons, as demand is high and booking online allows you to miss some of the queues.
The Roma Pass (www.romapass.it), MilanoCard (www.milanocard.it) and Venezia Unica (www.veneziaunica. it) provide unlimited (or in Rome, discounted) entry to public and some private museums in their respective cities, together with unlimited use of public transport and some other benefits, for a set period of time. Depending on how you organise your sightseeing, they can be a real bargain, especially in Milan, where the card costs just €19 for 3 days; Roma Pass costs €38,50 for 3 days, while the Venezia Unica pass is more expensive, starting at €40 for an adult 3-day travelcard which can be combined with other museum passes, tours and excursions as well as parking and other services (One day to one week options available). In towns and cities with more than one attraction there are often joint-ticket systems where admission to one also lets you into another (or gives a discount), which also saves you money.
Admission to churches and religious buildings is usually free, but some charge an entry fee (generally €5–12, with reductions for children) to cover maintenance costs. In addition, the number of visitors allowed per day to see some major sights in churches (such as Giotto's Scrovegni chapel in Padua) is limited for conservation reasons, so you

LANGUAGE

need to book a visit. This can often be done online, as well as through local tourist offices. Also, you need to carry some change when visiting churches, to feed the coin-in-slot machines that illuminate frescoes and other details.

B

Budgeting for your trip

The cost of travelling in Italy varies enormously depending on where you go and how you travel. Florence, Venice, the northern lakes, much of Tuscany, Capri, and beach areas like Rimini in high summer are notoriously expensive places, but in less prominent areas and cities – rural Emilia-Romagna, the Marche, Sicily, Sardinia, even parts of non-touristy Milan – prices can be lower by as much as half. Hotel prices also vary enormously by season. In general, though, prices overall, even in the countryside, tend to be a bit higher north of Rome than south of it and in the islands.

If you order a drink or a meal at an outside table you will always pay more than inside, and more if you have a coffee at any table than standing at the bar Italian-style. The amount added on for *terrazza* service varies, so the price of sitting on the most celebrated terraces of Rome, Florence or Venice is astronomical. Hence people take their time. Beer is peculiarly expensive in Italy, especially at outside tables, often at around €4–6 for a smallish glass, and so is drunk relatively little; wine bought by the glass is similarly expensive, often around €5, except in traditional basic wine bars (*enoteche* or in Venice *bacari*), so in many cases you might as well order a bottle or a carafe. To eat, in most cities – even well-touristed ones – you can find unfussy restaurants that provide *tavola calda* lunch menus for around €15–20, while a generous pizza costs around €8–10. An enjoyable three-course meal with wine in mid-range restaurants can be found in Venice or Florence for around €50, in less fashionable places for closer to €30. Gourmet restaurants will cost from around €70–80 per person and upwards, although again in less trodden spots you can often find remarkable food for much less.

Hotel rooms, especially attractive ones, are expensive in Rome, Florence, Venice and some other

areas, and it's hard to find a pleasant double room in a hotel for much under €80 a night. Comfortable mid-range rooms cost around €150, while these cities and some other areas – the northern lakes, rural Tuscany – conversely have a great deal of luxury accommodation for an indulgent splurge, with rooms for €400 and upwards. Hence travellers to the main cities seek out more economical options, such as monastery stays, apartment rentals, B&Bs or bland but good-value business hotels like those of the NH chain. In less expensive parts of Italy, there are plenty of decent rooms to choose from for around €100, and even some luxury hotels are a little cheaper. B&B rooms on farms (*agriturismi*) are economical in most areas, often around €60, but there are also luxurious variations.

For long-distance travel, train fares are very reasonable (see page 390). A daytime taxi journey within the centre of most cities should cost around €10. In most cities and towns a single transport ticket costs €1.50, but most have systems that allow you to buy multiple tickets, saving time and money. In Rome and Milan the tourist cards (see page 393, Admission Charges) include unlimited transport for a set time.

C

Children

Italy is a very child-friendly country and very few restaurants ever object to admitting them, even very grand ones (although they will be expected to behave and sit at table properly). Few restaurants have special children's menus, but then Italian cuisine is full of things kids like – pasta, pizza, ice cream. Accompanied small children (generally under 6, or more traditionally under 1 metre (3ft) tall) travel free on most public transport. Admission is also free to most public museums and monuments for EU citizens aged under 18, and there is usually a reduced price for non-EU under-18s (some museums now also offer free entry to non-EU citizens under 18).

Many hotels have family rooms, or offer the option of an additional bed in the parents' room. Hotel bedsitting services, however, are fairly scarce except in more expensive hotels. An exception are the family-oriented holiday hotels

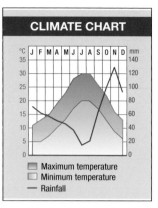

(often called a *centro de vacanze* rather than a hotel) around the Italian coasts, lakes and islands, usually open in summer only, which have play areas, kids' pools and many other facilities.

Climate

Italy experiences marked regional variations, from the more temperate north to the typically Mediterranean south, Sicily and Sardinia. The best time to visit Italy is between April and June when the weather is warming up but the crowds have not yet arrived. August can be very hot in the cities and the south – although more pleasant in the mountainous north – and many businesses close for the month. September to October is beginning to feel respite from the heat, although it is still hot in the far south. The winter can be ideal in the city but be prepared for rain, especially in the west.

Northern Italy Mountainous regions are popular with winter sports enthusiasts in winter. Summers are cool and ideal for walkers. Winters can be freezing across the foggy plains of Lombardy and Emilia-Romagna, or in the river cities such as Florence and Verona. Cities in the north do get snow and winters can be cold and rainy from November to March. Highs of 28°C/82.4°F (Florence) in summer and lows of -2°C/28.4°F (Milan) in winter; the Po Valley can reach as low as -14°C/6.8°F.

Southern Italy South of Florence the climate becomes more Mediterranean and the winters more moderate, but subject to rain in winter in the mid-region. Rome and Naples are stifling in high summer and the south of Italy and Sicily and Sardinia have long, hot and dry summers with a humid sirocco wind. Winter temperatures rarely drop below 10°C/50°F. Summer can reach as high as 45°C/113°F.

What to wear

Unless you are visiting mountain areas, the moderate climate makes heavy clothing unnecessary in summer. A light jacket should be adequate for summer evenings. In winter (November–March), the climate can be cold and wet throughout Italy, so pack warm clothes and waterproofs.

Crime and security

Violent crime, particularly involving foreigners, is in general relatively rare in Italy. The main problem for tourists is petty crime – pickpocketing, bag-snatching and theft from cars, of which, naturally, there is a greater risk in some cities than others; it is more of a problem in Rome, for example, than in Florence or Venice. All travellers should have travel insurance, covering loss or theft of all their possessions. The likelihood of street theft can also be reduced with a few basic, sensible precautions. Always lock your car and never leave luggage, cameras or other valuables inside. While walking around, always keep a shoulder bag closed, hold it at your front, not at the back, and keep a hand on the bag; when sitting at a table, especially outside, put your bag on your lap or the table in front of you, never on the ground or on the back of a chair. Only use atms in main streets, and during the day. Be extra-careful in big train stations, and avoid walking alone at night in deserted alleys of the historic centres of towns such as Bari, Genoa or Palermo, and stay where there are people. Special care is needed in Naples, where women especially should be wary of bag theft at all times, and if in doubt only visit the historic centre in a group. In small towns and rural areas, theft of any kind is very unlikely.

If you are the victim of a crime, or lose anything, it is essential to make a report at the nearest police station and get documentation to support an insurance claim. Italy has several police forces, the responsibilities of which are complex, but you can report a crime at any station of the national police (Polizia) or the semi-military Carabinieri. To phone for the police, dial **113** for the Polizia or **112** for the Carabinieri.

Customs regulations

Residents of EU countries can carry any amount of goods into and out of Italy without extra duty so long as they are for their personal use. Examples of amounts normally accepted to fit this criteria are 10 litres of spirits or strong liqueurs, 90 litres of wine, 800 cigarettes and 110 litres of beer.

For non-EU residents, duty-free allowances include: 200 cigarettes, 50 cigars or 250 grams tobacco, 1 litre of spirits and gifts worth up to €430. Any amount of currency exceeding €10,000 or equivalent must be declared on entry, and when leaving Italy.

Value-Added Tax (sales tax, currently 22 percent but likely to increase to 24 percent in 2017) can be reclaimed by non-EU residents when they leave Italy on single items costing more than €180. They must be bought in a shop with a "Euro Tax Free" sticker in the window; when buying the item, tell the shop staff that you want to do this and they should give you a "Tax Free Shopping Cheque" with your receipt, together with a form with instructions on how to claim the refund. When you leave Italy, take all these papers to a customs desk and get them stamped. This can take time, so get to the airport early.

D

Disabled travellers

Italy's older cities are not easily navigable for disabled travellers: cobblestones, narrow pavements and cramped lifts make getting around tricky. The Rome-based organisation co.in offers information (currently in Italian only) on disabled facilities in restaurants, shops and stations; www.coinsociale.it. In Rome, Roma Per Tutti is a useful information service for disabled travellers, again in Italian, although some staff may speak English; tel: 39-067 129 011; www.romapertutti.it.

Transport in Italy's larger cities is becoming more accessible, with increasing numbers of wheelchair-friendly buses and trams. For train travel check the Trenitalia website www.trenitalia.com; the wheelchair symbol denotes accessible trains, and there is a special helpline, tel: 199-303 060.

Accessible Italy is a non-profit body that organises accommodation and tours for people with disabilities; tel:

(Italy) 378-941 111; www.accessible italy.com.

E

Eating out

See the Walking Eye app for full restaurant listings.

Electricity

220 volts, with the standard European two-round-pin plugs. You will need adaptors to operate British three-pin equipment, and with older North American 110-volt flat-pin appliances, you may need a transformer as well as a plug adaptor.

Embassies and consulates

The following consulates and embassies are all based in Rome, but can put you in touch with other consulates. Dial the Rome code, even if calling from within Rome.
Australia: tel: 06-852 721
Canada: tel: 06-854 442 911)
France: tel: 06-686 011
Germany: tel: 06-492 131
Ireland: tel: 06-585 2381
New Zealand: tel: 06-853 7501
UK: tel: 06-4220 0001
US: tel: 06-46741

Etiquette

Italians are known for their sense of style, and if you stay or dine anywhere expensive, or try to get into any of the sleeker city clubs and bars, you will feel distinctly out of place (or be turned away) if you are unable to dress up at least a little. Elsewhere, dress can be much more casual. However, when sightseeing, both men and women are advised to cover their shoulders and avoid wearing shorts (or short skirts), as some churches, especially in Rome and Venice, bar visitors who are deemed unsuitably dressed.

Emergency Numbers

General Emergency Assistance and Carabinieri: 112 (24-hour service)
Police: 113
Fire Brigade: 115
Medical emergencies, ambulance: 118
Breakdown service: 803 116
Coast Guard: 1530

Newspaper kiosk in Rome.

G

Gay and lesbian travellers

Gay life in Italy is becoming more mainstream, helped by increasing numbers of club nights and festivals such as Rome's summer-long Gay Village. Attitudes are generally more tolerant in the north: Bologna is regarded as Italy's gay capital, and Milan, Turin and Rome all have a lively gay scene. The Bologna-based Arcigay network provides all kinds of information in Italian (tel: 051-095 7241; www.arcigay.it), while range of information in English is on www.gayfriendlyitaly.com.

H

Health and medical care

EU citizens should obtain a European Health Insurance Card (EHIC) before leaving home to be able to get emergency treatment from the Italian state health service. Some medicines may have to be paid for. However, this will not entitle you to repatriation in the event of serious illness, so you may wish to have private travel health insurance as well. Citizens of non-EU countries must pay for medical assistance and medicines, and so should always have full travel health insurance against all eventualities. Most hospitals have a 24-hour emergency department *(Pronto Soccorso)*, but a stay in an Italian hospital can be a grim experience, particularly in the south.

For minor complaints, seek out a *farmacia* (signs have a green cross). Normal opening hours are 9.30am–12.30pm and 3.30–7.30 or 8pm, Monday to Saturday. Outside these hours there is always at least one *farmacia* on duty in each town, and its address will be posted in the windows of all pharmacies in the area. In big cities there are pharmacies open 24 hours.

I

Internet

Many hotels and cafés now offer WiFi connections, usually for no extra charge. Most Italian cities also have plenty of public Wi-Fi hubs.

L

Lost property

Ask about lost items at the local lost property office *(ufficio oggetti smarriti)*, usually in the town hall. Items lost on public transport are generally directed to the transport authority's own lost property office. In Rome, you can enquire about items found on the city's buses, trams and metros at tel: 06 6769 3214. Alternatively, e-mail the Lost Property Office (oggettismarriti@comune. roma.it) located at Circonvallazione Ostiense 191.

M

Media

The Italian press is concentrated in Milan and Rome. The biggest papers are *La Repubblica* and *Il Corriere della Sera*, which publish regional editions.

However, *La Gazzetta dello Sport*, the pink sports paper, is probably the one you will notice most.

Most major cities have weekly listings magazines: *Roma C'e*, with a section in English at the back, is a guide to everything going on in Rome and is available from newsstands every Wednesday. Roma Today (www.romatoday.it) is a comprehensive online magazine in English. *La Repubblica* also publishes *Trovaroma*, a what's-on section, every Thursday, and Wednesday's Corriere della Sera has a listings supplement, *ViviMilano*.

Television stations include rai (the national network with three channels), the Vatican network, plus privately owned national channels, and over 450 local stations. Many European channels, CNN and other international channels can be seen in hotels.

Money

The currency in Italy is the euro (€), which is available in 500, 200, 100, 50, 20, 10 and 5 euro notes, and 2 euro, 1 euro, 50 cent, 20 cent, 10 cent, 5 cent, 2 cent and 1 cent coins. There are 100 cents to one euro.

Italy is a society that prefers cash to credit cards, except for large purchases, or, for instance, hotel bills. In modest restaurants and smaller shops, it is still usual to pay in cash. Check beforehand if there is any doubt, or at least have sufficient euro cash with you, just in case.

Banks are generally open 8.30am–1.30pm and for 1 hour or 90 minutes in the afternoon (usually 2.45–4.15pm), Monday to Friday only, so bear this in mind before each weekend. Travellers' cheques can still be useful in Italy, as they can be replaced if stolen or lost. Unfortunately, however, most banks are notoriously inefficient at changing cash or cheques, and currency conversion can turn into a tedious saga, so many travellers just use atms (cashpoints) wherever possible. There are also private bureaux de change in tourist cities, at airports and main railway stations, with more flexible hours. Avoid changing money in hotels, where commission will be high.

Cash machines and credit cards

Given the long queues for money-changing in Italy, it is simplest to get cash from ATM machines, which are widely available. Most *Bancomats* (cash machines) accept all major international credit and debit cards. In cities, many restaurants, hotels and larger stores will take major cards, and they can also be used to book train and museum tickets online, but in small shops and rural areas, as mentioned, you may be able to pay only in cash.

O

Opening hours

Smaller shops are usually open roughly 9am–1pm and 4pm–7.30 or 8pm, Monday to Saturday, although some work only a half-day on Saturdays, either morning or afternoon. Some traditional shops also close on Monday mornings. In cities, the only shops generally open on Sundays are big stores, supermarkets and malls, which also do not close for lunch during the week. In tourist areas many shops of all kinds also open on Sundays, especially during peak seasons. A special regime applies to pharmacies (see page 396, Health).

Offices traditionally work from around 8.30am–12.30 or 1pm and 3–6pm, Monday to Friday, although in major cities many now take a shorter lunch break. For bank hours, see page 396, Money. Nearly all museums close on one day each

Area codes

When dialling numbers inside or outside your area in Italy, the main number must always be preceded by the area code, including the zero. Area codes of some main cities are:
Bologna 051
Florence 055
Genoa 010
Milan 02
Naples 081
Palermo 091
Pisa 050
Rome 06
Turin 011
Venice 041
To call abroad from Italy, dial 00, followed by:
Australia 61
Canada 1
Irish Republic 353
New Zealand 64
South Africa 27
UK 44
US 1
Then dial the number, omitting the initial "0" if there is one.

week, usually Monday, although some close on Tuesday.

P

Postal services

Local post offices open 8am–1.30pm Mon–Sat only, but cities generally have a main post office that is open throughout the day, until about 7–8pm. Post offices provide a wide range of services such as *raccomandata* (registered post) and parcel post. Stamps *(francobolli)* can be bought at all tobacco shops *(tabacchi)* and in many bars.

Public holidays

January New Year's Day (1)
Epiphany (6)
March/April Easter Day, Easter Monday
April Liberation Day (25)
May Labour Day (1)
June Republic Day (2)
August Assumption of the Virgin Mary (15)
November All Saints' Day (1)
December Immaculate Conception (8), Christmas Day (25), St Stephen's Day (26)

In addition to these national holidays, almost all cities have a holiday to celebrate their own patron saint, for example St Mark, 25 April (Venice); St John the Baptist, 24 June (Turin, Genoa and Florence); SS Peter and Paul, 29 June (Rome); St Rosalia, 15 July (Palermo); St Gennaro, 19 September (Naples); St Petronius, 4 October (Bologna); St Ambrose, 7 December (Milan).

R

Religion

Roman Catholic Mass is celebrated every day and several times on Sundays in Italian. Some non-Catholic churches hold services in English; in Rome, you can find services in English at the Church of England All Saints (www.allsaintsrome.org), Via del Babuino 153B and at the Scottish Presbyterian St Andrew's (www.presbyterianchurchrome.org), Via XX Settembre 7. The Jewish Synagogue (http://jewisheurope.org) is at Lungotevere Cenci 9. The city's Great Mosque is in Via Anna Magnani. Ask at the local tourist office about places of worship in the area.

S

Smoking

Smoking is banned in all indoor public places in Italy, including all bars and restaurants except those that have a separate smoking room fairly tightly isolated from the rest of the establishment. Harsher rules aimed at curtailing the number of smokers (around 20 percent of the population) were introduced in 2016. These include a smoking ban in cars, hospitals and around hospitals as well as hefty fines (€300) for throwing cigarette butts on the ground.

Students

In the UK, the Italian Cultural Institute provides advice on courses in Italy, particularly language-based; tel: 020-7235 1461; www.icilondon.esteri.it. In the US, try the American Institute for Foreign Study; tel: 866-906 2437; www.aifs.org; and Study Abroad Italy, www.saiprograms.com.

To study in an Italian university, you will need to get your certificates translated and validated by the Italian consulate in your own country before making your application at the *ufficio stranieri* (foreign department) of the university of your choice in Italy; www.study-in-italy.it offers useful advice.

T

Telephones

Public telephones are plentiful, particularly in cities. Most accept phonecards *(carte telefoniche* or *schede telefoniche)*, available from tobacco shops, bars or post offices; few telephones accept coins. Post offices and many bars also have pay phones where you can make a call and then pay afterwards.

The cheapest time for long-distance calls is between 10pm and 8am Monday to Saturday, and all day Sunday.

For directory enquiries dial 12. For international enquiries call 176, and for the international operator and to make a reverse-charge (collect) call, dial 170.

Italy has an extremely high ownership of mobile (cell) phones, and in all cities and towns it's possible to buy or rent one on a cheap, short-term pay-as-you-go

TRANSPORT

A – Z

LANGUAGE

Top three tourist destinations – Rome, Florence and Venice

Rome

APT Rome: Piazza Campitelli; **tourist information phoneline**, daily 9am–9pm, tel: 06 06 08; www.turismoroma.it.

There are many tourist information points around the capital, most of them open daily 9.30am–7pm, with exceptions, including: at **Via Giovanni Giolitti** (outside Termini station); **Piazza Pia** (in front of Castel Sant'Angelo); **Via Minghetti** (near Fontana di Trevi); **Piazza delle Cinque Lune** (off Piazza Navona); **Via Nazionale** (near Palazzo dello Esposizioni); **Fiumicino** and **Ciampino** airports; and **Ostia Lido**.

The privately run tourist office **Enjoy Rome**, located near the railway station, is staffed by helpful English-speakers and provides a wide range of useful services, including guided tours round the city; Via Marghera 8A; tel: 06-445 1843; www.enjoyrome.com.

Florence

APT Florence (main office): Via Manzoni 16; www.firenzeturismo.it.

There are also information points run by the province or the city at Via Cavour 1r (tel: 055-290 832; just north of the Duomo; Mon–Fri 9am–1pm); **Piazza Stazione 4** (by the railway station; Mon–Sat 9am–7pm, Sun 9am–2pm); Piazza San Giovanni 1 (Mon–Sat 9am–7pm, Sun 9am–2pm)**;** and at **Peretola airport** (daily 9am–7pm).

Venice

APT Venice (main office): San Marco 2637; information phoneline tel: 041-529 8711; www.turismo venezia.it.

The main tourist office for the public is at **Piazza San Marco 71** (same phone; daily 9am–3.30pm, with extended hours in summer). There are other offices at **Stazione Santa Lucia** train station; **Piazzale Roma;** and **Marco Polo airport**, as well as in other parts of the province. Most these offices open daily between 9am–6pm, with exceptions. The tourist office also runs the **Venice Pavilion**, a bookshop and information centre dedicated to everything about Venice, at the Ex-Giardini Reale (on the waterfront, just west from San Marco); daily noon–6pm.

Venezia Unica, tel: 041-2424; www.veneziaunica.it, Venice's official tourist site, handles sales of the Venezia Unica Card which offers travel cards combined with museum passes, discounts and other attractions.

---

deal. The main mobile networks in Italy are TIM, Vodafone, Wind and 3, which have shops in every part of the country. Non-Italian mobiles will all work in Italy provided they have at least a tri- or quad-band system and have their roaming facility enabled, but always check with your home service provider on current charges before using a foreign mobile here. Many phone companies offer "bundles" of international calls for a set fee, which helps to limit costs.

Time zone

Italy follows Central European Time (GMT + 1 hour, EST + 6 hours: add one hour in summer).

Tipping

Italians generally tip very little or not at all. In restaurants, bills often include a cover and bread charge (coperto e pane) of around €5 per head, plus a 10 percent service charge (servizio), plus the extra charge if you sit outside, so there is no obligation to leave anything more. Some people (especially foreigners) leave a little extra as an acknowledgement if service has been particularly good. In taxis, it's common to add on around 5–10 percent for good service, but many people just round the fare up to the nearest euro. In Venice, water-taxi men expect fat tips because they are so used to dealing with wealthy foreigners. In hotels, an especially helpful concierge could be tipped around €10–15, a chambermaid €2–5.

Tourist information

Regions and provinces

Administratively, Italy is divided into regions (regioni) such as Tuscany and Sicily, then into provinces (provincie). Every provincial capital has an **Azienda Provinciale per il Turismo (apt)**, with subsidiary offices in many smaller towns, especially in popular tourist areas. As well as all kinds of helpful information, apt offices should provide free local maps. Tourist offices in main towns are listed below; many districts also have their own websites.

Italian State Tourist Board

The Italian State Tourist Board, enit (Ente Nazionale per il Turismo), provides general tourist information.
In the UK, enit, 1 Princes Street, London W1B 2AY; tel: 020-7408 1254; www.enit.it.
In the US, enit, 686 Park Avenue, New York, NY 10065; tel: 212-245 5618; www.italiantourism.com. There are also offices in Chicago, Los Angeles and, in Canada, Toronto.

Main tourist offices

Lombardy-Piedmont-Liguria

Bergamo: Bergamo Turismo, Piazzale Marconi (zone Stazione); tel: 035-210 204; www.visitbergamo.net.
Cinque Terre (La Spezia): tel: 0187-254 311; www.turismoliguria.it.

Genoa: tel: 010-557 2903; www.visitgenoa.it. Information offices in Via Garibaldi and at the airport.
Lake Como (Lago di Como): Piazza Cavour 17, Como; tel: 031-269 712; www.lakecomo.org. More information at www.provincia.como.it.
Lake Garda (Lago di Garda): Corso Repubblica 8, Gardone Riviera; tel; 030-374 8736; www.lagodigarda. it. Also offices in Desenzano, Lonato del Garda, Sirmione and other lake towns.
Lake Maggiore (Lago Maggiore): Piazza Marconi 16, Stresa; tel: 0323-30150; www.illagomaggiore.com.
Liguria: Via D'Annunzio 2/78, floor 16121, Genoa; tel: 010-530 821; www.agenziainliguria.com and www.turismoinliguria.it.
Lombardy: Città di Lombardia 1, Milan; tel: 02-6765 6099; www. turismo.regione.lombardia.it.
Milan: Piazza Castello 1; tel: 02-8058 0614; www.turismo.milano.it.
Piedmont: tel: (international toll-free number) 00-800-329 329; www. piemonteitalia.eu.
Turin: Piazza Castello 161; tel: 011-535 181; www.turismotorino.org. Also at the main train station and the airport.
Valle d'Aosta: Piazza Porta Praetoria 3, Aosta; tel: 0165-236 627; www.lovevda.it/turismo.

Veneto-Trentino-Emilia-Romagna

Alto Adige–South Tyrol: Südtiroler Straße/Via Alto Adige 60, , Bolzano/Bozen; tel: 0471-999 999; www.suedtirol.info.

Bologna: Piazza Maggiore 1e, Palazzo del Podestà; tel: 051-239 660; www.bolognawelcome.com. Also at the airport.
Bolzano (Bozen): Piazza Walther 8, Alto Adige; tel: 0471-307 000; www.bolzano-bozen.it.
Emilia-Romagna: www.emiliaromagnaturismo.it.
Friuli-Venezia Giulia: Villa Chiozza, Via Corso 3, Cervignano del Friuli; tel: 0431-387 130; www.turismofvg.it; also local offices.
Padua: Piazza Antenore 3; tel: 049-876 7911; www.turismopadova.it.
Parma: Piazza Garibaldi 1; tel: 0521-218 889; http://turismo.comune. parma.it.
Rimini: Piazzale Fellini 3; tel: 0541-704 587; www.riminiturismo.it.
Trentino: Via Manci 2; tel: 0461-216 000; www.visittrentino.it.
Veneto region: Palazzo Sceriman, Cannaregio 161, Venice; tel: 041-279 2644; www.veneto.to.
Verona: Via degli Alpini 9; tel: 045-806 8680; www.tourism.verona.it.
Vicenza: Via Montale 25; tel: 0444-994 770; www.vicenzae.org.

Tuscany-Umbria-Marche
Arezzo: Emiciclo Giovanni Paolo II; tel: 0575-182 2770; www.arezzoturismo. it.
Assisi: Piazza del Comune 12; tel: 075- 8138 680; www.visit-assisi.it.
Elba: Calata Italia 44, Portoferraio; tel: 0565-914 671; www.visitelba.info.
Lucca: Palazzo Ducale - Cortile Carrara 1; tel: 0583-4171; www.luccatourist.it.
Marche–Ancona: Via Thaon de Revel 4, Ancona; tel: 071-358 991; www.le-marche.com.

Palazzo Reale in Naples.

Orvieto: Piazza Duomo 24, tel: 0763-341 772; www.inorvieto.it. Information office Piazza Cahen (seasonal).
Perugia: Piazza Matteotti 18; tel: 075-573 6458; http://turismo. comune.perugia.it.
Pisa: Piazza Vittorio Emanuele II 14; tel: 050-929 777; www.pisaunicaterra. it.
San Gimignano: Piazza Duomo 1; tel: 0577-940 008; www.sangimignano. com.
Siena: apt Siena, Piazza Duomo 1; tel: 0577-280 551; www.terresiena.it.
Tuscany: www.turismo.intoscana.it.
Umbria: www.umbriatourism.it.
Urbino: Borgo Mercatale, Rampa di Francesco di Giorgio; tel: 0722-2631; www.turismo.pesarourbino.it.

Abruzzo-Molise
Abruzzo: Corso Vittorio Emanuele II 301, Pescara; tel: 800-502 520; www.abruzzoturismo.it.
Molise: Piazza della Vittoria 14, Campobasso; tel: 0874-415 662; www.discovermolise.com. More information at www.moliseturismo.eu.

Naples to Calabria
Calabria: Via San Nicola 8, Catanzaro; tel: 0961-856-882 001; www.turiscalabria.it.
Campania: Piazza dei Martiri 58, Naples; tel: 081-405 311; www.regione.campania.it.
Capri: P.tta I. Cerio 11; tel: 081-837 5308; www.capritourism.com. Also at Marina Grande and Anacapri.
Naples: Palazzo Reale; tel: 081-252 5711; www.inaples.it. Also at Via San Carlo 9 and Piazza del Gesù.
Puglia: Piazza Moro 33A, Bari; tel: 080-524 2361; www.viaggiareinpuglia.it.

Sorrento: Via Luigi De Maio 35; tel: 081-807 4033; www.sorrentotourism. com.

Sicily
Catania: Via Etnea 63/65; tel: 095-401 4070; http://turismo.provincia. ct.it.
Palermo: Piazza Castelnuovo 34; tel: 091-605 8351; www.palermotourism. com.
Sicily region: Via Notarbartolo 9, Palermo; tel: 091-707 8276; www.regione.sicilia.it/turismo.

Sardinia
Cagliari: Palazzo Civico, Via Roma 145; tel: 070 6778 173; www.cagliariturismo.it.
Sardinia region: Viale Trieste 105, Cagliari, tel: 070-606 7226; www.sardegnaturismo.it.

V

Visas and passports

EU citizens can enter Italy with only a national identity card, but those without them, such as UK and Irish citizens, must have full passports. Visitors from Australia, Canada, Japan, New Zealand, the United States and several other countries must have full passports but do not require visas for stays of no more than three months. All travellers to Italy are theoretically still supposed to register with the local police within three days of arrival. This will be taken care of by your hotel; if you are not staying in a hotel, supposedly you should contact the local police station, but virtually no one does.

Travelling with pets

Pets must be vaccinated against rabies, and you should obtain an official document stating that your animal is healthy no more than one month before you arrive in Italy.

W

Weights and measures

The metric system is used for all weights and measures.
For a quick conversion: 2.5cm is approximately 1 inch, 1 metre about a yard, 100g is just under 4oz and 1kg is 2lbs 2oz. Distance is quoted in kilometres. One kilometre equals 0.62 of a mile, so 100km is 62 miles.

TRANSPORT

A – Z

LANGUAGE

LANGUAGE

UNDERSTANDING THE LANGUAGE

Yes/No *Sì/No*
Thank you *Grazie*
Many thanks *Grazie mille/tante grazie/molte grazie*
You're welcome *Prego*
All right/OK/that's fine *Va bene*
Please *Per favore/Per cortesia*
Excuse me (to get attention) *Scusi* (singular), *Scusate* (plural)
Excuse me (to get through a crowd) *Permesso*
Excuse me (to attract attention, eg of a waiter) *Senta!*
Excuse me (sorry) *Mi scusi* (singular), *Scusatemi* (plural)
Wait a minute! (informal) *Aspetta!* (formal) *Aspetti!*
Could you help me? (formal) *Potrebbe aiutarmi?*
Certainly *Ma certo*
Can I help you? (formal) *Posso aiutarla?*
Can you help me? (formal) *Può aiutarmi, per cortesia?*
I'm sorry *Mi dispiace*
I don't understand *Non capisco*
Do you speak English/French/ German? *Parla inglese/francese/ tedesco?*
Could you speak more slowly, please? *Può parlare più lentamente, per favore?*
slowly/quietly *piano*
here/there *qui/là*
What? *Cosa?*
When/why/where? *Quando/perchè/ dove?*
Where is the lavatory? *Dov'è il bagno?*

Hello (good day) *Buon giorno*
Hello/hi/goodbye (familiar) *Ciao*
Good afternoon/evening *Buona sera*
Goodnight *Buona notte*
Goodbye *Arrivederci*

Pleased to meet you (formal) *Piacere di conoscerla*
I am English/American/Canadian *Sono inglese/americano/canadese*
Do you speak English? *Parla inglese?*
How are you? (formal) *Come sta* *come stai?* (informal)
Fine thanks *Bene, grazie*
See you soon *A presto*
Take care (formal) *Stia bene,* (informal) *Stammi bene*

IN THE HOTEL

Do you have a room free? *Avete camere libere?*
I have a reservation *Ho fatto una prenotazione*
I'd like... *Vorrei...*
a single/double room (with double bed) *una camera singola/doppia (con letto matrimoniale)*
a room with twin beds *una camera a due letti*
a room with a bath/shower *una camera con bagno/doccia*
for one night *per una notte*
for two nights *per due notti*
Could you show me another room? *Potrebbe mostrarmi un'altra camera?*
How much is it? *Quanto costa?*
on the first floor *al primo piano*
Is breakfast included? *È compresa la prima colazione?*
half/full board *mezza pensione/ pensione completa*
It's expensive *È caro*
Do you have a room with a balcony/ view of the sea? *C'è una camera con balcone/con vista sul mare?*
Can I see the room? *Posso vedere la camera?*
I'll take it *La prendo*
big/small *grande/piccola*
What time is breakfast? *A che ora è la prima colazione?*

Emergencies

Help! *Aiuto!*
I've had an accident *Ho avuto un incidente*
Call a doctor *Per favore, chiami un medico*
Call an ambulance/the police/ the fire brigade *Chiami un'ambulanza/la Polizia/i Carabinieri/i pompieri*
Where is the nearest hospital? *Dov'è l'ospedale più vicino?*
I want to report a theft *Voglio denunciare un furto*

Please give me a call at... *Mi può chiamare alle...*
Come in! *Avanti!*
Can I have the bill, please? *Posso avere il conto, per favore?*
dining room *la sala da pranzo*
key *la chiave*
lift *l'ascensore*
towel *l'asciugamano*

Bar snacks and drinks

I'd like... *Vorrei...*
coffee *un caffè* (espresso: small, strong and black)
un cappuccino (with hot, frothy milk)
un caffè latte (milky coffee)
un caffè lungo (weak)
uno corretto (laced with alcohol – usually brandy or grappa)
tea *un tè*
herbal tea *una tisana*
hot chocolate *una cioccolata calda*
orange/lemon juice (bottled) *un succo d'arancia/di limone*
fresh orange/lemon juice *una spremuta di arancia/di limone*
orangeade *un'aranciata*
water (mineral) *acqua (minerale)*
fizzy/still mineral water *acqua*

minerale gasata/naturale
with/without ice *con/senza ghiaccio*
red/white wine *vino rosso/bianco*
beer (draught) *una birra (alla spina)*
milk *latte*
a (half) litre *un (mezzo) litro*
bottle *una bottiglia*
ice cream *un gelato*
sandwich *un tramezzino*
Anything else? *Desidera qualcos'altro?*
Cheers *Salute*

In a restaurant

I'd like to book a table *Vorrei riservare un tavolo*
Have you got a table for... *Avete un tavolo per...*
I have a reservation *Ho fatto una prenotazione*
lunch/supper *il pranzo/la cena*
I'm a vegetarian *Sono vegetariano/a*
Is there a vegetarian dish? *C'è un piatto vegetariano?*
The menu, please? *Ci dà il menu, per favore?*
wine list *la lista dei vini*
What would you like? *Che cosa prende?*
What would you recommend? *Che cosa ci raccomanda?*
What would you like to drink? *Che cosa desidera da bere?*
a carafe of red/white wine *una caraffa di vino rosso/bianco*
fixed-price menu *il menu a prezzo fisso*
the dish of the day *il piatto del giorno*
VAT (sales tax) *IVA*
cover charge *il coperto/pane e coperto*
That's enough; no more, thanks *Basta (così)*
The bill, please *Il conto per favore*
Is service included? *Il servizio è incluso?*
Where is the toilet? *Dov'è il bagno?*

MENU DECODER

Antipasti (Hors d'oeuvres)

caponata **mixed aubergine, olives and tomatoes**
insalata caprese **tomato and Mozzarella salad**
insalata di mare **seafood salad**
insalata mista/verde **mixed/green salad**
melanzane alla parmigiana **fried or baked aubergine** (with Parmesan cheese and tomato)
mortadella/salame **salami**
pancetta **bacon**
peperonata **vegetable stew** (made with peppers, onions, tomatoes and sometimes aubergines)

Primi (first courses)

Typical first courses include soup, risotto, gnocchi or varieties of pasta in a wide range of sauces. Risotto and gnocchi are more common in the north.
il brodetto **fish soup**
il brodo **consommé**
gli gnocchi **potato dumplings**
la minestra **soup**
pasta e fagioli **pasta and bean soup**
il prosciutto (cotto/crudo) **ham**
i tartufi **truffles**
la zuppa **soup**

Secondi (main courses)

Main courses are typically fish-, seafood- or meat-based, with accompaniments *(contorni)* that vary greatly from region to region.

La Carne (meat)

arrosto **roast meat**
ai ferri **grilled**
al forno **baked**
al girarrosto **spit-roasted**
alla griglia **grilled**
stufato **braised, stewed**
ben cotto **well done** (steak, etc.)
al puntino **medium** (steak, etc.)
al sangue **rare** (steak, etc.)
l'agnello **lamb**
la bistecca **steak**
il capriolo/cervo **venison**
il cinghiale **wild boar**
il coniglio **rabbit**
il controfiletto **sirloin steak**
le cotolette **cutlets**
il fagiano **pheasant**
il fegato **liver**
il filetto **fillet**
il maiale **pork**
il manzo **beef**
l'ossobuco **shin of veal**
il pollo **chicken**
le polpette **meatballs**
la salsiccia **sausage**
il saltimbocca (alla romana) **veal**

escalopes with ham
le scaloppine **escalopes**
lo stufato **stew**
il sugo **sauce**
il tacchino **turkey**
la trippa **tripe**
il vitello **veal**

Frutti di Mare (seafood)

surgelati **frozen**
alla griglia **grilled**
fritto **fried**
ripieno **stuffed**
al vapore **steamed**
le acciughe **anchovies**
l'aragosta **lobster**
il baccalà **dried salted cod**
il branzino **sea bass**
i calamari **squid**
i crostacei **shellfish**
le cozze **mussels**
il fritto misto **mixed fried fish**
i gamberi **prawns**
i gamberetti **shrimps**
il granchio **crab**
il merluzzo **cod**
le ostriche **oysters**
il pesce **fish**
il pesce spada **swordfish**
il polipo **octopus**
il risotto di mare **seafood risotto**
le sarde **sardines**
la sogliola **sole**
la trota **trout**
il tonno **tuna**
le vongole **clams**

I Legumi/La Verdura (vegetables)

gli asparagi **asparagus**
le carote **carrots**
la cipolla **onion**
i fagioli **beans**
i fagiolini **French (green) beans**
il finocchio **fennel**
i funghi **mushrooms**
l'insalata mista **mixed salad**
l'insalata verde **green salad**

Pronunciation and Grammar Tips

Italian-speakers claim that pronunciation is easy – you pronounce it as it is written – but there are a few rules to bear in mind: *c* before *e* or *i* is pronounced "ch", eg *ciao, mi dispiace, la coincidenza*. *Ch* before *i* or *e* is pronounced as "k", eg *la chiesa*. Likewise, *sci* or *sce* are pronounced as in "sheep" or "shed" respectively. *Gn* in Italian is rather like the sound in "onion", while *gl* is softened to resemble the sound in "bullion".

Nouns are either masculine (*il*, plural *i*) or feminine (*la*, plural *le*). Plurals of nouns are most often formed by changing an *o* to an *i* and an *a* to an *e*, eg *il panino, i panini; la chiesa, le chiese.*

Words are generally stressed on the penultimate syllable unless an accent indicates otherwise.

Italian has formal and informal words for "You". In the singular, *Tu* is informal while *Lei* is more polite. It is best to use the formal form unless invited to do otherwise.

TRANSPORT

A – Z

LANGUAGE

la melanzana **aubergine**
le patate **potatoes**
le patatine fritte **chips/French fries**
i peperoni **peppers**
i pomodori **tomatoes**
il radicchio **red, bitter lettuce**
i ravanelli **radishes**
la rughetta **rocket**
gli spinaci **spinach**
la verdura **green vegetables**
gli zucchini **courgettes**

I Dolci (desserts)

al carrello **(desserts) from the trolley**
un semifreddo **semi-frozen dessert**
la cassata **Sicilian ice cream with candied peel**
le frittelle **fritters**
un gelato (di lampone/limone) **(raspberry/lemon) ice cream**
una granita **water ice**
una macedonia di frutta **fruit salad**
il tartufo (nero) **(chocolate) ice cream dessert**
il tiramisù **cold, creamy cheese and coffee dessert**
la torta **cake/tart**
lo zabaglione **sweet dessert made with eggs and Marsala wine**
la zuppa inglese **trifle**

La Frutta (fruit)

le albicocche **apricots**
le arance **oranges**
le banane **bananas**
il cocomero **watermelon**
le ciliegie **cherries**
i fichi **figs**
le fragole **strawberries**
i lamponi **raspberries**
la mela **apple**
il melone **melon**
la pesca **peach**
la pera **pear**
il pompelmo **grapefruit**
l'uva **grapes**

Basic foods

l'aceto **vinegar**
l'aglio **garlic**
il burro **butter**
il formaggio **cheese**
la frittata **omelette**
i grissini **bread sticks**
l'olio **oil**
la marmellata **jam**
il pane **bread**
il pane integrale **wholemeal bread**
il parmigiano **Parmesan cheese**
il pepe **pepper**
il riso **rice**
il sale **salt**
la senape **mustard**
le uova **eggs**
lo zucchero **sugar**

Days and dates

morning/afternoon/evening la mattina, il pomeriggio, la sera
yesterday/today/tomorrow ieri/oggi/domani
the day after tomorrow dopodomani
now/early/late adesso/presto/ritardo
Monday lunedì
Tuesday martedì
Wednesday mercoledì
Thursday giovedì
Friday venerdì
Saturday sabato
Sunday domenica

SIGHTSEEING

Si può visitare…? **Can one visit…?**
Suonare il campanello **ring the bell**
aperto/a **open**
chiuso/a **closed**
chiuso per la festa/ferie/restauro **closed for the festival/holidays/restoration**

AT THE SHOPS

What time do you open/close? A che ora apre/chiude?
Closed for the holidays Chiuso per ferie
Pull/push Tirare/spingere
Entrance/exit Entrata/uscita
Can I help you? Posso aiutarla?
What would you like? Che cosa desidera?
I'm just looking Stò soltanto guardando
How much is it? Quant'è, per favore?
How much is this? Quanto viene?
Do you take credit cards? Accettate carte di credito?
this one/that one questo/quello
Have you got…? Avete…?
We haven't got (any)… Non (ne) abbiamo…
Can I try it on? Posso provare?
the size (for clothes) la taglia
What size do you take? Qual'è la sua taglia?
the size (for shoes) il numero
Is there/do you have…? C'è…?
Yes, of course Sì, certo
That's too expensive È troppo caro
cheap economico
It's too small/big È troppo piccolo/grande
I (don't) like it (Non) mi piace
I'll take/leave it Lo prendo/lascio
Anything else? Altro?
Give me some of those Mi dia alcuni di quelli lì

a (half) kilo un (mezzo) chilo
100/200 grams un etto/due etti
more/less più/meno
with/without con/senza
a little un pochino
That's enough/No more Basta così

Types of shop

bakery/cake shop la panetteria/pasticceria
bank la banca
bookshop la libreria
boutique il negozio di moda
bureau de change il cambio
butcher la macelleria
chemist la farmacia
delicatessen la salumeria
department store il grande magazzino
fishmonger la pescheria
florist il fioraio
food shop l'alimentari
greengrocer il fruttivendolo
hairdresser il parrucchiere
ice-cream parlour la gelateria
jeweller il gioielliere
post office l'ufficio postale
shoe shop il negozio di scarpe
supermarket il supermercato

HEALTH

Is there a chemist nearby? C'è una farmacia qui vicino?
Which chemist is open at night? Quale farmacia fa il turno di notte?
I don't feel well Non mi sento bene
I feel ill Sto male/Mi sento male
Where does it hurt? Dov'è Le fa male?
It hurts here Ho dolore qui
I have a headache Ho mal di testa
I have a sore throat Ho mal di gola
I have stomach ache Ho mal di pancia
antiseptic cream la crema antisettica
sunburn scottatura da sole
sunburn cream la crema antisolare
insect repellent l'insettifugo
mosquitoes le zanzare

Numbers

1 uno		**16** sedici	
2 due		**17** diciassette	
3 tre		**18** diciotto	
4 quattro		**19** diciannove	
5 cinque		**20** venti	
6 sei		**30** trenta	
7 sette		**40** quaranta	
8 otto		**50** cinquanta	
9 nove		**60** sessanta	
10 dieci		**70** settanta	
11 undici		**80** ottanta	
12 dodici		**90** novanta	
13 tredici		**100** cento	
14 quattordici		**200** duecento	
15 quindici		**1,000** mille	

FURTHER READING

TRANSPORT

ART AND ARCHITECTURE

The Architecture of the Italian Renaissance, by Peter Murray. The classic guide to art and architecture of the Renaissance period.

Brunelleschi's Dome: The Story of the Great Cathedral in Florence, by Ross King. This book celebrates one of the greatest architectural feats ever accomplished, and its creator.

Fellini on Fellini, by Federico Fellini. Essays, letters and interviews charting the film director's life and work.

Italian Architecture from Michelangelo to Borromini, by Andrew Hopkins. A comprehensive guide tracing the background to the artistic patrimony of Florence and other Italian cities.

A New History of Italian Renaissance Art, by Stephen Campbell and Michael Cole. This book takes a fresh approach to a great period of art that is accessible to all.

The Stones of Florence and Venice Observed, by Mary McCarthy. A travel companion and an accessible introduction to art history.

CULTURE AND HISTORY

The Civilisation of the Renaissance in Italy, by Jacob Burckhardt. Published in 1860, this book effectively defined the concept of "Italian Renaissance", and remains enormously illuminating.

Florence: The Biography of a City, by Christopher Hibbert. Weaves together the history and culture of Florence, with excellent photographs and illustrations; equally fascinating are the same author's *The Rise and Fall of the House of Medici* and *Rome: The Biography of a City.*

A History of Sicily, by M.I. Finley and Dennis Mack Smith. The best overall Sicilian history.

The Merchant of Prato, by Iris Origo. An intimate and accessible account of the life of a 14th-century Italian merchant, pieced together from a huge cache of letters and documents unearthed in 1870.

Mussolini, by Dennis Mack Smith. Penetrating biography that illustrates clearly the viciousness and incompetence of Italy's dictator.

The Oxford Illustrated History of Italy, by George Holmes. An extensive, but still concise, insight into the whole of Italy's colourful past.

Renaissance Florence on Five Florins a Day, by Charles FitzRoy. Witty, very entertaining tour through Florence in its golden age written in the style of a contemporary guidebook.

The Twelve Caesars, by Suetonius. All the scandals and misdemeanours of the founders of the **Roman Empire,** by one of history's greatest gossips.

The Venetian Ghetto, by Roberta Curiel. A history of the city's Jewish community.

Venice: Pure City, by Peter Ackroyd. Grand history, anecdotes and endlessly surprising details from an always original writer.

Send Us Your Thoughts

We do our best to ensure the information in our books is as accurate and up-to-date as possible. The books are updated on a regular basis using local contacts, who painstakingly add, amend and correct as required. However, some details (such as telephone numbers and opening times) are liable to change, and we are ultimately reliant on our readers to put us in the picture.

We welcome your feedback, especially your experience of using the book "on the road". Maybe we recommended a hotel that you liked (or another that you didn't), or you came across a great bar or new attraction we missed.

We will acknowledge all contributions, and we'll offer an Insight Guide to the best letters received. Please write to us at:

**Insight Guides
PO Box 7910
London SE1 1WE**
Or email us at:
hello@insightguides.com

GENERAL

La Bella Figura – A Field Guide to the Italian Mind, by Beppe Severgnini. A wry look at the Italian psyche.

Bitter Almonds, by Mary Taylor Simeti and Maria Grammatico. Poignant memoir of a much-fêted Sicilian chef and former nun, and a collection of her recipes.

Cosa Nostra: A History of the Sicilian Mafia, by John Dickie. A comprehensive history.

The Dark Heart of Italy, by Tobias Jones. A provocative portrait of Italy highlighting the interplay between politics, society and crime.

The Leopard, by Giuseppe Tomasi di Lampedusa. A classic novel about the demise of the Sicilian aristocracy threatened by Garibaldi's revolution. This gripping tale focuses on the endless struggle between mortality and decay and abstraction and eternity.

Gomorrah, by Roberto Saviano. Terrifying, immensely brave insight into the world of organised crime in Naples.

The Italians, by Luigi Barzini. Originally published in the sixties, this is still worthwhile reading for the frankness of Barzini's portrait of his fellow countrymen.

Italian Ways: On and Off the Rails from Milan to Palermo, by Tim Parks. Exploring his adopted country through its trains. Also very worth finding are the same author are *A Season with Verona* (on football), and *An Italian Education.*

The Last Supper, by Rachel Cusk. Impressions of a summer in Tuscany and Naples.

Mafia Women, by Clare Longrigg. A courageous investigation into the changing role of women in Cosa Nostra.

The Prince, by Niccolò Machiavelli. The new Penguin translation by Tim Parks is the liveliest version in years of Machiavelli's classic treatise on power in the Renaissance.

Slow Food: The Case for Taste, by Carlo Petrini. A book that challenges our attitude to eating and shopping.

Venice for Pleasure, by J.G. Links. A guide to the city – not practical, but beautifully written by a man who is passionate about his subject.

A – Z

LANGUAGE

CREDITS

Insight Guide Credits

Distribution
UK, Ireland and Europe
Apa Publications (UK) Ltd;
sales@insightguides.com
United States and Canada
Ingram Publisher Services;
ips@ingramcontent.com
Australia and New Zealand
Woodslane; info@woodslane.com.au
Southeast Asia
Apa Publications (SN) Pte;
singaporeoffice@insightguides.com
Hong Kong, Taiwan and China
Apa Publications (HK) Ltd;
hongkongoffice@insightguides.com
Worldwide
Apa Publications (UK) Ltd;
sales@insightguides.com
**Special Sales, Content Licensing
and CoPublishing**
Insight Guides can be purchased in
bulk quantities at discounted prices.
We can create special editions,
personalised jackets and corporate
imprints tailored to your needs.
sales@insightguides.com
www.insightguides.biz

Printed in China by CTPS

All Rights Reserved
© 2017 Apa Digital (CH) AG and
Apa Publications (UK) Ltd

www.insightguides.com

Editor: Carine Tracanelli
Author: Lisa Gerard-Sharp
Updaters: Jackie Staddon, Hilary
Weston, Maciej Zglinicki
Head of Production: Rebeka Davies
Update Production: AM Services
Picture Editor: Tom Smyth
Cartography: original cartography
ERA Maptec Ltd, updated by Carte

Legend

City maps

	Freeway/Highway/Motorway
	Divided Highway
	Main Roads
	Minor Roads
	Pedestrian Roads
	Steps
	Footpath
	Railway
	Funicular Railway
	Cable Car
	Tunnel
	City Wall
	Important Building
	Built Up Area
	Other Land
	Transport Hub
	Park
	Pedestrian Area
	Bus Station
	Tourist Information
	Main Post Office
	Cathedral/Church
	Mosque
	Synagogue
	Statue/Monument
	Beach
	Airport

Regional maps

	Freeway/Highway/Motorway (with junction)
	Freeway/Highway/Motorway (under construction)
	Divided Highway
	Main Road
	Secondary Road
	Minor Road
	Track
	Footpath
	International Boundary
	State/Province Boundary
	National Park/Reserve
	Marine Park
	Ferry Route
	Marshland/Swamp
	Glacier
	Salt Lake
	Airport/Airfield
	Ancient Site
	Border Control
	Cable Car
	Castle/Castle Ruins
	Cave
	Chateau/Stately Home
	Church/Church Ruins
	Crater
	Lighthouse
	Mountain Peak
	Place of Interest
	Viewpoint

Contributors

Formerly an editor for RAI TV in
Rome, **Lisa Gerard-Sharp** is London
correspondent to Italian *Vogue* and a
contributor to *The Times* and *The
Telegraph*. Her partner, previously
head of the Italian tourist board,
claims he knows the country better
than he does. While researching this
book, Lisa was particularly struck by
the emergence of unsung regions,
such as Emilia Romagna, Liguria and
Puglia. But she was equally delighted
to find Florence, Rome and Turin
enjoying a renaissance, with
restored art museums, revamped
districts, better restaurants and, in
some cases, more eco-friendly
transport, from tram tours in Turin to
segway and bicycle tours in Florence
and Rome.

About Insight Guides

Insight Guides have more than
45 years' experience of publishing
high-quality, visual travel guides. We
produce 400 full-colour titles, in both
print and digital form, covering more
than 200 destinations across the
globe, in a variety of formats to meet
your different needs.

Insight Guides are written by
local authors, whose expertise is
evident in the extensive historical
and cultural background features.

Each destination is carefully
researched by regional experts to
ensure our guides provide the very
latest information. All the reviews
in **Insight Guides** are independent;
we strive to maintain an impartial
view. Our reviews are carefully
selected to guide you to the best
places to eat, go out and shop, so
you can be confident that when
we say a place is special, we really
mean it.

INDEX

Main references are in bold type

THE EGOIST

AN ANNOTATED TEXT
BACKGROUNDS
CRITICISM

heart- breaking -dance
dream waking -chance
one taken - seem to give
soul dying - live